THE
ROCK
YEARBOOK
1985

Managing Editor
ROXANE STREETER

Designed by
JON BARRACLOUGH and ANITA PLANK

Cover by
KEN ANSELL

THE ROCK YEARBOOK 1985

For information, address: St. Martin's Press, 175 Fifth Avenue,
New York, NY 10010.

Printed in Great Britain

First U.S. Edition

10 9 8 7 6 5 4 3 2 1

THE ROCK YEARBOOK 1985

EDITED BY

ALLAN JONES

St. Martin's Press
New York

CONTRIBUTORS

EDITOR

ALLAN JONES has been propping up bars in a variety of exotic locations, from Venezuela to Lapland, since 1974, when the *Melody Maker* rather foolishly offered him money to write about rock 'n' roll and the people who make it. He was once told by Boy George that he had the kind of face that made people laugh; ironically, this is precisely the effect the overweight crooner's voice has on him. He is presently editor of *Melody Maker* and married to an American.

CONTRIBUTORS

LYNDEN BARBER has been penning his diatribes for *Melody Maker* in earwax since 1980. Opinions differ as to the state of his mental health, but his mother thinks it's about time he "grew up and got a proper job". Lynden is handsome, single and wears Pagan Man aftershave.

RICHARD BARNES is a freelance writer and graphic designer. Among his books are *Mods!* and *The Who: Maximum R&B*. He is currently chairperson of the stone cladding, picture window and crimplene appreciation society and is campaigning to get Duran Duran to take themselves more seriously.

LLOYD BRADLEY contributed regularly for three years to the *NME* and four to *Look-In*, then sailed 600 miles down the river Nile, in nuptial bliss, to gaze upon the Great Pyramid of Cheops. He now knows there is more to life than living beyond your means.

GEOFF BROWN was a *Melody Maker* staff writer (1971-77) and editor of *Black Music* (1977-79) before working for two years as a freelance, during which time his first book, *Diana Ross*, was published. Subsequently *Time Out* music editor (1981-83), he is now its sports editor. In April 1984, his second book, *Michael Jackson: Body & Soul*, was published.

BRIAN CASE has been writing about jazz for the past ten years. His writing has appeared in *The Sunday Times, The Observer, The Guardian* and *The Times Literary Supplement*, as well as the music press. He is the author of a novel, *The Users*, and *The Illustrated Encyclopaedia Of Jazz*. He is a staff writer on *Melody Maker*.

IAN CRANNA is the quiet, shy, and retiring self-styled fourth member of XTC. Ian "Jocky" Cranna wrote for *NME* from Edinburgh, pioneered the pop magazine sensation *Smash Hits*, and when not managing the Virgin Prunes likes nothing better than to slip into a frogman's suit and be whipped with a copy of *Horse And Hovercraft* while listening to *The Sound Of Music*.

FRED DELLAR has been a regular contributor to *NME* and *Hi-Fi News* for several years. Books he has authored or co-authored include *The Illustrated Encyclopedia Of Country Music, The Essential Guide To Rock Records, The NME Guide To Rock Cinema* and *The Country Music Book Of Lists*.

ROBERT ELMS was born in North London in 1959, graduated through Ben Sherman shirts and his brother's soul collection to the LSE and the Blitz nightclub. He began writing for the fledgling style magazine, *The Face*, chronicling the colourful world of London nightlife and quickly established a reputation as a controversialist. Today, he continues to contribute to *The Face*, Fleet Street, the BBC and any bar that's open when the others are shut. And he listens to jazz.

JIM EVANS is currently special projects editor of the UK trade magazine *Music Week* and was previously news editor of the same organ. He is also UK correspondent of the US magazine *Pro Sound News* and once appeared on *Nationwide*.

DESSA FOX writes on video for *Video Maker* and *Time Out*.

PETE FRAME lives in remotest Buckinghamshire, isolated from reality. There he continues to convince himself that the world or rock is still exciting enough to write about. He is now bashing together a third volume of *Rock Family Trees*.

DAVID FRICKE is the American correspondent for *Melody Maker*. Based in New York, he is a frequent contributor to *Rolling Stone* and *Musician* and is currently the editor of *Star Hits*, the U.S. sister publication of *Smash Hits*. A firm believer in the power and integrity of American underground music, he thinks groups like Styx, Kansas and Toto owe the world an apology.

SIMON GARFIELD has appeared from nowhere to become assistant music editor on *Time Out*. He also writes regularly for *Blitz* and occasionally for the *Education Guardian*. He is still outrageously young, and hopes one day to read Charles Shaar Murray's imminent biography of Jimi Hendrix.

JOHN GILL *didn't* appear out of nowhere to become music editor of *Time Out*. After too many years freelancing as *Sounds'* captive pseud, he achieved professional status with a similar staff job on *Time Out*. Burroughs, Greenpeace, Karen Silkwood and gay rights are among the subjects he hopes have brought him to the attention of the CIA. He has now decided he doesn't *want* to know who the Residents are.

CHARLIE GILLETT is the author of *The Sound Of The City*, which has been described by the *New York Times* as "the best history yet written of rock and roll". He broadcasts regularly on Radio London, and runs his own Oval Records from an address in Wandsworth, South London.

ED HANEL is a serious record collector who writes a lot. He has yet to visit the South Pole or New Guinea in his never-ending quest for the great undiscovered Who record.

MICHAEL HEATLEY occupied the editor's chair at *The History Of Rock* (1983) and *Soundcheck* (1984) before retiring to write books and dust off his Fender bass. If he's not on *Top Of The Pops* by the time you read this, he's probably found another comfy chair somewhere.

BARNEY HOSKYNS is staff writer for *NME* and contributes to *The Guardian* and *The New Statesman*. Any ridiculously large advances for long-winded pop books will be considered.

COLIN IRWIN is a perfectly charming person who was born with a finger in his ear but is alright now. His collective passions include Southampton Football Club, Faye Dunaway and Siamese cats. When forced to pay the mortgage he is assistant editor of *Melody Maker*.

DREW MOSELEY is a New York-based writer who is presently perfecting her de-frosting technique. She lives with two sharks cleverly disguised to look like cats, and has been writing for *The Rock Yearbook* since it began. She is also the editor of *Rock World*.

BETTY PAGE is currently deputy editor of *Record Mirror*, having battled her way there in a male dominated arena via *Sounds* and *Noise!*, the greatest pop mag that never was. She boasts an extensive wardrobe of unusual clothing and once turned down the opportunity to sip hot cocoa back at Simon Le Bon's place.

JON SAVAGE is still at TVAM, for whom he claims to hae done everything but read the weather forecasts. He contributes regularly to *The Face*, and is occasionally present in the columns of the *Sunday Times* and *Time Out*. He has recently completed a book on the Kinks.

PAUL 'SCOOP' SIMPER is a writer who has been delighting his mother since New Year's Eve '81 when he began to write for *Melody Maker*. Later he became film editor for the free spirited *New Sounds, New Styles* before laying to rest – for the moment at least – with the mighty *No. 1*.

STEVE SUTHERLAND once pioneered the much-maligned alliterative style to the detriment of *Melody Maker* so the powers that be put him in charge of reviews. Consequently he spends too much time these days talking as his belly guides him, deluding himself that bald is beautiful and perfecting his impersonation of Richard Jobson.

ADAM SWEETING has contributed to numerous publications, many of which subsequently went into liquidation. He is fond of cricket, medieval alliterative poetry and Neil Young, and is therefore features editor of *Melody Maker*. He has already written a book, and hopes to write another one fairly soon.

JOHN TOBLER continues to write books about rock music and to drive a yellow car. He keeps a pet gannet who eats cheesecake and goes to Folk Festivals. Tobler slept under canvas this year for the first time since the Sixties, but has not shaved since 1970.

DAVE WALTERS, is a retired dolphin trainer who has spent far too long in the record industry. Seven years as a WEA Records press officer led to a gold medal and a switch to A&R, where he still holds the staff record for auditioning over 5,000 dodgy bands. By 1983 his talents were ensconced at Virgin Records HQ, where he excelled as resident tea-maker to Boy George. He contributes regularly to *Time Out*, and has never written for *Blitz* or *The Face*.

CONTENTS

ACKNOWLEDGEMENTS

As the curtain falls with its annual slap upon the completion of this formidable volume of information, opinion and sheerly ill-tempered invective, it's usual to offer thanks and praise to the individuals whose tireless enthusiasm turned its publication from a spurious possibility, which is what at times it seemed to be, into a viable reality.

This year will be no different.

Enormous thanks therefore, to Roxane Streeter for being in three places at the same time, trying to organise us all and still managing to be on the end of a telephone, often at quite unreasonable hours, with suggestions for improvement and words of reassurance when they were needed most; Adam Sweeting, who stopped by for a drink and stayed to finish the bottle; Jon Barraclough, who prevented the pandemonium of production from degenerating into pantomime, and Elvis Costello, whose *Get Happy!!* usually provided the late-night soundtrack for the reading of our contributors' copy. Thanks, too, of course, to each of *them*, for filling what otherwise would have been rather a lot of blank pages.

Again we relied heavily on the generosity of record companies, book publishers and the music papers for material, and would like to thank them profusely. The following kind-hearted individuals also bailed us out with their various talents and deserve credit here:

Keith Altham's gang, Peter Anderson, Brian Aris, Peter Ashworth, Joe Bangay, Tony Barratt, Adrian Boot, Brad Branson, Joel Brodsky, Central Television, Al Clark, Karen Collier, Anton Corbijn, Fin Costello, Paul Cox, Andre Csillag, Lynn Cumming, Ian Dickson, Graham Ewens, Simon Fowler, Chris Garnham, Debbie Geller, Geoff at Keyline, Lynn Goldsmith, Ross Halfin, Richard Haughton, Jeff Hornbaker, George Hurrel, Jayne, Stephanie Jones, Dennis Keeley, David Kennedy, Jak Kilby, Bill King, Sue Lanzon, Sue Latham, Mike Laye, David Levine, Terry Lott, MTV, Macioce, Gered Mankowitz, Linda McCartney, Stephen Meisel, Dennis Morris, Leon Morris, Clare Muller, Marguerite Nicholls, Dennis O'Regan, Pippa at PSA, Steve Rapport, David Redfern, Paul Rider, Robin Ridley, Robert at Stones Record Shop, Sheila Rock, Trevor Rogers, Howard Rosenberg, Red Saunders, Tom Sheehan, Chuck Sillery, Pennie Smith, Tom Smith at the Virgin Megastore, Ursula Steiger, David Sygal, Bruce W. Talamon, David Travis, Mary Volk, Eric Watson, Mark Weiss, Wolfgang Wesemer, Steve Wright, Richard Young.

A.J.

This one goes out to Steph and Russ

THE YEAR

AUGUST 83

1. *The United States increases its support to Chad, positioning an aircraft carrier and troops off the coast of Libya.*

2. James Jamerson, responsible for the basslines on countless Motown classics, dies in Los Angeles, aged 45.

4. *26 IRA men receive jail sentences as a result of information volunteered by "supergrass" Christopher Black.*

4. *Unemployment figures now total 3,231,720 – almost one in seven of the work force.*

5. CSN star David Crosby is sentenced to five years for cocaine possession and three years for illegal firearms possession by a Dallas judge. Crosby, who slept through most of the trial, gets bail, pending appeal.

6. Performance artist Klaus Nomi, known for his operatic voice, dies of AIDS in New York, aged 38.

10. Research reveals that in the United States, cassette sales, now accounting for 53 per cent of the market, are outstripping those of albums.

13. KC & The Sunshine Band rise to the top of the UK singles chart with 'Give It Up'.

K.C.

PHIL LYNOTT

17. Lyricist Ira Gershwin dies in New York, aged 86.

18. The only surviving pirate station, Radio Caroline, operating from a converted trawler 15 miles off the East Anglian coast, resumes broadcasting after a three-and-a-half year hiatus.

18. *For the first time in 18 months, trade union leaders hold talks with the Secretary of State for Industry, Norman Tebbit – discussing, among other things, the Youth Training Scheme.*

20. *Eighteen Greatest Hits*, a TV advertised Michael Jackson/Jackson 5 compilation, tops the UK album chart, displacing *The Very Best Of The Beach Boys*. Culture Club become the first group in 20 years to have three singles from their debut album enter the US Top Ten.

20. Johnny Ramone, guitarist with veteran NY punks The Ramones, suffers a near fatal head blow during a street fight over his girlfriend.

26. *President Andropov offers to destroy SS20 missiles "to the level equal in number to those in Britain and France" if the the US cancel their plans to deploy further missiles in Europe in December. The offer is rejected.*

27. Dub poet Michael Smith is stoned to death in a Jamaica street, a day after addressing a stormy political meeting.

28. Thin Lizzy play their farewell gig, headlining the last day of the annual Reading Rock Festival.

31. All 269 people on board a South Korean Boeing 747 are killed when Soviet fighters destroy the plane for violating Soviet airspace.

Marc Almond announces his disenchantment with the business, vowing to quit and never return to the forefront of pop. Kajagoogoo frontman Limahl leaves to go solo. Shakatak lose their keyboard player, Nigel Wright; AC/DC acquire a new drummer, Simon Wright. ELO drummer Bev Bevan joins Black Sabbath, replacing Bill Ward ("far too ill to tour"). Former Beat frontmen Dave Wakeling and Ranking Roger announce their new group, General Public. Ex-Bad Company guitarist Mick Ralphs starts low key gigging with his new band. Bauhaus, the Au Pairs, and Rip Rig & Panic all split up.

SEPTEMBER 83

1. *President Reagan orders an amphibious force, including 1600 marines, to sail to Lebanon following further outbreaks of fighting in Beirut.*

3. After 8 weeks at the top of the US singles chart, 'Every Breath You Take' by Police is ousted by the Eurythmics' 'Sweet Dreams'. 'Red Red Wine' returns UB40 to the top of the UK singles chart.

EURYTHMICS

8. *As Christian and Druze militia battle for control of Beirut, the British Embassy advises British citizens to leave Lebanon.*

10. Michael Jackson's *Thriller*, already a number one for 19 weeks, returns to the top of the US album chart, dislodging *Synchronicity* by The Police – but only for one week. 'Confusion' by New Order is UK's best selling independent single.

THE POLICE

12. *At the UN Security Council, the Soviet Union vetoes a resolution "deeply deploring" the shooting down of the South Korean airliner and calling for an UN enquiry.*

17. Paul Young tops the UK album chart with *No Parlez*.

18. *At a Hell's Angels rally at Cookham, Berkshire, two are stabbed to death and four seriously wounded with knives and axes.*

21. *As fighting in Lebanon escalates, President Reagan accuses Syria of blocking attempts to negotiate peace terms.*

22. At the Royal Albert Hall, The Everly Brothers play their first concert together for over ten years.

24. Billy Joel has the best selling US single, 'Tell Her About It'. In Britain, UB40 top the album chart with *Labour of Love*, while Culture Club's 'Karma Chameleon' starts a six week reign as number one single.

25. *38 IRA prisoners escape in a break-out from the Maze top security prison in Belfast. Half are recaptured within a few days; the rest go to ground.*

27. Reggae artist Prince Far I is assassinated by gunmen at his home in St. Catherine's Jamaica. Motives behind the murder remain obscure.

30. In an unprecedented move, the Royal Albert Hall removes all arena seats for Siouxsie & The Banshees' only London dates this year.

The Clash sack founder/guitarist Mick Jones; Bow Wow Wow sack their singer, Annabella Lwin. In a matter of weeks, Marillion drummer Andy Ward is replaced by John Marter, Jonathan Mover, and finally Ian Mosley.

OCTOBER 83

2. *Neil Kinnock is elected leader of the Labour Party.*

4. *Richard Noble beats the 13-year-old American record and regains the World Land Speed record for Britain, averaging 633 mph over a measured mile at Black Rock Desert, Nevada.*

5. *The 1983 Nobel Prize is awarded to Lech Walesa, leader of Poland's Solidarity Union, currently outlawed. British author Williams Golding wins the prize for literature.*

10. *Sir Ralph Richardson, the actor, dies, aged 80.*

14. *Following disclosures from his former secretary and mistress, Sara Keays, now expecting his child, Trade and Industry Secretary Cecil Parkinson resigns his post.*

GENESIS

15. *Genesis* enters the UK album chart at number one. Bonnie Tyler's 'Total Eclipse Of The Heart' is the best selling US single.

20. Merle Travis, innovative guitar picking C&W star, dies in Nashville aged 65.

22. *Massive anti-nuclear demonstrations take place in many European cities to protest against the imminent arrival of more US missiles.*

22. Sales of Culture Club's 'Karma Chameleon' top one million, making it only the third UK platinum single of the eighties (together with the Human League's 'Don't You Want Me' and 'Come On Eileen' by Dexy's Midnight Runners). Their album, *Colour By Numbers*, enters the UK album chart at number one; *Snap* by The Jam enters at number two.

25. *On President Reagan's orders, US troops invade Grenada "just in time to thwart a Soviet-backed take-over of the island by Cuba."*

26. *President Andropov warns that if NATO deploy more Cruise and Pershing 11 missiles in Europe in December, Geneva talks on nuclear arms reductions will be broken off.*

29. *Police arrest 102 women after an attack on Greenham Common nuclear missile base, in which the perimeter fence was cut and penetrated.*

Former Yazoo partner Vince Clarke unveils his new project, The Assembly. John Lydon returns to the UK stage, touring with Public Image Ltd. John Coghlan, ex-Status Quo, launches Stranger, Andde Leek, ex-Dexy's Midnight Runners, launches Fascination, Dave Mortimer, ex-Wham!, launches Grapes, and Don Snow, ex-Squeeze, launches Out. Greg Lake replaces John Wetton in

JOHN LYDON

Asia and former Ted Nugent singer Derek St. Holmes joins The Michael Schenker Group. Peter Wolf, singer with The J. Geils Band since their inception in the late sixties, leaves to go solo. Chris Stamey leaves the DBs, Mick Moody leaves Whitesnake. As bassist Kelly Groucutt is reportedly suing for 25 per cent of the group's gross profits since 1974, it would appear that ELO are no more. Roy Milton, R & B pioneer, dies of a stroke in Canoga Park, California aged 76.

3. *In South Africa, the acceptance of a referendum extends constitutional and political rights to "Indians" and "Coloureds", but no concessions are granted to the country's 20 million "Blacks".*

4. *Dennis Nilsen, who admitted killing 15 young men in Muswell Hill and Cricklewood, is sentenced to life imprisonment.*

5. 'Uptown Girl' takes Billy Joel to the top of the UK singles chart.

NOVEMBER 83

2. The surviving Doors fly to London for a convention at the ICA.

THE DOORS

BILLY JOEL

12. Lionel Richie has the number one US single with 'All Night Long'. His album *Can't Slow Down*, knocks Culture Club off the UK top spot, but only for one week.

14. *The first Cruise missiles to arrive in Britain are delivered to the Greenham Common air base by a US Starlifter aircraft.*

15. *Actor John Le Mesurier dies, aged 71.*

17. *Miss United Kingdom, Sarah-Jane Hutt, is elected Miss World.*

18. Barney Bubbles, 41, innovative sleeve designer/video director/illustrator, takes his life.

18. *An independent report commissioned by the Metropolitan Police finds racial intolerance, sexism and over-use of force common in a substantial minority of officers.*

19. Tom Evans, 36-year-old former bass player with Badfinger, is found hanged at his Surrey home.

23. *The Soviet Union breaks off peace talks in Geneva, as threats of nuclear superiority begin to fly.*

26. Quiet Riot's *Metal Health* becomes America's best selling album, dislodging the Police's *Synchronicity*, which first made number one back in July. 'PYT' becomes the sixth US Top Ten single drawn from Michael Jackson's album *Thriller*, which becomes the biggest selling album in the history of CBS – overtaking Simon and Garfunkel's *Greatest Hits*.

29. After the Court of Appeal orders the seizure of the NGA's entire ten million pound assets following a dispute over the Messenger Group Newspapers in Stockport, some 4000 pickets clash with 1000 police outside their printing factory in Warrington, demonstrating their opposition to current employment laws.

Stannard Ridgeway quits Wall Of Voodoo, guitarist Wayne Hussey leaves Dead Or Alive. Ex-Led Zeppelin frontman Robert Plant emerges with his new band to start a world tour.

DECEMBER 83

1. *The environmental protection group Greenpeace is fined £50,000 for failing to obey a court injunction preventing them from interfering with nuclear waste being discharged into the Irish Sea from the Sellafield reprocessing plant in Cumbria. Their claims of radioactive contamination were*

later seen to have been well founded.

3. Duran Duran enter the UK album chart at number one with *Seven And The Ragged Tiger;* U2 enter at number two with *Under A Blood Red Sky.*

DURAN DURAN

6. *A security officer at a warehouse near Heathrow is charged with complicity in the theft of gold bullion worth £26 million.*

8. Repeating their Albert Hall triumph, a superstar band organised by ex-Faces member and MS victim Ronnie Lane and led by Jeff Beck, Eric Clapton and Jimmy Page, plays the first of two benefit concerts at Madison Square Garden to raise money for Action Research Into Multiple Sclerosis. The trio also auction rare guitars.

10. 'Say Say Say' by Paul McCartney and Michael Jackson becomes the best selling single in US. *No Parlez* returns to the top of the UK album chart, while the Flying Pickets take over the singles chart with 'Only You'.

PAUL McCARTNEY AND MICHAEL JACKSON

11. *Some 25,000 women demonstrators converge on Greenham Common to protest against the siting of nuclear missiles.*

14. *The military leaders who ruled Argentina following the 1976 coup – including those who instigated the Falklands war – are charged with repression, torture and murder.*

17. *Following similar explosions at Woolwich barracks, Kensington High Street and Oxford Street, an IRA bomb kills six and injures almost 100 outside Harrods in Knightsbridge.*

17. *The vanquished PLO leader Yasser Arafat leads his loyal*

troops in their evacuation from Tripoli.

26. *Actress Violet Carson, better known as Ena Sharples in Coronation Street, dies, aged 85.*

28. Beach Boy Dennis Wilson drowns while diving near Marina del Rey, California, aged 39.

31. Michael Jackson's *Thriller* returns to the top of the US album chart again! Now selling even faster than in its first few weeks of release over a year ago, it becomes the third album in history to enjoy worldwide sales in excess of 20 million (along with *Grease* and *Saturday Night Fever*).

After 491 weeks, Pink Floyd's *Dark Side Of The Moon* overtakes Johnny Mathis' *Greatest Hits* as the longest running chart album in the history of *Billboard* magazine. 'Karma Chameleon' becomes the best selling British single of the Eighties. Brian Robertson, guitarist with Motorhead, leaves after 18 months. Eddie Jobson leaves Yes, replaced by original keyboard man Tony Kaye. Former Stiff Little Fingers leader Jake Burns returns with a new band, Jake Burns & The Big Wheel. Pete Townshend issues a statement confirming that The Who will never work as a unit again.

THE WHO

JANUARY 84

1. Alexis Korner, British R & B pioneer and champion, and inspiration behind the early sixties boom, dies of lung cancer, aged 55.

7. The compilation album *Now That's What I Call Music* ends its three week run as UK number one.

9. *Sterling falls below $1.40 for the first time.*

11. *French farmers seize lamb from container lorries and hold the drivers in protest against meat imports from Britain.*

14. In UK, *No Parlez* returns to the number one spot for the fourth time, as 'Pipes Of Peace' gives Paul McCartney the top single.

14. After playing it 15 times during the week, BBC Radio One stops playing 'Relax' by Frankie Goes To Hollywood because of "overtly obscene lyrics".

16. Britain's first cable TV station, Sky Channel, begins operation in Swindon.

17. Linda McCartney is charged with importing cannabis at Heathrow, and is subsequently fined £75. A few days earlier, she and Paul had each been fined £70 by Barbados magistrates for possession of marijuana.

21. Jackie Wilson, pioneer soul singer, dies in New Jersey, aged 49, He had been semi-comatose since suffering a stroke onstage in 1975.

21. In a dramatic comeback, Yes rise to the top of the US singles chart with 'Owner Of A Lonely Heart'.

22. *Blizzards and gales bring chaos to Scotland and the northern half of England. Eleven people die and thousands are stranded.*

24. Yoko Ono and Sean Lennon tour Liverpool, visiting landmarks made famous by The Beatles.

25. *The Government announces that all personnel at the Government Communications Headquarters at Cheltenham must renounce trade union membership. Under duress, most agree.*

26. Michael Jackson's hair catches fire while filming a Pepsi-Cola commercial, inflicting second degree burns to his crown and neck.

28. 'Relax' by Frankie Goes To Hollywood takes over the top spot on the UK singles chart – despite restricted airplay. The uncontrollable *Thriller* tops both UK and US album charts. The three singles released by The Smiths, their entire

FRANKIE GOES TO HOLLYWOOD

THE THOMPSON TWINS

SIMPLE MINDS

catalogue, take the top three places in the UK indie chart.

29. *President Reagan announces his intention to stand for a second term.*

Nine months after their introduction to the British market, research reveals that the sales of pop compact discs has been insignificant – less than 3 per cent of total record sales. The high cost of playing equipment and weak selection of titles are blamed. Island Records and Stiff Records join forces in a merger which sees Stiff founder Dave Robinson become UK MD of both companies. Neil Murray (bass, ex-Gary Moore) and John Sykes (guitar, ex-Thin Lizzy) join Whitesnake. Drummer B.P. Hurding quits Classix Nouveaux to join Two Minds Crack. Madness's original instigator, Mike Barson, leaves to live in Amsterdam with his wife. Orange Juice are reduced to a duo following the departure of David McClymont and Malcolm Ross. Bassist Dave Roberts and drummer Ray Mondo leave Sex Gang Children and John Williams leaves Sky. Altered Images split up; Clare Grogan goes solo. Bow Wow Wow change their name to Chiefs Of Relief. Terry Hall, who split the Fun Boy Three in July, unveils his new group, The Colour Field.

FEBRUARY
84

4. 'Karma Chameleon' takes Culture Club to the top of the US singles chart. The Eurythmics' *Touch* becomes

Britain's best selling album after eleven weeks on the charts.

7. *Captain Bruce McCandless emerges from the space shuttle 'Challenger' to walk in space 165 miles above the Earth, becoming the first human to enter space without a safety line.*

7. *As Lebanon erupts in civil war, US and British contingents of the peacekeeping force withdraw to ships off the coast. Embassy staff and civilians are also evacuated.*

8. *The winter Olympics start in Sarajevo, Yugoslavia. Six days later ice dancers Jayne Torvill and Christoper Dean take the gold to win Britain's only medal.*

9. *Soviet president Yuri Andropov dies, aged 69, after only 15 months in office. Konstantin Chernenko succeeds.*

13. *Buckingham Palace announces that the princess of Wales is expecting a second baby, due in late September.*

16. Broadway musical queen Ethel Merman dies, aged 75.

17. *French lorry drivers block main roads to the Alps after disputes with customs officers at the Franco-Italian border. The blockade, lasting over a week, brings havoc to all road users, including some 350 trapped British drivers.*

18. *Sparkle In The Rain*, the new album by Simple Minds, enters the UK chart at number one. 'She Was Hot' gives the Rolling Stones their 32nd UK hit – the most hits by any group (just ahead of the shadows – 31, Hot Chocolate – 30, the Hollies and Status Quo – 29).

25. 'Relax' by Frankie Goes To Hollywood celebrates its fourth week as UK number one. (Only 'Je t'aime' by Jane Birkin and Serge Gainsbourg shares the distinction of reaching the top in the face of a *Top Of The Pops* ban). 'Jump' by Van Halen is the new best-selling single in America. The Thompson Twins enter the UK album chart at number one with *Into The Gap*.

27. *Seven British mercenaries, imprisoned for attempting to overthrow the government regime in 1976, are released from Angola.*

28. *As the US presidential campaign gathers momentum, outsider Gary Hart unexpectedly catapults into second place behind Walter Mondale in the Democratic Candidacy race.*

28. At the annual Grammy Awards ceremony in Los Angeles, Police, Culture Club and Duran Duran demonstrate their integration into US establishment rock. Michael Jackson, as expected, gathers most awards, including Album Of The Year *(Thriller)* Record Of The Year ('Beat It'), and Best Male Pop Vocalist.

Old punks never die! The Clash (with new line-up) return to British stages for the first time in two years, the original Heartbreakers re-form for a UK visit, the Vibrators get back together for "a permanent reunion". Saxplayer Stephen Singleton, a founder member, leaves ABC – now down to the duo of Martin Fry and Mark White. Former Secret Affair frontman Ian Page launches his new band, Bop. Dee Harris (ex-Fashion) and Rick Wright (ex-Pink Floyd) combine to form Zee. Hugo Burnham (ex-Gang Of Four) and Robert Dean (ex-Japan) reappear in Illustrated Man. Gang Of Four, Sad Cafe and 1919 decide to pack up. New group rumours link John Wetton (ex-Asia) and Simon Kirke (ex-

Bad Company); Jimmy Page (ex-Led Zeppelin) and Paul Rodgers (ex-Bad Company); Mick Jones and Topper Headon (both ex-Clash). In an attempt to deter potential additions, the United Nations releases a list of some 200 entertainers who have worked in South Africa despite a UN boycott due to the country's racist policies. Rock names include Linda Ronstadt, the Beach Boys, Cher, Kenny Rogers, and Sha Na Na. Elton John marries German born studio engineer Renata Blauel in Sydney, Australia.

MARCH
84

1. Twenty years after the advent of Stateside Beatlemania, seven albums by the Fab Four re-enter the US charts.

THE BEATLES

1. *Tony Benn returns to Parliament after winning the Chesterfield by-election for Labour.*

3. The Smiths' eponymous debut album enters the UK chart at number two, ahead of Madness whose *Keep Moving* comes in at number six. '99 Red Balloons' makes Nena the fourth German act to achieve a number one UK single (after Kraftwerk, the Goombay Dance Band and Nicole). 24 of the US Top 50 singles are by British acts.

4. *Independent medical experts confirm that Iraqui forces have been using chemical weapons in their war against Iran.*

10. Michael Jackson's *Thriller*, 32 weeks at US number one, eclipses Harry Belafonte's *Calypso* (1956), the *South Pacific* soundtrack (1958) and Fleetwood Mac's *Rumours* (1977) – all dethroned after 31 weeks at the top. He still has some way to go to catch the *West Side Story* soundtrack (1962) – 54 weeks at number one.

12. *After the National Coal Board's decision to close some 20 pits, half the nation's miners go on strike. Protracted confrontations between police, flying pickets and miners ensue.*

13. *The prices of cigarettes, petrol, beer, spirits, road tax and take-away food are raised in Nigel Lawson's first budget.*

14. Found to be in breach of the British Phonographic Industry's code of conduct, EMI are fined £10,000 for offering free albums to chart-return shops – seen as an inducement to boost chart placings.

15. *Thriller* becomes the best selling record of all time. With over 30 million copies sold, and estimated to be shipping another million every 4½ days, it accounts for over 10% of CBS' entire income. They disclose that a follow-up album, *Victory*, ready for some time, has been shelved until sales begin to fall off.

17. Howard Jones' debut album, *Human's Lib*, enters the UK chart at number one. The following week it stays there, fending off The Style Council's debut, *Cafe Bleu* – in at number two.

18. *Oxford win the boat race – postponed for 24 hours after Cambridge hit a moored barge and wrote off their £7000 boat during a practice run.*

23. *Sarah Tisdall, a Foreign Office Clerk, is imprisoned for six months after admitting she leaked secret documents to* The Guardian *newspaper concerning the arrival of Cruise missiles.*

24. Motown's 302nd British hit, 'Hello' by Lionel Richie, displaces Nena at the top of the UK singles chart.

30. *Anti-apartheid organisations protest against the Rugby Football Union's decision to tour South Africa. A few days later, 17-year-old Zola Budd, unofficial world record breaking 5000 metres runner, is granted a British passport to allow her to compete in the Olympic games.*

31. Country rocker Kenny Loggins has the new number one single in America – the title track from the film *Footloose*. Back at the top of the UK album list after over four months – *Can't Slow Down* by Lionel Richie.

LIONEL RICHIE

Freez and Haysi Fantayzee confirm their dissolution. Bassist Colin Ferguson leaves H_2O, drummer Carmine Appice leaves Ozzy Osbourne's band (replaced by Tommy Aldridge), and Ray Sawyer leaves Dr. Hook. Peter Christopherson and Geoff Rushton leave Psychic TV to start Coil, and former Japan bassist Mick Karn joins ex-Bauhaus singer Peter Murphy in a new group project. Philthy Phil Taylor quits Motorhead and three new men come in to support sole survivor Lemmy – Pete Gill (ex-Saxon, drums), Phil Campbell (ex-Persian Risk, guitar) and Wurzel (no pedigree disclosed, guitar). Mick Jagger becomes a father again – to the daughter of Jerry Hall – and Annie Lennox gets married to a German Hare Krishna named Rhada.

APRIL 84

1. On the eve of his 45th birthday, soul giant Marvin Gaye, whose voice and compositions helped to create and define the distinctive Motown sound in the Sixties, is shot dead by his father, a retired minister, during a family argument at the latter's Los Angeles home.

4. *The Government announce plans to reduce the number of job centres from 1000 to 350.*

4. *A total of 59 women are arrested after bailiffs and police clear protesters from their 2½ year old camp outside Greenham Common.*

5. *The Civil Aviation Authority give Virgin Records boss Richard Branson the go-ahead to start Virgin Atlantic Airlines, providing cheap trans-Atlantic flights.*

7. In the second such case in a month, WEA Records are fined £6000 by the BPI for unethical practices.

9. *Renewed violence outside pits in Nottinghamshire and Yorkshire precedes NUM leader Arthur Scargill's refusal to hold a pithead ballot on the strike.*

10. *Stars Shirley MacLaine and Jack Nicholson win Oscars at the annual Academy Awards ceremony as* Terms Of Endearment *collects most major awards – including Best Film, Best Director and Best Adapted Screenplay.*

12. The Home Office reveals that plans are under consideration to legalise pirate radio stations before the end of the year.

14. Emulating its predecessor, Volume 2 of *Now That's What I Call Music*, a compilation double album, reaches number one in Britain.

15. *Comedian Tommy Cooper, 62, collapses and dies onstage during a live television show.*

16. *MI5 counter espionage officer Michael Bettaney is sentenced to 23 years imprisonment after being found guilty of offering information to the KGB.*

17. *Shots fired at demonstrators from a window of the Libyan People's Bureau in St. James Square, London, kill policewoman Yvonne Fletcher. All Libyan officials are subsequently ordered to leave the country as Britain breaks off diplomatic relations.*

21. Michael Jackson is bumped off the top of the US album chart by the movie sountrack *Footloose*. The new number one single is 'Against All Odds' by Phil Collins.

PHIL COLLINS

22. *President Reagan visits China to meet political leaders and discuss mutual concern over Soviet military expansion.*

26. Jazz bandleader Count Basie dies of pancreatic cancer in a Florida hospital, aged 79.

27. Elton John and Lech Walesa exchange autographs and chat about computers, politics and soccer after the former's concert in Gdansk.

Ian Gillan, who quit Black Sabbath last month, is singer in the re-formed Deep Purple – also featuring Ritchie Blackmore, Ian Paice, Jon Lord and Roger Glover, a line-up which originally dissolved in summer 1973. Ex-Thin Lizzy duo Phil Lynott and Brian Downey form a new five piece group, Grand Slam; ex-Motorhead pair Phil Taylor and Brian Robertson join Chris Glenn (ex-MSG) and Pete French (ex-Cactus) in a new project; and ex-Fun Boy Three singers Lynval Golding and Neville Staples join former Selector singer Pauline Black in Sunday Best. The re-vamped Cure embark on their first UK tour in two years, and Nick Cave & The Cavemen make their debut. After only a few weeks, John Wetton returns to Asia in place of Greg Lake. Pink Floyd's Roger Waters launches his solo career, while Mick Jagger starts work on his first solo album. Hard living rock 'n' roller Jerry Lee Lewis, 48, marries his sixth wife, sometime country and gospel singer Kerrie Lynn McCarver, 21.

MAY 84

1. Mick Fleetwood, drummer and founder of Fleetwood Mac, reportedly files for bankruptcy in America, with debts said to total two-and-a-half million pounds.

3. *With Glue sniffers dying at a rate of one every five days, the Home Secretary announces plans to ban the sale of solvents to children under 16.*

4. *Diana Dors, actress and media personality, dies aged 52.*

5. 'The Reflex' by Duran Duran becomes Britain's best selling single.

8. *The Soviet Union pulls out of the forthcoming Olympic Games because of "chauvinist sentiments and anti-Soviet hysteria" displayed by the Americans. Other Communist countries, including Vietnam and East Germany, follow their lead.*

9. *During traditional pre-game Locality Familiarisation, a Spurs supporter is shot dead in a Brussels bar. Two more are shot and wounded, over 150 arrested.*

19. The Bob Marley hit compilation *Legend* enters the UK chart at number one; the Human League's **Hysteria** at number three.

BOB MARLEY

23 *NUM and NCB leaders break off their first peace settlement talks within an hour of meeting, unable to resolve basic differences. Clashes between pickets and police escalate in intensity and frequency, as the miners' strike enters its twelfth week.*

26 New top US single is 'Let's Hear It For The Boy' by Deniece Williams, from the *Footloose* soundtrack – still the best selling album.

28. *Comedian Eric Morecambe dies, aged 58.*

A month of career re-launches: Ex-Jam man Bruce Foxton plays his first solo dates; Marc Almond and David Sylvian, former leaders of Soft Cell and Japan respectively, re-emerge as solo artists; ex-Squeeze frontmen, Difford and Tilbrook, return as a duo; former Undertones Mickey Bradley and Damian O'Neill unveil their new group, Eleven. Samson split up. Madness and Stiff Records sever their relationship after an unbroken run of 18 hit singles.

JUNE 84

2. 'Wake Me Up Before You Go Go' takes Wham! to the top of the UK singles chart for the first time.

2 *Margaret Thatcher greets South African Prime Minister Pieter Botha at Chequers.*

4 *President Reagan visits London for talks with Margaret Thatcher, following a three day visit to Ireland.*

9 Cyndi Lauper has the best selling US single, 'Time After Time'.

10 *England's footballers beat Brazil for the first time, 2-0.*

12 *Over 1000 die during a Sikh uprising at the Golden Temple in Amritsar.*

16 'Two Tribes' by Frankie Goes To Hollywood enters the UK singles chart at number one. Duran Duran's 'The Reflex' rises to the top of the US singles list.

18 *Over 100 arrests are made during the month's worst confrontation between police and NUM pickets, outside the Orgreave coking plant near Sheffield.*

20 As part of an extensive European tour, Stevie Wonder plays Britain for the first time in years.

22. *Virgin Atlantic, owned by Virgin Records boss Richard Branson, makes its first flight: Gatwick to New Jersey for £99.*

30 Huey Lewis & The News have the best selling US album, *Sports*. Ex-Pink Floyder Roger Waters plays his first solo concerts, backed by Eric Clapton among others. Robert Smith leaves The Banshees to concentrate on The Cure. John Carruthers, formerly of Clock DVA, replaces him. Former Yazoo singer Alison Moyet launches her solo career.

JULY 84

5 *Alhaji Dikko, former Transport Minister, is kidnapped outside his Bayswater home, drugged and bundled into a crate, ready to be transported back to Nigeria. Together with three other men, he is discovered by security officers at Stanstead Airport.*

7 'Relax' by Frankie Goes To Hollywood, now back up to number two, overhauls the Human League's 'Don't You Want Me' and Culture Club's 'Karma Chameleon' to become Britain's best selling single of the Eighties. In America, 'When Doves Cry' by Prince takes over as number one single; Bruce Springsteen has the number one album, *Born In The USA*.

7 *After the driest weather since the 1976 drought, water restrictions are imposed in some parts of Britain.*

8 *John McEnroe and Martina Navratilova take the singles trophies at Wimbledon.*

11 *The pound sinks to a new low of $1.32, and unemployment figures still show an underlying upward trend.*

14 The Bob Marley compilation *Legend* displaces Michael Jackson's long running *Making Of Thriller* at the top of the video chart, as the album begins its tenth week at number one.

19 *Walter Mondale is selected as the Democrats' presidential challenge to Ronald Reagan.*

21 Status Quo play their final gig, at Milton Keynes Bowl.

STATUS QUO

22 *Dockers resume work following a 21 day national strike.*

29 *The Olympic Games begin in Los Angeles.*

30 *13 are killed and at least 40 seriously injured in a rush hour train derailment near Falkirk, Scotland.*

Bob Dylan returns to the British stage, for gigs at Newcastle and Wembley; ELO front man Jeff Lynne launches his solo career; Sonja Kristina and Darryl Way resurrect Curved Air! Frankie Goes To Hollywood becomes the only act to hit platinum with its first two singles – both million sellers. Laser 558, a US backed pirate radio station moored in the North Sea, claims 9 million listeners in Europe. The Belle Stars split up.

ROCK

FRANKIE GOES TO HOLLYWOOD

Marvin Gaye was shot, Stevie Wonder and Bob Dylan came to Europe, and Van Morrison moved into London's Dominion Theatre, almost permanently. Compared to the media barrage surrounding Frankie Goes To Hollywood, these things might never have happened. Nobody could deny the potency of cheap publicity.

Frankie, though heavily indebted to banned videos for their success, essentially exploited all the oldest tricks in the book with an ease which bordered on the fatuous.

Effortlessly, they goaded Radio One dee-jay Mike Read into apoplexy simply by singing the word "come", and swiftly bustled to number one with 'Relax'. The accompanying video, about gay sex, was banned. . .and Frankie went to Hollywood.

As spring turned into summer and the West Indian batsmen began to develop a healthy appetite for the English bowling, Frankie issued 'Two Tribes', a devil of a din which this time shifted the emphasis from sex to politics.

The video, depicting Superpower hostility in terms of mud-wrestling, was previewed in fragments, cannily offering just enough to convey the notion that it was 'controversial'. The record vaulted to number one, while the video was 'discussed' on late-night TV. This was lucrative, a great scam and probably pop art.

So, have we learned anything in 25 years? Try the following: (1) Groups are made and not born. (2) The most commonplace news item

becomes treason when it is converted into pop, especially when aided and abetted by video. (3) Producers can and will make hit records. (4) People in the pop business think sex and politics are 'sensitive' subjects, and therefore presumably have a mental age measurable in single figures. (5) Paul Morley knows all this.

Frankie's logistical back-up was impressive. Producer Trevor Horn regularly turns out records which sound like continents cracking open, and

Frankie's discs were no exception. Morley, the group's irritant-theorist, blathered opaquely in words which only sociologists could understand. Sociologists accordingly filled many a column inch about him and the rather sordid Frankie Goes To Hollywood, and before long a 'pop phenomenon' had been created. Thanks to 'emerging technology', pop phenomena are no longer spontaneous freaks of nature, but the logical outcome of statistical probability. Human error? Who needs it.

But hold on there. It was Bob Dylan, now rather dated and increasingly peripheral after all these years, who observed rather acidly that most of the people who'd sprawled in the mud at Woodstock (1969) were now 'probably all in computers''. What he meant was, he is paralysed by techno-fear and is thus almost completely fossilised. Ironically, Dylan is still singing about nuclear war, political corruption and the lack of faith in this garbage-strewn world. These are quite serious topics, and strangely fashionable with today's young people. But Dylan has signally failed to make suppressible videos, so his message will remain mere nostalgia for a thinning-haired generation who went on the *original* CND marches. Lesson: moan all you like about upstart technowizardry, but *do it on MTV*.

Meanwhile, life went on and some people sold records and others didn't. Mainly, the year under surveillance offered lots of bits and pieces, but nothing as loud and ugly as punk. That might have been veering too close to creativity. Chaps aiming for a career in pop these days have it pretty soft. It's all been written down, analysed and anthologised, and even if you can't read, it's perfectly obvious that all you have to do is steal. People like Re-Flex, Howard Jones and APB are interchangeable, biodegradable dollops like those things you put in the cistern to make the water turn blue. Listen once and it's gone. Listen twice and you might as well be dead. Much the same might be said for The Lotus Eaters, Nena, The Thompson Twins, The Icicle Works and Nik Kershaw, blithering idiots to a man. Sadly, the list is endless.

Hell, it's been a *listless* twelvemonth, as almost any jaded old soak in the trade will

tell you for the price of a small Heineken. An ominous portent was the further advance on British television of programmes for 'young people'. *Ear Say* wasn't too bad despite Nicky Horne, but *Eight Days A Week* was fronted by a man in a chair and allowed waffling Bob Geldof into the studio *twice*, while numerous Euro-style satellite spectaculars only emphasised the shattering paucity of electrifying new talent. Most fantastic of all was the return of Steve Taylor, presumed dead of embarrassment after his *Loose Talk* debacle. No such luck! Back he came with the incredible youth talk-in *Crying Out Loud*, a spurious forum for the debating of 'young people's issues' populated exclusively by siblings of TV executives. Taylor is obviously half-witted, and will presumably end up as Director General of the BBC.

It was on *Ear Say* that wasp-tongued Phil Oakey of the slothful and overpaid Human League announced that there was now too much pop on television. He was absolutely right, though that didn't alter the fact that the much-anticipated League comeback album, an overpackaged affair called *Hysteria*, was anaemic and moribund. Never was such a limited grasp of how to work a computer hailed so sycophantically by so many deaf hacks eager to partake of Virgin Records' hospitality.

So did anyone do well, '83-'84? Wham!, charmingly idiotic as ever and wearing positively Nubian suntans, emerged from the old Tin Pan Alley standby The Legal Wrangle with a chart-topping single called 'Wake Me Up Before You Go-Go', and could thus claim a 'comeback'. Here, they had been greatly assisted by unscrupulous biz-wiz Simon Napier-Bell, the living embodiment of that old adage about old tricks which always work. Wham!, though utterly farcical, at least had the good sense to enlist good old-fashioned Blag on their behalf. In this they could be admired, though no further.

Something similar might be said of uncouth Spandau Ballet, a bunch of louts who got slick and struck oil (it is said they also struck Frankie Goes To Hollywood, who had disparaged them in print). The Spand's motto might be "if you've got it, flog it". There's something endearing about the Spands, nonetheless – maybe it's Tony Hadley's foghorn

SPANDAU BALLET

croon, or perhaps the group's exquisite instinctive grasp of kitsch. Keep it up, lads!

As usual, quite a few things stayed exactly the same, and I don't just mean hype. For instance, the 'new' album from Jerry Dammers and his Special AKA remained in a permanent state of being unfinished. The project began shortly after the Berlin airlift, and seemed at one point to be destined to run until the next vinyl shortage. Why put off until tomorrow what you could leave until the day after?

Also completely unchanging were the drab New Order, the world's worthiest rock group. Armed with backing tapes, millions of lights and a solitary sequencer riff, these faceless artisans managed to lodge the impenetrably forgettable 'Blue Monday' into the UK chart for months on end. Later, they replaced it with 'Thieves Like Us', though unstinting forensic analysis could discern no difference between it and its predecessor. Despite occasional flashes of brilliance in their murky past, New Order remain one of the great unsolved crimes.

Personally, I'd throw The Smiths in with them and lose the key, pronto. Does their shared Mancunian provenance have anything to do with it? By the time the over-inflated Smiths released their droning single 'God I'm A Miserable Bastard Now', even erstwhile fans were forced to confess that if singer Morrissey had learned another chord, they were damned if they could notice it. Morrissey, flowers sticking out of his rump like a Rampton inmate starring in his own imaginary one-man talent show, was quite simply

baffling. His supporters shifted uncomfortably in their seats and insisted that Morrissey did jolly good interviews. Margaret Thatcher probably mixes a demon Tequila Sunrise, but so what?

If we discount genuine nonentities like Specials/Funboy Three, The Colour Field (nearly as interesting as the average crime prevention officer) and Kitchenware Records prodigies Prefab Sprout (dyslexic Scrabble), we are left with almost nothing of interest. . .in a *whole year*. Bronski Beat seemed okay, while the Kane Gang weren't too bad either. Neither offered much hope of longevity, though, and much the same went for hopefuls like Bourgie Bourgie and Lloyd Cole And The Commotions, who turned out to be a false start and a feeble pun, respectively. Most people grew thoroughly sick of hearing about Boy George's voice and Duran Duran's enviable drug exploits.

Incredible to relate, it was the Americans who provided the most fun to be had while stupefied. Jason And The Scorchers came barrelling out of Hicksville, Tennessee like an electric twister, guitars blazing and invoking the ghosts of Gram Parsons and George Patton in about equal measure. They played several London shows, and each time left the audience for dead. Meanwhile, Georgia boys R.E.M. once referred to as an IRS tax dodge, made an album called *Reckoning* which wasn't as good as their debut LP *Murmur*, but then played some dates which reaffirmed that they'd re-established contact with the sort of Right Stuff unseen in a decade or more.

THE ROLLING STONES

This was both rare and encouraging. We'd like more, please.

Also American, also plugging into a few home truths, were Womack & Womack an outcrop of the endless Womack clan who'd never played live before but suddenly found they had a hit single called 'Love Wars'. The album of the same name looked like making its way into quite a few end-of-year favourite discs lists, judging by the glutinous reverence with which 'serious critics' greeted the pair's London performances. This wasn't the Womacks' fault, though, and they seem sussed enough to handle it.

Other older hands took advantage of the absence of convincing young upstarts to re-establish themselves. Queen, with Fred Mercury looking more like a Turkish waiter by the minute, came back with 'Radio Ga-Ga' and 'I Want To Break Free', both very respectable performances for people of their age. Roger Taylor appeared on every quiz show known to man.

Not nearly so old but still with plenty to prove was Paul Weller. His Style Council project weathered a firestorm of ridicule from certain quarters, and by the time they'd played some impressive British dates and released the convincing 'My Ever Changing Moods', Weller could afford a malicious smirk. America's *Soul Train* show offered the Council a slot, and history was rewritten. Scrap the cappuccino, though.

Another turn-up for the books was The Rolling Stones' surprise return to the limelight with the *Under Cover* album in late '83. The album was patchily impressive, greatly boosted by Julien Temple's rivetting video for the 'Under Cover' single. At a stroke, this illuminated most of the things lacking in the average glib pop video—it had a plot, it felt like a real movie, it had wit, imagination, several distinct characters and a stiff shot of violence. It was brilliant, and the BBC loathed it. It was somehow sad that it took the 40 year-old delinquents to teach the self-satisfied video industry some basic home truths.

But video is another country and they do things differently there (mostly by recording live shows badly and selling them at £20 each without compunction). Bruce Springsteen, a suspicious old rocker, toyed with the idea of making his very first promo video for his hit 'Dancing In The Dark'. Meanwhile, his *Born In The USA* album returned Bruce to his rock roots with a vengeance, and may well have been his best album to date with or without video-aid.

So far, the immense potential of video has been stunted by turning it mostly into a promotional treadmill. Clichés are what count, while genuine flair for narrative or visual texture make you Art House and therefore unbankable.

But time is short and I must rest my case. It's a year later, but I'm afraid we don't know any better. Once the element of surprise has been lost, your only options are recycle or be damned. Hmmmm.

ADAM SWEETING

BRUCE SPRINGSTEEN

QUEEN

REGGAE

July 1983: things look good. Bob Marley's *Confrontation* is still kicking around the pop charts after peaking at number five. On the bookshelves the demand for deep roots literature is ensuring that several worthy works are earning a decent living. In discoland all the best turntables are wearing the near perfect summer style of 'Go Deh Yaka', Monyaka's seamless mix of reggae syncopation and hard funk urgency. Yellowman is adding dates to a sold out UK tour...

The world, it appears, is the reggae musician's oyster—the same as it seems around this time every year, when the warm weather and pre-carnival *sensi*bilities can cause even the more than casual observer to float blissfully on the bright side.

Look again, look deeper.

Marley is even further out in front. The books, two of which are Bob Marley biographies, are tributes to better days. The hip kids' reaction to Monyaka's follow up, 'Reggae-Matic-Funk', showed that the fad had passed, while Yellowman was simply a repackaging of the same rhythms and delivery styles of last year and the year before, breaking new ground only in sheer offensiveness.

However, this bizarre looking albino dee-jay was to have a strong effect on the Jamaican music industry during the coming year.

Britain, where the majority of reggae is ultimately aimed, appeared to welcome him in a near frenzy. True to say that this was from a following largely too young to know better, a media fascinated by his physical appearance and sexual bravado, and in turn a major label (CBS) offered him a deal, but it was enough for the Caribbean power bases to shrug off the need for any radical progress with conviction. What the UK wanted was more of before.

Producers settled back into those comfortable old grooves, and new blood was moulded to fit, not encouraged to develop. The record buyer, through lack of any alternative with authentic J.A. credentials,

GREGORY ISAACS

accepted this as the right stuff. The circle was unbroken so the thrones were secure.

A couple of old masters put this stagnant state of affairs to good use. Johns Holt and Osbourne drew on experience and came up with 'Police In Helicopter' and 'Water Pumping' respectively, class albums standing out from the pack and proving that this particular style was best left to the singers and writers that understood it properly. Horses for courses.

A few did try to move on. Gregory Isaacs flirted with different rhythm patterns on *Out Deh*, but didn't seem happy (this might have something to do with his spell in chokey on gun and drugs charges, which concurred with the set's recording), opting for a finished article which mainly sounded like *Night Nurse Vol. II*. Dennis Brown's *The Prophet Rides Again* concluded that a soul/reggae blend meant one side of each but nothing with true conviction. On the success side, Bob Andy (remember Bob and Marcia?) came out of a five year retirement to express disgust

at the current scene and, aided by two fluent American musicians, cut *Friends*, a multi-faceted, gloriously forward looking album. Eek-A-Mouse continued his vocal adventures through both straight and scat to critical and peer group acclaim (he was the name most likely to be dropped by any young toaster asked

about influences) that did not translate to sales figures. The poets hung in there, a compilation album *Word Soun' 'Ave Power* lived up to its title, but the horrific politically motivated murder of Michael Smith (August 16, 1983) while underlining the importance of their work, also seemed to slow it down a little.

THE SPECIAL AKA

These were exceptions though. Jamaican reggae was cruising on autopilot; it was across the Atlantic that some serious shake-ups were going on.

The hip hop scene, bubbling under for some time, had burst through as the fashionable expression of black pride. Youths who two years ago would've been following sound systems, humping speaker boxes, were now donning track suits and baseball caps to body pop for tourists' loose change. Instant stardom with no loss of face.

The roots market was entering something of a decline, as youngsters discovered hip hop was more fun, and to each new generation Jamaica became further away with the South Bronx now showing at a cinema near you. The scene became more self-protective and insular as a result. Widening the already existing split between the cultural adopter and adapter.

Laurel and Hardy, two young London dee-jays typified the specialist reaction to the shifting beat.

In early '83, their style, which leant in equal amounts on Eastwood and Saint and their British birthright, had critics, public and a major label (CBS again) urging them on. By the end of that year they had left the record company by mutual agreement, performed a string of dismal dates backed up a superb but utterly wasted band, split with their manager and are now virtually unknown outside of a couple of South London sound systems and the aptly named Fashion Records.

The excuse that there was no market for them held no water, for even as I write the record

that everybody wants to do well is Smiley Culture's 'Cockney Translation'.

The UK dubmasters on the other hand, rose to the challenge. The likes of Groucho Smeckle, Mikey Dread and The Mad Professor revelled in the new technology and techniques – after all, it was only a much improved form of what had been filched from them years ago. Their explorations resulted in some electronic masterpieces, often so left-of-centre they became proficiency exercises rather than commercial propositions, but the beat went on.

One man who had been making such journeys for

years, Adrian Sherwood, was so taken by the sound that his 'Watch Yourself' by London gals Akabu became the first British recording to be released on Tommy Boy, New York's seminal hip hop firm.

At the time Sherwood said, "I don't care if it (reggae) shakes itself free or not. I'm not

EEK-A-MOUSE

carrying any banner for reggae." Savage words from the force behind Creation Rebel, New Age Steppers and The Crytuff Dub Encounter series, which featured Prince Far-I, the year's second tragic victim of Jamaica's political gunmen.

Steel Pulse, too, continued on a global perspective. The group touched home base long enough to record and release *Earth Crisis* and play a three week tour, serving to remind the British public of what they're missing, then it was back to Africa and America where they are appreciated.

In mainstream pop culture, reggae was becoming increasingly evident. Several big name producers were experimenting with reggae based rhythms and recording techniques while UB40's *Labour Of Love*, a collection of covers of classics was a fond gaze backwards at their rude boy beginnings, and their best selling album to date. The Special AKA felt the time was right to (at last) come out of the studio with *In The Studio*, and The Beat's passing was mourned as *What Is Beat* took

ASWAD

over from *Special Beat Service* as the band's epitaph.

Although this situation looked encouraging, it was really already established acts following up the trends of the past year rather than new reggae acts that stepped forward. The barrier there it seemed, still lay in a failure to understand the importance of as high a profile as possible in the pop machinery. Half a dozen brief interviews would not be enough.

Dennis Bovell's Dub Band tried to capitalize on their live successes and put out their first single, a light enough tune that died through lack of exposure. Marley siblings The Melody Makers released 'I Met Her On A Rainy Day' but suffered the same fate for much the same reasons, even Culture Club's Steve Levine's poppy production counted for nothing. Musical Youth were growing up quickly, and as they became less frequent on kids' TV so the sales of their second set *Different Style* tailed off. Linton Kwesi Johnson re-signed with Island, recorded his best album, featuring crisp backing from Bovell and Co., yet had to blow out a gig through disappointing advance ticket sales.

Unsurprisingly, it was Aswad who for so long had been the best that reggae had to offer – anywhere – who came to terms with this.

Now a trio after the departure of percussionist Levi and back under Chris Blackwell's wing, *Live And Direct* and *Chasing For The Breeze* showed them to have lost none of their edge, and recent TV appearances by Drummie (on *Eight Days A Week* and *Pop Quiz*) bore witness to a change in approach.

Front man Brinsley Forde told *Time Out*, "What reggae artists must do, is make sure they get into the homes of all the people – so that they *know* the artist."

That's what it takes, and with any luck more will follow the Grove Warriors' lead and realise that 25 minutes of buffoonery on a show like *Pop Quiz* is just a grain of sand in the grand scheme of a lasting career.

In the meantime, the stream of Bob Marley albums, singles, books and videos will keep things ticking over, and I'll continue to look forward with the kind of optimism that leaves a mug of cocoa out for Santa every Christmas eve.

LLOYD BRADLEY

ELECTRO

You probably recall the scene in *Annie Hall* where Woody Allen magics Marshall McLuhan from nowhere to set the adjacent pseud in the cinema queue straight.

Witnessing various conversations this year there were times when I dreamt of being able to conjure up *Private Eye's* Heath to draw one of his deflating Great Bores Of Our Time cartoons on the nearest wall, the caption to read: "Rock 'n' roll was great while it lasted may it rest in peace but youngsters these days they're not the slightest bit interested in buying

their hatred for their parents culture should have to suffer the nagging worry that their own kids might prove to be just as contrary.

Youth, meanwhile, was simply getting on with what was really the most obvious thing to do in the circumstances. Bred in classrooms where every other pupil owned a computer and spending many glazed hours at the consoles of pocket space games, kids were simply translating these experiences and fantasies into good old-fasioned dance, mime and music, enacting robotic dance

Clinton in a dance-club somewhere between New York and Neptune. Even at the height of that record's success in the States, when it was selling some 650,000 copies *a week,* Silverman, producer Arthur Baker, dee-jay/rapper Afrika Bambaataa and keyboard player John Robie couldn't have begun to have imagined the dimensions of the thing they were sparking off. Judged against the standards of some of the synthetic funk symphonies that have followed in its wake, 'Planet Rock' sounds positively prosaic these days. The electro

would tell you are physical impossibilities on a conventional kit; not to mention that they're smashed out at the kind of volumes that would make the average thunderstorm sound like lambs kissing. One of the most appealing aspects of electro is that it combines the pulse-racing thrill of virtuoso performances without simplicity and comparative egalitarianism. Anyone with strong musical instincts can learn how to do it in a fraction of the time it would take to perfect technique on conventional instruments. A tour around the backstreets of Brixton would show DIY rapping and scratching to electro discs challenging toasting as the favoured bedroom activity for the hip British black.

A measure of the vitality and importance of electro has been the level of vitriol and passionate controversy it's stirred up. If the essential requisite for a new, genuinely significant musical movement, be it be-bop or hip hop, is the capacity to make the shit hit the fan, electro has hit the stools for six. Like punk it has drawn howls of outrage from the guardians of the temple of mainstream conservatism, obsessed as they are with their court rituals and worship of the Gods of Worthiness, Dues-Paying and Musicianship.

One of *NME's* soul-boy writers summed up the sourpusses' mood with the words: "Electro looks like being the worst thing to hit music since Elvis Aaron Presley enlisted in 1958, it is such an easily formulated and ingested set of contrivances. Much of it mouths meaningless piffle, uses baby language and worn FX etc etc. . ." (Why the soul fraternity consider "baby language" and all round high spirited silliness respectable in George Clinton and not elsewhere is something you're probably scratching your head over as much as I am).

Tom Silverman had the following conversation at a jazz-funk marathon in Luton: "I asked 'What is the problem with my music and how come

AFRIKA BAMBAATAA

records they're too busy starting intercontinental nuclear war with their Sinclair home computers and playing Pacman with etc etc. . ."

The idea of that youth's obsession with the machinery of the electronic age was likely to soon turn the very idea of music into an obsolete, rusting heap of conceptual junk wasn't uncommon, and though a far from stupid notion, probably owed more to rampant paranoia than it did to perspicacity. It was, after all, only natural justice that the generation who defined themselves by the extremity of

gestures to the thunderous soundtrack of a printed circuit on overload. Technology hadn't swept music away, just changed it.

A couple of years ago the South Bronx's rapping scene was running around in depressingly predictable circles, its vacant solipsism mired in a dearth of musical inspiration. When Tom Silverman released 'Planet Rock' on his Tommy Boy label it slipped into the needs of the time like a crate of alcohol at a flaging party, pointing the way forward to a new electric synthesis of Kraftwerk and

movement has proven to be young urban black America's own punk. It's an analogy that shouldn't be drawn too literally (especially as it's questionable to measure a largely black culture against the yardstick of a white one), but the blinding intensity of some of the music and frenetic pace of musical events have thrown up parallels that are impossible to ignore.

Machines like the Linn Drum, the Clap Trap and the Oberheim DMX have made it possible to create drum patterns that even the sharpest session drummers people at Mafia-controlled marathons like this won't play it?' The guy said it wasn't soul music. I said 'What's your idea of soul music?' and he said 'Marvin Gaye, do I have to say more?' I said 'Well, maybe you have to say a little more. . .' "

While nobody would deny that much of the genre's output has been unintelligently mimetic, numbingly formulaic and just plain simple-minded, the best records have possessed a power and beauty that's been nothing less than awesome (check Bambaataa's titanic 'Looking For The Perfect Beat' or Keith LeBlanc's 'Malcolm X' blitzkrieg). Even the more run-of-the-mill releases like Sucker MC's 'Run DMC', Davey DMX's 'One For The Treble' and Rama's 'Don't Want You To Be' kick their way out of the Tannoys with a boundless exuberance.

It's the sheer *physicality* of the music that's been its most vital quality. The sound of electro is an invisible but almost palpable material careening through the oxygen like storm waves beating mercilessly at the foot of a cliff. This is the reason producers and mixing engineers have enjoyed such an important (and frequently authorial) role.

Records like Two Sisters' 'High Noon' (Raul Rodriguez), Beatmaster's 'Lipservice' (Keith LeBlanc), Time Zone's 'Wild Style' (Bambaataa and Bernard Zekri), Herbie Hancock's 'Rockit' (Bill Laswell and Michael Beinhorn aka Material), Cybotron's 'Techno City' (Ben Grosse), Shannon's 'Let The Music Play' and 'Give Me Tonight' and Filliponio's 'All 'Arrembaggio' (all Mark Liggett and Chris Barbosa) were minefields of sound; sudden detonations screamed blissfully at the listener from all directions over rhythms bearing the stunning impact of multiple hammer attacks.

Pumpkin's 'Here Comes That Beat' used studio gadgetry to create the effect of plate glass shattering six inches from the head amid Sly Stone references and the usual gamut of rap and scratch methods. More traditional instrumentation could find space too. Kurtis Blow's 'Nervous' slid to ecstasy on a peach of a Nile Rodgers soundalike guitar break and Steps Ahead's 'Radio Active' used saxophones to sound like The Thing stomping on the wimp-like corpse of jazz-funk.

Bass guitars weren't uncommon either.

Despite the music's embrace by young urban blacks, the involvement of whites like Baker, Silverman, Laswell and Man Parrish, plus the open acknowledgement of Kraftwerk as an influence, has doubtless led to suspicions in some quarters that electro is somehow not a truly *black* music. This is a ridiculously myopic observation, of course, because the music stands unambiguously in the funk tradition begun by James Brown in the mid-Sixties, its long dance workouts based on a startling sense of syncopation with a sense of fun and puerility clearly borrowed from George Clinton.

Like James Brown, electro turns every instrument into a drum. When Afrika Bambaataa picked his name and called his street gangs The

THE SYSTEM

Zulu Nation the choice was far from accidental. When Davey DMX named himself after the eponymous machine he probably wasn't thinking of microchips so much as 'drum kit' – albeit in a radical new form. If Africa is the home of the drum, electro has led to a re-emphasis on the African, percussive elements in the black tradition. Many 12-inchers have been little more than a rap spun over a hefty percussion workout.

What's probably confused people is the undeniable European element, though the idea of Bronx dwellers

carrying around Kraftwerk tapes in their ghetto blasters is less surprising when you remember that Dusseldorf's finest lifted black funk rhythms for their computer games. One of the healthiest aspects of the movement is the sense of cross-breeding it embodies, New York and Europe colliding somewhere south of Greenland. Whodini flew to Germany to record with Conny Plank for 'Rap Machine', Teutonic punks Die Töten Hosen collaborated with rapper Freddy Love for 'Hip Hop Bommi Bop' (a great record). Trevor Horn's Art of Noise reached number one in the US dance charts with 'Into Battle' and New Order funked out with Arthur Baker on 'Confusion'.

Meanwhile Baker's importance retreated long ago. His Temptations-ish 'Cheap Thrills' get-together with

fellow Bostonians Planet Patrol was an unsuccessful sop to the soul snobs and his work on Loleatta Holloway's 'Crash Goes Love' was just tarted-up Hi-Energy that peers like Carol Lynn Townes' '99½' knocked into the drain.

Two of my favourites in '84 were Shahid's 'Future Shock' and Grandmaster Funk's exquisite 'Don't Stop', long, slow and dirty funk grooves in the tradition of Clinton's 'Atomic Dog' (retrodden brilliantly as 'Dog Talk', a long rap by K-9 Corporation).

Special badges of commendation went to

Morgan Khan for his Streetsounds label's packaging of expensive US imports into the Electro series of LPs at affordable prices. These were big sellers in Britain, as were Rock Steady Crew's rotten 'Hey You etc' (though the album wasn't half as bad) and Break Machine's 'Breakdance Party' and 'Street Dance' singles on the small Record Shack label. Newtrament's fab 'London Bridge Is Falling Down' was Ladbroke Grove gone New York.

With the sudden rash of 'breaksploitation' movies reaching the UK by the summer it was obvious hip-hop was becoming big-business. As far as the specialist import shops were concerned, electro was about to be replaced by jazz in the dance floor hipsters' affections – "We're waiting for the Stan Getz twelve inchers," one assistant told me. By this time electro was already solidly ensconced in the mainstream, with everybody who was anybody hiring a beatbox operative and pile of synths to revitalize their careers – done particularly brilliantly by Doctor John with 'Jet Set' (authentic New Orleans hip-hop!)

The sound of soul had become the sound of electronic music. Chic's 'Believer', Earth, Wind & Fire's 'Electric Universe' (incredibly dispensing with horns in favour of a bank of synths), 'Boy Wonder' Jackson's 'Wanna Be Startin' Somethin'', Tom Browne's 'Rockin' Radio' . . .hell, it's easier just to say *everybody* was using some kind of electronic angle except Womack & Womack.

It's impossible to separate the influence of Electro from seminal electric soul records like The System's 'You Are In My System' (their *Sweat* album was disgracefully never issued in the UK) and the Peech Boys' 'Don't Make Me Wait', but only the most dogmatic would see these two strands as anything other than closely linked siblings in any case.

What's important is that electricity has sparked life back into music, bringing a decisive end to the arid torpor created by the collapse of the new wave into glib, manipulative 'new pop' a few years back. And for that we should be eternally grateful.

LYNDEN BARBER

19

SOUL

It wasn't a glum year and it certainly wasn't a bad year – actually it was quite interesting in its way. But somehow, looking back, two things loom over it all. The selling and selling and selling and selling of Michael Jackson and the shocking losses in the month of April.

The month started as badly as it could. On April Fool's Day, one day short of his 45th birthday, Marvin Gaye was shot dead by his father, the emphatic final deed in a domestic quarrel. Later in the month, Count Basie, the great jazz bandleader, composer and pianist, died after illness as did Frank 'Machito' Grillo, the legendary Cuban bandleader who'd done so much over the years to popularise Latin American music in North America and Europe.

At the end of the month, on the 27th, Z.Z. Hill, a fine R&B singer in the deep South tradition, died as the result of a blood clot caused by a car crash some two months earlier. Hill's demise was particularly sad because for the past three years he'd enjoyed an Indian summer in his career since signing with Malaco, the Jackson, Mississippi label.

All four artists left a strong, long legacy of music. Three of them – Gaye, Machito, Basie – influenced musics outside their own field while Hill had become a frontrunner within a resurgent field of black American music returning for nourishment to its old R&B and blues roots. That field, of course, was just one of many subdivisions into which black American music, 'soul', call it what you will, is now split largely for marketing purposes.

Ten years ago the divisions, regional and stylistic, which had always been apparent had begun to polarise and as they did so they proliferated, splitting and splitting not unlike a cell reproducing itself. Disco was exemplified by the Jackson Five's 'Dancing Machine', Philly by The Three Degrees' 'When Will I See You Again', Miami soul by Betty Wright's 'Shoorah! Shoorah!' and Latimore's 'Let's

JAMES INGRAM

Straighten It Out', funk by The Ohio Players' 'Fire' and Kool & The Gang's 'Hollywood Swinging', jazz-funk, the New Jersey sound. . .the catalogue of 1974's soul strata goes on and on.

The success of Michael Jackson's *Thriller*, with its mix of pop-soul, ballads and rock became, not surprisingly, a blueprint for many, many more singers. This finely-judged potpourri of styles is well-illustrated in black music terms by Deniece Williams' album *Let's Hear It For The Boy*, a real something-for-everyone LP. The title track and hit single was the best song in the movie *Footloose*, thus satisfying the soundtrack buffs. 'Haunting Me' was a similarly chiselled dance song. There were delicately painted ballads. at which Williams is so adept, a couple of hard rock guitar solos (obligatory since Jackson's 'Beat It'), a piece of amusing hokum titled 'Blind Dating' and a sparsely-arranged gospel song 'Whiter Than Snow' for the born-again market. That analysis makes the album seem cold and calculating. It is never that and it's to Williams great credit that she holds it all together. Few attempted to please quite as many tastes as she. Some,

indeed, seemed hardly to be trying at all.

Donna Summer, Diana Ross and Ray Parker have been in artistic decline. Earth Wind & Fire have been resting, their *Electric Universe* outshined by their vocalist Philip Bailey's *'Continuation'* set. Chic is in mothballs with Nile Rodgers off producing rock stars (Bowie, Jagger) and Lionel Richie has assumed the mantle of the hottest new black act to have crossed over into the big bucks, white MOR market. Shalamar split, Howard Hewett, the group's best singer, still has the band's name (and a couple of new singers) while Jeffrey Daniels, beloved in Britain, roller-skates his way around a theatre in London in a 'musical', *Starlight Express*.

The most successful producer in the past couple of years has, inevitably, been Quincy Jones. With no new Michael Jackson LP to work on he's kept busy by helping James Ingram, one of his session singers and composers, to step forward. Ingram's *It's Your Night* album and duets with Patti Austin, herself a graduate of the QJ School of Excellence, were among the more memorable musical moments of the soul year.

Much of the music heard on

the black charts, however, sounded lazily written – a simple riff, hook or lyric idea spread over three or more minutes. Not as numb-brained as Duran Duran or plagiaristic as Wham! but not the most imaginative either.

In that context, the emergence of Linda and Cecil Womack from hugely-respected writers and producers to hit album makers with their impressive debut *Love Wars* and Bobby Womack's re-established position as a major soul artist with *The Poet II* (not as good as its predecessor, *The Poet*, but still several grooves above most albums of the year) were among the most positive aspects.

The Womacks Bobby and Cecil, as part of the family gospel group and of the Valentinos R&B band, have a pedigree stretching back well over two decades. Linda, Cecil's wife, is the daughter of the legendary Soul Stirrer gospel singer turned R&B singer and pop star Sam Cooke and genealogy does not come better than that. When one listens to the work of people list this, who've learned and honed their trade over many years, it throws into sharp relief the work of the many soul parvenus who emerge from time to time. This is why it is never sensible to write off a proven soul or R&B artist like George Clinton.

WOMACK & WOMACK

GEORGE CLINTON

In the last couple of years Clinton has been able to put behind him the dreadful financial and legal complications which bedevilled and disrupted his professional and personal life at the end of the Seventies. He's reclaimed his position as a hard-funk leader with the follow-up to *Computer Games*, *You Shouldn't-Nuf Bit Fish*, and with the P. Funk All-Stars' *Urban Dancefloor Guerrillas*. Just as Clinton's sidemen and close friends broke out of his musical stable, so Prince, he of the mighty *1999* double LP, has seen his Minneapolitan mates like Andre Cymone and Time make some headway.

Clinton, of course, has had a major effect on a whole generation of self-contained bands. Of the Parliament-Funkadelic contemporaries, Kool & The Gang have lasted the course well in later years by moving with great success into the smooth pop-soul market. The recruitment of James Taylor as singer and the knowing writing of Robert Bell and his band on the *In The Heart* LP added up to some of the cutest pop-soul of the year. Of the other post-Clinton hard-funk bands, Cameo, The Gap Band, Salve and Brass Construction have been the

most worthy this last year, especially Larry Blackmon's slimmed-down Cameo whose *She's Strange* LP re-established them after a couple of indifferent sets.

For some, it paid to leave proven bands. Jeffrey Osborne's second solo album, *Stay With Me Tonight*, justified his departure from LTD – the title track's bass-line was the most emphatic of the year. And *Don't Look Any Further*, Dennis Edwards' first work away from the Temptations, was much, much better than a lot of the pop music press would have us believe.

Jazz-funk and Brit-funk were pretty mediocre all year. In the former, the most interesting development was the appearance of the Japanese band Casiopea and the emergence of the young Icelandic group Mezzoforte. Bassist Bill Laswell's LP was clever, Stanley Clarke edged back to jazzier work, the Marsalis brothers, Wynton and Branford, built on their already astounding reputation, but Miles Davis's *Decoy* put the competition in its place. As a musical organiser and innovator, he's still clearly the master.

In Brit-funk, a term distastful to all British

musicians playing 'funk', the successful bands like Level 42 and Shakatak were off to the United States to make their fortunes or existed in another state, that of limbo. The most prominent figure was Phil Fearon, whose Galaxy records were very functional pop 'n' dance pieces while Loose Ends, I-Level and Second Image all broadened their appeal. Those members of Second Image who backed Womack & Womack on the couple's first ever British tour, however, did much to confirm one's suspicions that British musicians still lack the sensitivity, breadth of technical expertise and sheer adaptability to match the best American band players.

The most telling British records in the domestic marketplace were, in fact, the compilations – series like *Street Sounds*, *Dance Mix* and *Wired For Clubs* were all basically a throwback to the perennially popular 'Motown Chart-busters' bargains with the innovation of remixes, greater frequency and so on. Rather more valuable have been the proliferating re-releases on Kent, Ace and Charly of Various Artists albums covering a certain era or style, or LPs of a particular singer or group. Kent did *The*

Impressions, Ace *The Jive 5*, for example. An ambitious project to re-release a sequence of classic Atlantic soul albums which had long been unavailable got under way. Perhaps the only cautionary note to strike here is that this type of market could easily become flooded with 'rediscovered classics'.

It's also been a year when more and more folks rediscovered their gospel roots. In the US, where the majority of soul stars cut their teeth singing in choirs, this is a continuous process of spiritual rejuvenation. In Britain, the gospel phenomenon is new. Gospel is the one form of black music which white rock musicians, certainly in the UK, have been unable to plunder wholesale. Here, the music is found in many churches in the West Indian Communities of the bigger cities and its choirs have youthful fervour, power and exuberance. They've yet to throw up the truly outstanding solo voice – a Mahalia Jackson, Sam Cooke, Al Green or Aretha Franklin – but this is surely to come. The London Gospel Community Choir and The Inspirational Choir have both made records ('Fill My Cup' and 'Clean Heart', respectively) and a pop-soul group such as Paradise, who covered the Lennon/McCartney song 'We Can Work It Out', make much of their gospel beginnings. They may not be as sanctified and downright upsettin' as American acts like The Winans or the O'Neals but it's a start.

One of the most 'gospelly' American singers, Chaka Khan, has had a good 12 months too. After a couple of uncertain years, she's made progress by recording a jazz album and followed it with *Stompin' At The Savoy*, a double album mixing live and studio tracks with her band Rufus. Aretha, despite her Luther Vandross-produced album, kept a low profile so perhaps the very best (and certainly the most unexpected) album from a woman during the year was Anita Baker's *The Songstress*, a very simple yet classically conceived set of songs delivered with the greatest of maturity and richness by the largely unknown singer. It was another feather in the cap of Beverly Glenn, the label which had recharged Bobby Womack's batteries.

The return to the virtues of a good singer and a good song were also reflected by two other

LPs this year – J. Blackfoot's *City Slicker* and Bobby Story's *Storyteller*, two albums on small independent labels from the South of the US which plugged into the reborn market for soul as the genuine article, a music which can drive out personal devils by expressing them or can uplift the spirit more fundamentally than any other music.

The antithesis of this area is electro. This has kept pace in popularity with other new styles. As befits any new form, a lot of rubbish passes as acceptable, exciting simply because it is new or different or gimmicky, not because it's of any lasting value. In this it has much in common with longer established fads or specialist markets like Northern Soul, where after honorable beginnings rarity and, second, danceability rather than the quality of a record was its main asset.

What will endure is the work of a writer and singer such as Luther Vandross, arguably the best soul vocalist to have emerged in the Eighties. His most recent LP, *Busy Body,* conclusively established him as a top recording artist and his ever-increasing list of composing and production credits confirm him as one of the most important figures in the field over the past four years. His only fault is that he may be tempted to spread himself too thin, to do too much. Vandross first came to attention with Change, the Italian-spawned studio band whose 1980 LP *The Glow Of Love* was distinguished by his singing of the title track and 'Searching'. Change have, in fact, come back well recently with *Change Of Heart,* a fine, varied, modern R&B-dance LP produced by the hot pairing of Jimmy Jam and Terry Lewis, who were also involved in the success of the SOS Band in the past year. A word too for Kashif, the songwriter turned producer turned artist, and Narada Michael Walden and George Duke who both seem to get more than their fair share of production credits.

Finally, the most touching album of the year was surely Teddy Pendergrass's – his first new recordings since his near-fatal car crash. His now frail vocals are coaxed through a series of ballads: The faster cuts requiring vocal power and expressions of urgency show just how restricted Pendergrass is as a result of the accident. He appears to have no power at all left in the diaphragm and sings solely from the throat, almost by instinct. But, unlike the great and lamented Marvin Gaye, Pendergrass is still here to share that impressive instinct for singing with us.

GEOFF BROWN

MARVIN GAYE

COUNTRY

YIP YIP COYOTE

It was the year of chrome on the range, a year in which Willie Nelson went international by buddying-up to Spanish heart-throb Julio Iglesias, a year that saw ex-Las Vegas croupier Lee Greenwood grab Nashville's Best Male Singer title, a period during which the Osmonds went country and helped fill Wembley Arena, home of the Silk Cut Festival, with many coachloads of over-age teenyboppers.

And if Nashville seemed to be nodding in the direction of things glitzy and Hollywood, then Tinsel Town equally had a thing going with Music City. One country music movie, *Tender Mercies*, gained an Oscar for its star, Robert Duvall, while screen queen Sissy Spacek moved on a notch from portraying a country star – which she did in the 1980 *Coal Miner's Daughter* – and actually *became* one, cutting *Hangin' Up My Heart*, a Rodney Crowell-produced debut album.

It was also the year of the gnome on the range, the year that saw Little Jimmy Dickens, diminutive recording star of 'May The Bird Of Paradise Fly Up Your Nose' fame, tearfully receive the CMA's coveted Hall Of Fame Award. Others honoured at the annual Opry House ceremony included Janie Fricke (female vocalist), Merle Haggard and Willie Nelson (vocal duo), The Ricky Scaggs Band (instrumental group), Chet Atkins (instrumentalist) and John Anderson (single of the year). Alabama, the four-piece country-rock outfit, grabbed three major CMA awards, including Entertainer Of The Year, and then went on to appear at various other awards ceremonies where they picked up laudits with all the alacrity of ultra-lucky competitors on TV give-away shows.

Dolly Parton, whose career seemed to have slowed a smidgen or two since making *The Best Little Whorehouse* movie, made exactly the right move by recording a Bee Gees song, 'Islands In The Stream', with Kenny Rogers. The resulting single eventually topped the US pop charts and even went Top 20 in Britain, providing the voluptuous one

with her first real trip into the UK charts since 'Jolene' in 1976.

Not that Dolly really needed the royalties. She'd already signed a contract to appear in (and provide a score for) *Rhinestone*, a Fox musical which teamed Sevier County's shapeliest with original *Rocky* Top Sylvester Stallone, this deal reportedly bringing in a nifty three million dollars.

Perhaps Waylon Jennings earned a few less shekels during his trip to Britain but he achieved something rare among country singers by gaining purple prose reviews from the attending rock mag hard hats. "The most simply-executed, lovingly-played show of the year," judged *NME's* Barney Hoskins. And though the UK rock press had warmed to stetson-toters on previous occasions (predominantly when Don Williams became acclaimed by Eric Clapton and when Joe Ely became chummy with The Clash) never had the in-print applause seemed quite so unanimous. Even so, the then current Jennings album, *Waylon And Company,* still failed to move many copies in Britain. At least it was available. RCA stood by their men (and women) and put out a respectable number of country albums in the UK during the year, as did MCA and CBS. But WEA copped out.

Despite having the rights to a series of outstanding albums by the likes of John Anderson, Hank Williams Jnr, The Whites and Guy Clark, WEA issued no more than a trickle of country releases, leaving the importers, plus such enterprising indie labels as

Waterfront, Sundown, Range and Charly, to fulfil the needs of the largely vinyl-starved British country music fan.

Onie Wheeler, Roy Acuff's mouth-harp man and sometime rockabilly, was one of those who headed for the sweet bye and bye, collapsing onstage at the opry while performing his gospel classic 'Mother Prays Loud In Her Sleep'. Country music lost several talents this year: Roy Hall, the country-rockabilly performer and publisher who wrote 'Whole Lotta Shakin' Goin' On', Australian great Tex Morton; Nudie, the Hollywood tailor who overdressed everyone from Hank Snow to Presley; Al Dexter, creator of the million-selling 'Pistol Packin' Mama'; and perhaps the greatest loss of all – Merle Travis, one of country's most influential guitarists and songwriters.

Meanwhile, back in Nashville, the living got on with the task of prying a few dollars more from the pockets of visiting tourists. Like Johnny Cash, Loretta Lynn, Conway Twitty and many others before them, Waylon Jennings, George Jones and Barbara Mandrell moved into the 'Fan Attractions' business, Jones opening his Country Music Park in Colmesneil, Jennings starting up Waylon's Private Collection (a tally of exhibits that includes Buddy Holly's motorbike), while Mandrell, who already runs a chain of one hour photo-developing shops in Music City, opened her contribution to the city's clutch of star-run museums.

TV-wise, things progressed promisingly. In Britain, the Wembley Festival was not only

allocated its usual quota of screenings by the Beeb but the CMA awards ceremony was also shown in most ITV regions, Channel 4 pitching in with a short season of country-oriented shows that included *Hank Williams – The Show He Never Gave*, a highly acclaimed fictionalised reconstruction of the legendary singer's last hours. In America too, country TV continued to make headway, Music City's Nashville Network winning many new friends and sponsors through such shows as *Bobby Bare And Friends*, a programme given the critical thumbs-up by *Rolling Stone* editor Chet Flippo, who, in a *People* magazine article, nominated it "the best country TV show".

Also, for once, country musicians seemed to be moving less into rock while rockers increasingly looked towards Nashville for inspiration. Such groups as America's Jason And the Scorchers and Rank And File, along with Britain's So You Think You're A Cowboy, Yip Yip Coyote, Helen And The Horns and The Boothill Foot Tappers, all donned checkshirts and adopted the best in country licks in an attempt to gain a fair slice of the youth audience.

However, amid all the comings and goings, the to-ings and fro-ings, the cow-punk and the country funk, much remained the same. Jerry Lee Lewis decided to get married (for the sixth time); British bands kept on playing 'Crystal Chandelier' (even the Hank Wangford Band kept a cock-eyed version on tap); the Everlys discovered they were brothers; the UK music industry kept up its claim that "country just isn't popular" as Don Williams and Charley Pride played sell-out tours; and Slim Whitman, named by Chet Flippo as "country's answer to Veg-O-Matic", headlined at Wembley and received a standing ovation.

Some things, like the tag on Minnie Pearl's hat, were never meant to change.

FRED DELLAR

ELECTRONIC

With Kraftwerk *still* silent and, at time of writing, no further word out of Dusseldorf, this year's laurels return home to entrants from Sheffield and the London district of Camberwell SE5. Sheffield was represented, perhaps unsurprisingly, by The Human League, making a sorely belated return with *Hysteria*, a troubled production but one which sees them ditching artifice for a gloriously simple (if still soul-influenced) one-finger-tapping electronic pop. Camberwell fielded newcomers Bronski Beat, a trio of gay 20-year-olds fronted by extraordinary falsetto Jimi Somerville. After little more than a dozen small club gigs, their debut single 'Smalltown Boy', entered the charts at 35, jumped to 4 and, as finger hits typewriter key, is sandwiched at number 3 between two Frankie Goes To Hollywood singles and the execrable Wham! All this while they were still plugging their gorgeous electro-soul around the club circuit.

The British gay community might in fact be something to keep an eye on. Protein, the Cabaret Voltaire to the Bronski's Human League, are following the Bronskis out of the gay clubs and may well have been signed by the time this reaches your see-bones. Interestingly, after a decade or more of manipulative old tarts in frocks telling the daily tabloids that, actually, they're bisexual, these two bands present a refreshing change; so 'out' that their sexuality becomes a boring subject and insistent that the noise, rather than the pose, is the thing that matters.

After their American and European tours, The Residents returned to Ralph Studios, seemed to put the *Mole* trilogy on hold and re-emerged with *George & James*, the first in a 16-year series of 'tributes' to Great American Composers, the victims here being Messrs Gershwin and Brown, respectively. Their mischievous re-arrangement job of Gershwin's 'Rhapsody In Blue' and others didn't particularly surprise, but their

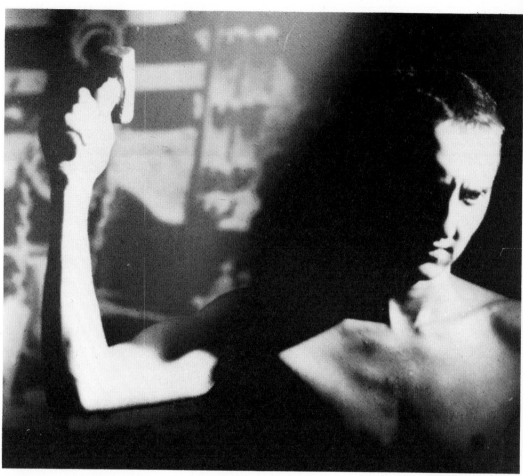

TEST DEPARTMENT

sassy trawl through Brown's classic *Live At The Apollo* did, displaying a dirty humanity and humour to the detractors who accuse them of being laboratory theorists. Their label, New Ralph, also released an album of tones 'n' drones from Rhythm & Noise, a comeback album from Canadian tacky-pop transcendentalist Nash The Slash and a charming collaboration, *Title In Limbo*, between The Residents and Portsmouth eccentrics Renaldo & The Loaf. Amusingly, The Residents themselves were signed to WEA in Europe, for the release of *George & James* and, possibly, a video of the never-completed 'Vileness Fats' movie. Watching this massive multinational trying to market these notorious oddballs should be as much fun as a Residents gig itself.

One of their old pals, Blaine Reininger of expatriates Tuxedomoon, presented probably the most interesting live date of the year; a duo with American keyboard-player and composer Mikel Rouse which played a few small club dates in London. With the two on live and pre-set keyboards, and Reininger occasionally picking up his violin, they played a gritty and enchanting brand of gentle DIY systems music, and one song from their *Colorado Suite* had Reininger cowboy-crooning "Yippy-i-ay-dee-o" over complex keyboard repetitions in a particularly boggling manner.

Apart from *Hysteria*, Blancmange's robust *Mange Tout* and the continuing ascendance of Thomas Dolby, the rest left me at best glassy-eyed, at worst, spitting and snarling. Two years ago I wrote that you could now buy

electronic music in Woolworth's. Now you can get it in *Bejam's*. Yazoo split, as did Soft Cell (Marc and I finally made it up. I think), and apart from Eurythmics and Cabaret Voltaire, neither of them deserving comparison to the legions of pretty-boy chart electronic acts, the rest is rank forgery. If they're not using synthesisers to fake Motown they're using them to fake pop orchestras. Why bother?

Far better (and, if you need it, hipper) to hang around with the eccentrics, maniacs, danger-freaks and mad foreigners. At least they're honest, and you stand a greater risk of plugging into the wild pop thrill that we sometimes forget is the only reason we're here, anyway.

Holger Czukay and Laurie Anderson held up the eccentrics' side very well, the former with his inspired synth/

ethnic mix-up *Der Osten Ist Rot,* the latter with *Mr. Heartbreak.* Some accused Anderson of moving away from 'performance art' and into straight pop, but the light and warmth of that follow-up to *Big Science* was very cheering after the ever-expanding grey drones of 'United States'. Frank Tovey, too, still stands like a beacon among all the wallies wiggling away behind their Rolands, and his *Under The Flag* deserves special mention.

Last year's main arrival, Test Department (who aren't maniacs but do sound as though they are) got signed by Some Bizzare, got arrested for staging sneak gigs on British Rail property, released an album, *Beating The Retreat* and video, *Program For Progress,* and by the time you see this may well have caused a riot when they played, of all things, the Kool (aka Newport) Jazz Festival in New York.

Their Berlin metal-bashing cousins Einsturzende Neubauten (some of whom actually *are* maniacs) got themselves in trouble when their *Concerto For Machinery And Voices* at the London ICA arts centre turned into a free-for-all, with the audience ripping up the lip of the stage, and musicians wielding pneumatic road-drills leaping into the audience to start digging up the floor. An awesome and at times frightening event. Negotiations over damages continue.

The third of the tin-can triumvirate, SPK – who in an earlier incarnation used to outdo Throbbing Gristle in the shockarama stakes – turned themselves into pop stars.

Systems music continued to penetrate the market; apart from a European tour, Phillip Glass was silent, presumably preparing the premiere of his third major opera in the *Einstein* trilogy, *Akhenaton.* But London can expect *Akhenaton* in the autumn of 1985, and the Brooklyn Academy of Music in New York is planning a new version of *Einstein,* which may also come to Europe.

Holland's Soft Verdict were silent, Britain's Lost Jockey orchestra collapsed under its own weight, but refugees were to be seen in a small-scale systems opera, *Mozart At Palm Springs,* in London, and the best news of all is the emergence of Man Jumping!, a smaller group out of Lost Jockey who, again, might have been signed by the time . . .

This leads interestingly into This year's Big Theory. While hundreds of grammar school boys wiled away their Chaucer revision to the accompaniment of Kitaro or some other blissed-out flying carpet salesman, I could be found making a spectacle of myself in various

THE HUMAN LEAGUE

nightclubs to the accompaniment of giddying New York hip-hop/scratch from the likes of Afrika Bambaataa, Grandmaster Flash, Grandmixer D. St., Shango, Material-mainman Bill Laswell's apocalyptic Praxis and others. This has happened before – Phil Glass's indirect influence on Giorgio Moroder, most notably – and although systems can't be called a direct influence on hip-hop/scratch (it might, in fact, be defined as 'de-structuralist', if you dared) – the reliance on fast, complexly rhythmic keyboards certainly assumes the shape. And they didn't expect you to discuss Hermann Hesse – merely dance! This was all that 1984 had to offer in the way of epiphanies.

Some great moments, though; New Order at their overwhelming peak with *Power, Corruption And Lies,* Shriekback's massive comeback with *Jam Science,* the dizzying speedy funk and shimmering pop of Section 25's *From The Hip* on Factory, the intermittent tape releases from the *Touch* magazine/artefact, Miles Davis's magisterial *Decoy* (Well . . .? Miles plays synth on a couple of tracks), return visits from Sun Ra, Trevor Horn's mixes for Frankie Goes To Hollywood, Eno's retro 10-album box set (but no new studio work) and, after years of resisting technology, my lover, a composer, bought a Roland polyphonic, but refuses to let me near it for fear that I might try and launch my own one-man synthfunk career.

SHRIEKBACK   JOHN GILL

JAZZ

SARAH VAUGHAN

Compared with the United States or Europe, jazz gets little airplay and less press coverage in Britain. If consumer surveys of comparative festival audiences place the British jazz fan as a real ale man with a bus map, overshadowed by the Fortnum's hampers of Glyndebourne and the hot dogs of rock, he is nevertheless a stubborn statistic. Something of an orphan for decades, jazz has been billeted on a succession of fickle publicans. This year sees the opening of the National Jazz Centre in a converted warehouse in London's Covent Garden, complete with workshops, lecture halls and performance space, a permanent home at last.

Perhaps because of the continuing doldrums on the pop scene, the past year has seen a growing curiosity among teenagers in the music of Louis Jordan and Cab Calloway, that whole hellzappoppin' period of Zoot Suits and surreal vouteroonie jive talk. The hippy era saw a fringe interest in Sun Ra and John Coltrane, the Seventies a fringe interest in the jazz-rock off-shoots of Miles Davis, and this decade's browsers have plumped for the Forties novelty number. Jazz has always commuted between the concert platform, the club and the dance floor, but whether the kids hoofing to 'Knock Me A Kiss' and 'Caldonia' will also check out the clubs and concerts remains to be seen.

The resurrection of the supergroups of yesteryear – MJQ, VSOP and the Mingus Dynasty – shows how far the nostalgia industry has penetrated the music. Jazz, once described as the sound of surprise, could be in danger of becoming the sound of reprise. Bandleader Chris Barber's dictum that the average jazz punter is probably really a Max Bygraves fan at heart is partly borne out of box-office figures: revivalism puts more bums on seats than improvisation. The old Duke Ellington song title, 'Things Ain't What They Used To Be', becomes an infinitely layered statment in this context: things are note-for-note what they used to be – and they shouldn't be.

The spread of the big packaged jazz festival now girdles the globe, and has seen promoters playing safe with commemorations. Kansas City Days and Bebop Revisited pageants figure on most festival bills, and require the ageing giants to rise no higher than typicality. Familiarity, even in jazz, spells bucks. That grand-pappy of jazz festivals, Kook, New York, set the tone with tributes to Ellington, Mingus, Coleman Hawkins and Bill Evans. Bob Wilber and the Bechet Legacy seemed to be on every festival bill, while VSOP II headlined at Nice, Northsea and Montreux.

VSOP II turned up too at the Royal Festival Hall, and gave a Rolls-Royce demonstration of how a supergroup meshes. One had almost forgotten how good Herbie Hancock can be in the straight-ahead bag on acoustic piano, and Tony Williams and Ron Carter have patented their particularly stylized patterns of prowling tension and release. Of course, the inescapable shadow of the great Miles Davis-Wayne Shorter group colours the music, which is perhaps unfair to the young Marsalis brothers. Despite overselling by the media, there hasn't been a critical backlash against Wynton Marsalis. Jazz had had many brilliant young trumpeters, but seldom one so young, gifted and backed. If he is not an innovator – and he seems stretched enough within the tradition – he is certainly proof that jazz can make news.

Innovation in general was thin on the ground this year. Jazz is still assimilating the upheavals of 25 years, and not looking for anyone to rock the boat. Just how distant the sound-and-fury of the New Thing seems today was illustrated by the Ganelin Trio from the USSR who toured Britain for Contemporary Music Network, and whose anarchy fell largely upon unreceptive ears. Actual '83, however, soldiered on undaunted with a postively truculent programme of Free Music.

Camden Jazz Week mixed it all up, ranging from the tough-tenor battles of Johnny Griffin and Arnett Cobb to a troupe of Bronx breakdancers. Apart from a seasonal rash of small festivals – Bracknell, Sheffield, Newcastle, Cardiff, Edinburgh – Britain also saw the circulation of American jazz stars. James Moody, Billy Mitchell, Teddy Edwards, Jimmy Witherspoon, Shorty Rogers, Bill Perkins, Abdullah Ibrahim and Carols Ward were just a few of those who toured to enthusiastic houses.

London clubs like Ronnie Scott's and The Pizza Express gave residencies to McCoy Tyner, Buddy Tate, Al Grey, Gil Evans and his All-British Orchestra, Sal Nistico, Al Cohn, Ernie Wilkins, Joe Newman, Warren Vache, Timeless All-Stars, Sphere, and Woody Herman And The Young Thundering Herd. An ambitious three-night vocal event, Jazz Greats, featured Sarah Vaughan, Billy Eckstine, Mel Torme, Rosemary Clooney, Buddy Greco, Brook Benton and Kay Starr.

Stan Tracey topped the Readers Poll in *Jazz Journal* as Musician of the Year, while Album of the Year was *The Rhythmakers Of 1932*, followed by Clifford Brown's *Pure Genius* and the David Murray Octet's *Home*. Prestige returned to the original packaging of its jazz catalogue, Capitol found a new market for reissued Sinatra, Peggy Lee and Nat King Cole, and Japanese Blue Notes took another price hike.

Obituaries included Count Basie, Harry James and Machito, with Britain particularly hard hit by the deaths of Alexis Korner and Harry Miller. In New York, Jimmy Ryan's finally folded, as did the shortlived Covent Garden Canteen. The economic recession doesn't seem to have made a great deal of difference to the British jazz scene – perhaps because it never received much help from anyone anyway. Some indication of the traditional neglect of the British jazzman can be seen in the career of saxophonist Peter King: voted *Melody Maker's* New Star in 1960, he put out his debut album as leader this year.

The concert of the year, according to reports, took place at Town Hall, New York, when Sonny Rollins felt sufficiently challenged by Wynton Marsalis to really pull out all the stops, and demonstrate his matchless improvisational genius.

SONNY ROLLINS   BRIAN CASE

FOLK

THE POGUES

On the first day of April, 1984 an extraordinary thing happened: Pogue Mahone played their first folk club.

It wasn't a wildly memorable night. The Oxford Club – home base for Jumpleads, themselves one of the more outrageous bands on the circuit – was rooting for them without totally obliterating the mutual suspicion between band and audience. Yet the mould of the British folk scene had surely been comprehensively broken.

Pogue Mahone – later to be The Pogues – were/are diabolical. Cheerfully diabolical, but diabolical nevertheless. Which is precisely the point. Singer Shane McGowan had only been in one folk club in his life before – to see Ewan MacColl – and was indignantly unimpressed; their raucous female bass player Caitlin confided that her favourite band was Orange Juice and her ambition was to be on the cover of Smash Hits. The only folk heroes they'd acknowledged were the much-ridiculed Dubliners.

Not for them, certainly, any reverence about traditions, nor any influence from the great revivalists. The Pogues turned to folk merely as a demonstration of their disillusionment with current rock forms and an expression of their own first generation London Irish upbringing. They feel no empathy with the established folk movement. It's taken a long time, but the punk mentality has finally touched folk and it might never be the same again, especially with the support of the extremely vocal 'rogue folk' faction who have long been battering away at the purist barriers and conservative attitudes that have traditionally protected folk from the big bad world outside.

Bracketed with The Pogues in a similar kind of acoustic ideology have been various other young London bands – The Boothill Foot-Tappers, The Hackney Five-O, The Shillelagh Sisters, Rough-House Allstars – all of them playing folk music of a sort, but none of them with any knowledge or interest in the existing folk club movement. There was a brief buzz of excitement when Dexys got a number one hit with 'Come On Eileen' on the back of a blaze of fiddles and accordions, and again when Malcolm McLaren scoured the world ripping off ethnic folk styles for his *Duck Rock* project; but here was a genuine grass roots movement born from pubs with none of the contrivance of other recent attempts to turn folk music into a going commercial concern. The ever-sensitive BBC banned Pogue Mahone on the grounds that we should be protected from the full horror of the Irish translation of their name (something to do with kissing buttocks) and the group simply milked the publicity for all it was worth, signed to Stiff and abbreviated their name. Smart band. And if they do succeed, by accident, in taking folk music out of the rarified atmosphere of the folk clubs and back into pubs and everyday usage, then this shambolic, irreverent bunch of loudmouths will have performed a service that professors, committees, conferences and professional singers have spent the last decade debating how to achieve.

It has been an opportune time in which to take folk back to the people because the last year has seen the old guard crumbling. With the recent deaths of A.L. Lloyd, Seamus Ennis, Bob Roberts and Joe Heaney, Ewan MacColl alone survies from the forward commando unit which launched the folk revival at the end of the Fifties, while the impetus of the brigade of innovative young singers which gave it its second wind has, for varying reasons, finally faltered. Nic Jones still recovers slowly from his horrific 1982 road accident; Chris Foster became disillusioned and drifted into semi-retirement; Martin Carthy chose to channel much of his mighty talent into the challenging band format of Brass Monkey; Bill Caddick has done the same with Home Service; Dave Burland supplemented the precariousness of life on the road with radio work; June Tabor became more interested in running an hotel; and Vin Garbutt stepped into a hail of scorn and abuse, sacrificing many of his female devotees, by vehemently stating his opposition to abortion via the Topic Album, *Little Innocents*.

And if Dick Gaughan could do no wrong in 1983, the early part of '84 at least was a nightmare for him. His long awaited follow-up to the brilliant *Handful Of Earth* album, *A Different Kind Of Love Song* earned almost as many insults as *Earth* had won awards. The political undercurrent which had given *Earth* such a bite, bubbled right over the surface, and Gaughan's radical politics, his move towards his own songs at the expense of traditional material, and several wholly rock-orientated arrangements combined to attract the critics' knives. The reaction perhaps confirmed the conservative attitude of the folk scene: the unexpected always puts the fear of God into folkies. Gaughan, in fact, had already predicted the album would inspire this sort of hostility, but wasn't around much for any eyeball to eyeball confrontations with his attackers, stricken for a large part of the year with a serious throat problem. By the summer of '84 Gaughan had also bailed out of Perform, the body he'd launched four years earlier in a flood of goodwill and optimism to give folk music a national voice. "It appears to me," said Dick, "that the vast bulk of folkies are more interested in playing 'my dad's bigger than your dad' than in actually doing anything about music."

A watershed time, then, for folk music on all levels. Even the Celtic surge felt the wind of change. The flower of Scotland's folk, The Battlefield Band, Tannahill Weavers, Ossian and Silly Wizard all underwent major personnel surgery and Ossian and Wizard decided to cut back drastically on gigs. Battlefield, though, more than compensated with the best album from the early part of '84, the majestic *Anthem For The Common Man*, itself full of politcal implications and at last fulfilling the promise they'd made several years earlier to make a classic Scottish album to rank alongside the great Irish records achieved by the likes of Planxty and The Bothy Band.

For Ireland, though, it was a curiously barren period. Moving Hearts marched on, but more in desperation than triumph, shedding key

members along the route and releasing a shoddy live album. There was a kind of appalling inevitability about their struggle – the most exciting, innovative band to have emerged for years in any musical form, forced to scrape a living in pubs due to the notoriously brainless nonentities who pull the strings in the radio and record industry. There are parallels here with Home Service, who splintered from the Albion Band in a blaze of publicity and anticipation a couple of years ago and whose career since then has been a wretched frustration. Finally, in the summer of '84, Jigsaw issued their debut album, and it was pretty good, even if the bold display of brass didn't wield quite the same clout it would have done when the group was first formed. It was still revelatory for Bill Caddick's raucous singing and Home Service certainly wiped the floor with the other main band using brass, the irritatingly erratic Brass Monkey.

If there was a group who saw the year through in total triumph, though, it was De Danann, fully recovering from the trail of disaster that had come within a bodhran beat of causing their total collapse a year earlier, giving Mary Black the platform to prove herself the finest female singer in Ireland and making a startlingly vibrant album,

Song For Ireland. With Clannad seemingly dedicating themselves to producing music for television, De Danann had very little competition from their home country, though the Canada-based Touchstone (featuring former Bothy Band-it Triona Ni Dhomhnaill) inspired a great deal of excitement with two outstanding albums. Ireland did, however, suffer grave losses in '84 with the deaths of Joe Heaney and Luke Kelly, lynchpin of The Dubliners. After 20 years on the road, The Dubliners decided to continue, co-opting Sean Cannon, as famous nowadays for his Kinetic Curry van as for his singing. The Dubliners immediately sounded fresher than they had done for years.

It was De Danann, though, who flew the Irish flag at the Cambridge festival, an event that held firm in a disaster-prone year for festivals. Norwich, for example, was cancelled following a 'Peace Festival' that all but wrecked the festival site, and the two major events of '83, Goodwood and Sheffield failed to re-emerge after the accounts had been studied. Folk did, however, finally make the big time with a surpisingly successful festival held during Easter at Butlin's Holiday Camp at Bognor Regis. Chalets were said to be rockin and a-reeling all weekend and Redcoats were observed fleeing

like Italians in the war.

While The Pogues were blowing the scene apart from the outside, there were plenty of subversive elements at work on the inside. Andrew Cronshaw, of course, the mad professor, twiddling for all his worth with a bunch of new toys and threatening to send us all to kingdom come with a new band and getting plenty of encouragement from cohorts like Ric Sanders and the incorrigible Martin Simpson (who came back to form with a superb album, *Grinning In Your Face*). The totally nutty Blowzabella also shattered a few purist hearts with their extraordinary mix of bagpipes, hurdy gurdie and strange Eastern European rhythms, while the original pioneers of the culture clash, The English Country Blues Band bowed out to make way for their larger, even more fearsome successors, Tiger Moth. The promising development of Cluster Of Nuts, Pyewackett and The Oyster Band demonstrate the strides now being made with English dance music.

Poignantly, another father of the folk club movement, Alex Campbell went into enforced retirement as a result of throat cancer and one of the artists he directly inspired, Richard Digance (now firmly esconced as a disc-jockey at Capitol Radio) fittingly announced he was forming a new record label, Dambuster, specifically designed to give an outlet to the emergent young talent he felt was being stifled by the lack of enterprise in folk clubs. The double compilation album of dance tunes, *Buttons And Bows* proved to be a formidable statement of intent from the label.

The lesson of the year, though, is that folk clubs are no longer necessarily the cornerstone of the folk movement and can by bypassed without undue trauma. One of the most highly-rated new bands, The Catsfield Steamers from Sussex, have blended their sound as a result of informal sessions in pubs and in common with a lot of ceilidh bands now, have rarely appeared in folk clubs which brings us back to The Pogues. And as long as *they* go on putting peoples' backs up The Pogues should be considered a positive force.

Banned by the BBC and despised by the EFDSS – now *this* is a band that deserves our undying admiration...

THE BATTLEFIELD BAND

COLIN IRWIN

BLUES

JOHNNY COPELAND

To the casual reader of the *Rock Yearbook,* an exhaustive study of the blues over the past year must seem as distant and obtuse as a weekend in Sumatra. In short, to the outsider, the blues has returned to a state of anonymity, a fond memory of something that used to be and, for some, a sad farewell to idealistic youth.

The passing of Alexis Korner this year robbed Britain not only of its pioneering elder statesman of the blues, but also the last link with a Radio One dee-jay who regularly programmed the likes of Muddy Waters, Big Bill Broonzy et al with the utmost degree of sympathy and respect. So where does an aspiring young blues collector start off in 1984? How does one ferret out the wheat from the chaff, as it were? Ultimately, is there any *real* alternative to Radio One's blitzkrieg Top 40 programming policy? The answer to the last question is certainly 'No', but there are ways around this problem.

A new monthly magazine was launched in July entitled *Blues & Rhythm – The Gospel Truth.* Edited by Paul Vernon (brother of Eric Clapton/John Mayall veteran producer Mike Vernon), the mag contains many features, lists new records and books, and carries a comprehensive breakdown of local UK radio stations programming blues/R&B, which will be regularly added to. (Available for 60p from 18 Maxwelton Close, Mill Hill, London NW7 3NA). It makes a fine companion to the highly authoritative *Blues Unlimited.*

The declining interest in blues of course goes hand-in-hand with the tragic but inevitable loss of some of its biggest names. I was lucky enough to have witnessed many of the giants in live performance: Muddy Waters, Sonny Boy Williamson, Lightnin' Hopkins, Little Walter, Magic Sam, and so on. All have died in the past fifteen years, yet all contributed immensely to the blues in its purest form. The stimulation and excitement of seeing these 'living legends' triggered off the infamous British Blues Boom of the Sixties in no uncertain terms. In fact, it's hard to believe now, but at that time the UK rock charts carried singles by the likes of Jimmy Reed and John Lee Hooker.

So, on reflection, it's not too surprising to discover an impasse in new recruits to the music, although for blues on record it's been yet another bumper crop. Johnny Copeland's much-acclaimed *Texas Twister* (Demon) really has all the style and panache promised by his previous two albums. A trifle more 'down-home' in its approach, Copeland sounds in fine fettle alongside such guests as Texas guitar wizard Stevie Ray Vaughan and tenorist Archie Shepp. The tracks are all originals with the exception of

THE ROBERT CRAY BAND

Louis Jordan's 'Early In The Morning', and Copeland sings with enough vigour to drive along his punchy brass-laden band at a respectable toe-tapping pace.

Sticking with Demon, the second album from The Robert Cray Band, (another hot favourite) *Bad Influence,* looks set to establish them as the West Coast's leading blues outfit. Guitarist Cray and his multi-racial five-piece were originally discovered by "Blues Brother" John Belushi, who gave them a bit part in *Animal House.* Now they've polished up the act, offering a smokin' set "where Stax left off," to quote Cray. Influenced by Bobby Bland and guitarist Albert Collins, Cray offers mostly self-penned tunes along with Johnny Guitar Watson's 'Don't Touch Me' and Eddie Floyd's 'Got To Make A Come Back'.

It's good to see Albert King's 'Laundromat Blues' collection (Edsel) back in catalogue. These are the original Stax sides from Memphis in the mid-Sixties; 'Born Under A Bad Sign', 'The Hunter', 'Cold Feet' and 'Personal Manager' are just the tip of the iceberg. King's aggressive southpaw guitar style perfectly complements the superb Stax

house band (actually Booker T & The MGs/Isaac Hayes/Memphis Horns).

Collectors of vintage Chicago blues should seek out *Chicago Boogie 1947* (St. George Records). Little Walter, Jimmy Rogers, Othum Brown, Johnny Young and others are featured on sides originally cut for the local Ora Nelle label. They provide a fascinating insight into the roots of urban blues in the city, especially when remembering that both Walter (harmonica) and Rogers (guitar) went on to become key sidemen to Muddy Waters during his most creative period in the early to mid-Fifties.

One of the year's most unusual releases must be *Nobody Knows My Name: Blues From South Carolina And Georgia 1924-1932* (Heritage), unusual in that the identity of the artists involved is completely unknown. The man responsible for the recordings was one Lawrence Gellert, and they are important as historical evidence, capturing black folk blues as it really was, without commercial interference. This is one for the student of blues research, a companion volume to the Alan Lomax field recordings of 1947, *Murderers' Home.*

Another oddity, but with the accent on humour, is *Copulatin' Blues Vol 2* (Stash). A decade on from the first *Copulatin!* eyebrow-raising album, Stash have now put together an even weirder compilation. The tracks were mostly recorded in the Thirties and Forties and include such delights as 'It's Too Big Papa' (Claude Hopkins & His Band), 'Take Out That Thing' (Cliff Edwards), 'She Squeezed My Lemon' (Art McKay), 'It's

Tight Like That' (Clara Smith) and finally, from the Fifties, The Clovers' acapella version of 'Rotten Cocksuckers Ball'. Volume one certainly sold in handsome amounts, and this time the sleeve's been over-stickered with the dubious legend "The Party Record For Adults!"

Other albums to note: Jimmy Witherspoon's *Who's Been Jivin' You* (Ace), spirited recordings from the Modern catalogue of the Forties/early Fifties featuring the bands of Maxwell Davis and Buddy Floyd; *Zydeco Blues Vol.2* (Flyright), yes, the Jay Miller sessions including Clifton Chenier's juke-box sides from 1958-59 plus Rockin' Dupsee and more; Guitar Junior's 'The Crawl' (Charly), better known as Lonnie Brooks, the Bayou boogieman presents a scorching selection from the Goldband label (plus liner notes from the legendary Ray Topping); other Charly re-issues including two Atlantic Records greats: Ruth Brown's 'Rockin' With Ruth' and LaVern Baker's 'Real Gone Gal', 16-tracks from each compiled by Cliff White and therefore faultless in the selection. (Ruth's 'This Little Girl's Gone Rockin' ' (1958) has been changing hands for telephone numbers!)

Combustive New Orleans-style R&B from the mid-Fifties is now available with Huey 'Piano' Smith & The Clown's self-titled collection on Ace. Chanting and shouting to a hot shuffle beat, Smith was an instant success and indeed the forerunner to Fats Domino, Allen Toussaint and the entire New Orleans rhythm and blues movement. Finally, for those lucky enough to possess a juke-box, Chess (US) has reissued almost fifty classic singles titles from the Fifties and Sixties ranging from several Chuck Berry's through Muddy Waters to Etta James to Bo Diddley in a goodly slice of the leading blues catalogue of the period.

Looking to the immediate future, we're promised a few brave ventures in the way of UK tours (after all, B. B. King played here *twice* in '84 and Al Green made his welcome comeback in a gospel setting), although the decline of the pound against the dollar hasn't helped encourage the more adventurous of promoters. Ah well, the current plethora of record releases will hold the blues in good stead for the next few years, at least.
DAVE WALTERS

THE YEAR'S VIDEOS

"When in the Sixties the record industry was waiting for the next Elvis they got the Beatles, when they were waiting for the next Beatles they got Led Zeppelin, when they were waiting for the next Led Zeppelin they got The Sex Pistols, and when they were waiting for the next Sex Pistols they got MTV."
– Pat Sweeney, *Independent Video*, March 1984.

In 1976 an innocent named Bruce Gowers became the Pandora of the Sony age, with the phantoms of old Beatles clips as his square-eyed accomplices. The Gowers-directed "Bohemian Rhapsody" was – aside from tailboned curiousities remaining from Ed Sullivan shows – undoubtedly the first and foremost of its kind, concentrating on "theme" over performance and passionate about not boy or girl or beat but *glamour*. For better or worse, Gower's work released the infinite images of 'Promo' into the upper airwaves. And there they remain, as permanent and kilowatt-encrusted as satellites and as numerous as mirrors in teen bedrooms. Recent observation tells us one thing: music videos will continue to proliferate as fast as fresh singles, and maybe even faster.

In 1984, virtually every aspect of promotional video got very big very quickly. *Everything* increased: the size of an average four-minute budget, the scope of the sets (witness 'Thriller'), the variety of music programmes on TV (and a parallel growth in audiences, since promo watchers proved to be as young as six and as old as 36), the sound of satellite titans clashing overhead, the publicity, the awards, the scandals, and the number of leather trousers per minute. Joining in the general blur of activity were advances from other areas, such as the soon-come promise of fully computerised video and the letters from Hollywooders with *Flashdance* writ large on their balance sheets.

Amid all this, some very good

MICHAEL JACKSON

videos got made, most of them unseen. The director Don Letts spoke for thousands when he stated, "My big complaint is the lack of distribution outlets. I'm sick of making videos which are never shown." There is as yet no visual equivalent of the indie charts, with the unhappy result that much of the adventurous camerawork that follows adventurous singles is at present languishing in BBC vaults. Which is not to say that all fringe productions were prizewinners – ZZT, for one, could profit by video directors as witty and zealous as their Fairlight programmers. Moreover, not all number ones were delivered bundled in floss. The continuing excellence of Mallet, Pope, Gibbins, (both) Barrons, and Godley and Creme did much to make music lovers happy to own a television.

This was also the year that video directors became auteurs. A recently-issued Banshees promo, for example, is commonly referred to as "The new Tim Pope", and people are probably still asking David Mallet to duplicate his enormously influential special effects in 'Ashes To Ashes'. Video directors have currently reached such prominence that Julien Temple must be the only man presently employed ever to have obscured a flannel-

mouthed Mick Jagger on television (The Tube's 'Undercover' interview). Video's still-unsettled relationship with film is evident in the stampede of crossovers from film to video and back again. Lindsay Anderson made a promo this year, as did John Landis, Tobe Hooper, Nicolas Roeg, and a rumoured Steven Spielberg (for Yes).

Meanwhile Temple, Mulcahy, and Barron are all working on their first feature films. Other non-cinematic climes also spawned directors, from photographers old and new (Bailey, Goude, Angus McBean's contributions to 'The Red Guitar') to musicians (Ultravox's Ure and Cross, David Byrne, the perenially wonderful Devo) and assorted nuts (artist John Sanborn) and bolts (Malcolm McLaren).

Before leaving the subject of direction, it is necessary to malign the reputation of video auteurism, a concept which may prove as leaky and unfair to promos as it was to film. Just as the director-as-main-artist theory ignored the efforts of others, so also is the video equivalent threatening to muffle the contributions of musicians. The makers of The Birthday Party's 'Nick The Stripper', for example, would probably be the first to

acknowledge that all would have amounted to cold soup without the ideas of the band. The wondrous 'Stripper' will forever be remembered not for its clever editing but for the sight of Nick Cave waking the dead in a tattered Mothercare outfit.

Stylistically, the year's headaches and garlands stemmed from two areas: the nature of TV and the screen treatment of live performances. One of video's more severe lessons to date is that promos are by and large unsuited to epic productions. An average TV screen is cubelike, which means that airports, massed dancers, armies and continental trains look less than effective on video, never minding the fact that they crowd the band. The same holds true for complex narratives, which are more suited to the unravelling of two hours than wedged between keyboard shots. Simplest remains best: The Police's stunning ('I'll Be) Wrapped Around Your Finger' succeeded with a lone, brilliant idea (Sting dancing in slow motion between rows of hundreds of candles) while in 'Union Of The Snake' Duran Duran looked overwhelmed amid the technoglamour, like salesmen in spacesuits.

1984 was also the year that musicians discovered they hated to act. They hated dropping past windows, gazing moodily at ponds, wearing pancake makeup under hot lights, and rollerskating with six foot model girls. But they also hated to look dull, so sometimes a little reasonable suffering became necessary (the 'Buffalo Soldiers' dreads looked surpisingly convincing in Confederate uniforms). TV veterans like Tracey Ullman and Alexei Sayle added unforeseeable delights to otherwise just-there singles, as did non-professionals like Talk Talk's Mark Hollis and all of Madness. And the 'Great Faces' – Robert Smith, Annie Lennox, Ian McCulloch – simply had to show up on set to launch a thousand distant sighs.

Videocassettes, for the most part, remained reproductions

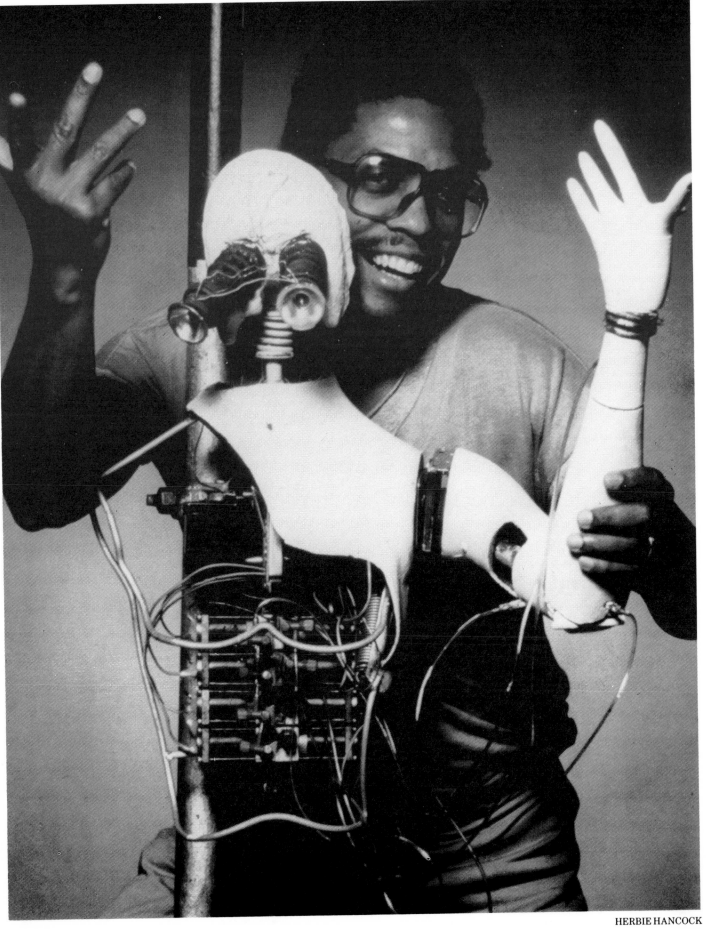

HERBIE HANCOCK

CABARET VOLTAIRE

of live dates, and therein lies a traitorous set of circumstances. For one thing, conventional stage lighting – stop-light red, go-light green, etc – almost always goes unheeded in a concert hall and later almost always looks terrible on TV. *A Night With Lou Reed*, 'Dexy's Midnight Runners: *The Bridge*' and '*Orchestral Manoeuvres In The Dark Live At The Theatre Royal Drury Lane*' all suffered from ill-considered lashings of red light. Curiously, plain, well-balanced white seemed to work just fine (see Bauhaus' opulently sharp live bits in '*Shadow Of Light*') And it has to be reiterated that musicians with an excess of personality fare best in a cool medium, especially over a period of 50-odd minutes. For this reason, Culture Club's '*A Kiss Across The Ocean*' and The Fall's '*Perverted By Language*' were standouts in the live area, together with Eurythmics' '*Sweet Dreams*' and '*Beating The Blues*' from The Redskins (a visual harangue, but an effective one).

Overall, humour proved to be Video 84's most prized party guest. From David Lee Roth's send-ups of himself in 'Jump' to Andy Partridge's Caesar Romero grimaces in XTC's 'Look Look' to Weird Al's uncannily excellent Jackson parody, 'Eat It' (featuring dance seizures over the bar stools), laughs saved a lot of musicians from looking overly content with themselves. Also lodging a non-ponderous grip on the imagination were archive tapes like MGM's *Girl Groups* and PMI's *Ready Steady Go*. These contained not only moments of weird levity (Cathy McGowan: 'Why do they call you The Animals then?' Eric Burdon: 'Cos we look like animals, hyuh'), but much-appreciated insights into musical history.

But the problems of unintelligible four-minute plots remain, together with too-numerous shots of decaying dungeons, waxen girls in limousines, five-year-olds running down hallways, and black and white studios with bits of melting sculpture propped up in one corner. The remedy, of course, is imagination. Thomas Dolby's 'Hyperactive' is a laudable example; it is, in effect, the acceptable face of 'art', being both fearlessly experimental and absolutely stunning to watch. Other independent-minded successes were Scritti Politti's 'Wood Beez', Orange Juice's 'What Presence?', and Everything But The Girl's 'Each And Every One' (all the efforts of underground film-makers).

The unstinting pioneers in the cassette field are the Nottingham-based Doublevision and Factory Records' visual offshoot Ikon. Both these organisations bypass wheezing stereotypes in favour of unpredictable attempts to recreate a mood. And, lest anyone suspect that 'alternative' tapes are snobbish and sleep-inducing, refer to Doublevision's winning *TV Wipeout*. *Wipeout*, with its mix of interviews, imported promos, and monster-movie clips is simply the way videos *ought* to be, in equal parts strange, funny and danceable (like a good record collection, in fact). *Wipeout*, deserves some competition in 1985.

DESSA FOX

THE FIVE BEST VIDEOS OF 1984

1 – NEIL YOUNG: Wonderin'

Tim Pope's wild gift. 'Wonderin' ' features a cheery, sorbet-tinted landscape with the ragged presence of Young providing unsettling counterpoint. Worth it just for Young's eerie, slurred smile.

2 – HERBIE HANCOCK: Rockit

The invasion of the domestic jitterbugs. Superb editing, masterful use of colour, and general air of motorised hysteria make 'Rockit' one of the best of all promos to date.

3 – COCTEAU TWINS: Pearly Dewdrops' Drops

Honey at the core, and in its avoidance of glitz and pyrotechnics an example to all.

4 – CABARET VOLTAIRE: The Crackdown

Still the finest argument for taking the 'art' train to a visual destination. Independent minds on both sides of the camera.

5 – MICHAEL JACKSON: Thriller

Fully deserving of all the printer's ink it received this year, 'Thriller' relates to the ordinary promo the way a hologram relates to bifocals. The ensemble dancing also remains unequalled.

THE FIVE WORST VIDEOS OF 1984

1 – SARA BRIGHTMAN – Rhythm Of The Rain

The visual equivalent of false eyelashes. Plot: naff chanteuse in naff alleyway lolls 'abandonedly' on every available car bonnet, accompanied by naff dancers. Naff.

2 – LIONEL RICHIE: Hello.

Risible. Probably well-meaning, but there are some matters that should be spared exposure on MTV.

3 – DURAN DURAN: The Reflex

Any production that spends half its budget on a staged tidal wave and then approximates said wave's effects by tossing a bucket of water over someone's head deserves the honour.

4 – WHAM: The Collected Works.

I feel I speak for millions here.

5 – THE POINTER SISTERS: Automatic

Worst lighting award. Pushed mercilessly against a pizza-coloured backdrop, the Sisters look uncomfortably ready for B-movie interrogation.

THE YEAR'S ALBUMS

A

ABC
Beauty Stab (Neutron)
ABC have become U2 with a Nelson Riddle production. A sickeningly smug revelation of over-30's rock, glossed over with a thin veneer of big band sound.
SOUNDS

Boy George has more soul in his little finger than Martin Fry's entire, awkward body.
MELODY MAKER

Get off the picket line, boys, and get back to the boudoir or the ballroom.
NME

AC/DC
Flick Of The Switch
(Atlantic)
AC/DC have got what's demanded of them. So you can leave 'progress' and 'development' right out of this issue...
MELODY MAKER

...the rapid, rabid riffs career through your living room like an amphetamine-fueled juggernaut.
SOUNDS

...believe it or not, all 10 tracks on the album end on the same note, played in the exact same manner.
CREEM

ACCEPT
Balls To The Wall (Portrait)
...will become even mightier than the Scorpions.
MELODY MAKER

...their singer sounds as stupid as Freddie Starr impersonating a camp commandant.
RECORD MIRROR

Does there exist a more powerful distillation of inarticulate misanthropic anomie than their 'Fight It Back'? 'I am forced to live that boring life/God, I hate the average/Go and nuke it out/Go, piss the accepted, screw them all.'
NME

THE ACCURSED
Up With The Punks
(Wreck 'Em)
...a ridiculously crass and incomprehensible

record that as a result is quite enjoyable...abominably played and recorded...

ADAM ANT
Strip (CBS)
Adam has an enjoyability and a craziness...that shines out like a beacon through po-faced 'contemporary pop'.
SOUNDS

Lumbering...in thought and tune and garb and move. Adam Ant is starting to look like pop's hopeless fat boy again...
NME

Obviously a giant piss-take.
RECORD MIRROR

Adam deserves a medal for his bravery. And also, apparently, for his virility.
MELODY MAKER

'Strip' is the most predictable Rod Stewart record ever released. It's the deadest drone Bananarama ever recorded.
CREEM

KING SUNNY ADE
Juju Music Of The 80's
(Sunny Alade)
Just how many of this man's discs can a poor boy collect? A lot if they're all as inspired as this one and you're willing to do without luxuries like food.
SOUNDS

Synchro System (Mango)
...if this is the way the King gets down, I can't wait to hear what the peasants are into.
CREEM

...an interesting blend of urgent percussive rhythms, mesmerising vocal chants, and non-steroidal guitar work. It makes a pleasant change from synthetic soulless pop...
RECORD MIRROR

AKENDENGUE
Mando (CBS)
...prowling African dance rhythms rub shoulders with chic French sophistication.
SOUNDS

THE ALARM
Declaration (IRS)
Who could hate such patent village idiots as these? I am convinced this band contribute more than any other to the derision of rock and roll.
NME

THE ALARM

...would be so easy to ridicule if it weren't for the unavoidable power of their songs. The Alarm make their point with style and dignity...
MELODY MAKER

...their rebellion may be spurious but it is at least listenable. Singalong hooks and boisterous backing vocals abound.
SOUNDS

...an album of slogans, power and promises – but promises that mean nothing. Behind the group's revolutionary stance, the thoughts are about as radical as the conversation at a Tupperware party.
RECORD MIRROR

ALIEN SEX FIEND
Who's Been Sleeping In My Brain? (Cherry Red)
ASF share the same artistic shallowness and stifled superiority of their Blitz predecessors....dreadful in a squalid, spastic unlistenable sort of way.
NME

..the sound of four pairs of feet stamping around in their own little puddle of piss.
SOUNDS

...most of all they're great fun.
MELODY MAKER

MOSE ALLISON
Lessons In Living
(Elektra-Musician)
...as unique an artist as jazz, blues and pop can

muster between them...shows him not just ageing, but getting better.
NME

ALTERED IMAGES
Collected Images (Epic)
...now is the time to realise that Altered Images were led up the garden path to lose on the roundabout what they had gained on the swings.
SOUNDS

AMERICA
Your Move (Capitol)
...a couple of old bores...
RECORD MIRROR

IAN ANDERSON
Walk Into Light (Chrysalis)
...sounds like third rate Genesis.:.
RECORD MIRROR

LAURIE ANDERSON
Mister Heartbreak (WEA)
Creative listeners will find it a multi-faceted meditation/examination of man-as-but-tourist in his universe.
NME

...more defined, less jerky, and ultimately more complete as a cohesive listening delight...
SOUNDS

Immerse yourself in this sublime record and

one day you'll wake and wonder if it really happened, and by then it won't matter anyway.
MELODY MAKER

BOB ANDY
Friends (I-Anka)
...to whisk you right back to those elysian days...when Crombies and Brogues were *de rigueur* and your sister's boyfriend was a genuine Bov boy skinhead and it was something to be proud of...
NME

...a sort of rootsy lovers' rock.
RECORD MIRROR

ANGELIC UPSTARTS
Angel Dust (Anagram)
...the Oi band who gave the movement justification and real moral fibre.
SOUNDS

...an intelligent, chronologically-ordered summary of their achievements...
MELODY MAKER

ANTHRAX
Fistful Of Metal (MFN)
They sum up what they're about with their own lines: 'Abandon all hope those who enter/Cos there ain't too much of that down here'.
SOUNDS

ANTI-PASTI
Anti-Pasti (Rondelet)
...a transparent band with no substance.

ANY TROUBLE
Wrong End Of The Race (EMI America)
...welcome home, boys.
NME

...after listening to four sides of Clive Gregson pouring his heart down his sleeve, even the most stalwart Any Trouble fan might be forgiven for feeling slightly exhausted.
MELODY MAKER

ARCANGEL
Arcangel (Portrait)
Good listening for anybody waiting for the third Boston LP.
SOUNDS

JOAN ARMATRADING
Track Record (A&M)
A bit cocktail parties, bridge and SDP, but good value all the same.
MELODY MAKER

...stuck up a cul-de-sac of formularised 'pop'...
NME

STEVE ARRINGTON'S HALL OF FAME
Positive Power (Atlantic)
Human rhythm is always welcome. Time these scions of Ohio got their butts onto a British stage.
NME

ARROW
Hot Hot Hot (Air)
As one of the leading soca masters, he creates a sound that is going to be a vital ingredient in the new music that's coming.
NME

ASIA
Alpha (Geffen)
Akin to bolting your way through a wedding cake.
NME

VIRGINIA ASTLEY
From Gardens Where We Feel Secure
(Happy Valley Records)
A vivid collection of pastoral tone poems based loosely around a childhood summer spent in the heart of the English countryside.
NME

...a momentary fragment of complete recollection. pregnant with all the fleetingly suggested emotional traumas of an induced *déjà vu*.
MELODY MAKER

ASWAD
Live And Direct (Island)
...a strangely dated reggae now...
MELODY MAKER

...a document of a great band doing what they do best.
NME

ATOMIC ROOSTER
Headline News
(Towerbell)
A complete dud.
SOUNDS

ATTILA THE STOCKBROKER
Sawdust And Empire
(Anagram)
The only thing he has got is monotony down to a fine art.
SOUNDS

AU PAIRS
Live In Berlin

ASWAD

(AKA Records)
...they're boxing themselves into a corner and marching themselves up a cul-de-sac.
MELODY MAKER

...a messy souvenir and cheap farewell...
NME

PATTI AUSTIN
Patti Austin (Qwest)
We're not talking Bacharach here, we're talking spirit of Bessie Smith meets Prince!
SOUNDS

...has about as much character as a flat pint of lager.
RECORD MIRROR

AUSTRALIAN CRAWL
Semantics (Geffen)
...reveals a chronic lack of inspiration. A failure to look further than their own backyards, to grow beyond the boundaries imposed by Australia's non-existent music history.
SOUNDS

AXE
Nemesis (Atco)
...immensely dull.
NME

AZTEC CAMERA
High Land, Hard Rain
(Rough Trade)
...sounds younger than yesterday and not necessarily stoned, just beautiful.
CREEM

JOAN ARMATRADING

B

THE B-52'S
Whammy (Warner Bros.)
The B's may think this is progress, and one can't blame them for not wanting to do the first album a third time, but never before has the band sounded like this...anonymous.
CREEM

BAD BRAINS
Rock For Light (Abstract)
...as close as they could hope to a recreation of their live outrage, the staggering pace, the jolting energy, the insane clanging of their no-holds-barred hard core punk shooting out of the speakers...
MELODY MAKER

...four USA rasta-types whose schtick is to do half-reggae songs and half-punk thrash, which makes them...yes! *Twice* as awful as you could possibly hope for!
SOUNDS

DAVE BALL
In Strict Tempo
(Some Bizarre)
A joke in search of a punch line.
MELODY MAKER

BANANARAMA
Bananarama (London)
I just wish they could SING...
NME

...you're left with a curiously empty feeling.
SOUNDS

BANANARAMA

PETER BAUMANN

THE BARRACUDAS
Live 1983 (Coyote)
...over the past three years, they've matured into an explosive rock 'n' roll garage combo.
SOUNDS

JOHN BARRY
Stringbeat (Cherry Red)
Music for intermissions.
NME

TONI BASIL
Toni Basil (Virgin)
...all the soul of a calculating machine.
RECORD MIRROR

...as infectious as AIDS but with far less damaging consequences to the body.
SOUNDS

Toni Basil personifies all that is wrong with the music industry. Not content with letting Boy George loose on a prurient nation, Virgin let an American *choreographer* sing.
MELODY MAKER

BAUHAUS
The Singles 1981-1983
(Beggar's Banquet)
...one of those second-division acts who only kept going because they were too stupid to realise they'd *always* been flogging a dead horse.
MELODY MAKER

PETER BAUMANN
Strangers In The Night
(Arista)
Ex-member of Tangerine Dream releases ropey techno-pop album...
SOUNDS

...his musical direction is heading down the plug.
MELODY MAKER

THE BEACH BOYS
Rarities (Capitol)
Only fanatics need apply.
NME

THE BEACH BOYS
The Very Best Of The Beach Boys, Vol. 1 and 2
(Capitol)
A LAST desperate attempt to mine a last few nuggets of gold from the Sixties El Dorado.
RECORD MIRROR

ADRIAN BELEW
Twang Bar King (Island)
...all the young twang bar kings *always* make albums like this: a collection of notes looking for a reason to be.
SOUNDS

Why can't guitarists stick to being guitarists and leave their grand and unrealistic pretensions in the basket of their daydreams?
MELODY MAKER

PAT BENATAR
Live From Earth (Chrysalis)
Most heavy rock fans over here are in their mid-teens and they don't want to go and see someone who looks like their mum wearing a mini-skirt strutting about.
RECORD MIRROR

GEORGE BENSON
In Your Eyes (Warner Bros.)
...'bland' would not be an overstatement.
RECORD MIRROR

BERLIN
Love Life (Mercury)
A shallow, glossy American group who want to be continental and risqué.
SOUNDS

BIG BROTHER AND THE HOLDING COMPANY
Cheaper Thrills (Edsel)
...pure psychedelic nitro glycerin...
SOUNDS

...only the fanatics are going to wet themselves over this one, chum.
NME

BIG COUNTRY
The Crossing (Mercury)

...frequently achieves the epic drama it's after.
CREEM

THE BIRTHDAY PARTY
Mutiny! (Mute)
...contains some of the dirtiest, loudest, gut-crunching, ear-wrenching cataclysmic music you ever heard.
MELODY MAKER

BITCH
Be My Slave (Metal Blade)
...a woman with a fetish for whips, chains and kinky pleasures.
SOUNDS

BLACK FLAG
My War (SST)
It wallows as compulsively as the Velvets in the scum around the bath-tub of The Great American Wash-Out. Depraved, disgusting – and essential.
NME

...scorches your brain and it hurts so GOOD!
SOUNDS

A concerned colleague wondered if I'd got the record on the wrong speed; I wondered if Black Flag will ever get their sanity back.
MELODY MAKER

BLACK SABBATH
Born Again (Vertigo)
...like Frankenstein's monster with a club foot. It snarls and growls but wanders around aimlessly.
RECORD MIRROR

If music had an IQ, then this monstrosity would clock in somewhere around zero.
MELODY MAKER

BLACK UHURU
Anthem (Island)
...set against 'Anthem' most reggae pales into insignificance.
NME

...a distinct step forward.
MELODY MAKER

J. BLACKFOOT
City Slicker (Sound Town)
...strictly for the tourists with too many cameras and disgusting check trousers.
MELODY MAKER

He testifies.
SOUNDS

BLANCMANGE
Mange Tout (London)
...excellent technicians, not great tunesmiths.
RECORD MIRROR

...a lobotomized Yazoo...
NME

Nowhere does their humour lapse or their altruism falter.
SOUNDS

...founders clumsily in their new-found desire for polish and perfection.
MELODY MAKER

THE BLASTERS
Non Fiction
(Slash/Warner Brothers)
...the most well-meaning band in the land has finally made a record worthy of its exemplary intentions.
CREEM

...the best; from the best...
MELODY MAKER

PETER BLEGVAD
The Naked Shakespeare (Virgin)
...probes into some weird and wonderful crevices of the imagination.
MELODY MAKER

BLUE AEROPLANES
Bop Art (Party Records)
Interesting, angry, sad, beautiful, rewarding, and bursting with very real emotion.
NME

What these aviators are about is anyone's guess; suffice to say 'Bop Art', although slightly flawed by its 'hey, we're being really creative man!' outbursts, is a little gem.
SOUNDS

THE BLUE NILE
A Walk Across The Rooftops (Linn)
The beauty is unassuming, the intelligence is uncontrived. Great music is still being made.
NME

Nostalgia romance, elation and reflection are woven into the fabric with gossamer-fine delicacy.
MELODY MAKER

BLUE OYSTER CULT
The Revolution By Night (CBS)
...a platter that just might please all factions of their worshippers.
SOUNDS

...starting to sound like folksongs from some extra-terrestrial prairies of the mind.
NME

BLANCMANGE

BLUE RONDO
Bees Knees & Chickens Elbows (Virgin)
This stuff is good.
SOUNDS

BODINE
Three Times Running
(Rhinoceros)
...nothing more than everyday excess.
SOUNDS

THE BOLLOCK BROTHERS
Live Performances
(Charly)
...a compendium of trash values and manic nostalgia like the Cramps, the Gun Club, the Doors, the Birthday Party and Screaming Lord Sutch rolled into one!
MELODY MAKER

BON JOVI
Bon Jovi (Vertigo)
...get wise to the American counter-attack.
SOUNDS

JAMES BOOKER
Classified (Demon)
...a major New Orleans talent...
MELODY MAKER

This marvellous music is here and now, bringing the tributaries that run through America's REALLY PROUD HERITAGE smack up to date.
NME

DAVID BOWIE
Ziggy Stardust: The Motion Picture (RCA)
...on a par with some of the greatest rock 'n' roll bands of all time, such as Eater or Flintlock.
MELODY MAKER

I can tell you it's crap, that's what.
NME

DAVID BOWIE
Fame And Fashion (RCA)
...a bland and unadventurous potted history of the pre-Serious Moonlight Bowie...
SOUNDS

I can't see who's going to buy this fraudulent example of corporations at their mercenary worst...
MELODY MAKER

...really nothing more than the latest in an exploitative line of RCA Bowie repackages.
NME

THE BOX
Great Moments In Big Slam (Go! Discs)
...fulfils all of the group's pre-pubescent promise.
SOUNDS

BILLY BRAGG
Life's A Riot With Spy Vs Spy (Go! Discs)
Hail the return of the street corner songwriter.
RECORD MIRROR

Billy Bragg is some kind of wonderful.
NME

BRAINTICKET
Cottonwoodhill
(Bellaphon)
...one of the greatest psychedelic meisterwerks of all time, starring the completely unlegendary Jane Free, acid housewife supreme.
SOUNDS

BREAK MACHINE
Break Machine (Record Shack)
More suited to the 'Des O'Connor Show' than the streets, Break Machine have turned electro funk into a particularly odious cabaret show.
RECORD MIRROR

BRONZE
Taken By Storm (Bronz)
...a heavy metal five piece from the West Country, specializing in tawdry Foreigner and Toto impressions...
RECORD MIRROR

...nothing more than a third-rate Uriah Heep rip-off.
SOUNDS

CLARENCE 'GATEMOUTH' BROWN
One More Mile (Demon)
...a cornucopia of sheer delight – cajun carouses with be-bop, big-band swing bustles with the blues and crosses into country.
NME

...one *hot* record.
MELODY MAKER

JAMES BROWN
Roots Of A Revolution
(Polydor)
I can honestly say I've never come across a record so lovingly put together and with such meticulous and informative sleeve notes...
MELODY MAKER

...an invaluable historical document...
RECORD MIRROR

JACKSON BROWNE
Lawyers In Love (Asylum)
...good soul-shattering cryptic, apocalyptic ballads...
MELODY MAKER

...the best record Browne has made.
NME

TOM BROWNE
Rockin' Radio (Arista)
...inconsequential sound, that's what this is.
NME

...pallid and cliché-ridden enough to send even the most ardent electro-spunker hot on the heels of a Steeleye Span revival.
MELODY MAKER

T-BONE BURNETT
Proof Through The Night
(Warner Bros.)
Never having measured America's decline by the willingness of its female citizens to take their clothes off, I find that some of Burnett's allegories fail to touch me as I know they should.
CREEM

It's 1983, on the doorstep of '84. All the last romantics are crowding into one room and this is the album under their arms.
NME

BUTTHOLE SURFERS
Butthole Surfers
(Alternative Tentacles)
...like a crow with brain disease that's sitting on an electric fence and too gone to fly away.
SOUNDS

T-BONE BURNETT

C

CABARET VOLTAIRE
Johnny Yes No (The Original Soundtrack From The Motion Picture)
(Doublevision)
Music for East Germans.
RECORD MIRROR

I reserve the right to...consign this release to the junkyard...
MELODY MAKER

CABARET VOLTAIRE
The Crackdown (Some Bizarre)
...a compulsive concoction that doesn't bleat to the beat.
SOUNDS

an entirely satisfying slice of metallic electropunk-phunk.
RECORD MIRROR

CABARET VOLTAIRE

THE JIM CARROLL BAND
I Write Your Name
(Atlantic)
...Carroll has the high IQ art/heart market all sewn up.
SOUNDS

THE CARS
Heartbeat City (Elektra)
...jerky, clichéd, pompous trash.
SOUNDS

CARLENE CARTER
C'est C Bon (Epic)
Her always innovative ancestors in the illustrious Carter Family can continue to be justly proud of Carlene.
SOUNDS

A gentle and revealing record that will, alas, find no toehold in this marketplace of fools and ruffians.
NME

At least Carlene is *singing* again.
MELODY MAKER

NICK CAVE
From Her To Eternity
(Mute)
Cave has inked a comic strip for the dark hours, a kind of Fungus The Bogeyman for those forbidden sick moments nobody likes to admit to but entertains with a guilty fascination all the same.
MELODY MAKER

Nick Cave has disappeared in the quicksand of his myth.
SOUNDS

...one of the greatest rock albums ever made.
NME

CARMEL

...a wider range of motifs to match their restricted range of themes would be welcome.
MELODY MAKER

J. J. CALE
8 (Phonogram)
Warning: sleeping rattlesnake.
NME

JOHN CALE
Caribbean Sunset
(Island/Ze)
...still in that sad position where the titles are better than the actual songs on his albums.
SOUNDS

...continues Cale's burpy ride through a bumpy, uneven career.
NME

CAPTAIN SENSIBLE
The Power Of Love (A&M)
...a bizarre rag-bag of semi-ideas and sort-of humour, leaving an overall impression of flimsy vagueness. Why would anyone bother?
MELODY MAKER

40 minutes of the Captain is still a tonic.
NME

...it's a dammed (sic) hard slog listening to this

album all at once.
RECORD MIRROR

IRENE CARA
What A Feelin' (Epic)
One great pop song...and 10 more or less mediocre attempts to follow it up.
MELODY MAKER

CARMEL
The Drum Is Everything
(London)
...a comparatively inchoate offering from someone who may turn out to be a giant.
MELODY MAKER

...this album has a lot more to offer than the Serge Clerc cartoon cover that makes it look like a Fifties table mat.
SOUNDS

...Carmel simply can't sing...
NME

KIM CARNES
Café Racers (Capitol)
Toffee-brain piffle from a woman of no importance. Even her laryngitis seems to have cleared up.
NME

CHAIRMEN OF THE BOARD
Salute The General
(H-D-H Records)
...stands as a great introduction to a vastly underrated group.
NME

THE CHAMELEONS
Script Of The Bridge
(Statik)
...a perfect record for 5am depression, or as the haunting background music for a tragic love story set in windswept Cornwall.
RECORD MIRROR

They could be the next underground cult, or the next U2.
SOUNDS

CHEAP TRICK
Next Position Please (Epic)
...efficient mainstream rock...
MELODY MAKER

The band that tries to be everything will invariably wind up being nothing.
CREEM

CHIC
Believer (Atlantic)
Its best moments aren't far short of classic Chic...
MELODY MAKER

Anyone for aural necrophilia?
SOUNDS

CHINA CRISIS
Working With Fire And Steel; Possible Pop Songs Vol 2 (Virgin)
More coffee and less Ovaltine is needed.
NME

Strength through fragility.
RECORD MIRROR

...the prize guys of the meaningful, morose and lachrymose bunch.
MELODY MAKER

THE CHOCOLATE WATCHBAND
The Best Of (Rhino import)
...the definitive psychedelic band...
SOUNDS

CHRIS & COSEY
Songs Of Love And Lust
(Rough Trade)
If the mood takes you, this record played very loud has a pleasing cathartic effect. It parades human feelings in bondage, overlaid with a sticky pallor, presenting an ultimately very sad world of starved emotions and brittle pains and pleasures.
NME

Diehard industrialists will scorn the commercial connotations of this record but, removing the scepticism, it's got to be the best thing C & C have done in their duo career.
SOUNDS

THE CHURCH
Seance (Carrere)

The Church...will never be irrelevant because they are quite simply timless.
SOUNDS

...The Church's acid edge has settled into marshmallow hippy gumbo.
MELODY MAKER

ANNE CLARK
Changing Places
(Red Flame)
...it really is impossible to escape Anne Clark's lugubriousness. It's not sensitivity this represents so much as depression.
MELODY MAKER

Anne's poetry doesn't provide any solutions: the message is that life/love is a pile of shit and there's not a lot we, as helpless individuals, can do about it.
SOUNDS

CLASSIX NOUVEAUX
Secret (Liberty/EMI)
After an encouraging 18 month absence, here they resume their place as the pompous fishes who provided early insipid inspiration for the Fixx, H₂O, Blue Zoo, Talk Talk, and so on.
NME

CLARENCE CLEMONS AND THE RED BANK ROBBERS
Rescue (CBS)
...flung together with little thought.
RECORD MIRROR

JIMMY CLIFF
The Power And The Glory
(CBS)
...selling himself short...
RECORD MIRROR

...defensive water treading.
NME

GEORGE CLINTON
You Shouldn't-Nuf Bit Fish
(Capitol)
Hot body pop from the hand of the master.
MELODY MAKER

...funky as a salamander stew...
NME

...a mild little record caught in a crossfire of half grasped ideas and lazy handshakes with current trends.
RECORD MIRROR

COCTEAU TWINS
Head Over Heels (4AD)
These songs are rhapsodies bled of desire, songs that posit nothing but an innocent Ineffable.
NME

...their magic is a fluid element that won't *ever* be explained.
MELODY MAKER

THE COMMODORES
Commodores 13
(Motown)
Turgid, drawn out and garish, it reveals the Commodores at their most complacent...

CHIC

MELODY MAKER

...what's been suspected since his departure is now achingly plain on this first full post-Richie set.
RECORD MIRROR

...A Motown rarity – a great soul *band*...
NME

COMSAT ANGELS
Land (Jive)
...eventually fails to deliver...strangely incomplete and less than satisfying.
SOUNDS

...since you only have to sell about nine copies of an album to dominate the LP chart for at least a fortnight, the Comsats can probably look forward to a decent chart placing.
MELODY MAKER

ALICE COOPER
DaDa (Warner Bros.)
...just pathetic parodies of his late '60s and early '70s work...
NME

...one of the original wild men of rock 'n' roll and the closest the USA has come to producing a real live punk, has become a dead boring wimp.
SOUNDS

JULIAN COPE
World Shut Your Mouth
(Phonogram)
...a sort of mixture in modern times of Syd Barrett and Gary Glitter.
SOUNDS

...merely erratic and dissatisfying.
MELODY MAKER

...the result of listening to all those Chocolate Watchband albums, eh Julian?
RECORD MIRROR

STEWART COPELAND
Rumble Fish (A&M)
Film unseen and titles ignored, it conjures up nothing and as a record, therefore, it fails.
MELODY MAKER

ELVIS COSTELLO AND THE ATTRACTIONS
Punch The Clock (F-Beat)
...probably represents the best collection of Elvis's songs on one album.
RECORD MIRROR

...a great deal of it is indispensable if you want to be a serious Costellobore.
MELODY MAKER

...this is adjudged a major letdown by Elvis's acolytes.
CREEM

ELVIS COSTELLO & THE ATTRACTIONS
Goodbye Cruel World
(F-Beat)
...consistently relevant and thought-provoking...
SOUNDS

ELVIS COSTELLO & THE ATTRACTIONS

...Elvis at his most biting, musically and lyrically. Even the cover is worth sticking on the wall just for itself. Sad, depressing, but brilliant.
RECORD MIRROR

JOSIE COTTON
From The Hip (Elektra)
...inside 'From The Hip' there is a real record trying to get out.
NME

...she manages to capture the sound of those great all-girl Sixties singing groups, she shines like a diamond.
SOUNDS

THE CRAMPS
Smell Of Female
(Enigma, US import)
...guaranteed enjoyment for pussycats with sharp claws and tigers with sabre teeth.
SOUNDS

...their long-promised live disc, showcases some of their most inspired ever moments.
NME

...a watered down version of the 'Off The Bone' singles collection released last year.
SOUNDS

THE CRAVATS
The Colossal Tunes Out
(Corpus Christi)
The Cravats' sound has matured and they're fighting back.
MELODY MAKER

A pumping, pulsing slice of aggression liberally smattered with gruff and gritty lyrics.
SOUNDS

RANDY CRAWFORD
Nightline (Warner Bros.)
...continues to uphold a standard that's inevitably classy but rarely remarkable.
MELODY MAKER

ROBERT CRAY BAND
Bad Influence (Demon)
...the best current evidence that there is still life in the blues...
SOUNDS

MARSHALL CRENSHAW
Field Day (Warner Bros.)
...while Marshall is writing his pop Annie Hall, Steve Lillywhite is producing Tarzan And The Leopard Woman.
CREEM

CULTURE CLUB
Colour By Numbers
(Virgin)
...so far '83's most consistently enjoabale LP...
NME

I somehow had more faith in Boy George and never expected him to go for the soft option in such a crass and weak fashion.
MELODY MAKER

...enough to sing in the shower at least through early next year.
CREEM

THE CURE
Japanese Whispers:
The Cure Singles
Nov. 82: Nov. 83 (Fiction)
...the *angst*-ridden *doppelgangers* of the pretty boys of pop.
NME

...the dark secret corners of 'A' Level rock (prerequisites: an appreciation of existentialism, a pale complexion and a miserable childhood)...
RECORD MIRROR

...this eight-track compilation demonstates in lingering detail where and how often The Cure went wrong.
MELODY MAKER

THE CURE
The Top (Fiction)
...a record of wicked originality and wit.
RECORD MIRROR

...isn't he a preposterous prat?
SOUNDS

...psychedelia that can't be dated, the sounds and shapes of somebody revelling in an identity crisis.
MELODY MAKER

...if it has any value it's only as a vivid illustration of the ease with which even the flagship bands of the cleansing turmoil of the late '70s can slide into the same miasma of self indulgence that nurtured the sickness we thought had been purged forever. In this case, The Cure is as painful as the disease.
NME

IVOR CUTLER AND LINDA HURST
Privilege (Rough Trade)

...a record of true wonder...
NME

I cannot see the point...
SOUNDS

THE CURE

HOLGER CZUKAY
Der Osten Ist Rot (Virgin)
Like the inventor of a series of private jokes, Czukay has manufactured a world impervious to the gaze of outsiders.
MELODY MAKER

IVOR CUTLER

D

DANSE SOCIETY

D.O.A.
Bloodied But Unbowed
(Alternative Tentacles)
...the biggest pile of whingeing tripe I have heard in a long, long time.
MELODY MAKER

DALEK I LOVE YOU
Dalek I Love You (Korova)
...an anachronism from the tail of the erstwhile Liverpool boom.
SOUNDS

Last year Dalek played the Futurama from behind a curtain; next year I fear they'll be able to do it from behind a pile of unsold copies of this album.
NME

ROGER DALTREY
Parting Should Be Painless (WEA)
Parting should be painless, not a long drawn out embarrassment for all concerned.
SOUNDS

'...amounts to no more than an early '70s singer-songwriter LP with Daltrey as a male Judie Tzuke.
NME

THE DAMNED
Live In Newcastle
(Damned)
...reaffirms just why the Damned are one of the most exciting bands in the country...
SOUNDS

DANSE SOCIETY
Heaven Is Waiting (Arista)
...a make-believe madness, a collection of the clichés of insanity, a psychedelic amusement but never an experience.
MELODY MAKER

It's not computer piss, not exactly anyway, but it just seems to have suffered a little over-production so it appears humourless and a wee bit too slick.
RECORD MIRROR

Po-faced and portentous on the surface, frail and unfocussed at the core, 'Heaven is Waiting' raids the back catalogue of Joy Division and the Cure...
SOUNDS

DAVID J
Etiquette Of Violence
...horribly oppressed by his own version of masculinity.
NME

...embarrassing-poetry-people-write-before-outgrowing-a-half-fare-on-the-bus...
SOUNDS

...a hearteningly perverse determination to investigate new ideas in his own style.
MELODY MAKER

DEAD CAN DANCE
Dead Can Dance (4AD)
...a spiritual beauty above and beyond the realms of the imagination... ...calls for our total immersion...
MELODY MAKER

...as new as we can get.
SOUNDS

DEAD OR ALIVE
Sophisticated Boom Boom (Epic)
...highly capable purveyors of extremely infectious kitsch pop and boystown bop.
RECORD MIRROR

...not a classic album.
NME

There is more to Dead Or Alive than you think.
MELODY MAKER

...thrusts a tongue into every cheek that's going and even dares to wiggle it about a bit.
SOUNDS

DeBARGE
All This Love (Motown)
Well tailored, competent and ultimately dull production line LP...
NME

DEEP FREEZE MICE
Saw A Ranch House Burning Last Night
(Mole Embalming Records)
Hooked in a mid-Sixties psychedelic pop quicksand...
SOUNDS

DEPECHE MODE
Construction Time Again
(Mute)
...grey, precious and indulgent.
MELODY MAKER

demonstrates how obsolete the term 'electro-pop' has now become.
NME

...the most surprising album this year. Quite simply, it's also one of the best.
SOUNDS

DETROIT SPINNERS
Crossfire (WEA)
...after 28 years of recording, maybe it's quite something they bothered to turn up at all.
RECORD MIRROR

HOWARD DEVOTO
Jerky Versions Of The Year (Virgin)
...the nastiest wimp since Ron Mael...
CREEM

DIAMOND HEAD
Canterbury (MCA)
Like Led Zeppelin and the god-like Deep Purple

DEAD OR ALIVE

before them...masters of authentic heavy rock brilliance.
SOUNDS

...they have bared their souls and laid their necks on the line...
MELODY MAKER

DIE HAUT WITH NICK CAVE
Burnin' The Ice (Illuminated Records)
...just...lacklustre middle ground...
SOUNDS

...an art-rock showband...
NME

Cave is rock's most powerful presence right now and, erratically, its most creative lyricist.
MELODY MAKER

DIO
Holy Diver (Warner Bros.)
...features back cover credits arranged under the headings 'Those Who Created', 'Those Who Laboured' and 'Those Who Supported'. Too bad they left out the category for us listeners – 'Those Who Suffered'.
CREEM

DIRE STRAITS
Alchemy (Vertigo)
...without purpose or fun.
NME

...what an audience! Arms raised, they look like born-again Christians at a Billy Graham rally or worse, clean-cut kids from one of those old 'I'd like to buy the world a Coke' adverts. I bet they're always in by midnight, never play the stereo too loud and are respectful to their parents.
SOUNDS

...Dire Straits play true progressive rock. And all available evidence shows that they can only get better.
MELODY MAKER

DISLOCATION DANCE
Midnight Shift
(Rough Trade)
Charming, though hardly crucial.
MELODY MAKER

...white folk messing with a music they don't understand.
SOUNDS

...colossally dull, dismally feeble, coy, trifling, bland beyond belief.
NME

DISORDER
The Singles Collection
(Disorder)
Musically, Disorder are hopeless. They show no competence whatsoever...
SOUNDS

THE DOOBIE BROTHERS
Farewell Tour (Warner Bros)
One for slack stomachs.
NME

THE DOORS
Alive She Cried (Elektra)
...an album for all those old bores who decry the music of today and bemoan the passing of a golden age.
MELODY MAKER

What was that he said? No time to wallow in the mire. Tell that to the folks who have somehow managed to turn a band that had maybe eight terrific months into a mini-industry.
CREEM

THOMAS DOLBY
The Flat Earth (Parlophone)
...Dolby is shaping up to become no less than an updated Peter Gabriel.
MELODY MAKER

...who would dare to question Dolby's navigation? He steers as much by magic as by plain common sense.
SOUNDS

...an elaborate exercise in mental engineering with no corresponding emotional commitment.
NME

DR. JOHN
The Brightest Smile In Town (Demon)
...one of those deliciously uncommon records which instigates a desire to (re)discover an artist's back catalogue...
SOUNDS

DURAN DURAN
Seven And The Ragged Tiger (EMI)
...restores danger and menace to a band that

DIRE STRAITS

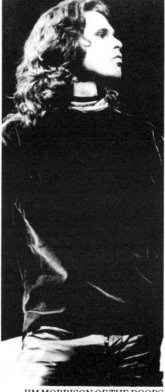

JIM MORRISON OF THE DOORS

was veering dangerously close to the insipid...
MELODY MAKER

...pathetic, useless, no good. It's pretentious, pompous and possibly the first chapter in their decline.
RECORD MIRROR

...so assuredly awful it breaks new ground in badness...
SOUNDS

I do not hesitate to recommend *Seven* heartily to all fans of the group and the occasional normal person who's got a taste for some yummy harmonies.
CREEM

THE DURUTTI COLUMN
Another Setting (Factory)
The law of diminishing returns can be applied to Reilly's pastoral delicacies with an unfortunate degree of accuracy.
MELODY MAKER

It's gruelling malevolence against drifting sorrow, a long groaning *chug* against one light breath of regret.
NME

IAN DURY & THE MUSIC STUDENTS
4000 Weeks' Holiday (Polydor)
...none of the open-hearted surgery of 'Panties' and therefore none of the bite.
SOUNDS

...the best thing he's done since 'New Boots And Panties'.
MELODY MAKER

Dury below form is still an improvement over at least half of pop on their best day.
NME

DYKE & THE BLAZERS
So Sharp (Kent)
...mandatory music for anyone tracing an evolution of the funk, and some of the sharpest dance power around.

...a little second division.
RECORD MIRROR

BOB DYLAN
Infidels (CBS)
...as stimulating as an evening in the launderette.
MELODY MAKER

There is a lot to be said for early retirement.
RECORD MIRROR

God knows (and I use that phrase advisedly) how far off the deep end he'll go if John Glenn becomes president.
CREEM

E

EARTH WIND & FIRE
Electric Universe (CBS)
...slick but ultimately mediocre...
RECORD MIRROR

ECHO AND THE BUNNYMEN
Ocean Rain (Korova)
...one of our most precious talents.
RECORD MIRROR

...he is wasted on one of contemporary rock's more worthless quests: to relocate The Chord The Moody Blues lost a decade ago. Sad to report Echo And The Bunnymen have found it.
NME

As the dinosaurs roam the earth and ultimately (hopefully) become extinct, all that will be left will be Bunnymen.
SOUNDS

ECHO & THE BUNNYMEN

...easily spans both sublime and ridiculous.
MELODY MAKER

DENNIS EDWARDS
Don't Look Any Further (Gordy)
...all rather routine background music in an Essex wine bar.
RECORD MIRROR

EEK·A·MOUSE
Mouseketeer (Greensleeves)

...the most distinctive voice in reggae whines through another selection of blistering tracks.
RECORD MIRROR

An eccentric character indeed and for this reason to be cherished all the more.
SOUNDS

EINSTURZENDE NEUBAUTEN
Strategies Against Architecture (Mute)
The noise that assaulted my horrified ears was

so loathesome, so vile, so fulsome, so feculent, so noisome, so odious...
MELODY MAKER

EINSTURZENDE NEUBAUTEN
Zeichnungen Des Patienten OT (Some Bizarre)
'Zeichnungen' makes the term 'difficult' obsolete; it makes music, as we're fed it, pedestrian.
SOUNDS

...its suffocating uniformity seems wilfully unlistenable...
NME

...the soundtrack for an exclusive club of miseries who take a misguided pride in the depths of their depressions.
MELODY MAKER

ELBOW BONES AND THE RACKETEERS
New York At Dawn (EMI America)
It's pointless dressing up in your penguin suit if you've got no stomach for the party.
MELODY MAKER

August Darnell does not own a dog. I can say this without fear of contradiction, because if August Darnell did have a dog it would have made a record by now.
NME

ELECTRIC LIGHT OR CHESTRA
SecretMessages (Jet/CBS)
I won't bore you with the details in regard to how the lyrics on this LP all kind of run together after a few tunes (and this one isn't a concept album, either).
CREEM

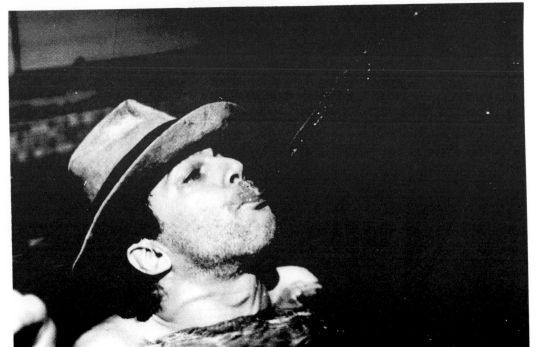

IAN DURY

THE ELECTRIC TOILET
In The Hands Of Karma
(Psycho 8)
...becomes powerfully obsessive, once it's worked its way into your cistern...
SOUNDS

ENDGAMES
Building Beauty (Virgin)
...they lack the hooks, the looks and the croon.
RECORD MIRROR

A limp art funk slouching after the euphoria of early '70s dance. Neuter funk for nowhere scenes.
NME

We can assume that the six players on this team all have day jobs posing for quattro-centro Italian artists with a liking for alabaster.
SOUNDS

ENGLISH DOGS
Invasion Of The Porky Men (Clay)
While the majority of punk bands sink lower and lower in the sewer of brain drain non-sensical gluebag thrashes, there still remains a notable minority of wickedly worthwhile outfits who sparkle with radiant fire.
SOUNDS

BRIAN ENO
Working Backwards 1983-1973 (Editions EG)
It is an unfortunate but not always inappropriate coincidence that the serial prefix to most of Eno's later records reads EG'ED.
NME

Containing ten LP's and an EP of rarities, this ten year retrospective of Brian Eno's recordings is a flickering kaleidoscope of inventiveness...
SOUNDS

...let's face it; Eno and the moon were made for each other.
CREEM

DAVID ESSEX
The Whisper (Mercury)
Give it up, David, and get back to acting.
RECORD MIRROR

THE EUROPEANS
Live (A&M)
...like an American adult-orientated rock version of Joy Division with riffs nicked from the Ten Years After museum of Antiquated Guitar Histrionics.
SOUNDS

THE EUROPEANS
Vocabulary (A&M)
...they've woven a safety net of overworked post '77 youth platitudes: communication, radial delineation, not forgetting obfuscation.
NME

They desperately want to be hip and modern, but 'Vocabulary' merely frustrates me with its lack of old-fashioned melodies and passion.
SOUNDS

...a rather unpleasant all-white athletic look, made worse by silly masks and the highly affected yodel...
MELODY MAKER

EURYTHMICS
Touch (RCA)
'Touch' promised the world. Promised, but failed to deliver.
RECORD MIRROR

It may lack the fluidity of a Hockney, but it *is* masterful, just the same. It's calming, and pleasing, and has no eyesores within its framework.
SOUNDS

...some of the finest-crafted pop tracks this year.
NME

...a perfect, carefully balanced tonic for the newly conscripted troops.
MELODY MAKER

If it was free, we might be talking.
RECORD MIRROR

GIL EVANS
Priestess (Antilles)
Not the great G. Evans album the world is waiting for, but it'll do for now .
CREEM

THE EVERLY BROTHERS
The Everly Brothers Reunion Concert (Impression)
...a shopping must ... for Everly excessives and nostalgia buffs, since none of these renditions outdoes those sublime originals.
NME

EVERYTHING BUT THE GIRL
Eden (Blanco Y Negro)
...floats pleasantly if rather inconsequentially overhead; as relaxing as a good dose of Quiet Life tablets.
RECORD MIRROR

...a very, very honest album.
SOUNDS

...supposed to be taken to heart as a confessional but we can never allay our suspicions that these tiny domestic traumas are really just academic exercises in emotional posturing.
MELODY MAKER

THE EX
Blueprints For A Blackout (Pig Brother Pig)
A real burner. Not to say that this is out and out, head down thrash. No, the Ex are far too subtle for that one.
SOUNDS

THE EXPLOITED
Let's Start A War (Said Maggie One Day) (Pax)
...predictable, tuneless, dated thrash...
SOUNDS

EYELESS IN GAZA
Rust Red September (Cherry Red)
...part terrifying angst, part soothing lullaby...
SOUNDS

...pleasant, but rather pointless. Boys, there are better places to waste your time than the recording studio.
RECORD MIRROR

FACE TO FACE
Face To Face (Epic)
...a fine selection of hard-edged pop songs which are elevated from the norm by the ace production and the sleekness and elegance of the band itself.
SOUNDS

FAD GADGET
Gag (Mute)
...sees him slipping back over old ground.
MELODY MAKER

...one hell of a companionable platter... tremendous gutteral verve.
NME

...too hip and intelligent for the denim bozos and too traditionally versed for the teeny masses.
SOUNDS

THE FALL
Perverted By Language (Rough Trade)
...often thought of as a latter-day answer to the Velvets; here they almost live up to the compliment – harsh, raging and utterly hypnotic.
MELODY MAKER

This is the Fall as always: slovenly, sick, self-satisfied, sarky.
NME

I can't understand what Mark Smith is going on about in nearly all of his lyrics here.
SOUNDS

...leaves you wanting to give the Fall a good kick up the arse.
RECORD MIRROR

FALLEN ANGELS
Fallen Angels (Fallout)
...a flash punk's story of razor knives and back street dives ... with the occasional cosmic intrusion...
SOUNDS

THE FARMER'S BOYS
Get Out & Walk (EMI)
The Boys' wilful pursuit of trivia continues unabated ... the infuriating fripperies of love, of tears, soft drinks, of waking up in the morning.
MELODY MAKER

...all their songs SOUND EXACTLY THE SAME.
SOUNDS

...preferable to the pre-packaged deep-frozen fare that forms so much of our staple diet.
NME

FASHION
Twilight of Idols (Epic/DeStijl)
...music for boudoirs; seductive, filmic ... warm and throbbing...
RECORD MIRROR

THE FARMER'S BOYS

Out of ten tracks, they haven't got a melody to rub together.
SOUNDS

FASTWAY
All Fired Up (CBS)
...this album can't boast two full sides of manic panic genius but there's enough class here to put most of the competition to sleep.
SOUNDS

FATBACK
Is This The Future (Polydor)
I'm afraid not lads! If this is the future, I've had a premonition and seen it all before.
SOUNDS

Socio-political awareness masqueraded in futuristic funk could already be termed a hackneyed cliché in itself – but at least Fatback are attempting to cut their teeth in a different direction. And even if a trendy social conscience ain't your bag – there's plenty in this package to ensure funky aerobics.
MELODY MAKER

FELT
The Splendour Of Fear
(Cherry Red)
...a contemplation piece, a companion to solitude ... Orthodox descriptions can't hope to capture the gorgeous effect of Felt.
MELODY MAKER

...much, much more than six strange titles with gaps in between ... this is rare, floating, tingling beauty of a music.
SOUNDS

TIM FINN
Escapade (Epic)
...a real dreary downer, an aural knock-out drop of unbelievable tedium ... actually manages to be blander than Men At Work...
SOUNDS

THE FIXX
Reach The Beach (MCA)
...agonized can-this-be-adulthood vocal style, influenced by everyone from Bryan Ferry to Lou Gramm...
CREEM

MICK FLEETWOOD'S ZOO
I'm Not Me (RCA)
Send these ga-ga timewasters back to Malibu, and let's hope we never hear from them again.
NME

THE FLESHTONES
Hexbreaker (IRS)
...relentlessly white R&B which is coloured by purposefully dated instrumentation, sleazy sax and manic guitars, and arcane lyrics packed with period hip language.
MELODY MAKER

...breakneck buffoonery quickly becomes tiresome and forces the conclusion that this is a fun package which has no real place outside the hep cat hideaways.
SOUNDS

...goes further than any previous Fleshtones record towards bringing the wild infectiousness of their stage shows to vinyl.
NME

FLUX OF PINK INDIANS
The F.C.'s Treat Us Like Pricks (Spiderleg)
At a time when speaking out of turn is itself close to a crime, we could even trace courage in this thrashing and very black tumult.
NME

Imagine a tape of previous Flux music, shredded and crushed, then Sellotaped back together at random, and you'll have some idea of how this sounds.
SOUNDS

FLYING PICKETS
Lost Boys (10 Records)
Anyone buying 'Lost Boys' for the preppy ba-ba-ba-boom will be surprised by the sociological seriousness.
MELODY MAKER

LITA FORD
Out For Blood (Phonogram)
Save your curiosity and salvage your self-respect.
NME

Dancin' On The Edge
(Phonogram)
My wildest dream has at last come true. Lita Ford has finally produced material to equal her

looks. The word 'stunning' can now be applied with total conviction.
MELODY MAKER

This particular Ford is hyper-charged, tanked up and ready to burn off challengers.
SOUNDS

FORREST
Forrest (CBS)
...slick 'n' slushy disco.
SOUNDS

...leaf it out, John.
RECORD MIRROR

45 GRAVE
Sleep In Safety (Enigma)
The main lead 45 Grave have over all the other minions of rock'n'roll hell lies with their singer Dinal Cancer...
SOUNDS

...Debbie Harry meets the Addams Family...
MELODY MAKER

THE 4 SKINS
From Chaos To 1984
(Syndicate)
...a basic, brutal, raucous racket.
SOUNDS

BRUCE FOXTON
Touch Sensitive (Arista)
Oh, this is hopeless music.
NME

...is it real music? NO, not really.
RECORD MIRROR

THE FLESHTONES

Bruce, sadly, is an also-ran.
MELODY MAKER

JOHN FOXX
The Golden Section
(Virgin)
...heavy, clumsy and claustrophobic...
SOUNDS

Foxx appears slavishly ensnared by his love of machinery, unable to generate more fruitful symbiosis with wider genres or third-party collaborations.
MELODY MAKER

Is he seeking ... a perfect balance of all pop's imperfections, an ultimate harmony in the pop universe of homage and plagiarism, of influence and input?
NME

FRANKIE AND THE KNOCKOUTS
Makin' The Point (MCA)
...streamlined mainstream blandness...
SOUNDS

ARETHA FRANKLIN
Get It Right (Arista)
...continues to surpass all imitation.
SOUNDS

FREEEZ
Gonna Get You
(Beggars Banquet)
A successful exercise in opportunism.
MELODY MAKER

Their songs are dumb without any redeeming merriment and their fizzy, fuzzy mixes are like a carnival for clockwork animals.
NME

FREUR
Doot Doot (CBS)
...more self-congratulatory arty echo-drenched piffle...
SOUNDS

BOBBY FULLER
The Bobby Fuller Tapes Volume One (Rhino)
...to hear music this carefully crafted, this vigorously realised, this damn cared about, is an unexpected treat.
NME

FURYO
Furyo (Fury Records)
...disquieting originality.
SOUNDS

GANG OF FOUR
Hard (EMI)
On this showing, fellow grand larcenists Heaven 17 have little to fear.
NME

GANG OF FOUR

Now that both fashion and the national political climate have declared dissidence to be a dirty word, the Gang can be seen galloping headlong into Mainstream Culture with such an unquestioning haste that the onlooker is forced to wonder if their commitment to anything bar 'Success' was ever that great in the first place.
MELODY MAKER

...a right little gem ... essential listening. Well crucial, man.
RECORD MIRROR

THE GAP BAND
Gap Band V Jammin'
(Total Experience)
It's all down to forced fun and shameless slush.
RECORD MIRROR

...oozes style, panache and confidence.
MELODY MAKER

GARDENING BY MOONLIGHT
Melody In The Madness
(Interdisc)
...the songs have a rich and fully rhythmic content which provides the same physical motivation as conventional dance music without resorting to conventional forms and structures.
SOUNDS

Sculpting almost visual images in the air, their only serious rivals at the art must be Swiss electronic eccentrics Yello, whose wackiness shadows their boldly innovative talent.
MELODY MAKER

GENE LOVES JEZEBEL
Promise (Situation)
...intrinsic howls of anguish and tortured betrayal.
SOUNDS

...Gene Loves Jezebel have the ability to take that ... muso element out of music by subverting the conventionally macho pop song with a more integral force of emotion and idea.
NME

'Promises' is stark, dense, eerie, almost unremittingly bleak. It is fragmented and uncomfortable, but often incongruously 'rockist'.
MELODY MAKER

GENESIS
Genesis (Charisma)
'Duke' was bad but this is appalling. Kill it now, Phil, put it out of its misery.
MELODY MAKER

...appallingly boring...
NME

...you certainly can't say they're stuck in a rut anymore.
SOUNDS

ROBIN GIBB
How Old Are You?
(Polydor)
Middle-aged Gibb trembles through his pile of sickly tunes in what is a pretty disgusting album.
SOUNDS

IAN GILLAN BAND
Live At The Budokan
(Virgin)
Basically, we're taking huge cash-in from Virgin here...
MELODY MAKER

DAVID GILMOUR
About Face (Harvest)
Staid, safe and predictable.
MELODY MAKER

...do you really think it was a good idea putting all these things on a record?
SOUNDS

GIRLSCHOOL
Play Dirty (Bronze)
...the album to pull Girlschool out of the doldrums and into the limelight once more.
SOUNDS

...as one of the most objectionable things about HM is the intense and very silly concentration on willies, there are one or two reasons why Girlschool are easier to take than most.
RECORD MIRROR

THE GLOVE
Blue Sunshine (Polydor)
It seems almost appallingly *obvious* to say it, but it is the truth that if the Glove weren't

those two, Mssrs (real messers!) Severin and Smith, then this album's worth of abject baloney would not have seen the light of day.
SOUNDS

...a collection of morbid, dragging songs peppered with words that any lyricist worth his salt ... would have discarded...
NME

...a phenomenally unique culmination of a partnership that promised nothing but intrigue from its inception, a prized possession and the best LP I've heard this year.
MELODY MAKER

ROGER GLOVER
Mask (Polydor)
Okay, this is an album which will mainly appeal to boring old farts, but so what?
SOUNDS

PETER GODWIN
Correspondence (Polydor)
...harmless, vapid, singalongablob gunk...
SOUNDS

THE GO GO'S
Talk Show (IRS)
...it's easy to see why the Go Go's are strictly no no's this side of the Atlantic...
RECORD MIRROR

...they must remain Porky's to REM's The Last Picture Show.
SOUNDS

...we're talking far more soignée suss than many a more musically adept or media-hyped outfit.
NME

ROBERT GORL
Night Full Of Tension (Mute)
Gorl proffers notes from a cold and lonely room about the sex theorem so beloved of DAF: his bleached aftermath of whatever passion they worked a sweat over, and it gathers a disappointing collection of only half-shaped ideas.
NME

...one of the most lightweight albums ever made.
RECORD MIRROR

GRANDMASTER FLASH AND THE FURIOUS FIVE
Greatest Messages (Sugarbill)
...a reminder of how clichéd and studied the art of rap became.
RECORD MIRROR

DAVID GRANT
David Grant (Chrysalis)
...he's created the perfect vehicle for his ever so obliging colourful pop personality. A record that doesn't get in the way of the new hairstyle or red track suit, but simply blends into the background.
RECORD MIRROR

If David Grant really wants to be Michael Jackson, maybe he should go the whole hog and

hire Quincy Jones. As it is, this album tries to approximate the Jackson effect with the latest digital gadgetry but only comes over as glossy and faintly vacuous, nine songs in search of a pigeonhole.
MELODY MAKER

...George Benson-meets-Mary Poppins...
SOUNDS

EDDY GRANT
Going For Broke (Ice)
Eddy's out of touch...
RECORD MIRROR

...he probably has the potential to become the black answer to Paul McCartney – but his senses seem temporarily dulled.
SOUNDS

GREAT WHITE
Great White (EMI America)
...none of the phoney spandex and stud-infested hype there whatsoever... the music is hard, fast and going somewhere.
SOUNDS

Even hardline devotees of sexist garbage are liable to be bored out of their studded jock-straps by this one.
NME

AL GREEN
I'll Rise Again (Myrrh)
...only if you share Green's intense Christian faith, and so find interest and inspiration in these sermons, will you find this record worth repeated listenings.
NME

GREEN ON RED
Gravity Talks (Slash)
It may sound oh-so Sixties and (snigger, snigger) old fashioned but the sentiments expressed are fiercely contemporary even if it is laced with some excruciating acid imagery.
SOUNDS

...wholly original, tempestuously brilliant and deserves your full attention.
SOUNDS

D. GREENFIELD AND J.J. BURNEL
Fire & Water (Ecoutez Vos Murs) (Epic)
...lacks unity, and would probably be more atmospheric without the vocals.
RECORD MIRROR

...probably the closest any of the Stranglers will come to making a comedy record.
SOUNDS

What Burnel fails to understand is you can't glory in absolute stupidity and quote Einstein formulae in the same breath with any integrity.
NME

...if you've got any sense you'd do well to avoid it.
MELODY MAKER

GRIM REAPER
See You In Hell (Ebony)
...committing acts of gross indecency, blowing

EDDY GRANT

up nuns and rampaging round the local graveyard on motorcycles.
MELODY MAKER

THE GUN CLUB
The Las Vegas Story (Animal)
Music to crash the hearse to.
RECORD MIRROR

The Birth, The Death, The Ghost (ABC)
Attempting to snare the fatalistic horror of Robert Johnson or Charley Patton in a setting of trash punk, he overloads a saturated myth until the ghosts are as bloated as he is.
NME

...Gun Club lack the musical charm of their mentors and the songs on this record deterio-

rate too often into an incomprehensible thrash.
RECORD MIRROR

...the Gun Club have never sounded so tiresome...
MELODY MAKER

This set of recordings ... beyond just being an historical document ... after a few plays, will haunt your turntable for weeks on end.
SOUNDS

GUS AND THE NEW BREED
On The Verge (Nemperor)
...if a bizarre amalgam of Mitch Ryder, Aerosmith, and Def Leppard had somehow been on top of the pop universe in 1967, and the killjoy Beverly Hillbillies writers wanted to satirize said pop phenomenon, they would've hired...

Gus & The New Breed!!!
CREEM

H

STEVE HACKETT
Bay Of Kings (Lamborghini)
...the kind of stuff you find as the background for nature programmes on flopsy bunnies or television serials.
RECORD MIRROR

...rich man's indulgence.
NME

NINA HAGEN
Fearless (CBS)
...comes across like the cod mysticism in a bad Hong Kong horror movie.
NME

attempts to pass herself off as a makeshift disco queen which she so clearly isn't.
SOUNDS

...sees her superior vocal talents raining down on us in a superhuman fashion.
MELODY MAKER

PAUL HAIG
Rhythm Of Life
(Crépuscule/Island)
...a shame — but the signs are that it is the sort of shame Haig is set to outlive.
NME

The face of '82, the star of '84; Paul Haig cannot, will not, fail.
MELODY MAKER

HAIRCUT ONE HUNDRED
Paint And Paint (Polydor)
...while Haircut One Hundred have been maturing, both as songwriters and as a band, it's a safe bet that their audience has moved on to pastures new.
RECORD MIRROR

HALL & OATES
Rock 'N Soul Part 1 (RCA)
...peerless state-of-the-art pop monsters...
RECORD MIRROR

PETER HAMMILL
Patience (Naive)
Two listens... reveal a marvellous mind at work.
SOUNDS

...now one of the most redundant men alive.
NME

HANOI ROCKS
All Those Wasted Years
(Johanna)
They could have made a great single album out of this, but what the hell?
MELODY MAKER

HERBIE HANCOCK

HERBIE HANCOCK
Future Shock (CBS)
...this record spells inventive construction and clear confidence to get out and do it. Poppa Herbie's clearly got a brand new bag...
NME

BARCLAY JAMES HARVEST
Victims Of Circumstance
(Polydor)
What is so horrible about this is that it has got into the British charts (as well as the Luxembourg Top Thirty, probably) and that they have got a sell-out tour at major venues.
SOUNDS

HALL & OATES

...pure unremitting boredom ... so limp it makes China Crisis sound like Led Zeppelin.
RECORD MIRROR

HAWKWIND
Zones (Flicknife)
...a marshmallow wilderness of cosmic twitterings and AOR synthesizers.
SOUNDS

HAZE
C'est La Vie (Gabadon)
...three-piece techno rock band lost in a dream; either that or a bad acid trip...
MELODY MAKER

HEADPINS
Line Of Fire (MCA)
...a masterful blend of rowdiness and restraint.
SOUNDS

...Darby Mills bellows away with the gruffness of Bonnie Tyler and the high-pitched velocity of Jon Anderson with his knackers trapped in a well-greased toasted sandwich maker.
MELODY MAKER

HEAVY PETTIN
Lettin Loose (Hep)
...someone, somewhere, is trying to clone the Leppard pop rock sensibility right down to the ragged street-cred image.
MELODY MAKER

HELSTAR
Burning Star
(Music For Nations)
...another trigger-happy bunch of metal yankees who run the gauntlet from early Rainbow to late Seventies Priest...
SOUNDS

FINIS HENDERSON
Finis (Motown)
...wincingly saccharine...
MELODY MAKER

...cannot be much more than a holding operation for Motown.
NME

NONA HENDRYX
The Art Of Defence (RCA)
...Hendryx has burst free with a joyous, inspired abandon.
SOUNDS

KEVIN HEWICK AND THE SOUND
This Cover Keeps Reality Unreal (Cherry Red)
...years between wistful philosophy and morose detachment from the antics of the world.
MELODY MAKER

HEY! ELASTICA
In On The Off Beat (Virgin)
...a frantic tumble dryer of ideas, a dispiriting mess of a record.
NME

...a draggy, saggy slab of sub rock music.
SOUNDS

NICK HEYWARD

NICK HEYWARD
North Of A Miracle (Arista)
He now tries to sing with dulled Weller seriousness about something as important as life.
NME

...confirms the suggestion that Heyward feels himself in the difficult transition from teeny-bop idol to Serious Artist...
SOUNDS

Much of it *is* misconceived and hopelessly idealistic ... Heyward has bitten off more than he can chew, setting himself heights he has little chance of reaching...
MELODY MAKER

JOHN HIATT
Riding With The King
(Geffen)
The 12 trax here offer such a rich mix that I fear it'll take many more listens to find how good, bad or indifferent they all are...
SOUNDS

This is the first great record of the year — and one of the last.
NME

...little more than a heartless clone, aping both Costello's lyrical and vocal styles to the point of dreary predictability.
MELODY MAKER

HI ENERGY
Various Artists
(Street Sounds)
The insipidness of this record has to be experienced to be understood.
MELODY MAKER

As an introduction to the ultra-fast Boys Town music, you need look no further than this LP.
RECORD MIRROR

...class and authenticity.
SOUNDS

HOLGER HILLER
A Bunch Of Foulness In The Pit (Cherry Red)
His utterly unique conception of music has produced a debut album brimming with fantastic illusions and aural extravagances; a magic box full of tricks so sublime they never cease to captivate.
MELODY MAKER

It embodies all the qualities of being a milestone ... this is THE record of 1984 ... the beast from the formalist fission of emotion and intellect. It is brazenly modern.
SOUNDS

HOT CHOCOLATE
Love Shot (RAK)
Another ten portions of the agreeably familiar concoction...
RECORD MIRROR

HSAS
Through The Fire (Geffen)
...remarkably limp and middle of the road ... the overall impact is minimised by the safety of it all.
SOUNDS

HULA
Cut From Inside
(Red Rhino)
...the pulsating equivalent of a musical sledge-hammer reshaping your cranium ... a crunching reminder which underlines, with great

JOHN HIATT

THE HUMAN LEAGUE

THE ICICLE WORKS
The Icicle Works
(Beggars Banquet)
...Prawn Again Rock ... That is, pink and crispy on the outside and soft on the inside.
NME

Really very dull indeed ... don't buy.
RECORD MIRROR

...a stunner of a debut album.
SOUNDS

...more than my album of the year – it might well be the album of my lifetime.
MELODY MAKER

ICON
Icon (Capitol)
...harks back to the halcyon days of Judas Priest...
SOUNDS

ICONS OF FILTH
Onward Christian Soldier
(Mortarhate)
...their madness explodes in a pained pogo of searing one chord energy bursts that carry the equally hard-hitting message of liberty and personal emancipation.
SOUNDS

...only a fifth generation of Punkyperson with the politics of a Flower Child and the musical taste of a lobotomised Tasmanian Devil could find anything even remotely appealing in this tuneless Wall of Migraine.
NME

BILLY IDOL
Rebel Yell (Chrysalis)
...Idol's hotch-potch (sic) of historical poses are as feasible as anything currently jockeying for national affection.
MELODY MAKER

Idol is all set to be a minor American star ... competent, full of desperate shouts, new-wavey riffs, rebel-romantic lyrics and the like, but it's so tame.
NME

About as rebellious as a Conservative Party Conference...
SOUNDS

Can't work up an emotional sweat either way.
CREEM

JOHN ILLSLEY
Never Told A Soul (Vertigo)
Like, I've got this burning desire to express myself and I don't think I can. What's wrong with me?
SOUNDS

IMAGINATION
Scandalous (R&B)
There's nothing particularly original or intelligent about this record.
MELODY MAKER

...as unremittingly and infectiously vacuous as ever...
SOUNDS

---

gusto, how average the majority of contemporary music is.
SOUNDS

...just another Sheffield group...
MELODY MAKER

THE HUMAN LEAGUE
Hysteria (Virgin)
...a triumph of natural, organic feel over hi-tech.
RECORD MIRROR

Human League have delivered.
MELODY MAKER

A jewel can only really sparkle in a muted setting, and to find one brilliant song, let alone two on anybody's album in these times is no mean discovery.
SOUNDS

...the proven formula as straitjacket ... as dreary as it seems.
NME

IAN HUNTER
All Of The Good Ones Are Taken (CBS)
...at least three of the songs on this album are among the best he's written in the last six or seven years...
NME

...something ... bursts out of this ... pulsating vigour, turning his stylised clichés ... into vital affirmations of old-time traditional values.
SOUNDS

HUNTERS & COLLECTORS
The Fireman's Curse
(Virgin)
Too often, their music sounds like a half-developed mess of good ideas, bad arrangements and outrageous arrogance...
SOUNDS

...there's more vitality and variety here than you'll find in the recent work of Shriekback, Killing Joke or Gang of Four, three bands they kinda resemble.
CREEM

IQ
Tales From The Lush Attic
(Major)
...far from settling on being a surrogate, feeble impersonation, IQ search for identity and do so with maximum musicianship.
SOUNDS

...nothing more than an accurate reproduction of early Yes, Greenslade, and Genesis licks.
MELODY MAKER

ICEHOUSE
Sidewalk (Chrysalis)
Nine out of 10 ... hacks refuse to believe that this isn't a Music for Pleasure LP featuring hit trax by Simple Minds, David Bowie, Roxy Music and Ultravox.
RECORD MIRROR

...a more than worthy addition to a catalogue of creative accomplishment...
SOUNDS

Worth their weight only in amusement value... walking down a sidewalk to nowhere.
MELODY MAKER

...another moderately enjoyable LP that lures Youth to its Doom.
NME

THE IMPRESSIONS
It's All Right (Kent)
The Never Ending/... (Kent)
Keep On Pushing (Kent)
People Get Ready (Kent)
...rarely emulated greatness.
NME

THE IMPRESSIONS
The Impressions (Kent)
...a record shot through with class, a timeless nugget of soul-pop.
MELODY MAKER

INCANTATION
Dance Of The Flames (Beggars Banquet)
...just right for the coffee table.
SOUNDS

IN DEEP
Pajama Party (PRT)
The Human League would die to make a record as simple and effective as this...
SOUNDS

THE INFAS
Sound And Fury (Panache)
...third-rate Heavy Metal and second-rate Oi.
SOUNDS

INXS
The Swing (Mercury)
...you look forward to the sound the needle makes, bumping in the run-off groove.
RECORD MIRROR

GREGORY ISAACS
Out Deh! (Island)
...as much a victim of its predecessor's lustre as it is of any shortcomings of its own.
NME

ISLEY BROTHERS
Between The Sheets (Epic)
People who make music as sensual, soulful and as moving as the Isleys' shouldn't be just liked, but *worshipped*.
MELODY MAKER

...rock-dressed-up-as-funk... Bland white creaminess...
SOUNDS

J

JERMAINE JACKSON
Dynamite (Arista)
...indulgent mush of the most cloying kind.
MELODY MAKER

...one of the latest in a long line of confused black musicians caught in a no man's land somewhere between synthetic rock and disco soul.
RECORD MIRROR

...ultimately unfulfilling helping of LA-cleansed electro pop soul.
NME

JOE JACKSON
Mike's Murder—The Motion Picture Soundtrack (A&M)
Middle of the road rock of the most laid-back kind that is totally and absolutely SAFE.
RECORD MIRROR

I don't know what the film's like, but the soundtrack's murder...
NME

JOE JACKSON
Body And Soul
If he's borrowed the big band sound he's personalised it to a degree way beyond any normal reference points.
MELODY MAKER

Ever since he got on this jazz kick, it was inevitable that he'd wind up here — in someone else's digitally recorded past life.
SOUNDS

...a man pursuing his own vision with stubborn independence.
NME

...so damn serious on content and intent you end up wanting to shake the man.
RECORD MIRROR

JOE JACKSON

ICEHOUSE

MICHAEL JACKSON
Farewell My Summer Love (Motown)
Miraculously, the people at Tamla have found yet another batch of Wacko Jacko's dirty laundry and thrown it out on the line to dry.
RECORD MIRROR

MILLIE JACKSON
ESP (Sire)
When it comes to innuendo, double entendre and just plain smut, Frankie Goes to Hollywood have a lot to learn.
MELODY MAKER

...would be little more than average soul were it not for the gratuitous lines about 'coming' and 'sitting on my face'.
SOUNDS

THE JACKSONS
Victory (Epic)
...prepare for disappointment...
SOUNDS

THE JAM
Snap (Polydor)
Simply a superb collection from the most compassionate and intelligent lyricist British pop music has ever known.
RECORD MIRROR

...will serve as a comprehensive memento of this perplexing tight-lipped trio.
MELODY MAKER

Running these singles back to back one is forced to concede, no matter how reluctantly, that there was more movement within the Jam than is apparent hearing them one at a time.
NME

RICK JAMES
Cold Blooded (Motown)
A big, hard sound that dispenses with all the excess baggage of post-Clinton funk, all the clicks and claptracks, crap and clicktraps, and goes straight for the backbone, to clear, hard essentials.
NME

...a competent slice of burning funk 'n' roll guaranteed to get you dancing and little else.
MELODY MAKER

As his head contines to expand, tricks that once seemed honorably functional begin to smack of expediency ... this is not a man who should criticize his peers for dressing funny.
CREEM

JANE AND BARTON
Jane And Barton (Cherry Red)
...the poet has his feet planted messily in the sub-Kerouac beat mud, pretentious and passé in the extreme.
SOUNDS

CHAZ JANKEL
Chazablanca (A&M)
More that a sideman but less than a solo star...
MELODY MAKER

MILLIE JACKSON

JASON AND THE SCORCHERS
Fervor (EMI America)
If there's one thing that stops these songs from being the cottonpickin' pearls they so very nearly are, it's the sub-HM wang-bar workouts.
SOUNDS

...the beginning of a new music, which may fuse country's confrontation with contemporary reality.
NME

Buy now, and fan with stetson...
MELODY MAKER

JAZZATEERS
Jazzateers (Rough Trade)
Jazzateers ate style manifestos and dance floors for breakfast. It's a shame they didn't stick around for lunch.
MELODY MAKER

So the Jazzateers are no more and on this evidence it's not exactly carpet-gnashing and Kleenex time.
NME

In which Lou Reed meets Orange Juice and comes up with ... well, not very much really.
RECORD MIRROR

JEREMY'S SECRET
The Snowball Effect (Deep Six)
Between the amateurish clumsiness lie pockets of inquisitive deviation that demand repeated investigation...
MELODY MAKER

JOAN JETT AND THE BLACKHEARTS
Album (MCA)
...just a salty, snazzy, good-humoured, hard 'n' fast action whoopee ticket down the old Teenage Highway.
NME

She's vehemently stayed at that hot spot where punk and heavy metal are the same leather clad brute...
CREEM

JOBOXERS
Like Gangbusters (RCA)
...their chosen style, melding together the hard masculinity of pub rock, the sweet melodies of Motown and the sharp regimentation of swing, is a creative cul-de-sac.
MELODY MAKER

...for the very young, who need to feel old, and for the very old, who need to feel young. But not for me.
NME

EDDIE JOBSON
Zinc (Capitol)
...a pitiful and embarrassing collection...

BILLY JOEL
An Innocent Man (CBS)
No redeeming features whatsoever.
NME

He's still got his trademark Piano Man sound, which means puke to me but will be appreciated by his many fans.
CREEM

ELTON JOHN
Breaking Hearts (Rocket)
God, this is dull.
RECORD MIRROR

...an afterthought of an album...
SOUNDS

LINTON KWESI JOHNSON
Making History (Island)
...as hauntingly evocative and stridently political as ever on his fourth LP...
MELODY MAKER

...the most vital reggae document I have ever heard.
SOUNDS

...an inherent feeling of a smugness that belongs in magnolia coloured flats with Habitat chairs and theatre posters rather than your average SE14 abode.
RECORD MIRROR

HOWARD JONES
Human's Lib (WEA)
Howard rests somewhere on a sliding scale between Nik Kershaw and Thomas Dolby, having neither the former's soft charm, the latter's innovative genius or the (Thompson) Twins' cosmopolitan appeal...
RECORD MIRROR

The synthesized Gilbert O'Sullivan revival starts here...
SOUNDS

The aural equivalent of painting by numbers... I can think only of a kid who's been given a Rolf Harris Stylophone for Christmas and thinks he's Gandhi.
MELODY MAKER

...not even exceptionally ordinary, he's just downright ordinary.
NME

LOUIS JORDAN & THE TYMPANY FIVE
Look Out! (Charly)
...gives a fuller picture of the man's career and development ... lovingly annotated and compiled and ... unreservedly recommended.
NME

JUDAS PRIEST
Defenders Of The Faith
(CBS)

...a giant brooding, almost Wagnerian atmosphere.
SOUNDS

Halford is beginning to develop a strange resemblance to Pope John Paul II, but the music is still in thundering good trim.
RECORD MIRROR

...a long way short of the mega ball bustin', power punchin' cacophony that had been promised.
MELODY MAKER

KAJAGOOGOO
Islands (EMI)
Precious little to suggest that the GooGoo guys have anything beyond sleight of hand when it comes to creating a feeling of depth, feeling and interest.
SOUNDS

...in reality a hyped-up bunch of glam Billy Grahams — forgive them Lord, for they have sinned.
MELODY MAKER

KALEIDOSCOPE
Bacon From Mars (Edsel)
...seldom touches the heights of psychedelic masterworks like 'Electric Music For The Mind And Body' but will remain an amusing diversion from the norms of druggy regurgitation.
NME

INI KAMOZE
Ini Kamoze (Island)
...there isn't one track that really cuts it in a manner that justifies all the hype.
NME

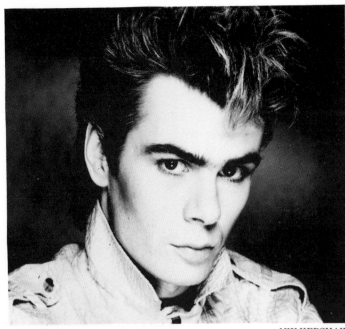

NIK KERSHAW

KC AND THE SUNSHINE BAND
All In A Night's Work (Epic)
...it probably rots your brain, but you try listening to it without your foot tapping.
RECORD MIRROR

KENNY G
G Force (Arista)
...when Channel Four grinds to a halt and you're too tired to write that novel you've been thinking about, 'G Force' will take away those aches and pains.
SOUNDS

NIK KERSHAW
Human Racing (MCA)
...somewhere between the heavyweight keyboard ramblings of Howard Jones and the glibber hack-pop of Nick Heyward.
MELODY MAKER

...like those shiny chrome things that turn to a dull green after a week or two's handling.
RECORD MIRROR

...would do best to stick to little records rather than big ones...
NME

It's just all a trifle pointless. He has nothing to say. Worse, he seems to think he has.
SOUNDS

KICK AXE
Vices (Pasha Records)
...thundering hard rock at its best ... as entertaining as it is skull-crushingly heavy.
SOUNDS

KID CREOLE AND THE COCONUTS
Doppleganger (Ze/Island)
Plainly the Creole vision is dimming but Darnell ... seems reluctant to let it drop. Like the Hope/Crosby vehicle, Darnell's Odyssey version of *The Road To...* series feels like it's going on forever.
NME

JOBOXERS

KING KURT

themselves in.
NME

LEW KIRTON
Talk To Me (Epic)
...a collection of mildly marketable clichés of
our time.
NME

KISS
Lick It Up (Phonogram)
...their musical brains are stuck somewhere at
the bottom of Black Sabbath's garbage can.
Except for the singer's, whose head seems to
be forever over a toilet bowl.
NME

DAVID KNOPFLER
Release (Peach River)
...a lucky dip of an album—only every time you
reach in for a song, you pluck out a winner.
MELODY MAKER

KNOX
Plutonium Express (Razor)
...sounds eerily like a bunch of rejected B-sides
by Lou Reed, Mink DeVille and Bruce
Springsteen.
NME

KOOL AND THE GANG
In The Heart (De-Lite)
It will be bought by couples who go out in
matching anoraks and sit happily next to the
Billy Joel albums.
MELODY MAKER

Listening to much of this remind me of my
dad's old Xavier Cugat albums.
MELODY MAKER

KING CRIMSON
Three Of A Perfect Pair (EG)
...a very sorry swamp indeed.
MELODY MAKER

I haven't heard such a dreadful din since I
tripped up over the cat last week and fell
downstairs.
RECORD MIRROR

KING KURT
Ooh Wallah Wallah (Stiff)
This is on a par with Neubauten and the Virgin
Prunes—bring on a Bourgie Bourgie quick!
SOUNDS

...the new nutty boys ... nobody's sure if they
will be bigger than Madness or remain as
quirky, toetapping and tepid as Tenpole.
MELODY MAKER

...drunken hillbilly music ... uncomplicated party
bozo primitives...
NME

CAROLE KING
Speeding Time (Atlantic)
Speeding time, eh? This new album never gets
out of first gear.
RECORD MIRROR

**JAMES KING AND THE LONE
WOLVES**
Texas Lullaby (Thrush)
...recorded proof of the magnificence and
genius of James King And The Lone Wolves...
SOUNDS

...about the bitterest reactionary rock's got
right now...
MELODY MAKER

EVELYN 'CHAMPAGNE' KING
Face To Face (RCA)
...as decorously superficial as the Fiorucci,
Henry Lehr threads she models on the cover.
NME

RICHARD H. KIRK
Time High Fiction
(Doublevision)
...suggests a nostalgia for the revolt against
form Cabaret Voltaire once readily immersed

LEW KIRTON

L

PATTI LABELLE
I'm In Love Again
(Philadelphia International)
...a record consistently sabotaged by the disappointing mediocrity of the chosen material.
MELODY MAKER

GREG LAKE
Manoeuvres (EMI)
...fascinatingly pointless songs.
NME

ANNABEL LAMB
The Flame (A&M)
Annabel Lamb is a great writer – even an important writer, given today's shoddy products of non-imagination.
MELODY MAKER

...little intrinsic worth.
RECORD MIRROR

LLOYD LANGTON GROUP
Outside The Law (Flicknife)
Bring back the Pink Fairies...
SOUNDS

BILL LASWELL
Baselines (Rough Trade)
Cerebral to be sure ... an expositionary approach to the bass.
SOUNDS

LAUGHING CLOWNS
Laughter Around The Table (Red Flame)
...the second compilation they've released in this country, yet the term 'ragbag' would be more accurate; their moments of triumph and worst excesses are placed cheek by jowl...
MELODY MAKER

CYNDI LAUPER
She's So Unusual (Portrait)
At least 75 per cent of this material has HIT branded on each and every note.
SOUNDS

How much can a man take of a squeaky voice that lies somewhere between Hilda Ogden singing and a cat being strangled half to death?
RECORD MIRROR

...imagine a cross between Kim Carnes and Patti Smith and you'd be almost there.
MELODY MAKER
She pursues the bimbo potential of her Betty Boop voice so single-mindedly that only two ... of these bright tunes really stand out...
CREEM

ANNABEL LAMB

JOHN LENNON & YOKO ONO
Milk And Honey (Polydor)
...jangly rock rhythms, simple emotions, very private feelings shared with the world for the last time.
RECORD MIRROR

It's a sad, poignant epitaph...
MELODY MAKER

Curtain Call For The Odd Couple.
NME

LEROI BROTHERS
Check This Action (Demon)
...the LeRois have enough humdingers between them to make the name worth watching.
MELODY MAKER

...Southern fried teen trance trashabilly ... twelve searing cuts that do their creators proud.
SOUNDS

HUEY LEWIS AND THE NEWS
Sports (Chrysalis)
An affable blend of Stax/Volt, doo-wop and good old common sense ... positively pus-filled with obvious and not-so-obvious hits.
CREEM

LEVEL 42
Standing In The Light (Polydor)
This American sojourn has made Level 42 flexible and let them flow to fit their best possible shape...
MELODY MAKER

...mid-paced easy listening at its most soothing.
RECORD MIRROR

More disco whitewash.
SOUNDS

This is probably the only record I have ever heard that makes me think of scampi.
NME

LITTLE STEVEN
Voice Of America
(EMI America)
...an excitement that nobody else in his field is coming near at the moment.
SOUNDS

NILS LOFGREN
Wonderland
(Backstreet/MCA)
It sounds like Lofgren has finally re-spelt 'cult' as 'hack'.
NME

...further signifies diminished horizons and loss of ambition.
MELODY MAKER

ROY LONEY
Fast And Loose
(Double Dare)
...if you're still buying Shakin' Stevens records, you can't do worse than check this.
NME

LONG PIG
Of Love And Addiction
(Anagram)
Half-baked arty ideas ... rub shoulders with a mild and unoriginal sci-fi fixation.
NME

...slightly reminiscent of the Psychedelic Furs on half-speed warped vinyl.
SOUNDS

LOOSE ENDS
A Little Spice (Virgin)
...hovering on the edge of something special.
RECORD MIRROR

...Loose Ends are as polite and undemanding as the new glossy pop boys, but lack their flair for cheap thrills and catchy tunes...
NME

BILL LASWELL

THE LOTUS EATERS

LORDS OF THE NEW CHURCH
Is Nothing Sacred? (IRS)
This is it: the confirmation that wherever you might be today, the Lords are always one step ahead.
MELODY MAKER

...let us not analyze their failings, let us close our eyes and hope they go away...
NME

This record is a sickening sell-out, a Miles Copeland sponsored nightmare, a defilement of street credibility, punk ethics and honest hard work and a rank plagiarism of James Jewel Osterburg, and I can't actually find any fault with it.
SOUNDS

LOS ILLEGALS
Internal Exile (A&M)
...a little of East LA's Hispanic music scene ... important for several reasons, not the least of which is that it's another testament to the *variety* inherent in that scene.
NME

THE LOTUS EATERS
No Sense Of Sin (Arista)
The most facile, fatuous face of Eighties pop... romantic music for kindergartens.
MELODY MAKER

They don't know how to have their hair cut.
SOUNDS

LOUNGE LIZARDS
Live From The Drunken Boat (Europa)
The Lounge Lizards have gone acoustic, reshuffled their line-up and come up with an album that's at least, oh, 20 times better than their Editions EG debut. In fact, a first-rate record by any criteria. 'Fake' jazz no more.
MELODY MAKER

LOVERBOY
Keep It Up (CBS)
Flying high and occasionally inspiring, it's a sound that can lift the heart and send it on an ecstatic journey of pseudo-discovery.
SOUNDS

MICHAEL LOVESMITH
I Can Make It Happen (Motown)
...a man of ideas and talent in absolute command searching for a soul sound that is at least a fraction different.
NME

...Anybody who dedicates his album to God and not the record company promotions department is in trouble.
RECORD MIRROR

NICK LOWE
Nick Lowe & His Cowboy Outfit (F-Beat)
...the cowboy who does bad things like riding around town stealing riffs but has a heart of gold and wins the girl in the end.
RECORD MIRROR

THE LURKERS
The Final Vinyl (Clay)
The Lurkers go out as they came in – sounding average.
SOUNDS

M

MC5
Babes In Arms (ROIR)
...probably the best American band of all time.
SOUNDS

This cassette ... whams along from one song to the next just like the 5 really did live: with spirit, enthusiasm, and euphoria as well as awesome overdrive.
NME

MADNESS
Keep Moving (Stiff)
...I can't help feeling that the formula is wearing a wee bit thin ... Madness are having to do a great deal of running on the spot just to keep warm.
MELODY MAKER

...an album of almost suffocating drabness. It's about as nutty as Leonard Cohen on a bad day.
SOUNDS

...I would say this is the best Madness record.
NME

THE MAHOTELLA QUEENS, MAHALATHINI AND OTHER GREAT STARS
Phezulu Equdeni (Earthworks/Rough Trade)
...classic black South African jive dating from '75.
SOUNDS

MAISONETTES
Maisonettes For Sale (Ready Steady Go!)
...textured but tepid ... consummate but colourless...
SOUNDS

Not as clever as the Rutles or Rundgren...
RECORD MIRROR

MAMA'S BOYS
Turn It Up (Spartan)
...it isn't the blockbuster that everyone's been looking forward to.
MELODY MAKER

...waxing poetic ... not inconsiderable ... a showcase ... superb guitar work ... shining example ... a potential biggie ... a skinbeat of no mean repute ... ripsnorter...
SOUNDS

MAN
Friday 13th (Picasso)
...a stunner, a dazzling effort from what by all rights should be a bunch of has-beens.
MELODY MAKER

THE MAISONETTES

MADNESS

MANFRED MANN'S EARTH BAND
Budapest (Bronze)
A live album ... Not surprisingly it's heavy on former glories.
SOUNDS

THE MANHATTAN TRANSFER

MANHATTAN TRANSFER
Bodies And Souls (Atlantic)
...it's tough to tell them from the Mike Sammes Singers.
NME

...as significant to pop as Lemmy is to classical music.
RECORD MIRROR

MANOWAR
Into Glory Ride
(Music For Nations)
Heavy-duty snores ... are littered with porky chestnuts about Armageddon, Satan's throne, and, well, death generally.
MELODY MAKER

I've the disturbing feeling that the band are starting to *sincerely believe* that they *are* barbarians from a bygone Hyborian Age...
SOUNDS

...Americans fuddled by years of ear-bleeding stadium rock, loopy demonology, buckets of soul-destroying sedatives and God knows what else.
NME

...a rumbling tumultuous chariot race of fast action and mayhem.
RECORD MIRROR

RAY MANZAREK
Carmina Burana (A&M)
The mix of classical and rock has never been much cop. 'Like grafting a tomato onto a hairbrush,' I think John Peel once said.
SOUNDS

MARC & THE MAMBAS
Torment & Toreros
(Some Bizarre)
The very real successes and breakthroughs Marc achieves amid the nightmare make it worth the time and considerable effort involved in listening to it.
MELODY MAKER

...an album to cherish, a testament of heartache and happiness...
SOUNDS

A right old crash and bang – and no mistake.
RECORD MIRROR

...an ambitious and ambivalent venture where Judy Garland meets Jean Genet and Liza Minelli sings the Marquis de Sade.
NME

MARILLION
Fugazi (EMI)
...prissy and pretentious English art rock...
NME

...full of passion, pain and pride. An album to see stars by.
RECORD MIRROR

...more irritating than stimulating, stubbornly clinging to outgrown limits...
MELODY MAKER

BOB MARLEY

HUGH MASEKELA
Techno-Bush
(Jive Afrika Hip)
...he's going to put Afrikan musics firmly back into the charts.
SOUNDS

BRIAN MAY & FRIENDS
Star Fleet Project (Capitol)
The idea of getting together outside their groups is great, but what did they end up playing? A TV theme and a couple of bloozejams.
CREEM

...about as much substance ... as in an average packet of sherbet dabs...
MELODY MAKER

...weedier than my back garden.
SOUNDS

PAUL McCARTNEY
Pipes Of Peace
(Parlophone)
...dull, tired and empty...
NME

...soppy...
SOUNDS

...slushy...
MELODY MAKER

JOHN McCOY
McCoy (LLM)
...boasts conviction and honesty, which is more than can be said of Ian Gillan's recent Deep Sabbath catastrophe.
MELODY MAKER

GEORGE McCRAE
One Step Closer To Love
(President Records)
His new album is crap. Bland isn't the word.
SOUNDS

CHRISTINE McVIE
Christine McVie
(Warner Bros)
Back in the Sixties, Christine McVie (then Christine Perfect) was a decent blues singer. Now she's just Stevie Nicks without the hairdressers.
MELODY MAKER

JOHN COUGAR MELLENCAMP
Uh-huh (Riva)
...Really awful ... music for hamburgers.
MELODY MAKER

Has the unsmudged force of modern sound around the snort of Cougar's superb band brawling through a rock'n'roll funhouse that everyone else has deserted.
NME

THE MEMBERS
Going West (Albion)
This isn't a slice of misplaced nostalgia, a remanant from a bygone age. They're a new, improved proposition...
SOUNDS

THE MEMBRANES
Crack House
(Criminal Damage)
...carefully discordant thrash-rants that land

GEORGE McCRAE

BOB MARLEY & THE WAILERS
In The Beginning (Trojan)
...has some ace moments and constantly serves to remind of some of the Wailers' finest hours; but those of us anxious for a proper document of these glories are still left waiting in vain.
NME

BOB MARLEY & THE WAILERS
Legend: The Best of Bob Marley & The Wailers
(Island)
...Island Records have maintained admirable dignity during the upsurge of the post-death Marley industry.
MELODY MAKER

'Legend' details only one side of this complex man: he knew everything was *not* gonna be

all right, but also that this smooth music could make it a bit sweeter.
NME

BERNIE MARSDEN'S ALASKA
Heart Of The Storm
(Music For Nations)
I can't really understand why Bernie's new outfit hasn't been greeted with more enthusiasm.
SOUNDS

MARY JANE GIRLS
Mary Jane Girls (Gordy)
...how a bunch of slatternly looking boilers is supposed to appeal to a Tesco's check-out girl is beyond me.
SOUNDS

BRIAN MAY AND FRIENDS

somewhere between the Birthday Party and the Fall.
NME

...second-rate stream of consciousness blurb; it must be all the magic mushrooms near the recording studios in North Wales.
SOUNDS

MEN WITHOUT HATS
Rhythm Of Youth (Statik)
...sounds like everything everybody was doing in the UK two years ago.
NME

...every tune here is a winner.
SOUNDS

MENTAL AS ANYTHING
Creatures Of Leisure (A&M)
As benign an evolutionary mishap as the koala bear, this displaced pub-rock band does its level best to act friendly and crazy despite disheartening life experiences.
CREEM

BETTE MIDLER
No Frills (Atlantic)
...trenchant relentless orchestrated sleaze, MOR for menopausal executives looking for a Bette on the side to revive sagging morales and bods.
NME

MIDNIGHT OIL
10,9,8,7,6,5,4,3,2,1 (CBS)
Life is full of disappointments. One day you're up ... the next you're listening to Midnight Oil.
NME

JOHN MILES
Play On (EMI)
...probably the most talented singer-songwriter in the whole known world of space and time ever.
NME

THE MILKSHAKES
Nothing Can Stop These Men (Milkshakes)
20 Rock And Roll Hits Of The 50's And 60's
(Big Beat)
In Germany (Wall City)
Showcase (Brain Eater)
Their trashy riproaring approach and bludgeoning energy combine superbly to create a fiery, raunchy raw sound.
SOUNDS

...records fuelled on a love-hate obsession with dusty, monochrome beat music...
NME

BETTE MIDLER

61

MINISTRY
Work For Love (Arista)
Not since 'Killer' have I heard an album so bristling with strong melodies, tight arrangements, intriguing lyrics, juicy chordwork and body-shaking bass riffs.
SOUNDS

...we should view it simply as a new force in the land.
MELODY MAKER

MINK DEVILLE
Where Angels Fear To Tread (Atlantic)
...a series of silly poses, the not-so-great grandaddy of cool strutting his smacked-out, hard-nut-with-a-poet's-heart stuff through a set of poorly-drawn street caricatures creaking with cliché.
MELODY MAKER

The angels in this case are simply treading water.
RECORD MIRROR

MIRRORS
Mirrors (Aura)
Mirrors ... would like very much to be the Police.
SOUNDS

MODERN ENGLISH
Richochet Days (4AD)
...once you've heard the record once or twice it provides as much satisfaction as a mouthful of fresh air.
MELODY MAKER

No expounding of the trash aesthetic can save this repulsively fat, rotting dead turkey.
SOUNDS

EDDIE MONEY
Where's The Party? (Columbia)
Maybe now that Rick Springfield has got a foothold in the British market, Eddie Money will begin to gain recognition as a major AOR star.
SOUNDS

MONSOON
Third Eye (Mobile Suit Corporation)
...goes the whole yawning way into the mystic—too much incense and nowhere near enough nonsense.
MELODY MAKER

THE MOODISTS
Thirsty's Calling (Red Flame)
...Melbourne's masters of diseased drama wear their hearts on their grimy cuffs.
SOUNDS

The Moodists are a product of ephemeral rock tribalism in that their expressive wherewithal lies in an unquestioning willingness to regurgitate the trappings and not the feeling of one hallowed rock tradition.
NME

THE MOODY BLUES
The Present (Decca/Threshold)
Melodic collection of nicely-sung observations about life, hindered only by massively stupid lyrics, pathetic synthesiser fills and the worst cover I have ever seen.
NME

Derek Jewell likes the new Moody Blues album.
MELODY MAKER

GARY MOORE
Dirty Fingers (Jet)
...rough 'n' ready rip-offs ... recommended for hardened fanatics only...
SOUNDS

Victims Of The Future (10 Records)
...remains one of the most accomplished axe acrobats in the country ... his most complete collection to date...
SOUNDS

The man with the flamethrower guitar will burn a highway from the top of your head to the tips of your toes.
RECORD MIRROR

...Listening to this album was one of the less pleasant half-hours spent in recent memory.
MELODY MAKER

PATRICK MORAZ AND BILL BRUFORD
Music For Piano And Drums (Editions EG)
...two masterful musicians doing what they do best ... an amalgam of styles rarely seen in today's over-specialised and fashion-conscious music.
MELODY MAKER

THE MORELLS
Shake And Push (Borrowed Records)
...authentic rock 'n' roll music with a special zing – the kind that can't be faked.
SOUNDS

VAN MORRISON

VAN MORRISON
Live At The Grand Opera House Belfast (Mercury)
...a reminder of how great this man is...
NME

For a man so allegedly imbued with mystical harmony, he comes on pretty arrogant and pompous ... and overweight too ... just like the music!
SOUNDS

A record as ponderous as the title, really.
RECORD MIRROR

MOTLEY CRUE
Shout At The Devil (Elektra)
...a sub Black Sabbath drone which can only be politely described as painful.
MELODY MAKER

MUSICAL YOUTH
Different Style (MCA)
...what's being paraded before us here is as much the result of worldwide acclaim and equal amounts of jetlag as any musical development.
SOUNDS

Musical Youth do not urge you to burn, loot or blather on about Jah. They'd much rather be pop stars, and are taking the shortest route to that end.
MELODY MAKER

The Pastoral Shepherdess/Earth Mother/Love-lorn Neo-Hippy formula might be a Laura Ashley type tragedy the first time round, but the second time it's a farce.
NME

N

NASH THE SLASH
American Bandages (Quality)
Living proof that Canadians never have and never will contribute anything worth having to pop's rich tapestry.
SOUNDS

NAZ NOMAD AND THE NIGHTMARES
Glve Daddy The Knife Cindy (Big Beat)
...in which various Dammed types once again piss heroically on the high altar or prove what an opportunist bunch of snot-nosed louts they are.
NME

NEATS
Neats (Ace Of Hearts)
...love songs that work the same coarse vein as ... R.E.M. ... Neat indeed.
NME

BILL NELSON
Savage Creatures For Charm's Sake (Cocteau)
...a pleasant collection of instrumental synthi-mood music. It's like a jaunty, less melancholy, more plastic rinky-dinky version of Eno's epochal doodlings...
NME

NENA
Nena (Epic)
...the usual terminal slobber which the Europeans seem to think passes as 'new wave'.
SOUNDS

NEW EDITION
Candy Girl (London/Streetwise)
...a Fast Food version of the Jackson 5 just isn't palatable in large doses.
RECORD MIRROR

For New Edition to say they don't want to be compared to the Jackson 5 would be as fatuous as Linda Kerridge saying she didn't want to be compred to Marilyn Monroe.
NME

I just hope that 'the kids' are making a bundle of cash out of this.
SOUNDS

...the kiddies don't sing that good. And they're not even related.
CREEM

NEW MODEL ARMY
Vengeance (Abstract)
...the most dynamic and exciting mesh of music

and personal politics since the first Clash bash...
SOUNDS

...when it comes to Balls, Bounce and Brutality, New Model Army have got a gobful ... a bull in an ideological china shop ...
NME

NEWTOWN NEUROTICS
Beggars Can Be Choosers (Razor)
...workmanlike tho' rarely scraping any heights of insight.
NME

...unexpectedly mature and, potentially, very enduring.
MELODY MAKER

NIGHTINGALES
Hysterics (Ink)
Here we have a logical extension of the English folk tradition ... wrapped up in a Brummie bonhomie that bites as hard as it barks.
SOUNDS

The Nightingales take the arid ground of creeping estates, chintzy pubs and drunken bores ... and make serious sprained ankle dance music out of it ... some of the best 'pop' sounds of the year.
MELODY MAKER

999
13th Floor Madness (Albion)
999 have gone soft! ... who the hell do they think is going to be interested in third-hand melodies and second-rate disco pop!
SOUNDS

NON
Physical Evidence (Mute)
...pure noise, crafted through echo, effects and all manner of extremities ... guaranteed to clear the house of unwanted guests ... excellent.
SOUNDS

Non's noise is a black hole absorbing energy and light, a negative force containing everything, but voluntarily giving off nothing.
NME

GARY NUMAN
Warriors (Beggars Banquet)
...one shouldn't deny that 'Warriors' is the most negatively attractive electronic pop muzak since Eno's influential 'Another Green World'
NME

...unfortunately his song writing is colourless, his singing whiney and his lyrics just plain embarrassing. This record is bereft of one exciting idea.
RECORD MIRROR

...Gary has sunk further into his make-believe world of ominous fantasy ... where sci-fi escapism can bolster insecurity.
MELODY MAKER

GARY NUMAN

O

CHIEF EBENEZER OBEY
Miliki Plus (Virgin)
If King Sunny Ade is the general of the first strike African invasion, Obey is his competitive colonel...
RECORD MIRROR

It's all too tempting to patronise this 'juju' music only because it makes one acutely aware And most ashamed of the dull, empty-hearted contrivance of contemporary Western dance music.
SOUNDS

Quite why he should forsake his own style for a format in which he is only mediocre remains a mystery...
SOUNDS

THE O'JAYS
Love And More
(Philadelphia International)
They've been at it for more than a quarter of a century and it doesn't seem a day too much.
RECORD MIRROR

ONE THE JUGGLER
Nearly A Sin (Regard)
...they can dress in every colour of their Romany-flavoured rainbow and allow a romantic wanderlust to pervade their atmosphere without ever seeming out of place in the grime of a Wardour Street.
MELODY MAKER

...who wants rock opera in 1984?
SOUNDS

OPPOSITION
Promises (Charisma)
...a prime example of White Boy Angst, grammar school department ... conjures up memories of Genesis and U2...
SOUNDS

...wades bodly into a tougher area and comments on how we've been duped by successive Governments...
MELODY MAKER

THE OPPRESSED
Oi! Oi! Music (Oppressed)
Their debut album is about three things: being skinheads, being violent and being working class.
SOUNDS

ORANGE JUICE
Texas Fever (Polydor)
...a very special record...
NME

...a gorgeous record...
SOUNDS

CHIEF EBENEEZER OBEY

ORANGE JUICE

...an absurdly ironic record, ironic as in self-mocking and self-celebratory.
MELODY MAKER

ORCHESTRAL MANOEUVRES IN THE DARK
Junk Culture (Virgin)
...finds OMD trapped between their overtly commercial senses and their desire to create their own awkward and upsetting niche. They never fully fulfil either function.
NME

JEFFREY OSBORNE
Stay With Me Tonight
(A&M)
...promising to go all the way and never really making it out of the hotel lift ... profoundly dull and sadly undistinguished.
MELODY MAKER

...an assured and astute play on the emotional susceptibilities of the middle-aged Manilow brigade...
SOUNDS

OZZY OSBOURNE
Bark At The Moon (Epic)
...this LP has the lot, proving Ozzy to be the Liberace of HM...
SOUNDS

...you just *know* he had more fun pretending to be a werewolf on the cover than he did laying down the vocals.
MELODY MAKER

...there isn't a musical move you haven't heard somewhere in some form already, many times over ... but you have to give the guy credit for having a bad attitude.
CREEM

JEFFREY OSBORNE

OZZY OSBOURNE

P

THE PALE FOUNTAINS
Pacific Street (Virgin)
...well worth the wait.
RECORD MIRROR

...they still manage to appear daring in the context of mid-Eighties pop.
MELODY MAKER

...a mighty album.
SOUNDS

...this cissy platter.
NME

PALLAS
The Sentinel (Harvest)
...re-constructed vintage Yes and Genesis, ideas you must have heard a zillion times before.
RECORD MIRROR

...they have about as much in common with Yes and Genesis as Black Sabbath have with the Smiths or JoBoxers.
MELODY MAKER

GRAHAM PARKER
The Real Macaw (RCA)
In his stridently unsubtle, tender-tough way, Graham Parker is a pretty good *soul* singer. But for the most part this disc is polly filler.
NME

...just old ground, learnt and revamped parrot fashion.
RECORD MIRROR

...he eloquently reveals poignant feelings of devotion that remind once again how deeply moving rock 'n' roll can be. Welcome back to the top, G.P...
CREEM

...a bunch of tepid compositions played with equally tepid enthusiasm.
MELODY MAKER

RAY PARKER JR
Woman Out Of Control (Arista)
...What a waste of time.
NME

VAN DYKE PARKS
Jump (Warner Bros)
...truly a breath of sweet Southern air in a musical smog ... beauty temptation, mystery and, once again, mischief.
SOUNDS

THE PARTISANS
The Time Was Right (Cloack and Dagger)
...a band reborn with tunes that Strummer and Jones would have been proud of.
SOUNDS

DOLLY PARTON
Burlap & Satin (RCA)
After a fortnight my awe at this LP's viruosity has done nothing but deepen with every listen and its purest moments haven't failed once to send a real shiver down my spine.
NME

The Great Pretender (RCA)
...Take away Dolly's brassy image and public

bar appeal and you're not left with a lot.
MELODY MAKER

Everybody needs a secret cache of Parton records: they're the only known antidote to the debilitating effects of cynicism.
NME

THE PASSAGE
Through The Passage
(Cherry Red)
The Passage, with pent-up passion, aggressive charm and grey charisma, just don't manage to consistently write *good* songs.
SOUNDS

FREDA PAYNE
Bands of Gold
(Demon/HDH)
...sprinkled with half remembered pleasures that handsomely reward reacquaintance. And it should be required listening at the offices of Respond Records.
NME

PEECH BOYS
Life Is Something Special
(Island)
...they seldom rise above providing shallow reflections of the past few years...
NME

The Peech Boys do better than most — at least half the music here deserves a place in your home.
MELODY MAKER

...virtually an encyclopedia of N.Y.C. dance music — no microchips anywhere carry so much verve, sex, or grit.
CREEM

TEDDY PENDERGRASS
Heaven Only Knows
(Philadelphia International)
...the man who inspired American housewives to throw their knickers on to the stage makes his quiet return.
MELODY MAKER

...very pretty.
RECORD MIRROR

...vacuous and insipid.
NME

JOE PERRY PROJECT
Once A Rocker, Always A Rocker (MCA)
...sounding like a pile of dustbins falling down a concrete staircase while a hot rod roars by with broken silencers ... a classy vinyl masterpiece.
SOUNDS

PET HATE
The Bride Wore Red
(Heavy Metal Records)
Pet Hate have tried for versatility at the expense of conviction and proper fire-power. In truth, the bride stripped bare has been caught with her knickers down.
MELODY MAKER

PETER AND THE TEST TUBE BABIES
The Mating Sounds Of South American Frogs
(Trapper)
The joke wears a little thin-like most metal thunders — and its too zomboid, too oafishly relentless for 'pop'.
NME

TEDDY PENDERGRASS

...they've grown up at last and their adulthood suits both them and me.
SOUNDS

PINK INDUSTRY
Who Told You You Were Naked? (Zulu)
This album is non-whimsical ... fairly friendly, and quite inarticulate. But as sound without a particular vision the record has quite a lot of ... *personality*.
NME

Pink Industry are going to develop into something really great.
SOUNDS

PLANET PATROL
Planet Patrol (21 Records)
...something like a private bet, a wager that Arthur Baker can smear and sluice together more FX than any mixmaster on his block.
NME

...the latest wooden dolls in the Baker/Robie playpen, a hand-me-down model of the Temptations clothed in a collection with New Order and Freez, pallid and cliché-ridden enough to send even the most ardent electrospunker hot on the heels of a Steeleye Span revival.
MELODY MAKER

RAY PARKER JR.

ROBERT PLANT
The Principle Of Moments
(Atlantic)
...not a bad album at all, as long as you don't expect too much excitement. Or coherence. Or adventure. Or any of that stuff.
CREEM

POINTER SISTERS
Break Out (Planet)
A vast talent, crying out for good material.
RECORD MIRROR

POPUL VUH
Agape-Agape/Love-Love
(Uniton)
Here we are in Egypt or Greece or heaven (and I don't mean the gay niteclub), with Florian caressing his ivories.
SOUNDS

PORTION CONTROL
Hite The Pulse (In Phaze)
Discordant noises, clattering synthesisers and people shouting a lot.
NME

A drooling derangement of modern music, a pulsating powerhouse of emotion...
SOUNDS

WILL POWERS
Dancing For Mental
Health (Island)
...fat plasticrap ... tarted up to the teeth in electronics and fake funk!
NME

The truly terrifying thing about Will Powers is that Lyn (sic) Goldsmith takes her paperback psychology SERIOUSLY.
SOUNDS

Every time he opens his mouth an idiot speaks.
RECORD MIRROR

It's an amazing album. Get out and improve yourself: buy it.
MELODY MAKER

PRAXIS
Praxis (Celluloid)
No harmony, melody, lyric or balance – just rhythm making sense and impact through its sheer unopposed physicality.
NME

PREFAB SPROUT
Swoon (Kitchenware)
The best pop album released by a British band so far this year.
RECORD MIRROR

...the first great album of 1984. It may yet gatecrash the towering trinity of 'Forever Changes.' 'Love Bites' and 'Before Hollywood'.
SOUNDS

It never excites or excels, is wildly harmless, consistently irksome and virtually passionless. Finally, it doesn't say much.
NME

...virtually unbearable ... this is drivel, mostly of the twee and gutless variety ... a gigantic folly, a *tour de force* of self indulgence.
MELODY MAKER

THE PRETENDERS
Learning To Crawl
(Real/WEA)
...a dead end; a drab collection of exhausted riffs, jaded lyrical conceits and palsied rhythms. Most of it sounds half-written, much of it sounds half-hearted.
MELODY MAKER

...the whole thing sounds both depressing and pathetic.
NME

The Pretenders appear much more at home in the pop singles field.
RECORD MIRROR

PRINCE AND THE
REVOLUTION
Purple Rain (Warner Bros)
In many ways, Prince is to 80's dance music what Hendrix was to 60's rock – a figure of great talent, showmanship, imagination and animalistic charisma...
SOUNDS

THE PRISONERS
Thewisermiserdemelza
(Big Beat)
...gives you the sinking feeling that the Prisoners are little more than early-Jam impersonators, hulking mods in dayglo clothing.
SOUNDS

THE PSYCHEDELIC FURS
Mirror Moves (CBS)
The explanation of just why the Psychedelic Furs are important lies firmly in the heart of this music.
SOUNDS

...an inspired and intelligent album out there on its own.
MELODY MAKER

...a disappointing and extremely patchy album...
NME

PSYCHIC TV
Dreams Less Sweet (CBS)
...an ungainly mass of spurious pretense ... ranging from ham-fisted mock classics to stumbling ruralistic hokum topped by a pathetic stream of pubescent drivel.
RECORD MIRROR

...an incredible con-job...
MELODY MAKER

...a colossal achievement...
SOUNDS

PUBLIC IMAGE LIMITED
Live In Tokyo (Virgin)
PiL's sound has become as formal and inelastic as elevator music: it is, again, noise – without heart or flesh of any sort.
NME

...in the best tradition of flogging dead horses ... Another chapter in the great rock 'n' roll swindle.
MELODY MAKER

John still sounds as if he'd far prefer to be down the pub with a lager in one hand a hamburger in the other.
RECORD MIRROR

This Is What You
Want...This Is What You
Get (Virgin)
...tiresome, meaningless whining and uninventive, mutant electro-funk and gibbering...
SOUNDS

...a record to baste the brainpot the same time as it's toasting the toes...
MELODY MAKER

THE PRETENDERS

THE Q-TIPS featuring PAUL YOUNG
Live At Last (Rewind)
...nothing ... actually justifies the reactivation of these recordings beyond the humble pursuit of hard cash ... fills in a few gaps in the story of Paul Young and not much more.
MELODY MAKER

QUEEN
The Works (EMI)
Awful, mainly. So from the average Queen fan's viewpoint, awful *good*!
SOUNDS

...there is even now occasionally a glimmer of deliberate self-parody and the suggestion of a smirk, a hint that they really know how ridiculous they are.
NME

Queen's career now depends on their refusal to commit themselves to anything but self-preservation...
MELODY MAKER

THE QUICK
International Thing (Epic)
...They don't know sweet fanny adams about soul ... sickly, flaccid arrangements and bland, derivative instrumentation.
MELODY MAKER

R.E.M.
Murmur (IRS)
R.E.M. have a claim to being one of the most evocative pop practitioners around.
NME

...so damn good, there isn't a hat size that will fit it ... a very loud cry for the most spectacular kind of attention.
MELODY MAKER

R.E.M.
Reckoning (IRS)
...one of the most beautifully exciting groups on the planet ... R.E.M. somehow transcend period fetishism to make music in tune with the times. In short, another classic.
NME

...the post-punk thrash is gone and its place the always present Byrds references are many and unashamed...
MELODY MAKER

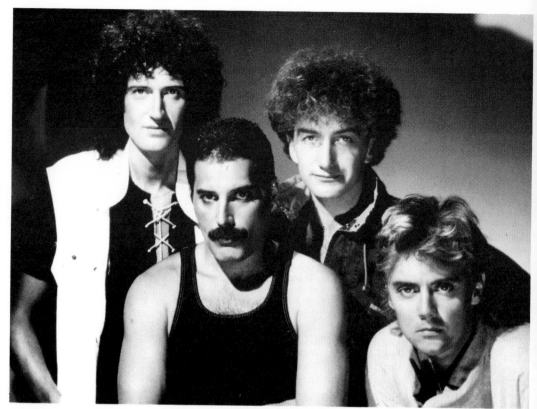

QUEEN

THE RAINCOATS

Largely gone is the twelve string guitar that ... helped fuel all those Byrds comparisons ...
SOUNDS

...when there's not much happening, pillage the past ... at times pleasant, but ultimately a pointless exercise.
RECORD MIRROR

THE RAIN PARADE
Emergency Third Rail Power Trip (Enigma)
...here is real brain tunnel music for today's and tomorrow's world, full of hope ... and glory.
SOUNDS

Whether they mean anything more than that psychedelics are once again sneaking into the suburbs I don't know, but the album as a whole comes off better than, say, the debut LP by the Electric Prunes.
CREEM

RAINBOW
Bent Out Of Shape (Polydor)
...another duff 'un...
RECORD MIRROR

...a virtual testament to the downfall of Ritchie Blackmore and his never ending Rainbow ... still searching for that pot of gold ... every time he releases a new album, he moves one step closer to total sellout.
MELODY MAKER

...an absolutely vital re-affirmation of Blackmore's prowess as both a guitarist and a songwriter.
SOUNDS

THE RAINCOATS
Moving (Rough Trade)
An assured, astute, even touching record that carries alongside its demure directness a lusty experimentalism...
SOUNDS

If the Incredible String Band had heard Bob Marley, they'd have sounded something like this...
MELODY MAKER

RANK AND FILE
Long Gone Dead (Slash)
...a record that will coil around you like the rattler squeezing out of the empty socket of the steer skull that's depicted on the album's jacket.
SOUNDS

RATT
Out Of The Cellar (Atlantic)
...one of the best US hard rock bands to emerge this decade ... Ratt will be metal monsters before you can scream and jump on the nearest chair.
SOUNDS

CHRIS REA
Wired to The Moon (Magnet)
Another one for those faithful then, everyone else will thumb past him once more.
RECORD MIRROR

He's proved to be one of our best exports in years, but I'm sure we can all make do with Barry and Julio.
SOUNDS

...probably his least offensive statement to date.
MELODY MAKER

THE RED CRAYOLA WITH ART & LANGUAGE
Black Snakes (Pure Freude)
...by far the Red Crayola's most cohesive and accessible outing.
SOUNDS

RED LONDON
This Is England (Razor)
...a magnificent, beautiful, heartrending masterpiece ... a light in the darkness, proud in adversity, strong in spirit ... the essence of punk, if the word ever meant anything at all.
SOUNDS

...weird and wonderful Folkwhimsy/Agit-prop/Punk hybrid...
NME

SHARON REDD
Love How You Feel (Prelude)
The staple formula is for Eric Matthew – her one-man band, writer and producer – to put a Linn drum on a loop while there's a whole lotta pantin' 'n' a-rantin', a-belchin' and a-squelchin'
from Miss Redd and her chorus.
NME

RE-FLEX
The Politics Of Dancing (EMI)
...oozes proud professionalism, raucous power and undeniable class ...
MELODY MAKER

They know as much about dancing as Norman Tebbit does about riding bicycles...
RECORD MIRROR

Re-Flex make the cardinal error of trying to make JOLLY SERIOUS STUFF out of their jar of candy. They probably imagine their title to be a very witty statement of the art – it's meaningless.
NME

...a very tasty flavour of the month.
SOUNDS

LOU REED
Live In Italy (RCA)
I've lost count of how many times Reed has damaged these tunes, but any one of the numerous Velvets bootleg performances around blows these into the middle of next *weak*.
SOUNDS

He seems to be operating in a limbo that's reserved solely for his own kind.
MELODY MAKER

RE-FLEX

LOU REED
New Sensations (RCA)
After all those years of parading his personal freak show, he now needs to show us how *ordinary* he can be...
RECORD MIRROR

It does have the power to put an electric thrill down your spine and Lou Reed *is* still worth listening to.
SOUNDS

THE RESIDENTS
George And James (Ralph)
...a clever way to mark time
MELODY MAKER

THE RESIDENTS AND RENALDO & THE LOAF
Title In Limbo (New Ralph)
...music that shocks, amuses, intrigues, and thoroughly entertains.
SOUNDS

PAUL REVERE & THE RAIDERS
Kicks (Edsel)
A fad rooted squarely (sic) in showbiz trad, the Raiders offer the same good fun on replay they always were in the flesh.
NME

...they should have never put on those stupid three-cornered hats.
SOUNDS

CLIFF RICHARD
Silver (EMI)
...his career has been going nearly as long as 'Coronation Street' but his enthusiasm is all there.
RECORD MIRROR

LIONEL RICHIE
Can't Slow Down
(Motown)
...the whole thing is entirely listenable and at least displays a consistent level of excellence in all departments...
MELODY MAKER

...stylish coffee-table soul.
RECORD MIRROR

...where the Commodores' funk often sounded a little forced, his jumpy international dance-pop comes to him naturally even when he's putting on that stupid West Indian accent.
CREEM

JONATHAN RICHMAN AND THE MODERN LOVERS
Jonathan Sings! (Sire)
...in his arrested infancy, Richman can still be articulate and strangely convincing, drawing simple but illuminating conclusions that swing with firm optimism.
MELODY MAKER

...an out' 'n' out winner ... the most satisfying Modern Lovers album of them all.
SOUNDS

Richman's surprising return to his senses...
CREEM

...songs about buzzy bees, flowers and trees ... I hate this.
RECORD MIRROR

MARC RILEY WITH THE CREEPERS
Cull (In Tape)
...mordant ditties that bounce with rude health and proudly proclaim the quintessential cool to be found only in stubborn unhipness.
NME

Gross Out (In Tape)
...music so unsophisticated as to make Crass sound like the London Symphony Orchestra.
SOUNDS

RIOT
Born In America (Quality)
...the best album Riot have made ... it harks back to the halcyon days of Rainbow's 'Rising'...
SOUNDS

ORIGINAL SOUNDTRACK
Risky Business (Virgin)
...outside of the movie theatre, the point of such an uneven set gets lost on all but *the* most obsessive soundtrack collector.
SOUNDS

SMOKEY ROBINSON
Blame It On Love & All The Great Hits (Motown)
Smokey could join Wham! tomorrow if he cared to and not lose an inch of stature in my eyes.
SOUNDS

ROCK GODDESS
Hell Hath No Fury (A&M)
...the fuel on which the rock and roll bonfire is

based ... a delightfully metallic pot-pourri...
SOUNDS

ROCK STEADY CREW
Ready For Battle
(Charisma)
...a very desperate dance album ... just perfect for late night parties, so long as no one over the age of 20 is going to be present.
MELODY MAKER

The breakdancing community is vital and quite refreshing, but that wonderful world just doesn't come through on vinyl.
RECORD MIRROR

ROCKWELL
Somebody's Watching Me (Motown)
Rockwell is a scared man: he doesn't know which of his many personalities to opt for.
NME

Apparently, growing up surrounded by the best possible musical influences doesn't necessarily mean they'll rub off.
SOUNDS

...we are going to be hearing a lot more from this young man. His dad might even be able to retire.
MELODY MAKER

SMOKEY ROBINSON

CLIFF RICHARD

ROCKY HORROR PICTURE SHOW
Audience Par-Tic-I-Pation
(Ode)

And you thought that 'The Rocky Horror Picture Show' could not possibly be milked for more cash. Wrong again, chump. Practically the whole movie, along with one audience's rehearsed responses, is here on vinyl, surely a first in the history of recorded sound.
MELODY MAKER

PAUL RODGERS
Cut Loose (Atlantic)

His voice is clapped out and the songs are trite and meaningless.
RECORD MIRROR

...this could've been one hell of a laff-riot at the expense of Paul Rodgers' credibility, but it's to the man's credit that he made good.
CREEM

THE RODS
Live (Music For Nations)

...a positively domestic effort. It limps when it should prowl, it whimpers when it should bang.
SOUNDS

...the only way of obtaining a decent sound out of this motley piece of metal is to crank up the volume to 10 and fiddle about with the tone knobs aimlessly like a gibbon playing an advanced video game ... worse than anything Ted Nugent has done recently.
MELODY MAKER

THE ROLLING STONES
Undercover
(Rolling Stones Records)

...The Stones are still capable of sounding younger than most studio-created chart fodder...
MELODY MAKER

...about as interesting as a Wednesday afternoon in Harrow.
RECORD MIRROR

They've done it again, folks. Yep, made an LP even worse than the one before ... it's abominable, inexcusable. Quite, quite dead.
NME

Not since 'Exile On Main Street' have they worked themselves into such an irrepressible mood...
SOUNDS

...the first Stones album I can recall where even Watts sounds asleep.
CREEM

ROCKWELL

THE ROLLING STONES

S

PAUL RODGERS

ROMAN HOLLIDAY
Cookin' On The Roof (Jive)
...as tight as a duck's arse and about as appetising.
SOUNDS

...Roman Holliday are stupid, sanitised, squeaky clean, cynically sold and cheapskate entertainment.
NME

Unashamedly prettifying a music that should rightfully ooze oil like an old car rag, Holliday reek of scent, not sweat, and hot sleaze, and have an existence that is strictly *superfluous*.
MELODY MAKER

THE ROMANTICS
In Heat (Epic)
You'd think that stutter-guitar riffs offset by split level vocal chants would grate after a few trax, but in fact the mood jus' grows 'n' grows ... they never get ambitious, tired *or* boring.
SOUNDS

RONNIE AND THE JITTERS
Roll Over (Nervous)
...American crap ... and the band are as ugly as sin.
NME

I've heard worse, but only from the likes of Quo.
SOUNDS

THE ROOM
Clear! (Red Flame)
It sparkles for its few brief minutes with an accomplished songwriting style but leaves no after-taste. No taste at all.
SOUNDS

The Room are not completely clueless but the ideas they do have are currently being submerged by a desire to continually allude to their influences.
NME

ROXY MUSIC
The Atlantic Years 1973-1980 (EG)
...a Christmas compilation designed to kid the Americans they've been missing out on something big by bundling together, willy nilly, some marketing person's idea of Roxy's most sellable assets.
MELODY MAKER
What began as tumultuous pulp, a jarring disorder of rock played by beautiful primitives hiding in the sophistry of 'art' ... became ... a smashed, compressed, resprayed and sumptuously unthreatening music of a mythical uptown, a melancholy cashcard paradise.
NME

RUBBER RODEO
Scenic Views (Mercury)
Since they're commenting on ... the fun of popular lobotomy, it's difficult to say whether hit singles are in store.
SOUNDS

RUDIMENTARY PENI
Death Church (Corpus Christi)
Sometimes tender, sometimes funny and sometimes savage, Rudimentary Peni, after nearly three years of relative obscurity, have finally disbanded. Their wonderful 'Death Church' LP is something to be extremely grateful for.
SOUNDS

RUSH
Grace Under Pressure (Vertigo)
...another selection of ugly, pompous songs ... completely and utterly contrived just so the musicians can show off.
RECORD MIRROR

...their most successful attempt at modernisation so far.
MELODY MAKER

MITCH RYDER
Never Kick A Sleeping Dog (Towerbell)
...excellent shotglass of backstreet US rock ... 'Sleeping Dog' will freshen up any ears it barks into.
NME

SADE
Diamond Life (Epic)
...more genuine romance than a dozen far-fetched Barbara Cartland novels.
SOUNDS

...she's not content simply to be Astrid Gilberto with a London accent and Nigerian grandparents...
MELODY MAKER

SAGA
Heads Or Tales (Portrait)
If you're under the illusion that Saga are just a limp, outdated pomp rock band, then think again.
SOUNDS

...they openly admit that their influences were probably some of the world's biggest musical bores ever...
MELODY MAKER

SAMSON
Don't Get Mad, Get Even (Polydor)
All previous efforts pale into insignificance ... Samson are now set to burn rubber with the biggest of them all.
MELODY MAKER

...it's difficult to see how this LP could further Samson's already negligible reputation.
SOUNDS

SAXON
Crusader (RCA)
...a quarter concept-album, quarter HM thrash, quarter MOR amphitheatre rock and quarter melodramatic bombast.
SOUNDS

...the Barnsley tea men, presumably out of sheer recalcitrance, have placed their balls once more on the chopping block.
MELODY MAKER

ALEXEI SAYLE
The Fish People Tapes (Island)
...I have chuckled once and deadpanned the second and the third time.
SOUNDS

I would rather be force-fed with prune juice ... than listen to this again.
RECORD MIRROR

His bursting suit, leather trilby, goggle-eyes, bullet head, piranha smirk and crazed cackle are funny. His jokes aren't.

How can you make a humorous LP that stands up to repeated listenings? Answer: you can't.
NME

SADE

dance music.
RED FLAME

The Heads play audio pornography: it's stimulating and essential.
SOUNDS

SEX GANG CHILDREN
Ectasy And Bendetta Over New York (ROIR)
A swansong from a dead duck ... they came, they made ripples, colours and noises, they went away again.
SOUNDS

...the Marillion of the Goths-in-the-belfry set ... Sex Gang Children fall far short of having a reason to exist.
NME

SEX GANG CHILDREN
Live (Sex Gang)
In these wrinkled days of antiseptic rock 'n' roll these boys provide the perfect antidote with their truly (com)passionate sex and soul.
MELODY MAKER

SHAKATAK
Out Of This World (Polydor)
Shakatak lakatak.
NME

SHANNON
Let The Music Play (Phonogram)
...a slick synthesis of the pop soul tradition and the fiercer electro funk...
MELODY MAKER

...reinstates smiles on faces and a spring into steps.
RECORD MIRROR

...doesn't gell as a whole...
SOUNDS

SHOCKABILLY
Colosseum (Rough Trade)
Shockabilly pick up and build with the stones rejected by other musical archeologists. They are the soundtrack to Ry Cooder's nightmares... Thoroughly brave and unprepossessing, this is the kind of record you return to when the daily grey grind and the bare-chested stadia-fillers threaten to suck all the faith and inspiration from you.
NME

...pretentious hippy bilge best suited to Cheapo's bargain bin.
MELODY MAKER

SHOOTING STAR
Burning (Virgin/Epic)
If Shooting Star ever do start 'Burning', I'm sure they'll produce a classic album.
SOUNDS

SILENT RUNNING
Shades Of Liberty (EMI)
...nowhere near the breathtaking vision of a heraldic 'Boy', but has obviously about 10 times more to say for itself than anything the Irish rock school have got up to since.
MELODY MAKER

MICHAEL SCHENKER GROUP
Built To Destroy (Chrysalis)
It looks like the time's come for the Michael Schenker Group to hang up their dancing shoes and to press the ... inbuilt self destruct button that has been cocked and primed for some time now.
MELODY MAKER

This totally forgettable collection of regurgitated ideas ... does achieve a rich cosmic status thanks to the hilarious sub-Bad News vocals of Gary Barden who yaps agitatedly through each non-song like a spaniel with its privates snapped in a mousetrap.
SOUNDS

SCORPIONS
Love At First Sting (Harvest)
...a corking collection of near cataclysmic proportions...
RECORD MIRROR

...explodes with sheer sensory crushing insanity...
MELODY MAKER

...they have never sounded better...
SOUNDS

SERIOUS DRINKING
The Revolution Starts At Closing Time (Upright)
...overall this is an exuberant, fun-loving album...
SOUNDS

...how can these lads sing about football when they come from Norwich?
RECORD MIRROR

SEVERED HEAD
Since The Accident (Red Flame)
...the attraction of this music is simply Ellard's manipulation of avant garde theory into an anarchic, lurching, dangerously-capsized

73

SHOCKABILLY

...the gritty rawness and spitfire energy doesn't quite cut through: it's all a bit too tasteful and sensitive to do them justice.
RECORD MIRROR

It dies prematurely within the confines of the speakers, leaving the poor listener blearyeyed and sober.
NME

PAUL SIMON

PAUL SIMON
Hearts And Bones
(Warner Brothers)
It's not Paul Simon's fault that the style that once spoke for a vivacious young generation now speaks to the same crowd in their thirties, preoccupied with the hassles of family living and able to spare little time for his in-genious lyrical subtleties.
SOUNDS

'60's teenage *angst* (the pastoral of the inner self) is a luxury in the '80's.
NME

As a grown up in the 1980's, Simon can't approach love or rock 'n' roll with unambiguous spontaneity, no matter what the songs of the Moonglows may have said to him more than 25 years ago.
CREEM

SIMPLE MINDS
Sparkle In The Rain (Virgin)
Ably conjuring elements of late 70's synth dreams, rock solid sweat and gristle and post art school whimsey...
RECORD MIRROR

...reeks of calculation.
SOUNDS

...they appear to have fallen under the unfortunate delusion that they actually *are* U2.
NME

Electrifyingly determined, exhilaratingly venomous, and so totally sure of themselves that it *wounds*. Simple Minds have come up with a stunner.
MELODY MAKER

SINGERS AND PLAYERS
Leaps And Bounds
(Cherry Red)
State of the art reggae from a group that less a band than a forum for some of the fine: talents the form has to offer.
MELODY MAKER

A playground of the mind welded to a futuristic electric temple full of stories of spirituality and resistance.
SOUNDS

SIOUXSIE AND THE BANSHEES
Nocturne (Polydor)
...the Banshees give themselves up to their music with a singlemindedness and dedication that is magnificent to behold. They care about every second that is passing by; they play their instruments like they are making love...
MELODY MAKER

Hearing this sad souvenir, you can imagine the sorry spectacle enacted in the auspicious portals of the Albert Hall — a spent group of people going through their irrelevant motions to the baying approval of an audience far more blindly entrenched in their blinkered enthusiasm than any HM crowd.
RECORD MIRROR

In all — from its messy, garish packaging to its accompanying video — this is one of the most pointless exercises imaginable. And it's a double!
SOUNDS

Once pioneers, Siouxsie And The Banshees are now no more than stylish but conservative entertainers. 'Which tunnel did *you* come through?' Siouxsie enquires of a truculent fan. Probably the same one as *she* did.
NME

Hyaena (Polydor)
...some of the most melodic utterings from the band for a long time.
RECORD MIRROR

'Hyaena' slowly turned its head, saw nothing worth shouting about, snaffled its breakfast and went back to sleep, to dream of the next album.
SOUNDS

...an immaculate conception.
MELODY MAKER

THE SKATALITES
Return Of The Big Guns
(Island)
It must be said that the decades have mellowed the Skatalites a bit.
SOUNDS

SLADE
The Amazing Kamikaze Syndrome (RCA)
Basically, it's all your average unemployed brickie's mate's thrash; high art it isn't, but it keeps the dandruff fanciers amused and doesn't stain the carpet or your brain.
NME

...no nonsense stuff to leave you with a throb in your pinkies...
RECORD MIRROR

Slade are still capable of rocking harder and catchier than most bands *half* their age.
SOUNDS

SLADE
Slade's Greats (Polydor)
A classic compilation guaranteed to make the ducks fall off your living room wall and leave cracks in the plaster.
RECORD MIRROR

...their definitively boisterous brand of Big Grin pop-with-balls has never been bettered...
SOUNDS

SLAVE
The Best Of Slave
(Cotillion)
As prime purveys of the ideal funk blueprint Slave have few peers.
RECORD MIRROR

...too often they settle for a pedestrian groove.
SOUNDS

GRACE SLICK
Software (RCA)
The original Starship Trooper would appear to have gone a bit off course.
MELODY MAKER

REX SMITH
Camouflage (CBS)
...it glides along like a high-performance Concorde ... floating and landing gracefully in a field of long grass, waiting for the sun to shine for those Californian beach parties...
SOUNDS

THE SMITHS
The Smiths (Rough Trade)
Musically the Smiths are little more than mildly regressive. What saves them is Morrissey's rare grasp of the myriad distortions of the pastel worlds of nostalgia.
NME

They're standing for attention here with their arms folded...
SOUNDS

There are moments here that float and shimmer with a spectacular inevitability, a timelessness, an opinion of their own enormous qualities that only the very best pop music can boast.
MELODY MAKER

THE SMITHS

SNATCH
Snatch (Pandemonium)
If this were a new group they'd be cited as innovative. Maybe a bit patchy, but superbly subversive.
SOUNDS

Spontaneity suited J&P, and spontaneous

combustion was the proper style for Snatch.
NME

SOFT CELL
This Last Night In Sodom
(Some Bizzare)
...reeks, more than ever, of promises turned bad, of worst anticipations fulfilled...
MELODY MAKER

This LP is a shambles. It sounds like it might have taken 37 minutes to record ... Piss off Soft Cell. So say all of us.
NME

...recommended as a fine farewell – a last and lasting comment on the human condition.
SOUNDS

THE SOUND
Shock Of Daylight (Statik)
...beautifully soulful rock music ... a classic.
SOUNDS

...plunging headlong into aggressively melodic territories with a positively heroic sense of its own momentum ... further evidence that the tide is changing, that the emphasis might at last be switching from the merely pretty, the glossily cosmetic.
MELODY MAKER

SPANDAU BALLET
Parade (Chrysalis)
A solemn march of twee songs, instilled with all the sincerity of a Bob Monkhouse chat show, laden with overblown melodies and superficial gloss.
SOUNDS

Surely this can't be premature middle-age already?
MELODY MAKER

SPEAR OF DESTINY
One Eyed Jacks (Epic)
...tough and bruising ... Kirk Brandon's hour

SLADE

THE SOUND

SPEAR OF DESTINY

SPECIMEN
Batastrophe (Sire)
...an essential buy for guttersnipe grave-diggers from Soho to San Francisco. Mascara'd mayhem for REAL men.
SOUNDS

SPIDER
Rough Justice (A&M)
The poor man's Status Quo have coughed up the dullest platter of their career.
RECORD MIRROR

...about as heavy as a milk bottle top.
SOUNDS

Imagine the bar-room boogie of Quo meeting a whole host of noises from Free to Foreigner and Samson to Styx.
MELODY MAKER

SPIRIT
The Thirteenth Dream
(Phonogram)
It boils down to one question – are the nouveau versions better than the originals? And yes, as usual, the answer's no.
NME

...what at first seemed dubious, integrity-wise, grows like a magic mushroom cloud.
SOUNDS

BRUCE SPRINGSTEEN
Born In The U.S.A. (CBS)
...bloody, unbowed, magnificent ... this might be the best Springsteen album ever.
SOUNDS

...show me a Brit into Bruce and I'll show you a misguided wally.
RECORD MIRROR

...the man's a walking museum piece ... he has more in common with Henry Fonda than with Boy George...
MELODY MAKER

SQUIRE
Get Smart (Hi-Lo Records)
...the last word in shallow nostalgia. Invest your fiver in a coupla pairs of white socks.
RECORD MIRROR

STATUS QUO
Back To Back (Vertigo)
...shows what a sorry state of affairs Quo have allowed themselves to slide into. From being one of the punchiest and most raucous bands in Britain, they've become a cheap circus act.
RECORD MIRROR

may even be at hand.
MELODY MAKER

Brandon has something interesting and worthwhile to sing about, deriving from his faith in the potential of youth for change.
SOUNDS

...has neither drive nor direction.
NME

THE SPECIAL AKA
In The Studio (2-Tone)
This is an essential purchase ... never perfect but always intriguing, the best long player so far this year...
RECORD MIRROR

...sublime agit-prop, a coolly sophisticated and masterfully varied modern pop cocktail ... with Dammers adding his haunting melodies and bucketloads of political suss.
SOUNDS

...displays a healthy disdain for the conservatism endemic in current rock...
MELODY MAKER

SPECIMEN

ROD STEWART

...rock 'n' roll with its face scrubbed so clean you can't even recognise it: only one teaspoonful of dirt per 10 gallons of water.
MELODY MAKER

AL STEWART
Russians and Americans (RCA)
Stewart's still got the fire, the lyrical prowess, the experience ... if only he wasn't such an old folkie!
SOUNDS

ROD STEWART
Camouflage (WEA)
Soppy love song follows arthritic groin-grinder follows love song and the whole thing splurges on like a particularly dull edition of 'Dynasty'.
RECORD MIRROR

...still only cruising music...
SOUNDS

THE STING-RAYS
Dinosaurs (Big Beat)
...not a cross between the Meteors and the Cramps, but an original combo much more diverse than their self-confessed influences...
SOUNDS

STRAY CATS
Rant And Rave With The Stray Cats (Arista)
...cardboard cut-out jobs...
SOUNDS

BRUCE SPRINGSTEEN

...inoffensive and gloriously happy. Tired of Status Quo and you're tired of life.
MELODY MAKER

STEEL PULSE
Earth Crisis
(Wiseman Doctrine)
Nobody else plays old-fashioned reggae with such effortless elegance.
MELODY MAKER

Maybe that's their plan: subvert through sugar-coating ... lamely likable.
SOUNDS

...a bright, polished and winningly confident affair...
NME

SHAKIN' STEVENS
The Bop Won't Stop (Epic)
...shoddy, completely lame but superficially attractive.
SOUNDS

...would make an excellent Christmas present for youthful grannies, teeny types and Shaky's mum.
NME

THE STRAY CATS

...content to hammer out a slavish copy of Fifties' jukebox rock without introducing one new angle or even a decent song.
MELODY MAKER

Their complete lack of irony or ability to laugh at the ludicrous nature of what they do puts them on a par with fellow American chart-topper jung Sting of the Police for pretentiousness.
NME

Only an idealogue would deny that these unlikely pop stars tear into rockabilly ready-mades with twice the gusto of any purists or authentics now recording.
CREEM

THE STYLE COUNCIL
Café Bleu (Polydor)
...fairly mediocre though reasonably agreeable...
MELODY MAKER

...too full of empty posturing and too short on good songs.
RECORD MIRROR

...only a partially successful experiment...
SOUNDS

I will counsel that Paul forgets his pole position, ignores the clamour for weighty rhetoric and 'vision', and restores the real vigour of his craft.
NME

STYX
Caught In The Act (A&M)
...mega American stadium rock at its best...
RECORD MIRROR

THE SUBHUMANS
From The Cradle To The Grave (Bluurg)
This is the record that Jimbo Pursey would have made had he been blessed with a less

THE STYLE COUNCIL

self obsessed world view and doubled IQ.
NME

DONNA SUMMER
A Hot Summer Night (Polygram)
...all very flat, very predictable, very Hollywood ... real overpriced champagne and chicken-in-a-basket stuff.
SOUNDS

DONNA SUMMER
She Works Hard For The Money (Mercury)

Donna Summer has done the mature American thing and got herself converted. But ... cynicism aside, this is really a very good record, as I'm sure it would have been, with or without His help.
MELODY MAKER

SWALLOW TONGUE
A Stain Upon The Silence (Cherry Red)
...they lack the honed-down clarity and simple enthusiasm that makes Carmel so appealing.
NME

This is dog food.
SOUNDS

SWANS
Filth (Zensor)
They remain true to their ugly selves, have the discipline to persevere beyond rock's self-imposed limits and the stamina to go on grinding until the end. 'Filth' is the closest yet a group has come to rendering the massive lurching, lumbering beast inert without bringing it to a complete halt. Therein lies the internal dynamic that snares and holds the listener, drawing him/her into complicity in Swan's

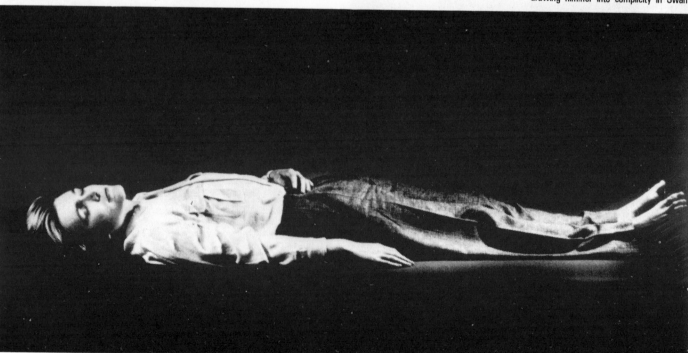

DAVID SYLVIAN

great blasting operation that might turn out to be rock's last remaining pleasure.
NME

Let's face it, this is crap.
MELODY MAKER

SYLVESTER
Call Me (Ecstasy Records)
Genuinely weird people shouldn't make ordinary records.
SOUNDS

SYLVESTER
Greatest Hits (Fantasy)
...a whole new era of chemically-propelled breakneck stomping.
RECORD MIRROR

DAVID SYLVIAN
Brilliant Trees (Virgin)
...glimmers with expectations and glows with success. He's left art school, gone through the grey and come out in a spectrum of pastel shades that enhance and enthral.
SOUNDS

...Sylvian is no longer petrified at the uncontrollable incomprehensibility of movement. A masterpiece...
MELODY MAKER

T

TSA
Spunk (Mega Ton)
...races out of the speakers with all the aplomb

of a runaway tank steered by a drug crazed Magnus Pike ... some superb meat-and-mash metal that will certainly garner them respect...
MELODY MAKER

...Poland's top heavy metal band ... raw, unpolished (no pun intended) ... next time Budgie venture to Poland they might have to pick a time when this bunch aren't gigging.
SOUNDS

T.S.O.L.
Change Today?
(Enigma U.S.)
...a timely reassertion that all is not lost with rock music across the Atlantic.
SOUNDS

TALK TALK
It's My Life (EMI)
...quickly fires vitriolic bullets of passion into your heart, opening up many wounds during its torrid journey.
MELODY MAKER

ROGER TAYLOR
Strange Frontier (EMI)
The product of a talented guy with no reason to do anything ever again...
SOUNDS

TELEVISION PERSONALITIES
The Painted Word
(Illuminated Jams)
Soul-saddening vignettes of sour adult life, innocent childish reflections, all sung in a quintessential English manner.
SOUNDS

...one of the most wanton and wilful cases of self-immolation you're ever likely to hear...
MELODY MAKER

Oh dear. This opus even made the cat cringe.
NME

THE TEMPEST
Five Against The House
(Anagram)
...next time around, they'll have to be bang on target if they intend to conquer anywhere other than their native Northampton.
SOUNDS

THE TEMPTATIONS
Back To Basics (Motown)
Temptations seldom touch on the deep and delicate mastery of their past. It is genius humbled, truly the work of fallen heroes.
NME

10CC
Windows In The Jungle
(Mercury)
Their music is virtually indistinguishable from the hum of the Xerox machine.
NME

TEX AND THE HORSEHEADS
Tex And The Horseheads
(Enigma)
With Rock Vodka pounding on drums and Smog Vomit thrashing his bass who can honestly hold them back?
SOUNDS

THE THE
Soul Mining (Some Bizzare)
...a classic slice of everyman's everyday music, ready made for the radio, the dancefloor and those thoughtful interludes late at night.
SOUNDS

Once again we must ask just why it is that this man is not phenomenally successful ... one of the year's rare heart-stopping moments.
NME

...the work of a massive but petrified ego... There's a schizoid sense of attempted and maybe failed exorcism, a congenitally frenzied

quest for self-discovery and ... the occasional stench of gratuitous sado-masochism...
MELODY MAKER

THIN LIZZY
Life (Vertigo)
A shameless rip-off and a fetid end for a once valued band.
NME

Lynott is still far more entertaining than most of the limp-wristed, whinging rubbish that now passes for 'heavy rock'.
SOUNDS

THIRD WORLD
All The Way Strong (CBS)
If Third World were honest, they'd call this long player, 'All The Way To The Bank'.
RECORD MIRROR

Cop this for instance: 'Wardrobe Coordination: Tara Posey (sic) ... Ibo's outfit by 'Shack's Executive Sportswear'! Honestly, would you trust a band who couldn't dress themselves?
SOUNDS

.38 SPECIAL
Tour De Force (A&M)
...if you like your music meaty but not so meaty as to be inedible, then this is for you.
SOUNDS

DAVID THOMAS & THE PEDESTRIANS
Variations On A Theme
(Sixth International/
Rough Trade)
Thomas works in more easily-digestible forms than he did in Pere Ubu ... I dunno what you'll make of Humpty Dumpty lounge jazz or fine feathered rockabilly and Western Swing salutes but these guys actually make interesting music out of 'em.
CREEM

THIN LIZZY

RON THOMPSON & THE RESISTORS
Treat Her Like Gold
(Takoma Records)
...Thompson may not be the same colour as Elmore James but he's close.
SOUNDS

THE THOMPSON TWINS
Into The Gap (Arista)
It's absolutely impossible to believe that any thought ever went into a TT song other than "what will make this sell?"!.. All they need now is the dog and I do believe they'd turn into the Archies.
MELODY MAKER

...for the most part the Twins are re-writing past hits or thieving from other people's...
SOUNDS

...guaranteed immediate high impact. I wish I was their bank manager.
RECORD MIRROR

THOR
Unchained (Ultra-Noise)
...most of this junk sounds as if recorded whilst jogging.
NME

An accumulation of all that is good and bad in heavy metal.
SOUNDS

You take three untalented musicians and match them with a singer whose arrogance will hopefully camouflage his lack of talent ... eminently forgettable.
MELODY MAKER

JOHNNY THUNDERS
Diary Of A Lover (PVC)
...for all its novelty value, this mixed bag doesn't really leave more than the most fleeting of half-baked impressions.
MELODY MAKER

Hurt Me (New Rose)
...there's very little that's brilliant about any of the songs on this collection. Thunders is certainly no poet, and a balladeer he definitely ain't.
MELODY MAKER

It'll give you the saddest laugh you've had for a long time.
NME

THUNDERSTRUCK
Beauty And The Beasts (Thunderbolt)
...this utterly horrible piece of plastic ... a muffled, indistinct boring mess...
SOUNDS

THE TIMES
I Helped Patrick McGoohan Escape (Artpop)
I'm talking about Ed Ball, one of the truly great song-writers of our time.
SOUNDS

TALK TALK

TOM TOM CLUB
Close To The Bone (Island)
...sloppy and childish, weak and uninspired. Most of the time ... they sound like Banarama or grown adults playing five year olds for the day...
NME

...suggests the kind of irresponsible exoticism cynics always suspect when rich white people find the meaning of life in the tropics.
CREEM

TONES ON TAIL
Pop (Beggars Banquet)
If this were the work of some new combo ... the culprits would have been banished to their bedrooms to think again.
SOUNDS

BERNIE TORME
Electric Gypsies (Zebra)
...far too much one-note bending and wobbly solos...
SOUNDS

BERNIE TORME
Live (Zebra)
...a dire and tiring mess of second-hand fuzzed guitaring pinched from Hendrix, Beck and Page.
MELODY MAKER

...lacerating axemanship.
SOUNDS

PETER TOSH
Mama Africa (EMI America)
A surprisingly good album from a man who's been acting the fool for years.
CREEM

TOYAH
Love Is The Law (Safari)
Never has anyone so safe presented themselves as being so dangerous.
NME

...proficient rock drivel ... drivel of the worst kind imaginable, because it is drivel so utterly dated that it ought properly to have been offered for public derision at least five ... years ago.
SOUNDS

Toyah has re-emerged with a refreshing maturity and a quiet sort of serenity.
RECORD MIRROR

TOYAH
Toyah! Toyah! Toyah! All The Hits (K-Tel)
Her voice always sounded like chalk squeaking down a blackboard...
RECORD MIRROR

Toyah is a product machine, and the goods are definitely sub-standard.
SOUNDS

Keep your daughter on the stage, Mrs Wilcox.
MELODY MAKER

TRASH
Watch Out (RCA)
Total sleaze is back fellers; and the teen tease of Trash ... are at the forefront of a wave that's guaranteed to start rolling...
MELODY MAKER

PAT TRAVERS
Hot Shot (Polydor)
...his best album to date.
SOUNDS

TROUBLE FUNK
In Times Of Trouble (D.E.T.T.)
...qualifies for a serious nomination for the 'hardest funk there is' trophy ... contains very few gems of verbal wit and wisdom, but it does feature an awful lot of blisteringly inventive and energetic music.
NME

TROUSER PRESS PRESENTS
The Best Of America Underground (Roir)
...a pile of bands ... who would have dearly lov-

ed to be the Knack, but didn't have it, their lack of success being the main contributory factor in their 'underground' status.
NME

ROBIN TROWER
Back It Up (Chrysalis)
...another episode of 1971 Revisited...
NME

I can't really recommend this album highly enough. It's a classic example of sheer professional excellence...
MELODY MAKER

TRUE WEST
Hollywood Holiday
(New Rose)
True West have already been glorified by me ... when they relesed their five track mini LP on Bring Out Your Dead Records.
SOUNDS

TINA TURNER
Private Dancer (Capitol)
Tina Turner has a wonderful voice, it's just a shame this album succeeds so well in hiding it.
RECORD MIRROR

The heartbeat is as shallow as the make-up, so it's difficult to get excited by either her or her music.
SOUNDS

TV SMITH
Channel Five (Expultion)
Where there should be menace and tension pushing the lyrics along, there is instead a formulated blandness to cushion them. Pop goes the TV, and a shame it is too.
NME

TWELFTH NIGHT
Live And Let Live
(Music For Nations)
...an album with clout, balls, and emotion.
MELODY MAKER

TWISTED SISTER
Stay Hungry (Atlantic)
...Dee Snider has surely got to be Alice Cooper's older, fatter brother.
RECORD MIRROR

...ten new reasons why they rule the Shock Rock roost.
SOUNDS

TWO SISTERS
Two Sisters (Sugarscoop)
Sceptical pundits may have scorned scratching, rap and electro for its lack of progression, but the opening two cuts here point an erect digit at the possibilities.
SOUNDS

THE TYGERS OF PAN TANG
The Best Of (MCA)
...lotsa distorted guitars, pummeling bass lines, drums that sound like a Volkswagen with terminal exhaust problems and a vocalist with a dangerous sense of vibrato – oops! There goes another decanter!
MELODY MAKER

TINA TURNER

TWISTED SISTER

...are you kiddin'? ... pussy cats rather than Tygers...
SOUNDS

JUDIE TZUKE
Ritmo (Chrysalis)
...brings Judie Tzuke bang up to date with a strongly contemporary feel that should open many eyes and ears.
SOUNDS

JUDIE TZUKE
Best Of Judie Tzuke
(Rocket)
A female Al Stewart with a touch of Joan Armatrading...
SOUNDS

U

U2
Under A Blood Red Sky
(Island)
...infinitely more welcome than some un-wieldy and overblown double album package.
SOUNDS

I find this record much more impressive than the last couple of their live shows I've seen. After all, you can't *hear* Bono climbing up the PA.
MELODY MAKER

Pity that this isn't the wall-of-heroics document it could and should've been. As a counter to the bootleggers it's paltry

pickings.
NME

UB40
Labour Of Love
DEP International)
...in fact nothing more than 10 versions done in typically flatulent UB40 fashion ... as little impact as a baked potato sent back to be reheated in Pizzaland.
RECORD MIRROR

The entire feel of the music reminds me of those toy dogs they used to have in the back window of cars, nodding. It is a music to nod to, which is the limit of its revolutionary *body* talk.
SOUNDS

Sometimes UB hit the spot of rock-reggae with absolute accuracy, and it's power to turn ears is far superior to the weight of their customary glum pamphleteering.
NME

It's beautiful.
MELODY MAKER

UFO
Headstone; The Best Of
UFO (Chrysalis)
...the bridging point between the old masters and the young apprentices; perhaps the proto-type professionals...
NME

...the definitive UFO compilation...
SOUNDS

UK DECAY
A Night For Celebration
Cassette (UK Decay Records)
...enough to send shivers down my spine...
NME

UK SUBS
Flood Of Lies (Scarlet)
A Skeletal Thatcher reclines on the album cover, surrounded by skulls and mutants and horrific images of death and destruction, as the UK Subs come back to reclaim their stall in the punk market-place...
MELODY MAKER

JAMES BLOOD ULMER

Certainly, change is needed; the roots may be secure, but the landscape is too flat. Full marks for playing in Poland, though.
SOUNDS

TRACEY ULLMAN
You Broke My Heart In Seventeen Places (Stiff)
I'm old-fashioned enough to believe that Ullman has something to say.
NME

...sounds uncomfortably close to one of those old Woolworth compilation jobs when they hired session guys to play identikit copies of the hits of the day.
MELODY MAKER

...an untalented, unfunny actress with a voice like a cheese-grater showing up the true roots of Stiff Records by doing cover versions of dreadful oldies with a backing that is, noticeably, stuck in 1970's-style country rock
SOUNDS

...Miss Ullman is set to charm the general public with an entertaining set of toe-tapping melodies.
RECORD MIRROR

JAMES BLOOD ULMER
Odyssey (CBS)
With the unprecedented challenges of his earlier records taken up by nobody, and with his own position of fringe acclaim at a nebulous standstill, Blood Ulmer simply goes back into his shell...
NME

...both severely uncompromising and circumspectly accessible to even the least informed listener ... creating a disorienting, affecting and acutely pleasurable world of possibilities.
SOUNDS

...a triumph, a record to *get really excited about*.
MELODY MAKER

...painfully beautiful stuff.
CREEM

ULTRAVOX
Lament (Chrysalis)
Bland, tuneless songs ... 'Lament' is nothing short of a flaccid placebo ... its contents prove Ultravox to be little more than a pimple on the arse of the industry.
SOUNDS

ULTRAVOX
Monument (The Soundtrack) (Chrysalis)
...this mini-album documents the live side of Ultravox without pretensions ... as it's longer than Neil Young's new album and considerably cheaper, it scarcely constitutes a rip-off.
SOUNDS

...absolutely crucial as a stereo enhancement to the gothic splendour of their vidshow.
RECORD MIRROR

...some of the daftest lyrics ever put to music ... the whole proceedings sound as dead as the proverbial dodo ... an overwhelming sense of

V

VDO
Music For The Assassins In Memoriam Of Hasan Sabbah (VDO)
...consists of 40 minute of wolves doing what they do *best*: howling, groaning and spitting...
SOUNDS

VAN HALEN
MCMLXXXIV (Warner Bros)
Amazingly, Van Halen actually seem to have put some positive *thought* into compiling this new album ... when you're used to having slops for dinner it *does* come as a surprise to be served up something out of the Robert Carrier cookbook.
SOUNDS

...songs stuffed with the crummiest cock-rock rubbish imaginable ... Next time, we want *more*.
MELODY MAKER

...it all sounds just *like* Van Halen.

ULTRAVOX

disappointment that a once-great band has slipped so far down the road to pomposity and dry-ice obsolescence.
MELODY MAKER

THE UNDEAD
Killing Of Reality (Riot City)
...a repetitive barrage of frenzied noise...
SOUNDS

THE UNDERTONES
All Wrapped Up (Ardeck)
...this LP (despite reeking of EMI cash-in) captures that essence of naive disquiet.
RECORD MIRROR

...they did write some great songs and they were great to have around. This K-Tel style requiem is an ideal way to hear it all again...
SOUNDS

The perfect finale for a juvenile pop fantasy, I suppose. Hit up, grow up and split up.
NME

UNITY
Heat Your Body Up (Charisma)
As commercial a proposition as a Big Mac...
RECORD MIRROR

UTOPIA
Oblivion (WEA)
...mostly Todd Rundgren at his finest in yonks ... right up there with some of his slightly-cracked-but-sparkling sub-classics...
SOUNDS

UTOPIA

VAN HALEN

VARIOUS ARTISTS
Bollox To The Gonads—Here's The Testicles (PAX)
Repulsive Alien keep things bouncing along...
SOUNDS

VARIOUS ARTISTS
Burning Up: Vols 1 and 2 (Burning Sounds)
A veritable goldmine from the Burning Sounds' archives...
NME

VARIOUS ARTISTS
Crew Cuts (Island)
...Island have cobbled together half a dozen of their hottest dancefloor cuts. Edited, mixed and given that little touch of magic dust, the resultant foot-tapping holocaust burns right to the bone.
SOUNDS

VARIOUS ARTISTS
Dance Mix Dance Hits Vol Four (Epic)
...brings back many happy memories of glorious party nights spent at the Canvey Island Goldmine, speeding on sulphate and grooving to the sounds...
SOUNDS

VARIOUS ARTISTS
Electro 3 (Streetsounds)

...the massed ranks of mediocrity that follow in the wake of any new movement...
MELODY MAKER

...the relentless rhythms, pulsing with electronic melodies, are breathtaking ... a more crucial album than 'Crucial Electro'...
SOUNDS

VARIOUS ARTISTS
Headline HIts (K-Tel)
The trend of padding out compilations whose whole excuse for existing is that they are lousy with HITS with realms of also-rans reaches an all time high with the duplicitly named 'Headline Hits', which, out of 20 tracks, boasts six un-hits.
NME

VARIOUS ARTISTS
Hi Energy 2 (Street Sounds)
The beats per minute go on and on.
RECORD MIRROR

Basically revamped disco for the gay scene ... a veritable Bacchanalian feast of amyl excess.
MELODY MAKER

VARIOUS ARTISTS
Let The Children Play (Panic)
...aimed at raising funds for the peace-camps ... What does any of this mean to an unemployed

Unfortunately, it also sounds like they're at home in the living room.
NME

LUTHER VANDROSS
Busy Body (Epic)
If you think 'soul' means Paul Young listen to this and maybe you'll understand what that much abused word really means.
MELODY MAKER

This sound tweaks your hat-brim, shines your shoes, and sprays a final dust of face powder before you saunter out to capture the night. These grooves are irresistible, even when heard spilling out of someone else's Walkman on the tube.
NME

...this time one feels the big man has spread his talents just a little bit too thin.
RECORD MIRROR

VARIOUS ARTISTS
American Heartbeat (Epic)
...recorded by very clever musicians with nice haircuts (approx 80 percent have perms) and nice expensive teeth.
SOUNDS

VARIOUS ARTISTS
Best Of Louie Louie (Rhino)
...here we have gathered from a reservoir of (at last count) 2,500 versions, timeless, priceless and thoroughly brainless arrangements of that terminal three-chord headbanger...
NME

LUTHER VANDROSS

17 year old in Wandsworth?
MELODY MAKER

...a collection that some will want to buy as a gesture of support.
NME

VARIOUS ARTISTS
Love The Reason
(Respond)
This shallow, weedy music is not the kind that restores pride and faith to a battered and stranded generation. This is the sound of a lot of slightly talented people murmuring, 'Let's go up Paul's house and play Motown'.
NME

This much is clear: Paul Weller is an appalling A&R man.
MELODY MAKER

Perhaps, after all, Rick Buckler was the genius in the Jam.
SOUNDS

VARIOUS ARTISTS
Mersey Beat (Parlophone)
...this entertaining double mostly catches the Beat.
NME

VARIOUS ARTISTS
Metal Battle (Neat)
The devil may have some good songs but none of them surface on this...
SOUNDS

VARIOUS ARTISTS
Motown Superstars Sing Motown Superstars
(Tamla Motown)
...Famous People single Other Famous People's songs ... A dumb idea, doomed to failure for the simple reason that nobody could add anything to 'Reach Out I'll Be There' or 'Tracks Of My Tears'...
NME

...worth a listen if only to show how much Michael Jackson has improved since his days as the black Jimmy Osmond.
SOUNDS

VARIOUS ARTISTS
Now That's What I Call Music II (EMI/Virgin)
If this album was a jukebox I'd play it to death in my local.
SOUNDS

VARIOUS ARTISTS
Piano Singer's Blues
(Rosetta Records)
...an album that had me sobbing with joy, an essential anthology of hug-to-your-heart recordings by a number of talented women...
NME

VARIOUS ARTISTS
20 Reggae Classics
(Trojan)
Twenty songs released between 1967 and 1974, all standing the test of time.
RECORD MIRROR

In comparison to the way UB40, the Specials and Bad Manners have treated them, the originals might sound pretty thin to casual listeners, but they have a plaintive quality that no amount of studio proficiency has been able to match.
SOUNDS

VARIOUS ARTISTS
Rockabilly Psychosis And The Garage Disease
(Big Beat)
...an admirable and invaluable collection of lunatic rockers spanning the last twenty years.
SOUNDS

VARIOUS ARTISTS
Roots Rockers
(Action Replay)
...these remnants of some of reggae's finest moments are a brutal eduction as to how the skill of crafty composition has degenerated in the form since the turn of the decade.
SOUNDS

VARIOUS ARTISTS
Son Of Oi! (Syndicate/Oi)
...a very fine confirmation of what Oi! was really all about – great punk tunes and working class points of view.
SOUNDS

...second rate and not very funny.
RECORD MIRROR

VARIOUS ARTISTS
The Sound Of Hollywood We Got The Power
(Mystic)
There is *no* conceivable justification for The Sound Of Hollywood: it's a sound which makes living here, in largely silent N22, seem just heavenly.
SOUNDS

VARIOUS ARTISTS
Staying Alive (RSO)
...makes staying awake a difficult task indeed.
NME

VARIOUS ARTISTS
Then Came Rock 'n' Roll
(EMI)
...well worn classics.
RECORD MIRROR

VARIOUS ARTISTS
This Are Two Tone
(2-Tone)
It sounds ancient, even older than punk.
NME

...on the whole, this strange phenomenon was little more than a quite pitiful re-gurgitation of a feeble, rather unlovable music–ska...
SOUNDS

...Dammers' intention to carry his audience to a more committed, experimental plane just didn't work.
RECORD MIRROR

This ... isn't an *epitaph* for the label, it's a

timely and hugely enjoyable reminder of the sheer vivacity and unquestionable excellence of some of the music it promoted. 2-Tone ain't dead, Jerry Dammers is just snoring very loudly. When he wakes up, so will we all.
MELODY MAKER

VARIOUS ARTISTS
Trash On Delivery
(Flicknife)
...suffers very strongly from an obsession with so-called 'trash' music; rock music more concerned with falling over ... a disaster, a car-crash for pop stars.
NME

VARIOUS ARTISTS
25 US No. 1 Hits
(Tamla Motown)
For a touch of authenticity they should have included some crackles and hiss to get that upfront 45 flavour that makes the original singles such classics.
SOUNDS

VARIOUS ARTISTS
UK/DK (Anagram)
...the soundtrack of the video of Cherry Red's beginner's guide to ... punk.
SOUNDS

VARIOUS ARTISTS
The Zulu Compilation
(Zulu)
A set of musical sketches from Merseyside ... a tantalising glimpse of the city's underground activity...
NME

A cottage industry in the heart of the city where everyone wants to be a pop star...
MELODY MAKER

THE VARUKERS
Another Religion Another War (Riot City)
These boys do not have musical ability, only a talentfor sounding like a twentieth rate Discharge thrown through a cement mixer.
SOUNDS

Bloodsuckers (Riot City)
...yet another cliché-ridden heavy-handed punk waxing.
SOUNDS

STEVIE RAY VAUGHAN AND DOUBLE TROUBLE
Texas Flood (Epic)
...amazingly powerful considering it involves only three musicians, eight days, and two overdubs ... real downhome Texas barbecue boogie.
NME

...has succeeded in capturing the verve and splendour ... of the original bluesmen in a set of standards and originals that owe nothing to stagnant revivalism.
SOUNDS

ALAN VEGA
Saturn Strip (Elektra)
Vega's best long-player yet, and a prime contender for this year's laurels ... A classic.
NME

USA radio may even succumb willingly .. What this boy would really like to hear, though, is something a bit more adventurous ...
SOUNDS

VELVET MONKEYS
Future (Fountain of Youth)
Bad Acid funsters...
SOUNDS

VENOM
At War With Satan (Neat)
An unrelenting holocaust of horror, this unmitigated racket relates the bitter battle betwixt Good and Evil over a chilling cascade of tempo changes garnished with savage soloing, anguished growling vocals and noises that defy human description.
SOUNDS

THE VIBRATORS
Alaska 127 (RAM)
...they suddenly seem to have really stretched out their style, which now encompasses everything from hillbilly to soulful balladeering.
MELODY MAKER

VIOLENT FEMMES
Violent Femmes
(Rough Trade)
...bitter heartache, petulant frustration, and torrid anger become scenic majesties .. the most impressive album released this year.
MELODY MAKER

...a thinking rockist's wet dream ... the touches of Verlaine's thoughtful guitar prose and suggestion of Lou Reed tackling Gershwin...
SOUNDS

VIRGIN STEELE
Guardians Of The Flame
(Music For Nations)
...hits some incredibly high notes, particularly during 'Burn The Sun', which sound almost unreal.
SOUNDS

...committed to resurrecting the grossness and downright splendour of the greatest American metal bands ever...
MELODY MAKER

VISAGE
Fade To Grey—The Singles Collection
(Polydor)
Visage aren't quite as bad as everybody remembers them. That is, of course, if anyone remembers them at all.
MELODY MAKER

Visage engendered an ugly, corrosive, collective mentality – the very antithesis of their necessarily vague manifesto ... they come out of this retrospective album seeming as enigmatic and alluring as a bunch of red-nosed clowns, whose only tears were shed on the

way to the bank.
SOUNDS

...electro-diskow at its most vacuous ... An overpainted speck on the history of pop and as they say, last year's make up was just some poor animal's bollocks.
RECORD MIRROR

VISIBLE TARGETS
Autistic Savant
(Park Avenue)
...a crisply-produced sensory representation of something frustratingly incomplete but happily abstract.
SOUNDS

W

TOM WAITS
Asylum Years (Asylum)
...the kind of record that'll appeal to twisted rockers, aged jazzers and connoisseurs of odd vocalists alike.
SOUNDS

TOM WAITS
Swordfishtrombones
(Island)
...Waits' latest work, is the scene of a most uncommon lustre...
NME

...it has beauty, pride, passion and excitement running through it. It shows Tom Waits still in the ascendant and brilliance being perfected.
SOUNDS

A good album, full of good lines and clever, original musical ideas.
MELODY MAKER

...after 10 years of making good records, Tom Waits has made his first great one.
CREEM

RICK WAKEMAN
Cost Of Living
(Virgin/Charisma)
And so it came to pass that the balding and overweight maestro donned his cloak yet again. Gathering a band of no-good dilettantes together, he hired a drinks cabinet — and a recording studio — and went to work.
SOUNDS

SCOTT WALKER
Climate Of Hunter
(Virgin)
This is *it*, the final fusion of free verse and New Music, a thoroughly modern album that gives not even half an inch to fashion. Bravo!
MELODY MAKER

...invites the listener to scream into the face of destiny.
NME

...the stutterings of a confused charlatan who believes his own myths and whose psyche is stretched too tautly over the wasteland

between past and present.
SOUNDS

WALL OF VOODOO
Granma's House (IRS)
...a testament to just how great a band they originally were.

JOE WALSH
You Bought It — You Name It (Asylum)
At the artists's request I shall name it: 'Asshole On The Moon'.
NME

TOM WAITS

WANG CHUNG

WANG CHUNG
Points On The Curve
(Geffen)
If this LP was a novel, it'd be serialised in *Women's Own.*
SOUNDS

...all a bit thin and lightweight...
RECORD MIRROR

We wouldn't be seen ... with a copy of this LP under our arms when we *could* be carrying the New Order 12-inch disco re-mix.
NME

WAR
Life (Is So Strange) (RCA)
...they're torn between disco and jazz trades, and masters of neither.
RECORD MIRROR

...the fulfilment of every promise and every threat the band made in those brooding pre-1975 years.
NME

WAS (NOT WAS)
Born To Laugh At Tornadoes (Geffen)
...as irreverent as two obsessive, talented men can be when they're dealing with something they have a deep love for: the endless rapids of American music, good and bad.
NME

Whereas the first album travelled most its lyrical distance on super-charged funk, 'Born ...' makes ample pit-stops to rip-off the coffin-clad chordal motifs which pervade AOR like inspirational leprosy – not always successfully.
SOUNDS

Marvellous.
RECORD MIRROR

If ever a record challenged musical assumptions, here it is: this sucker crosses over more musical boundaries than a bar mitzvah band.
CREEM

If Don and David Was were born to laugh at tornadoes, their greatest joy is still taking you along for the ride.
MELODY MAKER

WAS (NOT WAS)
The Woodwork Squeaks
(Ze/Island)
...in one snazzy package, you get all the meat and none of the gristle.
SOUNDS

If there was ever conceptual dance music, it's here. Often too long and always too smart. Was (Not Was) niggle and wheedle and demand to be heard.
MELODY MAKER

THE WATERBOYS
A Pagan Place
(Ensign/Island)
An odd record, wearing a mask of commerciality, but with something a little elusive at its core.
MELODY MAKER

...when ... an album like this embraces you and takes you where every sense is awakened and little else matters, *then* all it can be is innovative, magnificent and essential.
SOUNDS

ROGER WATERS
The Pros and Cons of Hitch Hiking (Harvest)
...full of endless ponderings on the meaning of life for rich hippies.
RECORD MIRROR

...I find it quite shocking that Waters has the temerity to continue to labour his guilt, neuroses and personal fuck-ups through this record.
NME

...the entire concept is conveyed with an expert conviction that only years of experience of premature genius could achieve.
SOUNDS

MUDDY WATERS
Hoochie Coochie Man
(Blue Sky)
Rollin' Stone (Blue Moon)
For those who weren't around at the time, this great man and his earth-shattering music will blow you clean away.
NME

WAYSTED
Vices (Chrysalis)
...an astonishingly powerful statement of intent.
SOUNDS

Too good to miss.
MELODY MAKER

THE WEATHER GIRLS
Success (CBS)
...makes ya wanna dance – and there's no better recommendation than that.
RECORD MIRROR

...just too much of the same...
MELODY MAKER

It's all 'woh oh oh' over 'bum bum bum' when it should and could be 'wow' and 'ow' over 'boom boom boom'.
SOUNDS

WEATHER REPORT
Domino Theory (CBS)
...awash with precious details.
NME

...quirky, jerky, mercurial music...
RECORD MIRROR

WEEKEND
Live At Ronnie Scott's
(Rough Trade)
...a pretty effective hammer for the last nail in Weekend's coffin.
RECORD MIRROR

...so weak it lacks the strength to actually be anything beyond the sum of its parts – five tunes on a groove in vinyl...
SOUNDS

Weekend never were worth caring about ... this is the weakest end.
NME

...leaves the listener wanting more...
MELODY MAKER

WENDY AND THE ROCKETTS
Dazed For Days (A&M)
As an example of its genre, this record is passably acceptable...
MELODY MAKER

WENDY AND THE ROCKETS

WEATHER REPORT

...something for everyone...
RECORD MIRROR

MATTHEW WILDER
I Don't Speak the Language (Epic)
Yet another of the faceless crop of singler/songwriters...
SOUNDS

...slips drearily into the back of your mind as esily as the kind of stuff they play at Tesco's.
RECORD MIRROR

WENDY O WILLIAMS
Wow (Music For Nations)
...no smoke and no fire.
SOUNDS

JACKIE WILSON
The Classic Jackie Wilson (Skratch Music)
This collection is indispensable for anyone with more than a passing interest in soul music.
SOUNDS

WITCHFINDER GENERAL
Friends Of Hell (Heavy Metal)
...*the* most tedious album I have *ever* heard ... epitomises all that stinks about bad hevy metal.
SOUNDS

Their future lies with sharp, smart pop; not with the Exploited.
SOUNDS

JAMES WHITE
James White's Flaming Demonics (Ze)
...leaves me neither shaken nor stirred.
NME

...staggeringly charmless ... a job lot of hot air.
MELODY MAKER

...has a rare passion and articulacy – of sound, style and delivery...
SOUNDS

SNOWY WHITE
White Flames (Towerbell)
...movingly mundane...
MELODY MAKER

WHITESNAKE
Slide It In (Liberty)
For reasons best known to his psychiatrist, he makes every lyric a vehicle for his senile sexual fantasies ... Can it really be true that when he went into hopsital with a groin pain they diagnosed a brain tumour?
SOUNDS

You could call it offensive sexist baloney, or you could see it all as being rather quaint and old-fashioned.
MELODY MAKER

KIM WILDE
Catch As Catch Can (RAK)
...a yawning imagintion in need of a fix...
SOUNDS

MATTHEW WILDER

JAH WOBBLE/THE EDGE/HOLGER CZUKAY
Snake Charmer (Island)
...a conglomeration of some of the healthiest musical trends in '83—steaming slabs of electrofunk, Islamic boogie and African pop...
MELODY MAKER

...displays more on and off the wall wit than erstwhile boss Lydon seems able to muster these days. *And* you can dance to it.
NME

THE WOLFGANG PRESS
The Burden Of Mules (4AD)
...a mish-mash of such modern sources as PiL, the Birthday Party and A Certain Ratio. Waves of electronic noise merge with wild sound effects battling with pseudo-ethnic beats.
NME

...likely to alienate through their far-reaching mixtures of experimentation ... does not lend itself to casual listening.
SOUNDS

BOBBY WOMACK
The Poet II (Beverley Glen)
...Womack rose from the dead and shocked us the sensuous brilliance of 'The Poet'. Amazingly, this follow-up surpasses even that.
SOUNDS

...one of the greatest and most neglected of black voices ... a record that's fabulously played and sung.
NME

WOMACK AND WOMACK
Love Wars (WEA)
The Womacks *'bring it on home'* with a verve and strength of character that overcomes any spurious revivalist tag. A massage for weary beleaguered hearts.
NME

...a sublime blend of gospel and soul full of fire and desire...
MELODY MAKER

THE WORLD
Break The Silence (WEA)
This is what happens when two Americans lock themselves away for five years with only a couple of Simple Minds LPs and a photo of Peter Gabriel for company.
SOUNDS

WRATHCHILD
Stakk Attack
(Heavy Metal Records)
...these hod-carrying angels with made-up faces are a cut above all the rest of the pretenders on the flam bandwagon.
SOUNDS

O.V. WRIGHT
Gone For Good (Charly)
...his voice ... practically burned a hole through the centre of my heart ... another extraordinary album of lost soul.
NME

YES

X
More Fun In The New World (Elektra)
...the rarest of all vinyl creatures, a commercial record that bites.
SOUNDS

...too derivative to truly qualify as the classic it has been heralded in some quarters.
NME

...if only they'd lay off the dope, the TV, the booze, the drive-ins, the neon, the cars, the self pity, the beach...
MELODY MAKER

X-MAL DEUTSCHLAND
Tocsin (4AD)
X-Mal could easily slip into the mundane. But, recognising their own vitality, they can still touch on new beauty.
SOUNDS

XTC
Mummer (Virgin)
...workshop pop ... sometimes suggests that this is a dumb show of some intelligence.
NME

...they now seem in danger of being reduced to fighting a parochial rearguard action, back-to-back on a small square of turf somewhere in Swindon.
SOUNDS

...lots of lovely, complex, richly-textured tunes and melodies and plenty of eccentric nooks and crannies to worm your way into.
RECORD MIRROR

I doubt if it'll make much of a dent in the album charts, but it deserves to be bought by the crateload.
MELODY MAKER

Y

Y & T
Mean Streak (A&M)
Pleasant, but hardly earth shattering.
MELODY MAKER

...wholly disappointing.
SOUNDS

WEIRD AL YANKOVIC
In 3-D (Scotti Brothers)
Weird Al is about as weird as Michael Parkinson.
RECORD MIRROR

YARBOROUGH & PEOPLES
Be A Winner
(Total Experience)
...surprisingly versatile ... suggests that Y&P are a long-term proposition.
RECORD MIRROR

An insistent, elevating record.
SOUNDS

YELLOWMAN
King Yellowman (CBS)
...a recipe that combines plagiarism with wit and insight whilst allowing the incorrigible one lots of freedom to explore his two favourite topics: himself and his relationship(s) with the opposite sex.
NME

With an ego the size of Sydney harbour (and about as deep) there's nothing actually wrong with him that a little death wouldn't cure.
MELODY MAKER

...trashcan fodder when ranked alongside the likes of I-Roy, U-Roy or the mighty Big Youth.
RECORD MIRROR

YELLOWMAN VERSUS JOSEY WALES
Two Giants Clash
(Greensleeves)
...an exercise in lyrical invention that blends humour, social insight and various pronunciations as to the nature of love and romance...
NME

There's nothing compelling about either Yellow's or Josey's tales. Hear them once and it's enough. Music for mugs with money to burn.
SOUNDS

YES
90125 (Atco)
...a remarkably good 'comeback' album.
SOUNDS

...they've recaptured the techno rock trophy. Big and hard hitting, they've built new empires under the guiding hand of Trevor Horn. Essential listening.
RECORD MIRROR

I promise to commit suicide if this one ever appears in the album chart.
NME

...full of shit...
CREEM

NEIL YOUNG & THE SHOCKING PINKS
Everybody's Rockin'
(Geffen)
He may look like an ageing Ted on the cover but believe me, he's Young at heart.
SOUNDS

For the first time, Young sounds middle-aged.
MELODY MAKER

Indubitably, rust never sleeps.
NME

It sucks, plain and simple ... Plainly speaking, a waste of money.
CREEM

YOUTH/BEN WATKINS
The Empty Quarter
(Illuminated)
...keep it for those uneasy moments when you're thinking of joining the Angry Brigade.
SOUNDS

Z

ZEE
Identity (Harvest)
...nondescript, hapless pap from zapless chaps.
SOUNDS

Polished, well produced, but ultimately sterile...
MELODY MAKER

SINGLES

The 1983 Virgin *Rock Year-Book* Singles Survey concluded with the bouyant news of a substantial increase in record sales (at least in the US), stimulating higher profit margins for the industry fat cats and, with this in mind, the overtly safe prediction of a hunky dory future for the record business in general. In the United States, UK acts were already spearheading the 'New Music' invasion (Duran Duran, Eurythmics, etc), spurred on by the promotional video explosion and the much-vaunted national MTV cable network. The worldwide music industry recession of 1978-81 had seemed all but over, a forcast that would be proved sadly incorrect.

By early '84 the world's economic climate was beginning to bite back in no uncertain terms. MTV, once a valuable promotional tool for the record companies, was suddenly losing money and impact as the novelty of viewing endless rock video repeats finally wore thin (Warners recently sold their 50 per cent stake in the company, along with their video games/ home computer subsidiary, Atari).

Not even the 'breakdance' phenomena (the only significant musical fad to emerge from the States in 12 months) could boost flagging sales figures on both sides of the Atlantic. Moreover, a recent news item in *Billboard* declared an "over-saturation" situation with breakin', the result of gross over-exposure through movies and TV. Independent labels like Sugar Hill, Profile and Streetwise have already reported a slowing down in sales of new product, while mass media interest in rap culture itself has still to convince radio stations to programme hard-core rap alongside the likes of Ollie & Jerry.

As regards any sweeping innovations in musical creativity and inventiveness, July '83–July '84 remained a year of solid predictability with the emergence of just a handful of hot new acts in terms of hard record sales

NIK KERSHAW

potential. The money-spinners of July '83 still dominate in '84: Wham!, Duran Duran, Blancmange, Spandau Ballet, Thompson Twins, Culture Club. The reasons for this stagnation can be placed fairly and squarely on the major record companies. Economic decline equals no-risk A & R policies, and while the independent charts are packed with adventurous new bands, few manage to break through without the marketing/distribution expertise of a major outlet. New order's 'Blue Monday', The Smiths 'This Charming Man' and the re-release of Joy Division's 'Love Will Tear Us Apart' are just three to successfully manipulate the system. Many major A&R decisions result from carefully monitoring the indie charts. A few thousand sales can be diligently swelled to 100,000 for the A&R man with enough insight into rock and roll demographics. Astute categorisation of the charts have made things even easier for the major record companies.

Gallup's computer now releases (through official trade journal *Music Week)* a separate chart for disco/dance alongside indies and the conventional Top 75. Let's scrutinize the best and worst of the hits in a mix of each section for the past year: Paul Young seemed to dominate the national chart for the latter half of '83; his blue-eyed treatment of an obscure Marvin Gaye song, 'Wherever I Lay My Hat (That's My Home)', stayed at number one throughout July, quickly followed by 'Come Back And Stay' and 'Love Of The Common People'. His record sales hit a sharp decline in '84, but CBS has more than recouped its (modest) outlay for the man. In September '83 the cultish UB40 finally topped the 75 with their worst ever, a clone-like work-out of Tony Tribe's Caribbean hit of the Sixties, the Neil Diamond-penned 'Red Red Wine'. They were thankfully replaced by '83s biggest selling single, Culture Club's 'Karma Chameleon'. Cleverly packaged alongside a snappy video of Boy George and chums cruising on a Mississippi riverboat (actually shot on the River Thames), it guaranteed maximum exposure and a much-needed bonus for the Virgin staff.

In fact, anyone strolling into Virgin's HQ at that time would

more than likely be confronted by George, either squabbling on the phone with Marilyn or organising the working day for each member of staff. All this of course prompted the showbiz launch of leggy Marilyn, to be duly awarded with a Top 20 hit in 'Calling Your Name', thus revealing the public's fascination with the homosexual lifestyle, later to manifest itself in the works of Bronski Beat and Frankie Goes To Hollywood.

Producer Trevor Horn's shrewd partnership move with retired *NME* hack Paul Morley certainly hit the pinnacle in rock 'n' roll alchemly. Their label, ZTT, was launched amidst a flurry of controversy and speculation. That initial release, FGTH's 'Relax' entered the 75 in November '83, and remained there for most of '84. Morley's erstwhile entrepreneurial flair came into full-flight in cultivating Frankie's devil-may-care obtrusiveness toward anyone dumb enough to question pointed references to gay sex in both the lyric to 'Relax' and in the band's much-publicised outlandish behaviour.

Superb timing by Radio One's breakfast dee-jay Mike Read effectively banned the single from the airwaves, thus providing the final accolade to ZTT for the year's sharpest piece of marketing expertise. The hype carries on, of course, in the shape of a million Frankie tee-shirts currently swamping the country, no doubt picking-up the 'Spin-Off

PRINCE

Of The Year' award.

A string of seasoned veterans continued to dominate the cross-over dancefloor hits of '83/'84: Herbie Hancock's irritating 'Rockit', Michael Jackson's regurgitated 'Thriller' (no

doubt to squeeze even more sales from the legendary video), Tina Turner's flirtation with Heaven 17 on 'Let's Stay Together', KC's infectious 'Give It Up', and Lionel Richie exploiting the extremes of dancefloor moods with 'Hello' and 'All Night Long'. Zappiest US-to-UK breakthrough in this category came in the shape of Prince, who sounded nothing like Prince on 'When Doves Cry'. Goodness knows, Warner Brothers had spent the best part of five years (and thousands of pounds) trying to break the mean and magnificent one in the colonies when lo, the answer was staring them right in the face. But just *who* will Prince sound like next year?

Grandmaster and Mell Mel, meanwhile, must pick up some sort of chart longevity award for their hedonistic melange, 'White Lines (Don't Do It)'. A Top Ten resident after 26 weeks on the chart, it met with some controversy over the drug reference in the lyric, though the artists insist it is an anti-drug song.

A few steps down the dance chart comes Shannon's joyous 'Give Me Tonight', Rufus (reunited with) Chaka Khan

UB40

MADONNA

CYNDI LAUPER

on 'Ain't Nobody', Madonna's obtuse 'Lucky Star' and Womack & Womack's finely-honed 'Love Wars'.

And the year's oddities? Well, they don't come much odder than Roland Rat Superstar. You either love or loath the little beast (a hero of TVAM maybe, but at that time of morning I can't tell the difference between Roland and Russell Grant), but he did manage three hits during the year, the most notable being 'Rat Rappin''. Coming a close second was Joe Fagin's awful 'That's Living Alright' along with the dreaded Torville & Dean's 'Bolero' ("Aren't you just sick of the buggers!" squirmed *Melody Maker* at the time). To finish the year, yes, boring old hippy Neil murdering the Traffic chestnut, 'Hole In My Shoe'.

Best of the rest? I liked, for reasons known and unknown, Fiction Factory's '(Feels Like) Heaven' for Kevin Patterson's vocal and Peter Wilson/Alan Rankine's spot-on production; Echo & The Bunnymen's 'The Killing Moon' for translating the raw, guitar-drenched traditions of pure rock 'n' roll into chilling originality; Bronski Beat's 'Smalltown Boy' for its sparkling wit, hidden away somewhere in the idealistic message; Sade's 'Your Love Is King' for weaving something new into the chanteause tradition;

Bananarama's 'Robert De Niro's Waiting' because I'm sure I could write a song just like it; Madness's 'Michael Caine' for Michael Caine; The Smiths 'Heaven Knows I'm Miserable Now' for local-lad-makes-good Morrissey battling with his conscience;

ZZ Top's 'Sharp Dressed Man' for sporting the best beards in the business.

Other significant chart movements: The Olympic-style launch of former Aylesbury hippie Howard Jones with 'What Is Love', 'New Song' and 'Hide And

Seek', thereby creating a whole new genre in the 'wimp' rock tradition. He is only equalled by diminutive Nik Kershaw, who also managed a triple with 'Wouldn't It Be Good', 'Dancing Girls' and 'I Won't Let The Sun Go Down On Me'.

ECHO & THE BUNNYMEN

Dancing', Prefab Sprout's 'Don't Sing' and Wang Chung's 'Dance Hall Days' (although I'm sure there'll be more from all four).

Looking to the future: as Frankie scores another million with 'Two Tribes' the band seem set for a lifetime of chart dominance. But they'll be hotly pursued by the Kane Gang ('Closest Thing To Heaven'), Alison Moyet ('Love Resurrection'), Red Guitars ('Good Technology'/ 'Steeltown'), The Cult ('Spiritwalker'), Sisters Of Mercy ('Temple Of Love'), Sid Presley Experience ('Hup Two Three Four'), Nick Cave ('In The Ghetto'). Then there's much talked about Shriekback, The Residents, the 'billy revival (Pogues, Boothill Foottappers, etc), and so on.

At present though, the old warhorses are in no threat of being toppled: Duran Duran ('New Moon On Monday', 'The Reflex'), Spandau Ballet ('Only When You Leave'), Wham! ('Wake Me Up Before You Go'), Human League ('Life On Your Own') have creamed off the biggest portion of the year's sales. But, with so many new bands demanding attention we await the next 12 months with, as they say interest and anticipation.

DAVE WALTERS

MADNESS

The rest: Ozzy Osbourne takes the Procol Harum award for plagiarism with 'So Tired'; bonnie Cyndi Lauper not for 'Girls Just Want To Have Fun' etc, but for the most overused/ over-retouched photograph of the year (wake up Epic!); the equally bonnie Tracey Ullman for singlehandly mounting a Sixties revival with the infectious 'They Don't Know' and 'Move Over Darling'.

On the resurgence front: Billy Joel with a bunch of classy Phil Ramone produced hits including 'Uptown Girl', 'Tell Her About It' and 'An Innocent Man'. There's no denying their catchiness, and the same goes for Queen and 'Radio Ga Ga', 'I Want To Break Free'.

One-hit wonders in '83-'84 include: Nena's silly '99 Red Balloons', Re-Flex with their percussive 'Politics Of

TRACEY ULLMAN

ALISON MOYET

EURYTHMICS

Eurythmics ended 1983 with a new album, *Touch*, and a sold-out British tour which culminated in a batch of deliriously-received dates around London. A string of hit singles, from 'Sweet Dreams (Are Made Of This)' to the Caribbean fizz of 'Right By Your Side,' had taken Eurythmics – Dave Stewart, Annie Lennox and a shifting crew of ancillary personnel – from faintly psychedelic obscurity to a position of pop pre-eminence surpassed only by the likes of Duran Duran and Culture Club.

With the American charts already breached (*Touch* would soon enter the US Top Ten), Eurythmics dedicated the first half of 1984 to a rigorous world tour, starting in Australia and New Zealand. Soon it became clear that Stewart and Lennox had *really* arrived – they'd even begun to *behave* like pop stars. Stories filtered back from their American dates that Annie had married a German chap with curious spiritual inclinations (true), while Dave was sighted with Nona Hendryx on his arm (a wind-up). Certainly they'd worked hard and long enough for a few inches of gossip column. Meanwhile, fans kept their fingers crossed and hoped that no permanent damage had been done.

It had been a long time coming. Dave Stewart, born in Sunderland in September 1952, had been a member of Longdancer at the start of the Seventies, and spent a great deal of money in a very short time. Then he busked around Europe, fell in and out of all sorts of groups, and took acid every day for a year. Finally he met a waitress called Annie Lennox in a Hampstead restaurant and formed The Tourists. It was the beginning of one of the weirdest relationships in pop.

Annie Lennox was from Aberdeen, and a strait-laced education at the Aberdeen High School For Girls went hand in hand with flute lessons, then performances with local orchestras and chamber music ensembles. But by the time the 17-year-old Annie came to London's Royal Academy of Music to study piano, harpsichord and flute in 1971, she'd discovered The Beatles, The Stones and Tamla Motown.

To cut a short story shorter, classical music couldn't compete. "There was no room for personal expression" Lennox lamented later. "I felt an overwhelming claustrophobia and I had to break away."

By the time Dave Stewart sauntered into the aforementioned Hampstead restaurant in 1977 to take Lennox away from all this, she'd been through an assortment of odd jobs, bedsits and dodgy bands. She had, however, discovered that she could sing. "The first words Dave said were 'will you marry me?'" she recalled. "I thought he was a serious nutter." It was time for The Tourists.

Despite a solid following and a hit single with Dusty Springfield's 'I Only Wanna Be With You,' The Tourists' main claim to fame was...Lennox. The press wrote things like this: "Annie's Day-Glo clothes and bleached white hair make her pop's freakiest pin-up." Penniless and embroiled in endless dog-fights with record companies, The Tourists eventually split up in Bangkok.

Horrific as life as a Tourist had been, it isn't too fanciful to detect within the band the seeds of what would eventually become Eurythmics – there was a clear grasp of what made pop tick, as well as a readiness to acknowledge the classic pop of earlier years as a means of nourishing forward motion. Mostly, of course, there was the Stewart/Lennox partnership.

All Dave and Annie had to show for their stint with The Tourists was £15,000 worth of debts. They decided to make a new start, only this time they decided to plan in detail. RCA showed cautious interest in Stewart's new songs, and a deal was signed. In October 1981, Eurythmics released their debut LP, *In The Garden*, recorded at Conny Plank's studio in Cologne. Conny was an old friend of Dave's, and he helped the duo to work towards the new sound they could hear in their heads, a sound which their new name reflected. "Eurythmics *sounded* good," said Stewart. "It also described what we wanted to be – European and rhythmical."

In The Garden, which featured contributions from Blondie drummer Clem Burke, Holger Czukay and Robert Gorl, didn't quite hit the spot but it contained most of the right clues. Annie explained that they wanted it to sound "melancholic, over-ripe...so the listener feels soothed but a little disconcerted at the same time." There in a nutshell was the essence of what would take Eurythmics onward and upward. Their combination of emotional involvement and simultaneous critical detachment would not take them far wrong.

Between the middle of 1981 and the autumn of 1983, Eurythmics released five singles without much success, while Dave and Annie quickly realised that they couldn't be full-time lovers as well as professional partners. "We'd become so close that the margins between us became blurred," Lennox admitted. "It was frightening – we both needed a break from each other." This decision only seemed to strengthen their music.

Indeed, perhaps this personal re-orientation formed the core of Eurythmics' hypnotic strength. Lennox, gifted, mercurial, wilful and fragile all at the same time, evidently needed the aura of faintly mystical calm which Stewart exuded. Dave had been through the mill, of course – addiction to amphetamines, experimentation with every drug known to man, victim of major surgery for a collapsed lung. He was a survivor, and it was no small part of his unlikely charisma that he was able to work with and apparently guide a creature as nervously thoroughbred as Annie Lennox.

In January 1983 they released the *Sweet Dreams (Are Made Of This)* LP and single. The single abruptly zoomed into the charts and the media began to buzz audibly. Eurythmics were airborne at last. Significantly, it was no small part of the success of *Sweet Dreams* that the tune was accompanied by a striking video, written and directed by Dave Stewart himself.

It's obvious now that Eurythmics were fortunate to be in striking distance of their musical ambitions at a time when video was becoming crucial to the pop process. America's MTV channel was beginning to transform the career prospects of countless chart hopefuls, while the coming of Channel 4 in Britain brought several new pop shows to British households.

But by any standards, Eurythmics' videos were exceptional. In the wake of the success of 'Sweet Dreams' they re-released 'Love Is A Stranger.' It had failed to register with the spending punter in September '82, but now, boosted by a spellbinding and controversial video, it caught fire pronto. On the screen, Lennox underwent several alarming metamorphoses – the society girl in diamonds and furs who tears off her wig to reveal cropped orange hair, brunette dominatrix in fishnets and leathers, asexual in suit and tie.

96

Stewart, meanwhile, played a sinister chauffeur with distinct voyeuristic tendencies. Love was indeed becoming stranger by the minute, and beneath the imagery lurked something both sophisticated and disturbing. Were the Eurythmics on video simply enacting their real-life roles? The thought prompted a shiver.

They took it a stage further in June with 'Who's That Girl?' another achingly haunting single, again taken into new dimensions via video. This time, Lennox played the Dietrich-style nightclub singer while Stewart, in white suit and Yorkshire terrier coiffeur, coolly paraded before the cameras with a dazzling array of girls – Bananarama, Kate Garner, Jay Aston, even *Marilyn*. To cap it, Lennox, disguised as male spiv-with-sideburns, *kissed herself*.

Eurythmics left Britain in the New Year with 'Here Comes The Rain Again' doing sterling chart duty, its success by this time a foregone conclusion. Not long before, Annie Lennox had told this correspondent about her attitude to image-manipulation. "Some people think you're doing it for real and they're even offended by it – 'How could you go into pop like this? You're selling out!' They don't see the intelligence behind it, the touch of irony.

"Our style statements are, a lot of the time, subconscious, what people choose to wear and how they choose to represent themselves. I find this very fascinating. I can't wear something and say 'this is me, this is what represents me, this is the sum total' – I couldn't represent myself like that."

Accusations that Eurythmics are simply "old hippies" cleaning up with electronic pop are approximately as accurate as a party political broadcast. They've grasped all the salient facts of modern pop marketing while remaining unpredictable, unsettling yet still profoundly musical. They also do great live shows. I've said it before and I'll say it again..."welcome to the complete modern pop group".

ADAM SWEETING

BIG COUNTRY

"Just as you sow shall you reap."

What if it's true? What if Big Country's biblical chant should suddenly assume the power of prophecy? Why, Wham! would sunburn to cinders for flaunting their obscene tans on *Top Of The Pops,* Maggie would die destitute on the dole, Boy George would perish from boredom, perpetually staring into a mirror, Ronnie would disintegrate in a nuclear accident. . .

Ah, daydreaming . . . When the smoke slowly clears from this ideal world, four avenging angels wearing check shirts and smiles would stand proud and free, knee-deep in smashed synthesisers and wasted eyeliner – all that remains of the shattered career of The Kershaw Twins. . . (Just wishful thinking).

So what do we find? The Alarm, scrabbling around among old Clash chords, rebels without a clue cashing in on sincerity, and creaky old Slade, slobbering over the bagpipe drone like there was no tomorrow.

Which, says Stuart Adamson, (wearing his CND badge) there won't be if we don't do something about it.

Adamson is one of those rare individuals who inadvertantly leads by example, an instinctive evangelist who inspires confidence simply because he lives the truth as he sees it; a man whose sole mission seems to be to make music that matters without making a big deal about it. That's why Big Country are here in the Acts Of The Year; not just because of the Highland flings and the lumberjack shirts or those rousing singles that sound like Wordsworth rewritten and set to music by Springsteen, but because they've made a success of challenging the status quo. Thanks to BC it's okay to rock again (hence the barely flattering imitations) but the terms, this time, are different.

Big Country aren't out to slay anybody, but to show what can be done. They're probably the first band for years who don't use their guitars like cocks or guns. Adamson and his Dunfermline sidekick Bruce Watson employ their instruments like outstretched hands or arms around shoulders, as gestures of friendship and solidarity. They scorn the others – the Simple Minds and the U2's whose grandeloquent gestures are nothing but pantomime – and claim kinship instead with Rank And File and R.E.M., the young American bands whose roots lie in common tradition, in the family feeling of well-being, in mining the motherlode.

The purpose: to communciate more honestly with an audience than any band in the world ever has, beyond mutual masturbation, sharing rather than strutting one's stuff. When it works – Hammersmith Odeon late '83 or Barrowlands Glasgow on New Year's Eve – the crowd takes up the songs like terrace anthems; when it doesn't Adamson's constant insistence on "sharing a song wi' us" can seem laboured and tiresome to the point of embarrassment.

Thus their relationship with an audience is crucial. They aren't just what they play, like Van Halen, but the way they play it and who they play it to, the way they mean it, the way it's given and the way it's received. They run a contact magazine called Country Club for their fans and Adamson feels strongly that if he is to play the reluctant hero (Americans won't allow him to be anything else) then he should at least be a responsible one – if not to set an example then presumably to assuage his conscience.

He's seen heroes act heroic roles before – your Strummers and your Rottens who betrayed the spirit of adventure for New York apartments and hastened in the era of complacent disillusion that allowed Howard Jones to have hits.

"Punk was the greatest thing ever," Adamson says. "A lot of the groups were crap but it didn't matter. It was the *feeling* that was important. It was young people having the chance to say what they wanted regardless of the dictates of fashion."

When punk turned sour, Adamson quit his first group, The Skids, in disgust: "I used to hate bands working me up to a fever pitch and then disappearing. It's not fair to share your ideals and emotions through your songs and then deny any close contact. I, personally, would like to destroy some of the barriers that have gone up over the years. If more groups did it in the same way as us, there'd be less of that celebrity bullshit going on."

Regrettably, such regular speeches in the press have moulded him a man of the people and he's become acutely aware of the irony of preaching "don't follow leaders."

"I always feel that I'm making a right fanny of myself when I explain myself in interviews. Y'know – the big rock 'n' roll star telling the kids where his head is at! I refuse to be seen as the spokesperson of a generation. All I want to be saying is the ideas that I think everyone feels. . ." Hence Big Country's debut album was called *The Crossing* to signify bridging the traditional gap between audience and performer.

"I've no respect for 95 per cent of the groups in the world," he explains, "not because of their music but because of their attitude. I really hate fascism and sexism in music but I think it's really scummy that we have to be portrayed as an 'attitude' band – it shouldn't be like that . . . There's fuck-all radical about us but over the past year we've realised just how important what we're doing is and I'm not joking, we're working alone."

Through Adamson's insistence that when you talk about pop, you talk about life, Big Country are unique. In the very week that Wham! insisted in Blitz magazine that escapism and self-aggrandisement were the be-all-and-end-all of pop, 'Wonderland' was in the British Top Ten, insisting on hope through community.

"There are no great ideologies in our songs," Adamson insists. "If there is one overall point worth emphasising, it is just the importance of people . . . The only guideline we set down was to make the band as honest as we can. . ."

In other words, the state of the art directly reflects the state of the world and Big Country's songs, along with rare gems like The Specials' 'Nelson Mandela', were the only political statements to reach a wide public via pop last year.

"Music is especially important at times like this because it's the only way that you can communicate between a mass of people. It's at times like this that the most vital music is made, when people feel a lack and a want and a need for someone who can go up there and say how they're feeling and not be scared of the consequences."

Big Country have fulfilled this role admirably and yet there are detractors. Some say Adamson lacks charisma, that 'Wonderland', 'Harvest Home' and 'In A Big Country' were essentially all the same song, that taking the missus and kiddie along on tour just ain't pop etiquette, that there's still something funny about peace, love and understanding, that their vindication of clichés have become clichés themselves.

These are fair points but, perhaps, premature. I once wrote that The Skids made songs that sounded like goals being scored. Well, Big Country have retained that emotional surge and now they're also making promises of better things to come. Whether they can prevent their rapidly established sound and identity from crystallising into self-parody, whether they can keep those promises remains to be seen. But if they fail it won't be for the want of trying.

STEVE SUTHERLAND

THE SMITHS

Faggots paved pop's way this year. With Boy George's wardrobe fully open, all the closet cases came spilling forth: Burns and The Bronskis, Frankie and NRG. The subtlest victory was Morrissey's—his the least fairy-tale, the least gaudily exhibitionist. Maybe it's because he conjured a ghost from all our pasts: the outsider, the Wierd One, the pariah you put at full-back so you didn't catch his leprosy.

When Morrissey refused to play "festive faggot", he was appealing to something fundamentally more lonely in us. He was making the outsider a star.

I met Morrissey just as 'This Charming Man' was peddling up the Top 30. I didn't warm to him; he seemed too bright to be a pop star. I see now that music had freed him from himself, that the unhappy invert who'd hidden away in a monastic Mancunian garret had found a complement in the music of Johnny Marr which was not simply stylistic but even, perhaps, spiritual.

Marr's music is Morrissey's fumigation. (It must have been awfully stuffy in Whalley Range). What he acts out in their brittle, brilliant vignettes is a sustained drama of self-pity. He indulges narcissism in order to overcome it. The Smiths' finest songs are a marriage of camp melancholoy – petulant distress – and musical grace.

Briefly to retrace: the first I heard of The Smiths was this dingbat character declaiming in ever so sententious tones that 'Hand In Glove' should be translated into all languages – that his whole life had been merely a process of crawling towards its three mighty minutes. I was impressed, and

the song duly swept into my heart. How to get close to it, other than to say it just seemed so proud, so heroically sad? (Something to do with the matting of bass and guitar, the injunction to "stay on my arm", the way the song hangs so absolutely between affirmation and desperation – hasn't Morrissey himself spoken of those songs that "speak with a biblical force?")

Next, I went to see them play: their first major engagement in the capital. Watching two dozen teenagers thrashing about onstage amidst shredded gladioli, with Morrissey louhaling 'Accept Yourself', I began to get a clearer picture of the group's mission. The music sounded like Tim Buckley backed by The Nightingales, but something purely their own pierced through. Maybe they *were* just a pop group, yet, as twits go, the tragic clown with Jimmy Hill's chin was so *confidently* out of place.

That night, too, The Smiths played a first take of the 'Charming Man', Mozart to 'Glove's Beethoven: did anything more sparkling, more kinkily witty ever rise so high through so much sludge? Well, a hit later and an album arrived. People said it was "dour", and two-thirds of it was. On the other hand, 'Reel Around The Fountain' was magnificent, and so was 'You've Got Everything Now'. The key to the resigned rebuke of 'Reel' is the perverse exactness of its "fifteen minutes with you": love has become a strange, sad ceremony. (Morrissey frequently plays the ornate off against the colloquial – "You can pin and mount me like a butterfly" is only two lines from "two lumps please/you're the

bees' knees" – so that there is always a kind of tension between courtship and contempt).

The marvellous 'Everything Now' follows in perfect sequence, pushed forward on one of Andy Rourke's most sturdily neutral bass lines. A great putdown anthem, it rails elegantly against the "oafish clods" who left Morrissey's school to become executives while he starved. So often music seems to be Morrissey's way of dealing with the pedestrian problems of his past, problems he doesn't try to turn into Greek tragedy but simply observes with humour and pathos.

Aside from these, 'I Don't Owe You Anything' is The Buzzcocks announcing their engagement to Burt Bacharach (to be intoned, cabaret-style, on a high stool). The remixed 'Glove' burns a shade less brightly. The hysterical Russ Mael falsetto of 'Miserable Lie' is tiresome by a third play. Long acoustic dirges like 'The Hand That Rocks The Cradle' and the Moors Murders saga 'Suffer Little Children' are meant to be sinister but do actually lull one into deep slumber. Finally, 'What Difference Does It Make?', the third single, is an unremarkable bonehead boogie stomp.

· A pity, *The Smiths*, since an album featuring the good songs and 'Charming Man', plus B-sides like 'Handsome Devil', 'Jeane', 'These Things Take Time', the achingly pretty 'Wonderful Woman' and the as yet unrecorded 'Night Has Opened My Eyes' would (hypothetically) have been a great record.

Further singles have followed which suggest that

Morrissey may have little left to report other than that misery is a state which can be celebrated with both humour and grace. It's hard to tell how easily he's slipped into the role of pop's intellectual village idiot. What is he if not the perverse creature who leapt out of "that horrible, stupid, sloppy Steven", the Steven Morrissey who was always "entwined" with pop but never part of it, and whose homo-erotic fascination with Angry Young Men led him to mistake Johnny Thunders for James Dean? (When it transpired that he'd written a whole book about The New York Dolls, I found it all but impossible to connect him with the hollowed-out "Coulda Binna Contender" Thunders whose heroin habit I was once obliged to subsidise for a day). What is Morrissey if not the critic become star?

One could say. . .one could say that The Smiths have made pop sound acute again. One could note that Morrissey breaks the codes of the Western love song, that he will never inhabit the body of a pop star, that he writes of an England that is ill and dying, an England of iron bridges over rivers of lead that comes gift-wrapped and video-taped from movies by Karel Reisz and Tony Richardson.

I feel he does more than this. He gives pop some point. "The only catharsis," he has said, "is to meet other people and to blend with them." The Smiths do this. If he can transcend his own finely ironic sense of himself as Lost Boy, there's no telling what further fruits the union of his mind with Marr's will bear.

BARNEY HOSKYNS

HOWARD JONES

Try and concoct an identikit chart pin-up to follow in the footsteps of the Durans, Whams and Spandaus, and the result would be something of a hunky, masculine pop vintage. But that's mere fantasy. Reality can play funny tricks on us, throwing preconceptions out the window. And who's done it? A mild-mannered, skinny, unexceptional looking 29-year-old from High Wycombe called Howard Jones. Strictly vin ordinaire in such tanned, jet-setting, womanising company, you might think. But it seems he occupies just as much previous adolescent wall space as the best of them.

So what's he got, this Howard Jones, if it's not immediate rabid drool appeal? He's got charisma – oodles of it – but not that distant, unavailable sort. His charm stems from being desperately normal, while proving to other desperately normal people that you can rise above it and be special. He articulates all those nagging thoughts and ideas that nestle constantly in the minds of Sharon and Wayne in Potters Bar, ones they daren't mention because it might sound silly. And he puts them in songs with damned catchy tunes. That's why 1984 has been Howard Jones's year.

He crept up and captured the nation's hearts without the support of the music press, rather like erstwhile writers' whipping boy Gary Numan had done before him. The press, of course, will never forgive either of them for this heinous crime. Not that this bothered Howard: he'd been waiting for so long 'to come here now and sing this song'.

Since the days of The Northern School Of Music in Manchester, in fact, where a bright-eyed Howard studied classical piano, grew sick of their stuffy attitudes, got rebellious and stomped off back to High Wycombe and a cling film factory, enriched with musical technique but embittered by the establishment.

Thus his inner frustration began to well, along with his much cherished notion of "challenging preconceived ideas". He started beavering away, writing songs with lyrics that dealt with the questions that plagued him – songs about life, society, people, love. Ordinary things. His determination to communicate his ideas to the public grew.

March 1983 bore fruit. Howard secured a Radio One session, then in May he played a key support on the China Crisis tour. Big ripples followed, and in June he signed to the giant WEA Records, after considerable persuasion by Howard and his manager, David Stopps (also the manager of the prestigious Friar's Aylesbury venue). But the bandwagon was already rolling; 'New Song', was released on August 19. The groundwork (over 200 gigs already) had more than paid off – the demand was there, the chart progress quick.

Smart move followed smart move – another tour support, this time to OMD, then, at last, his *Top Of The Pops*. He attracted as much attention as Jeffrey Daniel's bodypopping by performing with his mime artist friend Jed Hoile, who was bedecked in chains. 'New Song' rose to 22 and hard grafter Howie got his first taste of being mobbed. It peaked at three, and Mr. Jones returned triumphantly to home territory (Friary's) to be presented with a silver disc. 'New Song' went on to top sales of 400,000. Wowie, Howie.

Britain's fickle pop pickers seemed already hooked; 'What Is Love' made doubly sure they took the bait. Its dreamy, reflective mood suited the Christmas season and took Mr. and Mrs. Jones's boy to number two. Sure sounds like a fairytale so far. And it didn't end there. His impact was sufficient in such a short space of time to win his Best New Artist category in the respective readers' polls of *Smash Hits, No. 1* and *The Daily Express;* the sort of crossover appeal that's made in heaven.

The third single – time to take a bit of a chance and release a slightly uncommercial, epic ballad, name of 'Hide And Seek'. It didn't top the first two, but ensured that everyone saw Howard in a new light as a terribly versatile singer/songwriter. And then, just days before he started his first major headlining UK tour, Howard's debut album *Human's Lib* crashed into the charts at number one, going gold almost simultaneously.

Human's Lib saw Howard continuing to ask, gently, 'why?' in a musical context which drew influences from late Seventies English songwriting, made contemporary by the ubiquitous popsynth arrangement. On the one hand meaty, beaty and danceable, on the other soft, sparse and reflective, it found him sitting on a sliding scale with Nik Kershaw and The Thompson Twins at one extreme, Thomas Dolby and Eurythmics at the other.

Those who remained unmoved by his obscenely rapid achievements and unconvinced by his decidedly dodgy haircut found it difficult to be untouched by his live shows. In 3-D Howard expands in every direction; being in the flesh up on that stage is of much importance to the overall HJ make-up. Under the lights it's just one man and his banks of trusty technology, with visual diversions and mobile song interpretations provided by Hoile, now taking a key role in all Howard's shows and videos.

The inspiration lies in the field of good old-fashioned English folk rock, the Genesis/Gabriel school of troubadour theatrics, and Howard tops it off with his talent for the sort of audience communication not seen since last Christmas's Pantomime. He plays at being a Punch and Judy man and everyone ends up loving him for it. Bands constantly make a fuss about having 'no barriers' between themselves and their audience, but HJ is among the few who can genuinely claim to

project in a totally natural, unpretentious way. His fans respond by becoming totally absorbed in his pop visions and maintaining a deep rapport with this spiky-haired man-of-the-people.

He's not a sloganeer like Frankie, he just realises that even record buyers need food for thought; the sentiments in his songs proved right for the time. He would, we assume, like to see himself as a sort of Pied Piper (as in the 'New Song' video), leading people on to challenge ideas and think individual thoughts. Yes, ultimately, he is a bit of an old hippie, deep down wishing that everyone could be at peace with each other, love one another and at the same time realise their unique inner potential.

It's tempting to brand him naive, but maybe people need his sort of vulnerability. As he said himself, the public identify with feeling insecure, the 'one man against the world' syndrome. It's just that he doesn't feel embarrassed singing about it. But the one man crusade continued: 'Pearl In The Shell' got to number 12 with its story of not realising true potential. And in the light of the disunity that marred the Olympic Games, 'Like To Get To Know You' was Howard's statement about international harmony.

Howard Jones' simple pop philosophies are now spreading across the world. He can't claim to have started a new movement, forced a new chapter in musical history or indeed to be saying or playing anything that hasn't been said or played a hundred times before. But there must be something more to him than the synth and the funny haircut to have made him this year's pop mutant, the runt of the litter.

Maybe it's because he's challenging, but not threatening; soft but not soppy; danceable but not disco. He has the technology, but he also has the child in his eyes.

BETTY PAGE

FRANKIE GOES TO HOLLYWOOD

"Makes Wham! and Spandau look completely soft," was the slogan that trailed the release of 'Two Tribes', the second single by Frankie Goes To Hollywood. The boast of a big mouth, or the truth from the bold? A week later, we had the answer. 'Two Tribes' entered the British charts where it intended to stay – at the top. Frankie Goes To Hollywood were the unrivalled attractions of the summer of 1984. In fact, by the beginning of July, with Wham! and Spandau put firmly in their place, only one record even looked likely to challenge the dominance of 'Two Tribes'. And that was Frankie Goes To Hollywood's first single, 'Relax' which held down the second place in the UK chart, four months after its initial residency at number one. For the competition, it was all rather embarrassing.

It must have been said so often that people had begun to believe it: nothing would ever replace "punk", nothing would ever set the pop world alight in the same manner, inspire people with the same fervour, make the same kind of headlines, the same kind of history.

Frankie Goes To Hollywood refused, however, to agree.

"I say get off your arse and dance, we're all going to the same grave," Frankie's Paul Rutherford announced, providing the group with a loose manifesto.

This was typical of Frankie Goes To Hollywood's energetic iconoclasm: they were irreverent, provocative, plain-speaking. "The only thing we've got in common with groups like Duran Duran and Wham!" they claimed on the B-side of 'Two Tribes', "is that we've all got willies."

Despite the complaints of their detractors, it wasn't merely a talent for the outrageous or a calculating manipulation of controversy that brought Frankie such attention, such popular acclaim and two successive number ones. What suddenly made Frankie Goes To Hollywood so special, so very dangerous, was their disarming honesty, their incorrigible cheek.

'Relax' was a cheeky song. A song about gay sex (whatever Holly says about it being to do with motivation), a song with grunting, a sound to grunt to. When you got down to it (and boy weren't you meant to!) 'Relax' was a piece of throbbing disco good for only two things. And you couldn't dance *all* night.

And so enter the stuffy old BBC. The fusty, dusty, scatterbrained Beeb with its double standards and dodgy dee-jays. In fact enter Mike Read – a man who over night must have halved Mary Whitehouse's fan mail. The banning of 'Relax' by Read was, of course, a godsend for the band. The best publicity they could buy, the best publicity (in their heart of hearts) they could ever hope for from such a naughty disc. But Read didn't make Frankie. He simply played into their hands, gave them the number one they so richly deserved but would probably otherwise been deprived of.

'Relax' was banned. The boys drank champagne and threw up while their record company, ZTT, said they were beautiful and blameless. Then of course ZTT always did have something to say . . .

From the moment Frankie Goes To Hollywood signed on the dotted line to join ex-*NME* writer Paul Morley and wunderkid producer Trevor Horn at ZTT Records there was no way they were going to be simply allowed to amble on in their own merry way. Of course, that's what a record company is for – to help promote you, to help you sell records, and, like the wise men Horn and Morley have now undoubtedly shown themselves to be, they wanted to sell loads of records. *Millions.*

Thus, with Frankie's first single, 'Relax', came the 'hype' – the provocative S&M sleeve design, the 'saucy' sleeve notes, and the first real attention to the wild side, the *gay* side of Paul Rutherford and Holly Johnson's lives.

Morley was sly though. He wasn't out to wind up a few commuters or cause a snigger in the Indie charts. When 'Relax' was sent out to the dee-jays it was without the sleeve, without the lyrics.

Frankie had made it to *Top Of The Pops* before Mike Read had even checked "come" in the dictionary.

But are Frankie a con, then? A flight of Morley's fancy?

Certainly the band don't think so. "A lot of the songs we may use on our album, 'Welcome To The Pleasure Dome', we had before we signed to ZTT," says guitarist Nasher. "People say 'Oh they couldn't do it without Trevor Horn'. Why should we? We're both quite happy."

Perhaps that's why FGTH are so exciting. They're not just a band. They're a great idea. They make great records, tell fabulous tales, write a neat slogan. Get you going.

It is the application of Frankie which is so fine. The *way* they execute and *what* they execute.

Over the past couple of years several bands have tried with all their might to make history – and with even more might to make money. Once a formula's been found they've latched onto it. Watered-down disco, diluted soul, rock wrapped in ribbons – anything to keep them *there* (or thereabouts).

In the years since punk, mediocrity has reigned. Spandau Ballet and their cohorts made a bright stab at setting the world ablaze. But even they soon shifted their attention to matters of personal security and hefty chart returns.

In a land of wimp pop it seemed that nobody cared. Not enough to face the responsibility of grasping the greatest prizes, without lying through their teeth.

To a great extent Boy George changed all that – brought back that honesty. But it was left to Frankie to create the excitement.

Frankie have proved to be giantkillers. Not once but *twice* they've shaken the nation. And that's not just because their videos have been banned or because their record was banned. It's because they've shown the spirit and the determination to rise above the rest.

Which is what they've done. They've sailed to the top – not clawed and grafted like mere mortals, fumbling with their self doubts and guilt; Frankie's success has been shocking by it's *ease.*

Naturally there are bound to be a few disappointments ahead for Frankie. They won't keep hitting number one and doubtless some other enterprising act will manage to cook up some other scandal to momentarily steal their thunder. But their attitude so far, their resilience at coming through a *second* time, their restless nature, the subversive talents of Morley and the production genius of Horn suggest they'll be the most memorable band to emerge from the Eighties.

PAUL SIMPER

THE
THOMPSON TWINS

You have to go back a long way to find a band that has been as wilfully misconstrued by the press as The Thompson Twins. No one, it seems, is prepared to give their arguments a fair hearing – let alone an objective judgement – and regular trashings are administered by the critics, while others, who are not better than they are, get away with a quite staggering display of inane cavortings. Wishy-washy hippies one minute, rank opportunists the next – Tom Bailey could be forgiven for his rueful reflection that sometimes you just can't win.

Somehow the popular image has taken root that all was wonderfully well in those morally sound days before Eden fell and that The Thompson Twins were lionised by the music press for their innovative performances and political stance, both of which have now been cynically cast aside in favour of simplistic nursery rhymes in the calculated pursuit of wealth. The reality is somewhat different.

The Thompson Twins first saw the light of day in Chesterfield (near Sheffield) in 1977 when Tom Bailey and three friends performed at a friend's party. Taking their name from the bowler-hatted detectives in Herge's *Tin Tin* cartoon strip, they were a conventional two guitars, bass and drums outfit who played three minute pop songs and won a certain amount of local support by gigging in the immediate area. Classically trained and the black sheep of an established medical family, Bailey (then a reluctant music teacher in Sheffield) with guitarists John Roog and Pete Dodd then decided to head for London in search of bigger things, leaving behind them their dissenting drummer.

Once installed in a squat in London, the trio set about recruiting a new drummer – Chris Bell – and slowly the band began to drift from pop songs into a more experimental rhythmic sound. Also taken aboard as the group expanded to a somewhat rambling seven piece were bass player Matthew Seligman (currently with Thomas Dolby) and percussionists Joe Leeway and Alannah Currie.

Leeway was the son of an Irish woman and a Nigerian seaman and had been fostered out to an elderly couple in Dartford, Kent. Legend has it that he didn't speak to another black person until he was 21. Formerly with the Young Vic Theatre company in London where he was director of the youth wing on Monday nights, Leeway first joined the band as road manager after meeting Bailey at a party. One night he joined them on stage as well to play percussion and, after some to-ing and fro-ing, enlisted permamently.

The fiery Currie, meanwhile, was a New Zealander who had arrived in London via a spell of work in Australia in search of adventure. Having started with her brother's bongos while still at school, she now took up the saxophone to such effect (so the story goes) that neighbour Bailey came round to complain about the noise. They got talking and Currie was invited to join up.

The seven piece Thompson Twins was something of a musical curate's egg. They won considerable popularity for their energetic if somewhat chaotic live shows which featured a conscious attempt by the band to dissolve the barrier between artist and performer by handing out instruments and inviting the audience to join them on stage. They also took a strong political stance. Their first headlining tour was a shoestring budget 35 date "No Nukes" trek round Britain. Reviews, however, were not unanimously complimentary, and generally contained snide remarks about pop songs and unfavourable comparisons with XTC and Talking Heads.

Perhaps more relevant to their slow progress, however, was the fact that their songs were written for performance and did not translate well to the studio. After a couple of independent singles, The Thompson Twins had signed their own label deal with Ariola/Hansa and recorded two very patchy albums – *A Product Of (Participation)* (1981, with Jane Shorter on saxophone and Currie making guest appearances) and *Set* (1982). Steve Lillywhite's production lent a certain more professional air to the latter (which also featured contributions from an unknown Thomas Dolby) but the albums were untidy affairs that signally failed to capture the spirit of the gigs.

The turning point came with a song which Bailey had originally written as a filler for *Set*. His first specific shot at the dancefloor and the studio, 'In The Name Of Love' was sharp, simple and direct, and shot to the top of the *Billboard* dance chart where it reigned supreme for five weeks. Suddenly Bailey's eyes opened to the potential of communicating with more than just a small circle of friends. Deciding that he'd had

enough of aimless experimenting, he took the bull by the horns and opted to revert to shorter, simpler songs with Currie and Leeway. In fact, the three had already been working together for some time as Chaos PA – a kind of offshoot dub show based around hiring out the group's equipment – and had even considered releasing 'In The Name Of Love' themselves under the name Bermuda Triangle. After a final gig at London's Hammersmith Palais, the old line-up was disbanded and the bold threesome – having sold the idea to Arista Records – now faced the year of decision.

Initially the trio gave themselves 12 months in which to do or die. Each member was allocated a specific area of responsibility in which they were to have the final say. Bailey was given the province of arranging the music, both in the studio and with the backing musicians on tour; Currie – particularly alive to the importance of visuals – was given images and appearance; and Leeway was given the task of preparing the presentation of the live show. These days the lines aren't quite so defined. Currie, for example, now writes most of the lyrics, while the need for visual continuity means her working closely with Leeway. Current ideas are very much the product of a three way chemistry.

After announcing that they were off to Egypt to write songs (curiously they only got as far as mysterious Norfolk), the new look Thompson Twins chose Alex Sadkin as producer because of the clear, precise, exciting sound he had achieved with Grace Jones and for his interest in percussion, and headed for Compass Point studios in the Bahamas. The result – *Quickstep And Sidekick* – was released in February 1983. With its clean, energetic, danceable lines based around a simple formula of voice, percussion and synthesiser, it was the first full realisation of The Thompson Twins' rhythmic and melodic potential. It bulleted straight into the British charts at number two and although it never made it to the top spot, it stayed in the charts for over a year and contained the band's first Top Ten Singles – the classic 'Love On Your Side' and the more humorous 'We Are Detective'.

One year and a

phenomenally dedicated work schedule later came the release of *Into The Gap*. Again recorded in London and the Bahamas, it was less obviously dance-oriented but showed a quantum jump in the standard of songwriting and arranging so that the melodies were now as strong as the hook lines. With Bailey and Sadkin now sharing production credits, it also featured a greater range of instrumentation to achieve a warmth not possible with synthesiser alone. The stylish *Into The Gap* became a worldwide best-seller and spawned four further hit singles in 'Hold Me Now', 'Doctor, Doctor', 'You Take Me Up' and 'Sister Of Mercy'.

Clearly, the revitalised Thompson Twins are having no problem in their stated aim of mass communication. Where they do have a problem, however, is with their image (and no one is more image conscious than the music press.) After the reshuffle, it was taken for granted by all and sundry that Bailey was the real musical force – after all, he could play a whole range of traditionally acceptable instruments and had written most of the band's material to date. But Currie really *was* a true percussionist and not just serving a decorative function in hitting superfluous toys. Further, they should have reminded the world that Leeway could actually sing, play and write.

Such a song and dance was made about the fact that Currie and Leeway were involved in the videos and stage production, with no insight offered as to *how* they contributed that the Twins themselves seemed to be underlining the popular impression that they served no other useful function.

Worse, however, is their embarrassingly inane posing for the cameras – pulling all manner of silly faces and poses that are so clearly contrived and false that it robs them of their basic dignity and gives them a dreadful cartoon image that undermines their state-of-the-art intelligent pop far more effectively than any ill-informed sniping from the wings.

But the main charge to be levelled against the remamped Thompson Twins is one of intellectual slumming – that they are simply not extending themselves to their full capabilities as a matter of policy – and indeed there is an

element of truth in the accusation. The music – while superbly tuneful and faultlessly constructed – does lack a certain excitement that comes from taking risks. But it's lyrically, in their zeal to keep things simple in the interests of communicating beyond the traditional barriers of age, race and sex, that they sometimes don't aim high enough and come across (mistakenly) as patronising their audience. Some lines are clumsy and awkward, others embarrassingly arch, but they're certainly no worse than most and it's worth remembering that *Into The Gap* was effectively Currie's first as a lyricist.

Allied to that problem is the misconception that somehow some kind of political righteousness was sacrificed with the old line-up on the altar of the great god Commercial Success. While it is ironic that just as they are in a position to communicate their views to millions, the band should tone down their ideas, it's also to their credit that they haven't adopted a policy of anything goes in the pursuit of sales. Ever seen Currie – an ardent feminist who doesn't suffer fools gladly – in "girlie" pose for a paper? Ever seen Bailey in any orgy of conspicuous consumption in a nightclub? Ever seen Leeway adopting denims to court acceptance in the rock 'n' roll stakes? No, but you might well see them on an anti-nuclear march. Weightier topics are to be found in The Thompson Twins' songs, even if not in a particularly obvious or strident form, and the band are certainly one of the most aware in terms of personal politics.

All in all, it seems vaguely ludicrous that I should be penning "In Defence Of The Thompson Twins" when *Into The Gap* is, in the final analysis, such a bloody good record, but I'll go further. I reckon The Thompson Twins are a positive pointer for the future, demonstrating that not only can black and white, male and female actively get along together but also that it is possible to embrace the business side in a clear-headed manner *and* make accomplished, intelligent and invigorating records. And if there's still room for improvement then that's even better.

IAN CRANNA

PAUL YOUNG

Early in 1983, the folks at Workhouse Studios in London went wrong. Somehow they stitched together a spineless cover of Joy Division's 'Love Will Tear Us Apart', slammed it down as track two, side one of the first Paul Young album, and actually believed they'd done themselves a favour. They put the album out, watched it go platinum and sit for months at the top of the charts across Europe. Eventually they realized that what they'd done was pretty cruel. The version of 'Love Will Tear Us Apart' that Paul Young had recorded and included on *No Parlez,* his debut album, provided even his vaguest critics with enough ammunition to dismiss him virtually out-of-hand; even those critics who'd never even heard his version wondered at his temerity. His sterner critics, of course, had a field day.

The word "dare" figured prominently. How *dare* he cover such a brittle, private, cri-de-coeur of a song? How *dare* this blimp of a phoney soul imitator, this healthy, square block of a record company packaging exercise tackle not only black classics, but *that* song, the song that meant everything to hundreds of thousands of pale teenagers *and* treat it like it was some sort of sugar substitute on what was a producer's record anyway? How dare he leave a secure machinist's job at Vauxhall's, play a few routine dates with a soul band so orificially clean that they even termed themselves the Q-Tips, and then spend a few hours pussyfooting around with the work of a man who killed himself in the cause of art? At the very least he was. . .cheeky.

Paul Young smiled through most of it. He still liked his version, he reasoned, and at least people were paying attention to the music, at least people weren't bitching about his overstarched cuffs or something. And at least he had the uncertain accolade of

singing one of the most reviled (though, by many, adored) album cuts of the year. It was all a bit unlikely for a track sandwiched between two songs that received as much attention as 'Wherever I Lay My Hat' and 'Come Back And Stay'.

Along with "dare", the word "unlikely" featured with alarming regularity in connection with Young last year. It seemed unlikely, for example that a 28 year-old Luton soul-boy with a light stammer who had actually played near on 1,000 dates in five years, and who seemed to possess almost too old-fashioned a voice, could ever make it to the centrefold of *Woman* or *Smash Hits,* let alone the climax of *Top Of The Pops.* It seemed unlikely that unspectacular cover versions (versions, for example of fabled songs by Marvin Gaye and Nicky Thomas) would prove acceptable to a young market weaned on *personal* tales of love or incitements to rebel. It was also doubtful whether Young, essentially a shy, intelligent musician passionately concerned with the triumph of music over image and with deriving an unpressurized, wide-boy enjoyment of both, would emerge from the sudden media flush and mob rush clutching not only platinum records and Datsun Turbos, but also with his original ideals intact, unsullied by commercial compromise. It was always uncertain whether CBS could successfully package what most imaged to be a rather oily has-been as a suave, 'seasoned' and rather oily, leather-suited idol for millions of hearts in most of Europe.

However unlikely, this was nevertheless the kind of success Young achieved, but he wasn't carried away by it. He is, after all, old enough to acknowledge that the peak won't last long, if indeed it isn't already over. Accordingly he's paced things well and played it fairly cool. He worked harder

than most, but he cashed in less and indulged fairly little. It's hard to know if it was all pre-planned, but it now seems that it was his good sense and measured, candid integrity that appeals to a large crossover market almost as much as the slight outrage of a Frankie Goes To Hollywood or a Boy George. His looks prompted more dreams of adventure than lust, and if you were male you didn't really want to *be* Paul Young – you already *were* Paul Young, up there on the telly or stage, in spirit at least. And his voice? Well his voice didn't make him a star and he knows it: "I don't think a great vocal performance makes a good pop record now," he told the *NME,* "At least not as much as it used to."

Indeed the things that made success unlikely, now stand as a shining, twisted asset: ordinariness, a certain awkwardness, and an unmistakably old-guard appeal. It's all there on the sleeve of *No Parlez:* Paul Young sits pretty, slightly tense, and far from at home in his new environment. Uneasy in an ever-unfashionable collar, elbows on knees with far too much of an overstarched cuff showing. Young personified Cecil Gee in a year of Katharine Hamnett and Karl Lagerfeld. But at least it was simple. The record buyer said yes to the ordinary and eagerly sought out the uncoloured wax behind the counter.

And they found that his voice wasn't that special. What lifted it just above the norm was a gentle, mildly asthmatic croak, a rocker's lungs often buried in softer, soulful surroundings, a raw, slightly drowsy shake of your heart when you felt he was just dying to lunge for your throat. While the clean singles cleaned up – that half-sulky, half-chauvinist version of 'Wherever I Lay My Hat', that distinctly de-reggaed and pointedly reserved reading of "Love Of The Common People",

and the hammed-up plea of "Come Back And Stay" – the album still contained enough teenage friction ('Sex', 'Ku Ku Kurama') for him to maintain a slender hold on back-of-the-Cortina credibility.

Live, he resembled the classic Saturday night mike-hoisting twister – an unconscious mix of Rod Steward, Graham Parker and Big Country's Stuart Adamson. But on record he was only too prepared to tone down, sit back, and let producer Laurie Latham clicker through a decade of chart up-date.

Backed by The Royal Family and The Fabulous Wealthy Tarts, most of them calloused hands on the rails of the tour circuit, Young saw large chunks of the world and churned out many nights of plodding, grimly slick big-top rock combined with nights of more reassuring, steady pop strength that brought tears to teenies and brought it all back home for older boys.

It was clear he possessed an almost painful realism. "It'll level out," he suggested. "Why should it go as high as this after a musical lifetime of nothing?" One reason was because he was ordinary at just the right time. He was relatively non-pop, or at least non-image in a year when many British acts in the Top Ten still seemed more than content to put image first. As such he probably won't be remembered like some of his contemporaries. He changed few lives, and ultimately his own character changed little in relation to his circumstance.

Above all last year, he reassured. Not that a brilliant talent could make it with the dross: he didn't possess brilliance. We hadn't produced another eloquent spokesman – there were enough of those already. He was reassuring because he sang pretty good, and that was about it. He played his role straight. He was typical and untypical at once. And it was this that made him chart.

SIMON GARFIELD

MICHAEL JACKSON

There has, of course, been only one American pop star for the past year – the past two years, come to that. Everything he's touched has turned to double platinum. At least. Yes, we're talking Jackson. Michael Jackson. We're talking about someone whose personal fortune is by now almost impossible to estimate and whose picture seems to appear roughly once a week in every English language tabloid newspaper in the world, generally linked to a largely spurious piece of gossip.

The latter sadly, but in pop music terms inevitably, tends to obscure the fact that he's got where he is (i.e. The Top) on the back of a unique talent for singing and dancing, which in recent years has been enhanced by a maturing of his composing and record producing skills.

Before assessing his music and its effect on today's pop, let's briefly examine the aspects of his private life which so delight the gutter press. The stories, mostly, contradict themselves.

He is a recluse, they say. Yet he is often pictured by the same papers at a nightclub or official function or at the occasional pop concert wearing some ludicrously inefficient "disguise". He doesn't go to the local supermarket or McDonalds that often, but not many billionaires do.

He has a menagerie and a vast array of expensive "toys". That is, he has the money and time to indulge his childhood fantasies. Some people like to own football clubs, baseball teams, more cars than they could drive in a year, or half a mountain in Wales. Michael Jackson wants pets, cartoons and Laurel & Hardy films, a music room, a games room and a quiet place to retreat to.

He is not altogether 'with-it' mentally, we learn from various gossip sources. Yet he

...s recognised as a hard-headed businessman when it comes to managing his career, given to castigating his own father in the pages of Billboard when Joe made an ill-chosen remark about the white management firm which was, at the time, handling certain of his son's affairs.

Michael Jackson is not like you or I, of course. He is part of a large family – five brothers, three sisters – and began singing with several of his elder brothers when he was just four, back home in Gary, Indiana. Seven years later, when ordinary 11-year-olds usually have little else on their mind other than what to do when classes end for the day, the barely-teenage Jackson had his first American number one hit single, 'I Want You Back'. He spent the next six years as lead singer of the most popular black group in the world.

His only realities have been the tight family unit, Motown recording studios and the touring environment. His main source of non-musical learning was his tutor, Rose Fine. Although his elder brother Jermaine was the first major subject of teen adulation in the Jackson 5, Michael as lead singer (and, from 1971's 'Got To Be There', solo-hitmaker too) was the centre of artistic interest and the visual focus. And he loved it. Just watch again the sequence of home movie clips enshrined in the video The Making of Thriller showing the very early Jackson 5 rehearsals. A pre-teen Michael elbows brothers aside to hog the limelight with his accurate impersonation of James Brown dance-steps. One can see that when it comes to performance, no-one will ever upstage him.

When the amount of attention and focus of interest continued off-stage, however, the young age at which he was subjected to it betrayed him. After several attempts to deprive him of the odd arm, leg, or, at best, sizeable tufts of hair, he lost the innocent inquisitiveness of the child who first toured Britain in the early Seventies. A reticence, which developed and deepened as the crowds he faced got bigger and bigger, grew into something like paranoia.

Moreover, he'd been signed to Berry Gordy's Motown. The greatest black American corporation, it was built by Gordy on paternalistic lines. Because it was astutely aimed at the white record-buying market as much as at the black, Gordy was hyper-sensitive about how his acts conducted themselves in public. The grooming sessions run by the label for its artists are well known. Much of Gordy's attitude is apparent in Michael's wariness of the printed word and published photograph. He has taken great pains to look, as he sees it, 'the part'. Stringent diet, dance-as-exercise, a re-shaped nose, reputed hormone treatments to prevent his voice from altering too much when it broke, his skin tone apparently lightening. (The album sleeve portrait for Victory, the Jacksons latest LP, was re-done several times by the artist before Michael was satisfied that his colour was no more than lightly tanned.) These are the hallmarks one might expect of, well, a Hollywood actress holding down a part in Dallas or Dynasty. Or of Diana Ross, his mother-sister-lover-friend figure.

And, by all that's stars and stripes, he consorts with Ronnie and Nancy, the Reagans, ostensibly to launch a campaign against drunken driving but, by association, giving tacit support to the US President's re-election campaign. His punishment was to be hounded by White House staff, avid Jackson fans all, until even there he had to seek sanctuary by locking himself in a White House loo. This is, indeed, a superstar who has no escape from his fame.

Against all this, we have his magnificent pop music, which will endure. The sales figures for the Thriller album, its legion hit singles and its video are now so massive as to make the word astronomical barely adequate. The awards showered on him as a result have been indicative of the music industry's awe: Ten nominations at the American Music Awards (he took the prize in most of the categories as well) along with a special Award Of Merit, and eight Grammies, a record number.

Thriller has been so toweringly successful because in it the partnership between the singer and his producer Quincy Jones, which stretches back to their work on the soundtrack of The Wiz, reaches its apotheosis as pop teamwork. Although the preceding album, Off The Wall, is a better collection of pop-soul songs, thanks to composer Rod Temperton, and its overall performances, there's a shrewd breadth of appeal to Thriller that's become a blueprint for many, many other albums. There is novelty in the title track, hard rock through 'Beat It' with Eddie Val Halen's heavy metal guitar prominent, the nudging MOR schmaltz of 'The Girl Is Mine', the superstar duet with Paul McCartney – it all seems precisely designed for mass consumption.

But the match which ignited the fuse to the unending selling of Thriller was video. In the years between Off The Wall (1979) and Thriller three years later, video had assumed a strategic importance in the selling of records comparable to that of Henry Ford's notions about the manufacture and marketing of the family car. Jackson is tailor-made for the medium. A lithe, natural and inventive dancer not unlike a young, black Fred Astaire, he'd made an impression in his only major film role as The Scarecrow in The Wiz. In the videos for 'Billie Jean' and, especially, 'Beat It', he danced with the grace, energy, athleticism and expression of a graduate of a modern ballet school but without the sometimes obvious technical constraints of a 'taught' dancer. With 'Beat It' and 'Thriller', the art of the pop video was raised from high-class ads to that of cinema short, each song acted out with a relish for drama. Next to the mundane pop and rock videos which make up the bulk of American MTV and the UK pop shows, those two mini-movies looked like Citizen Kane. Thus did Thriller get its final, vital and unstoppable impetus.

Contrarily, although he's been seen almost constantly on TV and in the papers for the past two years, Jackson is an 'act of the year' who's been fairly inactive, quite remarkably so for someone who's loomed so influentially as a recording artist. He's cut the aforementioned album with his brothers, helped a few friends out on their recording projects (can anyone seriously believe that Rockwell, son of Gordy, would've had a hit with 'Somebody's Watching Me?' were it not for Michael's singing thereon?), had an unfortunate accident while filming an ad for Pepsi Cola, and picked up awards.

Jackson's return to live performance was (and here I'm understating wildly) eagerly anticipated. The Jacksons' US tour – 40 shows in 12 cities – was sponsored by Pepsi, co-promoted by boxing impressario Don King and characterised by continual wrangling between various businessmen culminating in a law suit from one (Don Russo) claiming 40 million dollars in damages, which is a lot of damage. The tour, like Thriller, was to be the biggest grosser of all-time.

Outside, all the world was dancing to his tunes. Has anyone in music ever actually done so little in a year and achieved so much?

GEOFF BROWN

WHERE ARE THEY NOW?

Now the most successful vocal duo ever, Hall & Oates spent most of the year after their step up into The Big League in their usual manner – working. Most of this time was spent on the road as they too joined the sponsorship league, their 107 date world tour being tied in with Canada Dry. Sadly their much anticipated British dates were a major disappointment, their lacklustre performances suggesting that the sophisticated duo were already on automatic pilot by this point on the itinerary. Elsewhere the tour was enlivened by a brush with machine-gun toting terrorists outside their hotel in Bangkok and by Hall nearly being refused entry into Japan for possession of a girlie mag.

On the record front, H_2O became their most successful album to date and the pot was kept boiling by the release of another (and somewhat unnecessary) compilation *Rock And Soul Part One* which spanned both their Atlantic and RCA years and included two new tracks – the wonderful 'Say It Isn't So' and the mediocre 'Adult Education' (both recorded with Nile Rodgers) – which duly became singles. A series of mellifluous, meticulous singles continued their US success while a cover version of Mike Oldfield's 'Family Man' provided them with a long overdue British Top Ten hit.

The usual noises were made about solo projects, though Hall did get as far as recording with Diana Ross and contributed vocals to the new Elvis Costello LP 'Goodbye Cruel World'. John Oates, however, preferred his beloved racing cars. Whilst in Britain he bought a £15,000 Tiga 2 litre model which he then shipped home and drove in the Formula 2000 race in Chicago where he came second. Happily the pair remain based in the New York which they find so inspirational, though they also bought country homes in Connecticut.

The twelve months ended as they had begun, this time recording an album in New York with noted dance producer Arthur Baker helping out on the arrangements and – if not actually touring, then preparing for one: another world venture planned to begin in October 1984 and taking them through to May 1985.

With their innate sense of style, street corner background and superbly crafted music, it's not difficult to see why Hall & Oates don't suffer from the complacency (a favourite Hall word) of their contemporaries and can maintain an all round credibility even in their mid-30s.

The focal point of the year for Musical Youth was clearly the release of their second album *Different Style!* Different it certainly was, indicating a move away from reggae towards disco-funk and featuring written contributions from Boy George and Stevie Wonder. Reviews showed widespread concern at what was seen as cramping of an emerging natural style and manupulation towards bubblegum and blandness. The general feeling that there was too much LA and not enough JA in *Different Style!* was summed up by the ever sharp Charles Shaar Murray. "'Youth Of Today' was a hot little pattie," he observed in *NME*. "This is a peanut butter and jelly sandwich." Even the group's own Michael Grant admitted on the quiet that it wasn't really like them and that they should have been in a more familiar place like Birmingham.

Greater cause for concern, however, was the disappointing standard of the band's own compositions after their sharpness of the first LP. Developing co-writing projects with the likes of Aswad is seen as a priority for the future but the feeling remains that founder figure Freddie Waite Snr. is still the band's greatest songwriting asset.

It was a mixed year, incidentally for Mr Waite Snr. On one hand he scored himself a singles deal with Virgin Records – 'Love Me' promptly sank without trace – and on the other he was given a 12 month conditional discharge in a court appearance on two charges of handling stolen guitars (and, curiously, a white tuxedo).

The singles from *Different Style!* met with mixed receptions from press and public alike. Versions of John Holt's 'Tell Me Why' and Desmond Dekker's '007' were followed by '16' (co-written by Freddie Waite Snr and

HALL & OATES

MUSICAL YOUTH

TOTO

Motown legend Lamont Dozier; an excellent song spoiled by a ludicrous and horribly patronising duet with Shalamar's Jody Watley).

British laws on child employment restrict the band's touring to a mere 39 days per year but Musical Youth certainly managed to cram a lot into them. At the Sunsplash reggae festival in Jamaica, Kelvin (who commands increasing respect) berated the 80,000 crowd for being too laid back. Taken aback, the crowd stood and applauded. In Los Angeles Stevie Wonder was reported miffed at not being invited to join them on stage; the boys were reported to be kicking themselves. They did however meet up with Wonder in his own studio, and also encountered Donna Summer (they appeared on her 'Unconditional Love' hit) and Michael Jackson. Amongst other places visited were Japan, the Montreux Jazz Festival in Switzerland, Germany, Israel and an island-hopping tour of the Caribbean.

Amongst other notable items crammed into a busy twelve months were writing the *Jim'll Fix It* theme tune for British TV, appearing in a road safety video, involvement in the marketing of the new "Now" range of clothes as part of the Mothercare chain, a guest appearance in UB40's 'Many Rivers To Cross' video, a fair share of less publicised charity work and – last but not least – only being beaten to the "Best Newcomers" Grammy by the all conquering Culture Club.

The band themselves remain pleasingly unaffected by all the razzamatazz surrounding them. At the time of writing Musical Youth were ensconsed in Eddy Grant's Blue Wave studios in Barbados – something to be viewed with mixed feelings. A bland, rootsless businessman like Grant is scarcely likely to restore their vitality or creativity, but they have time, talent and goodwill on their side; I'll echo last year's sentiments that Musical Youth deserve to survive.

The press file on Toto in their British record company offices is pleasingly slim – in fact, it's completely empty. Several phone calls to the States, however, establish that vocalist Bobby Kimball has left the group – nothing of course to do with his notorious cocaine bust that tarnished their Grammy grabbing act of 1982 – but due to "a change in direction" of the group.

Toto's principal activity over the past twelve months, however, has been the scoring and composition of the soundtrack to the film *Dune* (which also features Sting in an acting role).

The amount of individual session work – the proficient but faceless roles for which the individual members of Toto are best suited – consequently diminished considerably although the odd guest appearance can still be found with people like Lionel Richie, Joe Cocker and ex-Pink Floyd keyboard player Dave Gilmour.

Together Toto were also responsible for the boxing theme for the Olympics and mercifully that's about it. Happily soundtracks don't usually spawn many hits, so with a bit of luck the next twelve months will be as blissfully Toto-free as the last.

The worldwide exploits of Culture Club could fill this section of the book on their own. A good part of their last twelve months was taken up with touring, beginning with an American tour in September 1983 and moving on to Britain in December after a month's postponement when drummer Jon Moss broke a finger. The London dates at Christmas were also recorded for film and video release as *A Kiss Across The Ocean* which showed for all the world to see how band (especially George) and audience clearly adored one another. After a break for

recording, the touring resumed again in Summer 1984 with a trip to the Far East before returning to the studio to complete the band's third album.

The figure of Helen Terry also loomed large on the band's horizon in more ways than one. After sterling performances on backing vocals, she was invited to join the Culture Club organisation full time but tension developed between her and other band members – particularly Jon Moss – which the forthright Ms. Terry made little attempt to conceal. The obvious solution was adopted: Helen Terry signed a solo deal with Virgin, recorded a moderately successful single ('Love Lies Lost') and an album with much-publicised help from George and guitarist Roy Hay and the way was clear for her to bow out gracefully after the band's dates in the Far East.

On the record front, 'Karma Chameleon' was the one that finally established Culture Club with its five week reign at number one in Britain, selling well over a million copies in the process. After that, the choice of singles shrewdly became more challenging to avoid complete media overkill. 'Victims' – a fine dramatic ballad – made number four at Christmas while 'It's A Miracle' (astutely renamed from its original title of 'It's American') made the Top Ten in March 1984. Meanwhile across the Atlantic 'I'll Tumble 4 Ya' (with its heavy five times daily rotation on MTV) became the third US Top Ten single from *Kissing To Be Clever*. Even the establishment bowed as Culture Club walked off with one of the few Grammies – Best Newcomers – not cornered by Michael Jackson. Meanwhile the one that had started it all – 'Do You Really Want To Hurt Me?' – continued its triumphal march all over the globe, becoming number one in eighteen countries and clocking up sales of over four million in the process.

Culture Club's second album *Colour By Numbers* was released in October 1983 to instant platinum status. Reviews were predictably glowing, such was the magic charm that Boy George had cast over the press (except for *Melody Maker* who made unkind jibes about MOR).

Meanwhile Boy George had become a national institution. Although he was brave enough to point out that his credibility lay within the band, off stage the others were all but forgotten. Everyone, it seemed, who'd passed within a five mile radius of Boy George was interviewed for their memoirs of skinny dippings, fare dodging and even shop lifting, while the now

reported – not knowing who George was – to have asked who that "over-made-up tart" was

In fact Boy George wasn't really all that outrageous, especially given his commendable truthfulness. It's almost the reverse as he cuts a curiously old fashioned and moral figure these days with his advocacy of love and his anti-drugs stance. He carefully de-fused the threat of his sexual ambiguity by emphasising his masculinity without lying about is bisexuality – "a poof with muscles" was his own self-mocking description – and by playing down the sex element to the point of casual matter of factness. This provided another celebrated quote about preferring a cup of tea to sex, although what he actually

"encouraging transvestism" with his effeminate appearance. The Mormon Church forbade members to buy Culture Club records for much the same reason. Never at a loss, George's good humoured rejoinder was to quip that Mormons could have four wives but not a Culture Club album!

All in all, it seems entirely appropriate that Boy George's character should be recognised as much as Culture Club's music – the two seem indivisible. A Boy George waxwork was installed in Madame Tussauds, he won the *Daily Mirror* Personality Of The Year for the second year in succession and there was even a Parliamentary motion to congratulate Culture Club (among other bands) on their achievements in the land of

produced by Mike Nesmith and directed by former Monkees man Bob Rafelson, 'All Night Long' was an ambitious change of style – a reggae/funk/calypso cocktail – and an enormous success.

The single, however, proved to be a long way ahead of the parent album in terms of invention. Released in February, *Can't Slow Down* – although an improvement over its MOR predecessor – was once again guided by James Carmichael (though Richie now shared the credit) and reverted to the coffee-table soul and formularised ballads that had brought him thus far.

The album also featured a new look – a tapered haircut which suited him infinitely more than the previous pudding bowl effect. The flip side of this coin, unfortunately was the latest in the current deplorable trend of trying to make black artists look as white as possible. In fact, anxiety has been expressed in black music circles over Richie's increasingly white direction, both musically and in terms of the people employed by his business.

But whatever the image or content, the album sold – over five million copies in the US and over one million in the UK, making it Motown's best selling LP ever.

Subsequent singles pulled from the album met with mixed fortunes. The forgetable 'Running With The Night' was a comparative flop – it only made the Top Ten – despite being accompanied by a video in which Richie believed sufficiently to invest some £60,000 of his own money towards the total production costs of £175,000. The follow up, however, struck pay-dirt in no uncertain fashion as 'Hello' chalked up a six week reign at No.1 in Britain alone. More bluesy and uncertain than his usual optimistic dewy-eyed stuff, its emotional impact was undermined by a truly appalling video whose tasteless featuring of a blind girl (acted, of course) combined pure ham with hard core corn and stank of market research into cheap sentiment. Meanwhile in the US it became the seventh successive year that Richie had scored a No.1 single either as a writer or a performer.

CULTURE CLUB

infamous letter describing the young George as "argumentative and insolent" which accompanied his expulsion from school (for refusing to accept corporal punishment for violating the school dress code) also became public property.

A happy chatterbox with an opinion – usually thoroughly sensible – on virtually anything, Boy George cast a spell over young and old alike with a mixture of positive professionalism, sheer personal charm and an impeccable sense of timing as to when (and how much) to rock the boat. Consequently there were well publicised clashes with British Customs officials, French immigration and even the Royal Family when on one public occasion Princess Margaret was

said in his usual humorous style was that he preferred staying in with a cup of tea to going to a club to pick up someone for sex – which is altogether different!

But then we're dealing with an exceptional figure here. Boy George was also aware enough to turn down offers of advertising simply for the money and loyal enough to turn down working with Michael Jackson in favour of remaining within the Culture Club. Boy George takes nothing for granted.

Of course there were those who didn't wish to give him his chance. The loony Moral Majority press in the States trumpeted against letting Boy George turn your son into a homosexual (a ludicrous idea however you look at it) while Malaysia banned him for

Uncle Sam. Boy George's particular strengths lie in his openly emotional approach, his sense of humour, his sheer force of personality, his understanding that there is an intelligent way to do things, a refusal to see himself as glamorous and a determination not to be changed by money. With these qualities of character and the British appreciation of eccentrics, perhaps George will be named the *Daily Mirror's* Personality Of The Eighties.

After what seems like eons of solid – if somewhat uninspired building, Lionel Richie startled everybody by suddenly unleashing a bona fide classic. Complemented by an adventurous video

As usual, Richie spent much of the year hard at work. His first solo tour in America took in 50 dates and then in March 1984 he topped the sponsorship

LIONEL RICHIE

league in spectacular style. Sponsored by Pepsi, the deal included a movie, a TV special and a three month concert tour in return for composing a Pepsi theme and a series of commercials. The whole package was reckoned to be worth a cool eight million dollars – three million more than the previous biggest figure paid for a tie-in with the Jacksons. November 22, 1983 was declared 'Lionel Richie Day' in Los Angeles.

Underneath it all, however, the shy multi-millionaire seems to remain pretty much unchanged. He never forgets how life was before he became famous and continues to write songs with the specific intention of making people fall in love. He also retains his strong religious and moral convictions. "I'd love to give you some real dirt on him," his wife told one magazine, "but there is none." Which pretty much sums up Lionel Richie – clearly he isn't going to vanish with the dew in the morn either.

ABC, meanwhile, had a disastrous year. Things started going wrong even before the tour to pomote *Lexicon Of Love* with the departure of drummer David Palmer. Forced to choose between ABC and his own ideas, Palmer opted for the latter and left to work with Yellow Magic Orchestra's Yukihiro Takahashi. He has since formed a band called Person To Person and signed to CBS.

Palmer wasn't replaced and the remaining threesome

chose a sixteen piece backing group (including a string section) to accompany them on a world tour that took them to the Far East, Australia and the US, where the album had made a significant impact. Meanwhile the first cracks had started to appear at home as a series of increasingly weak singles were pulled from the LP and ABC's public stock began a downward drift.

The next step in what had once seemed an infallible plan for world domimation – the video – turned out to be an equivocal disaster. Opting for a pastiche of '60s spy films, 'Mantrap' was recorded in only ten days in February as a new setting for live footage. Starting by employing the grossly overrated Julien Temple as director, the project started badly and fell away. Featuring a transparently ridiculous plot based on the idea that those naughty, naughty Russkies were trying to kidnap Martin Fry (for reasons best known to themselves); to call the acting wooden would be an insult to trees. 'Mantrap' – even with tongue wedged firmly in cheek – was an embarrassment to all concerned.

The biggest mistake of all, however, was the band's second album *Beauty Stab*. Written and rehearsed in ABC's industrial home town in Sheffield, the self-produced album was supposed to be all about falling in love with the UK (faults and all). Stripping away the strings and sheen of the first album, it aimed to find something more abrasive. Lame was out and leather was in, along with guitars and "live

in the studio" performances to capture the spirit of the band.

So much for the theory – reality showed yet another grandiose idea failing en route to fruition. *Beauty Stab* was clichéd and old fashioned in the worst possible way. The riffs were ugly heavy metal, the ideas second hand Roxy Music – a comparison not helped by the employment of the former Roxy rhythm section of drummer Andy Newmark and bassist Alan Spenner – but worse still were the lyrics, whose suddenly acquired social conscience gave every impression of being a spray-on cosmetic after the previous pursuit of glamour. Not surprisingly, the record received universally poor reviews.

The singles pulled from the album fared no better. The awkward and ungainly 'That Was Then But This Is Now' struggled to reach number 18 in Britain. Poor in comparison to its predecessors, it was nevertheless the highlight of the album and the follow-up 'SOS' flopped miserably.

The whole unhappy episode in ABC's meteoric career was brought to a close with the announcement of yet another departure from the ranks; founder member and

saxophonist Steve Singleton declared that his departure had been gradual and for various reasons, mostly that he wanted to be true to himself and fulfill his creative ideas. Ho hum. Needless to say, he hasn't been heard of since.

Fry and White then announced auditions and the early recording of a third album. However, several months later, a long series of auditions had proved fruitless and the duo announced holidays to be followed by a trip to Los Angeles, of all places. Perhaps they plan a link up with Toto.

Whatever they come up with next, it had better amount to something more than a few glib slogans and a change of clothes if ABC are not to be remembered more for the selling than what they sold.

ABC

Flying as ever in the teeth of fashion, I refuse to join in the general chorus of jeering at Men At Work. Their professional (if not particularly original) brand of efficient white pop – neat uncomplicated songs, clever lyrics and able musicianship – their irreverent sense of humour and their unrepentant refusal to meekly accept British or American cultural colonialism all deserve better

MEN AT WORK

than ill-informed sneering.

The press file isn't exactly overflowing either, though their seven month world tour accounted for most of this. Britain was visited in May and June (with a return visit in July due to the success of 'Down Under') and the US followed in October. After this they retreated "utterly exhausted" to Australia where, apart from a brief tour there little has been heard of them since. In fact they've been taking their first break in three years to rest and gather fresh inspiration. Houses were bought. Colin Hay produced fellow Australian band Le Club Foote and, along with Greg Ham and Ron Strykert, was reported to be writing new material with a view to recording the third album in September or October.

Alarm bells will start ringing if this turns out to be as similar to the first as was the second, but Men At Work seem a sober and intelligent crew who have what it takes to survive the jibes of the ignorant.

I do not care for Duran Duran. At best they make functional dance music and dubious videos that range from exploitative to out-and-out pretentious, but it's difficult not to have at least some respect for a new band that can not only work together in a disciplined fashion under a phenomenal work-load but actually appear to thrive on it.

Seven And The Ragged Tiger took the best part of six months to make. Working under the direction of Alex Sadkin, they started in the South of France before moving to Montserrat in the West Indies. The album was eventually finished in Sydney, Australia, months behind schedule and leaving only ten days for the band to rehearse before they began the

Australian leg of their second world tour. Australia was followed by dates in Britain in December 1983 (sponsored by Sony and involving a blank C90 tape giveaway that left their record company EMI somewhat less than ecstatic). Japan and a 30 date tour of the US (sponsored this time by Coca Cola) took the band through to April 1984. After that the British were treated to the unusual sight of having Duran Duran around in their country for a while. No rest for the wicked of course – special concerts were filmed for a live video which will no doubt appear just in time for Christmas 1984.

Seven And The Ragged Tiger – a typically obscure piece of Le Bon imagery masquerading as art – was naturally a British album

chart topper and clocked up sales of one-and-a-quarter million within the first ten days of American release. Equally naturally, the band didn't receive a very warm welcome from the critics who accused it of being boring, bland and lacking in depth. Judging by John Taylor and Nick Rhodes' reviews of singles in the pop press, they seem to be intelligent and moderately tasteful so one

can't help but wish that they could curb the conceited Le Bon's vocal and verbal excesses. (Producer Sadkin apparently made Le Bon revise his lyrics several times. One dreads to think what the originals were like).

By contrast, the progress of the singles provided a hiccup in the seemingly unstoppable rise of Duran Duran, especially while they were resting on their laurels in the recording studio. Neither 'Union Of The Snake' nor 'New Moon On Monday' made the top slot in Britain (though the latter went Top Five in the States). A heavy duty re-mix of 'The Reflex' however captured the top slot in both countries.

Despite the work-load, the various members still found time to indulge in various solo projects. John Taylor did a session for ex-Thin Lizzy guitarist Scott Gorham and then together with Andy Taylor recorded with various members of Chic. Andy Taylor also opened a wine bar called Rio in his town of Whitley Bay, near Newcastle, and Nick Rhodes prepared his book of Polaroids called *Interference* for publication. Roger Taylor simply got married.

With their chocolate box good looks – the real secret of their success – the fivesome went on to become part of the national consciousness. They

even received a virtual "by appointment" seal from royalty when Princess Diana admitted they were her favourite band, and Duran Duran subsequently performed a distinctly under-rehearsed set to raise money for the Prince of Wales' Trust For Children. Princess Di herself (and her husband) actually left early during the concert.

Still, at least the concert did

raise £30,000 for charity, which was in marked contrast to the MENCAP fiasco. Held at Aston Villa's football ground in their native Birmingham, the concert was expected to raise around £75,000 on behalf of the mentally handicapped. Instead it brought them not a penny as expenses swallowed up even the exorbitant entry price of eight pounds per head. Eventually a frustrated and embarrassed Duran Duran paid MENCAP £5,000 out of their own pockets.

In general the press – particularly the tabloids – just couldn't get enough of Duran Duran. Their love lives were subjected to constant scrutiny and the subject of much ill-founded gossip. Mothers were interviewed and former girl friends persuaded to tell all in return for large cheques. The worst stitch-up came from two former employees who considered themselves hard done by and came up with a drugs scam that made the band look as if they had all but had nosebags of cocaine surgically attached. Indeed some of the writing verged on self-parody, describing Simon Le Bon as the "golden boy who can make girls fall unconscious with a flick of his hips."

Even the word "Durannie" passed into general usage to describe a breed of particularly obsessive and resourceful

DURAN DURAN

female fans who dogged their every move. This was even encouraged in the States where the arrival time of the band's incoming flight was repeatedly broadcast on MTV. Duran Duran swept the polls and the fan club struggled to cope. The critics might moan but the little girls understood all right. There can be few doubts that Duran Duran will be with us for some time to come.

RETURN TO GENDER

This year's thing is only ever last year's model; according to **Jon Savage,**
pop has always bent its genders

A middle aged man walks up to two boys on the Covent Garden street corner. He is wearing the traditional tourist gear of a tie, check pants with a camera slung around his neck. The two boys are dressed mainly in black, with a few glittering accessories. What is most striking about them is not their clothes, but their demeanour: their whole posture, their whole thrust is angular, shrill, deliberately effeminate. The man approaches them with a step that is both wary, but determined: "What are you?" he asks, in a Scandinavian accent. The two boys giggle and flounce for just an instant: "We're Gender Benders", they reply. The Scandinavian is confused, but takes his pictures anyway: this is, after all, one of the things – along with the Trooping Of The Colour and Buck House – that he came to England to capture: in pictures, to show the folks back home.

These two boys are only one obvious symptom – now reached a stage ready for the tourist guides – of one particular phenomenon that has been all over the charts and clubs over the last year: the outright expression of sexual confusion and divergence – of homosexuality, transvestism and even transexualism – that is now known as "gender bending" It has taken many forms, and has arisen for a multitude of reasons, but it is there, definable enough to create its own market and its own reaction.

A crucial episode in the current phase for 'men in frocks' was attained in *Smash Hits* during the month of May. There, in a spread that *The Sun* would have paid thousands of pounds for, four leading and not so leading exponents of the 'genre' slagged each other off in best fishwife style over a double page spread. Oh, it was wonderful! Tasty Tim slagged off Marilyn for being too serious; Marilyn slagged off

Pete Burns for being tasteless; Pete Burns slagged off Boy George for being conservative. Boy George remained above it all, but pained. So pained that he later wrote to the *NME* in a plea for transexual solidarity, or something. Meanwhile Mud Club doorman Philippa Sallon was moved to offer in *The Face:* "Boy George is on a sea food diet at the moment. He sees food and he eats it."

BOY GEORGE

An old joke, but all of this upped the ante on the usual pop tittle tattle about people's flared trousers. Suddenly all this frippery was developing an ideology. And there lies its paradox: for like most pop phenomena, the gender benders in all their forms are an index of something that is profoundly trivial – in some way, the waste products of pop's current cultural impotence – and yet alive: for despite their

transience and lack of weight, they have kept afloat pop's ability to offer up for discussion, in a wider arena than usual, ideas that fall outside society's mainstream. And that means, in our current society, anything that falls outside a very narrow and priviliged section of the population.

Male homosexuality and the various forms of camp attendant on it have been a vital part of British pop music since its beginning. I have never forgotten seeing footage of a British manager which began on his moccasined feet, wafted over his monogrammed door mat, and ended up opposite the sofa on which lounged five of his charges, scowling greasily. Marvellous camp, and stranger than fiction: Laurence Harvey didn't even come close to it in *Expresso*

Bongo, and MacInnes only hinted at it in *Absolute Beginners.* British pop's rather seedy beginnings on the fringes of an old industry – variety, cinema owners, and the music hall trade – made this sort of behaviour rampant. In its primitive acceptance of the prevailing sex codes, it contributed in part to the feebleness of early English pop. In America, freakishness like that of Little Richard could explode for a while, unharnessed; in the UK, it was translated into the way that these budding stars behaved. Malleable, bland, identikit, they displayed the passivity – the femininity, if you're being normative about these things – of the adored object, the idol: the only trouble was, very few of them were ever good enough to attain that state.

In the Sixties this androgyny became less passive, more overt and more aggressive. The English music business still ran on the same lines – seedy, yet quilty in its hidden pleasures – but the old order was cracking up. Groups like The Beatles, and later The Rolling Stones, and later still, The Kinks, The Pretty Things and all the little mod groups with their page boy bangs, used an implicit androgyny as part of a wider arsenal of shock effects. Mick Jagger would be photographed under the hair dryer, while Ray Davies rearranged his Dickensian jacket and crooned 'See My Friends', a world-weary evocation of sexual confusion.

The whole question of sexual divergence was raised, but rarely directly. Attention was focussed more on the more superficial aspects of the phenomenon – the groups' dollar earning capacities, or the 'profusion' of British beat talent. And the beat groups themselves were not concerned, primarily, with gender bending. What they were after was cultural and social freedom, and, if exploiting their sexual ambiguity got them what they wanted, then so be it. Yet these moves were historically correct: the relaxation of sexual roles that they implied, amongst other things, found its legal expression in the Sexual Offences Act of 1967, which made male homosexuality legal, with various strings attached.

All the mid-Sixties jokes about 'Are You A Boy Or A Girl?' (c *The Barbarians*, 1965) finally came to roost with the hippie. The crossover between mod and hippie had introduced some amusing side effects: formerly butch groups like the Pretty Things coming over all coy and sexless in songs like 'Defecting Grey', while early psychedelic heroes The Pink Floyd gave the sexual blurring that was a result of poly-drug abuse an explicit storyline in 'Arnold Layne'. By the time Mick Jagger wore a dress in Hyde Park in June 1969, the big word was unisex: it might just have meant hairdressers, but to the population at large – who remained untouched, as ever, by much of this tomfoolery – this was part of the 'permissive society', which they might read about from afar, in a national newspaper. Sexual freedom had been attained, and was unimportant, anyway, in comparison with pressing matters like the 'Revolution': the new face of pop was stern, earthy, heavy. Jeans, boots and beards, not the flowing scarves and foppish demeanour of the heroes of 1967.

The next generation of pop idols gave pop's implicit sexual ambiguity a new name: Glam. David Bowie's epochal announcement of his bisexuality in *Melody Maker* make severe camping de rigeur for the next of starlets that followed him. If Bowie had used his own sexual ambiguity as part of his distance – "I'm no mere pop star, but a moonage daydream" – and an implicit disgust with sex, then bricklayers like The Sweet turned it into farce. Stompers like 'Ballroom Blitz' denied the lisping introduction and their rent boy make-up with a strong lyric about heterosexual lust. As they winked behind their glitter eyeliner on *Top Of The Pops*, you *knew* they couldn't be serious. Pop was camp, but this was a kind of camp that avoided seriousness and flaunted its trashiness. The thrift-shop extravagance of the New York Dolls and the cool, deco ironies

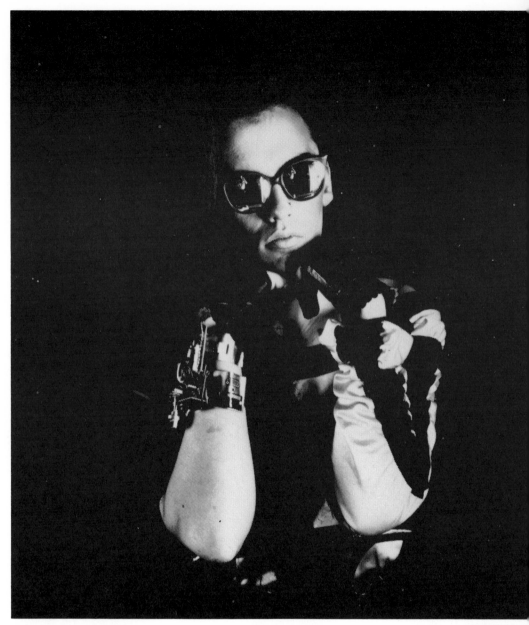

PETE BURNS

of Roxy Music defined the parameters of the genre. This was a reference ridden sophistication that went beyond pop's heart of a whore.

Yet this seediness, this sexual exploitation at the heart of pop which had found various expression to suit various generations, was implicitly understood and exploded by Malcolm McLaren. It was reduced to a series of gestures which, impinned on a Brian Epstein or a Cambridge rapist tee-shirt was part of a costume that was intended to make obvious the various forms of exploitation at the heart of our society. Yet punks weren't perverts, far from it: in their most public utterances they quoted a disgust with sex that was reminiscent of David Bowie. They knew that sexual

display shocked, and the more extreme the better, as Vivienne Westwood's tee-shirts ran the gamut of sexual exotica, yet the intent, and their use was strangely puritan. The punks were inheritors of the idea of kinky sex as decadent, just like Huysmans or *Cabaret,* and this decadence was part of the moral slime that had to be extirpated, along with Mr. Freedom and Elton John. As in 1968, these gestures that were part and parcel – even if rather more extreme – of what people expected from pop were used for a greater good: punk's social critique.

When that had turned out to be as ineffective as pop's critiques inevitably are, punk's style was suddenly re-examined and the demons flew out of Pandora's box. All that

bondage suddenly looked fun – and was played out for real by greater numbers of people in the sexual playgrounds of the United States. In the gap left by the failure of punk rhetoric pop went overboard for style above content – where it still remains in deep water. As the music industry re-established its control, pop stars lost their social and ideological assertiveness and were content to be young businessmen. Coincidentally, one saw the rise of pretty but passive stars like Adam of the Ants, an Eighties Jess Conrad and that passivity of the adored object all over again – a process which has now reached its nadir with 'idols' – stuck like by flypaper on the pages of the teen press – such as Nick Heyward and Nik Kershaw.

The outward face of current pop styles gives the hint of a circle turned in full and yet, in part, that is what people wish you to believe. What interests me about the current crop of androgynous mutants is both their ubiquity and their diversity: that, as in the more obvious area of youth styles, pop's past approaches to the question of sexual divergence have been thrown up into the air and are being revived at once in a mad whirl.

It's worth recounting some of what has exactly happened over the last couple of years: separate events that, in the lack of any coherent pop 'movement' have come to mean more than just the sum of their parts. The best selling record of 1982 in England was 'Tainted Love' a distinctly ambiguous love lament that set genders bending furiously; in 1983, Culture Club and Boy George made newspaper headlines across the world commensurate with their record sales – most of it concentrating on Boy George's "outrageous" cross dressing; the best selling record of 1984 so far is 'Relax' by Frankie Goes

To Hollywood, at the outset, a group with two explicitly gay members and a "raunchy" video set in a putative San Francisco gay bar; and the latest industry sensation is an avowedly homosexual pop group, Bronski Beat, whose 'Smalltown Boy' has personalised and made pop the club trend of the year: Hi Energy, the fast disco that gay men dance to. Never mind all the minnows swimming around scrabbling for a bite at the bender action – like Marilyn, Tasty Tim or even Pete Burns – these are the really big fish.

Yet what does it all add up to? The groups that have succeeded consistently have been those that fall within accepted pop codes, as they must. Frankie have now gone to war, widening their sexual outrage into political outrage; add a couple of banned videos and here you have a new, beautifully packaged, Rolling Stones. Despite the care of his music, Boy George has succeeded because he's turned himself, quite deliberately, into a living doll. His pleas for sexual tolerance encoded into

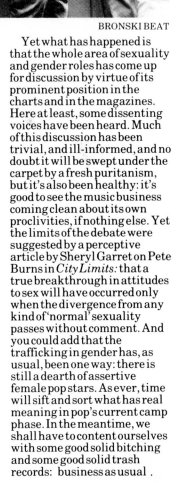

BRONSKI BEAT

MARILYN

his appearance – and songs like 'Do You Really Want To Hurt Me?' – have dovetailed into the wider pop liberalism of 'Karma Chameleon' – this generation's 'Melting Pot'. And yet George himself is without overt sexual threat, taking care to remove any aggressive sexuality; his fans, and the general public now, in general, accept him as they would Cliff Richard – no mean feat.

It would be a mistake to interpret this toleration in pop for a mood of toleration in the world outside, certainly not in its institutions – as the dismal litany of scandals, court cases, and police harassment attests. If you step over the line, you lose it: Marc Almond's career has dived in direct proportion to the extent that he refused to toe the line of what is acceptable. And even within pop's playpen, the tolerance only goes so far: Bronski Beat's appearance in the Top Ten was greeted by a *Top Of The Pops* segment where they were framed by a male and female dancer performing the perennial bumps and grinds of 'light entertainment' choreography. Just in case anybody got the wrong idea.

Yet what has happened is that the whole area of sexuality and gender roles has come up for discussion by virtue of its prominent position in the charts and in the magazines. Here at least, some dissenting voices have been heard. Much of this discussion has been trivial, and ill-informed, and no doubt it will be swept under the carpet by a fresh puritanism, but it's also been healthy: it's good to see the music business coming clean about its own proclivities, if nothing else. Yet the limits of the debate were suggested by a perceptive article by Sheryl Garret on Pete Burns in *City Limits:* that a true breakthrough in attitudes to sex will have occurred only when the divergence from any kind of 'normal' sexuality passes without comment. And you could add that the trafficking in gender has, as usual, been one way: there is still a dearth of assertive female pop stars. As ever, time will sift and sort what has real meaning in pop's current camp phase. In the meantime, we shall have to content ourselves with some good solid bitching and some good solid trash records: business as usual .

THE DECLARATION OF INDEPENDENTS

David Fricke rallies round the flag and salutes the new American underground

The new American underground has a lot to be thankful for – the mutinous spirit and daredevil programming of college radio, a supportive if sometimes stodgy press, a growing chain of small but musically alert record stores that can sell respectable numbers of the most obscure independent releases if, of course, it's in the grooves. Together they were strong enough to shoot R.E.M.'s 1984 album

Reckoning into the Top 30 only four weeks after release. They were certainly crucial in getting LA guitar brigands The Dream Syndicate a major label deal. Even chicano party band Los Lobos might not be the proud owners of an '84 Grammy for their Slash Records EP . . *And A Time To Dance* if it wasn't for the early patronage of the punks.

It seems strange, then, to think America's post-punk flowering also owes a debt of

begrudging thanks to the British fashion groove thing of Duran Duran, Culture Club and Spandau Ballet. The endless parade of comely English faces with their undisguised teen appeal and glossy soul inventions infuriated Yankee youngbloods. They felt it was practically their patriotic duty to play their *rock* – as opposed to pop's tick-tock electronics and casual disco glide – that much harder, to cut away

every ounce of naive fat from their songs.

The guitar, the weapon of choice by teen revolutionaries from Presley to The Pistols, made a big difference. Peter Buck gassed up the silky lyricism and Dixie mystery of R.E.M. with the Townshendian swipe and modal eccentricities of his Rickenbacker. D.Boon of Los Angeles trio The Minutemen blew the hardcore punk game wide open with his death-ray

R.E.M

VIOLENT FEMMES

distortion, kung-fu chord chop and abstract riffing, like some unholy communion of Pere Ubu and The Ramones. The rootsy vigor of punk-folk trio The Violent Femmes, whose two Slash LPs *Violent Femmes* and *Hallowed Ground* sound like the missing link between Jonathan Richman and Lou Reed, has a lot to do with singer-guitarist Gordon Gano's lusty acoustic strum.

So it is stranger still that the American upstarts should also benefit from Duran-demonium and Boy George's effortless US publicity sweep. Polar opposites in style and credo, they nevertheless have been perceived by many young teens hungry for some New Wave cool as part of the same Eighties pop coup. Sure, 'The Reflex' was Number One, and Boy George alternates weeks in *People* magazine with Michael Jackson, but the live bands playing between videos down at the rock discos in Everytown, USA have made that excitement seem much more real, brought it right around the block. Each city now has it own R.E.M., Jason And The Scorchers and Dream Syndicate. And the parallel appeal of Duran Duran's funk fantasies with the brash enthusiasm of the bratty Yanks is what finally broke once and for all the heavy doofus grip of the lumbering AOR giants (Styx, Journey, Boston, etc).

Which is not to say the new breed is simply reaping what The Ramones, Television and The Patti Smith Group sowed under great duress ten years ago. The cable music video channel MTV relegates most

alternative rock videos, like R.E.M.'s dreamlike 'Radio Free Europe' and The Scorchers' reading of Dylan's 'Absolutely Sweet Marie,' to the 4 a.m. graveyard shift. Commerical FM radio is no better. One promotion man for IRS Records in New York complained that blanket college airplay and serious crossover sales on R.E.M. didn't mean a thing to most big-time program directors. Their response to *Reckoning* was usually a chilly, "I just don't hear it."

That kind of brick-wall Philistine thinking, the impression that a new band has commercially little to gain and therefore artistically little to lose, has encouraged young America to take some hard turns to the left. True to their name, The Minutemen shoehorn their lightning pine angst into songs usually clocking two minutes and under, resulting in a barely suppressed fury that embarrasses the churlish sub-Pistols/Sham 69 melodrama that characterized late Seventies LA thrash. The follow-up to their explosive *Buzz Or Howl Under The Influence Of Heat* is supposed to be a 49-song double album.

Comparative old-timers Black Flag and The Dead Kennedys continue to make a glorious noise that annoys. Of late, most of the Kennedys' noise seems to be coming from singer Jello Biafra's mouth. A tireless promotor of alternative music, he has spent most of his time recently mouthing off on behalf of scrappy young worthies like San Francisco's Flipper, whose

Blow 'n' Chunks cassette on Reach Out International sounds like mega-Neubaten one minute and Hawkwind at 16 rpm the next. Black Flag (who once picketed Adam Ant gigs with the slogan "Black Flag Kills Ants dead!") have gone just as schizophrenic, dividing their '84 *My War* album between lengthy white noise blasts and 90-mile-an-hour protest-metal. In New York, No Wave descendants Sonic Youth and avant-guitar composer Glenn Branca are confounding punk expectations with music that is equal parts Motorhead, 'Sister Ray' Velvets and, in Branca's case, a grating industrial subersion of 'Tubular Bells.'

The Velvet Underground comparison, the last refuge of most critics, has been an especially difficult cross for The Dream Syndicate to bear.

The press hounds drooled over the group's 1982 debut EP and subsequent album *The Days Of Wine And Roses,* citing the abrasive scrape and long-distance jamming of guitarist Karl Precoda and Steve Wynn's acidic monotone as the rightful inheritance of *White Light/White Heat.* Wynn later spent a lot of time in interviews paying respects to the amphetamine shriek of Blue Cheer, The Fall's shambolic charm and the moody fuzz blues of Neil Young's Crazy Horse. That all of the above survived intact and uncompromised under producer Sandy Pearlman's heavy hand on *Medicine Show,* the Syndicate's 1984 major label debut, was a tribute to their absorbing perversity. (A vigorous slap on the wrist, however, to A&M Records for slicing down the original 25-minute version of 'John Coltrane Stereo Blues' to a teasing nine minutes).

The fact that *Medicine Show,* for all of its openly admitted precedents, doesn't sound the slightest bit retro (thanks in part to The Dream Syndicate's fearless approach to live improvisation) has a lot to do with the way new American bands view their influences. It would be cruel but fair to say that many English pop acts lazily ape American soul and disco sources, not to mention Kraftwerk electronics, without particularly improving on them. American neo-psychedelic and garage punk bands like Plasticland and the Chesterfield Kings are also shameless copycats. But they go about their Xeroxing

THE DREAM SYNDICATE

121

with such bold enthusiasm and fighting spirit in the face of major label inertia that it's hard to find fault with their lack of originality. The import *Plasticland* collection on France's Lolita label (talk about taking the long way home) is about as good as *erstatz* Syd Barrett will ever get. LA's Rain Parade go The Love/Tim Buckley/Beau Brummels route with liquid grace and quiet charm. And for a swinging '66 good time, it's hard to beat The Kings, whose authenticity – from their Prince Valiant hairdos to the tips of their custom-made Beatle boots – has the same six-pack kick of their Standells snarl.

The strange hold country music still has on young musicians in America no doubt has a lot to do with the forbidding quality of its rigid commerical styling (Dolly Parton's Nashville glitz, the cartoon hobo warble of Slim Whitman) and exaggerated romantic tone. Anything that cosmetic is ripe for overhaul. Expatriate Frisco punks Rank And File, who issued their second LP *Long Gone Dead* this year, picked up where Gram Parson left off with The Flying Burrito brothers, hot-rodding their campfire twang with a shiny pop finish. Jason And The Scorchers, Nashville boys raised on the real thing, took America and England by surprise with a dizzy guitar attack combining frantic *Sun Sessions* basics with an electric near-metal crunch. The band also had in singer Jason Ringenberg a songwriter of rare quality who was sensitive to the lyric mythology of country music while bringing it down to hard earth at the same time.

More extreme treatments of the form came from Rhode Island's Rubber Rodeo –

country *kitsch* treated with modern pop techniques – and Phoenix, Arizona's nervy Meat Puppets, a feisty little trio that turned critics' heads 180 degrees with their mix of frank unadorned prairie dog blues and hardcore growl on *Meat Puppets II*. In Los Angeles, Tex And The Horseheads were off on a more gritty blues tangent inspired by The Gun Club. England's answer to this, of course was stylish hypes like Yip Yip Coyote whose dabbling in country music was the best they could do in the face of rock's alleged spiritual bankruptcy. Yet in America, bands are finding in something as simple as country music new possibilities for energizing the old dog.

The miracle of R.E.M., easily the biggest thing out of Athens, Georgia since the B-52's, is that they succeeded beyond anyone's expectations by absorbing *all* of the above and sounding like none of it. Their indie single debut 'Sitting Still'/Radio Free Europe', dark horse winner in the 1981 *Village Voice* critics poll, inspired reviewers to lay on the Sixties/Love/Byrds comparisons real thick. The combination of Peter Buck's souped-up church bell guitar, Michael Stipe's inscrutably melted singing and the acoustic lilt of songs like 'Pilgrimage' and 'Moral Kiosk' on the '83 album *Murmur* made an alluring kind of folk-rock strangely born of the Pistols/Ramones uprising.

The second album *Reckoning* revealed the band's closer ties to mythic Seventies Dixie pop group Big Star. Like R.E.M., Big Star was a Southern band playing a gripping style of folk-rock. The friendly poppish structures of Alex Chilton's songs were quietly transformed by the confessional painfully inward

LOS LOBOS

tone of his lyrics and scorched nasal whine of his voice. The clarion ring of Big Star's guitars and those sunrise choruses were exhilarating, not unlike those of R.E.M.

But R.E.M. scored where Alex Chilton self-destructed because they were not afraid to show the courage of their convictions in the marketplace. While many new English bands still come prancing across the waters with 50-minute live shows padded out with repeats of the big 'hit', R.E.M. might play up to two hours nightly. A typical set could be 50 per cent covers and new, unrecorded originals. And the band has repeatedly turned down opening act slots on big arena tours to make friends in some of the strangest new music venues in America – like The Drumstick, an honest-to-God fried chicken restaurant in Lincoln, Nebraska.

"I don't mind devoting 70 hours a week to what I do," Peter Buck said in an early *Melody Maker* interview. "And I believe if you make good music over a series of years, people are going to get to know you no matter how commercial you are. The funny thing is all our friends think we're a commercial band because they're so uncommercial."

Well, commerciality is a matter of opinion, something you will find plenty of in the high recommended *OP*

magazine, a periodical totally devoted to independent music, American or otherwise. For anyone who wants to hear more of what this underground is throwing over, a decent shopping list would certainly include X (who took all the chances and all the lumps when punk was still a dirty word), the late great Mission Of Burma, R.Stevie Moore (a kind of one-man Super-Human League), singer-songwriters T-Bone Burnette and John Hiatt, New York area popsters Beat Rodeo and The Smithereens, Feelies offshoot The Trypes, and awesome hardcore trio Husker Du who did some remarkable things to 'Eight Miles High' on a single this year.

But giving Styx a vicious shove to the sidelines won't be the hardest thing the new US rock will ever do. Consider the dee-jay on Los Angeles' pioneering KROQ-FM last year who took a break from the station's usual diet of English synth-pop and cheap novelty records (howzabout a band called Killer Pussy?) to play a taste of The Dream Syndicate's 'Halloween' from *The Days Of Wine And Roses*. After only 30 seconds, he brusquely yanked the needle off the record and announced with misguided pride, "I like to give local bands a chance, but this is ridiculous. You won't be hearing more of that band on this station."

So near, and yet so far away.

JASON AND THE SCORCHERS

BRITTANIA WAIVES THE RULES

Drew Moseley has second thoughts about the current British infiltration of America's airwaves

This year marks the twentieth anniversary of the first musical British 'invasion'. 20 years ago, The Beatles first set their pointy-toed boots on American soil and conquered the nation. Now there are rumours of another invasion, but these rumours are greatly exaggerated.

It seems as if every time America turns around, someone claims to have invaded. Last year, it was the Australians. Since their first invasion in the Sixties, Britain has claimed at least three other invasions. It's a familiar public relations hype to allege 'invasion', and it has come to mean very little.

In the Sixties, The Beatles and The Rollings Stones brought back to the US all the blues they'd learned listening to American artists. It should be pointed out that many of these US artists could trace their roots back to the UK anyway, and a lot of the folk and blues music had evolved from old Scottish-Irish and English folk tunes. The difference between the way music evolved in America and the way it evolved in Britain was simply a matter of different mixing vats: blues and bluegrass and country had all rubbed up against the songs of slavery and the spirituals that are up in the black communities in the American south. America was a melting pot in the early part of the century, and music was one of the elements mixed into the stew. What made The Beatles and The Stones so important was that they had taken the mixture out of the melting pot and added their own interpretations to the genre. It was an invasion. Parents were deeply disturbed to discover their children crouched over mono record players, growing their hair, wearing mini skirts, sobbing at airports and hotels. Britain, via The Beatles, had a stranglehold on the US charts.

U2

In the Seventies, Britain claimed two more invasions: heavy metal and punk. Parents were disturbed at the volume of the music their children called heavy metal, but parents by then were veterans. They had noticed that although the decibel level was somewhat uncomfortable, their children still stood a good chance of growing up to be respectable people with decent jobs and families of their own. Heavy metal and punk, while harrowing for some, did not effect as much change in America as it did in the UK. It

is nearly impossible to get through a job interview with a safety pin stuck through one's cheek or a stud collar around one's neck.

'New Music' is the all-encompassing term which stretches out to include a recycling of US Sixties protest music (U2, Aztec Camera, The Clash), dashes of ancient Greek androgynism/post-Seventies David Bowie (Culture Club, Eurythmics), fashion-oriented MOR (Duran Duran), Thompson Twins) and reggae-inspired rock (Eddy Grant, The Police). Its roots

are multi-national, the bands that play this music are British. The question is, does it count as a British invasion?

The Police are definitely not 'new', but they are the only British band to come up with a number one LP this year in the US. Six British bands had number one singles: The Police ('Every Breath You Take') Bonnie Tyler ('Total Eclipse Of The Heart' with an American producer/writer), Yes ('Owner Of A Lonely Heart'), Culture Club ('Karma Chameleon'), Phil Collins (with the title song from the film 'Against All Odds') and Duran Duran ('The Reflex'). For an out and out invasion, this is hardly an impressive number – the combined weeks on the chart for British records is still less than half the year at number one. For LPs, the number is even bleaker. Maybe if this hadn't been the year of Michael Jackson (who broke several records established by The Beatles in the first British invasion) and *Footloose*, the sountrack to one of the most dreadful films in film history, Britain might have had a chance to lay claim to an invasion.

Goodness knows, the Brits behaved like invaders. Def Leppard's Joe Elliot refered to the Tex-Mex community in a very derogatory fashion, necessitating weeks of heartfelt apology on the part of his band. The Fixx got into a brawl over the size of a stage they were supposed to play on while ticket holders waited outside patiently. The Clash were habitually smarmy. Boy George charmed the nation by exclaiming that the US knew a good drag queen when it saw one. Rod Stewart still lounges here, even though the invasion that brought him is long over. Will someone please come and take him home?

Even MTV, that bulwark of pro-British programming, had an annual average of only nine British artists playing in

DURAN DURAN

heavy rotation out of a possible 23. Again, less than half. And without MTV, it seems highly probable that no claims of invasion would have been made at all; US radio would still be running its usual sure-fire throwbacks to the dark ages.

Certainly, there has been some sort of invasion fashion-wise. The East Village of New York City and the trendy areas of Los Angeles are acrawl with strange haircuts and Boy George designer clothes. But British fashion – or anti-fashion – was not created to be 'trendy'. It originated,

holds a job would think of going to the office with a head full of pink hair spikes.

Those who are too young to have jobs or worry about having them are dressing to look more human, thanks to Duran Duran, who seem to have left their more bizarre hair colours behind them. Others are trying desperately to look war-torn, a la U2 and The Fixx. Billy Idol and Adam Ant have given us the nuclear pirate mode, which has the added advantage of being very comfortable for summer and the hot lights of the stage. But the British fashion is not as

BILLY IDOL

THE POLICE

supposedly, to demonstrate British youth's disillusionment with the established order of things. Americans go along with the British mode to associate themselves more closely with their musical heroes, and they want to look good at the same time, which destroys the original intent. Most US youth is not on the dole, and office fashion is somewhat more restrictive here. Haircuts have been adapted to look responsible and upwardly mobile during the day and in vogue at night. No one who

pervasive as it might be and has been in the past. There are pockets in almost all the major cities, but the looks are not widespread. American artists had a hand in youth-oriented fashion as well – droves of high school students in New Jersey fought tooth and nail to be able to wear one white glove to school like Michael Jackson, and they lost. Whether or not young girls decide to get their hair cut into checkerboards like Cyndi Lauper remains to be seen, but she, too, is starting up her own fashion line.

America has the largest

music market in the world, and other countries are always claiming to have invaded it. But the phrase 'invasion', at this point in history, is inappropriate. Good music will be accepted and drawn into the culture of any country, whether it is born of the troubles in Ireland or the fantasy life of Boy George. There is no need to invade if no one is fighting against you. If

the music says something to the listener, if it imparts a thought or a feeling or evokes memories, it doesn't matter if it comes from England or Germany or Australia or America. Over time, it takes on the nationality of the listener and gives reference to a small part of the listener's life. That's why we listen in the first place, and why we will continue to listen.

CULTURE CLUB

RHYTHMS OF LIFE

Charlie Gillett describes his disenchantment with Western pop and his conversion to African music

In the middle of 1983 it looked as if African music was poised for a commercial breakthrough to the British market; in the middle of 1984, African music is still there, still poised.

In pop music, standing in the same place for more than a few minutes is perceived as running backwards, but in this case significant advances have been made in 12 months, even if they are mostly beneath the surface of the pop charts. There is now, as there was not then, a structure—of shops, gigs, labels, clubs—to carry the music into the middle of the pop mainstream.

A year ago, if you asked the mythical 'typical' pop fan—the reader of the *NME* or *Sounds,* the listeners of Peter Powell or Gary Crowley—to name some people who played 'African Music', the answer might have been "King Sunny Ade, Malcolm McLaren. . ." and an uncomfortable shuffle.

Sunny Ade and his 18-piece African beats had made an electrifying demonstration of the effect of Nigerian 'Ju Ju' music' on Channel Four-TV's *Midsummer Night's Tube.* Malcolm McLaren was in the Top Ten with 'Double Dutch', which galvanised dancers with the lurching rhythms of South African 'jive' music, and seduced everyone else with the ingenious use of a video that featured New York kids skipping ropes.

What lay beyond, behind, beneath, between? Not many knew then, but in the past year there's been a lot of scraping and digging, and the air has been shaken by the shouts of exultant explorers at each delicious new discovery.

The catalyst for all this sudden interest in the sounds of Africa was the extensive live performances by King Sunny Ade And His African Beats during 1983 throughout Britain, Europe, and the United States, following the arrangement he made to record

KING SUNNY ADE

125

an album a year for Island Records (to be released throughout the world outside his home territory of Nigeria).

One day, none of us had heard of Ju Ju music; the next, we were instant converts to this music which simultaneously managed to be both the inspiration and successor of every style of blues and rock we had ever known and loved. Suspicions that a couple of hours of live African music might be a bit repetitive and samey were dispelled by a band whose five guitarists each took a separate melodic line and

be glad; and hear the rest.

Those in the know assured the newcomers that there was much more to African music than Ju Ju, and that Sunny Ade was hardly known outside Nigeria in the rest of Africa, where the real King was Franco, the leader a band from Zaire called O.K. Jazz, who played a music full of melody and with a gentle 'Latin' rhythmic emphasis, known as 'soukous'.

It is a daunting prospect to try to catch up on such a huge area of music as African music but the whole murky picture

Charles, and Sam Cooke on black American music, you would begin to get the idea. His colossal recorded output on singles and albums approaches the quantity of those giants put together, and his career stretches back as far, to the early Fifties. Yet he has never had a release of any kind in Britain, not even one track on a compilation album.

The bill at The Palais was loaded with too many bands who used up valuable time and funds unnecessarily, and it was past midnight before Franco's band took the stage. The whole

paying in unison, coming in at certain moments during a song to give it a dynamic lift, instead of playing in the predictably-structured way of Western arrangements.

After a couple of numbers, onto the stage comes Franco himself, so big that the guitar looks like a toy mandolin against his chest. For a brief interlude, three girls come out to shimmy with so much frantic intensity we wonder what rhythm they can hear; hard and fast, something disturbingly seedy about their appearance – just like The Ikettes used to be with the Ike & Tina Turner Revue. And then they're gone and we're back to gazing at Franco. All meat, no fat, this man was once so fragile that his mother was afraid he might not survive his childhood. People say that he is a political exile, that he owns skyscrapers, that he is one of the richest men in all Africa, and that he is a tough man you had better not anger. There is a surprising dexterity to his big hands as his fingers move across the frets.

Franco smiles the benign smile of a ruler whose world is behaving itself, and when he dedicates a song to the dancers in the crowd we find that we are no longer staring at the stage in the way we are used to, but are hypnotically lost in a reverie created by this incomparable dance band.

There is an old-fashioned ambience to Franco's show which will not appeal to everyone, and it is certainly completely different from the bluesy aspect of Ju Ju; really, Soukous is nothing more or less than marvellous middle-of-the-road pop music, based on a repertoire of melodic ballads which may be about love ('Mabele'), or about political intrigues, or even in one case may be a straightforward commecial jingle for a motor car which has been extended into a ten-minute masterpiece called 'Azda'. All sung in a mixture of the local African dialect (Lingala) and French, it doesn't seem to matter much if we can't understand the words. There are any number of English-language pop songs which would probably sound better if we couldn't understand them.

Which leads to a question that Africans keep asking: why now, why, after all these years, has the West suddenly become so intrigued with African music? The music has been there all the time, and has not made any conspicuous change

FRANCO

wove it into an elaborate web which made us dizzy if we tried to untangle it. Better to surrender to the overall impact, and tremble at the effect of a close-miked set of talking drums. Nothing but guitars, voices, and percussion: the classic rock 'n' roll line-up, expanded beyond belief. How did an 18 piece band make ends meet on a worldwide tour, where previously the only economic solution for an unknown band had been to cut down from a four-piece to a three-piece, and make your roadie triple up on sound, lights, and driving? Don't ask;

became clearer during the first six months of 1984 with a succession of live concerts in London by some of the major names of African music; several of these were presented in a series at The Venue sponsored by the GLC as part of their Anti-Racism campaign, but a week or two earlier we had a chance to see Franco and O.K. Jazz at The Hammersmith Palais.

It is hard to calculate and explain the stature of Franco as an influence and inspiration throughout Africa, but if you were to imagine the combined influence of James Brown, Ray

aura was very reminiscent of the tours by American soul stars who came here during the Sixties, with the band in uniforms and a loud-mouthed emcee berating us to enjoy ourselves. Three vocalists stood at the front, middle-aged men whose faces showed that they have not spent all their lives in luxury hotels, and whose voices made our skin tingle: the Zaire technique of singing is to blend three voices in unison, all following an intricate and often sad melody line with telepathic precision. To their left, three horn players adopt a similar technique of to justify or explain this surge of interest. My own answer is tinged with guilt: I have no excuse except that I wasn't interested before, being happy enough with what I could find in American music through the Fifties and Sixties, and in British music during the late Seventies. But now that almost every young musician in the West sets out to be a businessman first and an artist second, I am not moved by the results of their market-oriented calculations: I am occasionally impressed, but that is not enough reason to listen to their records more than twice.

So, to some extent, it is by default that I am now searching through the music of the New World for music that lifts the spirit and tugs the heart. And now that I am listening, I hear and appreciate and think that I understand all kinds of stuff that before just sounded to me wierd or quaint or out-of-tune. But even now I retain a prejudice against anything that is self-consciously 'ethnic' or 'traditional'; I like best the African music which seeks to be unashamedly popular, and for most of the same reasons that I have previously liked Western pop.

Before we leave the Soukous music of Zaire, mention should be made of some of Franco's rivals and the spin-off musicians who have left his band over the years. The other long-established and generally-dependable bandleader from Zaire is Seigneur Rochereau (also known as Tabu Ley), who has maintained a comparatively prolific output since the early Sixties, including some particularly good records recently which feature his female vocalist Mbilia Bel (who is also his wife). Generally quicker in tempo than Franco's records, Rochereau's songs make more prominent use of horns, and at times his band sounds like a successor to the famous American big bands of the Forties.

Rivals for 20 years, Franco and Rochereau made records together in 1983 under the banner of Choc Choc Choc. Was this a new name to supplant soukous, much as the terms 'rock steady' and then 'reggae' replaced 'bluebeat' back in the Sixties? We'll find out, but in the meantime Franco has put out two more albums – both doubles – using the same generic title.

In 1983 Rochereau launched his Genida label, whose first releases were particularly good – *En Amour Y A Pas De Calcul* by Rochereau himself, and *L'Explosive Mbilia Bel*. Pamelo Mounk'a, another soukous star, also released an album on Genida, but it did not match the perfection of his previous *Samantha*, which had been released in France the year before but only surfaced here (as an import) during '83.

It turns out that the centre of soukous music is not Kinshasha (in Zaire) or Brazzaville (in Congo) but Paris (in France). It is there that most of the records are first recorded and then manufactured, before being distributed throughout Africa. And it is to Paris that many of the leading soukous musicians have migrated.

Only a couple of soukous bands retained a stable line-up in Europe; more commonly, records and gigs were played by a loose-knit group of session musicians who seemed to record practically every day, taking it in turns to be featured as the name on the cover, jumping from one label to another for each release. Inevitably, the standards are erratic, and few names guarantee satisfaction. But among those which crossed the channel to become favourites in every British club that gave them a chance were: Nyboma's *Double Double* and Bibi Den's Tshibaye's *The Best Ambiance*, most releases by Pablo, whose 'Madeleina' and 'Bo Manda' were among the highlights on Island's two sampler albums, *Amour Fou* all sustained a simple formula with disarming effectiveness.

Nyboma and Pablo (the latter unbilled) were among the star-studded cast who appeared at one of The Venue African Nights under the name of Les Quatre Etoiles, when they kept the entire place on its feet throughout their two-hour set. Also featuring Bopol, Syran, and Wuta May, the Four Stars charmed us with a music-oriented, almost-shy stage manner which did not conceal their delight at getting so much reaction from a supposedly staid British audience.

By contrast, the other highpoint of the series was the performance by Youssou N'Dour with Les Etoiles de Dakar, very theatrical and not conspicuously African. Instead the Senegal-based band displayed a confident familiarity with practically every Western idiom of the past 20 years, shifting with deceptive ease and evidently some internal logic from sounding like Steely Dan one moment to Genesis the next, and on through The Crusaders to The Wailers, all in a few bars. Over it all, Youssou wailed in his distinctive Arabic style, and made us realise the difficulty many African bands have in capturing their sound in the mostly primitive recording facilities of West

ORCHESTRE JAZIRA

Africa. It was hard to think of a more accomplished band than this, yet their records sound like cheap demos by comparison.

The task of spreading the gospel of African music in Britain lies with three sets of people: the musicians who live and work here (and the agents and promoters who book their gigs), the record companies based here, and the people who play records, on the radio and in dance clubs. A few pioneer dee-jays in clubs all around the country fork out small fortunes to stay on top of the latest sounds, some of them specialising almost totally in Afro-Caribbean rhythms, and others mixing African records into their standard fare of dance rock or jazz funk.

On the radio, John Peel is in front as ever with his four-nights-a-week show on Radio One, slipping African records into virtually every programme, and sticking with his favourites long enough to make sure the listeners have a chance to figure out the name and maybe even the title. I have an hour every Saturday night on London's Capital Radio which I devote entirely to 'tropical' music, mostly African but also some from the Caribbean and Latin America. Scattered through the local BBC stations is the occasional hero who somehow finds out what is what and who is who for the benefit of their fortunate listeners. But for the real breakthrough, African music will need the support of the live music scene and the record business.

The major labels have so far viewed African music with cautious scepticism. Having made such an effective start by signing King Sunny Ade, and releasing the two *Sound D'Afrique* albums, Island has not ventured further into the field. Virgin jumped in early with two excellent albums recorded in Kenya by Orchestra Makassy and Orchestra Super Mazembe but has since restricted its activities to releasing a disappointing album by Ebenezer Obey, who had seemed to be Sunny Ade's main contender as Ju Ju chief.

For many years, the African market was dominated by the colonial subsidiaries of EMI, Philips, and Decca based in most of the larger African countries, but most of these have closed down since the move to independence, and their British headquarters have shown little conviction in trying to sell the stuff here. EMI had an unsatisfactory reunion with Fela Kuti, the wayward innovator who reclaimed the James Brown guitar riff for Africa during the Seventies, when he evolved a powerful rhythmic basis for declamatory songs which he sang in pidgin-English in a style he called Afro-Beat. But by 1983 Fela seemed to have lost his sense of direction, and he certainly did not provide EMI with a record that could have sold tens of thousands of copies.

In the absence of any real interest from the companies with big marketing budgets, African musicians with recordings to release have made pacts with independent labels, and during the year four companies in particular put themselves on the line by committing a substantial part of their A&R time and money to African music.

Earthworks was the first, launched by Jumbo Van Reenen, a South African who had previously been a friendly presence in Virgin's A&R department for the ten years

THOMAS MAPFUMO

France and Africa to dealing with locally-based musicians, and among the highlights in its rapidly-expanding catalogue are two impressive albums by the strident, emotional Zimbabwe writer-singer Thomas Mapfumo, and three attractive compilations of the sort of South African and Zimbabwe Jive music that inspired Malcolm McLaren; in the case of one track by the Mahotella Queens on the album, *Phezulu Eqhudeni*,

CHIEF FELA KUTI

since the company began. Jumbo and his wife Mary took on the task of importing and distributing African records from whatever source could supply them, to any outlet that would stock them, and began to license material for release on their Earthworks label. Among the label's first releases was the first single by one of the leading African music groups based in Britain, Orchestre Jazira. 'Love', managed to set the skittering guitars of Ghanaian Highlife music around the steady throb of a bass drum without losing their essential flavour, and the group's only apparent weakness is the lack of a distinctive lead vocalist.

Since then Earthworks has preferred licensing from

'inspired' is hardly the word – Malcolm wrote new words to an existing tune and arrangement, and proceeded to credit himself as total author. Yet he still must be applauded for recognising the enormous appeal of this music, and for helping to familiarise us with its conventions.

During 1983 a new team took over the management of Sterns, the Tottenham Court Road electrical appliance shop whose tiny record department in the back room had for many years been the main outlet for African records in London. Relocating to cheaper premises a couple of blocks away on Whitfield Street, the new management renamed their shop Sterns African Record

Centre, and rapidly built up a stock of over 2,000 different titles.

The Sterns record label soon followed, and their first three releases had an immediate impact in both Britain and Europe. Mohammad Malcolm Ben's *African Feeling* is among the few records which successfully integrates English-language lyrics into the odd melodies and harmonies of 'highlife' music, notably in the impassioned plea for peace and understanding called 'Preservation Of Humanity'. Hardly an auspicious title for an entertaining dance anthem, but that is what it turns out to be.

Also from Ghana, but based in Britain, Hi Life International made a workmanlike album whose appeal mysteriously improved through the year, until initial reservations about the lack of bass frequencies gave way to pleasure in the many tuneful songs.

The third release on Sterns was from a young pretender to the title of JuJu chief being contested by Sunny Ade and Ebenezer Obey; Segun Adewale followed up the brilliant *Ase* on his own Nigerian-based label with a deliberate shot at what he

perceived to be British tastes with 'Yo Pop Music' on the Sterns album *Play For Me, Adewale*. Energetic and charismatic, he and his band left a lasting impression with their rousing set at The Venue.

Of the established indie labels, Cherry Red and my own Oval label changed course to cater for, and cultivate, the emergence of this market for African music. Cherry Red launched a new subsidiary called Africagram, whose most interesting releases were produced by John Collins in Ghana. British by birth but with many years of living in Africa behind him, John runs a remarkable Portastudio operation in the country, several miles from Accra, offering to record local bands, groups and singers in a neat symbiotic arrangement whereby they retain African rights in their recordings while John has the rights for the rest of the world. His first compilation on Africagram, *The Guitar And The Gun*, introduced us to the charms of the Genesis Gospel Singers, whose 'N' Tutu' was also released as a single; hardly tough enough at the bottom end to qualify for dance club play, one of John's records could easily become one of those freak radio novelty hits that keep so

many of us playing this game of pop roulette.

Oval's first African record came in as a tape made by African Connexion, a mix of Sierra Leone and British musicians led by Mwana Musa, whose adroit blend of soukous, rock and reggae made 'C'Est la Danse' one of the most-played African radio records of the year. At the time of writing, we have just released two records by Ghanaians based in Berlin: 'Highlife Time' by George

SEGUN ADEWALE

Darko, which has been widely played here as an import album track on his own Okoman label; and 'Asiko' by Kantata, whose lead singer Lee Dodou is also the vocalist on George's records. Influenced equally by the Ghanian master guitarist Ko Nimo and by American jazz funk hero George Benson, George Darko looks like the man most likely to infiltrate the world of the jazz funk clubs, who have previously been very suspicious of anything with an African tag. Meanwhile, Kantata have a more prominent Caribbean influence, and hope to penetrate the equally narrow world of reggae clubs, where even 'soca' music from Trinidad has had a hard time getting in.

The future depends on what happens on the live music front, up and down the country. By common consent, several of these African bands generate a more exciting atmosphere at gigs than your average technocrats can manage with drum machines and a bank of synths. Julian Bahula has done a marvellous job with his regular series of African Nights at The 100 Club in Oxford Street in London, enabling groups like Hi-Life International, African Connexion, and Super Combo to rise through the ranks of support bands to become crowd-pullers in their own right.

But the next move is up to the college secretaries across the country, without whose support the whole African movement could be stillborn. With that support, we could see a band emerge as an African-styled equivalent to UB40 or Dire Straits, a band with enough belief in its own musical principals to ignore the fashionable trends and sweep through the scene without even realising that there are any barriers. The way things are looking now, that band will make its break in partnership with an indie label.

CHIEF EBENEEZER OBEY

...AND THEN THERE WAS JAZZ

Jazz was the peg where every potential young hipster wanted to hang his hat last year, but as **Robert Elms** suggests, you had to be cool to be kind

CARMEL

Everybody came from different directions, but it was obvious they'd get there in the end. Ever since punk, with its pimply white trash pose (in reality usually more hackneyed than acned) detonated the entire rock myth, so all the fashionable young musical things have looked back to black music for a lead. The Eighties have seen, with varying degrees of subtlety, mock disco followed by mock funk, mock salsa, mock soul, then by 1984, as the decade progressed inexorably backwards, came jazz. Some of those fashionable young things may have taken their time getting there, but don't mock the turtle, there's been some good music this year.

It wasn't so much that you could hear any actual jazz on daytime radio, but that a wide selection of young British bands had dipped into the jazz bag and pulled out a variety of stylistic and musical influences which have tinted the pop charts ever so slightly blue.

Carmel was one of the first to see the word jazz used about her by journalists who didn't really know what it meant, but I suppose it's understandable. Miss McCourt and her two beefy Mancunian sidekicks – Jimmy Paris on double bass and Gerry Darby on drums – play a kind of attenuated, anarchic gospel. The boys roll the sleeves of their check shirts to the forearms and she shuts her eyes and belts out a mix of dark and arty originals and standards like 'Willow Weep For Me'.

Therefore, people who knew no better predictably called her the new Billy Holliday. Now Lady Day had one of the most shimmering, sensitive voices ever to pour out paeans to pain. Carmel is a belter with powerful lungs, but none too subtle. With stark, bluesy songs like 'Bad Day', her London Records debut single, she can make stirring, genuinely dramatic records, but stretched over an album, her limitations become apparent.

By walking into the Electric Ballroom in Camden Town on a Friday night Simon Booth had stumbled into an astonishing scene. Here were young kids, most of them black, dancing scorching steps to jazz. Not funk, or disco or electro but jazz by Art Blakey and Cecil McBee and Tito Puente, jazz pure and fast. So Booth decided to make music for them. Paul Murphy was the dee-jay playing music for them who decided to start Paladin, a jazz record label showcasing young British bands making jazz for young audiences. The two came together and 'Venceremos' was the first result of their union. Featuring Working Week plus Robert Wyatt, Chilean Claudio Figuero and Tracey Thorn (again) guesting on vocals, 'Venceremos' was instantly one of the finest, most moving records of the year.

The Paladin road to jazz was one that mystified rock critics who like to think of all those wailing sax solos and bass runs as somehow intellectual and worthy. But here were kids who'd graduated through jazz-funk and fushion, through Lonnie Liston Smith and Chick Corea to the wildest batucada and the bluest note.

They saw jazz as the ultimate dance challenge, a soundtrack to sharp steps and good times.

Working Week actually incorporated jazz dance into their live set. IDJ (I Dance Jazz) a crew made up of London's premiere Ballroom jazz boys who mix a frenetic blur of funk, modern, tap and acrobatics, choreographed stage routines to go with Working Week's strident, percussive sound. They provide the visual edge to live gigs and video that could just turn jazz into pop.

And while IDJ were busy breaking the image of jazz as museum music, so in Manchester there was a team of steppers with their own, very considerable style. The Jazz Defectors threw more graceful, balletic shapes than their lightning southern counterparts and boasted their own band to step to. Kalima, who used to be The Swamp Children, mirrored the difference between the northern and southern styles of dancing by concentrating on bossa novas and swaying mid-tempo shufflers. They released a fine, low-key single on Factory, 'The Smiling Hour', before joining the Paladin fold.

The Drum Is Everything, her debut LP is full of tracks that sound like somebody wailing in the bath while banging on the plumbing. Tunes are replaced by half-baked ideas about experimentation, Carmel's shout is remorseless and too often her band simply do not swing. The problem with improvised music is that you have to be damn good to cut it.

The Drum was jazz born out of punk, that 1976 notion of "anybody can do it," but Carmel could only do it every now and then. *Cafe Bleu* was jazz by an old punk who decided to do it after undergoing a miracle conversion. Paul Weller was the leader of The Jam, the great white hopes of the rock fraternity, forever topping *NME* polls – the Eighties version of Cream. Then suddenly he became a born again trendy, sacked his increasingly embarrassing band and formed the achingly hip Style Council.

Weller's arrival at the word jazz was perhaps the most predictable, but certainly the most tortuous of them all. For years he'd adopted the superficial trappings of the all-powerful Sixties mod myth. The Jam had the right

IDJ (I DANCE JAZZ)

haircuts, but apparently only one suit between them, and sounded like yet another rock band. It could only be so long before Weller actually studied the modernist lineage and 'discovered' R&B, soul, and at the dawn of it all, sweet and sharp modern jazz.

So he re-read Colin MacInnes' *Absolute Beginners*, bought a new mac and learned a couple of the correct names to drop – *Cafe Bleu* comes complete with a palid MacInnes parody booklet where Nina Simone, The

Plugged Nickel and "Miles' sad, lonely trumpet" are given clumsy plugs – and he had a go.

If it had been a debut album by a bunch of young unknowns *Cafe Bleu* would have been a nice try. In 'You're The Best Thing', it contains one soul song of genuine majesty, and, in touches, the hazy melancholy aimed at on side one is actually achieved, especially when Tracey Thorn breathes 'The Paris Match'. But it's so overburdened with ersatz 1961 continental cool, of the kind pretentious boys from

TRACIE THORN

SADE

Ilford went in for all those years ago, that it seems terribly contrived. Still, if it makes kids go out and listen to the real thing . . .

This genuine (dance) floor level resurgence in interest in "syncopated, strongly rhythmic music of American negro origin in which improvisation is much used" (Penguin English dictionary) was capped by Julien Temple's decision to direct a musical version of MacInnes' much talked about *Beginners*. Having told the world that rock 'n' roll was a swindle he decided to step back to 1958, a time of neat suits, cool tunes and hot, angry summers.

With IDJ and The Jazz Defectors set to spin across the screen and a soundtrack by Working Week, Sade and Paul Weller as well as Elvis Costello, The Kinks and The Rolling Stones, it was a veritable tribute to the year that bop became the hip hop. And one Mr. Gil Evans was flown in to make the arrangements. Just for one second England felt like Birdland.

And Jerry Dammers, that most English of modern musical institutions with his toothless grin, his loud shirts and baggy shorts, could often be seen at one of the new jazz

club nights grooving to the mix of salsa, bop, Cuban, African and R&B. And when his long awaited Special AKA album *In The Studio* finally appeared you could hear all those nights in there.

Moving on from reggae to the many rhythms of modern jazz, it even came complete with a duo-tone pastiche of a Fifties Impulse or Verve sleeve, oozing with jazz stylisation. Jazz-tinged is all you could really say about tracks like 'Girlfriend' and 'Lonely Crowd', but that was the tinge that made them sparkle. And Mr. Dammers became a vociferous spokesman for the new jazz.

If The Specials were 2-Tone turned polyrhythmic, then Swans Way were Birmingham futurists turned 52nd Street cool cats, from The Rum Runner to The Plugged Nickel. In 1983 JoBoxers pioneered a kind of Bowery boy and bar room jazz package, in 1984 Swans Way moved up town and slightly up-market with 'Soul Train', a moody method actor melodrama set somewhere in jazz mythology. It was quite a good record, too.

And it wasn't a bad start all round. Jazz is likely to go the way of most fads, and the trendies will move with the trend. But once touched, some

people will remain moved by the beautiful and powerful music they've been alerted to by the pop records they hear on the radio. And the pop records that this year have been laced with a shot of jazz are better pop records than most.

Tracey Thorn also weighed in with her own admirable effort. Along with her partner, lover and fellow Hull University undergraduate, guitarist Ben Watt, she made up Everything But The Girl whose 'Each And Every One' was one of the year's most surprising and pleasing single successes. A lazy, nagging bossa nova, it was Astrid Gilberto with lyrical barbs and a lovely floating arrangement. *Eden,* the album which followed, was more of the same, with an overriding sadness and a little Peter, Paul and Mary folkiness thrown in. That combined with their nouveau hippy obsession with not appearing on *Top Of The Pops* cast a few doubts about the future, but they certainly had a good year.

Using the same producer, Robin Millar, and the same studio, Powerplant in Sunny Willesden, came the other female voice to make jazzy sound waves this good year, Sade. But Tracey and Sade

were chalk and chocolate in more than just skin tones, Sade was jazz strictly where it slid into soul, style so refined it was almost invisible.

Much attention was paid to her obvious good looks, her exotic Nigerian background and name (Folasade Adu) and her hair, and they all forgot to mention that she could really sing. But then came the proof. The single 'Your Love Is King' was a fine soul ballad, while the album, *Diamond Life* was a remarkably mature and consistent debut both in terms of songwriting and performance. On tracks like 'Sally' and 'Frankies First Affair', her young band played with a light but incisive touch, while her voice is soft, dark and pliable. But then we do share a flat.

Working Week were the other band to share that studio and producer and they were the real jazzers of the lot. Metamorphosing out of Weekend, "a pop band with a jazz feel", into Working Week, "a jazz band with a pop approach", they're a fluid conglomeration of itinerant instrumentalists led by Simon Booth, a young guitarist and composer, who've come together to make latinate, danceable jazz.

WORKING WEEK

BOOK REVIEWS

AC/DC
HM Photo Book
(Omnibus)

This series of picture books of heavy metal groups is produced in Japan and commendable for the excellence of the colour printing. Usually half the 96 pages are in colour with a short biog taking up another 12 or so. Good stuff for heavy metal freaks. The AC/DC book for some reason has only one-third in colour, some fab shots nevertheless.

AN IDEAL FOR LIVING: AN HISTORY OF JOY DIVISION
Mark Johnson
(Proteus)

An obsessive chronological examination of the career of one of the new wave's least lovable bands. Paul Morley's interjections sit somewhat uneasily amidst a mass of facts and trivia that will fascinate the converted but mean very little to anyone else. A rock book that Takes Itself Seriously.

DEBORAH SPUNGEN
And I Don't Want To Live This Life
(Corgi)

The fact that this is a mass market paperback (albeit an expensive one) might suggest that some publishers have finally recognised the commercial viability of rock books. There isn't much about music here, however – this is the frequently harrowing account of the sad life of Nancy Spungen, who was probably killed by Sid Vicious, who was soon dead himself from a drug OD. It's a brave book for a mother who lost her obviously disturbed child in such a manner, but curiously provides insights into the human condition. Mrs. Spungen's interest in punk rock can be judged from the fact that the few mentions of Johnny Rotten refer to him as John Lyman – close, but no cigar. The book, however, deserves to be read by anyone with a problem child who seems devoted to the more appalling aspects of popular music.

BARRY
Howard Elson
(Proteus)

Barry Manilow fans apparently call themselves – wait for it – Barry Buddies

(yecch!) If you aren't one, keep a bucket by you if you read this cliché-ridden sycophantic biog. Written in severe over-schmaltz like a PR handout from a publicist on heat, it sketches his life and career ("So I learned all about loneliness and wrote songs about it.") and interviews some Barry Buddies ("I became so involved with Barry, that I forgot to take my anti-depressant tablets." "I sat there with tears streaming down my face – and he hadn't even sung a note.") Criticised elsewhere for his sugaryness, Manilow has an undoubted therapeutic effect on his many fans and has made millions from being mothered. But even he deserves something better designed and less obviously fawning than this – and that's saying something.

THE BEATLES: AN ILLUSTRATED DIARY
H.V.Fulpen
(Plexus)

After pretty well everyone else has cashed in on their Beatles memories and memorabilia, stand by for the former head of the Dutch Beatles Fan Club with the view from Amsterdam. Detailed diary-style format jostles for attention with short articles (The Beatles' Homes, Was Paul Dead?, Beatles Cartoons) and the odd interesting snap. Might well have lost something in the translation, though. . .

THE BEATLES COMPLETE – GUITAR/VOCAL EDITION
(Wise Publications)

Words and (guitar) music to 203 songs written by The Fabs up to 1970 or thereabouts, with an "appreciation" by Ray Connolly and some OK black and white pictures. Great for would-be coverers of Beatle songs, but if that's not your aim, the only possible use for this book would be as a door stop or to drop off tower blocks – it's weight and velocity would certainly be sufficient to kill anyone it hit.

BEFORE I GET OLD: THE STORY OF THE WHO
Dave Marsh
(Plexus)

The Who have to be God's gift to rock historians. Some groups never seem to change their style – the Who tried R & B and power pop, invented the dreaded rock opera and found the time to discover the synthesiser. Other bands lack personality – the Who had at least four of 'em, depending on how many you credit Keith Moon with. Rolling Stone alumnus Marsh makes the most of his subject, and it's his penetrating character analyses – particularly of guitarist/songwriter Pete Townshend – that graphically convey the band's unique creative tensions and make this book impossible to put down.

BILLBOARD BOOK OF US TOP 40 HITS – 1955 TO PRESENT
Joel Whitburn
(Guinness)

A kind of US equivalent of the highly successful Guinness books of hits, although

limited (for no good reason that I can see) to the Top 40. Whitburn, who also publishes books which do list all the Top 100 hits, has been lucky enough to acquire the rights from Billboard to reproduce their charts, for which I envy him, and is obviously squeezing the last drop out of this acquisition in the same way as Read, The Rices and Gambaccini are doing in this country. An invaluable resource book – and far cheaper than Whitburn's volumes!

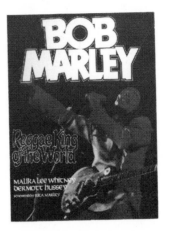

BOB MARLEY: REGGAE KING OF THE WORLD
Malika Lee Whitney & Dermott Hussey
(Plexus)

Weighing in with a foreword from Rita Marley came the latest book on Marley in a year when Island's posthumous Legend compilation album demonstrated that both that record and this book were aptly titled. Unlike the LP, though, this is a confusing and poorly put together volume. Particularly irritating is the extensive use of song lyrics, seemingly a prerequisite of 'authorised' biographies – for while Marley wrote some moving and noteworthy lyrics, lines taken in isolation often mean very little, especially without the music. Fails to rival either Stephen Davis' biography for detail or Viv Goldman/Adrian Boot's book for pictorial content. Disappointing.

BOWIEPIX
Pearce Marchbank
(Omnibus)

The sort of souvenir brochure that'll cost you an arm and a leg at a concert (Omnibus settle for £2.50). A classy 20-page picture record of Bowie's chameleon imagery laced with random quotes, presumably added to give the package some spice. A huge colour poster is probably its most vital selling point.

BOY GEORGE & CULTURE CLUB
Jo Dietrich
(Proteus)

Short but competent story of formation and development of Culture Club. Mostly about Boy George, of course. Relates his schooldays, nightclub-posing background, brief involvement with Bow Wow Wow, and

the formation and success of Culture Club. A sort of gladrags-to-riches fairytale summed up by George himself, "For someone like me to write a song and get to number three, just shows that anybody can do it." 40 pics, 32 pages, nice design on colour pages. Worth the price.

THE CLASH
Miles
(Omnibus)

Cuttings libraries throughout the land are raped to provide us with the story of the punk revolution one more time: Mick Jones saying how drugs had destroyed rock music in the mid-Seventies and within months himself being doped to the eyeballs, Mark P. claiming that punk died the day The Clash signed to CBS, the fights with CBS, the bemused reactions to Sandinista. But it is just an historical commentary. There are no fresh revelations, for example, about the sudden departure of Mick Jones and all the information is recycled from old quotes. It's okay as a reference point but its literary worth is negligible and like all books written in this manner ultimately leaves a feeling of frustration.

CULTURE CLUB – BOY GEORGE IN HIS OWN WORDS
(Omnibus)

The 'In Their Own Words' series have, arguably, done their bit towards the low standing of rock books generally. Too often they seem padded-out and dubiously designed. The titles suggest the artists were involved when they were not. The 'Words' were usually from interviews in other publications. Being the most widely available rock books they often took up bookshop-space at the expense of better products on the same artists. The theory was and is, no doubt, that fans will buy anything on their heroes, however naff. They've recently changed from 128-page bound books to a 32-page stapled magazine format like concert programmes. Bigger pages but far fewer quotes and pics, and printed in only two colours, sometimes not too successfully. Still it's kept the price down. Boy George has 50-odd quotes and 19 two colour pics, and a full colour pull-out poster.

DAKOTA DAYS
John Green
(St. Martin's Press)

Green was John Lennon's tarot card reader for the final six years and his account of them is little more than a reconstruction of conversations between himself and John and Yoko (credited to his own "fine memory") to the latter's great detriment. Green's integrity has recently been in question; apparently Yoko had to pay him $30,000 to move out of her loft building where he had been living rent-free, and where she kept Beatles artifacts, when she discovered he was charging admission to the loft. Would you buy a book from this man?

DAVID BOWIE BLACK BOOK
Miles
(Omnibus)

The enigmatic title is deceptive. Far from the juicy exposé of DB's innermost secrets intimated by the title, this is a straightforward historical biography lent its mood of exotica by virtue of being printed in white on black pages. Miles has done a reasonably comprehensive job without apparently having had the tedious bother of having to interview any of the luminary figures himself for the information; this results in an oddly abrupt portrayal of the facts. No insights then, but it is a weighty volume that *looks* outstanding with a genuinely impressive and exhaustive selection of photographs.

DAVID BOWIE – OUT OF THE COOL
Philip Kamin & Peter Goddard
(Virgin)

Picture book of Bowie's "Serious Moonlight" tour of 1983 that would like to think it's something more. Because, let's face it, there was very little remarkable about Bowie's stage show for the particular tour – and when rock's original Karma Chameleon lets you down, you gotta lotta ground to catch up. A few typically oblique snippets from the man himself, a snatched conversation with his rhythm guitarist and a load of waffle to justify an arty subtitle. If you could only afford a back-row seat for the tour it sets you closer to the action but at £5.95 it's no gift for the merely curious.

DEEP PURPLE
Chris Charlesworth
(Omnibus)

Very nice, but does anyone actually *care* any more that in April, 1970 Purple played the Central Hall, Chatham and were paid £400? Or that Roger Glover was disappointed with the *Fireball* album? Or that. . . Charlesworth hacks out the Purple story in professional, but coldly unemotional style. There is, however, a lavish array of pictures depicting various changing faces of wallydom – the book's one source of amusement.

DEEP PURPLE – HM PHOTO BOOK
(Omnibus)

96 pages of colour pics less exciting than rest of series – plus brief biog.

DIRE STRAITS
Michael Oldfield
(Sidgwick & Jackson)

Yes, it's the book of the album of the video of the compact disc. . .Oldfield, former *Melody Maker* editor, is probably the ideal author for a Dire Straits biography – both are great respectors of tradition. The resulting book was hardly *News Of The World* serialisation material, then, but who'd expect it? A worthy, if unexciting read in a coffee-table format that allows the reader to dip in at will. A bit like a Straits record, really – nice to have around for the occasional track but a bit too much all at one sitting.

THE DOORS
John Tobler & Andrew Doe
(Proteus)

Fact-filled book on a band that has never, it seems, gone out of fashion. Stranglers, Joy Division, Echo And The Bunnymen and Annabel Lamb notwithstanding, the originals have always retained their mystique – largely because of the mysterious death of singer Jim Morrison in 1971. Tobler and Doe wisely leave the is he/isn't he argument alone. The

one big disappointment is the photographs (all from the same period) and their unimaginative, sometimes incomprehensible use. Read *The Doors* with Jerry Hopkins' sensationalist Morrison biography *No One Here Gets Out Alive* for two sides of a fascinating story.

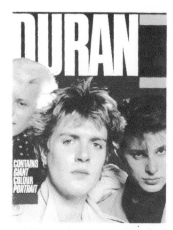

DURAN DURAN – IN THEIR OWN WORDS
(Omnibus)

32-page stapled magazine format, 24 large pics printed black and red or black and blue, 'giant' pull-out colour poster (which is cover pic turned the other way to look different) and over 100 quotes. Depending on your view, the quotes could either be a lot of egomaniacal coke-induced bullshit from five silly pratts or fascinating statements on their art and career. Still, even if you find their words a bit two-plankish, they look very pretty – even fatty Simon.

THE ESSENTIAL GUIDE TO ROCK BOOKS
Ed Hanel
(Omnibus)

A well-meaning, if sometimes irritatingly uncritical rock bibliography covering books from the mid Sixties to 1983. Suffers from lack of a title index which would certainly have complemented the thoughtful layout.

THE ESSENTIAL GUIDE TO ROCK RECORDS
Fred Dellar and Barry Lazell
(Omnibus)

Thorough, well-presented illustrated catalogue itemising every record released in the UK by 400 or so acts. Compulsive browsing material.

EURYTHMICS – IN THEIR OWN WORDS
(Omnibus)

30-page magazine format containing 18 large pics (some just a bit too arty and pretentious) plus 'giant' pull-out colour poster of cover shot. Quotes are a bit more interesting than usual in this series (see Duran Duran) reflecting no doubt the intelligence of this talented duo.

GRATEFUL DEAD – THE MUSIC NEVER STOPPED
Blair Jackson
(Plexus)

"Blair Jackson has attended roughly 75 Grateful Dead gigs in eight states since 1970." The above quote, which starts the "About The Author" section of this book, should indicate what this chunky volume is all about.

Dead Heads will almost certainly possess a copy already, and if you're curious about this neo-religion, this is as good a place as any to start – fairly well balanced and not too adulatory, but ultimately it's difficult to suggest who else would be interested in a group who seem to typify everything that was wrong with pre-punk rock music. There's even a very poor imitation of a Pete Frame family tree. . .

THE GREAT ROCK AND ROLL TRIVIA QUIZ
Dafydd Rees & Luke Crampton
(Virgin)

"From the compilers of the Radio 1 programme" says it all – but I'd rather be given this at a Radio 1 roadshow than pay £2.95 for it!

THE GUITAR – THE HISTORY, THE MUSIC, THE PLAYERS
Allan Kozinn, Pete Welding, Dan Forte & Gene Santoro
(Columbus Books)

Kozinn covers classical music, about which no comment, Welding contributes sections on jazz and blues, which seem up to his usual high standard, Dan Forte does a chunk on country and bluegrass, which may or may not be comprehensive – I was unaware that Willie Nelson was more than a workmanlike guitarist, and Red Rhodes is absent from the brief steel guitar section. Gene Santoro tries to cover thirty years worth of rock guitarists in just over forty pages. This is where the book falls down – Danny Kalb rates around three times as much copy as Carolos Santana, Joe Walsh is mentioned once en passant, well known Sex Pistols axeman Steve Cook (sic) rates a couple of lines, and Brian May isn't important enough to even get a name check. Without the rock section, this book might be rather good – pleasant layout, fair pictures, etc. Would have been oodles better in separate volumes.

HEAVY METAL IN JAPAN – HM PHOTO BOOK
(Omnibus)

Biggest and best of the HM Photo Books series. If you're into heavy metal and dig pics of hairy, leatherclad machos pulling faces and masturbating with guitars this is for you. 128 pages, half in superb colour on quality art paper. No biogs but some exceptionally good photos of – Iron Maiden, Van Halen, AD/DC, Whitesnake, Def Leppard, Motorhead, UFO, Thin Lizzy, Led Zeppelin, Saxon, Tygers of Pan Tang, Kiss, Twisted Sister, Aerosmith, Girlschool, Rainbow, Rush, Scorpions, Y&T, Deep Purple, Judas Priest, Ozzy Osbourne, Michael Schenker Group, Motley Crue, Graham Bonnet, Blackfoot, Black Sabbath . . . Makes you snarl as you go through it.

HENDRIX – AN ILLUSTRATED BIOGRAPHY
Victor Sampson
(Proteus)

Competent sympathetic biog, of one of the greatest rock guitarists. Outlines his unhappy, insecure childhood in Seattle, his army life, early gigs in various backing bands, discovery and move to swinging London, breakthrough and success, hit records and major tours, management double-dealing, problems, drugs and premature death. Text has fast exciting pace but design is a bit pedestrian. Extensive discography.

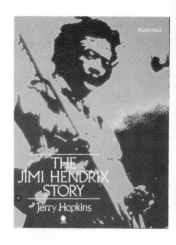

HIT AND RUN
Jerry Hopkins
(Sphere)

Another excellent biog from the man who brought us the two best most straightforward books on Presley plus the Jim Morrison book which Danny Sugerman turned into a rock version of 'Peyton Place'. Somewhat surprisingly, Hendrix hasn't yet been the subject of dozens of books, perhaps because his life and particularly his career were brief, and taken in conjunction with Chris Welch's now ancient (but perhaps recently updated) Hendrix book, this should tell you most things you need to know. Good pictures, co-operation from Jimi's family – a fitting tribute and a good read.

HIT PARADE
Harry Hammond & Gered Mankowitz
(Plexus)

A photo book, combining the work of Hammond from the '50s and '60s and the somewhat more arty Mankowitz from 1963 on. A few silly typos ('Petula Clarke', 'Six Pistols') threaten to mar what is otherwise an amusing and enjoyable book. Look for the amazing (and previously unseen) pic of Eddie Cochran.

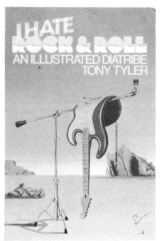

I HATE ROCK & ROLL – AN ILLUSTRATED DIATRIBE
Tony Tyler
(Vermilion)

Illustrated diatribe? Illiterate diarrohea more like. Ex-rock journalist Tyler's attempt to cash-in by ratting on whole rock phenomenon is very laudable really but the result is a dull, disappointing yawn. It drones on in a sort of third-rate pub-bore idiot-idiom, unsuccessfully attempting to be witty and padded out with minor facts and insignificant incidents, half-backed theories and weedy generalisations on rock music and personalities. Everybody is seemingly either a dork, nurd or pillock. An unfunny, uninteresting, unrevealing school-boyish sneer. Not much good to say about this book although the binding isn't bad.

I NEED MORE
Iggy Pop and Anne Wehrer
(Kaez-Cohl Publishing)
The front cover shows Iggy sucking the nipple of a statue, and one of the many (often rather repetitive) photos inside provides definite proof that Iggy doesn't just have the whanger of the week but the yardarm of the year. Full frontal! The words inside are split between song lyrics, a foreword by Andy Warhol (scream!), a couple of poems, an album discography, a short section by Ms. Wehrer (apparently a lady of 50 who somehow fell under Iggy's spell) and a lot of amusing, fragmentary and half-assed reminiscences which seem to conveniently skate over periods when the 'star' found his light extinguished. No mention of his child, Nijinsky, John Cale, etc, but still a quite undemanding fun read if you're interested.

THE ILLUSTRATED BOOK OF ROCK RECORDS: A BOOK OF LISTS VOLUME 2
Barry Lazell & Dafydd Rees
(Virgin)
Remaindering unwanted books has gone out of fashion: excess copies of Volume 1 were packaged inside a cardboard jukebox with an easter egg! The authors claim that the first volume provided many a lazy Dee Jay with a conversational crutch: in this reviewer's household it caused queues at the bathroom door. Unfortunately, the authors use their own charts as a source of positions for records – irritating for the rock historian or purist. But then Volume 2, as with its predecessor, will probably be better received by constipated radio personalities.

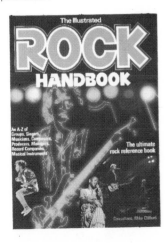

THE ILLUSTRATED ROCK HANDBOOK
(Salamander)
Attractively illustrated, mostly well researched biographies and discographies of most of the people you'd expect. Irritating in its inconsistencies, though: Adam and the Ants' "Kings Of The Wild Frontier" is referred to as a "minor hit" in their biography and is subsequently revealed to have reached No.2 in the charts.

THE INTERNATIONAL ENCYCLOPEDIA OF HARD ROCK & HEAVY METAL
Tony Jasper & Derek Oliver
(Sidgwick & Jackson)
Laughable example of a never-mind-the-quality – feel-the-width metal handbook. Tony Jasper may know something about Cliff Richard, but this 400 page paperback (no pics) will do his credibility with hard rockers very little good. The jacket claims he has an audience of 15 million for a heavy metal radio show he presents each week on SSVC Radio. Curiously, no one of our acquaintance has ever heard of it, but that's obviously our problem. Anyway, a good example of the precision with which this epic was written can be found under the entry for "Shanghai" which begins "Shanghai featured Mike Green (ex-Pirates) and drummer Pete Kirsher (now with Status Quo)." Two errors relating to names in one sentence...and the cover features a picture of Mick Box!

THE JAM: A BEAT CONCERTO – THE AUTHORIZED BIOGRAPHY
Paulo Hewitt
(Omnibus)
Paul Weller's intro claims: "...there is no more to be said on the Jam's formation and rise than is contained in this book." That's debatable; it's the official Weller line mostly, but at least that means that this interesting and easy-flowing biog comes from the inside and is free of opinionated rock-journalese and pretentious analyses. We're taken step-by-step through The Jam's evolution and Weller's influences. The Who, Kinks, Beatles, Dr. Feelgood, punk, The Clash all changed him. His parents even cut off the phone in order to buy him an amp. Pics could be better.

JIMMY PAGE – TANGENTS WITHIN A FRAMEWORK
Howard Mylett
(Omnibus)
Howard Mylett is magnificently obsessed with Jimmy Page, and has already penned a couple of Led Zep books which fail to provide much in the way of the insight that contact with the subject might suggest. For all his knowledge of his subject, without direct access to Page, Mylett is unable to penetrate the veil of secrecy that has traditionally surrounded the guitarist. If and when an authorised Jimmy Page biography is written, it'll probably tell a somewhat different story, but until then, this is impressively factual about the music without shedding any light on Page the man other than what is already known.

JOHN LENNON – IN MY LIFE
Pete Shotton and Nicholas Schaffner
(Coronet)
It's a logical fact of life that the best stories come not from ex-wives sacked band members, former business acquaintances or old managers. They come from mates. Pete Shotton claims to have been John Lennon's best friend and with anecdotes-a-go-go from childhood pranks to drug busts, there's plenty of evidence here to support the claim. No interrogation of schoolmasters or neighbours; no deep psychological analysis; no *conclusions*. Shotton and Schaffner just keep churning out the stories and they tell you more about Lennon than a million "in-depth" interviews. Like many others, Shotton ultimately fell foul of Yoko (she bore him a grudge and tried to prevent him visiting right up to Lennon's death) and subsequently there's little about the post-Beatle Lennon; but it is nevertheless a delightfully entertaining, unpretentious little effort.

JOHN WINSTON LENNON: VOLUME 1 1940-1966
Ray Coleman
(Sidgwick & Jackson)
Despite a pathological dislike of all self-proclaimed "definitive" biographies, it must be admitted that this is far, far more than just another Beatles book. Coleman's 20-year stint with *Melody Maker* coincided with Lennon's recording career and facilitated their friendship, but it's the well-researched and graphically descriptive early chapters covering Lennon's formative years that make this addictive reading. There surely can't be many more worthwhile books on the Fab Four still in the making, but this was worth the wait. Roll on Volume 2...

LADY SINGS THE BLUES
Billie Holiday with William Dufty
(Penguin)
First published in 1956, the autobiography of one of the jazz vocal greats does more than tell the sad story of a talent bedevilled by heroin addiction. Its powerful indictment of the racism endemic in US society of the Thirties and Forties make it particularly suitable that Diana Ross starred in the book's screenplay, *Lady Sings The Blues*; Holiday broke down the barriers for today's black superstars.

LED ZEPPELIN – HM PHOTO BOOK
(Omnibus)
96 pages, half in colour of OK pics of probably the first heavy metal group of the early

Seventies (apparently they hated to be categorised as HM). Short but competent biog.

THE LOVE YOU MAKE: AN INSIDER'S STORY OF THE BEATLES
Peter Brown and Steven Gaines
(Pan)
Beatle businessman Brown's semi-ghosted Beatle biog aroused instant interest with its controversial 'revelation' of a homosexual affair between Epstein and Lennon: will the boy who whispered necrophilia *please* leave the classroom? Page 84 apart, this provides a few new angles on an oft-told story, leaving the reader, like the hapless Eppy, "as hollow as before." Shout it ain't...a disappointment it most certainly is.

LOVING JOHN
May Pang and Henry Edwards
(Warner Books/Corgi)
The continuing posthumous demolition of John Lennon. Pan was the Lennons' secretary and, purportedly at Yoko's instruction, John's lover during the year he spent wasting time in Los Angeles. Her portrait of John is of an always self-pitying, occasionally violent drunk whom Yoko got to return to her through hypnosis. Very a-mistress-remembers in tone, its saving grace is that it provides the most thorough account to date of the grisly sessions with Phil Spector for the *Rock 'n' Roll* album.

KAJAGOOGOO – THE OFFICIAL LYRIC BOOK
Pearce Marchbank
(Omnibus)
Another stapled magazine-type book, with 17 smudgily-printed pics. Fawning introduction by Paul Gambaccini, 4-full colour pics and pull-out colour poster. Lyrics to nine songs. Dated as Limahl is in all the pics but left the group shortly after the book came out.

THE KINKS – THE SOUND AND THE FURY
Johnny Rogan
(Elm Tree)
The latest in Rogan's splendidly researched series about keynote acts of the '60s and '70s, this book provides an alternative to the 'official' story of a group who have rarely been granted the accolades so richly deserve in this country, although their status in the United States largely compensates. However, if there is more than a grain of truth in Rogan's assertions and conclusions, there is a dark and somewhat self-destructive streak pervading the frequently superb songs of Ray Davies. Some alarming suggestions are made (supported by first hand interviews, although not with either Ray or Dave Davies, of course). Heavy.

MICHAEL JACKSON – BODY AND SOUL
Geoff Brown
(Virgin)
If Michael Jackson can sell records and videos by the warehouseload, then surely a book should do likewise? If Michael could ever be persuaded to *say* anything, you'd have the best-selling rock book of all time. Until his authorised biog comes out, this one will do. There are few quotes, even from the early days; and *Time Out* critic Brown relies on a former Motown employee for most of his first-hand reminiscences. Photo-

graphically it's no more than adaquate, and wasting one and a half pages on pictures of the Patridge Family, "a manufactured rival to the J5", is nothing more than blatant padding.

MICHAEL! THE MICHAEL JACKSON STORY
Mark Bego
(Zomba)

Already a big seller, to some extent because it seems to have been the first MJ book to hit the shops, although this should not be allowed to detract from the fact that it seems superior to many of its rivals, if perhaps less informative than Geoff Brown's MJ book. Number two in a field of dozens isn't bad.

MICHAEL JACKSON
(Omnibus)

Tacky attempt to cash-in on Jacksonmania with stapled 32-page glossy mag containing 20 pics printed in bluish/reddish bilge. Pull-out poster in proper colour. Minimal history and brief "in his own words" type of hype. Surely even Jackson zealots will think twice about this grubby offering? Contender for "Rip-Off Of The Year" award.

MUSIC MANIA
Robyn Flans
(Starbooks)

A superficial, 96-page review of rock music since The Beatles put together with little regard for accuracy (John Lennon is pictured as a left handed guitarist, a very shortlived version of The Byrds has each of the four group members incorrectly indentified) or for anything other than the personal prejudices of the author. The information seems to include little that isn't already very well known, although a whole chapter on Journey seems a bit over the top in a book which doesn't mention The Pistols but does find room for The Go-Gos. Designed for America, obviously.

THE NEW ROCK 'N' ROLL
Stuart Coupe & Glenn A. Baker
(Omnibus)

An A-Z job on the post-punk bands, starting with ABC and going through to Moon Unit Zappa. There's a certain curiosity value in the fact that the authors are both based in Australia, which Miles' introduction attempts to persuade us gives them an enlightened perspective free of British and American chauvinistic consideration. It also means we have a lot of oddly-named Australian and Japanese bands included (try Deckchairs Overboard, or The Hoodoo Gurus, or RC Succession or Hajime Tachibana) while the sharp turnover of bands gives the book an inevitable built-in obsolesence. The information on the bands – factual and in no

way opinionated – seems sound enough, but the concept is full of holes.

OZZY OSBOURNE – HM PHOTO BOOK
(Omnibus)

Good pics – best colour pics of HM series – and short biog. 96 pages, 48 in quality colour.

PAPA JOE'S BOYS – THE JACKSONS STORY
Leonard Pitts Jr.
(Starbooks)

Another 96 pager from the same source as *Music Mania*, with lots of poorly reproduced pictures (blame the paper quality rather than the research). To give credit where its due, at least the jacket picture is of the group, and you-know-who isn't individually mentioned on the outside. File next to all the other MJ books – certainly no better, but no worse than several of the others.

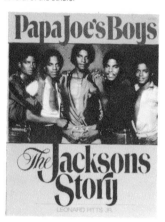

PHOTOGRAPHS
Annie Leibovitz
(Pantheon Books/Thames & Hudson)

As Tom Wolfe correctly notes in his introduction, photography has replaced folk singing as the favourite delusion of young Americans who want to change their lives; the star status accorded to Leibovitz by *Rolling Stone* over the past decade-and-a-half, has been a contributing factor. A fine orthodox photographer – her black-and-white portraits of the Stones are remarkable – and an inventive and obviously persuasive scene-setter, she is finally a little too self-conscious to be a great one yet.

PINK FLOYD
Miles
(Omnibus)

"The first major book on Pink Floyd and the nearest to an official biography of one of the world's biggest-selling bands." Maybe so, but it's *not* an official biography and is scarcely the tome hard-core Floydrophiles would claim their heroes' music merits. There are some fascinating stories, particularly from the early days, but no real insight or overview of the demons that drove Syd Barrett and Roger Waters. Well illustrated, but the whole thing has a disappointingly perfunctory air that's out of keeping with the nature of the band.

PHOTOGRAPHED BY LYNN GOLDSMITH

THE POLICE
Lynn Goldsmith
(Vermilion)

Similar to Pennie Smith's excellent photo book on The Clash, Lynn Goldsmith's large format book of black-and-white pics benefits greatly from her being on the inside. Split into pics of Sting, Stewart, and Andy, pics are linked to an aphorism (eg Sting sitting backstage has underneath, 'Somebody's boring me – I think it's me'/Dylan Thomas). This doesn't always work but pics do. Very droolable.

THE POLICE CHRONICLES
Philip Kamin & Peter Goddard
(Virgin)

"This is not a book about a tour" runs the intro blurb. "It's about one concert near the end of a tour." In which case, howcum Sting's golden countenance gazes out on the cover legend "From Beginning to End: The Story and Latest Photographs"? Sounds like a case for the Trades Description Act, right? Right!

THE RISE AND FALL OF ROCK
Jeff Kent
(Witan Books)

The right to publish your own book is one that should be defended to the death, although when reading a self published book (as this is), it sometimes becomes clear why self publication was necessary. Leaving aside the political bias of the introduction, Kent is less than accurate in the 'facts' which he states – for example, 'Ebony Eyes' was not a number one record, Marty Wilde's real name was not Reg Scott (it was Smith), Johnny Preston (of 'Running Bear' fame) was not English. But where the whole thing becomes ludicrous is when you read that "Greasy Bear was probably the greatest of all Country Rock bands and one of the top groups of all time." I rest my case.

THE ROCK ALBUM VOLUME TWO
Maxim Jakubowski
(Zomba)

The second volume (in slightly smaller format) of Jakubowski's often amusing series in which he reviews every album released during a year, in this case 1983. Just how valuable his criticism/praise may be is obviously for the individual to decide, but at a time when there's so much vinyl shovelled on the market (much of it doing little more than hastening the next petrol crisis), the serious collector can use this book for reference purposes.

ROCK EXPLOSION – THE BRITISH INVASION IN PHOTOS 1962-1967
Harold Bronson
(Rhino Books)

This is an example of the right way to put together a book of this type – Harold, the Anglophile who runs the very wonderful Rhino Records label in Los Angeles, has uncovered a tasty selection of historic and amusing photos of the notable and not so notable (like The Silkie or The Applejacks), along with less well known shots of The Beatles, The Stones and The Who. Thrill to the sight of Carol Wayne chopping up a TV set, Wayne Fontana with hair, David Jones on his way to becoming David Bowie. . . A few captioning errors (nothing serious), but overall a volume to treasure if you were there in those fabulous Sixties, and maybe if you weren't. Ace.

ROCK FAMILY TREES VOLUME 2
Pete Frame
(Omnibus)

Frame is the best historian of popular music in the world, simply by conveying the necessary information with the minimum of waffle. When he does give an opinion it's usually an interesting one, thrown in almost as an after-thought. Graphically labyrinthine and extraordinary as ever.

ROCK ODYSSEY
Ian Whitcomb
(Hutchinson)

An engaging and quite lengthy hardback written by erstwhile hitmaker and music historian Whitcomb, author of two or three other 'Rock History' volumes. This one seems to centre on the sixties, which so many people (this writer included) would like to see return, at least in spirit. Probably not a suitable purchase for those whose knowledge of the rock genre is limited, as there are tendencies towards over generalisation, but a good fun read for anyone who loves the era. Well written, but under illustrated.

ROCKSPEAK!
Tom Hibbert
(Omnibus)

Subtitled "the dictionary of rock terms", a dry, funny, revealing compendium of 30 years of pop slang, sometimes illustrated by examples. Compulsive reading which exercises a grisly fascination. In some circles, much more useful than an ordinary dictionary.

THE ROLLING STONE ENCYCLOPEDIA OF ROCK & ROLL
John Pareles & Patricia Romanowski
(Michael Joseph)

Unashamedly American-biased in its selection criteria, the *Encyclopedia* nevertheless affords an enormous amount of information in a handily-sized paperback volume. Blots its copybook rather with specious half-page 'category' entries (on death rock, one-hit wonders etc) and, irritatingly, with birthdates – the editors can't seem to make up their minds if they're important or not! Whatever, it's a fair bet that Duran Duran will improve on their current one paragraph in the reprint – and there'll undoubtedly be several of those.

SOFT CELL
Simon Tebbutt
(Sidgwick & Jackson)

An authorised biography by a writer from *Record Mirror* which, not surprisingly, includes a great many well reproduced pictures and not too much in the way of text. Chainsaws, dwarves, mutilated people, sub-Berlin sleaze and everything you might expect from a book about Marc Almond, including pictures of Marc with Warhol and Divine. Tebbut is described as "a close personal friend of the band", which gives some indication of his (lack of) objectivity, but then a heavy put-down would probably have been too obvious and simple.

THE SONGWRITER'S RHYMING DICTIONARY
Sammy Cahn
(Souvenir Press)

Veteran Sinatra songwriter Cahn donates his trade secrets to posterity in a witty introdcution before leaving the reader to get on with the job. An invaluable possession if music's your profession.

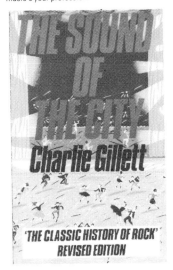

THE SOUND OF THE CITY
Charlie Gillet
(Souvenir)

First published in 1971 and now revised, this excellent fact-filled volume could easily claim to be the definitive history of rock. Examines the circumstances that produced rock 'n' roll and documents it's evolution over it's major period, 1954-1971. Its 500 pages of accurate, well-researched, well-informed information on styles, artists and record labels are both a good read and a valuable reference book. Well-indexed. In a class of its own.

SPANDAU BALLET – IN THEIR OWN WORDS
(Omnibus)

32-page stapled magazine format. Over 40 black-and-white pics, two colour, pull-out colour poster and lots of quotes revealing how highly they regard themselves. However no matter how much they go on about being stylish, they look distinctly wallyish in many of the photos.

THE STONES
Philip Norman
(Elm Tree/Hamish Hamilton)

Stylish, authoritative and painstakingly researched, this is clearly a determined crack at the definitive Stones biography. Hugely readable and much more engrossing than Norman's previous epic on The Beatles (*Shout*) – though with the Stones he *does* have rather more dramatic material to work on – the early years are especially well documented. There are some appetising revelations (Brian Jones was up for dumping Jagger at one point and Andrew Oldham was given to swanning around enjoying the protection of a bodyguard named Reg The Butcher!) but Norman's irritating verbosity often clouds the issue. He also shows an alarming habit of getting sidetracked by favourite members of the supporting cast, notably Oldham and Marianne Faithfull, who is dealt with in embarrassingly sympathetic detail, and occupies as much space as Bill Wyman, Charlie Watts, Ronnie Wood and Mick Taylor put together. Jagger, naturally, tends to be the main focus of the book and comes out of it as a spoilt brat, on an eternal quest for social status, which makes an admirable foil for the colourful narrative inspired by the Jones/Richard/Pallenburg triology. The clash of mountainous egos, violent death, drug busts, sickening decadence. . . Norman's commentary runs out of steam around the mid-Seventies, but it's still *the* classic rock 'n' roll story expertly told.

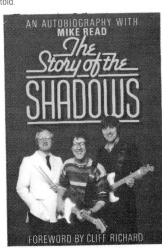

THE STORY OF THE SHADOWS
Mike Read
(Elm Tree)

114 pages on the period up to the end of 1961, 76 pages on '62 to '68, and 44 pages on '69 to '83, which is probably about the right weight in terms of the significance of Hank Marvin and his pals. A book that needed to be written, although without any dramatic new insights, especially in view of the fact that Marvin, Bruce Welch and Brian Bennett are credited on the copyright page, but with some good snaps from various family albums. Far too expensive as a hardback – wait until the paperback if you're really interested.

THOMPSON TWINS – IN THEIR OWN WORDS
Pearce Marchbank
(Omnibus)

32-page stapled magazine with 30 posey pics in black and red, plus usual selected quotes which seem to be soley about themselves. 'Giant' colour poster. Of interest only to Thompson Twins fans. Design a bit better than usual for this series (see Duran Duran).

THROB
Andy Summers
(William Morrow/Sidgwick & Jackson)

Large glossy of personal photographs taken by Police guitarist Andy Summers. Seems as though he's just bought all the Nikon accessories and gadgets, but this results in interesting experimental shots and delayed time pics of himself, etc. Impressive and varied collection ranging in mood from serious and reflective to quite comical, including extreme close-up of toothbrush, shadowy hotel rooms, the odd nude or two, exotic settings, foreign characters, and Sting. More of a real photography 'art' book than the rock 'n' roll life on the road account advertised. Well printed.

UP-TIGHT – THE VELVET UNDERGROUND STORY
Victor Bockris/Gerard Malanga
(Omnibus)

Follows career of Velvets mainly through collection of interesting and revealing interviews with main participants, particularly bassist Sterling Morrison, but also Lou Reed, John Cale, Andy Warhol and others. Good insight into characters involved with one of the first and most important American avant-garde rock groups. Successfully gets across flavour of times and the whole experimental NY art rock theatre period with mixed media events like Warhol's 'Exploding Plastic Inevitable'. Definitely the inside story. Well illustrated.

VAN MORRISON – A PORTRAIT OF THE ARTIST
Johnny Rogan
(Elm Tree)

Rogan's by now familiar style (previous subjects include The Byrds and Neil Young) zeroes in on the enigmatic Van, to its subject's intense disapproval apparently. Infinitely superior to Richie Yorke's pseudo authorised book of some years ago, but perhaps unfortunately over reliant on others who claimed to be friends of Van's rather than on the subject himself. Nevertheless, an exhaustive historical biography in many ways, and the most informative book thus far on one of the finest and most influential rock stars ever.

THE VIDEO YEARBOOK
Angela & Elkan Allan
(Virgin)

1983's 700 best tapes given the once-over in short order, but the fast-moving video market renders any publicatioon of this nature outdated as quickly as the copies roll off the press. A brave try.

WAITING FOR THE BEATLES
Carol Bedford
(Blandford)

The story of the "Apple Scruffs" by one of them, and a fairly fascinating read which illustrates the obsessional love for The Beatles which female American teenagers seemed uniquely to possess. This one apparently had the hots for George, although, like so many, she originally fancied Ringo. Once you've been through all the John Lennon biogs and the often pathetic kiss-and-tell books by close associates, a book like this comes as something of a relief.

WHEN CAMERAS GO CRAZY – CULTURE CLUB
Kasper de Graaf & Malcolm Garrett
(Virgin)

Success in 18 chapters – the time it takes to flick from George's baby pics (Chapter 3) to the Number 1 spot (Chapter 21). Press cuttings chronicle the Boy's triumphant procession from public enemy to media darling, while a couple of spreads of fan portraits and one of George lookalikes (female, as far as the eye can discern) add colour to what is mostly a monochrome volume. Real time-capsule stuff, this – if you consider it as a social document rather than a slim book of fan fodder, the £3.95 might seem a little more reasonable!

YARDBIRDS
John Platt, Chris Dreja, Jim McCarty
(Sidgwick & Jackson)

Based on memories of rhythm guitarist Dreja and drummer McCarty. Gives interesting inside story of one of the most influential Sixties club bands who took over coveted residency at Crawdaddy club vacated by The Stones in 1963. Successfully captures magical, exciting and promising atmosphere of period – one can almost taste the Richmond L'Auberge coffee bar frothy coffee and smell the sweat in the Eel Pie Island Hotel. Curiously for a group that boasted Clapton, Beck and Page as successive lead guitarists, their records seemed a bit of a pop-out compared to their great live R & B stage work. Good pics. Very readable insight into Sixties group life.

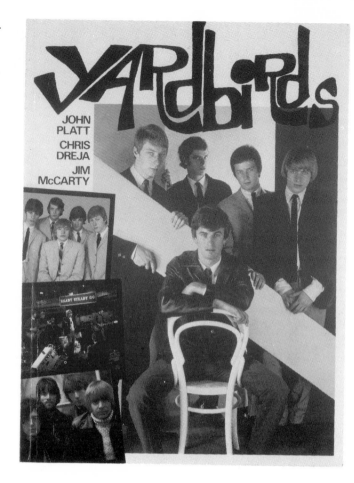

VIDEO REVIEWS
by Dessa Fox and Adam Sweeting

THE BAND
The Band Is Back
(Videoform, 90 minutes)
Well, *most* of The Band is back – missing is guitarist and key-man Robbie Robertson, presumably out on location somewhere with Martin Scorsese. Standing in on guitar is somebody called Earl Cate, who does a pretty fair impersonation of Robbie's spikey, cartwheeling lines. There are also additional men on bass and drums, which seems a little unnecessary when you already have Rick Danko and Levon Helm playing them. However, the old songs emerge sounding still pretty fine after all these years – among others, you'll find 'The Weight', 'Rag Mama Rag', 'King Harvest Is Surely Come', 'Long Black Veil' and 'Up On Cripple Creek'. The concert footage (shot in Vancouver) is intercut with interviews with the four remaining Bandsmen, suspiciously similar to Scorsese's technique in *The Last Waltz*. Actually, they seem a little less stoned here, though Levon Helm now seems to feel he's the leader of the group and consequently can't be made to shut up. A better cassette than might have been anticipated but still mainly of curiosity value.

AMERICAN HEARTBEAT
(CBS/Fox, 40 minutes)
A companion cassette to *Rock Cocktail*, and more US-style rock acts – Blue Oyster Cult's 'Don't Fear The Reaper', Toto's 'Africa', 'Eye Of The Tiger' from Survivor, 'Keep On Loving You' from REO Speedwagon...must I go on?

BAUHAUS
Shadow Of Light
(Kace International, 40 minutes)
I gather there may still be some Bauhaus fans at large, and if so, this is for them. *Shadow Of Light* comprises three tracks recorded live onstage at London's Old Vic theatre alongside promotional sequences for several of their best-loved numbers. The promo for 'Mask' takes Bauhausism about as far as it could go, with its shots of moonlight on ruined castles and corpses shedding skins. Also on display – 'Bella Lugosi's Dead', 'Telegram Sam', 'Ziggy Stardust' and 'She's In Parties'.

BIG COUNTRY
Big Country Live
(Polygram, 75 minutes)
Big Stuart Adamson and his tartan-clad rockers invade Glasgow's Barrowland Ballroom for a New Year's Eve rave-up, and see the fans go ape! Big Country's material is completely daffy when you look closely, but here onstage you can see why they get the crowd going. Songs like 'Chance', 'Porrohman' and 'Fields Of Fire' make full use of the simplest rock dynamics, lavishly decorated with huge droning guitars in the Celtic manner. Just add tartan shirts and scarves and a batch of pipers to play in the New Year and you've almost got a riot on your hands. Clearly an occasion, but how often could you sit through it?

DAVID BOWIE
Video EP
(EMI, 12 minutes)
You've probably seen the three promos collected here ad naseum, but for the record, you get David Mallet's efforts for 'Let's Dance' and 'China Girl' plus Jim Yukich's 'Modern Love' sequence. Some (like me) might argue that none of them lived up to their pre-publicity – 'Let's Dance' seems oddly scrappy, 'Modern Love' is basically the Serious Moonlight band onstage, while the few seconds of David's naked bottom in 'China Girl' hardly ranks as one of the great erotic moments of cinema.

DAVID BOWIE

DAVID BOWIE
Serious Moonlight
(Videoform, 50 minutes)
The album, the books, the tour...can you afford the video too? Being Bowie, *Moonlight* is breathtakingly slick. After all, the band were rehearsed to the hilt for live video-screen projection while playing, so naturally director David Mallet has little difficulty in making immaculate sense of lighting and camera angles. Let's face it, Bowie looks great and songs like 'Let's Dance', 'Fashion', 'Cat People' and 'China Girl' more than do justice to his haircut. This man has his whole life planned to the last detail.

DAVID BOWIE
Ziggy Stardust And The Spiders From Mars
(EMI, 97 minutes)
Well, what a time for Bowie – first the album and tour and movies, now a whole batch of videos. *Ziggy Stardust* is a movie of Bowie's final Hammersmith concert as the eponymous rock star, and is mostly band and audience apart from a few backstage glimpses of the glamorous rocker recovering from another exhausting costume change. Though Bowie apparently fussed endlessly over the sound mix, the music and The Spiders sound dreadful – clumsy, out of tune and unimaginative. Tracks include stuff like 'Rock'n'Roll

Suicide', 'Moonage Daydream' and 'Suffragette City', while David plays the camp narcissist to the hilt with Jacques Brel's dolorous 'My Death'. Strange tales from a strange time, most of them ludicrous. It all looks terribly dated now.

DAVID BOWIE
Love You Till Tuesday
(Polygram, 30 minutes)
Bowie as ex-hippie, 14 years before 'Serious Moonlight' and shortly after 'Laughing Gnome'. The primitive version of 'Space Oddity' included among the nine tracks here may hint at nascent superstar potential, but frankly you could have fooled me. Then again, his catastrophic efforts at mime would later become legendary too, so don't take my word for it. Time to fork out again, fans.

THE CHERRY RED VIDEO
Pillows And Prayers
(PVG, 31 minutes)
An entirely praiseworthy 'theme' cassette, the general frame of things being "the secure gardens, the warm evenings in front of the TV, the fond memories of your youth." Featuring – among others – Fantastic Something, Eyeless In Gaza, The Monochrome Set, The Marine Girls strolling by the beach, and Kevin Hewick at an existential tea party. Director Christopher Robin Collins balances the fairground and hedgerow shots with old Cadbury adverts and a lightheartedly psychosexual duet by Honor Blackman and Patrick MacNee, 'Kinky Boots'.

MONOCHROME SET

PHIL COLLINS
Video EP
(PMI, 16 minutes)
A four-bead strand of so-so promos: 'In The Air Tonight', 'I Missed Again', 'Through These Walls', and – the only real sparkler of the bunch – 'You Can't Hurry Love'. Collins is a poor actor but seems to genuinely agonise over his songs, which means you can forgive him for that hideous bathrobe in 'Through These Walls'.

COOL CATS
25 Years Of Rock'n'Roll Style
(MGM, 76 minutes)
Although lush with rivetting slices of history, this one makes the mistake of dwelling overlong on the views of 'pundits'. Nothing kills the subject of style quicker than sociological analyses, especially those of questionable experts like Vidal Sassoon (!). Phil Everly's definition of cool is all we ever needed: "anything that makes the girls scream". Still, fascination is delivered in the form of Elvis clips, very early Blondie, and Bowie's 'Boys Keep Swinging' video.

PATRICK MACNEE AND HONOR BLACKMAN

CULTURE CLUB
A Kiss Across The Ocean
(Virgin, 60 minutes)

A live recording of The Club onstage at Hammersmith Odeon, but director Keith MacMillan has taken extensive steps to ensure that this is a cut or two above the average in-concert cassette. An elaborate digital recording proves conclusively that Culture Club is a versatile and authoritative unit, while George's winsome crowd appeal is here in all its powder-and-lipstick close-up. You name 'em, they're here – 'Do You Really Want To Hurt Me', 'Black Money', 'Church Of The Poison Mind', 'It's A Miracle', 'Karma Chameleon' etc. Big, bold close-ups and exotic backdrops maintain visual interest, but it's George's show all the way. Even Helen Terry can't come close to upstaging him. I think this may be what they mean by 'entertainment'.

DIO
Live In Concert
(Polygram, 60 minutes)

Mr. Ronnie James Dio once appeared on the front cover of *Sounds*, which is where he should have stayed. Here, before a bunch of Dutch people in Utrecht, he bewilders us with his heavy metal band, gruff wailing voice and mock-Wagnerian stage sets (mountains made of tinsel). Songs include 'Stand Up And Shout', 'Shame On The Night' and the morose 'Children Of The Sea'. Everywhere, Viv Campbell plays very fast guitar solos and stands with his legs apart. Most peculiar.

DIRE STRAITS
Alchemy
(PVG, 90 minutes)

More than competent, but you have to be a D.S. fan to fully succeed in loving this one. 'Romeo And Juliet' and the theme from the film 'Local Hero' stir the blood a bit, but otherwise its gently weeping guitarists' night down at the Hammy Odeon.

THOMAS DOLBY
Live Wireless
(PMI, 58 minutes)

In which Dolby wisely re-invents himself. The stage performance feels old, dating as it does from the *Wireless* LP, and features the chalk-suit era Dolby, a strangely 2-D character whose wit and genuine inventiveness almost never travelled beyond the microphone. Fortunately, a newer, moodier Dolby pops up in a sub-plot. Said device saves the whole enterprise from gadgeteerism; the remodeled Dolby is an altogether looser guy, given to smoking in the shadows and letting the machines get out of control.

CULTURE CLUB

Overall, a funny, likeable, and extremely well-crafted tape, with just enough spicy technology to keep things ticking along. Bonus: not only does Dolby devise a snappy way of thanking his band, but the production crew are credited as well. A generous first.

EURYTHMICS
Sweet Dreams
(RCA, 66 minutes)

Eurythmics are one of a handful of acts who've really made video work for them, extending meaning and metaphor beyond their music, but this collection of live material from a gig at London's Heaven (very dated, too) plus a few promos doesn't do them justice. Stuff like 'Jennifer' and 'Somebody Told Me' are good enough, likewise the matchless promos for 'Who's That Girl' and 'Love Is A Stranger', but it's basically a mish-mash. Dave and Annie will undoubtedly do better than this when they get around to it.

THE FALL
Perverted By Language
(Ikon, 53 minutes. Available from Ikon F.C.L., 86 Palatine Road, West Didsbury, Manchester 20)

An insightful cassette from the Mancunian independents about more Mancunian independents. Quite possibly worth the price of admission for the live-in-New York version of the epic 'Totally Wired', but there's much more besides – Mark E. Smith talking rather cautiously about himself, a curious recital of 'The Confidence Of Henry Glaspance', and the mutant promo for 'Kicker Conspiracy'. Informal, informative and essential viewing for Fall fans.

THOMAS DOLBY

FAME LIVE AT THE ROYAL ALBERT HALL
(MGM/UA, 75 minutes)

Erica Gimpel, one of those charming girls from *Fame*, steps to the microphone and tells us about her time at The New York School For The Performing Arts. "I learned a really valuable lesson there...it's about believing in yourself..." This whole performance yells "ME!" at deafening volume, from Debbie Allen's brash and faintly lascivious Daisy Parker routine to Lori Singer's absurd attempts to play an electric cello during the backing band's version of 'Don't Stop Till You Get Enough'. And so on. It's difficult to say whether this lot actually have any talent or just a cringe-inducing lack of self-consciousness. Also includes 'Desdemona', 'Hi-Fidelity' and 'We Got The Power'. Not for the squeamish.

MARVIN GAYE
Marvin Gaye Live
(Videoform, 55 minutes)

Well, here's a surprise. The tragic demise of the great Marvin in early '84 seemed to pass with scandalously little furore, but this live performance filmed in Amsterdam is an astoundingly good requiem. Gaye, backed by a huge band, runs the whole gamut of his career, from a medley including the likes of 'Ain't That Peculiar', 'Heard It Through The Grapevine' and 'How Sweet It Is' to the epic, explosive 'What's Going On'. The band provides wonderfully agile and sympathetic support, ranging from the near-orchestral to the sinewy funk drive of 'Let's Get It On'. Gaye even re-enacts his various boy-girl duets in a medley with Florence Lyles which takes in 'You're All I Need To Get By', 'Ain't Nothin' Like The Real Thing' and the superb 'It Takes Two'. There's no 'Sexual Healing', unfortunately, but there's plenty to illustrate Gaye's remarkable ability to integrate that yearning voice into lush instrumental tapestries. A valuable recording indeed.

GIRL GROUPS
The Story Of A Sound
(MGM, 62 minutes)

Includes The Ronettes 'Shout', Martha And The Vandellas' 'Dancin' In The Streets', Little Eva's 'Locomotion', Mary Wells' 'My Guy', five tracks from The Supremes, The Dixie Cups, Dee Dee Sharp, The Shangri-Las, and The Marvelettes. With a playlist like this, you know the proceedings are going to be eminently danceable. But its not all zest, and

neither is it a catalogue of hairdos; laced skillfully between the performances are some tangible insights into The Way Things Were (Mary Wilson's memories of Florence Ballard's unhappy place in The Supremes are particularly compelling). Wholeheartedly recommended.

DARYL HALL & JOHN OATES
Rock'n'Soul Live
(RCA, 101 minutes)

Well-shot and recorded concert featuring the soul-boys in arena-sized live action in Montreal. Most of the stuff you'd expect – 'Italian Girls', 'You've Lost That Lovin' Feeling', even the tearful 'She's Gone' – plus some breathtaking swooping camerawork. They've more rock than soul these days, but this is a good thorough job.

HERBIE HANCOCK
Herbie Hancock And The Rockit Band
(CBS/Fox, 73 minutes)

Fusionaut Herbie leaves behind his more cerebral musical explorations in favour of scratch-mixes, rhythm machinery of many hues, and those creepy robot legs that look like something Terry Gilliam might have designed. This cassette was shot at the Hammersmith Odeon and Camden Palace, and brings on shocking spasms of late-night dancefloor déjà-vu (flashing lights and computer drums, aaargh). Also included are the videos for 'Autodrive' (many disconnected hands) and 'Rockit' (more robots). Hi-tech and very unfriendly. (*Dessa Fox challenges Adam's assessment in The Year In Video's Top Five, page 34 – ed*).

HERBIE HANCOCK

HANOI ROCKS
All Those Wasted Years
(Kace International, 55 minutes)

It appears that the Rocks boys themselves weren't too impressed with this offering, originally intended as a one-off TV special, but they shouldn't torture themselves *too* much over it. Hanoi Rocks are a noisy glam-rock throwback, great in small doses. This tape goes on a bit, and the setting (London's Marquee club) offers little room for manoeuvre for band or cameras, but 'Oriental Beat', 'Back To Mystery City' and The Stooges' 'I Feel Alright' prove that the Rocks are noisy, messy and make some splendid guitar noises. Try it – they might surprise you.

HEAVEN 17

HEAVEN 17
Heaven 17's Industrial
Revolution
(Virgin, 23 minutes)
This consists of six Heaven 17 promotional videos collected together, with various results. All these sequences are inevitably coloured by Heaven 17's analytical intelligence, though the jumble of chromakey effects and images of treadmills, typewriters, leisure and labour in 'Crushed By The Wheels Of Industry' suggests plenty of ideas but little ability to control them. However, 'Penthouse And Pavement', directed by Steve Barron, is a slick and intriguing piece about life at the top and espionage of both private and public kinds, while 'Let Me Go' makes fine monochrome use of a deserted City Of London. 'Temptation' and 'Come Live With Me' ring more changes on the themes of sexual ownership and identity, but 'We Live So Fast' is drab and disappointing. On the whole, though, a collection of a better class of promo.

BILLY IDOL
Dancing With Myself
(Palace, 12 minutes)
Sorry, can't see it meself. Three promos for three entirely merit-free songs. In 'White Wedding', we see girls' bottoms tightly encased in black plastic, while 'Hot In The City' is all about missiles being launched and H-bombs going off. All the while, Billy Idol pouts and poses as though this somehow *mattered*. The *piece-de-resistance* is supposedly the 'Dancing With Myself' promo itself, directed by Tobe Hooper and treated to mass media coverage in the States...but it's more second-hand after-the-holocaust stuff, all zombies in tatters. A bit like a jeans advertisement, in fact. Avoid.

BILLY IDOL

MICHAEL JACKSON
The Making Of Michael
Jackson's Thriller
(Vestron, 60 minutes)
One of the video events of the past year, young Michael's 'Thriller' extravaganza can now be shuddered at in the comfort of your own home. This cassette also gets behind the scenes (what Hollywood blockbuster doesn't have a "Making Of" to go with it these days?) and bungs in bits of 'Beat It', 'Billie Jean' (from the *Motown 25* special) and 'Can You Feel It' for good measure. What will the svelte trillionaire think of next?

THE JAM
Videosnap
(Polygram, 45 minutes)
A video accompaniment to the posthumous *Snap!* collection, *Videosnap* is mostly useful in demonstrating that The Jam delivered some peerless material in their time but usually made lousy videos to go with them. 'A Town Called Malice', for example, is accompanied by shots of Weller in a fog and Bruce Foxton playing bass next to a hat-stand, 'News Of The World' was filmed quite arbitrarily next to Battersea Power Station, and the least said about 'When You're Young' the better. Straightforward studio sequences, such as 'Going Underground' or 'In The City', work far more effectively with The Jam's hard, coiled attack. Stick to the record.

BILLY JOEL

BILLY JOEL
Live From Long Island
(CBS/Fox, 80 minutes)
Joel is apparently a native Long Islander, hence the ecstatic nature of his reception in front of an enormous home crowd. Joe, suit and sneakers akimbo, clearly thinks he's a pretty groovy kind of guy, and springs around the stage between keyboards to deliver the likes of 'My Life', 'Piano Man',

'Just The Way You Are' and 'Still Rock'n'Roll To Me'. It's noisy, theatrical and entertaining if you like that sort of thing. No sign of Christie Brinkley, unfortunately.

HOWARD JONES
Like To Get To Know
You Better
(Warner, 58 minutes)
Watch Howard Jones onstage in his home town High Wycombe, intercut with promotional videos for his hits like 'New Song', 'What Is Love' and 'Hide & Seek', and wonder what the hell happened to British pop, '84-style. Jones, a one-man bank of gadgetry and synths, writes watery little ditties about love and assorted other cosmic occurrences. Young girls seem to like him, but the reasons for this must remain shrouded in mystery.

HOWARD JONES

JUDAS PRIEST
Judas Priest Live
(CBS/Fox, 90 minutes)
How on earth (you might wonder) could you fill a 90 minute tape with Judas Priest? Good question. Answer: with dry ice, heavy metal thunder of the most oppressive kind, and the leathery cavortings of singer Rob Halford, who looks more like Python's Graham Chapman as the years tick cruelly by. Beats me.

KAJAGOOGOO
White Feathers Tour
(PMI, 59 minutes)
Recorded in May '83 at the Hammersmith Odeon, this Limahl-era performance pleased the ticketholders, anyway. Nick Beggs, as always, saves the proceedings from being just an exercise in stage lighting.

JERRY LEE LEWIS
Live
(CBS/Fox, 66 minutes)
The back of the package carries a prominent endorsement of the so-called "Killer" from the *NME*, but you'd be wise to ignore it. Lewis, live in London, is brash and confident to the point of complete indifference. His band is efficiently anonymous, and Jerry Lee attacks his piano remorselessly throughout endless rock'n'roll-style tunes. Staggeringly dull. .

LORDS OF THE NEW CHURCH

THE LORDS OF THE NEW CHURCH
Live From London
(Polygram, 60 minutes)
The unprepossessing Lords, an old tin can from the dustbin of time, may be studied here at leisure clanking their way through a set of such unmemorable songs as 'New Church', 'Johnny Too Bad', 'Black Girl! White Girl' and many more. Singer Stiv Bator, a kind of Bobby Bluebell from the wrong side of the tracks, barks his lyrics over the grinding metallic squawk of Brian James' lead guitar, sometimes appearing to be curiously out of synch. Could there be electrickery afoot? The audience, crushed into London's slippery Marquee, seem too numbed to notice. For addicts only.

MARILLION
Video EP
(EMI, 28 minutes)
Most of this cassette is taken up with a giant sprawling epic called *Grendel*, possibly a perfect summary of whatever the hell it is Marillion think they're playing at. Recorded live onstage at Hammersmith Odeon, it's got

KAJAGOOGOO

the lot – singer Fish's garish make-up, Steve Rothery's impassioned wailing guitar solo, mock-orchestral slow bits and loud bits in rotation. Also included is 'The Web', in which Fish destroys helpless plants and sucks his thumb. Help!

FISH

BOB MARLEY AND THE WAILERS
Legend – The Best Of Bob Marley And The Wailers
(Island, 57 minutes)

Released in conjunction with the LP of the same name, the video *Legend* gives you 13 video-assisted tracks charting the best-known stepping stones of Marley's career. In keeping with Island's commendably tactful treatment of the deceased superstar, the cassette has been put together with taste by Don Letts. Imagery ranges from the American Civil War setting of 'Buffalo Soldier', recording studios ('Redemption Song', 'Could You Be Loved') to the Wailers live onstage ('Jamming', 'I Shot The Sherriff'). It's a valuable memento and an excellent collection of music.

BOB MARLEY

NEW ORDER
Taras Shevchenko
(Ikon, 53 minutes)

A silent introductory collage of images gives way to an atmospheric tape of New Order live at New York's Ukrainian National Home in November '81. It's tastefully and atmospherically lit with fine sound quality, making 'Dreams Never End' tense, 'Everything's Gone Green' compelling and 'Temptation' as thrilling as ever. Sadly, New Order seem to have progressed little since, so treasure *Taras* while the going's good.

NOW THAT'S WHAT I CALL MUSIC
Vol. I
(Virgin/PMI, 75 minutes)
NOW THAT'S WHAT I CALL MUSIC
Vol. II
(Virgin/PMI, 78 minutes)

Vol. I includes Phil Collins' 'You Can't Hurry

Love', Duran Duran's 'Is There Something I Should Know', UB40's 'Red Red Wine', Heaven 17's 'Temptation', Freez's 'IOU', The Assembly's 'Never Never', Genesis' 'That's All', Howard Jones' 'New Song', Thompson Twins' 'Hold Me Now', Culture Club's 'Karma Chameleon', and Malcolm McLaren's 'Double Dutch'. Standouts: Will Powers' 'Kissing With Confidence' and UB40's unpretentiously dramatic 'Red Red Wine'.

Vol. II includes Nik Kershaw's 'Wouldn't It Be Good', China Crisis's 'Wishful Thinking', Thompson Twins' 'Doctor Doctor', Bourgie Bourgie's 'Breaking Point', Status Quo's 'Marguerita Time', Carmel's 'More More More', Shannon's 'Let The Music Play', Icicle Works' 'Birds Fly', Big Country's 'Wonderland', and Culture Club's 'Victims'. The cavalcade continues, with the only excessively painful bits being Marilyn's 'Cry And Be Free' and Re-Flex's 'Politics Of Dancing'.

GRAHAM PARKER
Live
(PGV, 60 minutes)

Dull, unfortunately (whatever happened to the 'Heat Treatment' Parker? This man could have been a contender). Parker and band seem stuck in beer-cellar bluesology: the whole thing is composed of blue jeans, blue light, and tarnished blue riffs. Much amplification, little satisfaction.

PICTURE MUSIC
A Compilation Of Contemporary Hit Videos
(PMI, 70 minutes)

A markedly elderly collection, 'Picture Music' includes Kim Carnes' 'Bette Davis Eyes', Undertones' 'It's Going To Happen', The Vapors' 'Turning Japanese', 'Abacab' from Genesis, and the Stranglers' 'Duchess'. Dr. Feelgood's 'Milk And Alcohol' is attractively

paranoid, while Bad Manners do a nice turn upending drinks over their heads in the rain. Archivist's lucky strike: Duran Duran's 'My Own Way' displays Andy Taylor with *blue hair*.

PIL
Live
(VIR, 40 minutes)

Featuring 'Public Image', 'Annalisa', 'Death Disco', 'This Is Not A Love Song' and 'Religion' (during which Lydon wears something that resembles a neon Polo mint around his neck – *and* manages to make this look like an enviable idea).

PiL play perfunctorily in front of two sets of audiences (Japanese and American), the members of which nosedive towards the stage in a vain effort to capture the camera crew's attention. Lydon, meanwhile, treats the camera like an insect about to be squashed. No one possesses an instinct for

being photographed like Lydon – its just too bad that three quarters of the music is plain tedious.

READY, STEADY, GO Vol. I
(PMI, 60 minutes)
READY, STEADY, GO Vol. II
(PMI, 55 minutes)

With The Who, Dusty Springfield, Cilla Black, The Beatles, Lulu, Gerry And The Pacemakers, Marvin Gaye, Gene Pitney, Them, Billy Fury, Cathy McGowan, Mick Jagger trying very hard not to be white, flower-shaped stickers on the walls, catwalks pre-dating *The Tube*, and a curiously un-slavish audience more interested in looking sharp than in looking at the bands. Bargains at twice the price.

THE REDSKINS
Beating The Blues
(Films At Work, 30 minutes, from Films At Work, 1a Terrace Road, London E9 7ES)

A rough-hewn but stimulating affair, this. X. Moore and his two fellow Redskins play what they refer to as "rebel soul" music, and the five numbers included here were recorded live in London for a broadcast by Capital Radio. 'Keep On Keeping On' is the best of them, but 'Kick Over The Statues' and 'Unionise' are also eloquent expositions of the band's guiding ideology. In between, fans and band get a chance to rant about music and politics, and the talk is kept refreshingly free of tedium thanks to the addition of assorted images and slogans. Altogether it's shrewd, provocative and good value for money.

LOU REED
A Night With Lou Reed
(RCA, 60 minutes)

All the fave hits, played with easy charm on the vocals but excessive power chording on the guitars. Reed receives a spinecurdlingly rude introduction: "the single most pervasive influence on new wave", etc. Ah, the American preoccupation with 'new wave'; y'mean Lou influenced A Flock Of Seagulls?

CLIFF RICHARD AND THE SHADOWS
Thank You Very Much
(PMI, 52 minutes)

A thoughtful, very well constructed tribute to twenty years of Cliff and The Shadows, incorporating a splashy (but not self-congratulatory) performance at the London Palladium in early '78. There are also views of a tight-trousered Cliff from the days of 'Oh Boy' and 'Expresso Bongo', together with some deftly edited cameo appearances from Adam Faith, Elton, and Olivia Newton-John. Cliff is eternally exuberant, and somehow also eternally puzzling.

ROCK COCKTAIL
(CBS/Fox, 36 minutes)

Presumably an MTV-inspired compilation of the kind of promo videos which run amok daily through American households – Journey's 'Chain Reaction', Quiet Riot's 'Come On Feel The Noise', Toto's 'Rosanna'. Best of the batch is Cyndi Lauper's busy, funny 'Girls Just Want To Have Fun', but Men At Work's 'Down Under' is surprisingly witty and much better than the group's music.

SHAKIN' STEVENS
Video Show
(CBS/Fox, 35 minutes)

In which we discover 12 promos for the singles which Shaky has sold to a gullible world since August 1980, and very foolish most of them are too. If 'Shirley', 'Give Me Your Heart Tonight' and 'It's Late' are uniformly ghastly, Shaky at least gets a helping hand from Bonnie Tyler in 'Rockin' Good Way', while the promo for 'I'll Be Satisfied' just lets the old boy get up on stage in front of some screaming kids. This clearly suits him much better than all this acting and dressing up business. Altogether, really rather silly.

SIOUXSIE AND THE BANSHEES
Nocturne
(Polygram, 60 minutes)

Recorded live at London's Royal Albert Hall in late summer '83, 'Nocturne' comprises a dozen prime Banshees cuts in Dolby stereo with occasional bits of slow motion and one or two rather curious coloured shapes dividing up the tracks. The gigs in question were allegedly of near-mystical proportions, though this isn't apparent from the video – camerawork is neither very imaginative nor versatile, while Siouxsie's limited vocal range and the band's restricted tonal palette swiftly become repetitive. 'Spellbound', 'Melt' and 'Israel' come off best. Elsewhere, you're sometimes hard-pressed to tell the songs apart. Disappointing.

SIOUXSIE AND THE BANSHEES

SPANDAU BALLET
Over Britain
(Palace Video, 60 minutes)

The Spands, having transformed themselves from loonies in kilts into a kind of suave lounge ensemble, have also demonstrated a canny grip on the importance of using video to its full advantage. *Over Britain*, recorded at London's Sadler's Wells Theatre on May Day 1983, captures something of the smoothly-organised live show the band were playing at the time in the wake of the successful *True* album, though not without some blatant tampering and overdubbing after the fact. In other words, some of this footage is genuinely live while other bits have been reconstructed, and musical blunders have been ruthlessly eliminated. But fans will doubtless thrill once more to the uplifting strains of 'Gold' or 'Lifeline', while 'Foundation' and 'Communication' give Tony 'Mario Lanza' Hadley full rein to indulge those platinum tonsils. This cassette is slick and professional, if lacking in real spark.

THE STYLE COUNCIL

keyboards person Jeff Hammer alongside Teardrop stalwarts Gary Dwyer, Troy Tate and of course the mercurial Julian Cope. Frankly, this cassette leaves several things to be desired. The sound is boxy and crashy, while the band's performances of songs like 'Ha Ha I'm Drowning' or 'Leila Khaled' are messy and lacklustre. There's little to suggest that there's actually an audience in attendance until shortly before the end, and even when you catch a glimpse of them they don't look very excited. 'Passionate Friend' is pretty good, though. Of course, nobody every accused the Teardrops of being professional.

TEST DEPARTMENT
Program For Progress
(43 minutes, mail order from Doublevision)

Born to be wild, 'Program' has been described as "arty", "mesmerising", "too loud", and "for industrial moodists only". This work should, if nothing else, nudge other bands into (a) thinking independently and (b) viewing video as a set of visual possibilities, like film. 'Program' utilises the videocassette as *medium*, not as a spool of fractured storylines. To this end, the various tracks – including 'Shockwork', 'Compulsion', and 'The Fall From Light' – are beautifully assembled behind a wave of industrial imagery. The editing throughout is brilliant, and equally praiseworthy is the painstaking concern over all aspects of production.
Caveats: some won't like the music, and some won't like its assembly-line romanticism. Nevertheless, a landmark.

THOMPSON TWINS
Side Kicks The Movie
(PMI, 60 minutes)

In print, The Twins are oft heard to complain that the music press treats them badly. They are perfectly right – reviewers *have* reached for the killing adjectives, and will probably continue to do so until two of these three performers justify their presence onstage.
Filmed live at the Liverpool Royal Court, *Side Kicks The Movie* makes it grotesquely apparent that Currie and Leeway have virtually nothing to do with the execution of the songs. And so, as in any overstaffed office, the water-cooler kids 'make busy'. There's a lot of hitting and skipping and eyepopping while Bailey rushes exhaustedly from one instrument to another. Meanwhile, the anonymous drummer, guitarist, and extra synth person – hard workers all – are never introduced to the audience.
Not a music tape.

PETER TOSH
Peter Tosh Live
(EMI Picture Music, 60 minutes)

Preceded by blasts of "Hallejujah", mystic and fire-eater Peter Tosh appears dressed like an OPEC potentate, brandishing some kind of crucifix, to deliver his growling sets of instructions to his disciples. How 'Johnny B. Goode' fits into all this is unclear, but 'Get Up, Stand Up' and 'African' fill the bill without difficulty. Perhaps it's the threat of impending brimstone which Tosh fans like so much.

PETER TOSH

TOYAH! TOYAH! TOYAH!
Video EP
(PGV, 20 minutes)

A mixture of good directors (Godley and Creme for 'I Want To Be Free', David Mallet for the Bowieish 'Brave New World'), but the cumulative effect is reminiscent of one long cosmetics advert.

TV WIPEOUT
(110 minutes on a three hour cassette, mail order from Doublevision)

Unquestionably the finest videocassette of the year, 'Wipeout' is pure entertainment. This tape has *longevity* – it can stand frequent replays because its contents are wholly absorbing and free from the cling of cliché. Included in the magazine-like format are words and music from Yello, The Fall, Test Department, Cabaret Voltaire, and Clock DVA, together with the most feverishly schizo promo ever made (Rennaldo And The Loaf) and clips from 'Plan Nine From Outer Space'.
The Nottingham-based Doublevision organisation has been responsible for three of the most adventurous releases of '84: 'Wipeout', 'Johnny YesNo', and CTI's 'Elemental Seventh'. Obtain at least one of these and be thankful for the invention of colour television.

THE STYLE COUNCIL
Far East & Far Out, Council Meeting In Japan
(Polygram, 60 minutes)

A whole hour of Paul Weller's Style Council ensemble zapping 'em in Japan, featuring all the hits – 'You're The Best Thing,' 'Long Hot Summer', 'My Ever Changing Moods', 'Money-Go-Round', 'Speak Like A Child' and a whole bunch more. Weller's ensemble has on occasion received a mauling from the press, but they undoubtedly start to fizz when the mood takes them. Not just for fans.

THE STYLE COUNCIL
What We Did On Our Holidays
(PGV, 20 minutes)

Forget – for a moment – that musician with the high forehead and the appealing smirk; let us now praise director Tim Pope. 'Holidays', comprising the promos 'Speak Like A Child', 'Money Go Round', 'Solid Bond In Your Heart', and the sublime 'Long Hot Summer', is a handy little package of pure viewing pleasure. From 'Child's dazzlingly simple special effects (think of the attack of the editing room caterpillars over the bus sequence) to 'Summer's swoon of an afternoon, these twenty minutes are a testament to Pope's tireless genius.
Besides the 'art' – which is considerable – Pope's greatest gift is in letting everyone enjoy themselves. There are a lot of unprompted grins here, so many that even viewers who are no friends of the Council will be hard pressed not to tap a toe or two in response.
A picnic in your living room.

STYX
Caught In The Act
(A&M, 87 minutes)

Is it a movie? Is it a gig? Both, in fact. The idea is great – use in-concert footage in conjunction with a science fiction plot to create an entire Audio-Visual Experience. Unfortunately, Styx are not the people to bring it off. The plot is sort of half-baked '1984-ism' – rock'n'roll has been banned by Dr. Everett Righteous and his Majority for Musical Morality, but ex-rock star Kilroy escapes from prison to reactivate his erstwhile musical career. The opening narrative section was filmed by *Breaking Glass* director Brian Gibson, and is fairly atmospheric despite blatant theft from the likes of Ridley Scott and John Carpenter. Unfortunately the potential tails off completely when we arrive at Styx onstage – they're mechanical, flat and unspeakably tedious. It's an ambitious project, but there's something rotten about Styx's ideology. Someone somewhere could take the idea a lot further. In case you're interested, songs include 'Rockin' The Paradise', 'Snowblind', 'Heavy Metal Poisoning' and 'Cold War'.

THE TEARDROP EXPLODES
Live In Concert
(Master Class, 28 minutes)

Available from Holiday Bros (Audio & Video) Ltd, 172 Finney Lane, Heald Green, Cheadle, Cheshire or Terry Blood Distributors.
This was shot at an unspecified gig in 1981, and features bassman Alfie Agius and

THE THOMPSON TWINS

THE CURE

JUDIE TZUKE
Live In Concert
(Master Class, 30 minutes)
Available from Holiday Bros (Audio
& Video) Ltd.
Never been able to see what anybody could
find alluring about either Ms. Tzuke or her
music, and this live video provides few
answers. It's been shot dutifully enough and
the sound tells you more than you want to
know about Judie's band and songs.
'Chinatown' is blundering sort-of funk,
'Sukarita' lumbers along rather painfully, and
the quicker 'Black Furs' is merely ugly,
largely because of the artiste's dreadful
bawling vocal. At least we are spared the
atrocious 'Stay With Me Till Dawn'. Pass.

U2
Under A Blood Red Sky
(Virgin, 61 minutes)
This is far and away the most exciting and
memorable chunk of concert footage seen on
video in a long time, for several reasons.
First, it was bagged under thunderstorm
conditions in Colorado's dramatic Red Rock
open-air auditorium in a temperature of
minus-two degrees. Secondly, U2's big,
simple dynamics and Bono's remarkable way
with an audience render the band ideal for
events on this scale. And last but equally
vital, the live sound was mixed by Jimmy
Iovine and Shelly Yakus and comes leaping
out at you in something like 3-D. Under a
lowering sky and lit by blazing torches, U2
deliver a taut cluster of their strongest
material, with '11 O'Clock Tick Tock', 'I Will
Follow' and 'New Year's Day' all hard
enough to get hairs rising up your neck. Fans
of guitarist The Edge won't be disappointed,
since the great man is in epic form here on
guitar, voice, piano and even bass (for the
closing '40'). Bono looks a bit of a prat at
times, but you can shut your eyes during
those bits. Hugely recommended.

THE UNDERTONES
(EMI, 20 minutes)
Despite much critical brouhaha, The
Undertones never received their full due
while they were still operative. Watch this,
therefore, and marvel at how much effortless
pop suss, wit and magic went begging. The
six tracks included run from 1978's dauntless
'Teenage Kicks' through to '83's 'Got To
Have You Back', the best record The Small
Faces never made. In between, there's Julien
Temple's fine promo for 'My Perfect Cousin'
(surely one of the wittiest pop lyrics ever), all
knobbly knees and Subbuteo, not to mention
Chris Gabrin's spellbinding sequence for the
mesmeric 'Love Parade'. The cassette has
plainly been assembled with care and
attention to detail, down to publicist Mick
Houghton's opening eulogy for the defunct
Derrymen. Well done, somebody at EMI –
shame it's too late. Consume.

VIDEO WAVES
Compilation
(PGV, 90 minutes)
Among the 25-odd clips are Blancmange
('That's Love That Is'), The Style Council ('A
Solid Bond In Your Heart'), Men Without
Hats ('Safety Dance'), Nick Heyward ('Blue
Hat For A Blue Day'), Status Quo ('A Mess Of
Blues'), Genesis ('Mama'), Marilyn ('Calling
Your Name'), Dire Straits ('Twistin' By The
Pool') etc. etc. A promo blizzard, and well
worth the price for both timeliness and the
inclusion of The Cure's 'Love Cats'. The
sleeve, however, scrimps on the ink by not
listing directorial credits.

WARREN ZEVON
Excitable Live
(Polygram, 68 minutes)
Mere in-concert footage this may be, but
there's enough happening to make you think
twice about what Ol' Warren really gets up
to behind that gingery stubble. "Heeeere's
Johnny" he roars amid the opening clamour
of 'When Johnny Strikes Up The Band', and
one half expects him to take a fire-axe to the
piano. Throughout, Warren looks
dangerously unhinged, especially during the
macabre 'Roland The Headless Thompson
Gunner' or the Roger Corman-style lighting
and dry ice of 'The Envoy'. The band is
chunky and powerful and recording quality is
excellent. Thrill, therefore, to Zevon classics
like 'Werewolves Of London' and 'Poor Poor
Pitiful Me', and even to the Springsteen-
penned 'Cadillac Ranch'. On this evidence,
Zevon is severely underrated.

BEST AND WORST

A section in which our editors camouflaged by anonymity, are encouraged to make all kinds of opinionated and boorish judgements about album covers. Some are included as a result of unanimous voting; others are just petty prejudices.

ALBUM COVERS OF THE YEAR

BEST **WORST**

SIOUXSIE AND THE BANSHEES
HYAENA (WONDERLAND, POLYDOR)
A Banshees/Da Gama design
Paintings: MARIA PENN
Typography: DAVID HOCKIN
The Banshees have been cultivating this look for a while, but this is the most effective example to date. The art nouveau inspiration is still apparent, but is increasingly a part of something more independent and individual to the group. This could have looked precious and pretentious. Instead it's sleek, colourful and appealing. A beautifully produced piece of work.

ROGER WATERS
THE PROS AND CONS OF HITCH HIKING (HARVEST, EMI)
Design: ROGER WATERS and GERALD SCARFE
Photography: ALEX HENDERSON
Waters' grubby, bullying misogyny and petulant misanthropy, which form the basis for this particularly repugnant LP, find their grotesque visual equivalents in Gerald Scarfe's crude, enormously offensive cover. That two supposedly intelligent men, of admittedly advancing years, could produce such an insensitive, insulting cover is simply reprehensible.

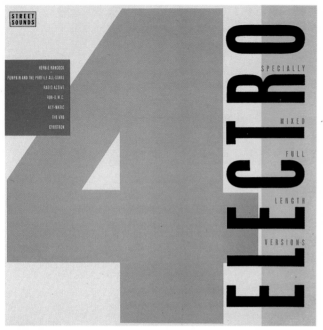

ELECTRO
(STREET SOUNDS)
Design: RED RANCH 4 CARVER'S
A bold and imaginative use of typography characterises this series of compilation albums. The sleeves are probably best seen in sequence, but this was our favourite. Excellent marketing.

GARY NUMAN
WARRIORS (BEGGARS BANQUET)
Photography: GEOFF HOWES
Make-up: PATTI BURRIS
The appalling Gary Numan has always deserved the heartiest ridicule, but rarely before has he looked such a comprehensive bone-head. The Road Warrior chic is a shameless rip-off from the Mad Max movies, but the Max factor here is purely cosmetic.

FRANKIE GOES TO HOLLYWOOD
RELAX (ZTT)
Illustration: ANNE YVONNE GILBERT
Sleeve Design: XL ZTT
Not an album sleeve, we know, but one of the year's most impressively conceived record sleeves and, as such, a valid card entry in our selection. The use of illustration is compelling and fresh, the dash of S&M tantalising enough to provoke the necessary controversy without getting the whole thing banned. Generally intelligent, really, with a sharp appreciation of the market-place that doesn't patronise its audience. Paul Morley's contentious sleeve jottings provide us with our only reservations, but you can probably scrape them off with a sharp enough scalpel.

DARK WIZARD
DEVIL'S VICTIM (MAUSOLEUM)
Illustration: ERIC PHILIPPE
What can you say? Conforming with a suicidal bravado to the stereotype of traditional HM artwork, this is ugly, daft and almost staggeringly inept. The airbrush technique resurrected here is so out-dated as to be positively pre-historic.

KING YELLOWMAN
KING YELLOWMAN (CBS)
Sleeve by IAN WRIGHT
Avoiding the usual militant didacticism of most reggae sleeves – there are no clenched fists, images of Babylon collapsing, Haile Selassie or rioting brethren – this is cheap and cheerful, boasting a carnival flair. Should appeal to his traditional audience and the kind of young white trendies who like to leave sleeves like this on their coffee tables to impress their friends with their liberal ethnic inclinations.

DAVE BROCK
EARTHED TO THE GROUND (FLICKNIFE)
Artwork: J. COULTHART
An example of a kind of portentous hippy cosmology, thought by experts to have expired in 1969, foolishly revived to utterly disastrous effect. The unspeakably mindless notion of the guitar turning into a machine gun in the veteran space-cadet's hands turns an idea that was originally only an ugly anachronism into something pitifully laughable.

ORANGE JUICE
TEXAS FEVER (POLYDOR)
Photography: ROBERT SHARP
Sleeve assembled at STYLO ROUGE
Orange Juice remain resolutely idiosyncratic on every level. This sleeve is wonderfully comic, teasing, full of sly references and an off-handed insolence. Its air of pleasant cynicism is as refreshing, amusing and stylish as the group's music.

DEAD OR ALIVE
SOPHISTICATED BOOM BOOM (EPIC)
Photography: PETER ASHWORTH
This is almost comical enough to be successful, but Pete Burns, desperately trying to look sleek and sensual, ends up, as usual, looking like a ravaged old tart. The sleeve finally collapses beneath the weight of its own obese sexual imagery. Very tacky.

THE THE
SOUL MINING (SOME BIZARRE, CBS)
Artwork: ANDY JOHNSON DOG
Typography: FIONA SKINNER
Despite a slight inclination towards a slick kind of hipness, this is bright, invigorating and enormously refreshing.

THE ROLLING STONES
UNDER COVER (ROLLING STONES RECORDS, EMI)
Cover concept and Art Direction: PETER CORRISTON
Cover Art: HUBERT KRETZSCHMAR
The Stones rarely do themselves any favours these days with their record sleeves. No doubt the intention here was to be stylishly outrageous, but the final effect is simply tawdry, rather cheap and faintly unpleasant.

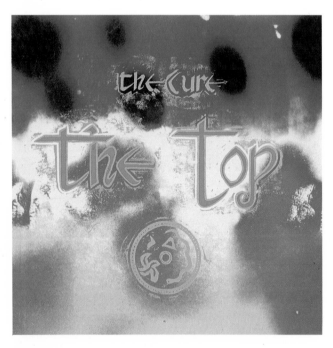

THE CURE
THE TOP (FICTION)
Design: PARCHED ART (ANDY VELLA and PORL THOMPSON)
The Cure's videos are invariably sharp and arresting, and so is this album sleeve. The colours and textures have the hallucinatory shimmer of an acid flashback, but the artwork owes little to the conceits of traditional hack psychedelia.

TWISTED SISTER
STAY HUNGRY (ATLANTIC)
Photography: MARK WEISS STUDIOS
Costume and Make-up design: SUZETTE GUILOT-SNIDER
T.S. Bone logo conceived and designed by: DEE SNIDER and SUZETTE GUILOT-SNIDER
Art Direction: BOB DEFRIN
Back Cover Concept: MARK MENDOZA
Genuinely repulsive. A witless original idea realised with a heavy-handedness that defies adequate description.

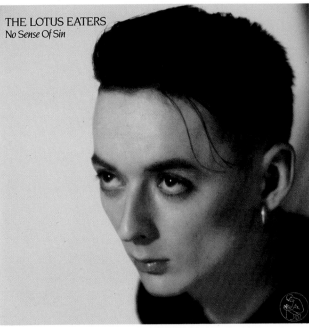

BIG COUNTRY
THE CROSSING (MERCURY)
Design: J. B. & Q. BRANCH
Photography: PAUL COX
An astute piece of marketing, this sells an image of the group without making them an obviously complicant element of the merchandising strategy. The embossed lettering is undeniably pompous, and the whole idea has a spuriously epic air about it, but no doubt the group's audience was suitably flattered by the apparent gravity of it all.

THE LOTUS EATERS
NO SENSE OF SIN (ARISTA)
Photography: CAMERON McVEY
Oh, dear! The thoroughly gormless Lotus Eaters have obviously aimed for an intense solemnity and a touch of vintage Berlin decadence with these enormously po-faced portraits, but the air of camp worldliness they were after has been reduced to a laughable sissiness.

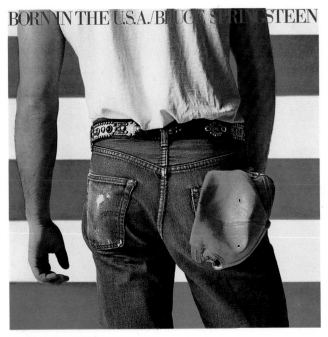

R.E.M.
RECKONING (IRS)
Art Direction: CARL GRASSO
Painting: HOWARD FINSTER
A daring sleeve, whose design owes nothing at all to any prevailing styles; its total individuality works supremely well, the intricacy of the cover art displaying an intuitive empathy with the group's teasing musical intrigues. Brave and successful.

BRUCE SPRINGSTEEN
BORN IN THE U.S.A. (CBS)
Art Direction and Design: ANDREA KLEIN
Photography: ANNIE LEIBOVITZ
Ridiculous. Springsteen has never been less than conspicuously overblown, but surely he should leave this sublimely pathetic butch posing to more genuine meat-heads like John Cougar Mellencamp. The whole idea should've been given the bum's rush before it got off the drawing board. It says little for Springsteen's idea of himself that he could even contemplate giving his approval to this kind of nonsense.

EURYTHMICS
TOUCH (RCA)
Photography: PETER ASHWORTH
Art and Design: LAURENCE STEVENS, with thanks to ANDREW CHRISTIAN
A bold, formidable image that still doesn't lack elegance and the stylish accomplishment one has now come to expect from Eurythmics. Annie Lennox has enormous presence, the photography is excellent and the typography sparse and unobtrusive. A confident, purposeful sleeve.

RAGE
RUN FOR THE NIGHT (CARRERE)
Art Direction/Design: DAVID LARKHAM, TORCHLIGHT
Photography: TREVOR ROGERS
This kind of soft-porn sleeve was always stupid, facile and offensive; it now looks stupid, facile, offensive and hopelessly old-fashioned. Even the group's potential audience must have winced at its colossal predictability and crude idiocy.

OZZY OSBOURNE
BARK AT THE MOON (CBS)
Design and Artwork: STEVE JOULE
Make-up: GREG CANNOM
Photography: FIN COSTELLO/TONY HARRISON
A classical example of how to go over-the-top and stay there. The sheer absurdity of the entire enterprise obviously hasn't escaped Ozzy, and he's clearly enjoying himself hugely. You could say that he's never looked better!

JUDIE TZUKE
WELCOME TO THE CRUISE (ROCKET)
Design: HIPGNOSIS/RICHARD DRAPER
Presumably intended to convey a mood of solemn romanticism and winsome mystery, the trite, pathetic imagery scales heights of pretentious comedy previously unknown beyond Moody Blues' sleeves. Complete nonsense.

BLANCMANGE
MANGE TOUT (LONDON)
Design: MARTYN ATKINS and MARCX, TOWN & COUNTRY PLANNING
This isn't as frivolous as some of the graphic imagery employed by this group, but it retains a characteristic charm and subtlety and is cheerfully devoid of the pompous solemnities usually associated with pairs of young men with severe haircuts who play synthesisers.

ALEXIS KORNER
JUVENILE DELINQUENT (CHARISMA)
Illustration: RALPH STEADMAN
A sad visual epitaph, entirely disrespectful to the memory of the man it seeks to celebrate. Steadman's caricature is extremely shoddy, clumsily irreverent and shamefully insensitive. The title says it all: this is juvenile *and* delinquent.

THE SMITHS
THE SMITHS (ROUGH TRADE)
Concept: MORRISSEY
Photography: JOE DALLESANDRO from Andy Warhol's *FLESH*
Although it appears initially to say comparatively little about The Smiths and their music, the choice of illustration here is in fact cunningly appropriate. The subtle use of colour and lettering enhance the mood of extravagant loneliness and heightened sexual tensions of Morrissey and Marr's songs.

IMAGINATION
SCANDALOUS (PRT)
Photography: NIGEL ASKEW
Artwork: CHESS CREATIVE SERVICES
There's invariably an entertaining element of pantomime about Imagination, but it never makes it as far as their album sleeves. Here they look like a trio of gay gladiators, and the effect is tacky, gaudy and eventually quite ghastly. The continued public appearances of Leee John's pubic hair, meanwhile, is massively unpleasant and really shouldn't be encouraged.

THE SPECIAL AKA
IN THE STUDIO WITH . . . (TWO TONE RECORDS)
Design: JERRY DAMMERS and DAVID STOREY
Photography: DAVIES/STARR
The cover shot somehow contrives to make a potentially forgettable image utterly memorable. The acceptable face of nostalgic design, it's period pastiche that works with an effective, atmospheric simplicity.

PAUL McCARTNEY
PIPES OF PEACE (PARLOPHONE)
Photography: LINDA McCARTNEY
'Van Gogh's Chair' Chrome sculpture by CLIVE BARKER, 1966
Just goes to show that money can't buy you a decent sleeve design. This suffers from an appalling literalness, a pedantic underlining of the album title.

WEEKEND
LIVE AT RONNIE SCOTT'S (ROUGH TRADE)
Cover by WENDY SMITH
Witty, deft and original. It looks like it may have been dashed off, but it's more likely the product of a lively, uncluttered imagination.

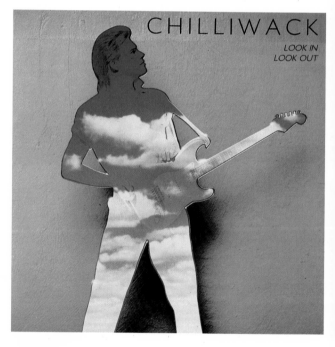

CHILLIWACK
LOOK IN LOOK OUT (SOLID GOLD)
Photography and Art Direction: JAMES O'MARA, assisted by BRENT DANIELS and PETER BISHOP
Mind-bogglingly dull, this would have looked like a period piece a decade ago. It couldn't do less to attract attention to, or interest in, a group whose passion for visual anonymity must surely be a cause for serious psychiatric concern.

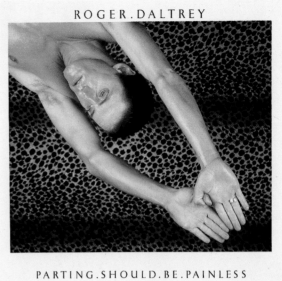

PUBLIC IMAGE LTD.
THIS IS WHAT YOU WANT . . . (VIRGIN)
Art Direction: JOHN VAN HAMERSVELD
Photography: NORMAN SEEFF
A visual confrontation, rather inevitably. Rotten's leering demeanour, his familiar sneer and the crude cut-up graphics aren't particularly novel, though they remain powerfully unmistakable. In the end, the eyes have it.

ROGER DALTREY
PARTING SHOULD BE PAINLESS (WEA)
Photography: GRAHAM HUGHES
Typography: RON BRINKWORTH
This shows an appalling lack of taste, an embarrassing lack of dignity. It's also catatonically dull.

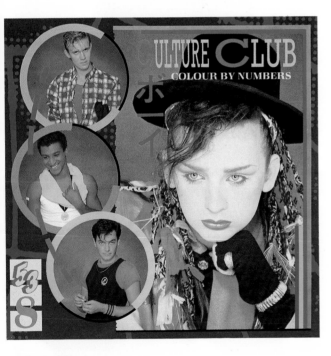

CULTURE CLUB
COLOUR BY NUMBERS (VIRGIN)
Sleeve produced by: ASSORTED iMaGes
A slick contrivance for the Smash Hits generation; brash, loud, but not too vulgar. The graphics and typography could have been tidied up, but it cleverly gets around the problem of what to do with the other members of the group without detracting from George's inevitably omnipotent visual presence. The kind of sleeve that definitely sells records. And whoever air-brushed out George's chin deserved a bonus.

FORCE
SET ME FREE . . . (HEAVY METAL)
Artwork: GARRY UNDERHILL
Just when you thought it was safe to go back in the record store, up pop Force with one of the most actively repulsive album sleeves in living memory. And the back cover is even worse. Gratuitously tasteless, its only redeeming feature is the distinct possibility that the record it contains will be even more brutal, pointless and stupid.

THANKS

THE IMPOSTER: For 'Pills And Soap', 'Peace In Our Time' and for making sure that The Special AKA's 'Nelson Mandela' got out in tune and on time.

R.E.M.: Most rock hacks favourite group in '84.

MORRISSEY AND JOHNNY MARR: The best new songwriting team.

WOMACK & WOMACK: For the year's coolest, most sophisticated soul album.

THE YOUNG ONES: The most hilarious and consistently outrageous television comedy show in years.

JOOLS HOLLAND: For refusing to pamper the egoes of a seemingly endless parade of pompous pop personalities.

VAN HALEN: Their 'Jump' video proved that even heavy metal bands can have a sense of humour.

TIM POPE: Director of the year's wittiest pop videos.

JERRY DAMMERS: The Special AKA finally released an album, and it was worth the wait.

PIRATE RADIOS: A bright alternative to the smug complacency of the BBC.

SPITTING IMAGE: A bunch of puppets, but nobody's dummies.

FRANKIE GOES TO HOLLYWOOD: For livening up the charts with a brazen mix of politics, entertainment and provocative bravado.

THE WHO: For finally calling it a day.

...BUT NO THANKS

MIKE READ: Self-appointed moral guardian.

JIM KERR: A talent sacrificed in the pursuit of the preposterous.

STORYBOOK VIDEOS: Lionel Richie's 'Hello' promo was the most tasteless extravaganza, but not the only offender.

EVERYTHING BUT THE GIRL: Why did they always look so damned miserable?

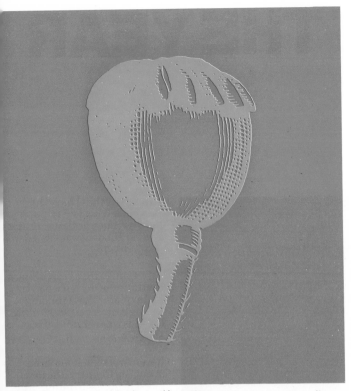

HEROIN: The price went down, but the casualties went up.

MTV: Unadventurous, prejudiced and conservative.

BREAKDANCING, BODY-POPPING AND FLASH DANCING . . . and everything else that involved spinning on your head.

JOE STRUMMER: He kept The Clash going when the sensible course was premature retirement.

YOKO ONO: For further exploiting John Lennon's murder.

QUOTES OF THE YEAR

"

OBVIOUSLY, I'M NO PARAGON OF VIRTUE. I'VE OFTEN BEEN CARRIED HOME IN THE LAST 30 YEARS.

Mick Jagger, Rolling Stones

If you're at ease with the technology, it becomes second nature. I mean, *On The Road* was written on a typewriter. The actual typing of it and the mechanical function of Jack Kerouac's typewriter did not play a big part in what you get from the book when you read it. The same thing should apply to music. I think studios are fascinating, but I keep my fascination for them out of my music as much as possible.
Thomas Dolby

If I was to wear tight satin, everybody would be able to see how fat I really am.
Ozzy Osbourne

With about one-eighth of my wealth now, I could live to 100 and have it pretty good.
Chuck Berry

I've been hallucinating. I just keep seeing faces . . . faces . . . everywhere.
Robert Smith, The Cure

Basically, I've got to relax until I've stored up enough artistic roughage, and then go and have a damned good artistic crap.
Andy Partridge, XTC, on conceiving a new album

No-one seems to be doing anything very innovative in stadium shows. I've seen David Bowie, I've seen Talking Heads and The Police, and, I mean, is that really all there is?
Mick Jagger, Rolling Stones

My sexual attitudes have changed. I used to say "if you don't want to fuck me, fuck off", but now I'll say "if you don't want to fuck me, okay, let's be friends".
Jayne County

Music now is full of immoral messages. 95 per cent of music being played now is full of these insidious messages. I'd like to separate myself from all that crazy stuff. I don't see why music has to thrive on sex and degradation and it's sick.
George Benson

If I heard myself come out of a jukebox somewhere, my face would probably turn red.
Tom Waits

I use Delia Smith's butcher for my sheep lungs. Otherwise, I like porridge, spaghetti and rabbit – preferably all mixed up.
Smeggy, King Kurt

I saw Andy Williams at the Barbican. He was wonderful. I met him afterwards and he said he liked my hair. The other thing I really want to do is get Kim Wilde to put a big custard pie in my face. It's got to be really gooey.
Limahl

At an art gallery, you wouldn't get 14 Van Gogh lookalikes all looking at a Van Gogh painting.
Dave Stewart, Eurythmics

I would say that I have three very close friends. The public tends to imagine that rock stars have millions of friends. I don't.
Sting, The Police

I always feel that I'm making a real fanny of myself when I try and explain what I'm doing – the big rock 'n' roll star telling the kids where his head is at.
Stuart Adamson, Big Country

Recently, I read something about Big Country, the new latest thing for 15 minutes in England. Stuart Adamson said that America was a joke, that everything here was borrowed from Europe. Now, is this guy in rock 'n' roll band? Who invented rock 'n' roll? Who invented blues? Country music? Jazz? Those are all American traditions and American artforms. And this stupid jerk from Glasgow is going to tell me what to think?
Brian Setzer, Stray Cats

There are still people who think that I'm the band's mother or manager, or even one of the cleaners, but now I can handle it. I just take the piss.
Vi Subversa, Poison Girls

IF ANYONE ELSE ASKS ME HOW I MAKE MY GUITAR SOUND LIKE BAGPIPES, I SWEAR I'LL FLATTEN THEM.

Bruce Watson, Big Country

My ideal would be to have a house in Liverpool and London and New York. Now that's not asking too much, is it?
Holly, Frankie Goes To Hollywood

We admit we've got very limited appeal. It's a kind of obscure piece of furniture that only one person in a thousand might want, as opposed to the Human League knocking out bright red plastic chairs that can be used anytime.
Andy Partridge, XTC

I think I'd get a bigger kick out of seeing our album on the record rack in The Cabin on *Coronation Street* than in a heap of rave reviews.
Garry Daly, China Crisis

I happen to think the most beautiful thing in the world is a woman, but I also look upon women as human beings. There's no question that they're equal to men – the only difference is that the lumps are in different places.
Adam Ant

I'm the most romantic person you could meet. When I fall for someone I go right over the top. I'm a real red roses and champagne man.
Roddy Frame, Aztec Camera

I THINK POLITICALLY I'M A LOT SHARPER NOW BECAUSE I THINK I KNOW MORE WHERE I STAND THAN I DID IN 1979 OR WHENEVER. I DIDN'T REALLY HAVE A FUCKING CLUE. I DON'T THINK I WAS NAIVE, I WAS JUST A BIT THICK REALLY.
Paul Weller, Style Council

I'm probably even less aware of what's going on now than I was two years ago. The only single I've bought this year has been 'Blue Monday' and the only album was Nico's. The only gig I went to was the Bunnymen. I'm not a consumer at all.
Robert Smith, The Cure

Degas said that everyone has talent at 25, but the difficulty is having it at 50.
Pete Townshend

I never lived the rock star myth and never had any desire to.
Sting, The Police

I always experimented with my hair, doing wild things with it. I wanted the effect of seeing a silhouette and not knowing what kind of weird beast it was – an owl, a unicorn, or what. It's great when all the little girls jump on stage trying to touch my locks.
Mike Score, Flock Of Seagulls

Siouxsie? She's doing Beatle numbers! The Stravinsky overture and the dry ice. Do we have to live through it all again? The Alarm? The wrapping on a chocolate bar. They're the imitation of a shadow of The Clash. That's why we're back. . .we're *needed* back.
Joe Strummer, The Clash

The Bunnymen were psychedelic, but, God, they nearly broke their bollocks trying to be. Walking around pretending they were on acid.
Pete Burns, Dead Or Alive

We have quite a few arguments about Einstein. Vince (Clarke) is convinced that he's wrong. The big problem is that Vince can get into the studio a lot earlier than me because he doesn't believe in time dilations.
Eric Radcliffe, The Assembly

The only black magic Sabbath ever got into was a box of chocolates.
Ozzy Osbourne

I think he (John Lydon) needs to see a psychiatrist. I don't think he's in touch with his feelings at all. John was my best friend for years; I thought he was great, so great. It was me, John and Sid. We all thought each other were great. Sid's dead and John has now died as far as I'm concerned.
Keith Levene

I WISH THERE WERE OTHER SONGWRITERS I COULD CLAIM KINSHIP WITH, BUT THERE IS NO-ONE. I CONSIDER MYSELF TO BE A GENIUS.
Morrissey, The Smiths

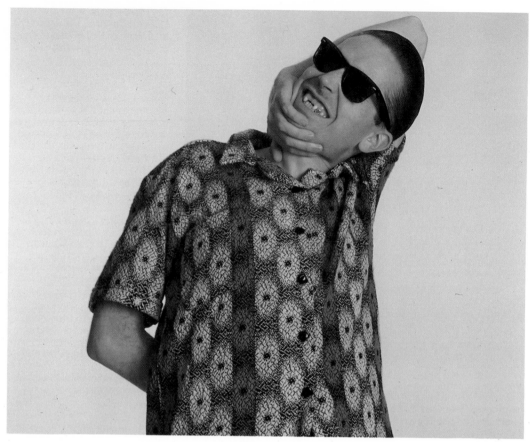

EVERYBODY GOES ON ABOUT US HAVING TO DEFEND OURSELVES AGAINST THE RUSSIANS INVADING, BUT THE AMERICANS HAVE ALREADY INVADED BRITAIN.

Jerry Dammers, The Specials

Heavy Metal is totally silly with all that macho posing. It meant something back in the early Seventies, but a lot of blokes in those bands are so old now that they should be reaching for their pension books.
Dennis Greaves, The Truth

I really do expect the highest critical praise for the album. I think it's a complete signal post in the history of popular music.
Morrissey, The Smiths

She has a flat, monotonous and boring voice.
Tracie on Carmel

LIZ TAYLOR'S SO FAT NOW THAT SHE TAKES MAYONNAISE WITH AN ASPIRIN.

Marilyn

Imagine in your mind an ELP number. Then imagine punk rock like a blow torch sweeping across it. That to me is what punk rock did. And that's what's got to happen again.
Joe Strummer, The Clash

I don't think I'll wilt quickly. We'll never be flavour of the month. I think we're just a little bit too clever for that.
Morrissey, The Smiths

IT CAN GET QUITE DANGEROUS, 'COS I'VE HAD PEOPLE GO FOR MY EARRINGS AND TRY TO PULL THEM OUT. I MEAN, IF YOUR EARRINGS GOT DRAGGED OUT, YOU'D RIP YOUR EAR, WOULDN'T YOU?

Steve Norman, Spandau Ballet

I've been working towards being a pop star since I was 14.
Matt Fretton

We can't walk anywhere without getting hassled non-stop. Sometimes I think it would be more fun to work in a factory.
Terry Hall, Fun Boy Three

I consider most producers wankers.
Phil Collen, Def Leppard

The song is about making love. Well, most songs are, aren't they?
Kate Garner, Haysi Fantayzee

To those who care now where Bob Dylan is at, they should listen to 'Shot Of Love' off the *Shot Of Love* album. It's my most perfect song. It defines where I'm at spiritually, musically, romantically and whatever else. It shows where my sympathies lie. No need to wonder if I'm this or that. I'm not hiding anything. It's all there in that one song.
Bob Dylan

I don't think anybody is going to remember The Thompson Twins at the end of the decade. The only bands to have left their mark will be the Mighty Wah! and about three others.
Pete Wylie, The Mighty Wah!

I say "Don't buy it. . .tape it!"
Chrissie Hynde, Pretenders on their new album

I have a very short attention span. I have a habit of falling in love with someone and then waking up and wondering what came over me. I'm dying to fall in love with someone and then stay with them.
Madonna

HOW CAN SHE BE FEMININE AND SEXY WHEN SHE'S GOT THE WHOLE OF THE NEW FOREST GROWING IN HER ARM PITS?
Tracie on Nena

We're fucking 43 year old men and we're behaving like children. It's silly, absolutely fucking idiotic. Retarded!
Eric Burdon on Animals re-formation

The doctors put me on valium. That was 14 years ago, and I'm still on it.
Knox, The Vibrators

The only way MTV will ever play the type of music I make is if it's on a major label and the faces are white.
Arthur Baker, producer

As far as I'm concerned, MTV is a step into the dark ages. It has completely failed to appreciate world wide music. It should be named 'MTV, The Caucasian Music Channel'.
August Darnell, Kid Creole & The Coconuts

I STILL HAVE DREAMS ABOUT BEING AT SCHOOL. I DON'T THINK I'M AN ADULT, I DON'T WANT TO GROW UP. I THINK MICHAEL JACKSON IS THE SAME, BUT I HAVEN'T SPOKEN TO HIM ABOUT IT RECENTLY.
Captain Sensible

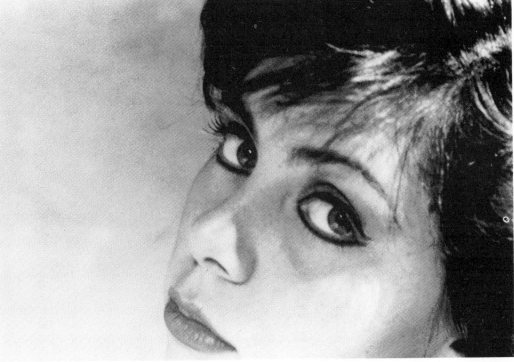
TRACIE

As long as somebody can get some joy or intense loathing from something I do, then I'm quite happy.
Marc Almond, Soft Cell

People say we should be grateful to be in the charts. Would you be grateful to get your coat back from the cleaners when it belongs to you?
Pete Burns, Dead Or Alive

When I'm at home, I play bingo all the time. I'll go seven nights a week if I have nothing else to do and twice on Saturday and Sunday.
Izora, The Weather Girls.

Music is very important to us but it's not our entire lives, however unfashionable that may sound. We're not part of the rock 'n' roll lifestyle.
Martyn Ware, Heaven 17

It's now gone up to five minutes. I've mastered the technique.
John Lydon, PIL, on his sexual prowess

I don't want to be like Van Morrison – just sit on a ranch and put out one record a year with a horrible cover.
Peter Buck, REM

I don't want to be associated with other people in groups. I think, rightly or wrongly, that what I'm doing is worth a bit more than the rest of them.
Paul Weller, Style Council

It's all very well to play in ridiculous time signatures, but it doesn't make a good pop song.
Nick Rhodes, Duran Duran

We're using the biggest PA system that's been used any-where in the world. . .it will make Cecil B. DeMille look like breakfast television.
David Coverdale, Whitesnake

I despair when I pass Oxford Street and see bondage and leather and studs everywhere. It's become quite acceptable to go to work like that. It's disgusting.
Siouxsie, Siouxsie And The Banshees

We're sick of people thinking that we're just three bubbly girls who only think about boys.
Keren, Bananarama

HE LEFT FOR MEDICAL REASONS – HE WAS MAKING ME SICK.
Ozzy Osbourne on drummer Carmine Appice's departure

OZZY OSBOURNE

We've nothing to offer nine years olds – unless they're rubber fetishists.
Pete Burns, Dead Or Alive

I've only ever been offered drugs once. A guy came up to me and said "Two speed for a pound" – and I said "What? What's speed?" and cocaine – well, I really wouldn't know what it looked like.
Susanne Sulley, the Human League

CAPTAIN SENSIBLE

ELVIS COSTELLO

THE THING IS, I AM A GOOD BLOKE. I DON'T ACTUALLY HATE MYSELF, AND I DON'T THINK I DESERVE ALL THE VITRIOL DEALT OUT TO ME.

Elvis Costello

People have always chased me down the street with Stanley knives—it's given me an edge.
Pete Burns, Dead Or Alive

If people choose not to like my music because I don't smoke ganja, then I say the hell with those people.
Eddy Grant

Black Sabbath was such a fucking bore for so many years it was untrue. The name is still a legend, like Robin Hood. . .it's like a pantomime now. I wish them all the luck in the world—I'm just glad I'm out of it.
Ozzy Osbourne

I've often looked out over an audience and thought that I'm old enough to be the father of most of them.
Dave Holland, Judas Priest

I think I'm a romantic fool, actually. I want to be proposed to at the top of the Statue of Liberty. . .or even the Empire State Building would do.
Clare Grogan

All the wee girls who used to turn up and scream, don't anymore. You can only be in rock 'n' roll for 7-and-a-half years.
Edwyn Collins, Orange Juice

Last week I was invited to a dinner with Michael Jackson and Quincy Jones—but those things are really kinda boring. It's more interesting to keep a low profile, not show up at everything.
Madonna

I don't think I'm gonna be really understood until maybe 100 years from now. What I've done, what I'm doing, nobody else does or has done. When I'm dead and gone maybe people will realise that, and then figure it out. There are all these interpreters around now, but they're not interpreting anything except their own ideas. Nobody's come close.
Bob Dylan

Andrew Lloyd Webber approached me when he'd just written *Jesus Christ Superstar* and asked me what I thought. I told him that if the job at the bank was still open, he should take it. Now he probably owns the bank.
John Peel

I'm really pleased I got married in Sydney because it meant none of my relatives could be here.
Elton John

Nick Beggs doesn't like us, he thinks we're morally wrong. I think he's a fucking idiot,—the guy's a fool. Another person who doesn't like us is Boy George. The guy's an idiot.
Paul Rutherford, Frankie Goes To Hollywood

I think all those peace campaigners are stupid. There hasn't been a major conflict since World War II. It's the terror of the bomb that keeps us safe. We're not all suddenly going to go up in a puff of smoke.
Gary Numan

We were just four lads, basically—four dumbos from Manchester. We never were saviours of the Human Race.
Bernie, New Order

Talking to me about music papers is like talking about the toilet.
Kirk Brandon, Spear Of Destiny

Apart from the girls at parties, who want to fuck you for Jesus, we're actually getting offered all sorts of things. Annie got offered something like three million dollars to put her name to Vidal Sassoon hair products. We just laughed at that one.
Dave Stewart, Eurythmics

My new album sounds more like Kajagoogoo than they do.
Limahl

In Glasgow, you're really cool if you're in a band for years and just slog away at it. As soon as you're on *Top Of The Pops*, you're uncool!
Ken McCluskey, The Bluebells

If I went to bed with either guy in the band, it would be the beginning of the end of us.
Alannah Currie, Thompson Twins

I don't want to come over as being the punk generation's Cliff Richard, a do-gooder. . .I hate that stuff.
Paul Weller, Style Council

I no longer wish to sing.
Marc Almond, Soft Cell

I DID ENJOY MY YOUTH TO THE MAXIMUM, I MUST SAY. IT WAS A PRETTY DIRTY, NASTY ONE, MAYBE.

Chrissie Hynde, Pretenders

CHRISSIE HYNDE

BILLY BRAGG

I've grown out of drugs. I've realised that there's no back door to heaven. You can't buy a religious experience for £3.
Roddy Frame, Aztec Camera

People have a laugh and say "Oh, she's just a hat stand". Ha, ha, ha. Very funny. I don't fucking care. I'll just get bigger and better hats. I wear a hat because I wanted to make a sex symbol out of it. It's my defence, if you like, against the whole fucking system. You see someone with a hat like that, you ain't looking at her tits, right? You ain't looking at her fanny.
Alannah, Thompson Twins

It was a combination of not being able to handle my success and too many drugs. One of them had to go, so I gave up being successful. My body was OK, but my mind was pretty gone. When I read interviews from that period, I can tell it was all rather dodgy.
Julian Cope

Everything we do is tongue in cheek. I think people should see immediately that it's all a bit of a joke to us. We just act at being pop stars for one and a half hours a day.
Andrew Ridgely, Wham!

I sat down with this oriental lady, just to please our record company. She told me she thought our image sucked – and I told her she had her face so far up her ass she couldn't hear me laughing at her.
Gregory Grey, Perfect Crime

What we feel we're doing makes sense when it's nestling shoulder to shoulder with Barry Manilow and REO Speedwagon. That's the context in which Gang Of Four should be heard.
Andy Gill, Gang Of Four

The record industry is going to die like the dinosaur which is so much resembles.
Peter Buck, REM

That man has such a high opinion of himself. I would love to go over to him, tweak him on the face and ask why his nose is so big and fat and ugly.
Tracie on Simon Le Bon

THERE ARE TWO WAYS TO HOLD YOUR GUITAR – OVER YOUR BOLLOCKS, OR UNDER YOUR CHIN LIKE A PRAT.

Billy Bragg

We don't have a major record company that gives us cocaine at the end of the tour.
Stephen Morris, New Order

There isn't any difference between Echo & The Bunnymen and Kajagoogoo – it's just that you need 'O' levels to appreciate that Echo & The Bunnymen are crap.
Pete Wylie, The Mighty Wah!

The synthesiser bands are already having problems: they can't really tour and they're very reliant on the floating market that buys hit records. They have no more longevity than their next song.
Adam Clayton, U2

I go to the ballpark in Detroit and I walk up to girls and say "Do you know who I used to be?"
Mitch Ryder

The sound of my own voice – I can't get used to it, never have. Makes you wanna hide.
Bob Dylan

Whenever we played, I always wanted to be in the audience.
Andy Partridge, XTC

I'm disgusted with elevator music, all this English synthetic Motown. Everything now is just so artificial and superficial. I'd like to see music get exciting again. I've had enough of all this shit, and I think the kids have too.
Joey Ramone, The Ramones

BEING A LIVING LEGEND IS SUCH A PRECARIOUS LIVELIHOOD. IT'S LIKE BEING A BAR OF SOAP IN A SHOWER WHICH DOESN'T HAVE ANY WATER IN IT.

John Cale

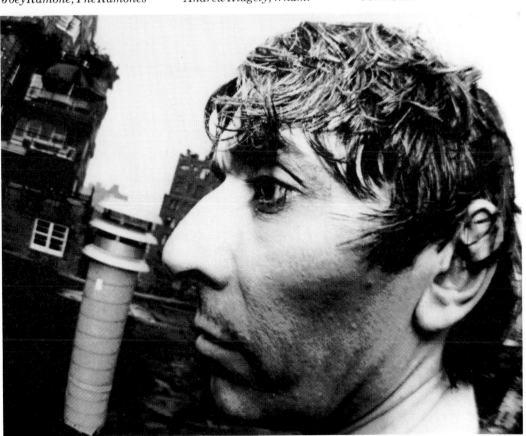

JOHN CALE

BRONSKI BEAT

WITH THREE QUEERS AND A COUPLE OF SYNTHS LYING AROUND, WE WERE BOUND TO COME UP WITH SOMETHING GOOD. WE'RE SUCH A CREATIVE LOT REALLY.

Larry Steinbachek, Bronski Beat

Once a girl asked me to autograph her breast, but the pen wouldn't work.
Nick Heyward

We are the best band in the world, simply. If we don't live up to people's expectations, they can fuck off, basically.
Billy, Death Cult

I'VE ALWAYS THOUGHT THAT I MANAGED QUITE WELL TO PORTRAY QUITE A SEXLESS IMAGE. I JUST REALLY DON'T HAVE THAT MUCH CONFIDENCE IN MY SEX APPEAL. I'VE GOT A 20 INCH CHEST AND I'M AS BLIND AS A BAT.

Clare Grogan

I'm normal; I get spots, I get the shits when I have curry.
Alison Moyet

Financially, I've been ripped to fuck. I've got all the respect in the world, but I ain't got tuppence.
John Lydon

It's not deliberate, but there's not much more we can sing about. Gay politics is obviously one of the most important things in our lives.
Jimi Somerville, Bronski Beat

Woodstock wasn't about anything. It was just a whole new market for tie-dyed tee-shirts. It was about clothes. All those people are in computers now.
Bob Dylan

I'VE NEVER ACTUALLY BEEN A BIG FAN OF OLD BOB. AS FAR AS I'M CONCERNED, HE'S JUST A JOB ON MY DATESHEET AT THE MOMENT.

Nick Lowe, on forthcoming gig, supporting Dylan.

It's always "Hey Ozzy, what do bats taste like?" or "Ozzy, is it true you blew a goat up?" I mean, it's incredible! They think I get up in the morning and go "mmmm. . .today's menu is going to be three cow's eyes and four cat's bollocks".
Ozzy Osbourne

We're talking total head removal here.
Ted Nugent

I work alone in the studio because then I have total concentration. I don't need a man mixing my paints or holding the easel up for me.
Eddy Grant

Although I wear silly sunglasses and bright trousers, underneath it all I'm still a very down-to-earth person from Sheffield. I could just as easily wear a flat cap.
Rick Savage, Def Leppard

There are more heterosexuals than gays in our group.
Holly, Frankie Goes To Hollywood

Your psyche is like your liver – you mustn't pour too much shit through it. If you do, you'll end up with a sweaty looking leather instead of a nice, big, receptive sponge like a sea anenome.
Ian Dury

JESUS HIMSELF ONLY PREACHED FOR THREE YEARS. I DON'T REGRET TELLING PEOPLE HOW TO GET THEIR SOULS SAVED. WHOEVER WAS SUPPOSED TO PICK UP ON IT, PICKED UP ON IT. NOW IT'S TIME FOR ME TO SAY SOMETHING ELSE.

Bob Dylan

A LOT OF PEOPLE THINK DAVID BOWIE GAVE ME ALL HIS DRESSES, BUT HE DIDN'T. I GET ALL MY DRESSES FROM EDNA EVERAGE.

Boy George, Culture Club

BOY GEORGE

The only people I don't respect are people on the right, because they're incredibly misguided, and, to be fair, most of them are motherfuckers. I mean, just look at Thatcher – she's a fascist. In every respect, she conforms to the definition: she's an authoritarian, a militarist, a materialist, a nationalist, and racist. At the very least you'd have to say she was a proto-fascist.
Jon King, Gang Of Four

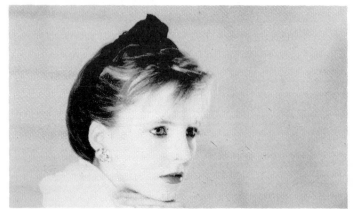

CLARE GROGAN

BOB DYLAN

The reason that we keep going is that we still like playing. We never rehearse much and we're not theatrical in the staging. I don't understand why a rock band rehearses for so long before it goes on tour.
Ray Davies, The Kinks

I would be false for me to be modest. I believe I'm a great singer and a great songwriter.
Sting, The Police

The reason I ran offstage that night is because my cock came out.
Graham Bonnet, Alcatrazz

I'm telling you, this substance cannabis is a whole lot less harmful than rum punch, whisky, nicotine or glue – all of which are perfectly legal. I would like to see it decriminalised.
Paul McCartney

IAN DURY

YOU KNOW THAT THING ANDY WARHOL SAID ABOUT EVERYBODY BEING FAMOUS FOR 15 MINUTES? WELL, I HAD 20 MINUTES, WHICH WAS PROBABLY MORE THAN MY FAIR SHARE ANYWAY.

Ian Dury

Television is taking away our ability to communicate. Everybody is becoming detached from reality. People are more worried about Sue Ellen running off with a teenager than about the state of Guatemala.
Ray Davies, The Kinks

I'm living in Tamworth; I've got a groovy domestic scene going with my girlfriend. Nothing happens in Tamworth, which is cool, because Liverpool and London were doing my head in.
Julian Cope

I like all types of music, but I'm tired of reading about the Shitheads on the Pinhead label from England. A lot of those bands don't deserve a chance, because they stink! Just because they're obscure doesn't mean they're good.
Brian Setzer, Stray Cats

Paul Weller seems to be in grave danger of making a total arsehole of himself.
Simon Le Bon, Duran Duran

You can't even call us weird, we're so weird.
Billy Gibbons, ZZ Top

We're talking total head removal here.
Ted Nugent

I've got past the stage of killing or badly hurting anyone just because the write something nasty about me.
Michael Schenker, MSG

WHAT MADE PERU AND PAKISTAN FAMOUS MADE A LOSER OUT OF UFO.

Pete Way, Waysted

PETE WAY

What I'd like to do is father 50 children in different countries all over the world. Then I could spend my spare time visiting them.
Simon Le Bon, Duran Duran

People talk about the pressure and the responsibility, but it's no worse than your average car worker. He's under pressure to pay the mortgage and make sure his wife has a coat. No, I don't subscribe to the theory of "Oh, the pressure".
Sting, The Police

There's a new breed of journalists who seem to hate me. One compared me to Heaven 17, another said it was Joy Division at the Seaside Special.
Matt Johnson, The The

My car insurance is pretty high. My insurance man said one of the reasons was because I might be driving with Adam Ant or Cliff Richard – but I said I didn't mix with those kind of people.
Gary Numan

THIS YEAR WE WENT TO TENERIFE AND IT WAS TERRIBLE BECAUSE EVERYBODY SAW ME TOPLESS. I KEPT HEARING BLOKES SAYING TO THEIR MATES "ERE, THAT'S TRACEY ULLMAN ISN'T IT? HASN'T SHE GOT TINY TITS?"

Tracey Ullman

T-BONE BURNETT

REDNECKS ON ACID ARE A LITTLE HARD TO TAKE, SO I LEFT TEXAS AND MOVED TO HOLLYWOOD, EXPECTING TO FIND SOPHISTICATES OR SOMETHING. I FOUND MORE REDNECKS ON ACID.

T-Bone Burnett

As far as I'm concerned, I'm trying to make enough money so that I don't have to work again ever.
Jim Brown, UB40

I was a loner as a teenager. I was fat and never had any hair on my face or my legs. And with a name like Derek Williams Dick, you can imagine the names I was called.
Fish, Marillion

TRACEY ULLMAN

JOE STRUMMER

Journey probably grossed more money in one year than the entire San Francisco music scene did in the five years between 1967 and 1972.
Walter Herbert, Manager of Journey

What I do isn't important. It's not exceptional. I'm just playing in a rock 'n' roll band.
Chrissie Hynde, Pretenders

I got a letter once from a young punk who said that since he heard the album *Hex* he'd been helping his mum with the washing up and the housework. That kind of change, which only seems to be a minor issue, is far more important to me than leading a crusade to change the world.
Vi Subversa, Poison Girls

I get annoyed when papers do interviews with me and all they want to do is get me to show my legs and ask me about sex. There's a lot more to me than just a fine pair of ankles.
Cyndi Lauper

Thank God for Boy George and Marilyn – they've made long hair fashionable again.
John Sykes, Whitesnake

Selina Scott on Breakfast TV was the worst. She said "and now it's time for an interview with the new Piaf" I felt my cup of tea shaking!
Carmel

I met a girl who taught me how to meditate properly. We used to sleep in the same bed, but we never had sex. It would have destroyed the purity of the moment and ruined our total state of relaxation. It must have been difficult controlling myself because I used to be such a randy wee bugger!
Mike Ogletree, Fiction Factory

I'VE SMOKED SO MUCH POT, I'M SURPRISED I HAVEN'T TURNED INTO A BUSH. THANK THE FUCK I HAVEN'T

Joe Strummer, The Clash

This place looks so normal and peaceful, but there is obviously trouble lurking just out of sight.
Linda Ronstadt on South Africa

I never pretended to be a sperm bank.
David Coverdale, Whitesnake

In America, audiences stick with things for ten years. In England, you're lucky to live more than a year. It's flavour of the month.
Dave Collard, JoBoxers

I never was an angry young man, I was always an angry old man. I always felt older, and always looked older, than I was.
Elvis Costello

Anything that smelled of compromise, I shot in the kneecap and sent home to mama.
Ted Nugent

The Clash were elected to do a job and it hasn't been done – because we were too self indulgent and made every mistake in the book.
Joe Strummer, The Clash

My father (Berry Gordy) is the kind of person who doesn't even know I'd signed to Motown.
Rockwell

The nation has taken me to its heart because I'm a bloody good geezer and my records are worth buying.
Captain Sensible

I wish we were simple enough people to be able to write something like Hank Williams. We know too much for our own good. When the media bombards you all the time, it soaks in. You can't help but know the ins and outs of what happened in Beirut or El Salvador or Grenada.
John Doe, X

We have to get away from the boring bank clerk image. It's been a real millstone around our necks. Really, we're a bundle of laughs.
Andy McClusky, Orchestral Manoeuvres In The Dark

Instead of watching bleeding TV, people ought to do something for themselves. I'm a shining example of that. I was thrown out of music lessons at school for being tone deaf, but music was my chosen thing and I made a point of doing it.
Captain Sensible

We've just seen too much, right from the early days of idiots like Stiff Little Fingers shooting way up beyond us when you could see they had no real ability and now dullards like Heaven 17 hitting the heights with the most pathetic versions of what The Fall did years ago.
Mark Smith, The Fall

The synthesiser should be symbollically burned.
Morrissey, The Smiths

You shouldn't treat the music business too seriously. It's all cotton wool.
Andy McCluskey, OMD

I once saw Al Green – that was pretty close to it.
Elvis Costello, asked if he believes in the supernatural

ONE DAY, I'D LIKE TO PLAY ON THE LIP OF AN ACTIVE VOLCANO, BUT THE ONLY TROUBLE IS, I DON'T THINK WE'D GET MANY PEOPLE IN THE AUDIENCE.
Simon Le Bon, Duran Duran

MARTIN FRY

SIMON LE BON

All I'm saying about music is this: here's pop today, millions of different people doing their thing whether they're motivated by money, glory, art, politics or pulling new girlfriends. And in the maelstrom of all that, occasionally somebody makes something which really touches you, it moves you.
Annie Lennox, Eurythmics

I THINK BRYAN FERRY IS SADLY LACKING IN STYLE. I SAW HIM ON TV; HE CAME ON IN A TUXEDO, THEN TOOK IT OFF. I THOUGHT, IS THIS THE SORT OF MAN WHO WALKS INTO A RESTAURANT AND ROLLS HIS SLEEVES UP?

Martin Fry, ABC

The trouble with people like Roddy Frame and Edwyn Collins is that they get sidetracked by the idea of being 'great songwriters'. Marc Bolan wrote classic songs automatically. Stuff like 'Metal Guru' doesn't make you sit around thinking about Yeats or Tennyson – you just think "Boogie!"
Bobby Bluebell, The Bluebells

I'm angry about a new white middle class male rock orthodoxy which seems to be establishing itself. After a couple of beers, I get very angry about it indeed.
Green, Scritti Politti

I think one of the quickest ways of getting a revolution in England overnight would be to ban beer and shut down pubs – people would be out on the streets, really militant.
Paul Weller, Style Council

I think we're successful, but I want to be more successful than this. I want to have a number one album all over the world at once for six months. And even then I'd want more!
Roy Hay, Culture Club

I can pretty well pull any girl I see in a bar or a restaurant. It's not something I ever talk about because I hate men who brag like that, but I've had more girls than any of the other Stones – more than all of them put together probably. I've had more than a thousand, while Charlie, our drummer, still has zero.
Bill Wyman, Rolling Stones

I'm coming back to Beethoven. To be quite honest, I've got sick of everything except classical music recently. If I go out, I tend to go and see the New York Philharmonic. I'm sick of popular music – it's quite horrible at the moment.
Joe Jackson

EMI moves at the pace of a slug on valium.
Beki Bondage, Ligotage

I could always take up a career in aviation.
Gary Numan

"

THE BUSINESS YEAR / UK

"The black disc will be dead by 1989," declared PolyGram's Jan Timmer early in 1983. In the year since he made this bold statement, much has happened to suggest that he might not have been very far from the truth.

This past year has seen major developments in sound-carrying technology, and the record companies, both small and large, while not always, one feels, understanding what's going on, are keeping pace.

The compact disc, the laser-read, digitally encoded miniature music carrier has been totally accepted by the recording industry as the ideal sound carrying medium. And the record companies have realised its marketing possibilities.

But manufacturers of vinyl are not as yet throwing themselves openly off the rooftops. The problem with CD is not so much that of public acceptance, but of a world shortage of manufacturing capacity. The CDs have to be produced in near-clinical conditions. And as yet, there's only one UK plant capable of producing them – the tiny Nimbus Records in South Wales which came on stream in July and claims to have a long waiting list of UK record companies queuing up to avail themselves of its services.

Until the manufacturing problems are sorted out, the releases of new product on CD look like continuing to be erratic. At the time of writing, CD deliveries to the trade were running at 30-40,000 a month, with the 1984 total predicted to settle at around 750,000 sales.

These encouraging figures, plus the improvements (albeit not of mammoth proportions) in sales of the traditional carriers, albums and pre-recorded cassettes, have seen the industry in a more buoyant mood than in recent years.

Pre-recorded cassettes now account for well over 40 per cent of the market. In the first three months of 1984, 7.2 million units were delivered, compared with 6.2 million for the same period in 1983, an increase of 16.5 per cent.

Sales of singles have declined slightly, but one or two mega-selling items have more than compensated for lower average sales. Michael Jackson (who?) has contributed handsomely to CBS's coffers, while Culture Club – as well as scoring a UK million-seller with 'Karma Chameleon' – have successfully flown the flag for home-grown UK talent in just about every territory of the world. And then there were the unexpected record-breaking achievements of Island's Frankie Goes To Hollywood. Both 'Relax' and 'Two Tribes' passed the million sales mark to contribute to Island's most successful period ever. And just for good measure, the West London label owned by Chris Blackwell, dominated the

album charts for weeks with Bob Marley's *Legend*. And with the video of *Legend*, knocked Michael Jackson off the top of the music video charts.

Video has continued to play an increasingly important part in record company business and in artist development. While the market for feature film videos has become established as a "rental situation", music videos, sensibly priced, have proved themselves commercially viable prospects.

Michael Jackson's *Making Of Thriller* opened a lot of doors (and a lot of wallets) and good business was enjoyed with titles from David Bowie, Culture Club, U2, Dire Straits, Eurythmics and other household names.

CHRIS BLACKWELL

The record companies continued to spend thousands – if not millions – on promo videos. While useful in breaking artists via *Top Of The Pops, The Tube* and the mushrooming cable and satellite TV companies, the returns to record companies from commercial exploitation of these promos can only, as yet, be measured in the hundreds of thousands of pounds. And this from an industry approaching a turnover of £10 million a year, largely funded by record companies.

But back to the records – and the chart that dominates the UK record industry and radio airwaves. Gallup, the research organisation responsible for compiling the industry-financed chart, continued to monitor computer returns with a fine tooth comb and weeded out the odd rotten apple. And the British Phonographic Industry (BPI) drew up a stricter "code of conduct" aimed at cutting out the numbers of "freebies" and other incentives given to chart return shops.

One of the more outrageous marketing ploys was undertaken by A&M who shrink-wrapped a promotional video to Annabel Lamb singles.

Marketing campaigns using free gifts and gimmicky versions of singles to achieve chart placings were denounced as "the scourge of the British music industry" by EMI Records UK managing director, Peter Jamieson. He continued: "There is such a fixation with achieving chart placings for a narrower and narrower range of product, that we are doing a dis-service to music as a whole."

Yet, a few months later, it was Jamieson's EMI that was fined £10,000 by the BPI for breaches in the chart code of conduct. A Gallup investigation revealed that EMI salesmen, promoting singles, offered dealers free albums by artists other than those whose records were being promoted, in direct contravention of the code.

Later in the year, WEA

Records was fined £6000 for offering free copies of the Van Halen album, *1984,* to shops including Gallup chart panel stores, conditional upon the Van Halen single, 'Jump', reaching the Top 30. This was the third time in less than four years that WEA had been implicated in chart hyping accusations.

That unhappy record aside, WEA UK, with new young management at the helm, headed by Rob Dickins and former Stiff person Paul Conroy, has been investing heavily in developing new talent, scoring its most notable success with Howard Jones.

The looming merger between the WEA parent company, Warners and the massive PolyGram group has hit a few legal snags and there would appear to be several hurdles to be crossed yet before the threatened PolyWarner conglomerate becomes a mammoth reality.

But another major merger looks certain to take place between RCA and Ariola. A preliminary agreement to merge the worldwide record, music publishing and music video interests has already been reached.

And the first big industry news headlines of 1984 were made by two of the UK's most innovative labels, Island and Stiff who announced the creation of a new joint venture. In typical bravado fashion, the deal was concluded just before Christmas after only 48 hours of negotiations between Island's Chris Blackwell and Stiff's Dave Robinson, with Island purchasing a 50 per cent share of Stiff.

Commenting on the move, Robinson said: "Now you could say that we are setting up the alternative Virgin. We will have two very separate companies which will be even better than they are now."

Whether you're talking about record companies, record retailing, recording studios, music publishing, computer games or even airlines, you can't review a business year without a cursory glance or two at the activities of the burgeoning Virgin empire and its chairman, Wing Commander Branson.

Headed by Culture Club, the Virgin record label soared to previously unscaled heights, while major record companies reeled back in their wake, and the subsidiary Ten label scored a number one with its debut release from The Flying

RICHARD BRANSON

Pickets.

And as well as the well-chronicled saga of Virgin Atlantic, the "pop millionaire" added just another two recording studios to his collection, and released a record-business game called "Hype".

One of the year's more interesting album/video marketing projects has been conducted with unusual co-operation between Virgin and EMI with assistance from other labels. Prompted perhaps by the proliferation of TV-merchandised chart compilation albums released by the likes of K-Tel and Ronco, the majors decided to keep this slice of the action for themselves and so far have released two double album sets of chart material and achieved most satsifactory sales figures. Compilation videos – under the same banner of *Now That's What I Call Music* have done as well in the respective market.

This action might well have contributed to TV album specialist Ronco finding itself in severe financial difficulties in mid-year.

At a jingoistic speech at the British Record Industry Awards Dinner, BPI chairman Maurice Oberstein (chairman of CBS Records) stated: "It is symbolic that we are gathered in The Great Room, because it has been a great year for our industry. The world is ours. By grit and determination we have come back – the British record industry is great."

Fair enough comment, especially when you look at the world's charts and see just how much UK-originated material has dominated over the past year.

But not everyone, it would appear, is quite so happy. At a London seminar in March, the International Federation of Phonogram and Videogram producers (IFPI) called for an international coalition to "save Europe's music" from "the dangers facing all those involved in the music business owing to the failure of copyright law to keep up with technical developments." The

new technology has brought forth a host of copyright problems which should make a lot of lawyers even wealthier.

On other favourite industry topics, the whole industry is still pushing for some kind of blank tape levy. Getting politicians interested in the subject is no problem, but getting any actual Parliamentary action instigated has proved rather more difficult. After all, it's not exactly a vote catching move to whack a tax on cassettes. And in Sweden, a levy – which was to be pooled and then redistributed to the music-makers – has produced far far less revenue than predicted. But smuggling blank tapes into the country is now a popular pastime.

Whatever, mid-way through the Eighties, the UK record industry, together with its associated leisure interests, is in good shape.

JIM EVANS

169

THE BUSINESS YEAR/US

Years from now, CBS Records president Walter Yetnikoff's distant offspring may or may not huddle around the hot tub on cold winter nights and tell the favourite family story of the black boy from Indiana who wore only one glove and single-handedly saved the music industry in America in 1983-84. But current CBS hype certainly reads to that effect and, to some extent, the hype is legitimate. Last year, record and tape sales boomed again in the US, just like they did back in the Seventies and Michael Jackson cracked records right and left, guiding record buyers back to the stores just like the Pied Piper of Hamelin. It would be a mistake, however, to predict the future success of the industry on the fluke success of one artist, and there is still a great deal to be done before all the executives start resting on their laurels.

Yes the Jacksons' long awaited family album did ship at last, with double platinum status. But the Jacksons' ballyhooed tour has been a fiasco from the start, with ticket prices at a whopping $30 each. No wonder America wants its MTV. New artists are getting more of a chance to prove themselves, but recording contracts for new acts are getting more constrictive and less lucrative. Many fledglings are shopping themselves to A&R executives via video tape.

This was also the year that saw MTV trying to buy exclusive rights to videos, Warner Brothers trying to merge with Polygram, and Arista and Buddah breaking up their distribution agreement. This was a year when corporate sponsors for US tours hit a new high. On radio, traditional FM broadcasting was dealt with a death blow – several of the most important FM stations determined that it was time to give 'Stairway To Heaven' a rest and give Boy George a chance at immortality, for which we must, again thank MTV. But despite MTV and radio's reviewed efforts to

breathe life into single records, it was still an album-oriented year.

The biggest story of the year is MTV's talks with the major labels about payment. A flurry of stories began in *Billboard* in February, and the issue is still building to a head. Are video clips a promotional device, or are they a means for achieving a profit? If the latter, who makes the profit? Do payments have to be made to SAG and AFTRA for acting? How are royalties paid on the songs? The whole thing is even more mind-boggling than it looks here, and it may take years to properly sort out.

On February 18, 1984 *Billboard* ran a story stating that Capitol and EMI-America were mulling over a one-and-a-quarter million dollar cash deal for the use of their video clips over a three-year period. The proposal included the guaranteed rotation of a "significant number" of the labels' videos in the "breakout" category and exclusivity for MTV. On March 31, it was reported that battle lines had been drawn between the business affairs people and the operations people at several record labels. The business

affairs people wanted the cash and the ability to better organize the distribution of video product. The operations people argued that the MTV deal might destroy the promotional value of videos and that the exclusivity clause would effectively cut the number of possible outlets.

As things stand at the time of writing, CBS will definitely be charging clip pools for the use of their clips in order to get back the costs of duplication and distribution, if not actually the cost of production. Atlantic will start changing if an industry standard is created. Elektra has indicated

WALTER YETNIKOFF

that they will not be signing any kind of deal with MTV and will not be charging for the use of their videos. As of June 23, 1984, MTV reported that it had signed deals with four majors "within the past ten days." Although the majors were not named, the general consensus is that they are CBS, RCA, Geffen and MCA. CBS will rceive eight million dollars over a two year period, according to industry insiders. RCA and MCA will receive two million for a three-year span. There are no provisions for giving any of the exclusivity

income to the artists at this time, which may make for more controversy unless some change is made in the current practice of charging artists for 50 per cent of each clip's production costs.

Also on the MTV front, Warner-Amex Satellite Entertainment Company has released a prospectus for the newly-formed corporate entity, MTV Networks. The prospectus reveals that MTV and Nickelodeon, a child-oriented cable channel, registered a profit for the first time in the first quarter of 1984, earning $2.8 million on a revenue of $20.5 million. The stock offering will raise about $80 million, which will be used to pay off $75 million in bank debts. Some of the money may also be used to help defray the cost of purchasing the exclusivity rights to video clips.

The PolyWarner merger, which shook the industry last year, appears to be at another standstill. In April of 1984, a federal appeals court forbade Warner Communications and Polygram to merge their recording interests pending review of a lower court ruling. The lower court had held that the Federal Trade Commission had failed to prove its charges of anti-trust violation.

The plan was to merge Polygram's and Warner's domestic record operations in a joint enterprise which would be owned 80 per cent by Warner and 20 per cent by Polygram. Other labels, most notably CBS, feared that a combined Warner-Polygram operation would dominate the marketplace and discourage competition. The merger would concentrate 26 per cent of the US record market in the hands of the joint venture, making PolyWarner the largest record company in the world. The coming year should see some interesting ramifications, either way.

On the corporate sponsor front, pointless debates have been rife. The question, apparently, is whether or not corporate identification with a musical group will have much of an effect on product sales. At the top of the list is PepsiCo's sponsorship of the Jackson tour: everyone knows that Michael Jackson drinks nothing but fruit juice, so will kids who identify with him buy Pepsi? Should beer companies be reprimanded for attaching themselves to bands who attract a younger audience? Should bands take money from beer and cigarette companies? Oh, for the good old days at Woodstock.

The good news is that sales are way up. Cassette sales topped LPs, accounting for almost 53 per cent of all album products shipped the year before. 1984 is off to a strong start in terms of gold and platinum albums. In the month of January, 20 albums were certified gold (as opposed to 12 the previous year) and seven were certified platinum (as opposed to five in 1983). In the first quarter, the gold album count was up 25 per cent over the last year, although gold singles are down a bit. The Christmas sales for 1983 averaged 15 per cent higher than the previous year, despite severe winter storms and sub-zero temperatures, and product seems to be continuing to sell on an upward scale.

CBS registered a 500 per cent increase in profits, Yetnikoff's great grandchildren may tell their own children some day, and the first quarter of 1984 saw a net income rise of 119 per cent over the same period last year. But will they also remember to whisper the 1983-84 was witness to the ARMS concert, instigated by Multiple Sclerosis victim Ronnie Lane? Probably not. On the business end, it's always and only the bottom line that counts.

DREW MOSELEY

RONNIE LANE AND A.R.M.S. BENEFIT PERFORMERS

UK INDEPENDENT

Will there, I wonder, still be an independent scene to write a resumé of this time next year? I offer this thought not because some dreadful financial holocaust is about to wipe out anything not able to attach itself limpet-like to a major label, but because the dominant trend over the past few years – for independents to make use of the majors' system for their own ends – has now come so far that in terms of new creative artists and pioneering spirits, the great gaps opened up by the punk movement have all but closed over again. No longer is there any sense of popular contempt for the major labels amongst the young bucks, nor even any hint of widespread indignation that the chart return system is preventing the big sellers on independent labels from receiving their due recognition in the public eye.

In fact, with the regeneration of the major

labels at the hands of a younger and more aware regime, the decline of the independent label seems to have set in to such a degree that any new act harbouring serious ambitions seems to regard putting out an independent record simply as a stepping stone to a deal with a major label. This time last year I mentioned two promising young bands with several releases to their credit on their own labels – Cook Da Books and Sisters Of Mercy. Both of them can now be found hand in hand with (or perhaps handcuffed to) a major company – Virgin/10 Records and WEA respectively. What's the betting that this time next year the Red Guitars (with several excellent singles like 'Good Technology' on their own Self Drive label) won't have joined them? Even now one can detect people feeling sorry for bands like Artery who don't have such a contract after

several years on the go. How long before the wheel turns full circle and acts like the Orson Family, who put out respectable records but don't get snapped up at once, are regarded as failures?

The reason for this evaporation of the independent *esprit de corps* is – the lure of instant cash aside – ironically chiefly due to the growing business awareness of those who have tasted not only a degree of success but also the problems and pressures in terms of time, energy and money that such success brings with it. Today's young moguls feel that the success of their artists is more important than independence for its own sake and that this success can be brought about more quickly by availing themselves of the majors' marketing muscle – or so they hope.

This time last year Go! Discs had made a stylish and eye-catching impact with their

energetic promotion of The Box. This year, after their alertness has rescued young Billy Bragg from the rubble that was Charisma, a similarly lively promotion campaign resulted in over 40,000 sales of his mid-price album *Life's A Riot With Spy Vs Spy*. This success, however, had been achieved on a shoe-string budget and had involved risking everything, while at the same time giving rise to frustration at not being able to compete more effectively with the big boys. Not only that but the label wouldn't be able to work equally effectively on, say, the Boothill Foot Tappers at the same time, let alone be able to offer something to new acts like The Redskins whom they wanted to sign. The result was almost inevitably that they link up with a major – in this instance Chrysalis, who Go! Discs offer almost apologetically, are only a bigger independent and not a

THE SMITHS

blanco y negro

AZTEC CAMERA

of pooling their knowledge and resources to form some kind of super-independent. As for deciding which act goes to which label, Travis says only that the contractual arrangements are very complex and that he's learned that it takes a lot of money to make a group successful. This could therefore well be the determining factor, since he could only hope to work on a couple of acts at a time at this level at Rough Trade. Would

Cherry Red have been able to launch Everything But The Girl into the Top 30 without such funding? Somehow I doubt it.

Overall, however, the general trend in sales is still a downward one, as Richard Scott of Rough Trade's wholesale outlet (and a fairly accurate weather vane in times past) confirms. Although Rough trade themselves have had their steadiest twelve months since they started, this has been partly due to accruing sufficient back catalogue (Aztec Camera's *High Land, Hard Rain* and New Order's *Power, Corruption And Lies* albums have been steady sellers, representing mostly profit since the initial investment of recording etc. has been recouped) and partly to the success of people like The Smiths at the top end of the market.

Rough Trade also moved to bigger premises which allowed them to become better organised. Given the current dearth of new independent labels of quality, Rough Trade have now started looking for more specialist catalogues of interest. European and post-copyist American imports are selling better, though again Scott attributes this to being better organised to handle it rather than any upsurge in public interest. African music, however, has not taken off as hoped. Clearly it is too broad in scope to be assimilated all at once and it will require some percolation down from the top by one or two big names before

multinational, and who have given them full artistic control and a budget to work within.

Similarly the independent sector lost Dave Kitson's Red Flame label to Virgin/10 Records (though retaining its subsidiary Ink), though Kitchenware chose to tackle the problem act by act with Prefab Sprout going to CBS and The Kane Gang and The Daintees going to London Records.

Even Rough Trade, committed as they are to the development of independent distribution through The Cartel, found themselves linking up with London Records to use the latter's sales force. The reason here, however, was quality rather than policy. The London sales force, with spare capacity, seemed to have a fair amount of affinity with Rough Trade in musical policy and was of better quality, in Geoff Travis' eyes, than alternatives like IDS. Given good records and a

strong base of live work, Travis feels that a good efficient sales force has been a key factor in The Smiths' success.

So what future then for Rough Trade? After all, they scored the major success of the year with The Smiths – confounding the norms with a string of hit singles that were far from polished techno-pop and an album that entered the UK LP charts at No.2. At last the potential which had been there with Aztec Camera and Scritti Politti had been realised; was this a blueprint for other acts? Sadly bands with the individuality of The Smiths are few and far between but for the future they've signed Jonathan Richman & The Modern Lovers, Float Up CP (Gareth Sager's new project) and Microdisney, welcomed back James Blood Ulmer from CBS and to show there's still a place for rank outsiders, signed Dishari (the Bangladesh group who previously appeared with

Robert Wyatt) and plan to release a lot more African material.

Pressing and distribution deals seem to be making a come-back as well with ex-Teardrop Dave Balfe's Food label (Brilliant, The Woodentops) and Earthworks (who hope to expand to include other ethnic musics). Sadly the OAO catalogue has been lost to Carrere (of all people) and the Slash catalogue has gone to London after a financial crisis in Los Angeles. (There was also a mutually agreed parting of the ways with The Go-Betweens who then signed to Sire).

Significantly, however, the potentially highly influential triumvirate of Geoff Travis, Mike Alway (who left Cherry Red, taking several acts with him including Everything But The Girl) and Michel Duval of Crepuscule chose to link up with the fiscal barons at Warner Brothers for their Blanco Y Negro label instead

173

real progress can be made.

Sadly, reggae continues in its present depressed state, even though public awareness and acceptance is higher now that at any time in the past. The big names are quiet and no new names are coming through to challenge them. The general opinion is that there simply isn't any good reggae about; the gap between the current scene and Marley's crown seems as wide as ever. On a more optimistic note, however, it is encouraging to see local authorities (especially in London) getting involved in helping to get local projects off the ground.

One interesting development on the distribution side is that IDS – who made such a dramatic impact last year with a string of impressive "assists" in making hits – have all but disappeared from this particular corner of the market and are now to be found principally working with the high energy disco releases of Record Shack, Proto etc. Experience seems to have shown that the marketing techniques they employ – those of the top end of the market: free records etc. – simply aren't cost effective in the current market conditions. (It is now possible to reach the Top 20 on sales that would have been out of the question eighteen months ago).

Meanwhile The Cartel – the centralised liaison between six regional distributors: Backs of Norwich, Fast Product of Edinburgh, Probe of Liverpool, Red Rhino of York, Revolver of Bristol and Rough Trade of London – having clung to life is now starting to grow slowly, offering both a local and a national service selling into stores like W.H.Smith, Boots, and the like. In fact, the market now seems oversubscribed with distributors – The Cartel, Pinnacle, IDS, Spartan and now PRT – and already Pinnacle and IDS have had merger talks. Scott considers there is room only for two or three and so expects one or more to fall by the wayside this year as retail outlets continue to shrink. Rough Trade, meanwhile, have set themselves the long term target of inching up their share of this declining market so that when the two graphs do cross, they will be able to survive even though that share may be quite modest.

This time last year I also suggested that future significant developments in this sector might lie in attitudes and ways of working rather than in generalised labels like 'independent' which are subject to the ebb and flow of public taste and opinion. This would seem to be being borne out as increasingly the independent labels of lasting significance can be attributed to the visions of one or two particularly committed invidivuals – people such as Ivo Watts-Russell and Daniel Miller.

Ivo Watts-Russell of 4AD considers that he's had a good year with the slow, uncontrived growth of the label and in particular with the success of The Cocteau Twins, whose band of followers has now taken these one time rank outsiders into the Top 30 with 'Pearly Dewdrops' Drops'. Another more personal pleasure (though equally significant) was his indulgence of recording Tim Buckley's haunting 'Song To The Siren' by This Mortal Coil (aka The Cocteau Twins) and seeing this wonderful, beautiful record become his label's then bestseller and hanging around the lower regions of the charts for months on end.

The success of the records, Watts-Russell considers, goes a long way to justifying his belief that it's faith in the long term and not necessarily hit singles that counts. "It's a means of attempting to change what is considered commercial without being contrived about it. Sales have increased because of that, because of having achieved that." Watts-Russell remains as opposed as ever to the manipulation of chart return shops with free records and similar incentives, although he confesses to have indulged himself in the case of 'Song To The Siren'. Ironically, however, though sales increased, the chart position the following week dropped and with 'Pearly Dewdrops' Drops' he stuck to his principles once more and had real success despite refusing to conform.

Ironically the success of The Cocteau Twins has been the label's biggest financial headache, causing cash flow problems as increasing numbers of records have to be paid for at the pressing plant but increased credit is extended to the system which sells those records, and leaving Watts-Russell wondering what he has to do to be able to spend extra money on ensuring that an independently made record is no less well made than one on a major label.

Significantly, Watts-Russell wants to concentrate his long term faith and energies on his small present roster – possibly decreasing it if anything – and has only taken on one new act in Dead Can Dance. Xmal Deutschland helped justify that approach with a number one independent album in Tocsin while overseas sales by Modern English helped the financial stituation. Also in America, Colour Box – whose superb 'Say You' single deserved better than it got – signed to Quincy Jones' Qwest label and are clearly a name to watch out for. Meanwhile Watts-Russell continues along his chosen path of aiming to sell as many records as possible without having to contrive at it and to enjoy doing so. More power to him.

Mute Records, meanwhile, continued their winning ways as the independent sector's most consistently successful label, blending hits that are dependent on intrinsic quality rather than big marketing spends (Depeche Mode, Vince Clarke) with Daniel Miller's own more esoteric line in experimental music (Einsturzende Neubauten, Non, the Throbbing Gristle back catalogue)

Bolstered by overseas sales (Depeche Mode, for instance, are huge in Germany) and by sensible housekeeping, Mute are not so constricted in their budgeting but Miller also sees it as important to keep the operation small and develop what he's got. He's thus only taken on two new acts – the easily accessible I Start Counting and the more challenging Mark Stewart & The Mafia, and is happy with the progress of newer signings like Nick Cave (ex-Birthday Party) with his surprisingly non-abrasive LP From Her To Eternity although the continued lack of success for Fad Gadget is a disappointment. Miller is even fairly happy with his twin distribution through Spartan and The Cartel, though he's still looking for improvement in overall efficiency. No prizes for guessing which label will still be in the top slot next year.

By contrast, Dick O'Dell's Y label seems to be all but dormant (although a new Sun Ra LP is rumoured to be on the way) as O'Dell pursues a career as a producer and their major asset, Shriekback, were bought out by Arista. Nor can one leave the subject of committed individuals without the traditional nod to Factory, whose energies seem mostly taken up with New Order these days although From The Hip, another album of tone poems by Section 25, also managed to sneak out. Crass, by comparison, seem to have faded from the scene somewhat and failed to outrage anybody this year.

Elsewhere The Cramps re-emerged to loud applause after their wranglings with the Copeland empire with their Smell Of Female live recording, and two interesting newcomers to the independent sector were The Damned, who proved their major label doubters wrong by successfully launching their own label, and the Carrere label, who left the world of major distribution and brought with them such diverse names as Golden Earring and Dollar.

Apart from genuine highlights like The Cramps, the independent charts were a distinctly unappealing dogs breakfast of hard-core punk (Flux Of Pink Indians, etc) and doom-laden Gothic bands (most of whom seem to incorporate the word "Dead" in their name), ageing hippies (Dave Brock, The Enid) and heavy metal (insert warlike name of your choice) each appealing to a minority interest and unlikely ever to do anything else. The only exception to this were some welcome archive re-releases from the Demon and Edsel labels in the F-Beat empire.

It is, I suppose, one of the more lasting appeals of the independent sector that you will still find there individuals whose ideas and ways of working cut right across the accepted modes of thought even with the 'alternative' sector themselves. Such a man is Ian McNay Of Cherry Red Records. Having seen his erstwhile partner Mike Alway depart for Blanco Y Negro with the lion's share of his artist roster, McNay had had rather a tough year of it but survives on other resources.

Cherry Red were – and still are – one of the few independent set-ups to appreciate the financial potential of publishing income, and not just with acts on their own label. Shrewd early signings like Blancmange, for example, have had

JONATHAN RICHMAN

international success to which Cherry Red have contributed like any other publisher and even though Everything But The Girl left Cherry Red Records with Alway, the fact that their publishing remains there means that Cherry Red will still see some reward for past efforts and being alert enough to spot their potential in the first place. Publishing income from The The and John Cale has also helped to bail out the operation and McNay now concludes that to stay independent without either hits or other interests is almost impossible.

McNay also remains the independents' spokesman on the BPI, the industry's governing body, where he has had the satisfaction of helping to implement one of this long-standing aims of tightening up on free gifts and the like to chart return shops. It was ironic, therefore, that – like Ivo Watts-Russell at 4AD – McNay should be finding himself this year breaking one of his firmly held principles – that of no free records – in a mail out desperate attempt to get Alien Sex Fiend into the chart return shops. It was, he considers, more a blow to his pride than anything else; he had to be realistic and compromise since he really had no alternative, and his ideals are still there.

A trained accountant, McNay nevertheless admires people like Geoff Travis, Daniel Miller and Tony Wilson (of Factory) – even though he doesn't always agree with their ideas – because they've found a formula which works for them within their own terms while he has not. Still, with the publishing on Thomas Leer (now with Arista), The Go-Betweens (now of Sire) and Red Box (now on WEA), he's still involved and it's still working out, even if it's not on Cherry Red Records.

"We're still here," he says with a mixture of optimism and relief that seems to reflect the times for most independent labels. "We're still in business and still putting out records. And to me, at the end of the day, if we can make a living out of doing that, that's the important thing."

IAN CRANNA

175

US INDEPENDENT

The past year has seen sales of cassettes surpass albums, the introduction of stereo video tapes, steady growth of video TV shows, and acceptance of compact discs. With such a technological upheaval, the industry sometimes seems to forget it is also supposed to create new music. Despite the efforts of American independents to keep music a primary consideration, several factors indicate serious problems for the non-majors.

Local record stores generally continue to cater to established acts, with little attention to independent record companies. At best, the typical chain store may have a small section for local bands. This causes more confusion than help as more and more stores reintegrate their inventory into a general 'Rock' category reminiscent of the Sixties and Seventies. The 'New Wave', 'Heavy Metal', and 'Punk' sections of recent years are fast disappearing.

Corporate machines have taken over the few areas once dominated by independent labels. In late July *Billboard* had just three indies charted on the current Dance/Disco Top 80. Only two years ago independents accounted for nearly 50 per cent of the chart. As dance clubs began playing more 're-mixed-master-extended-version-digital-dub-club' versions of the latest hit by ZZ Top or Bruce Springsteen, independent labels found it impossible to retain their once exclusive market.

This situation partly derives from the ever more monopolistic distribution system. When a large distributor the size of Pickwick sells out, the repercussions must be felt throughout the independent industry. Pickwick handled mostly majors, and a variety of business reasons account for the firm's demise. But the loss of Pickwick raises a serious

issue: What are the chances of survival for smaller, local distributors? Despite the mid-year formation of an organization such as Independent Distribution Network (IND), which hopes to give independent labels a means of national marketing, poor distribution remains the main obstacle to the average fan looking for new sounds.

To overcome the problem, efforts by Slash, I.R.S., Pasha and others to sign distribution deals with a major label seem

more the trend than ever before. Virgin Records, planning a second effort at the American market, is also following this course. Virgin will reopen a New York office, retain control over promotion/marketing, but hand over distribution to a national company.

Perhaps the best example of the state of American indies is the fate of Tom Silverman's Independent label Coalition (ILC). Established last year, and reported in this column of last year's *Rock Yearbook* as an encouraging development,

the ILC remains mostly a dream. As recently as March 1984, ILC could claim only 15 dues-paying members. The "one voice" for independents which ILC hopes eventually to become remains unheard (It would seem this goal is somewhat of a contradiction in terms for an industry made up of mavericks and free thinkers who, by definition, are independent).

These considerations should not obscure the many healthy aspects of the indie scene. In

many ways American music is more diverse, more open to something new, and more original than ever before.

There are more hard core fans to support more back alley record stores which cater to original, alternative types of music. This is reflected by the fact that almost every large town now supports some local music circuit. Places like Providence, Rhode Island, or Tacoma, Washington have venues for a wide variety of acts. Along with the clubs and bars are small local labels willing to press a limited run of

a few thousand records. That small local band section in chain stores throughout the country wouldn't have existed at all a year ago.

Reflecting a popular resurgence in hard rock and heavy metal, several indies have had a wider influence this past year. Pasha Records used company president, Spencer Proffer, to produce Quiet Riot's *Metal Health*. After the band travelled thousands of miles in a station wagon while slogging out interviews and recording local station ID's Pasha signed with CBS to gain national sales. Ratt sold 40,000 EP's on Time Coast Records which resulted in major label interest. Black And Blue, Great White, Warlord, and Pandemonium got started on indies such as Metal Blade Records, Shrapnel Records, and Par Records. This wide variety of heavy metal labels follows the same pattern set by punk/new wave a few years ago. This means there is absolutely no reason not to expect the major labels to overrun the field as bands prove their popularity (i.e. commercial worth). The independents will survive but without the extensive impact of this year.

The growing video industry promises some encouragement as major productions such as MTV provide "home video" contests. Unfortunately, many of the newer video formats (*Friday Night Videos, Hot Tracks*) rely solely on established Top 40 lists for their selections. Efforts such as Panacea Entertainment Management & Communications, owned by Todd Rundgren, may counter this tendency by attempting to identify new talent, and providing video support within reasonable costs. Panacea could foreshadow a whole new development: the independent video industry.

Indies continue to try the new and commercially

unacceptable. Reach Out Records (ROIR) produces only cassettes, and then limits itself to one release per act. With over 30 releases, ROIR has developed a reputation for innovative music. As a result, ROIR's status among fans has become deservedly a legend in the vein of the early Stiff label.

Interestingly, the home computer is supporting the growth of the indie industry. Direct Mail Catalogs are now simple and economical to put together. Even the smallest label, companies specializing in a particular brand of music find they reach new markets outside their local areas. For example, RAS (Washington, DC) used direct mail to boost sales and expand its reggae market on the East Coast. Down Home Records (El Cerrito, CA) used the same method, which may grow into a serious challenge to indie Rounder Records' domination of the R&B, folk market. Small record stores or collectors specialist shops such as Blue Meannie Records (Los Angeles) and Be-Bop Records (Philadelphia) have long used direct mail as a primary marketing tool for selling 'collectibles'. There is now a developing shift toward handling indie product as well.

Any summary of the past year would be incomplete without sadly noting the closing of *Trouser Press*. Editor Ira Robbins had built TP into one of the few national information sources on new bands, local scenes, and independent labels. To remain solvent he found the magazine had to pander to commercial bands in which he had little interest and he consequently stopped publication. The growth of American fanzines and interest in independent labels since 1974 is in large part due to *Trouser Press*. Its passing may be a dangerous indication of things to come.

ED HANEL

BECK · TORONTO NEW WAVE FESTIVAL · DEXY'S

Trouser Press

November 1980
No. 56
$1.50
UK 75p

THE CARS IN PROGRESS

APPROVED:
PUBLISHER
EDITOR NO
ART DIRECTOR NFW!

Entire Concept Weak!
Redo!!

ENLARGE PHOTO 20%

ISSN 0164-1883

EUROPE

PROPAGANDA

One name might typify, if not completely represent, Europe this year: Nena. Her transatlantic hit, '99 Red Balloons', annoyed me so much I grew to like it. Interestingly, while she needed a British translation to get to the top of our charts, in America it was the original German-language '99 Luftballons' that sailed up the charts. I'm not too sure what that says about the countries involved, although the insular British would come out of any interpretation in a bad light.

After Nena, the only thing to emerge from Europe that looked vaguely like becoming a phenomenon was Germany's Propaganda, and if their debut 45 'Dr. Mabuse' for Zang Tumb Tuum only got into the thirties, ZTT's guerilla ideas man Paul Morley proved keyboard-oriented German rock can be marketed/promoted on the chart scene where everyone in the past had failed. Pity it wasn't too hot a single, though.

Apart from the indie scene, everywhere it was still more schlager, schlager, schlager and most seemed to respond 'make mine a pint'. (Sorry). Even the blink-and-you'll-miss-it Die Neue Deutsche Welle ('new German wave') cobbled together by Phonogram is now but a brief, noisy memory. Berlin's Einsturzende Neubauten remain due largely to the media fuss (their actual audience of true fans is quite small), and the only others worth mentioning, the swinging, punky Abwarts are rumoured to have disbanded. Gonzo pop minimalists Trio apparently thrive in America. They recently got an album reviewed in Rolling Stone, although round our way that's equivalent to your relatives letting the doctor switch off your life-support system.

1984 might in retrospect be looked on as the year the old guard went quiet. There were exceptions – the third solo album from Holger Czukay, a double album of his Can-pal Irmin Schmidt's ravishing film music, and also from the Cologne stable, the third, and best so far, from Phantomband and, finally, a solo album from Micky Karoli, *Deluge*. Tangerine Dream were silent. Similarly, Kraftwerk and France's Richard Pinhas were nowhere to be seen/heard, Bernjard Szajner's deal with Island Records fell apart, Magma were still silent, and none of the French/Lowlands 'chamber music' axis – Univers Zero, Art Zoyd et al – could be found lurking in my post.

But the year wasn't without its pleasant surprises. Most notable was the appearance of Yugoslavian 'underground' group, Laibach. Admittedly, Yugoslavia is one of the more liberal Soviet satellites, but, even after the likes of The Plastic People Of The Universe (more of whom later) and Brygada Kryzys, that this group exists at all is quite extraordinary. They played a one-off London date at Christmas with Britain's own Last Few Days (with whom they had recently toured Yugoslavia) and shortly afterwards released a 12-inch EP, *Boji* on Crepuscule. Like a benign form of Futurism, they adopt a self-disciplining 'industrial' stance, strike a fine (if dangerous) balance between radical and totalitarian imagery, and produce a frightening sound disrupted by barked orders/shouts and clogged by slow, nightmare machinery. I still don't understand how this group's unflinching confrontationism can exist in Yugoslavia, but it does.

Crepuscule again proved itself probably the most productive and adventurous label of the year. While much music from the Lowlands tends to lean towards chamber/systems music – indeed, Crepuscule leads the pack with Soft Verdict – it also finds time for the less palatable adventures of the post-punk experimenters. *Deadly Weapons*, the second album for Minimal Compact, at times bristled with the violent edge of classic Pop Group. Crepuscule's 'neighbour' label, Crammed, run by Marc Hollander, was also to the fore, with work by The Honeymoon

NENA

Killers, Benjamin Lew and others, and the aforementioned became the first band from this axis to visit Britain when they played the ICA arts centre in London in August.

Although there's some geographical distance between the two, Sweden's Uniton Records find their way into Britain via the same channels as Crammed and Crepuscule, and so should perhaps be mentioned here. Apart from the long-silent Tasavallan Presidentii and Samla Mammas Manna, Scandinavia has made little impression on the international new wave, but Holy Toy and Fra Lippo Lippi, both units releasing albums and singles during the year, produce a strong (and in the former instance, highly politicised) brand of semi-electronic dance music.

Next up in my haphazard top ten was the guy from Auf Ruhr Records who wandered into my office one day. The 'stars' of this small German label are Vorgruppe, whose debut

album *Menschenkinder* and follow-up EP, *Das Sehnen Nach Dem Schein*, shadowbox with The Residents' style of production in a DIY, poppier fashion, using touches of rarefied jazz and funk to toughen up cluster-style keyboard music. Vorgruppe are threatening a second album this summer, and should be pursued in earnest. While you're at it, lend an ear to the unfortunately-named Bimbo Band, a more straightforward, politically-based version of their labelmates.

The most adventurous project of the year had to be *Film Noir – American Style*, the double-tape/magazine artefact released by Holland's Ding-Dong Records. Producer/compiler Ed van Kasteren wrote to around 60 bands and individuals in Europe and America asking for contributions to a cassette on and of film noir. The response was so great it had to be expanded to a double. 'Names' like Clock DVA, Der Plan,

Benjamin Lew, Richard Bone, Voice Farm and the ubiquitous Residents all contributed short musical vignettes offering their versions of or paying homage to film noir soundtracks, as did some strange wonders like Utilisation Du Vieux Port and The Doodooettes. Given the tendencies of rock trendies to bandy cinema terms around in the vain hope of looking intellectual, *Film Noir* might look pretentious on paper, but I've never come across a compilation (27 different acts in all) that is so consistently impressive. If I had one purchase to recommend, this is it, and it can be obtained from Ding-Dong, P.O. Box 115, 6801 BD Arnhem, Netherlands, for the equivalent of eight pounds sterling.

A couple of East European albums found their way onto my desk this year; *1984* by Republika, and *Spunk!* by TSA. Both were licensed from the Polish state record label Polton by Britain's Mega Records, and can safely be said

to number themselves among the 'official' bands sanctioned by the authorities. The former are an engaging, if soft-hearted new wave/skank outfit. The latter are a 'goodtime' hard rock band in the stadium band mould (they even call one of their tracks 'Black Sabbath'!) and while I sympathise with their enthusiasm their album left me glassy-eyed and twitching.

No such qualms attended the arrival of *Leading Horses*, the belated (they always are) third album from harrassed Czech underground band Plastic People Of The Universe. Recorded covertly and smuggled out independent of the band (their involvement would only cause further trouble) it's an album of passion and adventure, maybe even heroism. Cossetted Western hacks laugh at the term 'dangerous music', but by default, given what lengths the authorities go to to silence such music, this album has just started ticking. In comparison, the rest was just a false alarm.

JOHN GILL

IN MEMORIAM

ALEXIS KORNER

MARVIN GAYE

COUNT BASIE, pianist and bandleader, and one of the last great jazz legends, whose music spanned nearly five decades, died in Florida on April 26, 1984, aged 79. He had been suffering from pancreatic cancer.

BARNEY BUBBLES, the talented graphic artist who designed many of the early marketing campaigns and record sleeves for Stiff Records, committed suicide on November 18, 1983, aged 41.

TOM EVANS, former bass player and songwriter with Badfinger, hung himself at his home in Surrey on November 1983, compounding a tragic irony: several years previously, Pete Ham, another of the group's songwriters, hung himself after bitter legal wrangles over allegedly unpaid royalties had left him critically depressed.

MARVIN GAYE, one of soul music's great innovators and a founding inspiration behind Tamla Motown, was shot to death by his father on April 1, 1984, after a family row.

IRA GERSHWIN, the veteran Broadway lyricist, died, aged 86, in New York on August 17, 1983.

FRANK 'MACHITO' GRILLO, the veteran Cuban bandleader, died in London in April 1984, during a season of performances at Ronnie Scott's Soho jazz club.

Z.Z. HILL, the brilliant Texas soul singer, whose troubled career had been revived with a series of excellent recordings for the Mississippi-based R&B label, Malaco, died on April 27, 1984, from injuries sustained in a car-crash two months earlier.

ALEXIS KORNER, musician, writer, broadcaster and seminal figure in the evolution of British blues, died of lung cancer on January 1, 1984, aged 55.

ROY MILTON, the R&B singer, whose group the Solid Senders dominated the American R&B charts between 1946 and 1952 with a series of hits that included 'The Hucklebuck' and 'So Tired', died of a stroke in October, 1983. He was 76.

KLAUS NOMI, highly eccentric, operatically-trained German rock-cabaret artist, died in New York of AIDS on August 6, 1983: he was 38.

ESTHER PHILLIPS, the noted jazz, soul and blues singer, died on August 7, 1984, aged 48, after some months of ill health. Her last international hit was 1977's 'What A Difference A Day Makes'.

PRINCE FAR-I, another victim of Jamaica's political violence, was assassinated by gunmen in his home on September 27, 1983.

MICHAEL SMITH, the Jamaican dub poet, was stoned to death outside the Jamaican Labour Party headquarters in St. Andrews on August 27, 1983, allegedly by political opponents.

MERLE TRAVIS, country and western star of the Fifties, and writer of Tennessee Ernie Ford's 'Sixteen Tons', died in Nashville on October 20, 1983, aged 65.

JACKIE WILSON, the great American R&B singer, immortalised by Van Morrison on 'Jackie Wilson Says' and probably best-remembered for 'Reet Petite', 'Lonely Teardrops' and 'Higher And Higher'. He had been in a coma since suffering a stroke in 1975, and died on January 21, 1984, aged 49.

PHILIPPE WYNNE, lead singer of the Spinners from 1972-77 and latterly a solo artist, died on stage at a California nightclub of a heart attack on July 14, 1984. He was 43.

THE YEAR'S CHARTS

United Kingdom record chart information
© Music Week/BBC/Gallup 1983 & 1984
Reprinted with permission

United States record chart information
© Billboard Publications, Inc. 1983 & 1984
reprinted with permission

FEATURING THE
BILLBOARD
AND MUSIC WEEK
CHARTS

WEEK ENDING JULY 30 1983

US SINGLES	US ALBUMS	UK SINGLES	UK ALBUMS
1 EVERY BREATH YOU TAKE *The Police – A & M*	1 SYNCHRONICITY *The Police – A & M*	1 WHEREVER I LAY MY HAT… *Paul Young – CBS*	1 YOU AND ME BOTH *Yazoo – Mute*
2 ELECTRIC AVENUE *Eddy Grant – Portrait/Ice*	2 THRILLER *Michael Jackson – Epic*	2 I.O.U. *Freeez – Beggars Banquet*	2 THRILLER *Michael Jackson – Epic*
3 FLASHDANCE (WHAT A FEELING) *Irene Cara – Casablanca*	3 FLASHDANCE *Soundtrack – Casablanca*	3 WHO'S THAT GIRL? *Eurythmics – RCA*	3 SYNCHRONICITY *The Police – A&M*
4 NEVER GONNA LET YOU GO *Sergio Mendes – A & M*	4 PYROMANIA *Def Leppard – Mercury*	4 DOUBLE DUTCH *Malcolm McLaren – Charisma/Phonogram*	4 FANTASTIC *Wham! – Inner Vision*
5 IS THERE SOMETHING… *Duran Duran – Capitol*	5 THE WILD HEART *Stevie Nicks – Modern*	5 COME LIVE WITH ME *Heaven 17 – B.E.F./Virgin*	5 BEST OF THE BEACH BOYS *The Beach Boys – Capitol*
6 SWEET DREAMS… *Eurythmics – RCA*	6 LET'S DANCE *David Bowiie – EMI America*	6 THE CROWN *Gary Byrd & G.B. Experience – Motown*	6 NO PARLEZ! *Paul Young – CBS*
7 WANNA BE STARTIN'… *Michael Jackson – Epic*	7 KEEP IT UP *Loverboy – Columbia*	7 MOONLIGHT SHADOW *Mike Oldfield – Virgin*	7 THE LOOK *Shalamar – Solar*
8 SHE WORKS HARD FOR… *Donna Summer – Mercury*	8 CARGO *Men At Work – Columbia*	8 WRAPPED AROUND YOUR… *The Police – A & M*	8 JULIO *Julio Iglesias – CBS*
9 STAND BACK *Stevie Nicks – Modern*	9 1999 *Prince – Warner Bros.*	9 BABY JANE *Rod Stewart – Warner Bros.*	9 THE LUXURY GAP *Heaven 17 – Virgin*
10 OUR HOUSE *Madness – Geffen*	10 KILLER ON THE RAMPAGE *Eddy Grant – Portrait/Ice*	10 CRUEL SUMMER *Bananarama – London*	10 18 GREATEST HITS *Michael Jackson/Jackson 5 – Telstar*
11 MANIAC *Michael Sembello – Casablanca*	11 FRONTIERS *Journey-Columbia*	11 DO IT AGAIN/BILLIE JEAN *Club House – Island*	11 CRISES *Mike Oldfield - Virgin*
12 1999 *Prince – Warners Bros.*	12 H₂O *Daryl Hall & John Oates – RCA*	12 IT'S LATE *Shakin' Stevens – Epic*	12 LET'S DANCE *David Bowie – EMI America*
13 COME DANCING *The Kinks – Arista*	13 STATE OF CONFUSION *The Kinks – Arista*	13 FLASHDANCE (WHAT A FEELING) *Irene Cara – Casablanca/Phonogram*	13 PRINCIPLE OF MOMENTS *Robert Plant – WEA*
14 BABY JANE *Rod Stewart – Warner Bros.*	14 CUTS LIKE A KNIFE *Bryan Adams – A & M*	14 IT'S OVER *Funk Masters – Master-Funk Records*	14 FLASHDANCE SOUNDTRACK *Various – Casablanca/Phonogram*
15 IT'S A MISTAKE *Men At Work – Columbia*	15 PIECE OF MIND *Iron Maiden – Capitol*	15 DON'T TRY TO STOP IT *Roman Holiday – Jive*	15 IN YOUR EYES *George Benson – Warner Bros.*
16 CUTS LIKE A KNIFE *Bryan Adams – A & M*	16 DURAN DURAN *Duran Duran – Capitol*	16 THE WALK *The Cure – Fiction*	16 BODY WISHES *Rod Stewart – Warner Bros.*
17 (KEEP FEELING) FASCINATION *The Human League – A & M*	17 SPEAKING IN TONGUES *Talking Heads – Sire*	17 NEVER STOP *Echo & The Bunnymen – Korova*	17 HITS ON FIRE *Various – Ronco*
18 HOT GIRLS IN LOVE *Loverboy – Columbia*	18 REACH THE BEACH *The Fixx – MCA*	18 WAR BABY *Tom Robinson – Panic*	18 SWEET DREAMS … *Eurythmics – RCA*
19 ROCK OF AGES *Def Leppard – Mercury*	19 SHE WORKS HARD FOR… *Donna Summer – Mercury*	19 GIVE IT UP *KC & The Sunshine Band – Epic*	19 BURNING FROM THE INSIDE *Bauhaus – Beggars Banquet*
20 CHINA GIRL *David Bowie – EMI America*	20 ELIMINATOR *Z.Z. Top – Warner Bros.*	20 FORBIDDEN COLOURS *David Sylvian/Riuichi Sakamoto – Virgin*	20 TOO LOW FOR ZERO *Elton John – Rocket/Phonogram*

WEEK ENDING AUGUST 6 1983

US SINGLES	US ALBUMS	UK SINGLES	UK ALBUMS
1 EVERY BREATH YOU TAKE *The Police – A & M*	1 SYNCHRONICITY *The Police – A & M*	1 WHEREVER I LAY MY HAT *Paul Young – CBS*	1 THE VERY BEST OF … *The Beach Boys – Capitol*
2 SWEET DREAMS *Eurythmics – RCA*	2 THRILLER *Michael Jackson – Epic*	2 I.O.U. *Freeez – Beggars Banquet*	2 18 GREATEST HITS *Michael Jackson/Jackson 5 – Telstar*
3 SHE WORKS HARD … *Donna Summer – Mercury*	3 FLASHDANCE *Soundtrack – Casablanca*	3 DOUBLE DUTCH *Malcolm McLaren – Charisma/Phonogram*	3 NO PARLEZ! *Paul Young – CBS*
4 IS THERE SOMETHING … *Duran Duran – Capitol*	4 PYROMANIA *Def Leppard – Mercury*	4 WHO'S THAT GIRL? *Eurythmics – RCA*	4 THE CROSSING *Big Country – Mercury/Phonogram*
5 FLASHDANCE… *Irene Cara – Casablanca*	5 THE WILD HEART *Stevie Nicks – Modern*	5 GIVE IT UP *KC & The Sunshine Band – Epic*	5 YOU AND ME BOTH *Yazoo – Mute*
6 ELECTRIC AVENUE *Eddy Grant – Portrait/Ice*	6 LET'S DANCE *David Bowie – EMI America*	6 THE CROWN *Gary Byrd & The G.B.Experience – Motown*	6 THRILLER *Michael Jackson – Epic*
7 MANIAC *Michael Sembello – Casablanca*	7 KEEP IT UP *Loverboy – Columbia*	7 WRAPPED AROUND YOUR FINGER *The Police – A & M*	7 FANTASTIC *Wham! – Inner Vision*
8 NEVER GONNA LET YOU GO *Sergio Mendes – A & M*	8 CARGO *Men at Work – Columbia*	8 CRUEL SUMMER *Bananarama – London*	8 SYNCHRONICITY *The Police – A & M*
9 STAND BACK *Stevie Nicks – Modern*	9 1999 *Prince – Warner Bros.*	9 COME LIVE WITH ME *Heaven 17 – B.E.F./Virgin*	9 THE LOOK *Shalamar – Solar*
10 WANNA BE STARTIN' … *Michael Jackson – Epic*	10 FRONTIERS *Journey – Columbia*	10 CLUB TROPICANA *Wham! – Inner Vision*	10 THE LUXURY GAP *Heaven 17 – Virgin*
11 IT'S A MISTAKE *Men At Work – Columbia*	11 H₂O *Daryl Hall & John Oates – RCA*	11 IT'S LATE *Shakin' Stevens – Epic*	11 THE PRINCIPLE OF MOMENTS *Robert Plant – Swan Song*
12 OUR HOUSE *Madness – Geffen*	12 STATE OF CONFUSION *The Kinks – Arista*	12 MOONLIGHT SHADOW *Mike Oldfield – Virgin*	12 HITS ON FIRE *Various – Ronco*
13 (KEEP FEELING) FASCINATION *Human League – A & M*	13 REACH THE BEACH *The Fixx – MCA*	13 DO IT AGAIN/BILLIE JEAN *Club House – Island*	13 JULIO *Julio Iglesias – CBS*
14 HOT GIRLS IN LOVE *Loverboy – Columbia*	14 DURAN DURAN *Duran Duran – Capitol*	14 DON'T TRY TO STOP IT *Roman Holliday – Jive*	14 CRISES *Mike Oldfield – Virgin*
15 CUTS LIKE A KNIFE *Bryan Adams – A & M*	15 PIECE OF MIND *Iron Maiden – Capitol*	15 BIG LOG *Robert Plant – Swansong*	15 LET'S DANCE *David Bowie – EMI America*
16 COME DANCING *The Kinks – Arista*	16 SHE WORKS HARD … *Donna Summer – Mercury*	16 EVERYTHING COUNTS *Depeche Mode – Mute*	16 IN YOUR EYES *George Benson – Warner Bros.*
17 1999 *Prince – Warner Bros.*	17 SPEAKING IN TONGUES *Talking Heads*	17 FLASHDANCE… *Irene Cara – Casablanca/Phonogram*	17 FLASHDANCE *Soundtrack – Casablanca/Phonogram*
18 CHINA GIRL *David Bowie – EMI America*	18 CUTS LIKE A KNIFE *Bryan Adams – A & M*	18 THE WALK *The Cure – Fiction*	18 SWEET DREAMS … *Eurythmics – RCA*
19 ROCK OF AGES *Def Leppard – Mercury*	19 KILLER ON THE RAMPAGE *Eddy Grant – Portrait/Ice*	19 BABY JANE *Rod Stewart – Warner Bros.*	19 BODY WISHES *Rod Stewart – Warner Bros.*
20 I'LL TUMBLE 4 YA *Culture Club – Virgin/Epic*	20 SWEET DREAMS … *Eurythmics – RCA*	20 RIGHT NOW *The Creatures – Wonderland/Polydor*	20 TRUE *Spandau Ballet – Reformation/Chrysalis*

WEEK ENDING AUGUST 13 1983

US SINGLES

1 EVERY BREATH YOU TAKE
The Police – A & M

2 SWEET DREAMS
Eurythmics – RCA

3 SHE WORKS HARD ...
Donna Summer – Mercury

4 MANIAC
Michael Sembello – Casablanca

5 IS THERE SOMETHING ...
Duran Duran – Capitol

6 STAND BACK
Stevie Nicks – Modern

7 FLASHDANCE...
Irene Cara – Casablanca

8 IT'S A MISTAKE
Men At Work – Columbia

9 NEVER GONNA LET YOU GO
Sergio Mendes – A & M

10 (KEEP FEELING) FASCINATION
The Human League – A & M

11 ELECTRIC AVENUE
Eddy Grant – Portrait/Ice

12 PUTTIN' ON THE RITZ
Taco – RCA

13 HOT GIRLS IN LOVE
Loverboy – Columbia

14 CHINA GIRL
David Bowie – EMI America

15 I'LL TUMBLE 4 YA
Culture Club – Virgin/Epic

16 ROCK OF AGES
Def Leppard – Mercury

17 WANNA BE STARTIN' ...
Michael Jackson – Epic

18 1999
Prince – Warner Bros.

19 TAKE ME TO HEART
Quarterflash – Geffen

20 SAVED BY ZERO
The Fixx – MCA

US ALBUMS

1 SYNCHRONICITY
The Police – A & M

2 THRILLER
Michael Jackson – Epic

3 FLASHDANCE
Soundtrack – Casablanca

4 PYROMANIA
Def Leppard – Mercury

5 THE WILD HEART
Stevie Nicks – Modern

6 LET'S DANCE
David Bowie – EMI America

7 KEEP IT UP
Loverboy – Columbia

8 CARGO
Men At Work – Columbia

9 FRONTIERS
Journey – Columbia

10 STAYING ALIVE
Soundtrack – RSO

11 DURAN DURAN
Duran Duran – Capitol

12 SHE WORKS HARD ...
Donna Summer – Mercury

13 REACH THE BEACH
The Fixx – MCA

14 H$_2$O
Daryl Hall & John Oates – RCA

15 PIECE OF MIND
Iron Maiden – Capitol

16 1999
Prince – Warner Bros.

17 SPEAKING IN TONGUES
Talking Heads – Sire

18 SWEET DREAMS ...
Eurythmics – RCA

19 THE PRINCIPLE OF MOMENTS
Robert Plant – Swan Song

20 ALBUM
Joan Jett and the Blackhearts – Blackheart

UK SINGLES

1 GIVE IT UP
KC & The Sunshine Band – Epic

2 WHEREVER I LAY MY HAT
Paul Young – CBS

3 I.O.U.
Freeez – Beggars Banquet

4 DOUBLE DUTCH
Malcolm McLaren – Charisma/Phonogram

5 CLUB TROPICANA
Wham! – Inner Vision

6 THE CROWN
Gary Byrd & The G.B.Experience – Motown

7 WHO'S THAT GIRL?
Eurythmics – RCA

8 LONG HOT SUMMER
The Style Council – Polydor

9 I'M STILL STANDING
Elton John – Rocket/Phonogram

10 EVERYTHING COUNTS
Depeche Mode – Mute

11 BIG LOG
Robert Plant – Swan Song

12 GOLD
Spandau Ballet – Reformation/Chrysalis

13 CRUEL SUMMER
Bananarama – London

14 IT'S LATE
Shakin' Stevens – Epic

15 ROCKIT
Herbie Hancock – CBS

16 MOONLIGHT SHADOW
Mike Oldfield – Virgin

17 RIGHT NOW
The Creatures – Wonderland/Polydor

18 WRAPPED AROUND ...
The Police – A & M

19 COME LIVE WITH ME
Heaven 17 – B.E.F./Virgin

20 DON'T TRY TO STOP IT
Roman Holiday – Jive

UK ALBUMS

1 THE VERY BEST OF ...
The Beach Boys – Capitol

2 18 GREATEST HITS
Michael Jackson/Jackson 5 – Telstar

3 PUNCH THE CLOCK
Elvis Costello And The Attractions – F-Beat

4 FANTASTIC
Wham! – Inner Vision

5 NO PARLEZ!
Paul Young – CBS

6 THRILLER
Michael Jackson – Epic

7 THE CROSSING
Big Country – Mercury/Phonogram

8 YOU AND ME BOTH
Yazoo – Mute

9 THE PRINCIPLE OF MOMENTS
Robert Plant – Swan Song

10 SYNCHRONICITY
The Police – A & M

11 HITS ON FIRE
Various – Ronco

12 THE LUXURY GAP
Heaven 17 – Virgin

13 THE LOOK
Shalamar – Solar

14 TOO LOW FOR ZERO
Elton John – Rocket/Phonogram

15 JULIO
Julio Iglesias – CBS

16 IN YOUR EYES
George Benson – Warner Bros.

17 TRUE
Spandau Ballet – Reformation/Chrysalis

18 CRISES
Mike Oldfield – Virgin

19 LET'S DANCE
David Bowie – EMI – America

20 FLASHDANCE ...
Soundtrack – Casablanca/Phonogram

WEEK ENDING AUGUST 20 1983

US SINGLES

1 EVERY BREATH YOU TAKE
The Police – A & M

2 SWEET DREAMS
Eurythmics – RCA

3 SHE WORKS HARD ...
Donna Summer – Mercury

4 MANIAC
Michael Sembello – Casablanca

5 STAND BACK
Stevie Nicks – Modern

6 IT'S A MISTAKE
Men At Work – Columbia

7 IS THERE SOMETHING ...
Duran Duran – Capitol

8 (KEEP FEELING) FASCINATION
The Human League – A & M

9 PUTTIN' ON THE RITZ
Taco – RCA

10 I'LL TUMBLE 4 YA
Culture Club – Virgin/Epic

11 HOT GIRLS IN LOVE
Loverboy – Columbia

12 CHINA GIRL
David Bowie – EMI America

13 FLASHDANCE...
Irene Cara – Casablanca

14 TAKE ME TO HEART
Quarterflash – Geffen

15 HUMAN NATURE
Michael Jackson – Epic

16 NEVER GONNA LET YOU GO
Sergio Mendes – A & M

17 LAWYERS IN LOVE
Jackson Browne – Asylum

18 THE SAFETY DANCE
Men Without Hats – MCA

19 ROCK 'N' ROLL IS KING
ELO – Jet

20 ELECTRIC AVENUE
Eddy Grant – Portrait/Ice

US ALBUMS

1 SYNCHRONICITY
The Police – A & M

2 THRILLER
Michael Jackson – Epic

3 FLASHDANCE
Soundtrack – Casablanca

4 PYROMANIA
Def Leppard – Mercury

5 THE WILD HEART
Stevie Nicks – Modern

6 LET'S DANCE
David Bowie – EMI America

7 KEEP IT UP
Loverboy – Columbia

8 STAYING ALIVE
Soundtrack – RSO

9 REACH THE BEACH
The Fixx – MCA

10 DURAN DURAN
Duran Duran – Capitol

11 SHE WORKS HARD ...
Donna Summer – Mercury

12 CARGO
Men At Work – Columbia

13 FRONTIERS
Journey – Columbia

14 PIECE OF MIND
Iron Maiden – Capitol

15 THE PRINCIPLE OF MOMENTS
Robert Plant – Swan Song

16 SPEAKING IN TONGUES
Talking Heads – Sire

17 SWEET DREAMS ...
Eurythmics – RCA

18 H$_2$O
Daryl Hall & John Oates – RCA

19 1999
Prince – Warner Bros.

20 ALBUM
Joan Jett and the Blackhearts – Blackheart

UK SINGLES

1 GIVE IT UP
KC & The Sunshine Band – Epic

2 GOLD
Spandau Ballet – Reformation/Chrysalis

3 LONG HOT SUMMER
The Style Council – Polydor

4 CLUB TROPICANA
Wham! – Inner Vision

5 I'M STILL STANDING
Elton John – Rocket/Phonogram

6 EVERYTHING COUNTS
Depeche Mode – Mute

7 DOUBLE DUTCH
Malcolm McLaren – Charisma/Phonogram

8 ROCKIT
Herbie Hancock – CBS

9 WHEREVER I LAY MY HAT
Paul Young – CBS

10 I.O.U.
Freeez – Beggars Banquet

11 THE CROWN
Gary Byrd & The G.B.Experience – Motown

12 BIG LOG
Robert Plant – WEA

13 WHO'S THAT GIRL?
Eurythmics – RCA

14 RIGHT NOW
The Creatures – Wonderland/Polydor

15 THE FIRST PICTURE OF YOU
The Lotus Eaters – Sylvan/Arista

16 CRUEL SUMMER
Bananarama – London

17 WATCHING YOU, WATCHING ME
David Grant – Chrysalis

18 MOONLIGHT SHADOW
Mike Oldfield – Virgin

19 WINGS OF A DOVE
Madness – Stiff

20 WAIT UNTIL TONIGHT (MY LOVE)
Galaxy/Phil Fearon – Ensign/Island

UK ALBUMS

1 18 GREATEST HITS
Michael Jackson/Jackson 5 – Telstar

2 THE VERY BEST OF ...
The Beach Boys – Capitol

3 FANTASTIC
Wham! – Inner Vision

4 THRILLER
Michael Jackson – Epic

5 ALPHA
Asia – Geffen

6 NO PARLEZ
Paul Young – CBS

7 THE PRINCIPLE OF MOMENTS
Robert Plant – WEA

8 PUNCH THE CLOCK
Elvis Costello And The Attractions – F-Beat

9 TRUE
Spandau Ballet – Reformation/Chrysalis

10 YOU AND ME BOTH
Yazoo – Mute

11 TOO LOW FOR ZERO
Elton John – Rocket/Phonogram

12 SYNCHRONICITY
The Police – A & M

13 THE CROSSING
Big Country – Mercury/Phonogram

14 THE LUXURY GAP
Heaven 17 – Virgin

15 THE LOOK
Shalamar – Solar

16 STREET SOUNDS – EDITION 5
Various – Street Sounds

17 LET'S DANCE
David Bowie – EMI America

18 HITS ON FIRE
Various – Ronco

19 SWEET DREAMS ...
Eurythmics – RCA

20 CRISES
Mike Oldfield – Virgin

WEEK ENDING AUGUST 27 1983

US SINGLES

1. **EVERY BREATH YOU TAKE**
   The Police – A & M
2. **SWEET DREAMS**
   Eurythmics – RCA
3. **MANIAC**
   Michael Sembello – Casablanca
4. **SHE WORKS HARD ...**
   Donna Summer – Mercury
5. **PUTTIN' ON THE RITZ**
   Taco – RCA
6. **IT'S A MISTAKE**
   Men At Work – Columbia
7. **STAND BACK**
   Stevie Nicks – Modern
8. **(KEEP FEELING) FASCINATION**
   The Human League – A & M
9. **I'LL TUMBLE 4 YA**
   Culture Club – Virgin/Epic
10. **CHINA GIRL**
    David Bowie – EMI America
11. **THE SAFETY DANCE**
    Men Without Hats – Backstreet
12. **TELL HER ABOUT IT**
    Billy Joel – Columbia
13. **HUMAN NATURE**
    Michael Jackson – Epic
14. **LAWYERS IN LOVE**
    Jackson Browne – Asylum
15. **IS THERE SOMETHING ...**
    Duran Duran – Capitol
16. **DON'T CRY**
    Asia – Geffen
17. **HOT GIRLS IN LOVE**
    Loverboy – Columbia
18. **TAKE ME TO HEART**
    Quarterflash – Geffen
19. **ROCK 'N' ROLL IS KING**
    ELO – Jet
20. **TOTAL ECLIPSE OF THE HEART**
    Bonnie Tyler

US ALBUMS

1. **SYNCHRONICITY**
   The Police – A & M
2. **THRILLER**
   Michael Jackson – Epic
3. **FLASHDANCE**
   Soundtrack – Casablanca
4. **PYROMANIA**
   Def Leppard – Mercury
5. **THE WILD HEART**
   Stevie Nicks – Modern
6. **STAYING ALIVE**
   Soundtrack – RSO
7. **LET'S DANCE**
   David Bowie – EMI America
8. **KEEP IT UP**
   Loverboy – Columbia
9. **SHE WORKS HARD ...**
   Donna Summer – Mercury
10. **REACH THE BEACH**
    The Fixx – MCA
11. **DURAN DURAN**
    Duran Duran – Capitol
12. **FRONTIERS**
    Journey – Columbia
13. **LAWYERS IN LOVE**
    Jackson Brown – Asylum
14. **THE PRINCIPLE OF MOMENTS**
    Robert Plant – Swan Song
15. **SWEET DREAMS ...**
    Eurythmics – RCA
16. **SPEAKING IN TONGUES**
    Talking Heads – Sire
17. **CARGO**
    Men At Work – Columbia
18. **AN INNOCENT MAN**
    Billy Joel – Columbia/CBS
19. **1999**
    Prince – Warner Bros.
20. **KISSING TO BE CLEVER**
    Culture Club – Virgin/Epic

UK SINGLES

1. **GIVE IT UP**
   KC & The Sunshine Band – Epic
2. **GOLD**
   Spandau Ballet – Reformation/Chrysalis
3. **LONG HOT SUMMER**
   The Style Council – Polydor
4. **I'M STILL STANDING**
   Elton John – Rocket/Phonogram
5. **CLUB TROPICANA**
   Wham! – Inner Vision
6. **WINGS OF A DOVE**
   Madness – Stiff
7. **EVERYTHING COUNTS**
   Depeche Mode – Mute
8. **ROCKIT**
   Herbie Hancock – CBS
9. **RED RED WINE**
   UB40 – DEP International
10. **WATCHING YOU, WATCHING ME**
    David Grant – Chrysalis
11. **DOUBLE DUTCH**
    Malcolm McLaren – Charisma/Phonogram
12. **COME DANCING**
    The Kinks – Arista
13. **WALKING IN THE RAIN**
    Modern Romance – WEA
14. **THE SUN GOES DOWN ...**
    Level 42 – Polydor
15. **THE FIRST PICTURE OF YOU**
    The Lotus Eaters – Sylvan/Arista
16. **I.O.U.**
    Freeez – Beggars Banquet
17. **BIG LOG**
    Robert Plant – WEA
18. **THE CROWN**
    Gary Byrd & The G.B. Experience – Motown
19. **RIGHT NOW**
    The Creatures – Wonderland/Polydor
20. **WHEREVER I LAY MY HAT**
    Paul Young – CBS

UK ALBUMS

1. **18 GREATEST HITS**
   Michael Jackson/Jackson 5 – Telstar
2. **THE VERY BEST OF ...**
   The Beach Boys – Capitol
3. **FANTASTIC**
   Wham! – Inner Vision
4. **TRUE**
   Spandau Ballet – Reformation/Chrysalis
5. **THRILLER**
   Michael Jackson – Epic
6. **ALPHA**
   Asia – Geffen
7. **TOO LOW FOR ZERO**
   Elton John – Rocket/Phonogram
8. **THE PRINCIPLE OF MOMENTS**
   Robert Plant – WEA
9. **NO PARLEZ!**
   Paul Young – CBS
10. **PUNCH THE CLOCK**
    Elvis Costello And The Attractions – F-Beat
11. **THE LOOK**
    Shalamar – Solar
12. **THE CROSSING**
    Big Country – Mercury/Phonogram
13. **SYNCHRONICITY**
    The Police – A & M
14. **YOU AND ME BOTH**
    Yazoo – Mute
15. **THE LUXURY GAP**
    Heaven 17 – Virgin
16. **LET'S DANCE**
    David Bowie – EMI America
17. **STREET SOUNDS – EDITION 5**
    Various – Street Sounds
18. **SWEET DREAMS ...**
    Eurythmics – RCA
19. **FLASHDANCE**
    Soundtrack – Casablanca/Phonogram
20. **IN YOUR EYES**
    George Benson – Warner Bros.

WEEK ENDING SEPTEMBER 3 1983

US SINGLES

1. **SWEET DREAMS ...**
   Eurythmics – RCA
2. **MANIAC**
   Michael Sembello – Casablanca
3. **EVERY BREATH YOU TAKE**
   The Police – A & M
4. **PUTTIN' ON THE RITZ**
   Taco – RCA
5. **SHE WORKS HARD ...**
   Donna Summer – Mercury
6. **THE SAFETY DANCE**
   Men Without Hats – Backstreet
7. **TELL HER ABOUT IT**
   Billy Joel – Columbia
8. **IT'S A MISTAKE**
   Men At Work – Columbia
9. **I'LL TUMBLE 4 YA**
   Culture Club – Virgin/Epic
10. **HUMAN NATURE**
    Michael Jackson – Epic
11. **(KEEP FEELING) FASCINATION**
    The Human League – A & M
12. **CHINA GIRL**
    David Bowie – EMI America
13. **DON'T CRY**
    Asia – Geffen
14. **LAWYERS IN LOVE**
    Jackson Browne – Asylum
15. **TOTAL ECLIPSE OF THE HEART**
    Bonnie Tyler – Columbia
16. **STAND BACK**
    Stevie Nicks – Modern
17. **(SHE'S) SEXY + 17**
    Stray Cats – EMI America
18. **MAKING LOVE ...**
    Air Supply – Arista
19. **TAKE ME TO HEART**
    Quarterflash – Geffen
20. **HUMAN TOUCH**
    Rick Springfield – RCA

US ALBUMS

1. **SYNCHRONICITY**
   The Police – A & M
2. **THRILLER**
   Michael Jackson – Epic
3. **SOUNDTRACK**
   Flashdance – Casablanca
4. **PYROMANIA**
   Def Leppard – Mercury
5. **THE WILD HEART**
   Stevie Nicks – Modern
6. **SOUNDTRACK**
   Staying Alive – RSO
7. **AN INNOCENT MAN**
   Billy Joel – Columbia
8. **ALPHA**
   Asia – Geffen
9. **LAWYERS IN LOVE**
   Jackson Browne – Asylum
10. **REACH THE BEACH**
    The Fixx – MCA
11. **KEEP IT UP**
    Loverboy – Columbia
12. **LET'S DANCE**
    David Bowie – EMI America
13. **THE PRINCIPLE OF MOMENTS**
    Robert Plant – Es Paranza
14. **SHE WORKS HARD ...**
    Donna Summer – Mercury
15. **SWEET DREAMS ...**
    Eurythmics – RCA
16. **FRONTIERS**
    Journey – Columbia
17. **CARGO**
    Men At Work – Columbia
18. **SPEAKING IN TONGUES**
    Talking Heads – Sire
19. **METAL HEALTH**
    Quiet Riot – Pasha
20. **KISSING TO BE CLEVER**
    Culture Club – Virgin/Epic

UK SINGLES

1. **RED RED WINE**
   UB40 – DEP International
2. **GIVE IT UP**
   KC & The Sunshine Band – Epic
3. **GOLD**
   Spandau Ballet – Reformation/Chrysalis
4. **WINGS OF A DOVE**
   Madness – Stiff
5. **I'M STILL STANDING**
   Elton John – Rocket/Phonogram
6. **CLUB TROPICANA**
   Wham! – Inner Vision
7. **LONG HOT SUMMER**
   The Style Council – Polydor
8. **WHAT AM I GONNA DO ...**
   Rod Stewart – Warner Bros.
9. **WALKING IN THE RAIN**
   Modern Romance – WEA
10. **WATCHING YOU, WATCHING ME**
    David Grant – Chrysalis
11. **THE SUN GOES DOWN ...**
    Level 42 – Polydor
12. **ROCKIT**
    Herbie Hancock – CBS
13. **COME DANCING**
    The Kinks – Arista
14. **EVERYTHING COUNTS**
    Depeche Mode – Mute
15. **BAD DAY**
    Carmel – London
16. **TONIGHT I CELEBRATE MY LOVE**
    Peabo Bryson/Roberta Flack – Capitol
17. **CONFUSION**
    New Order – Factory
18. **DISAPPEARING ACT**
    Shalamar – Solar
19. **DOUBLE DUTCH**
    Malcolm McLaren – Virgin/Charisma
20. **MAMA**
    Genesis – Virgin/Charisma

UK ALBUMS

1. **18 GREATEST HITS**
   Michael Jackson/Jackson 5 – Telstar
2. **THE VERY BEST OF ...**
   The Beach Boys – Capitol
3. **FANTASTIC**
   Wham! – Inner Vision
4. **FLICK OF THE SWITCH**
   AC/DC – Atlantic
5. **TRUE**
   Spandau Ballet – Reformation/Chrysalis
6. **CONSTRUCTION TIME AGAIN**
   Depeche Mode – Mute
7. **THRILLER**
   Michael Jackson – Epic
8. **TOO LOW FOR ZERO**
   Elton John – Rocket/Phonogram
9. **STANDING IN THE LIGHT**
   Level 42 – Polydor
10. **NO PARLEZ!**
    Paul Young – CBS
11. **THE CROSSING**
    Big Country – Mercury/Phonogram
12. **THE PRINCIPLE OF MOMENTS**
    Robert Plant – WEA
13. **ALPHA**
    Asia – Geffen
14. **SYNCHRONICITY**
    The Police – A & M
15. **THE LOOK**
    Shalamar – Solar
16. **YOU AND ME BOTH**
    Yazoo – Mute
17. **BODY WISHES**
    Rod Stewart – Warner Bros.
18. **THE LUXURY GAP**
    Heaven 17 – Virgin
19. **LET'S DANCE**
    David Bowie – EMI America
20. **PUNCH THE CLOCK**
    Elvis Costello And The Attractions – F-Beat

WEEK ENDING SEPTEMBER 10 1983

US SINGLES

1. **MANIAC**
Michael Sembello – Casablanca
2. **SWEET DREAMS ...**
Eurythmics – RCA
3. **THE SAFETY DANCE**
Men Without Hats – Backstreet
4. **PUTTIN' ON THE RITZ**
Taco – RCA
5. **TELL HER ABOUT IT**
Billy Joel – Columbia
6. **EVERY BREATH YOU TAKE**
The Police – A & M
7. **SHE WORKS HARD ...**
Donna Summer – Mercury
8. **TOTAL ECLIPSE OF THE HEART**
Bonnie Tyler – Columbia/CBS
9. **HUMAN NATURE**
Michael Jackson – Epic
10. **I'LL TUMBLE 4 YA**
Culture Club – Virgin/Epic
11. **DON'T CRY**
Asia – Geffen
12. **(KEEP FEELING) FASCINATION**
Human League – A & M
13. **LAWYERS IN LOVE**
Jackson Browne – Asylum
14. **(SHE'S) SEXY + 17**
Stray Cats – EMI America
15. **MAKING LOVE ...**
Air Supply – Arista
16. **IT'S A MISTAKE**
Men At Work – Columbia/CBS
17. **FAR FROM OVER**
Frank Stallone – RSO
18. **HUMAN TOUCH**
Rick Springfield – RCA
19. **PROMISES, PROMISES**
Naked Eyes – EMI America
20. **HOW AM I SUPPOSED TO LIVE ...**
Laura Branigan – Atlantic

US ALBUMS

1. **THRILLER**
Michael Jackson – Epic
2. **SYNCHRONICITY**
The Police – A & M
3. **FLASHDANCE**
Soundtrack – Casablanca
4. **PYROMANIA**
Def Leppard – Mercury
5. **AN INNOCENT MAN**
Billy Joel – Columbia
6. **ALPHA**
Asia – Geffen
7. **STAYING ALIVE**
Soundtrack – RSO
8. **LAWYERS IN LOVE**
Jackson Browne – Asylum
9. **THE WILD HEART**
Stevie Nicks – Modern
10. **REACH THE BEACH**
The Fixx – MCA
11. **THE PRINCIPLE OF MOMENTS**
Robert Plant – Swan Song
12. **LET'S DANCE**
David Bowie – EMI America
13. **KEEP IT UP**
Loverboy – Columbia
14. **SHE WORKS HARD ...**
Donna Summer – Mercury
15. **SWEET DREAMS ...**
Eurythmics – RCA
16. **SPEAKING IN TONGUES**
Talking Heads – Sire
17. **METAL HEALTH**
Quiet Riot – Pasha
18. **GREATEST HITS**
Air Supply – Arista
19. **ELIMINATOR**
ZZ Top – Warner Bros.
20. **RHYTHM OF YOUTH**
Men Without Hats – Backstreet

UK SINGLES

1. **RED RED WINE**
UB40 – DEP International
2. **WINGS OF A DOVE**
Madness – Stiff
3. **WHAT AM I GONNA DO ...**
Rod Stewart – Warner Bros.
4. **GIVE IT UP**
KC & The Sunshine Band – Epic
5. **MAMA**
Genesis – Virgin/Charisma
6. **GOLD**
Spandau Ballet – Reformation/Chrysalis
7. **TONIGHT I CELEBRATE MY LOVE**
Peabo Bryson/Roberta Flack – Capitol
8. **I'M STILL STANDING**
Elton John – Rocket/Phonogram
9. **WALKING IN THE RAIN**
Modern Romance – WEA
10. **THE SUN GOES DOWN ...**
Level 42 – Polydor
11. **CLUB TROPICANA**
Wham! – Inner Vision
12. **CONFUSION**
New Order – Factory
13. **LONG HOT SUMMER**
The Style Council – Polydor
14. **WATCHING YOU, WATCHING ME**
David Grant – Chrysalis
15. **CHANCE**
Big Country – Mercury/Phonogram
16. **BAD DAY**
Carmel – London
17. **ROCKIT**
Herbie Hancock – CBS
18. **COME DANCING**
The Kinks – Arista
19. **DISAPPEARING ACT**
Shalamar – Solar
20. **WARRIORS**
Gary Numan – Beggars Banquet

UK ALBUMS

1. **THE VERY BEST OF ...**
The Beach Boys – Capitol
2. **18 GREATEST HITS**
Michael Jackson/Jackson 5 – Telstar
3. **FANTASTIC**
Wham! – Inner Vision
4. **TRUE**
Spandau Ballet – Reformation/Chrysalis
5. **THRILLER**
Michael Jackson – Epic
6. **NO PARLEZ!**
Paul Young – CBS
7. **CONSTRUCTION TIME AGAIN**
Depeche Mode – Mute
8. **THE CROSSING**
Big Country – Mercury/Phonogram
9. **FLICK OF THE SWITCH**
AC/DC – Atlantic
10. **STANDING IN THE LIGHT**
Level 42 – Polydor
11. **TOO LOW FOR ZERO**
Elton John – Rocket/Phonogram
12. **THE LOOK**
Shalamar – Solar
13. **SUNNY AFTERNOON**
Various – Impression
14. **BODY WISHES**
Rod Stewart – Warner Bros.
15. **SYNCHRONICITY**
The Police – A & M
16. **THE PRESENT**
The Moody Blues – Threshold
17. **THE PRINCIPLE OF MOMENTS**
Robert Plant – WEA
18. **ALPHA**
Asia – Geffen
19. **LET'S DANCE**
David Bowie – EMI America
20. **YOU AND ME BOTH**
Yazoo – Mute

WEEK ENDING SEPTEMBER 17 1983

US SINGLES

1. **MANIAC**
Michael Sembello – Casablanca
2. **TELL HER ABOUT IT**
Billy Joel – Columbia
3. **THE SAFETY DANCE**
Men Without Hats – Backstreet
4. **TOTAL ECLIPSE OF THE HEART**
Bonnie Tyler – Columbia
5. **SWEET DREAMS**
Eurythmics – RCA
6. **EVERY BREATH YOU TAKE**
The Police – A & M
7. **HUMAN NATURE**
Michael Jackson – Epic
8. **PUTTIN' ON THE RITZ**
Taco – RCA
9. **MAKING LOVE ...**
Air Supply – Arista
10. **DON'T CRY**
Asia – Geffen
11. **SHE WORKS HARD ...**
Donna Summer – Mercury
12. **(SHE'S) SEXY + 17**
Stray Cats – EMI America
13. **LAWYERS IN LOVE**
Jackson Browne – Asylum
14. **FAR FROM OVER**
Frank Stallone – RSO
15. **PROMISES, PROMISES**
Naked Eyes – EMI America
16. **KING OF PAIN**
The Police – A & M
17. **TRUE**
Spandau Ballet – Chrysalis
18. **I'LL TUMBLE 4 YA**
Culture Club – Virgin/Epic
19. **HOW AM I SUPPOSED TO LIVE ...**
Laura Branigan – Atlantic
20. **(KEEP FEELING) FASCINATION**
Human League – A & M

US ALBUMS

1. **SYNCHRONICITY**
The Police – A & M
2. **THRILLER**
Michael Jackson – Epic
3. **FLASHDANCE**
Soundtrack – Casablanca
4. **PYROMANIA**
Def Leppard – Mercury
5. **AN INNOCENT MAN**
Billy Joel – Columbia
6. **ALPHA**
Asia – Geffen
7. **STAYING ALIVE**
Soundtrack – RSO
8. **LAWYERS IN LOVE**
Jackson Browne – Asylum
9. **THE WILD HEART**
Stevie Nicks – Modern
10. **REACH THE BEACH**
The Fixx – MCA
11. **THE PRINCIPLE OF MOMENTS**
Robert Plant – Es Paranza
12. **KEEP IT UP**
Loverboy – Columbia
13. **LET'S DANCE**
David Bowie – EMI America
14. **RHYTHM OF YOUTH**
Men Without Hats – Backstreet
15. **METAL HEALTH**
Quiet Riot – Pasha
16. **GREATEST HITS**
Air Supply – Arista
17. **ELIMINATOR**
ZZ Top – Warner Bros.
18. **SHE WORKS HARD ...**
Donna Summer – Mercury
19. **SPEAKING IN TONGUES**
The Talking Heads – Sire
20. **FLICK OF THE SWITCH**
AC/DC – Atlantic

UK SINGLES

1. **RED RED WINE**
UB40 – DEP International/Virgin
2. **TONIGHT I CELEBRATE MY LOVE**
Peabo Bryson/Roberta Flack – Capitol
3. **KARMA CHAMELEON**
Culture Club – Virgin
4. **MAMA**
Genesis – Charisma/Virgin
5. **DOLCE VITA**
Ryan Paris – Carrere
6. **COME BACK AND STAY**
Paul Young – CBS
7. **WHAT AM I GONNA DO ...**
Rod Stewart – Warner Bros.
8. **WINGS OF A DOVE**
Madness – Stiff
9. **WALKING IN THE RAIN**
Modern Romance – WEA
10. **THE SUN GOES DOWN ...**
Level 42 – Polydor
11. **OL' RAG BLUES**
Status Quo – Vertigo/Phonogram
12. **CHANCE**
Big Country – Mercury/Phonogram
13. **GIVE IT UP**
KC & The Sunshine Band – Epic
14. **CONFUSION**
New Order – Factory
15. **I'M STILL STANDING**
Elton John – Rocket/Phonogram
16. **GOLD**
Spandau Ballet – Reformation/Chrysalis
17. **CRUSHED BY THE WHEELS ...**
Heaven 17 – B.E.F./Virgin
18. **CLUB TROPICANA**
Wham! – Inner Vision
19. **WATCHING YOU, WATCHING ME**
David Grant – Chrysalis
20. **NEVER SAY DIE ...**
Cliff Richard – EMI

UK ALBUMS

1. **NO PARLEZ!**
Paul Young – CBS
2. **THE VERY BEST OF ...**
The Beach Boys – Capitol
3. **18 GREATEST HITS**
Michael Jackson/Jackson 5 – Telstar
4. **FANTASTIC**
Wham! – Inner Vision
5. **HEADLINE HITS**
Various – K-Tel
6. **THRILLER**
Michael Jackson – Epic
7. **THE CROSSING**
Big Country – Mercury/Phonogram
8. **TRUE**
Spandau Ballet – Reformation/Chrysalis
9. **STANDING IN THE LIGHT**
Level 42 – Polydor
10. **CONSTRUCTION TIME AGAIN**
Depeche Mode – Mute
11. **BENT OUT OF SHAPE**
Rainbow – Polydor
12. **TOO LOW FOR ZERO**
Elton John – Rocket/Phonogram
13. **FLICK OF THE SWITCH**
AC/DC – Atlantic
14. **THE LUXURY GAP**
Heaven 17 – Virgin
15. **THE PRESENT**
The Moody Blues – Threshold
16. **BODY WISHES**
Rod Stewart – Warner Bros.
17. **THE LOOK**
Shalamar – Solar
18. **SUNNY AFTERNOON**
Various – Impression
19. **LET'S DANCE**
David Bowie – EMI America
20. **SYNCHRONICITY**
The Police – A & M

WEEK ENDING SEPTEMBER 24 1983

US SINGLES	US ALBUMS	UK SINGLES	UK ALBUMS
1 TELL HER ABOUT IT *Billy Joel – Columbia*	1 SYNCHRONICITY *The Police – A & M*	1 KARMA CHAMELEON *Culture Club – Virgin*	1 LABOUR OF LOVE *UB40 – DEP International/Virgin*
2 TOTAL ECLIPSE OF THE HEART *Bonnie Tyler – Columbia*	2 THRILLER *Michael Jackson – Epic*	2 RED RED WINE *UB40 – DEP International/Virgin*	2 NO PARLEZ! *Paul Young – CBS*
3 THE SAFETY DANCE *Men Without Hats – Backstreet*	3 FLASHDANCE *Soundtrack – Casablanca*	3 TONIGHT I CELEBRATE MY LOVE *Peabo Bryson/Roberta Flack – Capitol*	3 THE CROSSING *Big Country – Mercury/Phonogram*
4 MANIAC *Michael Sembello – Casablanca*	4 PYROMANIA *Def Leppard – Mercury*	4 COME BACK AND STAY *Paul Young – CBS*	4 BORN AGAIN *Black Sabbath – Vertigo/Phonogram*
5 MAKING LOVE … *Air Supply – Arista*	5 AN INNOCENT MAN *Billy Joel – Columbia*	5 MAMA *Genesis – Charisma/Virgin*	5 FANTASTIC *Wham! – Inner Vision*
6 SWEET DREAMS *Eurythmics – RCA*	6 ALPHA *Asia – Geffen*	6 DOLCE VITA *Ryan Paris – Carrere*	6 TRUE *Spandau Ballet – Reformation/Chrysalis*
7 HUMAN NATURE *Michael Jackson – Epic*	7 THE WILD HEART *Stevie Nicks – Modern*	7 WALKING IN THE RAIN *Modern Romance – WEA*	7 THE VERY BEST OF … *The Beach Boys – Capitol*
8 PUTTIN' ON THE RITZ *Taco – RCA*	8 LAWYERS IN LOVE *Jackson Browne – Asylum*	8 MODERN LOVE *David Bowie – EMI America*	8 THRILLER *Michael Jackson – Epic*
9 (SHE'S) SEXY + 17 *Stray Cats – EMI America*	9 REACH THE BEACH *The Fixx – MCA*	9 OL' RAG BLUES *Status Quo – Vertigo/Phonogram*	9 18 GREATEST HITS *Michael Jackson/Jackson 5 – Telstar*
10 DON'T CRY *Asia – Geffen*	10 THE PRINCIPLE OF MOMENTS *Robert Plant – Es Paranza*	10 WHAT AM I GONNA DO … *Rod Stewart – Warner Bros.*	10 HEADLINE HITS *Various – K-Tel*
11 KING OF PAIN *The Police – A & M*	11 STAYING ALIVE *Soundtrack – RSO*	11 CHANCE *Big Country – Mercury/Phonogram*	11 THE HIT SQUAD *Various – Ronco*
12 FAR FROM OVER *Frank Stallone – RSO*	12 METAL HEALTH *Quiet Riot – Pasha*	12 BIG APPLE *Kajagoogoo – EMI*	12 WARRIORS *Gary Numan – Beggars Banquet*
13 TRUE *Spandau Ballet – Chrysalis*	13 RHYTHM OF YOUTH *Men Without Hats – Backstreet*	13 WINGS OF A DOVE *Madness – Stiff*	13 UNFORGETTABLE *Johnny Mathis & Natalie Cole – CBS*
14 PROMISES, PROMISES *Naked Eyes – EMI America*	14 GREATEST HITS *Air Supply – Arista*	14 THE SUN GOES DOWN … *Level 42 – Polydor*	14 STANDING IN THE LIGHT *Level 42 – Polydor*
15 EVERY BREATH YOU TAKE *The Police – A & M*	15 LET'S DANCE *David Bowie – EMI America*	15 NEVER SAY DIE … *Cliff Richard – EMI*	15 CONSTRUCTION TIME AGAIN *Depeche Mode – Mute*
16 HOW AM I SUPPOSED TO LIVE … *Laura Branigan – Atlantic*	16 KEEP IT UP *Loverboy – Columbia*	16 GO DEH YAKA (GO TO THE TOP) *Monyaka – Polydor*	16 LET'S DANCE *David Bowie – EMI America*
17 ISLANDS IN THE STREAM *Kenny Rogers & Dolly Parton – RCA*	17 FASTER THAN THE SPEED OF … *Bonnie Tyler – Columbia*	17 CRUSHED BY THE WHEELS … *Heaven 17 – B.E.F./Virgin*	17 BENT OUT OF SHAPE *Rainbow – Polydor*
18 SHE WORKS HARD … *Donna Summer – Mercury*	18 FLICK OF THE SWITCH *AC/DC – Atlantic*	18 GIVE IT UP *KC & The Sunshine Band – Epic*	18 TOO LOW FOR ZERO *Elton John – Rocket/Phonogram*
19 LAWYERS IN LOVE *Jackson Browne – Asylum*	19 SPEAKING IN TONGUES *Talking Heads – Sire*	19 TAHITI *David Essex – Mercury/Phonogram*	19 THE LUXURY GAP *Heaven 17 – Virgin*
20 I'LL TUMBLE 4 YA *Culture Club – Virgin/Epic*	20 COLD BLOODED *Rick James – Gordy*	20 BLUE MONDAY *New Order – Factory*	20 LIKE GANGBUSTERS *JoBoxers – RCA*

WEEK ENDING OCTOBER 1 1983

US SINGLES	US ALBUMS	UK SINGLES	UK ALBUMS
1 TOTAL ECLIPSE OF THE HEART *Bonnie Tyler – Columbia*	1 SYNCHRONICITY *The Police – A & M*	1 KARMA CHAMELEON *Culture Club – Virgin*	1 NO PARLEZ! *Paul Young – CBS*
2 TELL HER ABOUT IT *Billy Joel – Columbia*	2 THRILLER *Michael Jackson – Epic*	2 RED RED WINE *UB40 – DEP International/Virgin*	2 LABOUR OF LOVE *UB40 – DEP International/Virgin*
3 THE SAFETY DANCE *Men Without Hats – Backstreet*	3 FLASHDANCE *Soundtrack – Casablanca*	3 MODERN LOVE *David Bowie – EMI America*	3 THE CROSSING *Big Country – Mercury/Phonogram*
4 MAKING LOVE … *Air Supply – Arista*	4 PYROMANIA *Def Leppard – Mercury*	4 TONIGHT I CELEBRIGHT MY LOVE *Peabo Bryson/Roberta Flack – Capitol*	4 THE HIT SQUAD *Various – Ronco*
5 (SHE'S) SEXY + 17 *Stray Cats – EMI America*	5 AN INNOCENT MAN *Billy Joel – Columbia*	5 COME BACK AND STAY *Paul Young – CBS*	5 UNFORGETTABLE *Johnny Mathis & Natalie Cole – CBS*
6 KING OF PAIN *The Police – A & M*	6 ALPHA *Asia – Geffen*	6 MAMA *Genesis – Charisma/Virgin*	6 LET'S DANCE *David Bowie – EMI America*
7 TRUE *Spandau Ballet – Chrysalis*	7 METAL HEALTH *Quiet Riot – Pasha*	7 DOLCE VITA *Ryan Paris – Carrere*	7 FANTASTIC *Wham! – Inner Vision*
8 MANIAC *Michael Sembello – Casablanca*	8 FASTER THAN THE SPEED OF … *Bonnie Tyler – Columbia*	8 BIG APPLE *Kajagoogoo – EMI*	8 THRILLER *Michael Jackson – Epic*
9 ISLANDS IN THE STREAM *Kenny Rogers & Dolly Parton – RCA*	9 REACH THE BEACH *The Fixx – MCA*	9 CHANCE *Big Country – Mercury/Phonogram*	9 BORN AGAIN *Black Sabbath – Vertigo/Phonogram*
10 FAR FROM OVER *Frank Stallone – RSO*	10 THE PRINCIPLE OF MOMENTS *Robert Plant – Es Paranza*	10 OL' RAG BLUES *Status Quo – Vertigo/Phonogram*	10 TRUE *Spandau Ballet – Reformation/Chrysalis*
11 DON'T CRY *Asia – Geffen*	11 LAWYERS IN LOVE *Jackson Browne – Asylum*	11 WALKING IN THE RAIN *Modern Romance – WEA*	11 18 GREATEST HITS *Michael Jackson/Jackson 5 – Telstar*
12 PROMISES, PROMISES *Naked Eyes – EMI America*	12 THE WILD HEART *Stevie Nicks – Modern*	12 BLUE MONDAY *New Order – Factory*	12 THE VERY BEST OF … *The Beach Boys – Capitol*
13 HOW AM I SUPPOSED TO LIVE … *Laura Branigan – Atlantic*	13 RHYTHM OF YOUTH *Men Without Hats – Backstreet*	13 TAHITI *David Essex – Mercury/Phonogram*	13 THE LUXURY GAP *Heaven 17 – Virgin*
14 PUTTIN' ON THE RITZ *Taco – RCA*	14 GREATEST HITS *Air Supply – Arista*	14 GO DEH YAKA (GO TO THE TOP) *Monyaka – Polydor*	14 CONSTRUCTION TIME AGAIN *Depeche Mode – Mute*
15 HUMAN NATURE *Michael Jackson – Epic*	15 STAYING ALIVE *Soundtrack – RSO*	15 THIS IS NOT A LOVE SONG *Pil – Virgin*	15 WARRIORS *Gary Numan – Beggars Banquet*
16 SWEET DREAMS *Eurythmics – RCA*	16 LET'S DANCE *David Bowie – EMI America*	16 SOUL INSIDE *Soft Cell – Some Bizzare/Phonogram*	16 STANDING IN THE LIGHT *Level 42 – Polydor*
17 ONE THING LEADS TO ANOTHER *The Fixx – MCA*	17 FLICK OF THE SWITCH *AC/DC – Atlantic*	17 DEAR PRUDENCE *Siouxsie And The Banshees – Wonderland*	17 TOO LOW FOR ZERO *Elton John – Rocket/Phonogram*
18 BURNING DOWN THE HOUSE *Talking Heads – Sire*	18 RANT 'N' RAVE WITH THE… *Stray Cats – EMI America*	18 CRUSHED BY THE WHEELS … *Heaven 17 – B.E.F./Virgin*	18 LIKE GANGBUSTERS *JoBoxers – RCA*
19 TELEFONE … *Sheena Easton – EMI America*	19 COLD BLOODED *Rick James – Gordy*	19 BODY WORK *Hot Streak – Polydor*	19 HEADLINE HITS *Various – RCA*
20 DELIRIOUS *Prince – Warner Bros.*	20 KEEP IT UP *Loverboy – Columbia*	20 WHAT AM I GONNA DO … *Rod Stewart – Warner Bros.*	20 SUNNY AFTERNOON *Various – Impression*

WEEK ENDING OCTOBER 8 1983

US SINGLES

1. **TOTAL ECLIPSE OF THE HEART**
   Bonnie Tyler – Columbia
2. **MAKING LOVE …**
   Air Supply – Arista
3. **KING OF PAIN**
   The Police – A & M
4. **TRUE**
   Spandau Ballet – Chrysalis
5. **(SHE'S) SEXY + 17**
   Stray Cats – EMI America
6. **ISLANDS IN THE STREAM**
   Kenny Rogers & Dolly Parton – RCA
7. **TELL HER ABOUT IT**
   Billy Joel – Columbia
8. **THE SAFETY DANCE**
   Men Without Hats – Backstreet
9. **ONE THING LEADS TO ANOTHER**
   The Fixx – MCA
10. **FAR FROM OVER**
    Frank Stallone – RSO
11. **PROMISES, PROMISES**
    Naked Eyes – EMI America
12. **HOW AM I SUPPOSED TO LIVE …**
    Laura Branigan – Atlantic
13. **MANIAC**
    Michael Sembello – Casablanca
14. **ALL NIGHT LONG (ALL NIGHT)**
    Lionel Richie – Motown
15. **BURNING DOWN THE HOUSE**
    Talking Heads – Sire
16. **TELEFONE …**
    Sheena Easton – EMI America
17. **DELIRIOUS**
    Prince – Warner Bros.
18. **PUTTIN' ON THE RITZ**
    Taco – RCA
19. **DON'T CRY**
    Asia – Geffen
20. **TONIGHT I CELEBRATE MY LOVE**
    Peabo Bryson/Roberta Flack – Capitol

US ALBUMS

1. **SYNCHRONICITY**
   The Police – A & M
2. **THRILLER**
   Michael Jackson – Epic
3. **FLASHDANCE**
   Soundtrack – Casablanca
4. **AN INNOCENT MAN**
   Billy Joel – Columbia
5. **PYROMANIA**
   Def Leppard – Mercury
6. **METAL HEALTH**
   Quiet Riot – Pasha
7. **FASTER THAN THE SPEED OF …**
   Bonnie Tyler – Columbia
8. **THE PRINCIPLE OF MOMENTS**
   Robert Plant – Es Paranza
9. **REACH THE BEACH**
   The Fixx – MCA
10. **GREATEST HITS**
    Air Supply – Arista
11. **THE WILD HEART**
    Stevie Nicks – Modern
12. **ALPHA**
    Asia – Geffen
13. **LAWYERS IN LOVE**
    Jackson Browne – Asylum
14. **RHYTHM OF YOUTH**
    Men Without Hats – Backstreet
15. **LET'S DANCE**
    David Bowie – EMI America
16. **RANT 'N' RAVE WITH THE …**
    Stray Cats – EMI America
17. **FLICK OF THE SWITCH**
    AC/DC – Atlantic
18. **COLD BLOODED**
    Rick James – Gordy
19. **KEEP IT UP**
    Loverboy – Columbia
20. **EYES THAT SEE IN THE DARK**
    Kenny Rogers – RCA

UK SINGLES

1. **KARMA CHAMELEON**
   Culture Club – Virgin
2. **MODERN LOVE**
   David Bowie – EMI America
3. **RED RED WINE**
   UB40 – DEP International/Virgin
4. **DEAR PRUDENCE**
   Siouxsie And The Banshees – Wonderland
5. **THIS IS NOT A LOVE SONG**
   Pil – Virgin
6. **COME BACK AND STAY**
   Paul Young – CBS
7. **TONIGHT I CELEBRATE MY LOVE**
   Peabo Bryson/Roberta Flack – Capitol
8. **TAHITI**
   David Essex – Mercury/Phonogram
9. **THEY DON'T KNOW**
   Tracey Ullman – Stiff
10. **BLUE MONDAY**
    New Order – Factory
11. **MAMA**
    Genesis – Charisma/Virgin
12. **BIG APPLE**
    Kajagoogoo – EMI
13. **NEW SONG**
    Howard Jones – WEA
14. **CHANCE**
    Big Country – Mercury/Phonogram
15. **IN YOUR EYES**
    George Benson – Warner Bros.
16. **SUPERMAN (GIOCA JOUER)**
    Black Lace – Flair
17. **DOLCE VITA**
    Ryan Paris – Carrere
18. **GO DEH YAKA (GO TO THE TOP)**
    Monyaka – Polydor
19. **68 GUNS**
    The Alarm – I.R.S.
20. **OL' RAG BLUES**
    Status Quo – Vertigo/Phonogram

UK ALBUMS

1. **NO PARLEZ!**
   Paul Young – CBS
2. **LABOUR OF LOVE**
   UB40 – DEP International/Virgin
3. **THE CROSSING**
   Big Country – Mercury/Phonogram
4. **LET'S DANCE**
   David Bowie – EMI America
5. **FANTASTIC**
   Wham! – Inner Vision
6. **THE HIT SQUAD**
   Various – Ronco
7. **LICK IT UP**
   Kiss – Casablanca/Phonogram
8. **THRILLER**
   Michael Jackson – Epic
9. **UNFORGETTABLE**
   Johnny Mathis & Natalie Cole – CBS
10. **THE LUXURY GAP**
    Heaven 17 – B.E.F./Virgin
11. **A TOUCH MORE MAGIC**
    Barry Manilow – Arista
12. **18 GREATEST HITS**
    Michael Jackson/Jackson 5 – Telstar
13. **TRUE**
    Spandau Ballet – Reformation/Chrysalis
14. **IN YOUR EYES**
    George Benson – Warner Bros.
15. **CONSTRUCTION TIME AGAIN**
    Depeche Mode – Mute
16. **STAYING ALIVE**
    Soundtrack – RSO
17. **BORN AGAIN**
    Black Sabbath – Vertigo/Phonogram
18. **THE VERY BEST OF …**
    The Beach Boys – Capitol
19. **FLIGHTS OF FANCY**
    Paul Leoni – Nouveau Music
20. **STANDING IN THE LIGHT**
    Level 42 – Polydor

WEEK ENDING OCTOBER 15 1983

US SINGLES

1. **TOTAL ECLIPSE OF THE HEART**
   Bonnie Tyler – Columbia
2. **MAKING LOVE …**
   Air Supply – Arista
3. **KING OF PAIN**
   The Police – A & M
4. **TRUE**
   Spandau Ballet – Chrysalis
5. **ISLANDS IN THE STREAM**
   Kenny Rogers & Dolly Parton – RCA
6. **ONE THING LEADS TO ANOTHER**
   The Fixx – MCA
7. **ALL NIGHT LONG (ALL NIGHT)**
   Lionel Richie – Motown
8. **THE SAFETY DANCE**
   Men Without Hats – Backstreet
9. **TELL HER ABOUT IT**
   Billy Joel – Columbia
10. **(SHE'S) SEXY + 17**
    Stray Cats – EMI America
11. **TELEFONE …**
    Sheena Easton – EMI America
12. **BURNING DOWN THE HOUSE**
    Talking Heads – Sire
13. **DELIRIOUS**
    Prince – Warner Bros.
14. **FAR FROM OVER**
    Frank Stallone – RSO
15. **PROMISES, PROMISES**
    Naked Eyes – EMI America
16. **HOW AM I SUPPOSED TO LIVE …**
    Laura Branigan – Atlantic
17. **SUDDENLY LAST SUMMER**
    The Motels – Capitol
18. **IF ANYONE FALLS IN LOVE**
    Stevie Nicks – Modern
19. **TONIGHT I CELEBRATE MY LOVE**
    Peabo Bryson/Roberta Flack – Capitol
20. **BIG LOG**
    Robert Plant – Es Paranza

US ALBUMS

1. **SYNCHRONICITY**
   The Police – A & M
2. **THRILLER**
   Michael Jackson – Epic
3. **FLASHDANCE**
   Soundtrack – Casablanca
4. **AN INNOCENT MAN**
   Billy Joel – Columbia
5. **PYROMANIA**
   Def Leppard – Mercury
6. **METAL HEALTH**
   Quiet Riot – Pasha
7. **FASTER THAN THE SPEED OF …**
   Bonnie Tyler – Columbia
8. **REACH THE BEACH**
   The Fixx – MCA
9. **GREATEST HITS**
   Air Supply – Arista
10. **THE PRINCIPLE OF MOMENTS**
    Robert Plant – Es Paranza
11. **THE WILD HEART**
    Stevie Nicks – Modern
12. **EYES THAT SEE IN THE DARK**
    Kenny Rogers – RCA
13. **RHYTHM OF YOUTH**
    Men Without Hats – Backstreet
14. **RANT 'N' RAVE WITH THE …**
    Stray Cats – EMI America
15. **FLICK OF THE SWITCH**
    AC/DC – Atlantic
16. **ELIMINATOR**
    ZZ Top – Warner Bros.
17. **COLD BLOODED**
    Rick James – Gordy
18. **SPEAKING IN TONGUES**
    Talking Heads – Sire
19. **LET'S DANCE**
    David Bowie – EMI America
20. **WHAT'S NEW**
    Linda Ronstadt – Asylum

UK SINGLES

1. **KARMA CHAMELEON**
   Culture Club – Virgin
2. **THEY DON'T KNOW**
   Tracey Ullman – Stiff
3. **DEAR PRUDENCE**
   Siouxsie And The Banshees – Wonderland
4. **MODERN LOVE**
   David Bowie – EMI America
5. **NEW SONG**
   Howard Jones – WEA
6. **THIS IS NOT A LOVE SONG**
   Pil – Virgin
7. **IN YOUR EYES**
   George Benson – Warner Bros.
8. **RED RED WINE**
   UB40 – DEP International/Virgin
9. **BLUE MONDAY**
   New Order – Factory
10. **TAHITI**
    David Essex – Mercury/Phonogram
11. **(HEY YOU) …**
    The Rocksteady Crew – Charisma/Virgin
12. **SUPERMAN (GIOCA JOUER)**
    Black Lace – Flair
13. **COME BACK AND STAY**
    Paul Young – CBS
14. **TONIGHT I CELEBRATE MY LOVE**
    Peabo Bryson/Roberta Flack – Capitol
15. **BLUE HAT FOR A BLUE DAY**
    Nick Heyward – Arista
16. **ALL NIGHT LONG (ALL NIGHT)**
    Lionel Richie – Motown
17. **68 GUNS**
    The Alarm – I.R.S.
18. **BIG APPLE**
    Kajagoogoo – EMI
19. **MAMA**
    Genesis – Charisma/Virgin
20. **DOLCE VITA**
    Ryan Paris – Carrere

UK ALBUMS

1. **GENESIS**
   Genesis – Charisma/Virgin
2. **NO PARLEZ!**
   Paul Young – CBS
3. **LABOUR OF LOVE**
   UB40 – DEP International/Virgin
4. **THE CROSSING**
   Big Country – Mercury/Phonogram
5. **FANTASTIC**
   Wham! – Inner Vision
6. **LET'S DANCE**
   David Bowie – EMI America
7. **SILVER**
   Cliff Richard – EMI
8. **THRILLER**
   Michael Jackson – Epic
9. **IN YOUR EYES**
   George Benson – Warner Bros.
10. **A TOUCH MORE MAGIC**
    Barry Manilow – Arista
11. **VOICE OF THE HEART**
    Carpenters – A & M
12. **THE HIT SQUAD**
    Various – Ronco
13. **UNFORGETTABLE**
    Johnny Mathis & Natalie Cole – CBS
14. **STAYING ALIVE**
    Soundtrack – RSO
15. **18 GREATEST HITS**
    Michael Jackson/Jackson 5 – Telstar
16. **CONSTRUCTION TIME AGAIN**
    Depeche Mode – Mute
17. **FLIGHTS OF FANCY**
    Paul Leoni – Nouveau Music
18. **TRUE**
    Spandau Ballet – Reformation/Chrysalis
19. **BORN TO LOVE**
    Peabo Bryson/Roberta Flack – Capitol
20. **THE LUXURY GAP**
    Heaven 17 – Virgin

WEEK ENDING OCTOBER 22 1983

US SINGLES	US ALBUMS	UK SINGLES	UK ALBUMS
1 **TOTAL ECLIPSE OF THE HEART** *Bonnie Tyler – Columbia*	1 **SYNCHRONICITY** *The Police – A & M*	1 **KARMA CHAMELEON** *Culture Club – Virgin*	1 **COLOUR BY NUMBERS** *Culture Club – Virgin*
2 **MAKING LOVE …** *Air Supply – Arista*	2 **THRILLER** *Michael Jackson – Epic*	2 **THEY DON'T KNOW** *Tracey Ullman – Stiff*	2 **SNAP!** *The Jam – Polydor*
3 **ISLANDS IN THE STREAM** *Kenny Rogers & Dolly Parton – RCA*	3 **METAL HEALTH** *Quiet Riot – Pasha*	3 **NEW SONG** *Howard Jones – WEA*	3 **GENESIS** *Genesis – Charisma/Virgin*
4 **TRUE** *Spandau Ballet – Chrysalis*	4 **AN INNOCENT MAN** *Billy Joel – Columbia*	4 **ALL NIGHT LONG (ALL NIGHT)** *Lionel Richie – Motown*	4 **LABOUR OF LOVE** *UB40 – DEP International/Virgin*
5 **ALL NIGHT LONG (ALL NIGHT)** *Lionel Richie – Motown*	5 **FLASHDANCE** *Soundtrack – Casablanca*	5 **DEAR PRUDENCE** *Siouxsie And The Banshees – Wonderland*	5 **NO PARLEZ!** *Paul Young – CBS*
6 **ONE THING LEADS TO ANOTHER** *The Fixx – MCA*	6 **FASTER THAN THE SPEED OF …** *Bonnie Tyler – Columbia*	6 **(HEY YOU) …** *The Rocksteady Crew – Charisma/Virgin*	6 **VOICE OF THE HEART** *Carpenters – A & M*
7 **KING OF PAIN** *The Police A & M*	7 **PYROMANIA** *Def Leppard*	7 **IN YOUR EYES** *George Benson – Warner Bros.*	7 **FANTASTIC** *Wham! – Inner Vision*
8 **DELIRIOUS** *Prince – Warner Bros.*	8 **REACH THE BEACH** *The Fixx – MCA*	8 **MODERN LOVE** *David Bowie – EMI America*	8 **LET'S DANCE** *David Bowie – EMI America*
9 **BURNING DOWN THE HOUSE** *Talking Heads – Sire*	9 **GREATEST HITS** *Air Supply – Arista*	9 **SUPERMAN (GIOCA JOUER)** *Black Lace – Flair*	9 **THE CROSSING** *Big Country – Mercury/Phonogram*
10 **TELEFONE …** *Sheena Easton – EMI America*	10 **THE PRINCIPLE OF MOMENTS** *Robert Plant – Es Peranza*	10 **SAY SAY SAY** *McCartney/Jackson – Parlophone*	10 **SILVER** *Cliff Richard – EMI*
11 **THE SAFETY DANCE** *Men Without Hats – Backstreet*	11 **WHAT'S NEW?** *Linda Ronstadt – Asylum*	11 **THIS IS NOT A LOVE SONG** *Pil – Virgin*	11 **MONUMENT** *Ultravox – Chrysalis*
12 **SUDDENLY LAST SUMMER** *The Motels – Capitol*	12 **EYES THAT SEE IN THE DARK** *Kenny Rogers – RCA*	12 **BLUE MONDAY** *New Order – Factory*	12 **THRILLER** *Michael Jackson – Epic*
13 **TELL HER ABOUT IT** *Billy Joel – Columbia*	13 **THE WILD HEART** *Stevie Nicks – Modern*	13 **THE SAFETY DANCE** *Men Without Hats – Statik*	13 **IN YOUR EYES** *George Benson – Warner Bros.*
14 **(SHE'S) SEXY + 17** *Stray Cats – EMI America*	14 **RANT 'N' RAVE WITH THE …** *Stray Cats – EMI America*	14 **BLUE HAT FOR A BLUE DAY** *Nick Heyward – Arista*	14 **THE TWO OF US** *Various – K-Tel*
15 **UPTOWN GIRL** *Billy Joel – Columbia*	15 **FLICK OF THE SWITCH** *AC/DC – Atlantic*	15 **PLEASE DON'T MAKE ME CRY** *UB40 – DEP International/Virgin*	15 **BORN TO LOVE** *Peabo Bryson/Robert Flack – Capitol*
16 **IF ANYONE FALLS IN LOVE** *Stevie Nicks – Modern*	16 **ELIMINATOR** *ZZ Top – Warner Bros.*	16 **RED RED WINE** *UB40 – DEP International/Virgin*	16 **STAYING ALIVE** *Soundtrack – RSO*
17 **TONIGHT I CELEBRATE MY LOVE** *Peabo Bryson/Roberta Flack – Capitol*	17 **COLD BLOODED** *Rick James – Gordy*	17 **MIDNIGHT AT THE LOST & FOUND** *Meat Loaf – Cleveland International/Epic*	17 **FLIGHTS OF FANCY** *Paul Leoni – Nouveau Music*
18 **MODERN LOVE** *David Bowie – EMI America*	18 **SPEAKING IN TONGUES** *Talking Heads – Sire*	18 **SUPERSTAR** *Lydia Murdock – Korova*	18 **STREET SOUNDS ELECTRO 1** *Various – Street Sounds*
19 **SAY SAY SAY** *McCartney/Jackson – Columbia*	19 **RHYTHM OF YOUTH** *Men Without Hats – Backstreet*	19 **TAHITI** *David Essex – Mercury/Phonogram*	19 **A TOUCH MORE MAGIC** *Barry Manilow – Arista*
20 **BIG LOG** *Robert Plant – Es Peranza*	20 **LET'S DANCE** *David Bowie – EMI America*	20 **68 GUNS** *The Alarm – I.R.S.*	20 **UNFORGETTABLE** *Johnny Mathis & Natalie Cole – CBS*

WEEK ENDING OCTOBER 29 1983

US SINGLES	US ALBUMS	UK SINGLES	UK ALBUMS
1 **ISLANDS IN THE STREAM** *Kenny Rogers & Dolly Parton – RCA*	1 **SYNCHRONICITY** *The Police – A & M*	1 **KARMA CHAMELEON** *Culture Club – Virgin*	1 **COLOUR BY NUMBERS** *Culture Club – Virgin*
2 **TOTAL ECLIPSE OF THE HEART** *Bonnie Tyler – Columbia*	2 **THRILLER** *Michael Jackson – Epic*	2 **ALL NIGHT LONG (ALL NIGHT)** *Lionel Richie – Motown*	2 **SNAP!** *The Jam – Polydor*
3 **ALL NIGHT LONG (ALL NIGHT)** *Lionel Richie – Mowtown*	3 **METAL HEALTH** *Quiet Riot – Pasha*	3 **THEY DON'T KNOW** *Tracey Ullman – Stiff*	3 **CAN'T SLOW DOWN** *Lionel Richie – Motown*
4 **TRUE** *Spandau Ballet – Chrysalis*	4 **AN INNOCENT MAN** *Billy Joel – Columbia*	4 **UNION OF THE SNAKE** *Duran Duran – EMI*	4 **GENESIS** *Genesis – Charisma/Virgin*
5 **ONE THING LEADS TO ANOTHER** *The Fixx – MCA*	5 **FASTER THAN THE SPEED OF …** *Bonnie Tyler – Columbia*	5 **NEW SONG** *Howard Jones – WEA*	5 **LABOUR OF LOVE** *UB40 – DEP International/Virgin*
6 **MAKING LOVE …** *Air Supply – Arista*	6 **PYROMANIA** *Def Leppard – Mercury*	6 **(HEY YOU) …** *The Rocksteady Crew – Charisma/Virgin*	6 **VOICE OF THE HEART** *Carpenters – A & M*
7 **KING OF PAIN** *The Police – A & M*	7 **FLASHDANCE** *Soundtrack – Casablanca*	7 **UPTOWN GIRL** *Billy Joel – CBS*	7 **THE TWO OF US** *Various – K-Tel*
8 **DELIRIOUS** *Prince – Warner Bros.*	8 **GREATEST HITS** *Air Supply – Arista*	8 **THE SAFETY DANCE** *Men Without Hats – Statik*	8 **NO PARLEZ!** *Paul Young – CBS*
9 **TELEFONE …** *Sheena Easton – EMI America*	9 **EYES THAT SEE IN THE DARK** *Kenny Rogers – RCA*	9 **IN YOUR EYES** *George Benson – Warner Bros.*	9 **MONUMENT** *Ultravox – Chrysalis*
10 **UPTOWN GIRL** *Billy Joel – Columbia*	10 **WHAT'S NEW** *Linda Ronstadt – Asylum*	10 **SUPERMAN (GIOCA JOUER)** *Black Lace – Flair*	10 **NORTH OF A MIRACLE** *Nick Heyward – Arista*
11 **SAY SAY SAY** *McCartney/Jackson – Columbia*	11 **REACH THE BEACH** *The Fixx – MCA*	11 **DEAR PRUDENCE** *Siouxsie And The Banshees – Wonderland*	11 **THRILLER** *Michael Jackson – Epic*
12 **SUDDENLY LAST SUMMER** *The Motels – Capitol*	12 **THE PRINCIPLE OF MOMENTS** *Robert Plant – Es Paranza*	12 **PLEASE DON'T MAKE ME CRY** *UB40 – DEP International/Virgin*	12 **IN YOUR EYES** *George Benson – Warner Bros.*
13 **BURNING DOWN THE HOUSE** *Talking Heads – Sire*	13 **ELIMINATOR** *ZZ Top – Warner Bros.*	13 **SAY SAY SAY** *McCartney/Jackson – Parlophone*	13 **FANTASTIC** *Wham! – Inner Vision*
14 **CUM ON FEEL THE NOIZE** *Quiet Riot – Pasha*	14 **THE WILD HEART** *Stevie Nicks – Modern*	14 **SUPERSTAR** *Lydia Murdock – Korova*	14 **LET'S DANCE** *David Bowie – EMI America*
15 **IF ANYONE FALLS IN LOVE** *Stevie Nicks – Modern*	15 **SPEAKING IN TONGUES** *Talking Heads – Sire*	15 **BLUE MONDAY** *New Order – Factory*	15 **THE CROSSING** *Big Country – Mercury/Phonogram*
16 **MODERN LOVE** *David Bowie – EMI America*	16 **COLD BLOODED** *Rick James – Gordy*	16 **MODERN LOVE** *David Bowie – EMI America*	16 **SILVER** *Cliff Richard – EMI*
17 **TONIGHT I CELEBRATE MY LOVE** *Peabo Bryson/Roberta Flack – Capitol*	17 **FLICK OF THE SWITCH** *AC/DC – Atlantic*	17 **MIDNIGHT AT THE LOST & FOUND** *Meat Loaf – Cleveland International/Epic*	17 **TOO LOW FOR ZERO** *Elton John – Rocket/Phonogram*
18 **THE SAFETY DANCE** *Men Without Hats – Backstreet*	18 **LIVE FROM EARTH** *Pat Benatar – Chrysalis*	18 **THIS IS NOT A LOVE SONG** *Pil – Virgin*	18 **FLIGHTS OF FANCY** *Paul Leoni – Nouveau Music*
19 **HEART AND SOUL** *Huey Lewis And The News – Chrysalis*	19 **TRUE** *Spandau Ballet – Chrysalis*	19 **BLUE HAT FOR A BLUE DAY** *Nick Heyward – Arista*	19 **UNFORGETTABLE** *Johnny Mathis & Natalie Cole – CBS*
20 **LOVE IS A BATTLEFIELD** *Pat Benatar – Chrysalis*	20 **THE CROSSING** *Big Country – Mercury*	20 **RED RED WINE** *UB40 – DEP International/Virgin*	20 **STREET SOUNDS ELECTRO 1** *Various – Street Sounds*

US SINGLES

1. **ISLANDS IN THE STREAM**
   Kenny Rogers & Dolly Parton – RCA
2. **ALL NIGHT LONG (ALL NIGHT)**
   Lionel Richie – Motown
3. **TOTAL ECLIPSE OF THE HEART**
   Bonnie Tyler – Columbia
4. **ONE THING LEADS TO ANOTHER**
   The Fixx – MCA
5. **UPTOWN GIRL**
   Billy Joel – Columbia
6. **SAY SAY SAY**
   McCartney/Jackson – Columbia
7. **MAKING LOVE …**
   Air Supply – Arista
8. **DELIRIOUS**
   Prince – Warner Bros.
9. **TELEFONE …**
   Sheena Easton – EMI America
10. **TRUE**
    Spandau Ballet – Chrysalis
11. **SUDDENLY LAST SUMMER**
    The Motels – Capitol
12. **CUM ON FEEL THE NOIZE**
    Quiet Riot – Pasha
13. **KING OF PAIN**
    The Police – A & M
14. **IF ANYONE FALLS IN LOVE**
    Stevie Nicks – Modern
15. **MODERN LOVE**
    David Bowie – EMI America
16. **TONIGHT I CELEBRATE MY LOVE**
    Peabo Bryson/Roberta Flack – Capitol
17. **LOVE IS A BATTLEFIELD**
    Pat Benatar – Chrysalis
18. **HEART AND SOUL**
    Huey Lewis And The News – Chrysalis
19. **SAY IT ISN'T SO**
    Daryl Hall & John Oates – RCA
20. **PYT (PRETTY YOUNG THING)**
    Michael Jackson – Epic

US ALBUMS

1. **SYNCHRONICITY**
   The Police – A & M
2. **THRILLER**
   Michael Jackson – Epic
3. **METAL HEALTH**
   Quiet Riot – Pasha
4. **FASTER THAN THE SPEED OF …**
   Bonnie Tyler – Columbia
5. **AN INNOCENT MAN**
   Billy Joel – Columbia/CBS
6. **PYROMANIA**
   Def Leppard – Mercury
7. **EYES THAT SEE IN THE DARK**
   Kenny Rogers – RCA
8. **GREATEST HITS**
   Air Supply – Arista
9. **FLASHDANCE**
   Soundtrack – Casablanca
10. **WHAT'S NEW**
    Linda Ronstadt – Asylum
11. **ELIMINATOR**
    ZZ Top – Warner Bros.
12. **REACH THE BEACH**
    The Fixx – MCA
13. **THE PRINCIPLE OF MOMENTS**
    Robert Plant – Es Paranza
14. **LIVE FROM EARTH**
    Pat Benatar – Chrysalis
15. **SPEAKING IN TONGUES**
    Talking Heads – Sire
16. **GENESIS**
    Genesis – Atlantic
17. **THE WILD HEART**
    Stevie Nicks – Modern
18. **THE CROSSING**
    Big Country – Mercury
19. **COLD BLOODED**
    Rick James – Gordy
20. **FLICK OF THE SWITCH**
    AC/DC – Atlantic

UK SINGLES

1. **UPTOWN GIRL**
   Billy Joel – CBS
2. **ALL NIGHT LONG (ALL NIGHT)**
   Lionel Richie – Motown
3. **UNION OF THE SNAKE**
   Duran Duran – EMI
4. **KARMA CHAMELEON**
   Culture Club – Virgin
5. **THEY DON'T KNOW**
   Tracey Ullman – Stiff
6. **THE SAFETY DANCE**
   Men Without Hats – Statik
7. **NEW SONG**
   Howard Jones – WEA
8. **(HEY YOU) …**
   The Rocksteady Crew – Charisma/Virgin
9. **PUSS'N BOOTS**
   Adam Ant – CBS
10. **PLEASE DON'T MAKE ME CRY**
    UB40 – DEP International/Virgin
11. **SUPERMAN (GIOCA JOUER)**
    Black Lace – Flair
12. **THE LOVE CATS**
    The Cure – Fiction
13. **IN YOUR EYES**
    George Benson – Warner Bros.
14. **SAY SAY SAY**
    McCartney/Jackson – Parlophone
15. **DEAR PRUDENCE**
    Siouxsie And The Banshees – Wonderland
16. **SUPERSTAR**
    Lydia Murdock – Korova
17. **KISSING WITH CONFIDENCE**
    Will Powers – Island
18. **BLUE MONDAY**
    New Order – Factory
19. **CRY JUST A LITTLE BIT**
    Shakin' Stevens – Epic
20. **KISS THE BRIDE**
    Elton John – Rocket/Phonogram

UK ALBUMS

1. **COLOUR BY NUMBERS**
   Culture Club – Virgin
2. **CAN'T SLOW DOWN**
   Lionel Richie – Motown
3. **SNAP!**
   The Jam – Polydor
4. **GENESIS**
   Genesis – Charisma/Virgin
5. **LABOUR OF LOVE**
   UB40 – DEP International/Virgin
6. **THE TWO OF US**
   Various – K-Tel
7. **VOICE OF THE HEART**
   Carpenters – A & M
8. **NO PARLEZ!**
   Paul Young – CBS
9. **THRILLER**
   Michael Jackson – Epic
10. **NORTH OF A MIRACLE**
    Nick Heyward – Arista
11. **FANTASTIC**
    Wham! – Inner Vision
12. **TOO LOW FOR ZERO**
    Elton John – Rocket/Phonogram
13. **IN YOUR EYES**
    George Benson – Warner Bros.
14. **MONUMENT**
    Ultravox – Chrysalis
15. **LET'S DANCE**
    David Bowie – EMI America
16. **ROCK 'N' SOUL PART 1**
    Daryl Hall & John Oates – RCA
17. **ZIGGY STARDUST**
    Soundtrack – RCA
18. **IMAGINATIONS**
    Various – CBS
19. **THE CROSSING**
    Big Country – Mercury/Phonogram
20. **AN INNOCENT MAN**
    Billy Joel – CBS

US SINGLES

1. **ALL NIGHT LONG (ALL NIGHT)**
   Lionel Richie – Motown
2. **ISLANDS IN THE STREAM**
   Kenny Rogers & Dolly Parton – RCA
3. **UPTOWN GIRL**
   Billy Joel – Columbia
4. **SAY SAY SAY**
   McCartney/Jackson – Columbia
5. **TOTAL ECLIPSE OF THE HEART**
   Bonnie Tyler – Columbia
6. **ONE THING LEADS TO ANOTHER**
   The Fixx – MCA
7. **CUM ON FEEL THE NOIZE**
   Quiet Riot – Pasha
8. **DELIRIOUS**
   Prince – Warner Bros.
9. **MAKING LOVE …**
   Air Supply – Arista
10. **SUDDENLY LAST SUMMER**
    The Motels – Capitol
11. **TELEFONE …**
    Sheena Easton – EMI America
12. **TRUE**
    Spandau Ballet – Chrysalis
13. **LOVE IS A BATTLEFIELD**
    Pat Benatar – Chrysalis
14. **MODERN LOVE**
    David Bowie – EMI America
15. **HEART AND SOUL**
    Huey Lewis and The News – Chrysalis
16. **TONIGHT I CELEBRATE MY LOVE**
    Peabo Bryson/Roberta Flack – Capitol
17. **SAY IT ISN'T SO**
    Daryl Hall & John Oates – RCA
18. **PYT (PRETTY YOUNG THING)**
    Michael Jackson – Epic
19. **CRUMBLIN' DOWN**
    John Cougar Mellencamp – Riva
20. **KING OF PAIN**
    The Police – A & M

US ALBUMS

1. **SYNCHRONICITY**
   The Police – A & M
2. **METAL HEALTH**
   Quiet Riot – Pasha
3. **THRILLER**
   Michael Jackson – Epic
4. **INNOCENT MAN**
   Billy Joel – Columbia
5. **FASTER THAN THE SPEED OF …**
   Bonnie Tyler – Columbia
6. **EYES THAT SEE IN THE DARK**
   Kenny Rogers – RCA
7. **PYROMANIA**
   Def Leppard – Mercury
8. **GREATEST HITS**
   Air Supply – Arista
9. **ELIMINATOR**
   ZZ Top – Warner Bros.
10. **WHAT'S NEW**
    Linda Ronstadt – Asylum
11. **GENESIS**
    Genesis – Atlantic
12. **FLASHDANCE**
    Soundtrack – Casablanca
13. **REACH THE BEACH**
    The Fixx – MCA
14. **LIVE FROM EARTH**
    Pat Benatar – Chrysalis
15. **CAN'T SLOW DOWN**
    Lionel Richie – Motown
16. **SPEAKING IN TONGUES**
    Talking Heads – Sire
17. **THE PRINCIPLE OF MOMENTS**
    Robert Plant – Es Paranza
18. **THE CROSSING**
    Big Country – Mercury
19. **THE WILD HEART**
    Stevie Nicks – Modern
20. **COLOUR BY NUMBERS**
    Culture Club – Virgin/Epic

UK SINGLES

1. **UPTOWN GIRL**
   Billy Joel – CBS
2. **ALL NIGHT LONG (ALL NIGHT)**
   Lionel Richie – Motown
3. **SAY SAY SAY**
   McCartney/Jackson – Parlophone
4. **CRY JUST A LITTLE BIT**
   Shakin' Stevens – Epic
5. **PUSS'N BOOTS**
   Adam Ant – CBS
6. **UNION OF THE SNAKE**
   Duran Duran – EMI
7. **THE SAFETY DANCE**
   Men Without Hats – Statik
8. **KARMA CHAMELEON**
   Culture Club – Virgin
9. **THE SUN AND THE RAIN**
   Madness – Stiff
10. **THE LOVE CATS**
    The Cure – Fiction
11. **PLEASE DON'T MAKE ME CRY**
    UB40 – DEP International/Virgin
12. **(HEY YOU) …**
    The Rocksteady Crew – Charisma/Virgin
13. **THEY DON'T KNOW**
    Tracey Ullman – Stiff
14. **NEW SONG**
    Howard Jones – WEA
15. **A MESS OF BLUES**
    Status Quo – Vertigo/Phonogram
16. **UNCONDITIONAL LOVE**
    Donna Summer – Mercury/Phonogram
17. **SYNCHRONICITY II**
    The Police – A & M
18. **THAT WAS THEN …**
    ABC – Neutron/Phonogram
19. **IN YOUR EYES**
    George Benson – Warner Bros.
20. **ONLY FOR LOVE**
    Limahl – EMI

UK ALBUMS

1. **CAN'T SLOW DOWN**
   Lionel Richie – Motown
2. **COLOUR BY NUMBERS**
   Culture Club – Virgin
3. **THE TWO OF US**
   Various – K-Tel
4. **PIPES OF PEACE**
   Paul McCartney – Parlophone
5. **LABOUR OF LOVE**
   UB40 – DEP International/Virgin
6. **SNAP!**
   The Jam – Polydor
7. **GENESIS**
   Genesis – Charisma/Virgin
8. **VOICE OF THE HEART**
   Carpenters – A & M
9. **INFIDELS**
   Bob Dylan – CBS
10. **THRILLER**
    Michael Jackson – Epic
11. **NO PARLEZ!**
    Paul Young – CBS
12. **AN INNOCENT MAN**
    Billy Joel – CBS
13. **TOO LOW FOR ZERO**
    Elton John – Rocket/Phonogram
14. **FANTASTIC**
    Wham! – Inner Vision
15. **IMAGINATIONS**
    Various – CBS
16. **ROCK 'N SOUL PART 1**
    Daryl Hall & John Oates – RCA
17. **ZIGGY STARDUST …**
    Soundtrack – RCA
18. **MONUMENT**
    Ultravox – Chrysalis
19. **NORTH OF A MIRACLE**
    Nick Heyward – Arista
20. **LET'S DANCE**
    David Bowie – EMI America

WEEK ENDING NOVEMBER 19 1983

US SINGLES

1. **ALL NIGHT LONG (ALL NIGHT)**
Lionel Richie – Motown
2. **SAY SAY SAY**
McCartney/Jackson – Columbia
3. **UPTOWN GIRL**
Billy Joel – Columbia
4. **ISLANDS IN THE STREAM**
Kenny Rogers and Dolly Parton – RCA
5. **CUM ON FEEL THE NOIZE**
Quiet Riot – Pasha
6. **TOTAL ECLIPSE OF THE HEART**
Bonnie Tyler – Columbia
7. **LOVE IS A BATTLEFIELD**
Pat Benatar – Chrysalis
8. **ONE THING LEADS TO ANOTHER**
The Fixx – MCA
9. **SUDDENLY LAST SUMMER**
The Motels – Capitol
10. **SAY IT ISN'T SO**
Daryl Hall & John Oates – RCA
11. **DELIRIOUS**
Prince – Warner Bros.
12. **HEART AND SOUL**
Huey Lewis And The News – Chrysalis
13. **PYT (PRETTY YOUNG THING)**
Michael Jackson – Epic
14. **CRUMBLIN' DOWN**
John Cougar Mellencamp – Riva
15. **TELEFONE …**
Sheena Easton – EMI – America
16. **MAKING LOVE …**
Air Supply – Arista
17. **CHURCH OF THE POISON MIND**
Culture Club – Virgin/Epic
18. **TONIGHT I CELEBRATE MY LOVE**
Peabo Bryson/Roberta Flack – Capitol
19. **MODERN LOVE**
David Bowie – EMI America
20. **WHY ME?**
Irene Cara – Geffen/Network

US ALBUMS

1. **SYNCHRONICITY**
The Police – A & M
2. **METAL HEALTH**
Quiet Riot – Pasha
3. **THRILLER**
Michael Jackson – Epic
4. **CAN'T SLOW DOWN**
Lionel Richie – Motown
5. **AN INNOCENT MAN**
Billy Joel – Columbia
6. **EYES THAT SEE IN THE DARK**
Kenny Rogers – RCA
7. **GREATEST HITS**
Air Supply – Arista
8. **PYROMANIA**
Def Leppard – Mercury
9. **WHAT'S NEW**
Linda Ronstadt – Asylum
10. **GENESIS**
Genesis – Atlantic
11. **FASTER THAN THE SPEED OF …**
Bonnie Tyler – Columbia
12. **COLOUR BY NUMBERS**
Culture Club – Virgin/Epic
13. **LIVE FROM EARTH**
Pat Benatar – Chrysalis
14. **ELIMINATOR**
ZZ Top – Warner Bros.
15. **REACH THE BEACH**
The Fixx – MCA
16. **FLASHDANCE**
Soundtrack – Casablanca
17. **UH-HUH**
John Cougar Mellencamp – Riva
18. **THE PRINCIPLE OF MOMENTS**
Robert Plant – Es Paranza
19. **THE CROSSING**
Big Country – Mercury
20. **THE BIG CHILL**
Soundtrack – Motown

UK SINGLES

1. **UPTOWN GIRL**
Billy Joel – CBS
2. **SAY SAY SAY**
McCartney/Jackson – Parlophone
3. **CRY JUST A LITTLE BIT**
Shakin' Stevens – Epic
4. **ALL NIGHT LONG (ALL NIGHT)**
Lionel Richie – Motown
5. **THE SUN AND THE RAIN**
Madness – Stiff
6. **PUSS'N BOOTS**
Adam Ant – CBS
7. **THE LOVE CATS**
The Cure – Fiction
8. **THE SAFETY DANCE**
Men Without Hats – Statik
9. **KARMA CHAMELEON**
Culture Club – Virgin
10. **NEVER NEVER**
The Assembly – Mute
11. **UNDERCOVER OF THE NIGHT**
The Rolling Stones – Rolling Stones
12. **A SOLID BOND IN YOUR HEART**
The Style Council – Polydor
13. **UNION OF THE SNAKE**
Duran Duran – EMI
14. **UNCONDITIONAL LOVE**
Donna Summer – Mercury/Phonogram
15. **PLEASE DON'T MAKE ME CRY**
UB40 – DEP International/Virgin
16. **ONLY FOR LOVE**
Limahl – EMI
17. **LOVE OF THE COMMON PEOPLE**
Paul Young – CBS
18. **(HEY YOU) …**
The Rocksteady Crew – Charisma/Virgin
19. **LOVE WILL TEAR US APART**
Joy Division – Factory
20. **A MESS OF BLUES**
Status Quo – Vertigo/Phonogram

UK ALBUMS

1. **COLOUR BY NUMBERS**
Culture Club – Virgin
2. **CAN'T SLOW DOWN**
Lionel Richie – Motown
3. **UNDERCOVER**
The Rolling Stones – Rolling Stones
4. **AN INNOCENT MAN**
Billy Joel – CBS
5. **THRILLER**
Michael Jackson – Epic
6. **LABOUR OF LOVE**
UB40 – DEP International/Virgin
7. **NO PARLEZ!**
Paul Young – CBS
8. **THE TWO OF US**
Various – K-Tel
9. **GENESIS**
Genesis – Charisma/Virgin
10. **PIPES OF PEACE**
Paul McCartney – Parlophone
11. **STAGES**
Elaine Paige – K-Tel/WEA
12. **CHART HITS '83**
Various – K-Tel
13. **VOICE OF THE HEART**
Carpenters – A & M
14. **SNAP!**
The Jam – Polydor
15. **INFIDELS**
Bob Dylan – CBS
16. **TOO LOW FOR ZERO**
Elton John – Rocket/Phonogram
17. **FANTASTIC**
Wham! – Inner Vision
18. **HIT SQUAD**
Various – Ronco
19. **IMAGINATIONS**
Various – CBS
20. **STRIP**
Adam Ant – CBS

WEEK ENDING NOVEMBER 26 1983

US SINGLES

1. **ALL NIGHT LONG (ALL NIGHT)**
Lionel Richie – Motown
2. **SAY SAY SAY**
McCartney/Jackson – Columbia
3. **UPTOWN GIRL**
Billy Joel – Columbia
4. **ISLANDS IN THE STREAM**
Kenny Rogers & Dolly Parton – RCA
5. **CUM ON FEEL THE NOIZE**
Quiet Riot – Pasha
6. **LOVE IS A BATTLEFIELD**
Pat Benatar – Chrysalis
7. **SAY IT ISN'T SO**
Daryl Hall & John Oates – RCA
8. **HEART AND SOUL**
Huey Lewis And The News – Chrysalis
9. **CRUMBLIN' DOWN**
John Cougar Mellencamp – Riva
10. **P.Y.T. (PRETTY YOUNG THING)**
Michael Jackson – Epic
11. **CHURCH OF THE POISON MIND**
Culture Club – Virgin/Epic
12. **TOTAL ECLIPSE OF THE HEART**
Bonnie Tyler – Columbia
13. **SUDDENLY LAST SUMMER**
The Motels – Capitol
14. **UNION OF THE SNAKE**
Duran Duran – Capitol
15. **ONE THING LEADS TO ANOTHER**
The Fixx – MCA
16. **WHY ME?**
Irene Cara – Geffen/Network
17. **TELEFONE…**
Sheena Easton – EMI America
18. **DELIRIOUS**
Prince – Warner Bros.
19. **TONIGHT I CELEBRATE MY LOVE**
Peabo Bryson & Roberta Flack – Capitol
20. **MAKING LOVE …**
Air Supply – Arista

US ALBUMS

1. **METAL HEALTH**
Quiet Riot – Pasha
2. **CAN'T SLOW DOWN**
Lionel Richie – Motown
3. **THRILLER**
Michael Jackson – Epic
4. **SYNCHRONICITY**
The Police – A&M
5. **AN INNOCENT MAN**
Billy Joel – Columbia
6. **EYES THAT SEE IN THE DARK**
Kenny Rogers – RCA
7. **WHAT'S NEW**
Linda Ronstadt – Asylum
8. **GREATEST HITS**
Air Supply – Arista
9. **COLOUR BY NUMBERS**
Culture Club – Virgin/Epic
10. **GENESIS**
Genesis – Atlantic
11. **PYROMANIA**
Def Leppard – Mercury
12. **FASTER THAN THE SPEED OF…**
Bonnie Tyler – Columbia
13. **LIVE FROM EARTH**
Pat Benatar – Chrysalis
14. **ELIMINATOR**
ZZ Top – Warner Bros.
15. **ROCK 'N' SOUL, PART I**
Daryl Hall & John Oates – RCA
16. **UH-HUH**
John Cougar Mellencamp – Riva
17. **REACH THE BEACH**
The Fixx – MCA
18. **FLASHDANCE**
Soundtrack – Casablanca
19. **THE BIG CHILL**
Soundtrack – Motown
20. **PIPES OF PEACE**
Paul McCartney – Columbia

UK SINGLES

1. **UPTOWN GIRL**
Billy Joel – CBS
2. **SAY SAY SAY**
McCartney/Jackson – Parlophone
3. **CRY JUST A LITTLE BIT**
Shakin' Stevens – Epic
4. **NEVER NEVER**
The Assembly – Mute
5. **LOVE OF THE COMMON PEOPLE**
Paul Young – CBS
6. **ALL NIGHT LONG (ALL NIGHT)**
Lionel Richie – Motown
7. **THE SUN AND THE RAIN**
Madness – Stiff
8. **THE LOVE CATS**
The Cure – Fiction
9. **CALLING YOUR NAME**
Marilyn – Mercury/Phonogram
10. **THRILLER**
Michael Jackson – Epic
11. **A SOLID BOND IN YOUR HEART**
The Style Council – Polydor
12. **PUSS'N BOOTS**
Adam Ant – CBS
13. **UNDERCOVER OF THE NIGHT**
The Rolling Stones – Rolling Stones
14. **HOLD ME NOW**
Thompson Twins – Arista
15. **RIGHT BY YOUR SIDE**
Eurythmics – RCA
16. **LET'S STAY TOGETHER**
Tina Turner – Capitol
17. **ONLY FOR LOVE**
Limahl – EMI
18. **KARMA CHAMELEON**
Culture Club – Virgin
19. **THE SAFETY DANCE**
Men Without Hats – Statik
20. **OBLIVIOUS**
Aztec Camera – WEA

UK ALBUMS

1. **COLOUR BY NUMBERS**
Culture Club – Virgin
2. **CAN'T SLOW DOWN**
Lionel Richie – Motown
3. **THRILLER**
Michael Jackson – Epic
4. **STAGES**
Elaine Paige – K-Tel/WEA
5. **UNDERCOVER**
The Rolling Stones – Rolling Stones
6. **CHART HITS '83**
Various – K-Tel
7. **NO PARLEZ!**
Paul Young – CBS
8. **TOUCH**
Eurythmics – RCA
9. **AN INNOCENT MAN**
Billy Joel – CBS
10. **FANTASTIC**
Wham! – Inner Vision
11. **GENESIS**
Genesis – Charisma/Virgin
12. **BEAUTY STAB**
ABC – Neutron/Phonogram
13. **LABOUR OF LOVE**
UB40 – DEP International/Virgin
14. **HIT SQUAD**
Various – Ronco
15. **PIPES OF PEACE**
Paul McCartney – Parlophone
16. **19025**
Yes – Atco
17. **THE TWO OF US**
Various – K-Tel
18. **VOICE OF THE HEART**
Carpenters – A & M
19. **HAVE YOU EVER BEEN IN LOVE**
Leo Sayer – Chrysalis
20. **TOO LOW FOR ZERO**
Elton John – Rocket/Phonogram

WEEK ENDING DECEMBER 3 1983

	US SINGLES	US ALBUMS	UK SINGLES	UK ALBUMS
1	**ALL NIGHT LONG (ALL NIGHT)** *Lionel Richie – Motown*	**CAN'T SLOW DOWN** *Lionel Richie – Motown*	**UPTOWN GIRL** *Billy Joel – CBS*	**SEVEN AND THE RAGGED TIGER** *Duran Duran – EMI*
2	**SAY SAY SAY** *McCartney/Jackson – Columbia*	**METAL HEALTH** *Quiet Riot – Pasha*	**LOVE OF THE COMMON PEOPLE** *Paul Young – CBS*	**UNDER A BLOOD RED SKY** *U2 – Island*
3	**UPTOWN GIRL** *Billy Joel – Columbia*	**SYNCHRONICITY** *The Police – A & M*	**SAY SAY SAY** *McCartney/Jackson – Parlophone*	**COLOUR BY NUMBERS** *Culture Club – Virgin*
4	**ISLANDS IN THE STREAM** *Kenny Rogers & Dolly Parton – RCA*	**THRILLER** *Michael Jackson – Epic*	**CALLING YOUR NAME** *Marilyn – Mercury/Phonogram*	**STAGES** *Elaine Paige – K-Tel/WEA*
5	**SAY IT ISN'T SO** *Daryl Hall & John Oates – RCA*	**AN INNOCENT MAN** *Billy Joel – Columbia*	**HOLD ME NOW** *Thompson Twins – Arista*	**NO PARLEZ!** *Paul Young – CBS*
6	**LOVE IS A BATTLEFIELD** *Pat Benatar – Chrysalis*	**EYES THAT SEE IN THE DARK** *Kenny Rogers – RCA*	**NEVER NEVER** *The Assembly – Mute*	**THRILLER** *Michael Jackson – Epic*
7	**CUM FEEL THE NOIZE** *Quiet Riot – Pasha*	**WHAT'S NEW** *Linda Ronstadt – Asylum*	**LET'S STAY TOGETHER** *Tina Turner – Capitol*	**CHART HITS '83** *Various – K-tel*
8	**HEART AND SOUL** *Huey Lewis And The News – Chrysalis*	**COLOUR BY NUMBERS** *Culture Club – Virgin/Epic*	**CRY JUST A LITTLE BIT** *Shakin' Stevens – Epic*	**CAN'T SLOW DOWN** *Lionel Richie – Motown*
9	**CRUMBLIN' DOWN** *John Cougar Mellencamp – Riva*	**GENESIS** *Genesis – Atlantic*	**ONLY YOU** *Flying Pickets – 10 Records/Virgin*	**BACK TO BACK** *Status Quo – Vertigo/Phonogram*
10	**CHURCH OF THE POISON MIND** *Culture Club – Virgin/Epic*	**PYROMANIA** *Def Leppard – Mercury*	**RIGHT BY YOUR SIDE** *Eurythmics – RCA*	**FANTASTIC** *Wham! – Inner Vision*
11	**UNION OF THE SNAKE** *Duran Duran – Capitol*	**GREATEST HITS** *Air Supply – Arista*	**THRILLER** *Michael Jackson – Epic*	**TOUCH** *Eurythmics – RCA*
12	**PYT (PRETTY YOUNG THING)** *Michael Jackson – Epic*	**UH-HUH** *John Cougar Mellencamp – Riva*	**A SOLID BOND IN YOUR HEART** *The Style Council – Polydor*	**HIT SQUAD** *Various – Ronco*
13	**WHY ME?** *Irene Cara – Geffen/Network*	**UNDERCOVER** *The Rolling Stones – Rolling Stones*	**WATERFRONT** *Simple Minds – Virgin*	**GENESIS** *Genesis – Charisma/Virgin*
14	**OWNER OF A LONELY HEART** *Yes – Atco*	**ROCK 'N' SOUL PART I** *Daryl Hall & John Oates – RCA*	**THE LOVE CATS** *The Cure – Fiction*	**AN INNOCENT MAN** *Billy Joel – CBS*
15	**UNDERCOVER OF THE NIGHT** *The Rolling Stones – Rolling Stones*	**ELIMINATOR** *ZZ Top – Warner Bros.*	**MY OH MY** *Slade – RCA*	**UNDERCOVER** *The Rolling Stones – Rolling Stones*
16	**TWIST OF FATE** *Olivia Newton-John – MCA*	**LIVE FROM EARTH** *Pat Benatar – Chrysalis*	**ALL NIGHT LONG (ALL NIGHT)** *Lionel Richie – Motown*	**ROCK'N SOUL PART 1** *Daryl Hall & John Oates – RCA*
17	**IN A BIG COUNTRY** *Big Country – Mercury*	**PIPES OF PEACE** *Paul McCartney – Columbia*	**THE SUN AND THE RAIN** *Madness – Stiff*	**THANK YOU FOR THE MUSIC** *Abba – Epic*
18	**SUDDENLY LAST SUMMER** *The Motels – Capitol*	**THE BIG CHILL** *Soundtrack – Motown*	**OBLIVIOUS** *Aztec Camera – WEA*	**CHAS 'N' DAVE'S KNEES UP …** *Chas 'n' Dave – Rockney/Towerbell*
19	**SYNCHRONICITY II** *The Police – A & M*	**FASTER THAN THE SPEED OF …** *Bonnie Tyler – Columbia*	**UNDERCOVER OF THE NIGHT** *The Rolling Stones – Rolling Stones*	**HAVE YOU EVER BEEN IN LOVE** *Leo Sayer – Chrysalis*
20	**MAJOR TOM (COMING HOME)** *Peter Schilling – Elektra*	**INFIDELS** *Bob Dylan – Columbia*	**PLEASE DON'T FALL IN LOVE** *Cliff Richard – EMI*	**VOICE OF THE HEART** *Carpenters – A & M*

WEEK ENDING DECEMBER 10 1983

	US SINGLES	US ALBUMS	UK SINGLES	UK ALBUMS
1	**SAY SAY SAY** *McCartney/Jackson – Columbia*	**CAN'T SLOW DOWN** *Lionel Richie – Motown*	**ONLY YOU** *The Flying Pickets – 10 Records/Virgin*	**NO PARLEZ!** *Paul Young – CBS*
2	**ALL NIGHT LONG (ALL NIGHT)** *Lionel Richie – Motown*	**SYNCHRONICITY** *The Police – A & M*	**LOVE OF THE COMMON PEOPLE** *Paul Young – CBS*	**STAGES** *Elaine Paige – K-Tel/WEA*
3	**UPTOWN GIRL** *Billy Joel – Columbia*	**THRILLER** *Michael Jackson – Epic*	**UPTOWN GIRL** *Billy Joel – CBS*	**THRILLER** *Michael Jackson – Epic*
4	**SAY IT ISN'T SO** *Daryl Hall & John Oates – RCA*	**UNDERCOVER** *The Rolling Stones – Rolling Stones*	**HOLD ME NOW** *Thompson Twins – Arista*	**COLOUR BY NUMBERS** *Culture Club – Virgin*
5	**LOVE IS A BATTLEFIELD** *Pat Benatar – Chrysalis*	**AN INNOCENT MAN** *Billy Joel – Columbia*	**MY OH MY** *Slade – RCA*	**SEVEN AND THE RAGGED TIGER** *Duran Duran – EMI*
6	**ISLANDS IN THE STREAM** *Kenny Rogers & Dolly Parton – RCA*	**METAL HEALTH** *Quiet Riot – Pasha*	**LET'S STAY TOGETHER** *Tina Turner – Capitol*	**UNDER A BLOOD RED SKY** *U2 – Island*
7	**UNION OF THE SNAKE** *Duran Duran – Capitol*	**WHAT'S NEW** *Linda Ronstadt – Asylum*	**CALLING YOUR NAME** *Marilyn – Mercury/Phonogram*	**NOW THAT'S WHAT I CALL MUSIC** *Various – EMI/Virgin*
8	**CUM ON FEEL THE NOIZE** *Quiet Riot – Pasha*	**EYES THAT SEE IN THE DARK** *Kenny Rogers – RCA*	**MOVE OVER DARLING** *Tracey Ullman – Stiff*	**FANTASTIC** *Wham! – Inner Vision*
9	**CRUMBLIN' DOWN** *John Cougar Mellencamp – Riva*	**COLOUR BY NUMBERS** *Culture Club – Virgin/Epic*	**PLEASE DON'T FALL IN LOVE** *Cliff Richard – EMI*	**CAN'T SLOW DOWN** *Lionel Richie – Motown*
10	**CHURCH OF THE POISON MIND** *Culture Club – Virgin/Epic*	**ROCK 'N' SOUL PART 1** *Daryl Hall & John Oates – RCA*	**NEVER NEVER** *The Assembly – Mute*	**CHART HITS '83** *Various – K-Tel*
11	**OWNER OF A LONELY HEART** *Yes – Atco*	**GENESIS** *Genesis – Atlantic*	**VICTIMS** *Culture Club – Virgin*	**GENESIS** *Genesis – Charisma/Virgin*
12	**TWIST OF FATE** *Olivia Newton-John – MCA*	**UH-HUH** *John Cougar Mellencamp – Riva*	**SAY SAY SAY** *McCartney/Jackson – Parlophone*	**CHAS 'N' DAVE'S KNEES UP …** *Chas 'n' Dave – Rockney/Towerbell*
13	**WHY ME?** *Irene Cara – Geffen/Network*	**PYROMANIA** *Def Leppard – Mercury*	**CRY JUST A LITTLE BIT** *Shakin' Stevens – Epic*	**TOUCH** *Eurythmics – RCA*
14	**UNDERCOVER OF THE NIGHT** *The Rolling Stones – Rolling Stones*	**ELIMINATOR** *ZZ Top – Warner Bros.*	**RIGHT BY YOUR SIDE** *Eurythmics – RCA*	**AN INNOCENT MAN** *Billy Joel – CBS*
15	**HEART AND SOUL** *Huey Lewis And The News – Chrysalis*	**90125** *Yes – Atco*	**ISLANDS IN THE STREAM** *Kenny Rogers & Dolly Parton – RCA*	**HIT SQUAD** *Various – Ronco*
16	**SYNCHRONICITY II** *The Police – A & M*	**PIPES OF PEACE** *Paul McCartney – Columbia*	**THRILLER** *Michael Jackson – Epic*	**BACK TO BACK** *Status Quo – Vertigo/Phonogram*
17	**IN A BIG COUNTRY** *Big Country – Mercury*	**GREATEST HITS** *Air Supply – Arista*	**WATERFRONT** *Simple Minds – Virgin*	**LABOUR OF LOVE** *UB40 – DEP International/Virgin*
18	**MAJOR TOM (COMING HOME)** *Peter Schilling – Elektra*	**THE BIG CHILL** *Soundtrack – Motown*	**CLUB FANTASTIC MEGAMIX** *Wham! – Inner Vision*	**TRACK RECORD** *Joan Armatrading – A & M*
19	**BREAK MY STRIDE** *Matthew Wilder – Private*	**LIVE FROM EARTH** *Pat Benatar – Chrysalis*	**THAT'S ALL** *Genesis – Charisma/Virgin*	**THANK YOU FOR THE MUSIC** *Abba – Epic*
20	**PYT (PRETTY YOUNG THING)** *Michael Jackson – Epic*	**INFIDELS** *Bob Dylan – Columbia*	**OBLIVIOUS** *Aztec Camera – WEA*	**VOICE OF THE HEART** *Carpenters – A & M*

WEEK ENDING DECEMBER 17 1983

US SINGLES	US ALBUMS	UK SINGLES	UK ALBUMS
1 **SAY SAY SAY** *McCartney/Jackson – Columbia*	1 **CAN'T SLOW DOWN** *Lionel Richie – Motown*	1 **ONLY YOU** *The Flying Pickets – 10 Records/Virgin*	1 **NOW THAT'S WHAT I CALL MUSIC** *Various – EMI/Virgin*
2 **SAY IT ISN'T SO** *Daryl Hall & John Oates – RCA*	2 **THRILLER** *Michael Jackson – Epic*	2 **LOVE OF THE COMMON PEOPLE** *Paul Young – CBS*	2 **NO PARLEZ!** *Paul Young – CBS*
3 **ALL NIGHT LONG (ALL NIGHT)** *Lionel Richie – Motown*	3 **SYNCHRONICITY** *The Police – A & M*	3 **MY OH MY** *Slade – RCA*	3 **COLOUR BY NUMBERS** *Culture Club – Virgin*
4 **UPTOWN GIRL** *Billy Joel – Columbia*	4 **UNDERCOVER** *The Rolling Stones – Rolling Stones*	4 **VICTIMS** *Culture Club – Virgin*	4 **STAGES** *Elaine Paige – K-Tel/WEA*
5 **UNION OF THE SNAKE** *Duran Duran – Capitol*	5 **WHAT'S NEW** *Linda Ronstadt – Asylum*	5 **HOLD ME NOW** *Thompson Twins – Arista*	5 **THRILLER** *Michael Jackson – Epic*
6 **LOVE IS A BATTLEFIELD** *Pat Benatar – Chrysalis*	6 **METAL HEALTH** *Quiet Riot – Pasha*	6 **LET'S STAY TOGETHER** *Tina Turner – Capitol*	6 **SEVEN AND THE RAGGED TIGER** *Duran Duran – EMI*
7 **OWNER OF A LONELY HEART** *Yes – Atco*	7 **EYES THAT SEE IN THE DARK** *Kenny Rogers – RCA*	7 **PLEASE DON'T FALL IN LOVE** *Cliff Richard – EMI*	7 **UNDER A BLOOD RED SKY** *U2 – Island*
8 **ISLANDS IN THE STREAM** *Kenny Rogers & Dolly Parton – RCA*	8 **COLOUR BY NUMBERS** *Culture Club – Virgin/Epic*	8 **TELL HER ABOUT IT** *Billy Joel – CBS*	8 **FANTASTIC** *Wham! – Inner Vision*
9 **TWIST OF FATE** *Olivia Newton-John – MCA*	9 **AN INNOCENT MAN** *Billy Joel – Columbia*	9 **MOVE OVER DARLING** *Tracey Ullman – Stiff*	9 **CHAS 'N' DAVE'S KNEES UP …** *Chas 'n' Dave – Rockney/Towerbell*
10 **CHURCH OF THE POISON MIND** *Culture Club – Virgin/Epic*	10 **ROCK 'N' SOUL PART 1** *Daryl Hall & John Oates – RCA*	10 **UPTOWN GIRL** *Billy Joel – CBS*	10 **GENESIS** *Genesis – Charisma/Virgin*
11 **UNDERCOVER OF THE NIGHT** *The Rolling Stones – Rolling Stones*	11 **GENESIS** *Genesis – Atlantic*	11 **ISLANDS IN THE STREAM** *Kenny Rogers & Dolly Parton – RCA*	11 **CAN'T SLOW DOWN** *Lionel Richie – Motown*
12 **CUM ON FEEL THE NOIZE** *Quiet Riot – Pasha*	12 **UH-HUH** *John Cougar Mellencamp – Riva*	12 **THRILLER** *Michael Jackson – Epic*	12 **TOUCH** *Eurythmics – RCA*
13 **WHY ME** *Irene Cara – Geffen/Network 7*	13 **90125** *Yes – Atco*	13 **CALLING YOUR NAME** *Marilyn – Mercury/Phonogram*	13 **FORMULA 30** *Various – Decca*
14 **CRUMBLIN' DOWN** *John Cougar Mellencamp – Riva*	14 **PYROMANIA** *Def Leppard – Mercury*	14 **WHAT IS LOVE?** *Howard Jones – WEA*	14 **CHART HITS '83** *Various – K-Tel*
15 **MAJOR TOM (COMING HOME)** *Peter Schilling – Elektra*	15 **PIPES OF PEACE** *Paul McCartney – Columbia*	15 **CLUB FANTASTIC MEGAMIX** *Wham! – Inner Vision*	15 **HAVE YOU EVER BEEN IN LOVE** *Leo Sayer – Chrysalis*
16 **SYNCHRONICITY II** *The Police – A & M*	16 **ELIMINATOR** *ZZ Top – Warner Bros.*	16 **THAT'S ALL** *Genesis – Charisma/Virgin*	16 **AN INNOCENT MAN** *Billy Joel – CBS*
17 **IN A BIG COUNTRY** *Big Country – Mercury*	17 **SEVEN AND THE RAGGED TIGER** *Duran Duran – Capitol*	17 **CRY JUST A LITTLE BIT** *Shakin' Stevens – Epic*	17 **LABOUR OF LOVE** *UB40 – DEP International/Virgin*
18 **BREAK MY STRIDE** *Matthew Wilder – Private*	18 **THE BIG CHILL** *Soundtrack – Motown*	18 **SAY SAY SAY** *McCartney/Jackson – Parlophone*	18 **VOICE OF THE HEART** *Carpenters – A & M*
19 **I GUESS THAT'S WHY …** *Elton John – Geffen*	19 **YENTL** *Barbra Streisand – Columbia*	19 **RIGHT BY YOUR SIDE** *Eurythmics – RCA*	19 **TRACK RECORD** *Joan Armatrading – A & M*
20 **TALKING IN YOUR SLEEP** *The Romantics – Nemperor*	20 **INFIDELS** *Bob Dylan – Columbia*	20 **READ 'EM AND WEEP** *Barry Manilow – Arista*	20 **GREATEST HITS** *Marvin Gaye – Telstar*

WEEK ENDING DECEMBER 24 1983

US SINGLES	US ALBUMS	UK SINGLES	UK ALBUMS
1 **SAY SAY SAY** *McCartney/Jackson – Columbia*	1 **THRILLER** *Michael Jackson – Epic*	1 **ONLY YOU** *The Flying Pickets – 10 Records/Virgin*	1 **NOW THAT'S WHAT I CALL MUSIC** *Various – EMI/Virgin*
2 **SAY IT ISN'T SO** *Daryl Hall & John Oates – RCA*	2 **CAN'T SLOW DOWN** *Lionel Richie – Motown*	2 **MY OH MY** *Slade – RCA*	2 **NO PARLEZ!** *Paul Young – CBS*
3 **UNION OF THE SNAKE** *Duran Duran – Capitol*	3 **WHAT'S NEW** *Linda Ronstadt – Asylum*	3 **VICTIMS** *Culture Club – Virgin*	3 **COLOUR BY NUMBERS** *Culture Club – Virgin*
4 **OWNER OF A LONELY HEART** *Yes – Atco*	4 **SYNCHRONICITY** *The Police – A & M*	4 **LOVE OF THE COMMON PEOPLE** *Paul Young – CBS*	4 **THRILLER** *Michael Jackson – Epic*
5 **ALL NIGHT LONG (ALL NIGHT)** *Lionel Richie – Motown*	5 **UNDERCOVER** *The Rolling Stones – Rolling Stones*	5 **MARGUERITA TIME** *Status Quo – Vertigo*	5 **STAGES** *Elaine Paige – K-Tel/WEA*
6 **UPTOWN GIRL** *Billy Joel – Columbia*	6 **METAL HEALTH** *Quiet Riot – Pasha*	6 **HOLD ME NOW** *Thompson Twins – Arista*	6 **FORMULA 30** *Various – Decca*
7 **LOVE IS A BATTLEFIELD** *Pat Benatar – Chrysalis*	7 **90125** *Yes – Atco*	7 **TELL HER ABOUT IT** *Billy Joel – CBS*	7 **CHAS 'N' DAVE'S KNEES UP …** *Chas 'n' Dave – Rockney/Towerbell*
8 **TWIST OF FATE** *Oliva Newton-John – MCA*	8 **AN INNOCENT MAN** *Billy Joel – Columbia*	8 **ISLANDS IN THE STREAM** *Kenny Rogers & Dolly Parton – RCA*	8 **SEVEN AND THE RAGGED TIGER** *Duran Duran – EMI*
9 **UNDERCOVER OF THE NIGHT** *The Rolling Stones – Rolling Stones*	9 **COLOUR BY NUMBERS** *Culture Club – Virgin/Epic*	9 **LET'S STAY TOGETHER** *Tina Turner – Capitol*	9 **CAN'T SLOW DOWN** *Lionel Richie – Motown*
10 **BREAK MY STRIDE** *Matthew Wilder – Private*	10 **ROCK 'N' SOUL PART 1** *Daryl Hall & John Oates – RCA*	10 **PLEASE DON'T FALL IN LOVE** *Cliff Richard – EMI*	10 **GENESIS** *Genesis – Charisma/Virgin*
11 **I GUESS THAT'S WHY …** *Elton John – Geffen*	11 **EYES THAT SEE IN THE DARK** *Kenny Rogers – RCA*	11 **WHAT IS LOVE?** *Howard Jones – WEA*	11 **FANTASTIC** *Wham! – Inner Vision*
12 **TALKING IN YOUR SLEEP** *The Romantics – Nemperor*	12 **SEVEN AND THE RAGGED TIGER** *Duran Duran – Capitol*	12 **MOVE OVER DARLING** *Tracey Ullman – Stiff*	12 **TOUCH** *Eurythmics – RCA*
13 **CHURCH OF THE POISON MIND** *Culture Club – Virgin/Epic*	13 **GENESIS** *Genesis – Atlantic*	13 **CALLING YOUR NAME** *Marilyn – Mercury/Phonogram*	13 **AN INNOCENT MAN** *Billy Joel – CBS*
14 **MAJOR TOM (COMING HOME)** *Peter Schilling – Elektra*	14 **YENTL** *Barbra Streisand – Columbia*	14 **UPTOWN GIRL** *Billy Joel – CBS*	14 **THE ESSENTIAL …** *Jean Michel Jarre – Polystar*
15 **CUM ON FEEL THE NOIZE** *Quiet Riot – Pasha*	15 **UH-HUH** *John Cougar Mellencamp – Riva*	15 **2000 MILES** *The Pretenders – Real*	15 **PIPES OF PEACE** *Paul McCartney – Parlophone*
16 **SYNCHRONICITY II** *The Police – A & M*	16 **ELIMINATOR** *ZZ Top – Warner Bros.*	16 **MANY RIVERS TO CROSS** *UB40 – DEP International*	16 **LABOUR OF LOVE** *UB40 – DEP International/Virgin*
17 **KARMA CHAMELEON** *Culture Club – Virgin/Epic*	17 **PYROMANIA** *Def Leppard – Mercury*	17 **READ 'EM AND WEEP** *Barry Manilow – Arista*	17 **UNDER A BLOOD RED SKY** *U2 – Island*
18 **ISLANDS IN THE STREAM** *Kenny Rogers & Dolly Parton – RCA*	18 **THE BIG CHILL** *Soundtrack – Motown*	18 **THAT'S ALL** *Genesis – Charisma/Virgin*	18 **GREEN VELVET** *Various – Ronco*
19 **WHY ME?** *Irene Cara – Geffen/Network*	19 **PIPES OF PEACE** *Paul McCartney – Columbia*	19 **STRAIGHT AHEAD** *Kool & The Gang – De-Lite*	19 **GREATEST HITS** *Phil Spector – Impression*
20 **IN A BIG COUNTRY** *Big Country – Mercury*	20 **INFIDELS** *Bob Dylan – Columbia*	20 **MERRY XMAS EVERYBODY** *Slade – Polydor*	20 **TRACK RECORD** *John Armatrading – A & M*

WEEK ENDING JANUARY 7 1984

US SINGLES	US ALBUMS	UK SINGLES	UK ALBUMS
1 **SAY SAY SAY** *McCartney/Jackson – Columbia*	1 **THRILLER** *Michael Jackson – Epic*	1 **ONLY YOU** *The Flying Pickets – 10 Records/Virgin*	1 **NOW THAT'S WHAT I CALL MUSIC** *Various – EMI/Virgin*
2 **SAY IT ISN'T SO** *Daryl Hall & John Oates – RCA*	2 **CAN'T SLOW DOWN** *Lionel Richie – Motown*	2 **MY OH MY** *Slade – RCA*	2 **NO PARLEZ!** *Paul Young – CBS*
3 **UNION OF THE SNAKE** *Duran Duran – Capitol*	3 **WHAT'S NEW** *Linda Ronstadt – Asylum*	3 **LOVE OF THE COMMON PEOPLE** *Paul Young – CBS*	3 **THRILLER** *Michael Jackson – Epic*
4 **OWNER OF A LONELY HEART** *Yes – Atco*	4 **SYNCHRONICITY** *The Police – A & M*	5 **VICTIMS** *Culture Club – Virgin*	4 **COLOUR BY NUMBERS** *Culture Club – Virgin*
5 **TWIST OF FATE** *Olivia Newton-John – MCA*	5 **METAL HEALTH** *Quiet Riot – Pasha*	5 **MARGUERITA TIME** *Status Quo – Vertigo/Phonogram*	5 **STAGES** *Elaine Paige – K-Tel/WEA*
6 **TALKING IN YOUR SLEEP** *The Romantics – Nemperor*	6 **90125** *Yes – Atco*	6 **TELL HER ABOUT IT** *Billy Joel – CBS*	6 **GREEN VELVET** *Various – Ronco*
7 **BREAK MY STRIDE** *Matthew Wilder – Private*	7 **COLOUR BY NUMBERS** *Culture Club – Virgin/Epic*	7 **ISLANDS IN THE STREAM** *Kenny Rogers & Dolly Parton – RCA*	7 **AN INNOCENT MAN** *Billy Joel – CBS*
8 **I GUESS THAT'S WHY …** *Elton John – Geffen*	8 **AN INNOCENT MAN** *Billy Joel – Columbia*	8 **HOLD ME NOW** *Thompson Twins – Arista*	8 **PIPES OF PEACE** *Paul McCartney – Parlophone*
9 **UNDERCOVER OF THE NIGHT** *The Rolling Stones – Rolling Stones*	9 **YENTL** *Barbra Streisand – Columbia*	9 **PIPES OF PEACE** *Paul McCartney – Parlophone*	9 **CAN'T SLOW DOWN** *Lionel Richie – Motown*
10 **ALL NIGHT LONG (ALL NIGHT)** *Lionel Richie – Motown*	10 **ROCK 'N' SOUL PART 1** *Daryl Hall & John Oates – RCA*	10 **WHAT IS LOVE?** *Howard Jones – WEA*	10 **CHAS 'N' DAVE'S KNEES UP …** *Chas 'n' Dave – Rockney Towerbell*
11 **UPTOWN GIRL** *Billy Joel – Columbia*	11 **UNDERCOVER** *The Rolling Stones – Rolling Stones*	11 **THRILLER** *Michael Jackson – Epic*	11 **FORMULA 30** *Various – Decca*
12 **LOVE IS A BATTLEFIELD** *Pat Benatar – Chrysalis*	12 **SEVEN AND THE RAGGED TIGER** *Duran Duran – Capitol*	12 **LET'S STAY TOGETHER** *Tina Turner – Capitol*	12 **FANTASTIC** *Wham! – Inner Vision*
13 **KARMA CHAMELEON** *Culture Club – Virgin/Epic*	13 **UH-HUH** *John Cougar Mellencamp – Riva*	13 **PLEASE DON'T FALL IN LOVE** *Cliff Richard – EMI*	13 **GENESIS** *Genesis – Charisma/Virgin*
14 **MAJOR TOM (COMING HOME)** *Peter Schilling – Elektra*	14 **EYES THAT SEE IN THE DARK** *Kenny Rogers – RCA*	14 **UPTOWN GIRL** *Billy Joel – CBS*	14 **THE ESSENTIAL …** *Jean Michel Jarre – Polystar*
15 **RUNNING WITH THE NIGHT** *Lionel Richie – Motown*	15 **GENESIS** *Genesis – Atlantic*	15 **MOVE OVER DARLING** *Tracey Ullman – Stiff*	15 **TOUCH** *Eurythmics – RCA*
16 **CHURCH OF THE POISON MIND** *Culture Club – Virgin/Epic*	16 **ELIMINATOR** *ZZ Top – Warner Bros*	16 **2000 MILES** *The Pretenders – Real*	16 **SEVEN AND THE RAGGED TIGER** *Duran Duran – EMI*
17 **JOANNA** *Kool & The Gang – De-Lite*	17 **PYROMANIA** *Def Leppard – Mercury*	17 **MANY RIVERS TO CROSS** *UB40 – DEP International/Virgin*	17 **PORTRAIT** *Diana Ross – Telstar*
18 **READ 'EM AND WEEP** *Barry Manilow – Arista*	18 **THE BIG CHILL** *Soundtrack – Motown*	18 **RAT RAPPING …** *Roland Rat Superstar – Magnet*	18 **LABOUR OF LOVE** *UB40 – DEP International/Virgin*
19 **SYNCHRONICITY II** *The Police – A & M*	19 **PIPES OF PEACE** *Paul McCartney – Columbia*	19 **STRAIGHT AHEAD** *Kool & The Gang – De-Lite*	19 **UNDER A BLOOD RED SKY** *U2 – Island*
20 **CUM ON FEEL THE NOIZE** *Quiet Riot – Pasha*	20 **GREATEST HITS** *Air Supply – Arista*	20 **MERRY XMAS EVERYBODY** *Slade – Polydor*	20 **BACK TO BACK** *Status Quo – Vertigo/Phonogram*

WEEK ENDING JANUARY 14 1984

US SINGLES	US ALBUMS	UK SINGLES	UK ALBUMS
1 **SAY SAY SAY** *McCartney/Jackson – Columbia*	1 **THRILLER** *Michael Jackson – Epic*	1 **PIPES OF PEACE** *Paul McCartney – Parlophone*	1 **NO PARLEZ!** *Paul Young – CBS*
2 **OWNER OF A LONELY HEART** *Yes – Atco*	2 **CAN'T SLOW DOWN** *Lionel Richie – Motown*	2 **WHAT IS LOVE?** *Howard Jones – WEA*	2 **NOW THAT'S WHAT I CALL MUSIC** *Various – EMI/Virgin*
3 **SAY IT ISN'T SO** *Daryl Hall & John Oates – RCA*	3 **WHAT'S NEW** *Linda Ronstadt – Asylum*	3 **MARGUERITA TIME** *Status Quo – Vertigo/Phonogram*	3 **THRILLER** *Michael Jackson – Epic*
4 **UNION OF THE SNAKE** *Duran Duran – Capitol*	4 **SYNCHRONICITY** *The Police – A & M*	4 **TELL HER ABOUT IT** *Billy Joel – CBS*	4 **COLOUR BY NUMBERS** *Culture Club – Virgin*
5 **TWIST OF FATE** *Olivia Newton-John – MCA*	5 **METAL HEALTH** *Quiet Riot – Pasha*	5 **LOVE OF THE COMMON PEOPLE** *Paul Young – CBS*	5 **AN INNOCENT MAN** *Billy Joel – CBS*
6 **TALKING IN YOUR SLEEP** *The Romantics – Nemperor*	6 **90125** *Yes – Atco*	6 **RELAX** *Frankie Goes To Hollywood – ZTT/Island*	6 **UNDER A BLOOD RED SKY** *U2 – Island*
7 **BREAK MY STRIDE** *Matthew Wilder – Private*	7 **COLOUR BY NUMBERS** *Culture Club – Virgin/Epic*	7 **VICTIMS** *Culture Club – Virgin*	7 **CAN'T SLOW DOWN** *Lionel Richie – Motown*
8 **I GUESS THAT'S WHY …** *Elton John – Geffen*	8 **AN INNOCENT MAN** *Billy Joel – Columbia*	8 **ISLANDS IN THE STREAM** *Kenny Rogers & Dolly Parton – RCA*	8 **PORTRAIT** *Diana Ross – Telstar*
9 **KARMA CHAMELEON** *Culture Club – Virgin/Epic*	9 **YENTL** *Barbra Streisand – Columbia*	9 **HOLD ME NOW** *Thompson Twins – Arista*	9 **TOUCH** *Eurythmics – RCA*
10 **RUNNING WITH THE NIGHT** *Lionel Richie – Motown*	10 **ROCK 'N' SOUL PART 1** *Daryl Hall & John Oates – RCA*	10 **ONLY YOU** *The Flying Pickets – 10 Records/Virgin*	10 **PIPES OF PEACE** *Paul McCartney – Parlophone*
11 **ALL NIGHT LONG (ALL NIGHT)** *Lionel Richie – Motown*	11 **SEVEN AND THE RAGGED TIGER** *Duran Duran – Capitol*	11 **MY OH MY** *Slade – RCA*	11 **FANTASTIC** *Wham! – Inner Vision*
12 **UNDERCOVER OF THE NIGHT** *The Rolling Stones – Rolling Stones*	12 **UH-HUH** *John Cougar Mellencamp – Riva*	12 **THRILLER** *Michael Jackson – Epic*	12 **GENESIS** *Genesis – Charisma/Virgin*
13 **JOANNA** *Kool & The Gang – De-Lite*	13 **UNDERCOVER** *The Rolling Stones – Rolling Stones*	13 **A ROCKIN' GOOD WAY** *Shaky & Bonnie – Epic*	13 **LABOUR OF LOVE** *UB40 – DEP International/Virgin*
14 **UPTOWN GIRL** *Billy Joel – Columbia*	14 **EYES THAT SEE IN THE DARK** *Kenny Rogers – RCA*	14 **RAT RAPPING …** *Roland Rat Superstar – Magnet*	14 **YOU BROKE MY HEART …** *Tracey Ullman – Stiff*
15 **LOVE IS A BATTLEFIELD** *Pat Benatar – Chrysalis*	15 **PYROMANIA** *Def Leppard – Mercury*	15 **STRAIGHT AHEAD** *Kool & The Gang – De-Lite*	15 **BACK TO BACK** *Status Quo – Vertigo/Phonogram*
16 **THE CURLY SHUFFLE** *Jump'n The Saddle – Atlantic*	16 **ELIMINATOR** *ZZ Top – Warner Bros*	16 **UPTOWN GIRL** *Billy Joel – CBS*	16 **FORMULA 30** *Various – Decca*
17 **THAT'S ALL** *Genesis – Atlantic*	17 **GENESIS** *Genesis – Atlantic*	17 **LET'S STAY TOGETHER** *Tina Turner – Capitol*	17 **STAGES** *Elaine Paige – K-Tel/WEA*
18 **READ 'EM AND WEEP** *Barry Manilow – Arista*	18 **THE BIG CHILL** *Soundtrack – Motown*	18 **THAT'S LIVING ALRIGHT** *Joe Fagin – Towerbell*	18 **THE ESSENTIAL …** *Jean Michel Jarre – Polystar*
19 **MAJOR TOM (COMING HOME)** *Peter Schilling – Elektra*	19 **GREATEST HITS** *Air Supply – Arista*	19 **BIRD OF PARADISE** *Snowy White – Towerbell*	19 **SEVEN AND THE RAGGED TIGER** *Duran Duran – EMI*
20 **I STILL CAN'T GET OVER …** *Ray Parker Jr – Arista*	20 **PIPES OF PEACE** *Paul McCartney – Columbia*	20 **MANY RIVERS TO CROSS** *UB40 – DEP International/Virgin*	20 **CHART TREK** *Various – Ronco*

WEEK ENDING JANUARY 21 1984

US SINGLES

1. **OWNER OF A LONELY HEART**
Yes – Atco
2. **SAY SAY SAY**
McCartney/Jackson – Columbia
3. **KARMA CHAMELEON**
Culture Club – Virgin/Epic
4. **TALKING IN YOUR SLEEP**
The Romantics – Nemperor
5. **BREAK MY STRIDE**
Matthew Wilder – Warner Bros
6. **I GUESS THAT'S WHY ...**
Elton John – Geffen
7. **TWIST OF FATE**
Olivia Newton-John – MCA
8. **JOANNA**
Kool & The Gang – De-Lite
9. **RUNNING WITH THE NIGHT**
Lionel Richie – Motown
10. **SAY IT ISN'T SO**
Daryl Hall & John Oates – RCA
11. **UNION OF THE SNAKE**
Duran Duran – Capitol
12. **GENESIS**
Genesis – Atlantic
13. **PINK HOUSES**
Joh Cougar Mellencamp – Riva
14. **THINK OF LAURA**
Christopher Cross – Warner Bros.
15. **THE CURLY SHUFFLE**
Jump'n The Saddle – Atlantic
16. **I STILL CAN'T GET OVER ...**
Ray Parker Jr – Arista
17. **HOLIDAY**
Madonna – Sire
18. **TIME WILL REVEAL**
DeBarge – Gordy
19. **IF I'D BEEN THE ONE**
38 Special A&M
20. **UNDERCOVER OF THE NIGHT**
The Rolling Stones – Rolling Stones

US ALBUMS

1. **THRILLER**
Michael Jackson – Epic
2. **CAN'T SLOW DOWN**
Lionel Richie – Motown
3. **WHAT'S NEW**
Linda Ronstadt – Asylum
4. **COLOUR BY NUMBERS**
Culture Club – Virgin/Epic
5. **90125**
Yes – Atco
6. **SYNCHRONICITY**
The Police – A & M
7. **METAL HEALTH**
Quiet Riot – Pasha
8. **AN INNOCENT MAN**
Billy Joel – Columbia
9. **ROCK 'N' SOUL PART 1**
Daryl Hall & John Oates – RCA
10. **SEVEN AND THE RAGGED TIGER**
Duran Duran – Capitol
11. **YENTL**
Barbra Streisand – Columbia
12. **UH-HUH**
John Cougar Mellencamp – Riva
13. **ELIMINATOR**
ZZ Top – Warner Bros
14. **GENESIS**
Genesis – Atlantic
15. **PYROMANIA**
Def Leppard – Mercury
16. **EYES THAT SEE IN THE DARK**
Kenny Rogers – RCA
17. **THE BIG CHILL**
Soundtrack – Motown
18. **UNDERCOVER**
The Rolling Stones – Rolling Stones
19. **PIPES OF PEACE**
Paul McCartney – Columbia
20. **GREATEST HITS**
Air Supply – Arista

UK SINGLES

1. **PIPES OF PEACE**
Paul McCartney – Parlophone
2. **RELAX**
Frankie Goes To Hollywood – ZTT/Island
3. **WHAT IS LOVE?**
Howard Jones – WEA
4. **THAT'S LIVING ALRIGHT**
Joe Fagin – Towerbell
5. **A ROCKIN' GOOD WAY**
Shaky & Bonnie – Epic
6. **BIRD OF PARADISE**
Snowy White – Towerbell
7. **MARGUERITA TIME**
Status Quo – Vertigo/Phonogram
8. **TELL HER ABOUT IT**
Billy Joel – CBS
9. **RUNNING WITH THE NIGHT**
Lionel Richie – Motown
10. **ISLANDS IN THE STREAM**
Kenny Rogers & Dolly Parton – RCA
11. **NOBODY TOLD ME**
John Lennon – Polydor
12. **HOLD ME NOW**
Thompson Twins – Arista
13. **WONDERLAND**
Big Country – Mercury/Phonogram
14. **LOVE OF THE COMMON PEOPLE**
Paul Young – CBS
15. **LOVE IS A WONDERFUL COLOUR**
The Icicle Works – Beggars Banquet
16. **WISHFUL THINKING**
China Crisis – Virgin
17. **KING OF PAIN**
The Police – A & M
18. **THRILLER**
Michael Jackson – Epic
19. **STRAIGHT AHEAD**
Kool & The Gang – De-Lite
20. **HERE COMES THE RAIN AGAIN**
Eurythmics – RCA

UK ALBUMS

1. **NOW THAT'S WHAT I CALL MUSIC**
Various – EMI/Virgin
2. **THRILLER**
Michael Jackson – Epic
3. **NO PARLEZ!**
Paul Young – CBS
4. **PIPES OF PEACE**
Paul McCartney – Parlophone
5. **AN INNOCENT MAN**
Billy Joel – CBS
6. **TOUCH**
Eurythmics – RCA
7. **CAN'T SLOW DOWN**
Lionel Richie – Motown
8. **UNDER A BLOOD RED SKY**
U2 – Island
9. **PORTRAIT**
Diana Ross – Telstar
10. **COLOUR BY NUMBERS**
Culture Club – Virgin
11. **LABOUR OF LOVE**
UB40 – DEP International/Virgin
12. **LEARNING TO CRAWL**
The Pretenders – Real
13. **GENESIS**
Genesis – Charisma/Virgin
14. **STAGES**
Elaine Paige – K-Tel/WEA
15. **BACK TO BACK**
Status Quo – Vertigo/Phonogram
16. **YOU BROKE MY HEART ...**
Tracey Ullman – Stiff
17. **GREEN VELVET**
Various – Ronco
18. **FORMULA 30**
Various – Decca
19. **THE ESSENTIAL ...**
Jean Michel Jarre – Polystar
20. **SOMETIMES WHEN WE TOUCH**
Various – Ronco

WEEK ENDING JANUARY 28 1984

US SINGLES

1. **OWNER OF A LONELY HEART**
Yes – Atco
2. **KARMA CHAMELEON**
Culture Club – Virgin/Epic
3. **TALKING IN YOUR SLEEP**
The Romantics – Nemperor
4. **I GUESS THAT'S WHY ...**
Elton John – Geffen
5. **BREAK MY STRIDE**
Matthew Wilder – Private
6. **JOANNA**
Kool & The Gang – De-Lite
7. **SAY SAY SAY**
McCartney/Jackson – Columbia
8. **RUNNING WITH THE NIGHT**
Lionel Richie – Motown
9. **TWIST OF FATE**
Olivia Newton-John – MCA
10. **THAT'S ALL**
Genesis – Atlantic
11. **THINK OF LAURA**
Christopher Cross – Warner Bros
12. **PINK HOUSES**
John Cougar Mellencamp – Mercury
13. **UNION OF THE SNAKE**
Duran Duran – Capitol
14. **I STILL CAN'T GET OVER ...**
Ray Parker – Arista
15. **SAY IT ISN'T SO**
Daryl Hall & John Oates – RCA
16. **HOLIDAY**
Madonna – Sire
17. **THE CURLY SHUFFLE**
Jump'n The Saddle – Atlantic
18. **LET THE MUSIC PLAY**
Shannon – Mirage
19. **AN INNOCENT MAN**
Billy Joel – Columbia
20. **JUMP**
Van Halen – Warner Bros

US ALBUMS

1. **THRILLER**
Michael Jackson – Epic
2. **CAN'T SLOW DOWN**
Lionel Richie – Motown
3. **COLOUR BY NUMBERS**
Culture Club – Virgin/Epic
4. **WHAT'S NEW**
Linda Ronstadt – Asylum
5. **90125**
Yes – Atco
6. **SYNCHRONICITY**
The Police – A & M
7. **ROCK 'N' SOUL PART 1**
Daryl Hall & John Oates – RCA
8. **AN INNOCENT MAN**
Billy Joel – Columbia
9. **UH-HUH**
John Cougar Mellencamp – Riva
10. **SEVEN AND THE RAGGED TIGER**
Duran Duran – Capitol
11. **METAL HEALTH**
Quiet Riot – Pasha
12. **ELIMINATOR**
ZZ Top – Warner Bros
13. **GENESIS**
Genesis – Atlantic
14. **PYROMANIA**
Def Leppard – Mercury
15. **YENTL**
Barbra Streisand – Columbia
16. **IN HEAT**
The Romantics – Nemperor
17. **THE BIG CHILL**
Sountrack – Motown
18. **1984**
Van Halen – Warner Bros
19. **BARK AT THE MOON**
Ozzy Osbourne – CBS
20. **EYES THAT SEE IN THE DARK**
Kenny Rogers – RCA

UK SINGLES

1. **RELAX**
Frankie Goes To Hollywood – ZTT/Island
2. **PIPES OF PEACE**
Paul McCartney – Parlophone
3. **THAT'S LIVING ALRIGHT**
Joe Fagin – Towerbell
4. **WHAT IS LOVE?**
Howard Jones – WEA
5. **A ROCKIN' GOOD WAY**
Shaky & Bonnie – Epic
6. **NOBODY TOLD ME**
John Lennon – Polydor
7. **BIRD OF PARADISE**
Snowy White – Towerbell
8. **WONDERLAND**
Big Country – Mercury/Phonogram
9. **WISHFUL THINKING**
China Crisis – Virgin
10. **GIRLS JUST WANT TO HAVE FUN**
Cyndi Lauper – Portrait/Epic
11. **HERE COMES THE RAIN AGAIN**
Eurythmics – RCA
12. **(FEELS LIKE) HEAVEN**
Fiction Factory – CBS
13. **I AM WHAT I AM**
Gloria Gaynor – Chrysalis
14. **BREAK MY STRIDE**
Matthew Wilder – Epic
15. **MARGUERITA TIME**
Status Quo – Vertigo/Phonogram
16. **RUNNING WITH THE NIGHT**
Lionel Richie – Motown
17. **THE KILLING MOON**
Echo & The Bunnymen – Korova
18. **TELL HER ABOUT IT**
Billy Joel – CBS
19. **LOVE IS A WONDERFUL COLOUR**
The Icicle Works – Beggars Banquet
20. **SPEED YOUR LOVE TO ME**
Simple Minds – Virgin

UK ALBUMS

1. **THRILLER**
Michael Jackson – Epic
2. **NO PARLEZ!**
Paul Young – CBS
3. **NOW THAT'S WHAT I CALL MUSIC**
Various – EMI/Virgin
4. **AN INNOCENT MAN**
Billy Joel – CBS
5. **TOUCH**
Eurythmics – RCA
6. **PIPES OF PEACE**
Paul McCartney – Parlophone
7. **CAN'T SLOW DOWN**
Lionel Richie – Motown
8. **UNDER A BLOOD RED SKY**
U2 – Island
9. **PORTRAIT**
Diana Ross – Telstar
10. **COLOUR BY NUMBERS**
Culture Club – Virgin
11. **LEARNING TO CRAWL**
The Pretenders – Real
12. **SOMETIMES WHEN WE TOUCH**
Various – Ronco
13. **THE CROSSING**
Big Country – Mercury/Phonogram
14. **BACK TO BACK**
Status Quo – Vertigo/Phonogram
15. **THE ESSENTIAL ...**
Jean Michel Jarre – Polystar
16. **LABOUR OF LOVE**
UB40 – DEP International/Virgin
17. **GENESIS**
Genesis – Charisma/Virgin
18. **SYNCHRONICITY**
The Police – A & M
19. **DEFENDERS OF THE FAITH**
Judas Priest – CBS
20. **YOU BROKE MY HEART ...**
Tracey Ullman – Stiff

WEEK ENDING FEBRUARY 4 1984

US SINGLES

1 **KARMA CHAMELEON**
Culture Club – Virgin/Epic

2 **OWNER OF A LONELY HEART**
Yes – Atco

3 **TALKING IN YOUR SLEEP**
The Romantics – Nemperor

4 **JOANNA**
Kool & The Gang – De-Lite

5 **BREAK MY STRIDE**
Matthew Wilder – Private

6 **I GUESS THAT'S WHY ...**
Elton John – Geffen

7 **RUNNING WITH THE NIGHT**
Lionel Richie – Motown

8 **THAT'S ALL**
Genesis – Atlantic

9 **THINK OF LAURA**
Christopher Cross – Warner Bros.

10 **PINK HOUSES**
John Cougar Mellancamp – Riva

11 **JUMP**
Van Halen – Warner Bros.

12 **I STILL CAN'T GET OVER ...**
Ray Parker – Arista

13 **SAY SAY SAY**
McCartney/Jackson – Columbia

14 **LET THE MUSIC PLAY**
Shannon – Mirage

15 **AN INNOCENT MAN**
Billy Joel – Columbia

16 **HOLIDAY**
Madonna – Sire

17 **TWIST OF FATE**
Olivia Newton-John – MCA

18 **99 LUFTBALLONS**
Nena – Epic

19 **WRAPPED AROUND ...**
The Police – A & M

20 **MIDDLE OF THE ROAD**
The Pretenders – Sire

US ALBUMS

1 **THRILLER**
Michael Jackson – Epic

2 **COLOUR BY NUMBERS**
Culture Club – Virgin/Epic

3 **CAN'T SLOW DOWN**
Lionel Richie – Motown

4 **1984**
Van Halen – Warner Bros.

5 **90125**
Yes – Atco

6 **SYNCHRONICITY**
The Police – A & M

7 **ROCK 'N' SOUL PART 1**
Daryl Hall & John Oates – RCA

8 **AN INNOCENT MAN**
Billy Joel – Columbia

9 **WHAT'S NEW**
Linda Ronstadt – Asylum

10 **SEVEN AND THE RAGGED TIGER**
Duran Duran – Capitol

11 **UH-HUH**
John Cougar Mellencamp – Riva

12 **METAL HEALTH**
Quiet Riot – Pasha

13 **ELIMINATOR**
ZZ Top – Warner Bros.

14 **GENESIS**
Genesis – Atlantic

15 **IN HEAT**
The Romantics – Nemperor

16 **YENTL**
Barbra Streisand – Columbia

17 **PYROMANIA**
Def Leppard – Mercury

18 **SPORTS**
Huey Lewis And The News – Chrysalis

19 **BARK AT THE MOON**
Ozzy Osbourne – CBS

20 **EYES THAT SEE IN THE DARK**
Kenny Rogers – RCA

UK SINGLES

1 **RELAX**
Frankie Goes To Hollywood – ZTT/Island

2 **GIRLS JUST WANT TO HAVE FUN**
Cyndi Lauper – Portrait/Epic

3 **THAT'S LIVING ALRIGHT**
Joe Fagin – Towerbell

4 **RADIO GA GA**
Queen – EMI

5 **BREAK MY STRIDE**
Matthew Wilder – Epic

6 **(FEELS LIKE) HEAVEN**
Fiction Factory – CBS

7 **PIPES OF PEACE**
Paul McCartney – Parlophone

8 **HERE COMES THE RAIN AGAIN**
Eurythmics – RCA

9 **THE KILLING MOON**
Echo & The Bunnymen – Korova

10 **WONDERLAND**
Big Country – Mercury/Phonogram

11 **A ROCKIN' GOOD WAY**
Shaky & Bonnie – Epic

12 **NEW MOON ON MONDAY**
Duran Duran – EMI

13 **HOLIDAY**
Madonna – Sire

14 **NOBODY TOLD ME**
John Lennon – Polydor

15 **WISHFUL THINKING**
China Crisis – Virgin

16 **WHAT IS LOVE?**
Howard Jones – WEA

17 **I AM WHAT I AM**
Gloria Gaynor – Chrysalis

18 **DOCTOR! DOCTOR!**
Thompson Twins – Arista

19 **BIRD OF PARADISE**
Snowy White – Towerbell

20 **WHAT DIFFERENCE ...**
The Smiths – Rough Trade

UK ALBUMS

1 **TOUCH**
Eurythmics – RCA

2 **THRILLER**
Michael Jackson – Epic

3 **MILK AND HONEY**
John Lennon & Yoko Ono – Polydor

4 **NO PARLEZ!**
Paul Young – CBS

5 **AN INNOCENT MAN**
Billy Joel – CBS

6 **NOW THAT'S WHAT I CALL MUSIC**
Various – EMI/Virgin

7 **CAN'T SLOW DOWN**
Lionel Richie – Motown

8 **UNDER A BLOOD RED SKY**
U2 – Island

9 **PIPES OF PEACE**
Paul McCartney – Parlophone

10 **THE CROSSING**
Big Country – Mercury/Phonogram

11 **COLOUR BY NUMBERS**
Culture Club – Virgin

12 **SOMETIMES WHEN WE TOUCH**
Various – Ronco

13 **LEARNING TO CRAWL**
The Pretenders – Real

14 **PORTRAIT**
Diana Ross – Telstar

15 **LABOUR OF LOVE**
UB40 – DEP International/Virgin

16 **QUICK STEP & SIDE KICK**
Thompson Twins – Arista

17 **GENESIS**
Genesis – Charisma/Virgin

18 **1984**
Van Halen – Warner Bros.

19 **FANTASTIC**
Wham! – Inner Vision

20 **STAGES**
Elaine Paige – K-Tel/WEA

WEEK ENDING FEBRUARY 11 1984

US SINGLES

1 **KARMA CHAMELEON**
Culture Club – Virgin/Epic

2 **JOANNA**
Kool & The Gang – De-Lite

3 **TALKING IN YOUR SLEEP**
The Romantics – Nemperor

4 **OWNER OF A LONELY HEART**
Yes – Atco

5 **JUMP**
Van Halen – Warner Bros.

6 **THAT'S ALL**
Genesis – Atlantic

7 **RUNNING WITH THE NIGHT**
Lionel Richie – Motown

8 **PINK HOUSES**
John Cougar Mellencamp – Riva

9 **THINK OF LAURA**
Christopher Cross – Warner Bros.

10 **I GUESS THAT'S WHY ...**
Elton John – Geffen

11 **BREAK MY STRIDE**
Matthew Wilder – Private

12 **99 LUFTBALLONS**
Nena – Epic

13 **LET THE MUSIC PLAY**
Shannon – Mirage

14 **AN INNOCENT MAN**
Billy Joel – Columbia

15 **GIRLS JUST WANT TO HAVE FUN**
Cyndi Lauper – Portrait

16 **I STILL CAN'T GET OVER ...**
Ray Parker Jr – Arista

17 **NOBODY TOLD ME**
John Lennon – Polydor

18 **WRAPPED AROUND ...**
The Police – A & M

19 **MIDDLE OF THE ROAD**
The Pretenders – Sire

20 **THRILLER**
Michael Jackson – Epic

US ALBUMS

1 **THRILLER**
Michael Jackson – Epic

2 **COLOUR BY NUMBERS**
Culture Club – Virgin/Epic

3 **CAN'T SLOW DOWN**
Lionel Richie – Motown

4 **1984**
Van Halen – Warner Bros.

5 **90125**
Yes – Atco

6 **SYNCHRONICITY**
The Police – A & M

7 **AN INNOCENT MAN**
Billy Joel – Columbia

8 **SEVEN AND THE RAGGED TIGER**
Duran Duran – Capitol

9 **ROCK 'N' SOUL PART 1**
Daryl Hall & John Oates – RCA

10 **LEARNING TO CRAWL**
The Pretenders – Sire

11 **UH-HUH**
John Cougar Mellencamp – Riva

12 **WHAT'S NEW**
Linda Ronstadt – Asylum

13 **METAL HEALTH**
Quiet Riot – Pasha

14 **GENESIS**
Genesis – Atlantic

15 **IN HEAT**
The Romantics – Nemperor

16 **ELIMINATOR**
ZZ Top – Warner Bros.

17 **SPORTS**
Huey Lewis And The News – Chrysalis

18 **PYROMANIA**
Def Leppard – Mercury

19 **BARK AT THE MOON**
Ozzy Osbourne – CBS

20 **THE BIG CHILL**
Soundtrack – Motown

UK SINGLES

1 **RELAX**
Frankie Goes To Hollywood – ZTT/Island

2 **RADIO GA GA**
Queen – EMI

3 **GIRLS JUST WANT TO HAVE FUN**
Cyndi Lauper – Portrait/Epic

4 **BREAK MY STRIDE**
Matthew Wilder – Epic

5 **DOCTOR! DOCTOR!**
Thompson Twins – Arista

6 **THAT'S LIVING ALRIGHT**
Joe Fagin – Towerbell

7 **HOLIDAY**
Madonna – Sire

8 **(FEELS LIKE) HEAVEN**
Fiction Factory – CBS

9 **NEW MOON ON MONDAY**
Duran Duran – EMI

10 **HERE COMES THE RAIN AGAIN**
Eurythmics – RCA

11 **THE KILLING MOON**
Echo & The Bunnymen – Korova

12 **LOVE THEME ...**
Juan Martin – WEA

13 **WHAT DIFFERENCE ...**
The Smiths – Rough Trade

14 **WONDERLAND**
Big Country – Mercury/Phonogram

15 **I AM WHAT I AM**
Gloria Gaynor – Chrysalis

16 **A ROCKIN' GOOD WAY**
Shaky & Bonnie – Epic

17 **WISHFUL THINKING**
China Crisis – Virgin

18 **PIPES OF PEACE**
Paul McCartney – Parlophone

19 **SPICE OF LIFE**
The Manhattan Transfer – Atlantic

20 **HYPERACTIVE**
Thomas Dolby – Parlophone

UK ALBUMS

1 **TOUCH**
Eurythmics – RCA

2 **THRILLER**
Michael Jackson – Epic

3 **AN INNOCENT MAN**
Billy Joel – CBS

4 **NO PARLEZ!**
Paul Young – CBS

5 **MILK AND HONEY**
John Lennon & Yoko Ono – Polydor

6 **CAN'T SLOW DOWN**
Lionel Richie – Motown

7 **NOW THAT'S WHAT I CALL MUSIC**
Various – EMI/Virgin

8 **UNDER A BLOOD RED SKY**
U2 – Island

9 **SLIDE IT IN**
Whitesnake – Liberty

10 **THE CROSSING**
Big Country – Mercury/Phonogram

11 **SOMETIMES WHEN WE TOUCH**
Various – Ronco

12 **PIPES OF PEACE**
Paul McCartney – Parlophone

13 **COLOUR BY NUMBERS**
Culture Club – Virgin

14 **QUICK STEP & SIDE KICK**
Thompson Twins – Arista

15 **PORTRAIT**
Diana Ross – Telstar

16 **LABOUR OF LOVE**
UB40 – DEP International/Virgin

17 **LEARNING TO CRAWL**
The Pretenders – Real

18 **CRUSADER**
Saxon – Carrere

19 **GENESIS**
Genesis – Charisma/Virgin

20 **WORKING WITH FIRE AND STEEL**
China Crisis – Virgin

WEEK ENDING FEBRUARY 18 1984

	US SINGLES		US ALBUMS		UK SINGLES		UK ALBUMS
1	**KARMA CHAMELEON** *Culture Club – Virgin/Epic*	1	**THRILLER** *Michael Jackson – Epic*	1	**RELAX** *Frankie Goes To Hollywood – ZTT/Island*	1	**SPARKLE IN THE RAIN** *Simple Minds – Virgin*
2	**JUMP** *Van Halen – Warner Bros.*	2	**COLOUR BY NUMBERS** *Culture Club – Virgin/Epic*	2	**RADIO GA GA** *Queen – EMI*	2	**TOUCH** *Eurythmics – RCA*
3	**JOANNA** *Kool & The Gang – De-Lite*	3	**1984** *Van Halen – Warner Bros.*	3	**DOCTOR! DOCTOR!** *Thompson Twins – Arista*	3	**THRILLER** *Michael Jackson – Epic*
4	**99 LUFTBALLONS** *Nena – Epic*	4	**CAN'T SLOW DOWN** *Lionel Richie – Motown*	4	**GIRLS JUST WANT TO HAVE FUN** *Cyndi Lauper – Portrait/Epic*	4	**AN INNOCENT MAN** *Billy Joel – CBS*
5	**TALKING IN YOUR SLEEP** *The Romantics – Nemperor*	5	**SYNCHRONICITY** *The Police – A & M*	5	**BREAK MY STRIDE** *Matthew Wilder – Epic*	5	**NO PARLEZ!** *Paul Young – CBS*
6	**THAT'S ALL** *Genesis – Atlantic*	6	**AN INNOCENT MAN** *Billy Joel – Columbia*	6	**HOLIDAY** *Maddona – Sire*	6	**CAN'T SLOW DOWN** *Lionel Richie – Motown*
7	**THRILLER** *Michael Jackson – Epic*	7	**LEARNING TO CRAWL** *The Pretenders – Sire*	7	**THAT'S LIVING ALRIGHT** *Joe Fagin – Towerbell*	7	**THE CROSSING** *Big Country – Mercury/Phonogram*
8	**OWNER OF A LONELY HEART** *Yes – Atco*	8	**SEVEN AND THE RAGGED TIGER** *Duran Duran – Capitol*	8	**MY EVER CHANGING MOODS** *The Style Council – Polydor*	8	**SOMETIMES WHEN WE TOUCH** *Various – Ronco*
9	**GIRLS JUST WANT TO HAVE FUN** *Cyndi Lauper – Portrait*	9	**90125** *Yes – Atco*	9	**NEW MOON ON MONDAY** *Duran Duran – EMI*	9	**NOW THAT'S WHAT I CALL MUSIC** *Various – EMI/Virgin*
10	**LET THE MUSIC PLAY** *Shannon – Mirage*	10	**ROCK 'N' SOUL PART 1** *Daryl Hall & John Oates – RCA*	10	**LOVE THEME …** *Juan Martin – WEA*	10	**THE VERY BEST OF MOTOWN …** *Various – Telstar*
11	**RUNNING WITH THE NIGHT** *Lionel Richie – Motown*	11	**UH-HUH** *John Cougar Mellencamp – Riva*	11	**99 RED BALLOONS** *Nena – Epic*	11	**UNDER A BLOOD RED SKY** *U2 – Island*
12	**NOBODY TOLD ME** *John Lennon – Polydor*	12	**ELIMINATOR** *ZZ Top – Warner Bros.*	12	**WHAT DIFFERENCE …** *The Smiths – Rough Trade*	12	**VICTIMS OF THE FUTURE** *Gary Moore – 10 Records/Virgin*
13	**AN INNOCENT MAN** *Billy Joel – Columbia*	13	**GENESIS** *Genesis – Atlantic*	13	**MICHAEL CAINE** *Madness – Stiff*	13	**MILK AND HONEY** *John Lennon & Yoko Ono – Polydor*
14	**WRAPPED AROUND …** *The Police – A & M*	14	**IN HEAT** *The Romantics – Nemperor*	14	**WOULDN'T IT BE GOOD** *Nik Kershaw – MCA*	14	**COLOUR BY NUMBERS** *Culture Club – Virgin*
15	**THINK OF LAURA** *Christopher Cross – Warner Bros.*	15	**METAL HEALTH** *Quiet Riot – Pasha*	15	**SOMEBODY'S WATCHING ME** *Rockwell – Motown*	15	**QUICK STEP & SIDE KICK** *Thompson Twins – Arista*
16	**PINK HOUSES** *John Cougar Mellencamp – Riva*	16	**SPORTS** *Huey Lewis And The News – Chrysalis*	16	**(FEELS LIKE) HEAVEN** *Fiction Factory – CBS*	16	**THE FLAT EARTH** *Thomas Dolby – Parlophone*
17	**BREAK MY STRIDE** *Matthew Wilder – Private*	17	**MILK AND HONEY** *John Lennon & Yoko Ono – Polydor*	17	**HYPERACTIVE** *Thomas Dolby – Parlophone*	17	**PIPES OF PEACE** *Paul McCartney – Parlophone*
18	**I GUESS THAT'S WHY …** *Elton John – Geffen*	18	**WHAT'S NEW** *Linda Ronstadt – Asylum*	18	**HERE COMES THE RAIN AGAIN** *Eurythmics – RCA*	18	**SLIDE IT IN** *Whitesnake – Liberty*
19	**MIDDLE OF THE ROAD** *The Pretenders – Sire*	19	**DEFENDERS OF THE FAITH** *Judas Priest – Columbia*	19	**LET THE MUSIC PLAY** *Shannon – Club/Phonogram*	19	**CRUSADER** *Saxon – Carrere*
20	**YAH MO B THERE** *James Ingram/Michael McDonald – Qwest*	20	**TOUCH** *Eurythmics – RCA*	20	**SOUL TRAIN** *Swans Way – Exit International/Phonogram*	20	**LABOUR OF LOVE** *UB40 – DEP International/Virgin*

WEEK ENDING FEBRUARY 25 1984

	US SINGLES		US ALBUMS		UK SINGLES		UK ALBUMS
1	**JUMP** *Van Halen – Warner Bros.*	1	**THRILLER** *Michael Jackson – Epic*	1	**RELAX** *Frankie Goes To Hollywood – ZTT/island*	1	**INTO THE GAP** *Thompson Twins – Arista*
2	**KARMA CHAMELEON** *Culture Club – Virgin/Epic*	2	**COLOUR BY NUMBERS** *Culture Club – Virgin/Epic*	2	**99 RED BALLOONS** *Nena – Epic*	2	**SPARKLE IN THE RAIN** *Simple Minds – Virgin*
3	**99 LUFTBALLONS** *Nena – Epic*	3	**1984** *Van Halen – Warner Bros.*	3	**DOCTOR! DOCTOR!** *Thompson Twins – Arista*	3	**AN INNOCENT MAN** *Billy Joel – CBS*
4	**GIRLS JUST WANT TO HAVE FUN** *Cyndi Lauper – Portrait*	4	**CAN'T SLOW DOWN** *Lionel Richie – Motown*	4	**RADIO GA GA** *Queen – EMI*	4	**THRILLER** *Michael Jackson – Epic*
5	**THRILLER** *Michael Jackson – Epic*	5	**LEARNING TO CRAWL** *The Pretenders – Sire*	5	**MY EVER CHANGING MOODS** *The Style Council – Polydor*	5	**TOUCH** *Eurythmics – RCA*
6	**JOANNA** *Kool & The Gang – De-Lite*	6	**AN INNOCENT MAN** *Billy Joel – Columbia*	6	**BREAK MY STRIDE** *Matthew Wilder – Epic*	6	**DECLARATION** *The Alarm – I.R.S.*
7	**NOBODY TOLD ME** *John Lennon – Polydor*	7	**SYNCHRONICITY** *The Police – A & M*	7	**SOMEBODY'S WATCHING ME** *Rockwell – Motown*	7	**THE CROSSING** *Big Country – Mercury/Phonogram*
8	**LET THE MUSIC PLAY** *Shanon – Mirage*	8	**SEVEN AND THE RAGGED TIGER** *Duran Duran – Capitol*	8	**GIRLS JUST WANT TO HAVE FUN** *Cyndi Lauper – Portrait/Epic*	8	**CAN'T SLOW DOWN** *Lionel Richie – Motown*
9	**WRAPPED AROUND …** *The Police – A & M*	9	**90125** *Yes – Atco*	9	**WOULDN'T IT BE GOOD** *Nik Kershaw – MCA*	9	**SOMETIMES WHEN WE TOUCH** *Various – Ronco*
10	**AN INNOCENT MAN** *Billy Joel – Columbia*	10	**UH-HUH** *John Cougar Mellencamp – Riva*	10	**JOANNA/TONIGHT** *Kool & The Gang – De-Lite/Phonogram*	10	**NO PARLEZ!** *Paul Young – CBS*
11	**THAT'S ALL** *Genesis – Atlantic*	11	**SPORTS** *Huey Lewis And The News – Chrysalis*	11	**MICHAEL CAINE** *Madness – Stiff*	11	**THE VERY BEST OF MOTOWN…** *Various – Telstar*
12	**SOMEBODY'S WATCHING ME** *Rockwell – Motown*	12	**ROCK 'N' SOUL PART 1** *Daryl Hall & John Oates – RCA*	12	**AN INNOCENT MAN** *Billy Joel – CBS*	12	**UNDER A BLOOD RED SKY** *U2 – Island*
13	**I WANT A NEW DRUG** *Huey Lewis And The News – Chrysalis*	13	**MILK AND HONEY** *John Lennon & Yoko Ono – Polydor*	13	**HOLIDAY** *Madonna – Sire*	13	**NOW, THAT'S WHAT I CALL MUSIC** *Various – EMI/Virgin*
14	**TALKING IN YOUR SLEEP** *The Romantics – Nemperor*	14	**GENESIS** *Genesis – Atlantic*	14	**LET THE MUSIC PLAY** *Shannon – Club/Phonogram*	14	**THE FLAT EARTH** *Thomas Dolby – Parlophone*
15	**HERE COMES THE RAIN AGAIN** *Eurythmics – RCA*	15	**ELIMINATOR** *ZZ Top – Warner Bros.*	15	**HIDE AND SEEK** *Howard Jones – WEA*	15	**MILK AND HONEY** *John Lennon & ｀oko Ono – Polydor*
16	**NEW MOON ON MONDAY** *Duran Duran – Capitol*	16	**IN HEAT** *The Romantics – Nemperor*	16	**STREET DANCE** *Break Machine – Record Shack*	16	**COLOUR BY NUMBERS** *Culture Club – Virgin*
17	**RUNNING WITH THE NIGHT** *Lionel Richie – Motown*	17	**TOUCH** *Eurythmics – RCA*	17	**THAT'S LIVING ALRIGHT** *Joe Fagin – Towerbell*	17	**VICTIMS OF THE FUTURE** *Gary Moore – 10 Records/Virgin*
18	**THINK OF LAURA** *Christopher Cross – Warner Bros.*	18	**DEFENDERS OF THE FAITH** *Judas Priest – Columbia*	18	**WHAT DIFFERENCE …** *The Smiths – Rough Trade*	18	**LEARNING TO CRAWL** *The Pretenders – Real*
19	**OWNER OF A LONELY HEART** *Yes – Atco*	19	**METAL HEALTH** *Quiet Riot – Pasha*	19	**RUN RUNAWAY** *Slade – RCA*	19	**STAGES** *Elaine Paige – K-Tel/WEA*
20	**YAH MO B THERE** *James Ingram/Michael McDonald – Qwest*	20	**SHOUT AT THE DEVIL** *Motley Crue – Elektra*	20	**NEW MOON ON MONDAY** *Duran Duran – EMI*	20	**LABOUR OF LOVE** *UB40 – DEP International/Virgin*

WEEK ENDING MARCH 3 1984

US SINGLES

1 **JUMP**
Van Halen – Warner Bros.

2 **99 LUFTBALLONS**
Nena – Epic

3 **GIRLS JUST WANT TO HAVE FUN**
Cyndi Lauper – Portrait

4 **THRILLER**
Michael Jackson – Epic

5 **NOBODY TOLD ME**
John Lennon – Polydor

6 **KARMA CHAMELEON**
Culture Club – Virgin/Epic

7 **SOMBODY'S WATCHING ME**
Rockwell – Motown

8 **WRAPPED AROUND …**
The Police – A & M

9 **LET THE MUSIC PLAY**
Shannon – Mirage

10 **I WANT A NEW DRUG**
Huey Lewis And The News – Chrysalis

11 **HERE COMES THE RAIN AGAIN**
Eurythmics – RCA

12 **JOANNA**
Kool & The Gang – De-Lite

13 **NEW MOON ON MONDAY**
Duran Duran – Capitol

14 **AN INNOCENT MAN**
Billy Joel – Columbia

15 **THAT'S ALL**
Genesis – Atlantic

16 **FOOTLOOSE**
Kenny Loggins – Columbia

17 **GOT A HOLD ON ME**
Christine McVie – Warner Bros.

18 **THE LANGUAGE OF LOVE**
Dan Fogelberg – Full Moon/Epic

19 **YAH MO B THERE**
James Ingram/Michael McDonald – Qwest

20 **TALKING IN YOUR SLEEP**
The Romantics – Nemperor

US ALBUMS

1 **THRILLER**
Michael Jackson – Epic

2 **COLOUR BY NUMBERS**
Culture Club – Virgin/Epic

3 **1984**
Van Halen – Warner Bros.

4 **CAN'T SLOW DOWN**
Lionel Richie – Motown

5 **LEARNING TO CRAWL**
The Pretenders – Sire

6 **AN INNOCENT MAN**
Billy Joel – Columbia

7 **SYNCHRONICITY**
The Police – A & M

8 **SEVEN AND THE RAGGED TIGER**
Duran Duran – Capitol

9 **90125**
Yes – Atco

10 **SPORTS**
Huey Lewis And The News – Chrysalis

11 **UH-HUH**
John Cougar Mellencamp – Riva

12 **MILK AND HONEY**
John Lennon & Yoko Ono – Polydor

13 **ELIMINATOR**
ZZ Top – Warner Bros.

14 **ROCK 'N' SOUL PART 1**
Daryl Hall & John Oates – RCA

15 **TOUCH**
Eurythmics – RCA

16 **GENESIS**
Genesis – Atlantic

17 **IN HEAT**
The Romantics – Nemperor

18 **DEFENDERS OF THE FAITH**
Judas Priest – Columbia

19 **SHOUT AT THE DEVIL**
Motley Crue – Elektra

20 **SHE'S SO UNUSUAL**
Cyndi Lauper – Portrait

UK SINGLES

1 **99 RED BALLOONS**
Nena – Epic

2 **RELAX**
Frankie Goes To Hollywood – ZTT/Island

3 **JOANNA/TONIGHT**
Kool & The Gang – De-Lite/Phonogram

4 **WOULDN'T IT BE GOOD**
Nik Kershaw – MCA

5 **DOCTOR! DOCTOR!**
Thompson Twins – Arista

6 **SOMEBODY'S WATCHING ME**
Rockwell – Motown

7 **RADIO GA GA**
Queen – EMI

8 **AN INNOCENT MAN**
Billy Joel – CBS

9 **MY EVER CHANGING MOODS**
The Style Council – Polydor

10 **RUN RUNAWAY**
Slade – RCA

11 **STREET DANCE**
Break Machine – Record Shack

12 **BREAK MY STRIDE**
Matthew Wilder – Epic

13 **GIRLS JUST WANT TO HAVE FUN**
Cyndi Lauper – Portrait/Epic

14 **HIDE AND SEEK**
Howard Jones – WEA

15 **LET THE MUSIC PLAY**
Shannon – Club/Phonogram

16 **MICHAEL CAINE**
Madness – Stiff

17 **GET OUT OF YOUR LAZY BED**
Matt Bianco – WEA

18 **HOLIDAY**
Madonna – Sire

19 **I GAVE YOU MY HEART (DIDN'T I)**
Hot Chocolate – RAK

20 **JUMP**
Van Halen – Warner Bros.

UK ALBUMS

1 **INTO THE GAP**
Thompson Twins – Arista

2 **THE SMITHS**
The Smiths – Rough Trade

3 **AN INNOCENT MAN**
Billy Joel – CBS

4 **TOUCH**
Eurythmics – RCA

5 **THRILLER**
Michael Jackson – Epic

6 **KEEP MOVING**
Madness – Stiff

7 **SPARKLE IN THE RAIN**
Simple Minds – Virgin

8 **NO PARLEZ!**
Paul Young – CBS

9 **THE CROSSING**
Big Country – Mercury/Phonogram

10 **CAN'T SLOW DOWN**
Lionel Richie – Motown

11 **NOW THAT'S WHAT I CALL MUSIC**
Various – EMI/Virgin

12 **UNDER A BLOOD RED SKY**
U2 – Island

13 **THE VERY BEST OF MOTOWN…**
Various – Telstar

14 **SOMETIMES WHEN WE TOUCH**
Various – Ronco

15 **DECLARATION**
The Alarm – I.R.S.

16 **COLOUR BY NUMBERS**
Culture Club – Virgin

17 **SEVEN AND THE RAGGED TIGER**
Duran Duran – EMI

18 **QUICK STEP & SIDE KICK**
Thompson Twins – Arista

19 **PIPES OF PEACE**
Paul McCartney – Parlophone

20 **IN THE HEART**
Kool & The Gang – De-Lite/Phonogram

WEEK ENDING MARCH 10 1984

US SINGLES

1 **JUMP**
Van Halen – Warner Bros.

2 **GIRLS JUST WANT TO HAVE FUN**
Cyndi Lauper – Portrait

3 **99 LUFTBALLONS**
Nena – Epic

4 **THRILLER**
Michael Jackson – Epic

5 **SOMEBODY'S WATCHING ME**
Rockwell – Motown

6 **NOBODY TOLD ME**
John Lennon – Polydor

7 **I WANT A NEW DRUG**
Huey Lewis And The News – Chrysalis

8 **HERE COMES THE RAIN AGAIN**
Eurythmics – RCA

9 **FOOTLOOSE**
Kenny Loggins – Columbia

10 **KARMA CHAMELEON**
Culture Club – Virgin/Epic

11 **WRAPPED AROUND …**
The Police – A & M

12 **NEW MOON ON MONDAY**
Duran Duran – Capitol

13 **LET THE MUSIC PLAY**
Shannon – Mirage

14 **GOT A HOLD ON ME**
Christine McVie – Warner Bros.

15 **AUTOMATIC**
Pointer Sisters – Planet

16 **THE LANGUAGE OF LOVE**
Dan Fogelberg – Full Moon/Epic

17 **ADULT EDUCATION**
Daryl Hall & John Oates – RCA

18 **AN INNOCENT MAN**
Billy Joel – Columbia

19 **JOANNA**
Kool & The Gang – De-Lite

20 **GIVE IT UP**
K.C. – Meca/Alpha

US ALBUMS

1 **THRILLER**
Michael Jackson – Epic

2 **COLOUR BY NUMBERS**
Culture Club – Virgin/Epic

3 **1984**
Van Halen – Warner Bros.

4 **CAN'T SLOW DOWN**
Lionel Richie – Motown

5 **LEARNING TO CRAWL**
The Pretenders – Sire

6 **AN INNOCENT MAN**
Billy Joel – Columbia

7 **SYNCHRONICITY**
The Police – A & M

8 **SPORTS**
Huey Lewis And The News – Chrysalis

9 **90125**
Yes – Atco

10 **SEVEN AND THE RAGGED TIGER**
Duran Duran – Capitol

11 **MILK AND HONEY**
John Lennon & Yoko Ono – Polydor

12 **UH-HUH**
John Cougar Mellencamp – Riva

13 **TOUCH**
Eurythmics – RCA

14 **ROCK 'N' SOUL PART 1**
Daryl Hall & John Oates – RCA

15 **WINDOWS AND WALLS**
Dan Fogelberg – Full Moon/Epic

16 **SHE'S SO UNUSUAL**
Cyndi Lauper – Portrait

17 **ELIMINATOR**
ZZ Top – Warner Bros.

18 **DEFENDERS OF THE FAITH**
Judas Priest – Columbia

19 **SHOUT AT THE DEVIL**
Motley Crue – Elektra

20 **GENESIS**
Genesis – Atlantic

UK SINGLES

1 **99 RED BALLOONS**
Nena – Epic

2 **JOANNA/TONIGHT**
Kool & The Gang – De-Lite/Phonogram

3 **RELAX**
Frankie Goes To Hollywood – ZTT/Island

4 **WOULDN'T IT BE GOOD**
Nik Kershaw – MCA

5 **STREET DANCE**
Break Machine – Record Shack

6 **SOMEBODY'S WATCHING ME**
Rockwell – Motown

7 **RUN RUNAWAY**
Slade – RCA

8 **AN INNOCENT MAN**
Billy Joel – CBS

9 **DOCTOR! DOCTOR!**
Thompson Twins – Arista

10 **JUMP**
Van Halen – Warner Bros.

11 **THE MUSIC OF TORVILL & DEAN**
Various – Safari

12 **HIDE AND SEEK**
Howard Jones – WEA

13 **I GAVE YOU MY HEART (DIDN'T I)**
Hot Chocolate – RAK

14 **LET THE MUSIC PLAY**
Shannon – Club/Phonogram

15 **GET OUT OF YOUR LAZY BED**
Matt Bianco – WEA

16 **RADIO GA GA**
Queen – EMI

17 **MY EVER CHANGING MOODS**
The Style Council – Polydor

18 **BREAK MY STRIDE**
Matthew Wilder – Epic

19 **BREAKIN' DOWN …**
Julia & Company – London

20 **GIRLS JUST WANT TO HAVE FUN**
Cyndi Lauper – Portrait/Epic

UK ALBUMS

1 **INTO THE GAP**
Thompson Twins – Arista

2 **THE WORKS**
Queen – EMI

3 **AN INNOCENT MAN**
Billy Joel – CBS

4 **THRILLER**
Michael Jackson – Epic

5 **THE SMITHS**
The Smiths – Rough Trade

6 **TOUCH**
Eurythmics – RCA

7 **KEEP MOVING**
Madness – Stiff

8 **CAN'T SLOW DOWN**
Lionel Richie – Motown

9 **SPARKLE IN THE RAIN**
Simple Minds – Virgin

10 **HUMAN RACING**
Nik Kershaw – MCA

11 **THE CROSSING**
Big Country – Mercury/Phonogram

12 **NO PARLEZ!**
Paul Young – CBS

13 **SOMETIMES WHEN WE TOUCH**
Various – Ronco

14 **THE VERY BEST OF MOTOWN…**
Various – Telstar

15 **UNDER A BLOOD RED SKY**
U2 – Island

16 **NOW THAT'S WHAT I CALL MUSIC**
Various – EMI/Virgin

17 **1984**
Van Halen – Warner Bros.

18 **COLOUR BY NUMBERS**
Culture Club – Virgin

19 **OFF THE WALL**
Michael Jackson – Epic

20 **DECLARATION**
The Alarm – I.R.S.

WEEK ENDING MARCH 17 1984

	US SINGLES		US ALBUMS		UK SINGLES		UK ALBUMS
1	**JUMP** *Van Halen – Warner Bros.*	1	**THRILLER** *Michael Jackson – Epic*	1	**99 RED BALLOONS** *Nena – Epic*	1	**HUMAN'S LIB** *Howard Jones – WEA*
2	**GIRLS JUST WANT TO HAVE FUN** *Cyndi Lauper – Portrait*	2	**1984** *Van Halen – Warner Bros.*	2	**JOANNA/TONIGHT** *Kool & The Gang – De-Lite/Phonogram*	2	**INTO THE GAP** *Thompson Twins – Arista*
3	**SOMEBODY'S WATCHING ME** *Rockwell – Motown*	3	**COLOUR BY NUMBERS** *Culture Club – Virgin/Epic*	3	**STREET DANCE** *Break Machine – Record Shack*	3	**AN INNOCENT MAN** *Billy Joel – CBS*
4	**99 LUFTBALLONS** *Nena – Epic*	4	**CAN'T SLOW DOWN** *Lionel Richie – Motown*	4	**WOULDN'T IT BE GOOD** *Nik Kershaw – MCA*	4	**THRILLER** *Michael Jackson – Epic*
5	**FOOTLOOSE** *Kenny Loggins – Columbia*	5	**LEARNING TO CRAWL** *The Pretenders – Sire*	5	**HELLO** *Lionel Richie – Motown*	5	**THE WORKS** *Queen – EMI*
6	**THRILLER** *Michael Jackson – Epic*	6	**SPORTS** *Huey Lewis And The News – Chrysalis*	6	**RELAX** *Frankie Goes to Hollywood – ZTT/Island*	6	**THE SMITHS** *The Smiths – Rough Trade*
7	**I WANT A NEW DRUG** *Huey Lewis And The News – Chrysalis*	7	**SYNCHRONICITY** *The Police – A&M*	7	**JUMP** *Van Halen – Warner Bros.*	7	**CAN'T SLOW DOWN** *Lionel Richie – Motown*
8	**HERE COMES THE RAIN AGAIN** *Eurythmics – RCA*	8	**AN INNOCENT MAN** *Billy Joel – Columbia*	8	**AN INNOCENT MAN** *Billy Joel – CBS*	8	**TOUCH** *Eurythmics – RCA*
9	**NOBODY TOLD ME** *John Lennon – Polydor*	9	**FOOTLOOSE** *Soundtrack – Columbia*	9	**SOMEBODY'S WATCHING ME** *Rockwell – Motown*	9	**HUMAN RACING** *Nik Kershaw – MCA*
10	**NEW MOON ON MONDAY** *Duran Duran – Capitol*	10	**SEVEN AND THE RAGGED TIGER** *Duran Duran – Capitol*	10	**THE MUSIC OF TORVILL & DEAN** *Various – Safari*	10	**SPARKLE IN THE RAIN** *Simple Minds – Virgin*
11	**GOT A HOLD ON ME** *Christine McVie – Warner Bros.*	11	**TOUCH** *Eurythmics – RCA*	11	**IT'S RAINING MEN** *The Weather Girls – CBS*	11	**OFF THE WALL** *Michael Jackson – Epic*
12	**AUTOMATIC** *Pointer Sisters – Planet*	12	**90125** *Yes – Atco*	12	**HIDE AND SEEK** *Howard Jones – WEA*	12	**THE CROSSING** *Big Country – Mercury/Phonogram*
13	**ADULT EDUCATION** *Daryl Hall & John Oates – RCA*	13	**MILK AND HONEY** *John Lennon & Yoko Ono – Polydor*	13	**WHAT DO I DO?** *Galaxy/Phil Fearon – Ensign/Island*	13	**KEEP MOVING** *Madness – Stiff*
14	**THE LANGUAGE OF LOVE** *Dan Fogelberg – Full Moon/Epic*	14	**SHE'S SO UNUSUAL** *Cyndi Lauper – Portrait*	14	**RUN RUNAWAY** *Slade – RCA*	14	**UNDER A BLOOD RED SKY** *U2 – Island*
15	**WRAPPED AROUND …** *The Police – A&M*	15	**WINDOWS AND WALLS** *Dan Fogelberg – Full Moon/Epic*	15	**BREAKIN' DOWN …** *Julia and Company – London*	15	**1984** *Van Halen – Warner Bros.*
16	**KARMA CHAMELEON** *Culture Club – Virgin/Epic*	16	**UH-HUH** *John Cougar Mellencamp – Riva*	16	**I GAVE YOU MY HEART (DIDN'T I)** *Hot Chocolate – RAK*	16	**THE VERY BEST OF MOTOWN …** *Various – Telstar*
17	**LET THE MUSIC PLAY** *Shannon – Mirage*	17	**ROCK 'N' SOUL PART 1** *Daryl Hall & John Oates – RCA*	17	**TO BE OR NOT TO BE …** *Mel Brooks – Island*	17	**NO PARLEZ!** *Paul Young – CBS*
18	**GIVE IT UP** *K.C. – Meca/Alpha*	18	**DEFENDERS OF THE FAITH** *Judas Priest – Columbia*	18	**'ULLO JOHN! …** *Alexei Sayle – Island*	18	**IN THE HEART** *Kool & The Gang – De-Lite/Phonogram*
19	**HOLD ME NOW** *Thompson Twins – Arista*	19	**SHOUT AT THE DEVIL** *Motley Crue – Elektra*	19	**DOCTOR! DOCTOR!** *Thompson Twins – Arista*	19	**COLOUR BY NUMBERS** *Culture Club – Virgin*
20	**AGAINST ALL ODDS** *Phil Collins – Atlantic*	20	**GENESIS** *Genesis – Atlantic*	20	**YOUR LOVE IS KING** *Sade – Epic*	20	**SOMETIMES WHEN WE TOUCH** *Various – Ronco*

WEEK ENDING MARCH 24 1984

	US SINGLES		US ALBUMS		UK SINGLES		UK ALBUMS
1	**JUMP** *Van Halen – Warner Bros.*	1	**THRILLER** *Michael Jackson – Epic*	1	**HELLO** *Lionel Richie – Motown*	1	**HUMAN'S LIB** *Howard Jones – WEA*
2	**SOMEBODY'S WATCHING ME** *Rockwell – Motown*	2	**1984** *Van Halen – Warner Bros.*	2	**99 RED BALLOONS** *Nena – Epic*	2	**CAFE BLEU** *The Style Council – Polydor*
3	**GIRLS JUST WANT TO HAVE FUN** *Cyndi Lauper – Portrait*	3	**COLOUR BY NUMBERS** *Culture Club – Virgin/Epic*	3	**STREET DANCE** *Break Machine – Record Shack*	3	**ALCHEMY – DIRE STRAITS LIVE** *Dire Straits – Vertigo/Phonogram*
4	**FOOTLOOSE** *Kenny Loggins – Columbia*	4	**CAN'T SLOW DOWN** *Lionel Richie – Motown*	4	**JOANNA/TONIGHT** *Kool & The Gang – De-Lite/Phonogram*	4	**AN INNOCENT MAN** *Billy Joel – CBS*
5	**HERE COMES THE RAIN AGAIN** *Eurythmics – RCA*	5	**FOOTLOOSE** *Soundtrack – Columbia*	5	**IT'S RAINING MEN** *The Weather Girls – CBS*	5	**FUGAZI** *Marillion – EMI*
6	**I WANT A NEW DRUG** *Huey Lewis And The News – Chrysalis*	6	**SPORTS** *Huey Lewis And The News – Chrysalis*	6	**WOULDN'T IT BE GOOD** *Nik Kershaw – MCA*	6	**CAN'T SLOW DOWN** *Lionel Richie – Motown*
7	**99 LUFTBALLONS** *Nena – Epic*	7	**LEARNING TO CRAWL** *The Prentenders – Sire*	7	**WHAT DO I DO?** *Galaxy/Phil Fearon – Ensign/Island*	7	**INTO THE GAP** *Thompson Twins – Arista*
8	**AUTOMATIC** *Pointer Sisters – Planet*	8	**SYNCHRONICITY** *The Police – A&M*	8	**ROBERT DE NIRO'S WAITING** *Bananarama – London*	8	**THRILLER** *Michael Jackson – Epic*
9	**ADULT EDUCATION** *Daryl Hall & John Oates – RCA*	9	**TOUCH** *Eurythmics – RCA*	9	**YOUR LOVE IS KING** *Sade – Epic*	9	**THE WORKS** *Queen – EMI*
10	**GOT A HOLD ON ME** *Christine McVie – Warner Bros.*	10	**AN INNOCENT MAN** *Billy Joel – Columbia*	10	**JUMP** *Van Halen – Warner Bros.*	10	**HUMAN RACING** *Nik Kershaw – MCA*
11	**THRILLER** *Michael Jackson – Epic*	11	**SEVEN AND THE RAGGED TIGER** *Duran Duran – Capitol*	11	**AN INNOCENT MAN** *Billy Joel – CBS*	11	**THE SMITHS** *The Smiths – Rough Trade*
12	**AGAINST ALL ODDS** *Phil Collins – Atlantic*	12	**SHE'S SO UNUSUAL** *Cyndi Lauper – Portrait*	12	**TO BE OR NOT TO BE…** *Mel Brooks – Island*	12	**TOUCH** *Eurythmics – RCA*
13	**THE LANGUAGE OF LOVE** *Dan Fogelberg – Full Moon/Epic*	13	**90125** *Yes – Atco*	13	**THE MUSIC OF TORVILL & DEAN** *Various – Safari*	13	**SPARKLE IN THE RAIN** *Simple Minds – Virgin*
14	**MISS ME BLIND** *Culture Club – Virgin/Epic*	14	**MILK AND HONEY** *John Lennon & Yoko Ono – Polydor*	14	**IT'S A MIRACLE** *Culture Club – Virgin*	14	**THE CROSSING** *Big Country – Mercury/Phonogram*
15	**HOLD ME NOW** *Thompson Twins – Arista*	15	**WINDOWS AND WALLS** *Dan Fogelberg – Full Moon/Epic*	15	**'ULLO JOHN! …** *Alexei Sayle – Island*	15	**OFF THE WALL** *Michael Jackson – Epic*
16	**NEW MOON ON MONDAY** *Duran Duran – Capitol*	16	**SOMEBODY'S WATCHING ME** *Rockwell – Motown*	16	**RELAX** *Frankie Goes To Hollywood – ZTT/Island*	16	**THE VERY BEST OF MOTOWN…** *Various – Telstar*
17	**HELLO** *Lionel Richie – Motown*	17	**UH-HUH** *John Cougar Mellencamp – Riva*	17	**SOMEBODY'S WATCHING ME** *Rockwell – Motown*	17	**LOVE AT FIRST STING** *Scorpions – Harvest*
18	**EAT IT** *Weird Al Yankovic – Rock 'n' Roll*	18	**SHOUT AT THE DEVIL** *Motley Crue – Elektra*	18	**HIDE AND SEEK** *Howard Jones – WEA*	18	**KEEP MOVING** *Madness – Stiff*
19	**NOBODY TOLD ME** *John Lennon – Polydor*	19	**ROCK 'N' SOUL PART 1** *Daryl Hall & John Oates – RCA*	19	**BREAKIN' DOWN …** *Julia & Company – London*	19	**THE DRUM IS EVERYTHING** *Carmel – London*
20	**BACK WHERE YOU BELONG** *38 Special – A&M*	20	**DEFENDERS OF THE FAITH** *Judas Priest – Columbia*	20	**RUN RUNAWAY** *Slade – RCA*	20	**NO PARLEZ!** *Paul Young – CBS*

WEEK ENDING MARCH 31 1984

US SINGLES	US ALBUMS	UK SINGLES	UK ALBUMS
1 **FOOTLOOSE** Kenny Loggins – Columbia	1 **THRILLER** Michael Jackson – Epic	1 **HELLO** Lionel Richie – Motown	1 **CAN'T SLOW DOWN** Lionel Richie – Motown
2 **SOMEBODY'S WATCHING ME** Rockwell – Motown	2 **1984** Van Halen – Warner Bros.	2 **IT'S RAINING MEN** The Weather Girls – CBS	2 **HUMAN'S LIB** Howard Jones – WEA
3 **JUMP** Van Halen – Warner Bros.	3 **FOOTLOOSE** Soundtrack – Columbia	3 **ROBERT DE NIRO'S WAITING** Bananarama – London	3 **ALCHEMY – DIRE STRAITS LIVE** Dire Straits – Vertigo/Phonogram
4 **HERE COMES THE RAIN AGAIN** Eurythmics – RCA	4 **COLOUR BY NUMBERS** Culture Club – Virgin/Epic	4 **IT'S A MIRACLE** Culture Club – Virgin	4 **THRILLER** Michael Jackson – Epic
5 **GIRLS JUST WANT TO HAVE FUN** Cyndi Lauper – Portrait	5 **CAN'T SLOW DOWN** Lionel Richie – Motown	5 **WHAT DO I DO?** Galaxy/Phil Fearon – Ensign/Island	5 **AN INNOCENT MAN** Billy Joel – CBS
6 **I WANT A NEW DRUG** Huey Lewis And The News – Chrysalis	6 **SPORTS** Huey Lewis And The News – Chrysalis	6 **YOUR LOVE IS KING** Sade – Epic	6 **INTO THE GAP** Thompson Twins – Arista
7 **AGAINST ALL ODDS** Phil Collins – Atlantic	7 **LEARNING TO CRAWL** The Pretenders – Sire	7 **A LOVE WORTH WAITING FOR** Shakin' Stevens – Epic	7 **CAFE BLEU** The Style Council – Polydor
8 **AUTOMATIC** Pointer Sisters – Planet	8 **TOUCH** Eurythmics – RCA	8 **STREET DANCE** Break Machine – Record Shack	8 **FUGAZI** Marillion – EMI
9 **ADULT EDUCATION** Daryl Hall & John Oates – RCA	9 **SYNCHRONICITY** The Police – A&M	9 **PEOPLE ARE PEOPLE** Depeche Mode – Mute	9 **THE SMITHS** The Smiths – Rough Trade
10 **MISS ME BLIND** Culture Club – Virgin/Epic	10 **SHE'S SO UNUSUAL** Cyndi Lauper – Portrait	10 **JOANNA/TONIGHT** Kool & The Gang – De-Lite/Phonogram	10 **THE WORKS** Queen – EMI
11 **99 LUFTBALLONS** Nena – Epic	11 **AN INNOCENT MAN** Billy Joel – Columbia	11 **99 RED BALLOONS** Nena – Epic	11 **HUMAN RACING** Nik Kershaw – MCA
12 **HOLD ME NOW** Thompson Twins – Arista	12 **UH-HUH** John Cougar Mellencamp – Riva	12 **WOULDN'T IT BE GOOD** Nik Kershaw – MCA	12 **THIS LAST NIGHT IN SODOM** Soft Cell – Some Bizarre/Phonogram
13 **HELLO** Lionel Richie – Motown	13 **SEVEN AND THE RAGGED TIGER** Duran Duran – Capitol	13 **YOU TAKE ME UP** Thompson Twins – Arista	13 **THE VERY BEST OF MOTOWN…** Various – Telstar
14 **EAT IT** Weird Al Yankovic – Rock 'n' Roll	14 **90125** Yes – Atco	14 **THE MUSIC OF TORVILL & DEAN** Various – Safari	14 **OFF THE WALL** Michael Jackson – Epic
15 **THRILLER** Michael Jackson – Epic	15 **SOMEBODY'S WATCHING ME** Rockwell – Motown	15 **CHERRY OH BABY** UB40 – DEP International/Virgin	15 **TOUCH** Eurythmics – RCA
16 **GOT A HOLD ON ME** Christine McVie – Warner Bros.	16 **LOVE AT FIRST STING** Scorpions – Polygram	16 **JUMP** Van Halen – Warner Bros.	16 **LABOUR OF LOVE** UB40 – DEP International/Virgin
17 **THE LANGUAGE OF LOVE** Dan Fogelberg – Full Moon/Epic	17 **SHOUT AT THE DEVIL** Motley Crue – Elektra	17 **AN INNOCENT MAN** Billy Joel – CBS	17 **SPARKLE IN THE RAIN** Simple Minds – Virgin
18 **NEW MOON ON MONDAY** Duran Duran – Capitol	18 **MILK AND HONEY** John Lennon & Yoko Ono – Polydor	18 **TO BE OR NOT TO BE…** Mel Brooks – Island	18 **COLOUR BY NUMBERS** Culture Club – Virgin
19 **RADIO GA GA** Queen – Capitol	19 **WINDOWS AND WALLS** Dan Fogelberg – Full Moon/Epic	19 **'ULLO JOHN!** Alexei Sayle – Island	19 **UNDER A BLOOD RED SKY** U2 – Island
20 **BACK WHERE YOU BELONG** 38 Special – A&M	20 **ELIMINATOR** ZZ Top – Warner Bros.	20 **P.Y.T. (PRETTY YOUNG THING)** Michael Jackson – Epic	20 **THE DRUM IS EVERYTHING** Carmel – London

WEEK ENDING APRIL 7 1984

US SINGLES	US ALBUMS	UK SINGLES	UK ALBUMS
1 **FOOTLOOSE** Kennly Loggins – Columbia	1 **THRILLER** Michael Jackson – Epic	1 **HELLO** Lionel Richie – Motown	1 **CAN'T SLOW DOWN** Lionel Richie – Motown
2 **SOMEBODY'S WATCHING ME** Rockwell – Motown	2 **FOOTLOOSE** Soundtrack – Columbia	2 **A LOVE WORTH WAITING FOR** Shakin' Stevens – Epic	2 **HUMAN'S LIB** Howard Jones – WEA
3 **AGAINST ALL ODDS** Phil Collins – Atlantic	3 **1984** Van Halen – Warner Bros.	3 **ROBERT DE NIRO'S WAITING** Bananarama – London	3 **…THAT'S WHAT I CALL MUSIC II** Various – Virgin/EMI
4 **HERE COMES THE RAIN AGAIN** Eurythmics – RCA	4 **COLOUR BY NUMBERS** Culture Club – Virgin/Epic	4 **YOU TAKE ME UP** The Thompson Twins – Arista	4 **THRILLER** Michael Jackson – Epic
5 **JUMP** Van Halen – Warner Bros	5 **CAN'T SLOW DOWN** Lionel Richie – Motown	5 **PEOPLE ARE PEOPLE** Depeche Mode – Mute	5 **AN INNOCENT MAN** Billy Joel – CBS
6 **AUTOMATIC** Pointer Sisters – Planet	6 **SPORTS** Huey Lewis And The News – Chrysalis	6 **IT'S RAINING MEN** The Weather Girls – CBS	6 **INTO THE GAP** The Thompson Twins – Arista
7 **MISS ME BLIND** Culture Club – Virgin/Epic	7 **TOUCH** Eurythmics – RCA	7 **IT'S A MIRACLE** Culture Club – Virgin	7 **ALCHEMY – DIRE STRAITS LIVE** Dire Straits – Vertigo/Phonogram
8 **ADULT EDUCATION** Daryl Hall & John Oates – RCA	8 **LEARNING TO CRAWL** The Pretenders – Sire	8 **WHAT DO I DO?** Galaxy/Phil Fearon – Ensign/Island	8 **CAFE BLEU** The Style Council – Polydor
9 **GIRLS JUST WANT TO HAVE FUN** Cyndi Lauper – Portrait	9 **SYNCHRONICITY** The Police – A&M	9 **THE MUSIC OF TORVILL & DEAN** Various – Safari	9 **COLOUR BY NUMBERS** Culture Club – Virgin
10 **HELLO** Lionel Richie – Motown	10 **SHE'S SO UNUSUAL** Cyndi Lauper – Portrait	10 **YOUR LOVE IS KING** Sade – Epic	10 **BEST OF MOTOWN LOVE SONGS** Various – Telstar
11 **HOLD ME NOW** Thompson Twins – Arista	11 **LOVE AT FIRST STING** Scorpions – Mercury	11 **P.Y.T. (PRETTY YOUNG THING)** Michael Jackson – Epic	11 **HUMAN RACING** Nik Kershaw – MCA
12 **I WANT A NEW DRUG** Huey Lewis And The News – Chrysalis	12 **UH-HUH** John Cougar Mellencamp – Riva	12 **CHERRY OH BABY** UB40 – DEP International/Virgin	12 **THE SMITHS** The Smiths – Rough Trade
13 **EAT IT** Weird Al Yankovic – Rock'n'Roll	13 **AN INNOCENT MAN** Billy Joel – Columbia	13 **STREET DANCE** Break Machine – Record Shack	13 **TOUCH** Eurythmics – RCA
14 **99 LUFTBALLONS** Nena – Epic	14 **SEVEN AND THE RAGGED TIGER** Duran Duran – Capitol	14 **NELSON MANDELA** The Special AKA – 2-Tone	14 **SPARKLE IN THE RAIN** Simple Minds – Virgin
15 **THEY DON'T KNOW** Tracey Ullman – MCA	15 **SOMEBODY'S WATCHING ME** Rockwell – Motown	15 **GLAD IT'S ALL OVER** Captain Sensible – A&M	15 **THE WORKS** Queen – EMI
16 **RADIO GA-GA** Queen – Capitol	16 **90125** Yes – Atco	16 **LUCKY STAR** Madonna – Sire	16 **OFF THE WALL** Michael Jackson – Epic
17 **GIRLS** Dwight Twilley – EMI America	17 **SHOUT AT THE DEVIL** Motley Crue – Elektra	17 **JOANNA/TONIGHT** Kool & The Gang – De-Lite/Phonogram	17 **LABOUR OF LOVE** UB40 – DEP International/Virgin
18 **GOT A HOLD ON ME** Christine McVie - Warner Bros.	18 **AMMONIA AVENUE** The Alan Parsons Project – Arista	18 **AIN'T NOBODY** Rufus And Chaka Khan – Warner Bros.	18 **FUGAZI** Marillion – EMI
19 **YOU MIGHT THINK** The Cars – Elektra	19 **WINDOWS AND WALLS** Dan Fogelberg – Full Moon/Epic	19 **AN INNOCENT MAN** Billy Joel – Motown	19 **UNDER A BLOOD RED SKY** U2 – Island
20 **LOVE SOMEBODY** Rick Springfield – RCA	20 **ELIMINATOR** ZZ Top – Warner Bros.	20 **99 RED BALLOONS** Nena – Epic	20 **STAGES** Elaine Paige – K-Tel/WEA

WEEK ENDING APRIL 14 1984

US SINGLES	US ALBUMS	UK SINGLES	UK ALBUMS

US SINGLES

1 FOOTLOOSE
Kenny Loggins – Columbia

2 AGAINST ALL ODDS
Phill Collins – Atlantic

3 SOMEBODY'S WATCHING ME
Rockwell – Motown

4 HELLO
Lionel Richie – Motown

5 AUTOMATIC
Pointer Sisters – Planet

6 MISS ME BLIND
Culture Club – Virgin/Epic

7 HERE COMES THE RAIN AGAIN
Eurythmics – RCA

8 HOLD ME NOW
Thompson Twins – Arista

9 ADULT EDUCATION
Daryl Hall & John Oates – RCA

10 JUMP
Van Halen – Warner Bros.

11 GIRLS JUST WANT TO HAVE FUN
Cyndi Lauper – Portrait

12 EAT IT
Weird Al Yankovic – Rock'n'Roll

13 LOVE SOMEBODY
Rick Springfield – RCA

14 THEY DON'T KNOW
Tracey Ullman – MCA

15 YOU MIGHT THINK
The Cars – Elektra

16 I WANT A NEW DRUG
Huey Lewis And The News – Chrysalis

17 GIRLS
Dwight Twilley – EMI America

18 RADIO GA-GA
Queen – Capitol

19 TO ALL THE GIRLS …
Julio Iglesias and Willie Nelson – Columbia

20 TONIGHT
Kool & The Gang – De-Lite

US ALBUMS

1 THRILLER
Michael Jackson – Epic

2 FOOTLOOSE
Soundtrack – Columbia

3 1984
Van Halen – Warner Bros.

4 CAN'T SLOW DOWN
Lionel Richie – Motown

5 SPORTS
Huey Lewis And The News – Chrysalis

6 COLOUR BY NUMBERS
Culture Club – Virgin/Epic

7 TOUCH
Eurythmics – RCA

8 LOVE AT FIRST STING
Scorpions – Mercury

9 LEARNING TO CRAWL
The Pretenders – Sire

10 SHE'S SO UNUSUAL
Cyndi Lauper – Portrait

11 AN INNOCENT MAN
Billy Joel – Columbia

12 SYNCHRONICITY
The Police – A&M

13 HEARTBEAT CITY
The Cars – Elektra

14 SEVEN AND THE RAGGED TIGER
Duran Duran – Capitol

15 INTO THE GAP
Thompson Twins – Arista

16 UH-HUH
John Cougar Mellencamp – Riva

17 AMMONIA AVENUE
The Alan Parsons Project – Arista

18 AGAINST ALL ODDS
Soundtrack – Atlantic

19 SOMEBODY'S WATCHING ME
Rockwell – Motown

20 IN 3-D
Weird Al Jankovic – Rock'n'Roll

UK SINGLES

1 HELLO
Lionel Richie – Motown

2 A LOVE WORTH WAITING FOR
Shakin' Stevens – Epic

3 YOU TAKE ME UP
Thompson Twins – Arista

4 PEOPLE ARE PEOPLE
Depeche Mode – Mute

5 ROBERT DE NIRO'S WAITING
Banaarama – London

6 GLAD IT'S ALL OVER/DAMNED …
Captain Sensible – A&M

7 IT'S A MIRACLE
Culture Club – Virgin

8 IT'S RAINING MEN
The Weather Girls – CBS

9 NELSON MANDELA
The Special AKA – 2-Tone

10 AGAINST ALL ODDS
Phil Collins – Virgin

11 WHAT DO I DO?
Galaxy/Phil Fearnon – Ensign/Island

12 P.Y.T. (PRETTY YOUNG THING)
Michael Jackson – Epic

13 AIN'T NOBODY
Rufus And Chaka Khan – Warner Bros.

14 LUCKY STAR
Madonna – Sire

15 YOUR LOVE IS KING
Sade – Epic

16 CHERRY OH BABY
UB40 – DEP International/Virgin

17 WOOD BEEZ …
Scritti Politti – Virgin

18 I WANT TO BREAK FREE
Queen – EMI

19 STREET DANCE
Break Machine – Record Shack

20 THE CATERPILLAR
The Cure – Fiction/Polydor

UK ALBUMS

1 …THAT'S WHAT I CALL MUSIC II
Various – Virgin/EMI

2 CAN'T SLOW DOWN
Lionel Richie – Motown

3 INTO THE GAP
Thompson Twins – Arista

4 THRILLER
Michael Jackson – Epic

5 HUMAN'S LIB
Howard Jones – WEA

6 ALCHEMY – DIRE STRAITS LIVE
Dire Straits – Vertigo/Phonogram

7 AN INNOCENT MAN
Billy Joel – CBS

8 LAMENT
Ultravox – Chrysalis

9 CAFE BLEU
The Style Council – Polydor

10 COLOUR BY NUMBERS
Culture Club – Virgin

11 THE SMITHS
The Smiths – Rough Trade

12 THE WORKS
Queen – EMI

13 GREATEST HITS
Marvin Gaye – Telestar

14 HUMAN RACING
Nik Kershaw – MCA

15 BODY AND SOUL
Joe Jackson – A&M

16 SPARKLE IN THE RAIN
Simple Minds – Virgin

17 TOUCH
Eurythmics – RCA

18 THE VERY BEST OF MOTOWN…
Various – Telstar

19 OFF THE WALL
Michael Jackson – Epic

20 UNDER A BLOOD RED SKY
U2 – Island

WEEK ENDING APRIL 21 1984

US SINGLES

1 AGAINST ALL ODDS
Phil Collins – Atlantic

2 FOOTLOOSE
Kenny Loggins – Columbia

3 HELLO
Lionel Richie – Motown

4 HOLD ME NOW
Thompson Twins – Arista

5 MISS ME BLIND
Culture Club – Virgin/Epic

6 AUTOMATIC
Pointer Sisters – Planet

7 SOMEBODY'S WATCHING ME
Rockwell – Motown

8 LOVE SOMEBODY
Rick Springfield – RCA

9 HERE COMES THE RAIN AGAIN
Eurythmics – RCA

10 THEY DON'T KNOW
Tracey Ullman – MCA

11 YOU MIGHT THINK
The Cars – Elektra

12 ADULT EDUCATION
Daryl Hall & John Oates – RCA

13 TO ALL THE GIRLS …
Julio Iglesias & Willie Nelson – Columbia

14 JUMP
Van Halen – Warner Bros.

15 EAT IT
Weird Al Yankovic – Rock 'n' Roll

16 GIRLS
Dwight Twilley – EMI America

17 GIRLS JUST WANT TO HAVE FUN
Cyndi Lauper – Portrait

18 TONIGHT
Kool & The Gang – De-Lite

19 DON'T ANSWER ME
Alan Parsons Project – Arista

20 HEAD OVER HEELS
The Go Go's – IRS

US ALBUMS

1 FOOTLOOSE
Soundtrack – Columbia

2 1984
Van Halen – Warner Bros.

3 THRILLER
Michael Jackson – Epic

4 CAN'T SLOW DOWN
Lionel Richie – Motown

5 SPORTS
Huey Lewis And The News – Chrysalis

6 COLOUR BY NUMBERS
Culture Club – Virgin/Epic

7 TOUCH
Eurythmics – RCA

8 LOVE AT FIRST STING
Scorpions – Mercury

9 HEARTBEAT CITY
The Cars – Elektra

10 SHE'S SO UNUSUAL
Cyndi Lauper – Portrait

11 LEARNING TO CRAWL
The Pretenders – Sire

12 INTO THE GAP
Thompson Twins – Arista

13 AN INNOCENT MAN
Billy Joel – Columbia

14 SYNCHRONICITY
The Police – A&M

15 AGAINST ALL ODDS
Soundtrack – Atlantic

16 UH-HUH
John Cougar Mellencamp – Riva

17 AMMONIA AVENUE
Alan Parsons Project – Arista

18 IN 3-D
Weird Al Yankovic – Rock 'n' Roll

19 SEVEN AND THE RAGGED TIGER
Duran Duran – Capitol

20 SOMEBODY'S WATCHING ME
Rockwell – Motown

UK SINGLES

1 HELLO
Lionel Richie – Motown

2 YOU TAKE ME UP
Thompson Twins – Arista

3 A LOVE WORTH WAITING FOR
Shakin' Stevens – Epic

4 AGAINST ALL ODDS
Phil Collins – Virgin

5 I WANT TO BREAK FREE
Queen – EMI

6 PEOPLE ARE PEOPLE
Depeche Mode – Mute

7 GLAD IT'S ALL OVER/DAMNED…
Captain Sensible – A&M

8 AIN'T NOBODY
Rufus And Chaka Khan – Warner Bros.

9 NELSON MANDELA
The Specia AKA – 2-Tone

10 WOOD BEEZ…
Scritti Politti – Virgin

11 … IN THE HEART
Kool & The Gang – De-Lite/Phonogram

12 ROBERT DE NIRO'S WAITING
Bananarama – London

13 JUST BE GOOD TO ME
S.O.S. Band – Tabu/Epic

14 THE CATERPILLAR
The Cure – Fiction/Polydor

15 DON'T TELL ME
Blancmange – London

16 IT'S A MIRACLE
Culture Club – Virgin

17 SOMEDAY
The Gap Band – Phonogram

18 IT'S RAINING MEN
The Weather Girls – CBS

19 LOCOMOTION
OMD – Virgin

20 LUCKY STAR
Madonna – Sire

UK ALBUMS

1 …THAT'S WHAT I CALL MUSIC II
Various – EMI/Virgin

2 CAN'T SLOW DOWN
Lionel Richie – Motown

3 INTO THE GAP
Thompson Twins – Arista

4 THRILLER
Michael Jackson – Epic

5 ALCHEMY – DIRE STRAITS LIVE
Dire Straits – Vertigo/Phonogram

6 HUMAN'S LIB
Howard Jones – WEA

7 AN INNOCENT MAN
Billy Joel – CBS

8 THE WORKS
Queen – EMI

9 LAMENT
Ultravox – Chrysalis

10 OFF THE WALL
Michael Jackson – Epic

11 HUMAN RACING
Nik Kershaw – MCA

12 COLOUR BY NUMBERS
Culture Club – Virgin

13 GREATEST HITS
Marvin Gaye – Telstar

14 BODY AND SOUL
Joe Jackson – A&M

15 THE SMITHS
The Smiths – Rough Trade

16 LABOUR OF LOVE
UB40 – DEP International/Virgin

17 CAFE BLEU
The Style Council – Polydor

18 TOUCH
Eurythmics – RCA

19 UNDER A BLOOD RED SKY
U2 – Island

20 SPARKLE IN THE RAIN
Simple Minds – Virgin

WEEK ENDING APRIL 28 1984

US SINGLES	US ALBUMS	UK SINGLES	UK ALBUMS
1 **AGAINST ALL ADDS** *Phil Collins – Atlantic*	1 **FOOTLOOSE** *Soundtrack – Columbia*	1 **HELLO** *Lionel Richie – Motown*	1 **…THAT'S WHAT I CALL MUSIC II** *Various – Virgin/EMI*
2 **HELLO** *Lionel Richie – Motown*	2 **1984** *Van Halen – Warner Bros.*	2 **AGAINST ALL ODDS** *Phil Collins – Virgin*	2 **CAN'T SLOW DOWN** *Lionel Richie – Motown*
3 **FOOTLOOSE** *Kenny Loggins – Columbia*	3 **CAN'T SLOW DOWN** *Lionel Richie – Motown*	3 **I WANT TO BREAK FREE** *Queen – EMI*	3 **INTO THE GAP** *Thompson Twins – Arista*
4 **HOLD ME NOW** *Thompson Twins – Arista*	4 **THRILLER** *Michael Jackson – Epic*	4 **YOU TAKE ME UP** *Thompson Twins – Arista*	4 **THRILLER** *Michael Jackson – Epic*
5 **MISS ME BLIND** *Culture Club – Virgin/Epic*	5 **COLOUR BY NUMBERS** *Culture Club – Virgin/Epic*	5 **THE REFLEX** *Duran Duran – EMI*	5 **GRACE UNDER PRESSURE** *Rush – Vertigo/Phonogram*
6 **LOVE SOMEBODY** *Rick Springfield – RCA*	6 **SPORTS** *Huey Lewis And The News – Chrysalis*	6 **A LOVE WORTH WAITING FOR** *Shakin' Stevens – Epic*	6 **THE WORKS** *Queen – EMI*
7 **YOU MIGHT THINK** *The Cars – Elektra*	7 **HEARTBEAT CITY** *The Cars – Elektra*	7 **… IN THE HEART** *Kool & The Gang – De-Lite/Phonogram*	7 **AND I LOVE YOU SO** *Howard Keel – Warwick*
8 **THEY DON'T KNOW** *Tracey Ullman – MCA*	8 **LOVE AT FIRST STING** *Scorpions – Mercury*	8 **GLAD IT'S ALL OVER /DAMNED…** *Captain Sensible – A&M*	8 **HUMAN'S LIB** *Howard Jones – WEA*
9 **AUTOMATIC** *Pointer Sisters – Planet*	9 **TOUCH** *Eurythmics – RCA*	9 **PEOPLE ARE PEOPLE** *Depeche Mode – Mute*	9 **AN INNOCENT MAN** *Billy Joel – CBS*
10 **TO ALL THE GIRLS …** *Julio Iglesias & Willie Nelson – Columbia*	10 **SHE'S SO UNUSUAL** *Cyndi Lauper – Epic*	10 **LOCOMOTION** *OMD – Virgin*	10 **ALCHEMY – DIRE STRAITS LIVE** *Dire Straits – Vertigo/Phonogram*
11 **SOMEBODY'S WATCHING ME** *Rockwell – Motown*	11 **INTO THE GAP** *Thompson Twins – Arista*	11 **DON'T TELL ME** *Blancmange – London*	11 **HUMAN RACING** *Nik Kershaw – MCA*
12 **LET'S HEAR IT FOR THE BOY** *Deniece Williams – Columbia*	12 **AGAINST ALL ODDS** *Soundtrack – Atlantic*	12 **AIN'T NOBODY** *Rufus and Chaka Khan – Warner Brothers*	12 **FOOTLOOSE** *Soundtrack – CBS*
13 **HEAD OVER HEELS** *The Go-Go's – IRS*	13 **LEARNING TO CRAWL** *The Pretenders – Sire*	13 **WHEN YOU'RE YOUNG …** *The Flying Pickets – 10 Records/Virgin*	13 **OFF THE WALL** *Michael Jackson – Epic*
14 **TONIGHT** *Kool & The Gang – De-Lite*	14 **AN INNOCENT MAN** *Billy Joel – Columbia*	14 **WOOD BEEZ…** *Scritti Politti – Virgin*	14 **COLOUR BY NUMBERS** *Culture Club – Virgin*
15 **ADULT EDUCATION** *Daryl Hall & John Oates – RCA*	15 **AMMONIA AVENUE** *The Alan Parsons Project – Arista*	15 **I'M FALLING** *The Bluebells – London*	15 **LAMENT** *Ultravox – Chrysalis*
16 **DON'T ANSWER ME** *Alan Parsons Project – Arista*	16 **UH-HUH** *John Cougar Mellencamp – Riva*	16 **NELSON MANDELA** *The Special AKA – 2-Tone*	16 **BANANARAMA** *Bananarama – London*
17 **OH SHERRIE** *Steve Perry – Columbia*	17 **IN 3-D** *Weird Al Yankovic – Rock'n'Roll*	17 **JUST BE GOOD TO ME** *S.O.S. Band – Tabu/Epic*	17 **GREATEST HITS** *Marvin Gaye – Telstar*
18 **HERE COMES THE RAIN AGAIN** *Eurythmics – RCA*	18 **SYNCHRONICITY** *The Police – A&M*	18 **DANCING GIRLS** *Nik Kershaw – MCA*	18 **BODY AND SOUL** *Joe Jackson – A&M*
19 **THE AUTHORITY SONG** *John Cougar Mellancamp – Riva*	19 **HARD TO HOLD** *Soundtrack – RCA*	19 **THE CATERPILLAR** *The Cure – Fiction/Polydor*	19 **THE SMITHS** *The Smiths – Rough Trade*
20 **GIRLS** *Dwight Twilley – EMI America*	20 **90125** *Yes – Atco*	20 **AUTOMATIC** *Pointer Sisters – Planet*	20 **LABOUR OF LOVE** *UB40 – DEP International/Virgin*

WEEK ENDING MAY 5 1984

US SINGLES	US ALBUMS	UK SINGLES	UK ALBUMS
1 **AGAINST ALL ODDS** *Phil Collins – Atlantic*	1 **FOOTLOOSE** *Soundtrack – Columbia*	1 **THE REFLEX** *Duran Duran – EMI*	1 **…THAT'S WHAT I CALL MUSIC II** *Various – EMI*
2 **HELLO** *Lionel Richie – Motown*	2 **CAN'T SLOW DOWN** *Lionel Richie – Motown*	2 **AGAINST ALL ODDS** *Phil Collins – Virgin*	2 **CAN'T SLOW DOWN** *Lionel Richie – Motown*
3 **HOLD ME NOW** *Thompson Twins – Arista*	3 **1984** *Van Halen – Warner Bros.*	3 **I WANT TO BREAK FREE** *Queen – EMI*	3 **INTO THE GAP** *Thompson Twins – Arista*
4 **FOOTLOOSE** *Kenny Loggins – Columbia*	4 **THRILLER** *Michael Jackson – Epic*	4 **HELLO** *Lionel Richie – Motown*	4 **THRILLER** *Michael Jackson – Epic*
5 **LOVE SOMEBODY** *Rick Springfield – RCA*	5 **COLOUR BY NUMBERS** *Culture Club – Virgin/Epic*	5 **AUTOMATIC** *Pointer Sisters – Planet*	5 **THE WORKS** *Queen – EMI*
6 **TO ALL THE GIRLS…** *Julio Iglesias & Willie Nelson – Columbia*	6 **SPORTS** *Huey Lewis And The News – Chrysalis*	6 **LOCOMOTION** *OMD – Virgin*	6 **AND I LOVE YOU SO** *Howard Keel – Warwick*
7 **YOU MIGHT THINK** *The Cars – Elektra*	7 **HEARTBEAT CITY** *The Cars – Elektra*	7 **WHEN YOU'RE YOUNG …** *The Flying Pickets – 10 Records/Virgin*	7 **FOOTLOOSE** *Soundtrack – CBS*
8 **THEY DON'T KNOW** *Tracey Ullman – MCA*	8 **LOVE AT FIRST STING** *The Scorpions – Mercury*	8 **DON'T TELL ME** *Blancmange – London*	8 **ALCHEMY - DIRE STRAITS LIVE** *Dire Straits – Vertigo/Phonogram*
9 **LET'S HEAR IT FOR THE BOY** *Deniece Williams – Columbia*	9 **SHE'S SO UNUSUAL** *Cyndi Lauper – Portrait*	9 **ONE LOVE/PEOPLE GET READY** *Bob Marley & The Wailers – Island*	9 **HUMAN'S LIB** *Howard Jones – WEA*
10 **MISS ME BLIND** *Culture Club – Virgin/Epic*	10 **INTO THE GAP** *Thompson Twins – Arista*	10 **YOU TAKE ME UP** *Thompson Twins – Arista*	10 **GRACE UNDER PRESSURE** *Rush – Vertigo/Phonogram*
11 **OH SHERRIE** *Steve Perry – Columbia*	11 **TOUCH** *Eurythmics – RCA*	11 **I'M FALLING** *The Bluebells – London*	11 **AN INNOCENT MAN** *Billy Joel – CBS*
12 **HEAD OVER HEELS** *The Go Go's – IRS*	12 **AGAINST ALL ODDS** *Soundtrack – Atlantic*	12 **IN THE HEART** *Kool & The Gang – De-Lite/Phonogram*	12 **HUMAN RACING** *Nik Kershaw – MCA*
13 **TONIGHT** *Kool & The Gang – De-Lite*	13 **LEARNING TO CRAWL** *The Pretenders – Sire*	13 **AIN'T NOBODY** *Rufus and Chaka Khan – Warner Bros.*	13 **COLOUR BY NUMBERS** *Culture Club – Virgin*
14 **TIME AFTER TIME** *Cyndi Lauper – Portrait*	14 **AN INNOCENT MAN** *Billy Joel – Columbia*	14 **DANCING GIRLS** *Nik Kershaw – MCA*	14 **OFF THE WALL** *Michael Jackson – Epic*
15 **DON'T ANSWER ME** *Alan Parsons Project – Arista*	15 **UH-HUH** *John Cougar Mellencamp – Riva*	15 **A LOVE WORTH WAITING FOR** *Shakin' Stevens – Epic*	15 **GREATEST HITS** *Marvin Gaye – Telstar*
16 **THE AUTHORITY SONG** *John Cougar Mellencamp – Riva*	16 **HARD TO HOLD** *Soundtrack – RCA*	16 **GLAD IT'S ALL OVER/DAMNED** *Captain Sensible – A&M*	16 **LAMENT** *Ultravox – Crysalis*
17 **THE LONGEST TIME** *Billy Joel – Columbia*	17 **IN 3-D** *Weird Al Yankovic – Rock 'n' Roll*	17 **JUST BE GOOD TO ME** *S.O.S. Band – Tabu/Epic*	17 **BODY AND SOUL** *Joe Jackson – A&M*
18 **BREAKDANCE** *Irene Cara – Geffen/Network*	18 **AMMONIA AVENUE** *Alan Parsons Project – Arista*	18 **THIEVES LIKE US** *New Order – Factory*	18 **BANANARAMA** *Bananarama – London*
19 **AUTOMATIC** *Pointer Sisters – Planet*	19 **TALK SHOW** *Go-Go's – IRS*	19 **THE LEBANON** *Human League – Virgin*	19 **THE SMITHS** *The Smiths – Rough Trade*
20 **SISTER CHRISTIAN** *Night Ranger – MCA*	20 **SEVEN AND THE RAGGED TIGER** *Duran Duran – Capitol*	20 **PEOPLE ARE PEOPLE** *Depeche Mode – Mute*	20 **NOW THAT'S WHAT I CALL MUSIC** *Various – EMI/Virgin*

WEEK ENDING MAY 12 1984

US SINGLES	US ALBUMS	UK SINGLES	UK ALBUMS
1 **HELLO** *Lionel Richie – Motown*	1 **FOOTLOOSE** *Soundtrack – Columbia*	1 **THE REFLEX** *Duran Duran – EMI*	1 **…THAT'S WHAT I CALL MUSIC II** *Various – Virgin/EMI*
2 **AGAINST ALL ODDS** *Phil Collins – Atlantic*	2 **CAN'T SLOW DOWN** *Lionel Richie – Motown*	2 **AGAINST ALL ODDS** *Phil Collins – Virgin*	2 **CAN'T SLOW DOWN** *Lionel Richie – Motown*
3 **HOLD ME NOW** *Thompson Twins – Arista*	3 **THRILLER** *Michael Jackson – Epic*	3 **I WANT TO BREAK FREE** *Queen – EMI*	3 **THRILLER** *Michael Jackson – Epic*
4 **LET'S HEAR IT FOR THE BOY** *Deniece Williams – Columbia*	4 **1984** *Van Halen – Warner Bros.*	4 **AUTOMATIC** *Pointer Sisters – Planet*	4 **OCEAN RAIN** *Echo And The Bunnymen – Korova*
5 **LOVE SOMEBODY** *Rick Springfield – RCA*	5 **COLOUR BY NUMBERS** *Culture Club – Virgin/Epic*	5 **LOCOMOTION** *OMD – Virgin*	5 **THE WORKS** *Queen – EMI*
6 **TO ALL THE GIRLS …** *Julio Iglesias & Willie Nelson – Columbia*	6 **HEARTBEAT CITY** *The Cars – Elektra*	6 **ONE LOVE/PEOPLE GET READY** *Bob Marley & The Wailers – Island*	6 **AND I LOVE YOU SO** *Howard Keel – Warwick*
7 **YOU MIGHT THINK** *The Cars – Elektra*	7 **SPORTS** *Huey Lewis and the News – Chrysalis*	7 **WHEN YOU'RE YOUNG …** *The Flying Pickets – 10 Records/Virgin*	7 **FOOTLOOSE** *Soundtrack – CBS*
8 **FOOTLOOSE** *Kenny Loggins – Columbia*	8 **LOVE AT FIRST STING** *Scorpions – Mercury*	8 **DON'T TELL ME** *Blancmange – London*	8 **INTO THE GAP** *Thompson Twins – Arista*
9 **OH SHERRIE** *Steve Perry – Columbia*	9 **SHE'S SO UNUSUAL** *Cyndi Lauper – Portrait*	9 **FOOTLOOSE** *Kenny Loggins – CBS*	9 **JUNK CULTURE** *OMD – Virgin*
10 **TIME AFTER TIME** *Cyndi Lauper – Portrait*	10 **INTO THE GAP** *Thompson Twins – Arista*	10 **HELLO** *Lionel Richie – Motown*	10 **THE TOP** *The Cure – Fiction*
11 **THEY DON'T KNOW** *Tracey Ullman – MCA*	11 **TOUCH** *Eurythmics – RCA*	11 **THE LEBANON** *Human League – Virgin*	11 **ALCHEMY – DIRE STRAITS LIVE** *Dire Straits – Vertigo/Phonogram*
12 **HEAD OVER HEELS** *The Go Go's – I.R.S.*	12 **AGAINST ALL ODDS** *Soundtrack – Atlantic*	12 **LOVE GAMES** *Belle And The Devotions – CBS*	12 **AN INNOCENT MAN** *Billy Joel – CBS*
13 **TONIGHT** *Kool & The Gang – De-Lite*	13 **GRACE UNDER PRESSURE** *Rush – Mercury*	13 **DANCING GIRLS** *Nik Kershaw – MCA*	13 **THE PROS AND CONS …** *Roger Waters – Harvest*
14 **THE LONGEST TIME** *Billy Joel – Columbia*	14 **AN INNOCENT MAN** *Billy Joel – Columbia*	14 **I'M FALLING** *The Bluebells – London*	14 **HUMAN'S LIB** *Howard Jones – WEA*
15 **BREAKDANCE** *Irene Cara – Network/Geffen*	15 **UH-HUH** *John Cougar Mellencamp – Riva*	15 **IN THE HEART** *Kool & The Gang – De-Lite/Phonogram*	15 **HUMAN RACING** *Nik Kershaw – MCA*
16 **THE AUTHORITY SONG** *John Cougar Mellencamp – Riva*	16 **HARD TO HOLD** *Soundtrack – RCA*	16 **SOMEBODY ELSE'S GUY** *Jocelyn Brown – Fourth & Broadway/Island*	16 **GRACE UNDER PRESSURE** *Rush – Vertigo/Phonogram*
17 **SISTER CHRISTIAN** *Night Ranger – MCA*	17 **IN 3-D** *Weird Al Yankovic – Scotti Bros.*	17 **TO ALL THE GIRLS …** *Julio Iglesias & Willie Nelson – CBS*	17 **GREATEST HITS** *Marvin Gaye – Telstar*
18 **MISS ME BLIND** *Culture Club – Virgin/Epic*	18 **AMMONIA AVENUE** *The Alan Parsons Project – Arista*	18 **LET'S HEAR IT FOR THE BOY** *Deniece Williams – CBS*	18 **OFF THE WALL** *Michael Jackson – Epic*
19 **THE REFLEX** *Duran Duran – Capitol*	19 **TALK SHOW** *Go Go's – I.R.S.*	19 **AIN'T NOBODY** *Rufus And Chaka Khan – Warner Bros.*	19 **LEGEND** *Clannad – RCA*
20 **DANCING IN THE SHEETS** *Shalamar – Columbia*	20 **LEARNING TO CRAWL** *The Pretenders – Sire*	20 **JUST BE GOOD TO ME** *S.O.S. Band – Tabu/Epic*	20 **SEVEN AND THE RAGGED TIGER** *Duran Duran – EMI*

WEEK ENDING MAY 19 1984

US SINGLES	US ALBUMS	UK SINGLES	UK ALBUMS
1 **HELLO** *Lionel Richie – Motown*	1 **FOOTLOOSE** *Soundtrack – Columbia*	1 **THE REFLEX** *Duran Duran – EMI*	1 **LEGEND** *Bob Marley & The Wailers – Island*
2 **LET'S HEAR IT FOR THE BOY** *Deniece Williams – Columbia*	2 **CAN'T SLOW DOWN** *Lionel Richie – Motown*	2 **AUTOMATIC** *Pointer Sisters – Planet*	2 **…THAT'S WHAT I CALL MUSIC II** *Various – Virgin/EMI*
3 **AGAINST ALL ODDS** *Phil Collins – Atlantic*	3 **THRILLER** *Michael Jackson – Epic*	3 **AGAINST ALL ODDS** *Phil Collins – Virgin*	3 **HYSTERIA** *Human League – Virgin*
4 **HOLD ME NOW** *Thompson Twins – Arista*	4 **1984** *Van Halen – Warner Bros.*	4 **I WANT TO BREAK FREE** *Queen – EMI*	4 **THE WORKS** *Queen – EMI*
5 **TO ALL THE GIRLS …** *Julio Iglesias & Willie Nelson – Columbia*	5 **SPORTS** *Huey Lewis And The News – Chrysalis*	5 **ONE LOVE/PEOPLE GET READY** *Bob Marley & The Wailers – Island*	5 **CAN'T SLOW DOWN** *Lionel Richie – Motown*
6 **TIME AFTER TIME** *Cyndi Lauper – Portrait*	6 **HEARTBEAT CITY** *The Cars – Elektra*	6 **FOOTLOOSE** *Kenny Loggins – CBS*	6 **THRILLER** *Michael Jackson – Epic*
7 **LOVE SOMEBODY** *Rick Springfield – RCA*	7 **COLOUR BY NUMBERS** *Culture Club – Virgin/Epic*	7 **LOCOMOTION** *OMD – Virgin*	7 **FOOTLOOSE** *Soundtrack – CBS*
8 **OH SHERRIE** *Steve Perry – Columbia*	8 **LOVE AT FIRST STING** *Scorpions – Mercury*	8 **LET'S HEAR IT FOR THE BOY** *Deniece Williams – CBS*	8 **OCEAN RAIN** *Echo and The Bunnymen – Korova*
9 **YOU MIGHT THINK** *The Cars – Elektra*	9 **SHE'S SO UNUSUAL** *Cyndia Lauper – Portrait*	9 **DON'T TELL ME** *Blancmange – London*	9 **AN INNOCENT MAN** *Billy Joel – CBS*
10 **FOOTLOOSE** *Kenny Loggins – Columbia*	10 **GRACE UNDER PRESSURE** *Rush – Mercury*	10 **WHEN YOU'RE YOUNG …** *The Flying Pickets – 10 Records/Virgin*	10 **INTO THE GAP** *Thompson Twins – Arista*
11 **HEAD OVER HEELS** *The Go Go's – IRS*	11 **INTO THE GAP** *Thompson Twins – Arista*	11 **LOVE GAMES** *Belle and The Devotions – CBS*	11 **AND I LOVE YOU SO** *Howard Keel – Warwick*
12 **THE REFLEX** *Duran Duran – Capitol*	12 **AGAINST ALL ODDS** *Soundtrack – Atlantic*	12 **THE LEBANON** *Human League – Virgin*	12 **ALCHEMY – DIRE STRAITS** *Dire Straits – Vertigo/Phonogram*
13 **BREAKDANCE** *Irena Cara – Geffen/Network*	13 **AN INNOCENT MAN** *Billy Joel – Columbia*	13 **SOMEBODY ELSE'S GUY** *Jocelyn Brown – Fourth & Broadway/Island*	13 **MAN ON THE LINE** *Chris De Burgh – A&M*
14 **THE LONGEST TIME** *Billy Joel – Columbia*	14 **UH-HUH** *John Cougar Mellencamp – Riva*	14 **DANCING GIRLS** *Nik Kershaw – MCA*	14 **JUNK CULTURE** *OMD – Virgin*
15 **THE AUTHORITY SONG** *John Cougar Mellencamp – Riva*	15 **TOUCH** *Eurythmics – RCA*	15 **HELLO** *Lionel Richie – Motown*	15 **MIRROR MOVES** *Psychedelic Furs – CBS*
16 **SISTER CHRISTIAN** *Night Ranger – MCA*	16 **HARD TO HOLD** *Soundtrack – RCA*	16 **BREAK DANCE PARTY** *Break Machine – Record Shack*	16 **THE TOP** *The Cure – Fiction*
17 **THEY DON'T KNOW** *Tracey Ullman – MCA*	17 **STREET TALK** *Steve Perry – Columbia*	17 **I'LL BE AROUND** *Terri Wells – Philly World/London*	17 **HUMAN RACING** *Nik Kershaw*
18 **DANCING IN THE SHEETS** *Shalamar – Columbia*	18 **SEVEN AND THE RAGGED TIGER** *Duran Duran – Capitol*	18 **STAY WITH ME TONIGHT** *Jeffrey Osborne – A&M*	18 **HUMAN'S LIB** *Howard Jones – WEA*
19 **I'LL WAIT** *Van Halen – Warner Bros.*	19 **TALK SHOW** *Go Go's – IRS*	19 **I'M FALLING** *The Bluebells – London*	19 **SEVEN AND THE RAGGED TIGER** *Duran Duran – EMI*
20 **TONIGHT** *Kool & The Gang – De-Lite*	20 **LEARNING TO CRAWL** *The Pretenders – Sire*	20 **JUST BE GOOD TO ME** *S.O.S. Band – Tabu/Epic*	20 **OFF THE WALL** *Michael Jackson – Epic*

US SINGLES

1 **LET'S HEAR IT FOR THE BOY**
Deniece Williams – Columbia
2 **HELLO**
Lionel Richie – Motown
3 **TIME AFTER TIME**
Cyndi Lauper – Portrait
4 **AGAINST ALL ODDS**
Phil Collins – Atlantic
5 **OH SHERRIE**
Steve Perry – Columbia/CBS
6 **TO ALL THE GIRLS I'VE LOVED**
Julio Iglesias & Willie Nelson – Columbia
7 **THE REFLEX**
Duran Duran – Capitol
8 **SISTER CHRISTIAN**
Night Ranger – MCA
9 **BREAKDANCE**
Irene Cara – Geffen/Network
10 **HOLD ME NOW**
Thompson Twins – Arista
11 **HEAD OVER HEELS**
The Go Go's – IRS
12 **YOU MIGHT THINK**
The Cars – Elektra
13 **THE HEART OF ROCK'N'ROLL**
Huey Lewis And The News – Chrysalis
14 **THE LONGEST TIME**
Billy Joel – Columbia
15 **LOVE SOMEBODY**
Rick Springfield – RCA
16 **I'LL WAIT**
Van Halen – Warner Bros.
17 **DANCING IN THE SHEETS**
Shalamar – Columbia
18 **BORDERLINE**
Madonna – Sire
19 **SELF CONTROL**
Laura Branigan – Atlantic
20 **IT'S A MIRACLE**
Culture Club – Virgin/Epic

US ALBUMS

1 **FOOTLOOSE**
Soundtrack – Columbia
2 **CAN'T SLOW DOWN**
Lionel Richie – Motown
3 **THRILLER**
Michael Jackson – Epic
4 **SPORTS**
Huey Lewis And The News – Chrysalis
5 **1984**
Van Halen – Warner Bros.
6 **COLOUR BY NUMBERS**
Culture Club – Virgin/Epic
7 **SHE'S SO UNUSUAL**
Cyndi Lauper – Portrait
8 **LOVE AT FIRST STING**
Scorpions – Mercury
9 **HEARTBEAT CITY**
The Cars – Elektra
10 **GRACE UNDER PRESSURE**
Rush – Mercury
11 **INTO THE GAP**
Thompson Twins – Arista
12 **AN INNOCENT MAN**
Billy Joel – Columbia
13 **UH-HUH**
John Cougar Mellencamp – Riva
14 **STREET TALK**
Steve Perry – Columbia
15 **AGAINST ALL ODDS**
Soundtrack – Atlantic
16 **TOUCH**
Eurythmics – RCA
17 **SEVEN AND THE RAGGED TIGER**
Duran Duran – Capitol
18 **TALK SHOW**
Go Go's – IRS
19 **ELIMINATOR**
ZZ Top – Warner Bros.
20 **BODY AND SOUL**
Joe Jackson – A&M

UK SINGLES

1 **THE REFLEX**
Duran Duran – EMI
2 **AUTOMATIC**
Pointer Sisters – Planet
3 **LET'S HEAR IT FOR THE BOY**
Deniece Williams – CBS
4 **WAKE ME UP BEFORE …**
Wham! – Epic
5 **I WANT TO BREAK FREE**
Queen – EMI
6 **ONE LOVE/PEOPLE GET READY**
Bob Marley & The Wailers – Island
7 **FOOTLOOSE**
Kenny Loggins – CBS
8 **AGAINST ALL ODDS**
Phil Collins – Virgin
9 **BREAK DANCE PARTY**
Break Machine – Record Shack
10 **DANCING WITH TEARS IN MY…**
Ultravox – Chrysalis
11 **GROOVIN'**
The Style Council – Polydor
12 **LOCOMOTION**
OMD – Virgin
13 **SEARCHIN'**
Hazell Dean – Proto
14 **LOVE WARS**
Womack & Womack – Elektra
15 **DON'T TELL ME**
Blancmange – London
16 **YOUNG AND IN LOVE**
The Flying Pickets – 10 Records
17 **I FEEL LIKE BUDDY HOLLY**
Alvin Stardust – Chrysalis
18 **I'LL BE AROUND**
Terri Wells – Philly World/London
19 **STAY WITH ME TONIGHT**
Jeffrey Osbourne – A&M
20 **SOMEBODY ELSE'S GUY**
Jocelyn Brown – Fourth & Broadway/Island

UK ALBUMS

1 **LEGEND**
Bob Marley And The Wailers – Island
2 **…THAT'S WHAT I CALL MUSIC II**
Various – Virgin/EMI
3 **THE WORKS**
Queen – EMI
4 **CAN'T SLOW DOWN**
Lionel Richie – Motown
5 **HYSTERIA**
Human League – Virgin
6 **THRILLER**
Michael Jackson – Epic
7 **FOOTLOOSE**
Soundtrack – CBS
8 **MANGE TOUT**
Blancmange – London
9 **AN INNOCENT MAN**
Billy Joel – CBS
10 **INTO THE GAP**
Thompson Twins – Arista
11 **MAN ON THE LINE**
Chris De Burgh – A & M
12 **HUNGRY FOR HITS**
Various – K-Tel
13 **ALCHEMY – DIRE STRAITS LIVE**
Dire Straits – Vertigo/Phonogram
14 **OCEAN RAIN**
Echo And The Bunnymen – Korova
15 **AND I LOVE YOU SO**
Howard Keel – Warwick
16 **LEGEND**
Clannad – RCA
17 **SEVEN AND THE RAGGED TIGER**
Duran Duran – EMI
18 **HUMAN'S LIB**
Howard Jones – WEA
19 **DON'T STOP DANCING**
Various – Telstar
20 **HUMAN RACING**
Nik Kershaw – MCA

US SINGLES

1 **LET'S HEAR IT FOR THE BOY**
Deniece Williams – Columbia
2 **TIME AFTER TIME**
Cyndi Lauper – Portrait
3 **HELLO**
Lionel Richie – Motown
4 **OH SHERRIE**
Steve Perry – Columbia
5 **THE REFLEX**
Duran Duran – Capitol
6 **SISTER CHRISTIAN**
Night Ranger – MCA
7 **AGAINST ALL ODDS**
Phil Collins – Atlantic
8 **THE HEART OF ROCK 'N' ROLL**
Huey Lewis And The News – Chrysalis
9 **BREAKDANCE**
Irene Cara – Network/Geffen
10 **TO ALL THE GIRLS I'VE LOVED**
Julio Iglesias & Willie Nelson – Columbia
11 **SELF CONTROL**
Laura Branigan – Atlantic
12 **BORDERLINE**
Madonna – Sire
13 **I'LL WAIT**
Van Halen – Warner Bros.
14 **JUMP (FOR MY LOVE)**
Pointer Sisters – Planet
15 **THE LONGEST TIME**
Billy Joel – Columbia
16 **IT'S A MIRACLE**
Culture Club – Virgin/Epic
17 **DANCING IN THE SHEETS**
Shalamar – Columbia
18 **DANCING IN THE DARK**
Bruce Springsteen – Columbia
19 **HEAD OVER HEELS**
The Go-Go's – I.R.S.
20 **YOU CAN'T GET WHAT YOU…**
Joe Jackson – A & M

US ALBUMS

1 **FOOTLOOSE**
Soundtrack – Columbia
2 **CAN'T SLOW DOWN**
Lionel Richie – Motown
3 **SPORTS**
Huey Lewis And The News – Chrysalis
4 **SHE'S SO UNUSUAL**
Cyndi Lauper – Portrait
5 **HEARTBEAT CITY**
The Cars – Elektra
6 **THRILLER**
Michael Jackson – Epic
7 **1984**
Van Halen – Warner Bros.
8 **COLOUR BY NUMBERS**
Culture Club – Virgin/Epic
9 **LOVE AT FIRST STING**
Scorpions – Mercury
10 **GRACE UNDER PRESSURE**
Rush – Mercury
11 **AN INNOCENT MAN**
Billy Joel – Columbia
12 **INTO THE GAP**
The Thompson Twins – Arista
13 **STREET TALK**
Steve Perry – Columbia
14 **UH-HUH**
John Cougar Mellencamp – Riva
15 **SEVEN AND THE RAGGED TIGER**
Duran Duran – Capitol
16 **TOUCH**
Eurythmics – RCA
17 **MIDNIGHT MADNESS**
Night Ranger – Camel/MCA
18 **TALK SHOW**
The Go-Go's – I.R.S.
19 **ELIMINATOR**
ZZ Top – Warner Bros.
20 **BODY AND SOUL**
Joe Jackson – A & M

UK SINGLES

1 **WAKE ME UP BEFORE …**
Wham! – Epic
2 **LET'S HEAR IT FOR THE BOY**
Deniece Williams – CBS
3 **REFLEX**
Duran Duran – EMI
4 **AUTOMATIC**
Pointer Sisters – Planet
5 **GROOVIN'**
The Style Council – Polydor
6 **DANCING WITH TEARS IN MY…**
Ultravox – Chrysalis
7 **I FEEL LIKE BUDDY HOLLY**
Alvin Stardust – Chrysalis
8 **SEARCHIN'**
Hazell Dean – Proto
9 **I WANT TO BREAK FREE**
Queen – EMI
10 **AGAINST ALL ODDS**
Phil Collins – Virgin
11 **HIGH ENERGY**
Evelyn Thomas – Record Shack
12 **ONE LOVE/PEOPLE GET READY**
Bob Marley & The Wailers – Island
13 **BREAK DANCE PARTY**
Break Machine – Record Shack
14 **FOOTLOOSE**
Kenny Loggins – CBS
15 **PEARL IN THE SHELL**
Howard Jones – WEA
16 **LOVE WARS**
Womack & Womack – Elektra
17 **RELAX**
Frankie Goes To Hollywood – ZZT/Island
18 **LOCOMOTION**
OMD – Virgin
19 **HEAVEN KNOWS I'M MISERABLE**
The Smiths – Rough Trade
20 **GOING DOWN TOWN TONIGHT**
Status Quo – Vertigo/Phonogram

UK ALBUMS

1 **LEGEND**
Bob Marley And The Wailers – Island
2 **THE WORKS**
Queen – EMI
3 **…THAT'S WHAT I CALL MUSIC II**
Various – Virgin/EMI
4 **CAN'T SLOW DOWN**
Lionel Richie – Motown
5 **THRILLER**
Michael Jackson – Epic
6 **HUNGRY FOR HITS**
Various – K-Tel
7 **THEN CAME ROCK 'N' ROLL**
Various – EMI
8 **FOOTLOOSE**
Soundtrack – CBS
9 **MANGE TOUT**
Blancmange – London
10 **AN INNOCENT MAN**
Billy Joel – CBS
11 **HYSTERIA**
Human League – Virgin
12 **DON'T STOP DANCING**
Various – Telstar
13 **HUMAN'S LIB**
Howard Jones – WEA
14 **INTO THE GAP**
Thompson Twins – Arista
15 **CAFE BLEU**
The Style Council – Polydor
16 **LEGEND**
Clannad – RCA
17 **MAN ON THE LINE**
Chris De Burgh – A & M
18 **ALCHEMY – DIRE STRAITS LIVE**
Dire Straits – Vertigo/Phonogram
19 **SEVEN AND THE RAGGED TIGER**
Duran Duran – EMI
20 **HUMAN RACING**
Nik Kershaw – MCA

WEEK ENDING JUNE 9 1984

	US SINGLES	US ALBUMS	UK SINGLES	UK ALBUMS
1	**TIME AFTER TIME** *Cyndi Lauper – Portrait*	**FOOTLOOSE** *Soundtrack – Columbia/CBS*	**WAKE ME UP BEFORE YOU...** *Wham! – Epic*	**LEGEND** *Bob Marley And The Wailers*
2	**LET'S HEAR IT FOR THE BOY** *Deniece Williams – Columbia/CBS*	**CAN'T SLOW DOWN** *Lionel Richie – Motown*	**LET'S HEAR IT FOR THE BOY** *Deniece Williams – CBS*	**THE WORKS** *Queen – EMI*
3	**OH SHERRIE** *Steve Perry – Columbia/CBS*	**SPORTS** *Huey Lewis And The News – Chrysalis*	**DANCING WITH TEARS IN MY...** *Ultravox – Chrysalis*	**...THAT'S WHAT I CALL MUSIC II** *Various – Virgin/EMI*
4	**THE REFLEX** *Duran Duran – Capitol*	**SHE'S SO UNUSUAL** *Cyndi Lauper – Portrait*	**THE REFLEX** *Duran Duran – EMI*	**HUNGRY FOR HITS** *Various – K-Tel*
5	**SISTER CHRISTIAN** *Night Ranger – MCA*	**HEARTBEAT CITY** *The Cars – Elektra*	**ONLY WHEN YOU LEAVE** *Spandau Ballet – Reformation/Chrysalis*	**CAN'T SLOW DOWN** *Lionel Richie – Motown*
6	**THE HEART OF ROCK 'N' ROLL** *Huey Lewis And The News – Chrysalis*	**COLOUR BY NUMBERS** *Culture Club – Virgin/Epic*	**SEARCHIN'** *Hazell Dean – Proto*	**THRILLER** *Michael Jackson – Epic*
7	**HELLO** *Lionel Richie – Motown*	**LOVE AT FIRST STING** *Scorpions – Mercury*	**GROOVIN'** *The Style Council – Polydor*	**AN INNOCENT MAN** *Billy Joel – CBS*
8	**BREAKDANCE** *Irene Cara – Geffen/Network*	**THRILLER** *Michael Jackson – Epic*	**PEARL IN THE SHELL** *Howard Jones – WEA*	**THEN CAME ROCK 'N' ROLL** *Various – EMI*
9	**SELF CONTROL** *Laura Branigan – Atlantic*	**1984** *Van Halen – Warner Bros.*	**HIGH ENERGY** *Evelyn Thomas – Record Shack*	**HUMAN'S LIB** *Howard Jones – WEA*
10	**JUMP (FOR MY LOVE)** *Pointer Sisters – Planet*	**GRACE UNDER PRESSURE** *Rush – Mercury*	**HEAVEN KNOWS I'M MISERABLE** *The Smiths – Rough Trade*	**FOOTLOOSE** *Soundtrack – CBS*
11	**BORDERLINE** *Madonna – Sire*	**AN INNOCENT MAN** *Billy Joel – Columbia/CBS*	**I FEEL LIKE BUDDY HOLLY** *Alvin Stardust – Chrysalis*	**DON'T STOP DANCING** *Various – Telstar*
12	**AGAINST ALL ODDS** *Phil Collins – Atlantic*	**STREET TALK** *Steve Perry – Columbia/CBS*	**SAD SONGS (SAY SO MUCH)** *Elton John – Rocket/Phonogram*	**LOST BOYS** *The Flying Pickets – Virgin 10*
13	**I'LL WAIT** *Van Halen – Warner Bros.*	**INTO THE GAP** *Thompson Twins – Arista*	**SMALLTOWN BOY** *Bronski Beat – Forbidden Fruit/London*	**MANGE TOUT** *Blancmange – London*
14	**DANCING IN THE DARK** *Bruce Springsteen – Columbia/CBS*	**SEVEN AND THE RAGGED TIGER** *Duran Duran – Capitol*	**AUTOMATIC** *Pointer Sisters – Planet*	**CAFE BLEU** *The Style Council – Polydor*
15	**IT'S A MIRACLE** *Culture Club – Virgin/Epic*	**ELIMINATOR** *ZZ Top – Warner Bros.*	**I WANT TO BREAK FREE** *Queen – EMI*	**SEVEN AND THE RAGGED TIGER** *Duran Duran – EMI*
16	**TO ALL THE GIRLS I'VE LOVED** *Julio Iglesias & Willie Nelson – Columbia*	**REBEL YELL** *Billy Idol – Chrysalis*	**RELAX** *Frankie Goes To Hollywood – ZZT/Island*	**LEGEND** *Clannad – RCA*
17	**YOU CAN'T GET WHAT YOU...** *Joe Jackson – A & M*	**MIDNIGHT MADNESS** *Night Ranger – Camel/MCA*	**RED GUITAR** *David Sylvian – Virgin*	**LAMENT** *Ultravox – Chrysalis*
18	**EYES WITHOUT A FACE** *Billy Idol – Chrysalis*	**TALK SHOW** *Go-Go's – I.R.S.*	**ONE BETTER DAY** *Madness – Stiff*	**INTO THE GAP** *Thompson Twins – Arista*
19	**ALMOST PARADISE...** *Mike Reno/Anne Wilson – Columbia/CBS*	**UH-HUH** *John Cougar Mellencamp – Riva*	**THINKING OF YOU** *Sister Sledge – Cotillion/Atlantic*	**HYSTERIA** *Human League – Virgin*
20	**DANCING IN THE SHEETS** *Shalamar – Columbia/CBS*	**BODY AND SOUL** *Joe Jackson – A & M*	**BREAK DANCE PARTY** *Break Machine – Record Shack*	**MASTERPIECES** *Sky – Telstar*

WEEK ENDING JUNE 16 1984

	US SINGLES	US ALBUMS	UK SINGLES	UK ALBUMS
1	**TIME AFTER TIME** *Cyndi Lauper – Portrait*	**FOOTLOOSE** *Soundtrack – Columbia/CBS*	**TWO TRIBES** *Frankie Goes To Hollywood – ZZT/Island*	**LEGEND** *Bob Marley And The Wailers – Island*
2	**THE REFLEX** *Duran Duran – Capitol*	**SPORTS** *Huey Lewis And The News – Chrysalis*	**WAKE ME UP BEFORE...** *Wham! – Epic*	**BORN IN THE USA** *Bruce Springsteen – CBS*
3	**LET'S HEAR IT FOR THE BOY** *Deniece Williams – Columbia/CBS*	**CAN'T SLOW DOWN** *Lionel Richie – Motown*	**ONLY WHEN YOU LEAVE** *Spandau Ballet – Reformation/Chrysalis*	**THE WORKS** *Queen – EMI*
4	**OH SHERRIE** *Steve Perry – Columbia/CBS*	**SHE'S SO UNUSUAL** *Cyndi Lauper – Portrait*	**SMALLTOWN BOY** *Bronski Beat – Forbidden Fruit/London*	**AN INNOCENT MAN** *Billy Joel – CBS*
5	**SISTER CHRISTIAN** *Night Ranger – MCA*	**HEARTBEAT CITY** *The Cars – Elektra*	**HIGH ENERGY** *Evelyn Thomas – Record Shack*	**...THAT'S WHAT I CALL MUSIC II** *Various – Virgin/EMI*
6	**THE HEART OF ROCK 'N' ROLL** *Huey Lewis And The News – Chrysalis*	**LOVE AT FIRST STING** *Scorpions – Mercury*	**DANCING WITH TEARS IN MY EYES** *Ultravox – Chrysalis*	**CAN'T SLOW DOWN** *Lionel Richie – Motown*
7	**SELF CONTROL** *Laura Branigan – Atlantic*	**COLOUR BY NUMBERS** *Culture Club – Virgin/Epic*	**PEARL IN THE SHELL** *Howard Jones – WEA*	**HUMAN'S LIB** *Howard Jones – WEA*
8	**JUMP (FOR MY LOVE)** *Pointer Sisters – Planet*	**THRILLER** *Michael Jackson – Epic*	**SAD SONGS (SAY SO MUCH)** *Elton John – Rocket/Phonogram*	**THRILLER** *Michael Jackson – Epic*
9	**DANCING IN THE DARK** *Bruce Springsteen – Columbia/CBS*	**1984** *Van Halen – Warner Bros.*	**LET'S HEAR IT FOR THE BOY** *Deniece Williams – CBS*	**THEN CAME ROCK 'N' ROLL** *Various – EMI*
10	**BORDERLINE** *Madonna – Sire*	**SEVEN AND THE RAGGED TIGER** *Duran Duran – Capitol*	**HEAVEN KNOWS I'M MISERABLE** *The Smiths – Rough Trade*	**HUNGRY FOR HITS** *Various – K-Tel*
11	**EYES WITHOUT A FACE** *Billy Idol – Chrysalis*	**GRACE UNDER PRESSURE** *Rush – Mercury*	**RELAX** *Frankie Goes To Hollywood – ZZT/Island*	**LOST BOYS** *The Flying Pickets – Virgin 10*
12	**BREAKDANCE** *Irene Cara – Geffen/Network*	**STREET TALK** *Steve Perry – Columbia/CBS*	**SEARCHIN'** *Hazell Dean – Proto*	**DON'T STOP DANCING** *Various – Telstar*
13	**IT'S A MIRACLE** *Culture Club – Virgin/Epic*	**AN INNOCENT MAN** *Billy Joel – Columbia/CBS*	**GROOVIN'** *The Style Council – Polydor*	**FOOTLOOSE** *Soundtrack – CBS*
14	**ALMOST PARADISE...** *Mike Reno/Ann Wilson – Columbia CBS*	**INTO THE GAP** *The Thompson Twins – Arista*	**THINKING OF YOU** *Sister Sledge – Cotillion/Atlantic*	**EDEN** *Everything But The Girl – WEA*
15	**HELLO** *Lionel Richie – Motown*	**MIDNIGHT MADNESS** *Night Ranger – Camel/MCA*	**FAREWELL MY SUMMER LOVE** *Michael Jackson – Motown*	**HYAENA** *Siouxsie And The Banshees – Wonderland*
16	**YOU CAN'T GET WHAT YOU...** *Joe Jackson – A & M*	**REBEL YELL** *Billy Idol – Chrysalis*	**I FEEL LIKE BUDDY HOLLY** *Alvin Stardust – Chrysalis*	**FAREWELL MY SUMMER LOVE** *Michael Jackson – Motown*
17	**WHEN DOVES CRY** *Prince – Warner Bros.*	**ELIMINATOR** *ZZ Top – Warner Bros.*	**ONE BETTER DAY** *Madness – Stiff*	**CAFE BLEU** *The Style Council – Polydor*
18	**I'LL WAIT** *Van Halen – Warner Bros.*	**BREAK OUT** *Pointer Sisters – Planet*	**I WON'T LET THE SUN...** *Nik Kershaw – MCA*	**BREAK MACHINE** *Break Machine – Record Shack*
19	**STAY THE NIGHT** *Chicago – Full Moon/Warner Bros.*	**JERMAINE JACKSON** *Jermaine Jackson – Arista*	**THE REFLEX** *Duran Duran – EMI*	**AMERICAN HEARTBEAT** *Various – Epic*
20	**RUN RUNAWAY** *Slade – CBS Associated*	**BODY AND SOUL** *Joe Jackson – A & M*	**SUSANNA** *The Art Company – Epic*	**MASTERPIECES – BEST OF SKY** *Sky – Telstar*

WEEK ENDING JUNE 23 1984

	US SINGLES	US ALBUMS	UK SINGLES	UK ALBUMS
1	**THE REFLEX** *Duran Duran – Capitol*	**FOOTLOOSE** *Soundtrack – Columbia/CBS*	**TWO TRIBES** *Frankie Goes To Hollywood – ZZT/Island*	**LEGEND** *Bob Marley And The Wailers – Island*
2	**TIME AFTER TIME** *Cyndi Lauper – Portrait*	**SPORTS** *Huey Lewis And The News – Chrysalis*	**WAKE ME UP BEFORE…** *Wham! – Epic*	**AN INNOCENT MAN** *Billy Joel – CBS*
3	**LET'S HEAR IT FOR THE BOY** *Deniece Williams – Columbia/CBS*	**CAN'T SLOW DOWN** *Lionel Richie – Motown*	**SMALL TOWN BOY** *Bronski Beat – Forbidden Fruit/London*	**BORN IN THE USA** *Bruce Springsteen – CBS*
4	**DANCING IN THE DARK** *Bruce Springsteen – Columbia/CBS*	**SHE'S SO UNUSUAL** *Cyndi Lauper – Portrait*	**I WON'T LET THE SUN …** *Nik Kershaw – MCA*	**THE WORKS** *Queen – EMI*
5	**SELF CONTROL** *Laura Branigan – Atlantic*	**HEARTBEAT CITY** *The Cars – Elektra*	**RELAX** *Frankie Goes To Hollywood – ZTT/Island*	**THEN CAME ROCK 'N' ROLL** *Various – EMI*
6	**THE HEART OF ROCK 'N' ROLL** *Huey Lewis And The News – Chrysalis*	**LOVE AT FIRST STING** *Scorpions – Mercury*	**ONLY WHEN YOU LEAVE** *Spandau Ballet – Reformation/Chrysalis*	**CAN'T SLOW DOWN** *Lionel Richie – Motown*
7	**JUMP (FOR MY LOVE)** *Pointer Sisters – Planet*	**1984** *Van Halen – Warner Bros.*	**SAD SONGS (SAY SO MUCH)** *Elton John – Rocket/Phonogram*	**AMERICAN HEARTBEAT** *Various – Epic*
8	**WHEN DOVES CRY** *Prince – Warner Bros.*	**THRILLER** *Michael Jackson – Epic*	**FAREWELL MY SUMMER LOVE** *Michael Jackson – Motown*	**CAMOUFLAGE** *Rod Stewart – Warner Bros.*
9	**OH SHERRIE** *Steve Perry – Columbia/CBS*	**BORN IN THE USA** *Bruce Springsteen – Columbia*	**HIGH ENERGY** *Evelyn Thomas – Record Shack*	**FAREWELL MY SUMMER LOVE** *Michael Jackson – Motown*
10	**EYES WITHOUT A FACE** *Billy Idol – Chrysalis*	**SEVEN AND THE RAGGED TIGER** *Duran Duran – Capitol*	**PEARL IN THE SHELL** *Howard Jones – WEA*	**…THAT'S WHAT I CALL MUSIC II** *Various – Virgin/EMI*
11	**BORDERLINE** *Madonna – Sire*	**COLOUR BY NUMBERS** *Culture Club – Virgin/Epic*	**THINKING OF YOU** *Sister Sledge – Cotillion/Atlantic*	**HUMAN'S LIB** *Howard Jones – WEA*
12	**ALMOST PARADISE…** *Mike Reno/Ann Wilson – Columbia/CBS*	**STREET TALK** *Steve Perry – Columbia/CBS*	**SUSANNA** *The Art Company – Epic*	**THRILLER** *Michael Jackson – Epic*
13	**IT'S A MIRACLE** *Culture Club – Virgin/Epic*	**AN INNOCENT MAN** *Billy Joel – Columbia/CBS*	**HEAVEN KNOWS I'M MISERABLE** *The Smiths – Rough Trade*	**BREAKDANCE** *Soundtrack – Polydor*
14	**SISTER CHRISTIAN** *Night Ranger – MCA*	**REBEL YELL** *Billy Idol – Chrysalis*	**DANCING WITH TEARS IN MY…** *Ultravox – Chrysalis*	**LOST BOYS** *The Flying Pickets – Virgin 10*
15	**YOU CAN'T GET WHAT YOU…** *Joe Jackson – A & M*	**MIDNIGHT MADNESS** *Night Ranger – Camel/MCA*	**SEARCHIN'** *Hazell Dean – Proto*	**MASTERPIECES – BEST OF SKY** *Sky – Telstar*
16	**STAY THE NIGHT** *Chicago – Full Moon/Warner Bros.*	**GRACE UNDER PRESSURE** *Rush – Mercury*	**LET'S HEAR IT FOR THE BOY** *Deniece Williams – CBS*	**EDEN** *Everything But The Girl – WEA*
17	**BREAKDANCE** *Irene Cara – Geffen/Network*	**BREAK OUT** *Pointer Sisters – Planet*	**GROOVIN'** *The Style Council – Polydor*	**BREAK MACHINE** *Break Machine – Record Shack*
18	**HELLO** *Lionel Richie – Motown*	**BREAKIN'** *Soundtrack – Polydor*	**I FEEL LIKE BUDDY HOLLY** *Alvin Stardust – Chrysalis*	**CAFE BLEU** *The Style Council – Polydor*
19	**LEGS** *ZZ Top – Warner Bros.*	**JERMAINE JACKSON** *Jermaine Jackson – Arista*	**CHANGE OF HEART** *Change – WEA*	**FOOTLOOSE** *Soundtrack – CBS*
20	**MAGIC** *The Cars – Elektra*	**ELIMINATOR** *ZZ Top – Warner Bros.*	**SO TIRED** *Ozzy Osbourne – Epic*	**HUNGRY FOR HITS** *Various – K-Tel*

WEEK ENDING JUNE 30 1984

	US SINGLES	US ALBUMS	UK SINGLES	UK ALBUMS
1	**THE REFLEX** *Duran Duran – Capitol*	**SPORTS** *Huey Lewis And The News – Chrysalis*	**TWO TRIBES** *Frankie Goes To Hollywood – ZTT/Island*	**LEGEND** *Bob Marley And The Wailers – Island*
2	**DANCING IN THE DARK** *Bruce Springsteen – Columbia/CBS*	**FOOTLOOSE** *Soundtrack – Columbia/CBS*	**I WON'T LET THE SUN…** *Nik Kershaw – MCA*	**BREAKING HEARTS** *Elton John – Rocket/Phonogram*
3	**WHEN DOVES CRY** *Prince – Warner Bros.*	**BORN IN THE USA** *Bruce Springsteen – Columbia/CBS*	**RELAX** *Frankie Goes To Hollywood – ZTT/Island*	**AN INNOCENT MAN** *Billy Joel – CBS*
4	**SELF CONTROL** *Laura Branigan – Atlantic*	**CAN'T SLOW DOWN** *Lionel Richie – Motown*	**SMALL TOWN BOY** *Bronski Beat – Forbidden Fruit/London*	**AMERICAN HEARTBEAT** *Various – Epic*
5	**JUMP (FOR MY LOVE)** *Pointer Sisters – Planet*	**HEARTBEAT CITY** *The Cars – Elektra*	**WAKE ME UP BEFORE…** *Wham! – Epic*	**CAN'T SLOW DOWN** *Lionel Richie – Motown*
6	**THE HEART OF ROCK 'N' ROLL** *Huey Lewis And The News – Chrysalis*	**SHE'S SO UNUSUAL** *Cyndi Lauper – Portrait*	**JUMP (FOR MY LOVE)** *Pointer Sisters – Planet*	**BREAKDANCE** *Soundtrack – Polydor*
7	**TIME AFTER TIME** *Cyndi Lauper – Portrait*	**1984** *Van Halen – Warner Bros.*	**FAREWELL MY SUMMER LOVE** *Michael Jackson – Motown*	**BORN IN THE USA** *Bruce Springsteen – CBS*
8	**EYES WITHOUT A FACE** *Billy Idol – Chrysalis*	**THRILLER** *Michael Jackson – Epic*	**…THERE'S NO STOPPING US** *Ollie & Jerry – Polydor*	**THE WORKS** *Queen – EMI*
9	**LET'S HEAR IT FOR THE BOY** *Deniece Williams – Columbia/CBS*	**LOVE AT FIRST STING** *Scorpions – Mercury*	**SAD SONGS (SAY SO MUCH)** *Elton John – Rocket/Phonogram*	**FAREWELL MY SUMMER LOVE** *Michael Jackson – Motown*
10	**ALMOST PARADISE…** *Mike Reno/Ann Wilson – Columbia/CBS*	**SEVEN AND THE RAGGED TIGER** *Duran Duran – Capitol*	**TIME AFTER TIME** *Cyndi Lauper – Portrait/Epic*	**CAMOUFLAGE** *Rod Stewart – Warner Bros.*
11	**OH SHERRIE** *Steve Perry – Columbia/CBS*	**REBEL YELL** *Billy Idol – Chrysalis*	**THINKING OF YOU** *Sister Sledge – Cotillion/Atlantic*	**THRILLER** *Michael Jackson – Epic*
12	**BORDERLINE** *Madonna – Sire*	**STREET TALK** *Steve Perry – Columbia/CBS*	**WHITE LINES (DON'T DO IT)** *Grandmaster & Melle Mel – Sugar Hill*	**THEN CAME ROCK 'N' ROLL** *Various – EMI*
13	**LEGS** *ZZ Top – Warner Bros.*	**COLOUR BY NUMBERS** *Culture Club – Virgin/Epic*	**SUSANNÁ** *The Art Company – Epic*	**HUMAN'S LIB** *Howard Jones – WEA*
14	**IT'S A MIRACLE** *Culture Club – Virgin/Epic*	**AN INNOCENT MAN** *Billy Joel – Columbia/CBS*	**HIGH ENERGY** *Evelyn Thomas – Record Shack*	**…THAT'S WHAT I CALL MUSIC II** *Various – Virgin/EMI*
15	**MAGIC** *The Cars – Elektra*	**MIDNIGHT MADNESS** *Night Ranger – Camel/MCA*	**TALKING LOUD AND CLEAR** *OMD – Virgin*	**HUMAN RACING** *Nik Kershaw – MCA*
16	**STAY THE NIGHT** *Chicago – Full Moon/Warner Bros.*	**BREAKIN'** *Soundtrack – Polydor*	**ONLY WHEN YOU LEAVE** *Spandau Ballet – Reformation/Chrysalis*	**PRIVATE DANCER** *Tina Turner – Capitol*
17	**DOCTOR! DOCTOR!** *The Thompson Twins – Arista*	**BREAK OUT** *Pointer Sisters – Planet*	**CHANGE OF HEART** *Change – WEA*	**BREAK OUT** *Pointer Sisters – Planet*
18	**INFATUATION** *Rod Stewart – Warner Bros.*	**ELIMINATOR** *ZZ Top – Warner Bros.*	**STUCK ON YOU** *Lionel Richie – Motown*	**FOOTLOOSE** *Soundtrack – CBS*
19	**DANCE HALL DAYS** *Wang Chung – Geffen*	**GERMAINE JACKSON** *Germaine Jackson – Arista*	**ABSOLUTE** *Scritti Politti – Virgin*	**CAFE BLEU** *The Style Council – Polydor*
20	**SAD SONGS (SAY SO MUCH)** *Elton John – Geffen*	**MADONNA** *Madonna – Sire*	**HEAVEN KNOWS I'M MISERABLE** *The Smiths – Rough Trade*	**LOST BOYS** *The Flying Pickets – Virgin 10*

WEEK ENDING JULY 7 1984

US SINGLES

1 **WHEN DOVES CRY**
Prince – Warner Bros.

2 **DANCING IN THE DARK**
Bruce Springsteen – Columbia/CBS

3 **JUMP (FOR MY LOVE)**
Pointer Sisters – Planet

4 **SELF CONTROL**
Laura Branigan – Atlantic

5 **THE REFLEX**
Duran Duran – Capitol

6 **EYES WITHOUT A FACE**
Billy Idol – Chrysalis

7 **TIME AFTER TIME**
Cyndi Lauper – Portrait

8 **ALMOST PARADISE…**
Mike Reno/Ann Wilson – Columbia/CBS

9 **THE HEART OF ROCK 'N' ROLL**
Huey Lewis And The News – Chrysalis

10 **LEGS**
ZZ Top – Warner Bros.

11 **LET'S HEAR IT FOR THE BOY**
Deniece Williams – Columbia/CBS

12 **MAGIC**
The Cars – Elektra

13 **DOCTOR! DOCTOR!**
The Thompson Twins – Arista

14 **INFATUATION**
Rod Stewart – Warner Bros.

15 **BORDERLINE**
Madonna – Sire

16 **DANCE HALL DAYS**
Wang Chung – Geffen

17 **SAD SONGS (SAY SO MUCH)**
Elton John – Geffen

18 **OH SHERRIE**
Steve Perry – Columbia/CBS

19 **GHOST BUSTERS**
Ray Parker Jr – Arista

20 **…THERE'S NO STOPPING US**
Ollie & Jerry – Polydor

US ALBUMS

1 **BORN IN THE USA**
Bruce Springsteen – Columbia/CBS

2 **SPORTS**
Huey Lewis And The News – Chrysalis

3 **FOOTLOOSE**
Soundtrack – Columbia/CBS

4 **HEARTBEAT CITY**
The Cars – Elektra

5 **CAN'T SLOW DOWN**
Lionel Richie – Motown

6 **SHE'S SO UNUSUAL**
Cyndi Lauper – Portrait

7 **1984**
Van Halen – Warner Bros.

8 **LOVE AT FIRST STING**
Scorpions – Mercury

9 **REBEL YELL**
Billy Idol – Chrysalis

10 **SEVEN AND THE RAGGED TIGER**
Duran Duran – Capitol

11 **BREAKIN'**
Soundtrack – Polydor

12 **THRILLER**
Michael Jackson – Epic

13 **ELIMINATOR**
ZZ Top – Warner Bros.

14 **AN INNOCENT MAN**
Billy Idol – Chrysalis

15 **MIDNIGHT MADNESS**
Night Ranger – Camel/MCA

16 **COLOUR BY NUMBERS**
Culture Club – Virgin/Epic

17 **BREAK OUT**
Pointer Sisters – Planet

18 **MADONNA**
Madonna – Sire

19 **STREET TALK**
Steve Perry – Columbia/CBS

20 **OUT OF THE CELLAR**
Ratt – Atlantic

UK SINGLES

1 **TWO TRIBES**
Frankie Goes To Hollywood – ZTT/Island

2 **RELAX**
Frankie Goes To Hollywood – ZTT/Island

3 **I WON'T LET THE SUN…**
Nik Kershaw – MCA

4 **TIME AFTER TIME**
Cyndi Lauper – Portrait/Epic

5 **…THERE'S NO STOPPING US**
Ollie & Jerry – Polydor

6 **JUMP (FOR MY LOVE)**
Pointer Sisters – Planet

7 **SMALLTOWN BOY**
Bronski Beat – Forbidden Fruit/London

8 **FAREWELL MY SUMMER LOVE**
Michael Jackson – Motown

9 **WAKE ME UP BEFORE…**
Wham! – Epic

10 **WHITE LINES (DON'T DO IT)**
Grandmaster & Melle Mel – Sugar Hill

11 **TALKING LOUD AND CLEAR**
OMD – Virgin

12 **STUCK ON YOU**
Lionel Richie – Motown

13 **THINKING YOU YOU**
Sister Sledge – Cotillion/Atlantic

14 **LOVE RESURRECTION**
Alison Moyet – CBS

15 **SAD SONGS (SAY SO MUCH)**
Elton John – Rocket/Phonogram

16 **LIFE ON YOUR OWN**
Human League – Virgin

17 **ABSOLUTE**
Scritti Politti – Virgin

18 **WHAT'S LOVE GOT TO DO WITH IT**
Tina Turner – Capitol

19 **CHANGE OF HEART**
Change – WEA

20 **YOUNG AT HEART**
The Bluebells – London

UK ALBUMS

1 **LEGEND**
Bob Marley And The Wailers – Island

2 **PARADE**
Spandau Ballet

3 **BREAKING HEARTS**
Elton John – Rocket/Phonogram

4 **BRILLIANT TREES**
David Sylvian – Virgin

5 **AMERICAN HEARTBEAT**
Various – Epic

6 **AN INNOCENT MAN**
Billy Joel – CBS

7 **CAN'T SLOW DOWN**
Lionel Richie – Motown

8 **HUMAN RACING**
Nik Kershaw – MCA

9 **BREAKDANCE**
Soundtrack – Polydor

10 **GOODBYE CRUEL WORLD**
Elvis Costello And The Attractions – F-Beat

11 **THRILLER**
Michael Jackson – Epic

12 **BREAK OUT**
Pointers Sisters – Planet

13 **THE WORKS**
Queen – EMI

14 **HUMAN'S LIB**
Howard Jones – WEA

15 **DISCOVERY**
Mike Oldfield – Virgin

16 **…THAT'S WHAT I CALL MUSIC II**
Various – Virgin/EMI

17 **FAREWELL MY SUMMER LOVE**
Michael Jackson – Motown

18 **BORN IN THE USA**
Bruce Springsteen – CBS

19 **PRIVATE DANCER**
Tina Turner – Capitol

20 **CAMOUFLAGE**
Rod Stewart – Warner Bros.

WEEK ENDING JULY 14 1984

US SINGLES

1 **WHEN DOVES CRY**
Prince – Warner Bros.

2 **DANCING IN THE DARK**
Bruce Springsteen – Columbia

3 **JUMP (FOR MY LOVE)**
The Pointer Sisters – Planet

4 **EYES WITHOUT A FACE**
Billy Idol – Chrysalis

5 **THE REFLEX**
Duran Duran – Capitol

6 **SELF CONTROL**
Laura Branigan – Atlantic

7 **ALMOST PARADISE…**
Mike Reno/Ann Wilson – Columbia

8 **GHOSTBUSTERS**
Ray Parker Jr – Arista

9 **THE HEART OF ROCK 'N' ROLL**
Huey Lewis And The News – Chrysalis

10 **LEGS**
ZZ Top – Warner Bros

11 **INFATUATION**
Rod Stewart – Warner Bros.

12 **MAGIC**
The Cars – Elektra

13 **DOCTOR! DOCTOR!**
The Thompson Twins – Arista

14 **TIME AFTER TIME**
Cyndi Lauper – Portrait

15 **STATE OF SHOCK**
The Jacksons – Epic

16 **SAD SONGS (SAY SO MUCH)**
Elton John – Geffen

17 **…THERE'S NO STOPPING US**
Ollie And Jerry – Polydor

18 **DANCE HALL DAYS**
Wang Chung – Geffen

19 **BORDERLINE**
Madonna – Sire

20 **I CAN DREAM ABOUT YOU**
Dan Hartman – MCA

US ALBUMS

1 **BORN IN THE USA**
Bruce Springsteen – Columbia

2 **SPORTS**
Huey Lewis And The News – Chrysalis

3 **HEARTBEAT CITY**
The Cars – Elektra

4 **FOOTLOOSE**
Soundtrack – Columbia

5 **CAN'T SLOW DOWN**
Lionel Richie – Motown

6 **REBEL YELL**
Billy Idol – Chrysalis

7 **1984**
Van Halen – Warner Bros.

8 **SEVEN AND THE RAGGED TIGER**
Duran Duran – Capitol

9 **BREAKIN'**
Soundtrack – Polydor

10 **ELIMINATOR**
ZZ Top – Warner Bros.

11 **PURPLE RAIN**
Prince And The Revolution – Warner Bros.

12 **SHE'S SO UNUSUAL**
Cyndi Lauper – Portrait

13 **LOVE AT FIRST STING**
Scorpions – Mercury

14 **THRILLER**
Michael Jackson – Epic

15 **OUT OF THE CELLAR**
Ratt – Atlantic

16 **BEAT STREET**
Soundtrack – Atlantic

17 **BREAK OUT**
The Pointers Sisters – Planet

18 **MADONNA**
Madonna – Sire

19 **STREET TALK**
Steve Perry – Columbia

20 **MIDNIGHT MADNESS**
Night Ranger – Camel/MCA

UK SINGLES

1 **TWO TRIBES**
Frankie Goes To Hollywood – ZTT/Island

2 **RELAX**
Frankie Goes To Hollywood – ZTT/Island

3 **TIME AFTER TIME**
Cyndi Lauper – Portrait/Epic

4 **I WON'T LET THE SUN…**
Nik Kershaw – MCA

5 **HOLE IN MY SHOE**
Neil – WEA

6 **…THERE'S NO STOPPING US**
Ollie & Jerry – Polydor

7 **JUMP (FOR MY LOVE)**
Pointer Sisters – Planet

8 **WHEN DOVES CRY**
Prince – Warner Bros

9 **WHITE LINES (DON'T DO IT)**
Grandmaster & Mell Mel – Sugar Hill

10 **WHAT'S LOVE GOT TO DO IT**
Tina Turner – Capitol

11 **SISTER OF MERCY**
The Thompson Twins – Arista

12 **SMALLTOWN BOY**
Bronski Beat – Forbidden Fruit/London

13 **LOVE RESURRECTION**
Alison Moyet – CBS

14 **YOUNG AT HEART**
The Bluebells – London

15 **TALKING LOUD AND CLEAR**
OMD – Virgin

16 **FAREWELL MY SUMMER LOVE**
Michael Jackson – Motown

17 **STUCK ON YOU**
Lionel Richie – Motown

18 **WAKE ME UP BEFORE…**
Wham! – Epic

19 **THINKING OF YOU**
Sister Sledge – Cotillion/Atlantic

20 **STATE OF SHOCK**
The Jacksons/Mick Jagger – Epic

UK ALBUMS

1 **LEGEND**
Bob Marley And The Wailers – Island

2 **PARADE**
Spandau Ballet – Reformation/Chrysalis

3 **BREAKING HEARTS**
Elton John – Rocket/Phonogram

4 **CAN'T SLOW DOWN**
Lionel Richie – Motown

5 **HUMAN RACING**
Nik Kershaw – MCA

6 **AN INNOCENT MAN**
Billy Joel – CBS

7 **AMERICAN HEARTBEAT**
Various – Epic

8 **BREAKDANCE**
Various – Polydor

9 **BREAK OUT**
Pointer Sisters – Planet

10 **THRILLER**
Michael Jackson – Epic

11 **BRILLIANT TREES**
David Sylvian – Virgin

12 **GOODBYE CRUEL WORLD**
Elvis Costello And The Attractions – F-Beat

13 **HUMAN'S LIB**
Howard Jones – WEA

14 **THE WORKS**
Queen – EMI

15 **…THAT'S WHAT I CALL MUSIC II**
Various – Virgin/EMI

16 **PRIVATE DANCER**
Tina Turner – Capitol

17 **DISCOVERY**
Mike Oldfield – Virgin

18 **INTO THE GAP**
Thompson Twins – Arista

19 **FAREWELL MY SUMMER LOVE**
Michael Jackson – Motown

20 **BORN IN THE USA**
Bruce Springsteen – CBS

WEEK ENDING JULY 21 1984

US SINGLES	US ALBUMS	UK SINGLES	UK ALBUMS
1 WHEN DOVES CRY *Prince – Warner Bros.*	**1 BORN IN THE USA** *Bruce Springsteen – Columbia/CBS*	**1 TWO TRIBES** *Frankie Goes To Hollywood – ZZT/Island*	**1 LEGEND** *Bob Marley And The Wailers – Island*
2 DANCING IN THE DARK *Bruce Springsteen – Columbia/CBS*	**2 SPORTS** *Huey Lewis And The News – Chrysalis*	**2 HOLE IN MY SHOE** *Neil – WEA*	**2 PARADE** *Spandau Ballet – Reformation/Chrysalis*
3 GHOSTBUSTERS *Ray Parker Jr – Arista*	**3 PURPLE RAIN** *Prince And The Revolution – Warner Bros.*	**3 RELAX** *Frankie Goes To Hollywood – ZTT/Island*	**3 VICTORY** *The Jacksons – Epic*
4 EYES WITHOUT A FACE *Billy Idol – Chrysalis*	**4 HEARTBEAT CITY** *The Cars – Elektra*	**4 TIME AFTER TIME** *Cyndi Lauper – Portrait*	**4 THE LAST IN LINE** *Dio – Vertigo*
5 JUMP (FOR MY LOVE) *Pointer Sisters – Planet*	**5 CAN'T SLOW DOWN** *Lionel Richie – Motown*	**5 WHEN DOVES CRY** *Prince – Warner Bros.*	**5 CAN'T SLOW DOWN** *Lionel Richie – Motown*
6 STATE OF SHOCK *The Jacksons/Mick Jagger – Epic*	**6 REBEL YELL** *Billy Idol – Chrysalis*	**6 WHAT'S LOVE GOT TO DO WITH IT** *Tina Turner – Capitol*	**6 AN INNOCENT MAN** *Billy Joel – CBS*
7 ALMOST PARADISE *Mike Reno/Ann Wilson – Columbia/CBS*	**7 FOOTLOOSE** *Soundtrack – Columbia/CBS*	**7 I WON'T LET THE SUN...** *Nik Kershaw – MCA*	**7 BREAKING HEARTS** *Elton John – Rocket*
8 LEGS *ZZ Top – Warner Bros.*	**8 BREAKIN'** *Soundtrack – Polydor*	**8 WHITE LINES (DON'T DO IT)** *Grandmaster & Melle Mel – Sugarhill*	**8 HUMAN RACING** *Nick Kershaw – MCA*
9 SAD SONGS (SAY SO MUCH) *Elton John – Geffen*	**9 1984** *Van Halen – Warner Bros.*	**9 JUMP (FOR MY LOVE)** *Pointer Sisters – Planet*	**9 BREAKDANCE** *Original Soundtrack – Polydor*
10 INFATUATION *Rod Stewart – Warner Bros.*	**10 ELIMINATOR** *ZZ Top – Warner Bros.*	**10 YOUNG AT HEART** *The Bluebells – London*	**10 PRIVATE DANCER** *Tina Turner – Capitol*
11 DOCTOR! DOCTOR! *The Thompson Twins – Arista*	**11 SEVEN AND THE RAGGED TIGER** *Duran Duran – Capitol*	**11 SISTER OF MERCY** *Thompson Twins – Arista*	**11 THRILLER** *Michael Jackson – Epic*
12 MAGIC *The Cars – Elektra*	**12 OUT OF THE CELLAR** *Ratt – Atlantic*	**12 LOVE RESURRECTION** *Alison Moyet – CBS*	**12 BREAK OUT** *Pointer Sisters – Planet*
13 ...THERE'S NO STOPPING US *Ollie & Jerry – Polydor*	**13 SHE'S SO UNUSUAL** *Cyndi Lauper – Portrait*	**13 ...THERE'S NO STOPPING US** *Ollie & Jerry – Polydor*	**13 AMERICAN HEARTBEAT** *Various – Epic*
14 THE REFLEX *Duran Duran – Capitol*	**14 BEAT STREET** *Soundtrack – Atlantic*	**14 STATE OF SHOCK** *The Jacksons/Mick Jagger – Epic*	**14 THE WORKS** *Queen – EMI*
15 SELF CONTROL *Laura Branigan – Atlantic*	**15 MIDNIGHT MADNESS** *Night Ranger – Camel/MCA*	**15 EVERYBODY'S LAUGHING** *Phil Fearon & Galaxy – Ensign*	**15 INTO THE GAP** *The Thompson Twins – Arista*
16 WHAT'S LOVE GOT TO DO WITH IT *Tina Turner – Capitol*	**16 BREAK OUT** *Pointer Sisters – Planet*	**16 TALKING LOUD AND CLEAR** *OMD – Virgin*	**16 DISCOVERY** *Mike Oldfield – Virgin*
17 I CAN DREAM ABOUT YOU *Dan Hartman – MCA*	**17 VICTORY** *Jacksons – Epic*	**17 SEVEN SEAS** *Echo And The Bunnymen – Korova*	**17 ...THAT'S WHAT I CALL MUSIC II** *Various – EMI/Virgin*
18 STUCK ON YOU *Lionel Richie – Motown*	**18 LOVE AT FIRST STING** *Scorpions – Mercury*	**18 STUCK ON YOU** *Lionel Richie – Motown*	**18 HUMAN'S LIB** *Howard Jones – WEA*
19 THE HEART OF ROCK 'N' ROLL *Huey Lewis And The News – Chrysalis*	**19 STREET TALK** *Steve Perry – Columbia/CBS*	**19 SMALLTOWN BOY** *Bronski Beat – Forbidden Fruit*	**19 SHE'S SO UNUSUAL** *Cyndi Lauper – Portrait*
20 DANCE HALL DAYS *Wang Chung – Geffen*	**20 THRILLER** *Michael Jackson – Epic*	**20 FAREWELL MY SUMMER LOVE** *Michael Jackson – Motown*	**20 BRILLIANT TREES** *David Sylvian – Virgin*

WEEK ENDING JULY 28 1984

US SINGLES	US ALBUMS	UK SINGLES	UK ALBUMS
1 WHEN DOVES CRY *Prince – Warner Bros.*	**1 BORN IN THE USA** *Bruce Springsteen – Columbia*	**1 TWO TRIBES** *Frankie Goes To Hollywood – ZTT/Island*	**1 LEGEND** *Bob Marley & The Wailers – Island*
2 GHOSTBUSTERS *Ray Parker Jr – Arista*	**2 PURPLE RAIN** *Prince And The Revolution – Warner Bros.*	**2 HOLE IN MY SHOE** *Neil – WEA*	**2 DIAMOND LIFE** *Sade – Epic*
3 DANCING IN THE DARK *Bruce Springsteen – Columbia*	**3 SPORTS** *Huey Lewis And The News – Chrysalis*	**3 RELAX** *Frankie Goes To Hollywood – ZTT/Island*	**3 CAN'T SLOW DOWN** *Lionel Richie – Motown*
4 STATE OF SHOCK *The Jacksons/Mick Jagger – Epic*	**4 HEARTBEAT CITY** *The Cars – Elektra*	**4 WHEN DOVES CRY** *Prince – Warner Bros.*	**4 PARADE** *Spandau Ballet – Chrysalis*
5 EYES WITHOUT A FACE *Billy Idol – Chrysalis*	**5 CAN'T SLOW DOWN** *Lionel Richie – Motown*	**5 WHAT'S LOVE GOT TO DO WITH IT** *Tina Turner – Capitol*	**5 PRIVATE DANCER** *Tina Turner – Capitol*
6 INFATUATION *Rod Stewart – Warner Bros.*	**6 REBEL YELL** *Billy Idol – Chrysalis*	**6 TIME AFTER TIME** *Cyndi Lauper – Portrait*	**6 AN INNOCENT MAN** *Billy Joel – CBS*
7 SAD SONGS (SAY SO MUCH) *Elton John – Geffen*	**7 VICTORY** *The Jacksons – Epic*	**7 WHITE LINES (DON'T DO IT)** *Grandmaster & Melle Mel Sugarhill*	**7 PRIMITIVE** *Neil Diamond – CBS*
8 LEGS *ZZ Top – Warner Bros.*	**8 BREAKIN'** *Soundtrack – Polydor*	**8 YOUNG AT HEART** *Bluebells – London*	**8 THRILLER** *Michael Jackson – Epic*
9 WHAT'S LOVE GOT TO DO WITH IT *Tina Turner – Capitol*	**9 FOOTLOOSE** *Soundtrack – Columbia*	**9 I WON'T LET THE SUN . . .** *Nik Kershaw – MCA*	**9 VICTORY** *Jacksons – Epic*
10 JUMP (FOR MY LOVE) *Pointer Sisters – Planet*	**10 1984** *Van Halen – Warner Bros.*	**10 LOVE RESURRECTION** *Alison Moyet – CBS*	**10 THE LAST IN LINE** *Dio – Vertigo*
11 ...THERE'S NO STOPPING US *Ollie & Jerry – Polydor*	**11 OUT OF THE CELLAR** *Ratt – Atlantic*	**11 JUMP (FOR MY LOVE)** *Pointer Sisters – Planet*	**11 THE WORKS** *Queen – EMI*
12 ALMOST PARADISE... *Mike Reno/Ann Wilson – Columbia*	**12 ELIMINATOR** *ZZ Top – Warner Bros.*	**12 EVERYBODY'S LAUGHING** *Galaxy/Phil Fearon – Ensign*	**12 HUMAN RACING** *Nik Kershaw – MCA*
13 I CAN DREAM ABOUT YOU *Dan Hartman – MCA*	**13 SEVEN AND THE RAGGED TIGER** *Duran Duran – Capitol*	**13 SISTER OF MERCY** *The Thompson Twins – Arista*	**13 BREAKDANCE** *Soundtrack – Polydor*
14 DOCTOR! DOCTOR! *The Thompson Twins – Arista*	**14 BEAT STREET** *Soundtrack – Atlantic*	**14 ...THERE'S NO STOPPING US** *Ollie & Jerry Polydor*	**14 BREAKING HEARTS** *Elton John – Rocket*
15 STUCK ON YOU *Lionel Richie – Motown*	**15 MIDNIGHT MADNESS** *Night Ranger – Camel/MCA*	**15 DOWN ON THE STREET** *Shakatak – Polydor*	**15 BREAK OUT** *Pointer Sisters – Planet*
16 MAGIC *The Cars – Elektra*	**16 BREAK OUT** *The Pointer Sisters – Planet*	**16 SEVEN SEAS** *Echo And The Bunnymen – Korova*	**16 INTO THE GAP** *The Thompson Twins – Arista*
17 SELF CONTROL *Laura Branigan – Atlantic*	**17 LOVE AT FIRST STING** *Scorpions – Mercury*	**17 YOU THINK YOU'RE A MAN** *Divine – Proto*	**17 AMERICAN HEARTBEAT** *Various – Epic*
18 IF EVER YOU'RE IN MY ARMS... *Peabo Bryson – Elektra*	**18 PRIVATE DANCER** *Tina Turner – Capitol*	**18 CLOSEST THING TO HEAVEN** *Kane Gang – Kitchenware*	**18 SHE'S SO UNUSUAL** *Cyndi Lauper – Portrait*
19 SUNGLASSES AT NIGHT *Corey Hart – EMI America*	**19 GHOSTBUSTERS** *Soundtrack – Arista*	**19 STATE OF SHOCK** *The Jacksons Mick Jagger Epic*	**19 ...THAT'S WHAT I CALL MUSIC II** *Various – EMI/Virgin*
20 PANAMA *Van Halen – Warner Bros.*	**20 THRILLER** *Michael Jackson – Epic*	**20 COME BACK** *Mighty Wah! – Beggars Banquet*	**20 HUMAN'S LIB** *Howard Jones – WEA*

ROCK REFERENCE

 RECORD COMPANIES/UK

A&M Records
(01) 736-3311
136-140 New Kings Road
London SW6 4LZ
Labels: Respond, IRS, Fascination, Piggy
Bank

Abstract Records
(01) 969-4018
35 Kempe Road
London NW6 6SP

Ace Records
(01) 267-5192
132-34 Grafton Road
Kentish Town
London N5

Albion Records Ltd
(01) 243-0011, 221-3113
119-21 Freston Road
London W11 4BD

Anagram Records
(01) 727-0346
53 Kensington Gardens Square
London W2 4BA

Arista/Ariola
(01) 580-5566
3 Cavendish Square
London W1

Aura Records And Music Ltd
(01) 486-5288
1 Kendall Place
London W1H 3AG

Backs Recording Company Ltd
(0603) 26221
St Mary's Works
St Mary's Plain
Norwich NR3 3AF

Bam-Caruso Records
(0727)) 32109
9 Ridgmont Road
St Albans
Herts

BBC Records And Tapes
(01) 580-4468
The Langham
Portland Place
London W1A 1AA

Beggars Banquet
(01) 870-9912
17-19 Alma Road
London SW18

Big Bear Records
(021) 454-7020
190 Monument Road
Birmingham B16 8UU

Bridge House Records Ltd
(01) 476-9947
15 Tinto Road
London E16 4BB

Bright Records
(01) 408-0288
34-36 Maddox Street
London W1R 9PD

Bronze Records
(01) 267-4499
100 Chalk Farm Road
London NW1 8EH

Burning Rome Records Ltd
(01) 240-7453
25 Denmark Street
London WC2

Carrere Records
(01) 437-7581
3rd Floor
Mutual House
193-97 Regent Street
London W1

CBS
(01) 734-8181
17-19 Soho Square
London W1
Labels: Epic, Geffen, Portrait, Full Moon,
Kitchenware, Monument, Philadelphia
International, Kirshner, Tabu, Caribou,
Unlimited Gold, Boardwalk, Prelude, Blue
Sky, Alfa, Scotti Bros, Inner Vision.

Charisma Records
(01) 434-1351
90 Wardour Street
London W1

Charly Records Ltd
(01) 639-8603/4/5/6
156-77 Ilderton Road
London SE15 1NT

Cherry Red Records
(01) 229-8854/5
53 Kensington Gardens Square
London W2 4BA

Chrysalis
(01) 408-2355
12 Stratford Place
London W1N 9AF
Labels: Two Tone, Reformation, Air

Clay Records Ltd
(0782) 273324/261990
26 Hope Street
Stoke-On-Trent

Cocteau Records
(01) 398-6413
P.O.Box 134A
Thames Ditton
Surrey

Compact-Organization
(01) 580-1617
Compact House
31 Riding House Street
London W1P 7PG

Crass Records
(01) 888-8949
10 Myddleton Road
London N22 4NS

Creole Records Ltd
(01) 965-9223
91-93 High Street
Harlesden
London NW10
Labels: Polo, Dynamic, Ecstasy, Replay,
Ocean, Cactus, Blast From The Past, Silver
Screen, Everest Europa, Timeless
Treasures

Demon Records
(01) 847-2481
Western House
Harlequin Avenue
Great West Road
Brentford
Middlesex TW8 9EW

Dep International
(021) 643-1321
92 Fazeley Street
Digbeth
Birmingham B5 5RD

DJM Records
(01) 242-6886
James House
5-11 Theobalds Road
London WC1X 8SE

Don't Fall Off The Mountain
(01) 870-9912
17-19 Alma Road
Wandsworth
London SW5

EG Records
(01) 730-2162
63a Kings Road
London SW3 4NT

EMI Records
(01) 486-4488
20 Manchester Square
London W1A 1ES
Labels: Harvest, Parlophone, Columbia,
Rolling Stones, Capitol, Liberty, HMV, EMI
America, MFP, LFP, CFP, World Records,
Sunset, Zonophone, Starline

Ensign Records Ltd
(01) 727-0527
3 Monmouth Place
Off Monmouth Road
London W2 5SH

Factory Communications Limited
(061) 434-3876
86 Palatine Road
Manchester 20

Fast Product
(031) 661-5811
3-4 East Norton Place
Edinburgh
Labels: Pop Aural, Accessory

F-Beat
(01) 847-2481
Western House
Harlequin Avenue
Great West Road
Brentford
Middlesex TW8 9EW

Flicknife
(01) 743-9412
82 Adelaide Grove
London W12

Glass Records
(01) 740-9268
The Metrostore
231 The Vale
Acton
London W3

The Go! Label
(01) 743-3845/3919
Go! Mansions
8 Wendell Road
London W12

Graduate Records Ltd
(0384) 59048/211159
196 Wolverhampton Street
Dudley
West Midlands
Labels: Ready Steady Go!, Assorted
Images

Greensleeves Records Ltd
(01) 749-3277/8
44 Uxbridge Road
Shepherds Bush
London W12

Hannibal Records
(01) 370-6166
3 Logan Place
London W8

Heartbeat Productions
(0272) 730458
14c Lansdown Place
Clifton
Bristol BS8 3AF

Ice Record Company
(01) 730-7291
P.O.Box 212
London SW1 4PU

Illuminated Records
(01) 381-1393
452 Fulham Road
London SW6

Imperial Recordings
(01) 969-9414
Kensaltown Works
Kensal Road
London W10

IRS (International Recording Syndicate)
(01) 727-0734
194 Kensington Park Road
London W11 2ES
Labels: Illegal

Island Records
(01) 741-1551
22 St Peter's Square
London W6 9NW
Labels: Ensign, Genetic, Island, Visual Arts, Ze, Zang Tuum Tumb, Stiff

Jamming Records
(01) 602-0048
69 Hammersmith Road
London W14

Jet
(01) 637-2111
35 Portland Place
London W1N 3AG

Kitchenware Records
(0632) 618036
62 Clayton Street
Newcastle-Upon-Tyne 1

K-Tel International Ltd
(01) 992-8055
K-Tel House
620 Western Avenue
London W3 0TU

Lamborghini Records
(0491) 34340
Brook Lodge
North Stoke
Wallingford
Oxfordshire

Lightning Records
(01) 969-5255
841 Harrow Road
London NW10 5N4

London Records
(01) 491-4600
15 St George Street
London W1

MCA
(01) 439-9951
72-74 Brewer Street
London W1

Magnet Records
(01) 486-8151
Magnet House
22 York Street
London W1H 1FD

Music For Pleasure
(01) 561-3125
1-3 Uxbridge Road
Hayes
Middlesex UB4 0SY

Mute Records
(01) 221-4840
49-53 Kensington Gardens Square
London W2

Neat Records
(091) 262-4999
71 High Street
East Wallsend
Tyne And Wear NE28 7RJ
Labels: Wudwink, Rigid, Completely Different, Floating World

Oily Records
(0224) 632749
6 Cedar Place
Aberdeen

Old Gold Records
(01) 884-2220
Unit 1
Langhedge
Edmonton N18 2TQ

Oval Records
(01) 622-0111
11 Liston Road
London SW4

People Unite Musicians Co-op And Publications
(01) 574-1718/1453
2a Dudley Road
Southall
Middlesex

Phonogram Limited
(01) 491-4600
50 New Bond Street
London W1Y 9HA
Labels: Mercury, Vertigo, Phillips, De-Lite, Casablanca, Some Bizarre, Rocket, Neutron, Club

Pickwick International Inc.Ltd
(01) 200-7000
The Hyde Industrial Estate
The Hyde
London NW9 6JU
Labels: Hallmark, Contour, Camden, Countour Classics, Spot, Ditto, Scoop.

Polydor
(01) 499-8686
13-14 St George Street
London W1R 9DE
Labels: RSO, MGM, Verve, Fiction, Obscure, Dreamland, Wonderland, 21 Records

Pop Aural
(031) 661-5811
3-4 East Norton Place
Edinburgh

President Records Ltd
(01) 839-4672/5
Broadmead House
21 Panton Street
London SW1 4DR
Labels: Bulldog, Crystal, Dart, Energy, Enterprise, Gemini, Jayboy, Joy, Max's Kansas City, New World, Rhapsody, Seville, Spiral

Probe Records
(051) 227-5646
8-12 Rainford Gardens
Liverpool 2

PRT Records
(01) 262-8040
ACC Huse
17 Great Cumberland Place
London W1A 1AG
Labels: Blueprint, Caliber, Caliber/Plus, Collector, Flashback, Golden House, Golden Guinea, Precision, Piccadilly, Spotlight, Top Brass, Becket, Compleat, GNP Crescendo, Sunnyview, Personal, Teresa, Hi-Cream

Radicalchoice
(01) 853-5899
17 Nelson Road
London SE1

RAK Records
(01) 586-2012
42 Charlbert Street
London NW8

RCA/Motown
(01) 636-8311
1 Bedford Avenue
London WC1
Labels: Ice, Regard, Salsoul, KR Records, Red Seal, Total Experience, F-Beat, Tamla Motown, Gordy, Morocco

Reachout International Records (Europe)
(01) 274-2025
1 Clarence House
Rushcroft Road
London SW2

Red Flame
(01) 743-0006
The Metrostore
231 The Vale
Acton
London W3 7QS

Red Lightnin' Records Blues And R&B Specialists
(0379) 88693
The White House
North Lopham
Diss
Norfolk

The Rocket Record Company Ltd
(01) 938-1741
125 Kensington High Street
London W8 5SN

Ronco Teleproducts
(01) 274-7761
Ellerslie Park
11 Lyham Road
London SW2

Rough Trade Records
(01) 833-2133/2561/2/3
61-71 Collier Street
London N1

Safari Records
(01) 723-8464
44 Seymour Place
London W1
Label: Singing Dog Records

Saga Records Ltd
(01) 969-6651
326 Kensal Road
London W10 5BL
Label: Trojan, B&C, Mooncrest

Satril Records Ltd
(01) 435-8063
444 Finchley Road
London NW2
Labels: Crash, Topaz, Service

Secret Records
(01) 870-8522
363 York Road
London SW15 1SP

Shout Records
(01) 381-1393
452 Fulham Road
London SW6

Situation 2
(01) 870-9912
17-19 Alma Road
London SW18

Solid Gold Records
(01) 734-3251
14 New Burlington Street
London W1X 2LR

Small Wonder Records Ltd
(0787) 76206
P.O.Box 23
Sudbury
Suffolk

Some Bizarre
(01) 734-9411
17 St Anne's Court
Wardour Street
London W1

Sonet Records
(01) 229-7267
121 Ledbury Road
London W11
Labels: Speciality, Alligator, Kicking Mule, Red Stripe, Titanic, Stone

Statik Records
(01) 381-0116, 385-0567
1a Normand Gardens
Greyhound Road
London W14

Stiff Records
(01) 741-1511
22 St Peters Square
London W6 9NW

Superville Records
(0904) 55584
9-10 Bridge Street
York YO1 1DD
Labels: Supermusic, Exploited

Towerbell Records
(01) 431-2770
32-34 Gondar Gardens
London NW6
Labels: Rockney, Shelf, Cockerel

Two Tone
(01) 408-2355
12 Stratford Place
London W1N 9AF

Upright Records
(01) 229-8856
49-53 Kensington Gardens Square
London W2 4BA

Virgin Records Ltd
(01) 968-6688
Kensal House
533-79 Harrow Road
London W10 4RH
Labels: Caroline, Charisma, Paladin, Dep
International, Statik, Beggars Banquet,
WMOT, 10/Virgin

WEA Records Ltd
(01) 434-3232
20 Broadwick Street
London W1V 2BH
Labels: Asylum, Atlantic, Elektra, Reprise,
Warner Brothers, Sire, Cotillion, Korova

Y.Records
(01) 743-2318/2336
70a Uxbridge Road
London W12
Labels: New York Connexion

Zang Tumb Tuum Records
(01) 229-1229
ZTT Building
8-10 Basing Street
London W11 1ET

Zomba Productions Ltd
(01) 459-8899
Zomba House
165-67 Willesden High Road
London NW10 2SG
Label: Jive

 # RECORD COMPANIES/US

A&M Records
(213) 469-2411
1416 North La Brea.
Hollywood, CA 90028.
New York office:
(212) 826-0477
595 Madison Avenue
New York, NY 10022.
Labels: I.R.S., Gold Mountain, Windham Hill

Arista Records
(212) 489-7400
6 West 57 Street
New York, NY 10019.
Labels: Jive, Africa, Electro, Zomba

Atlantic Recording Corp.
(212) 484-6000
75 Rockefeller Plaza
New York, NY 10019.
L.A. office:
(213) 205-7450
9229 West Sunset Boulevard,
Los Angeles, CA 90069.
Labels: Atco, Cotillion, Finnadar, Mirage,
Modern, Swansong, Duke, Island, Philly
World, Little David, Bronze.

Bearsville Records
(914) 679-7303
P.O. Box 135,
Bearsville, NY 12409.

Bomp Records
(213) 227-4141
2702 San Fernando Road
Los Angeles, CA 99065.
Labels: Voxx.

Buddah Records Inc.
(212) 582-6900
1790 Broadway
New York, NY 10019.
Label: Sutra, Beckett.

Cachalot Records
(212) 254-1979
611 Broadway
New York, NY 10012.

Capitol Records
(213) 462-6252
1750 Vine Street
Hollywood, CA 90028.
New York office:
(212) 757 7470
1370 Avenue of the Americas
New York, NY 10019.
Labels: Angel, Blue Note, EMI America,
Harvest, Seraphim, Manhattan.

CBS Records
(212) 975-4321
51 West 52 Street
New York, NY 10019.
L.A. office:
(213) 556-4700
1801 Century Park West
Los Angeles, CA 90067.
Labels: Epic, Columbia, Portrait, CBS
Masterworks, Odyssey CBS.
BID, Bang, Blue Sky, Caribou, Coast To
Coast, Chrysalis, Curb, Johnston, Kirshner,
Lynx, Nemperor, Pasha, Pavillion,
Philadelphia Int'l; Precision: Rock'n'Roll,
Scotti Brothers, T-Neck, TSOP, Uncle Jam,
Unlimited Gold, John Hammond.

Chrysalis Records
(212) 758-3555
645 Maidson Avenue
New York, NY 10022.
Labels: Animal, 2 Tone, Radialchoice, Air.

Columbia Records
Same as CBS Records.
labels: ARC, Stiff-Columbia, 415.

Compendium Inc.
(404) 873-3918
450 14th St. NW
Atlanta, GA 30318
Labels: DB, Press.

Cream Records
(818) 905-6344
13103 Ventura Blvd.
Studio City, CA 91604
label: Hi.

Elektra/Asylum/Nonesuch Records
(212) 355-7610
665 Fifth Avenue
New York, NY 10022.
L.A. office:
(213) 205-7400
9229 West Sunset Blvd.
Los Angeles, CA 90069.
Labels: Beserkley, Solar, Musicians, Ze,
Qwest.

EMI America/Liberty Records
(213) 462-6252
1750 Vine Street
Hollywood, CA 90028.
New York office:
(212) 757-7470
1370 Avenue of Americas
New York, NY 10019.
Labels: United Artists, Blue Note,
Manhattan.

Enigma Records
(213) 328-9407
PO Box 2896,
20445 Gramercy Place,
Torrance, CA 90509.

Epic/Portrait/Associated Labels
Same as CBS.
Labels: City Lights, Cleveland Int'l, Full
Moon, Park Lane, Lorimar, Stiff-Epic, Virgin,
Carrere.

Fantasy/Prestige/Milestone/Stax
(415) 549-2500
2600 10th St.
Berkeley, CA 94710.
Labels: Galaxy.

Fever Records
621 South 4th Street
Philadelphia, PA 19147
Label: Original Jazz Classics.

Folkways Records and Service Corp.
(212) 777-6606
632 Broadway
New York, NY 10012.
Labels: Asch, Broadsides, RBF

415 Records
(415) 621-3415
P.O. Box 14563
San Francisco, CA 94114.

Frontier Records
(213) 766-3374
Box 22
Sun Valley, CA 91352.

Geffen Records
(213) 278-9010
9130 West Sunset Blvd.
Los Angeles, CA 90069.
New York office:
(212) 484-7170
75 Rockefeller Plaza
New York, NY 10019.

Gold Mountain
(212) 840-6011
2 West 45th St.
New York, NY 10036

Hanibal Records
(212) 420-1780
61 Broadway
New York, NY 10012.

Island Records
(212) 477-8000
14 East 4th St.
New York, NY 10012
Labels: Mango, Antilles.

Jem Records Inc.
(201) 753-6100
3619 Kennedy Road
South Plainfield, NJ 07080.
West Coast office:
(213) 996-6754
18629 Topham Street,
Reseda, CA 91335.
Labels: Passport, PVC, Visa, Editions EG.

Landslide Records Inc.
(404) 873-3918
450 14 Street NW
Atlanta, GA 30318.

MCA Records Inc.
(818) 508-4000
100 Universal City Plaza,
Universal City, CA 91608.
New York office:
(212) 684-3377
51 Madison Ave.
New York, Ny 10010.
Labels: Coral, Impulse, Motown, Permian,
Sold Gold, Churchill, Rockshire, Sparrow,
AVI, Nashborough, Excello, Kenwood,
Creed, Booman, Out Of Town, Chess,
Checker.

Mobile Fidelty Sound Lab.
(213) 709-8440
21040 Nordhoff Street,
Chatsworth, CA 91311.

Motown Record Corp.
(213) 468-3500
6255 Sunset Boulevard
Los Angeles, CA 90028.
Labels: Gordy, Natural Resources, Prodigal,
Rare Earth, Soul, Tamla.

99 Records
(212) 777-4610
99 MacDougal Street
New York, NY 10012.

PolyGram Records Inc.
(212) 399-7100
810 Seventh Avenue
New York, NY 10019.
L.A. office:
(213) 656-3003
8335 West Sunset Blvd.
Los Angeles, CA 90069.
Labels: Casablanca, Mercury, London,
Verve, Chocolate City, DeLite, RSO, Riva,
Polydor, Atlanta Artists, Compleat, Deram,
Emarcy, Enja Gramavision, Lection,
Millenium, MPS, Oasis, Parachute, Phillips,
Treshold, Total Experience, 21, Vertigo.

Propellor Records
Box 658,
Allston Station
Boston, MA 02134.

Ralph Records
(415) 543-4085
109 Minna Street
San Francisco, CA 94105.

RCA Records
(212) 930-4000
1133 Avenue of the Americas
New York, NY 10036.
L.A. office:
(213) 468-4000
6363 Sunset Boulevard
Hollywood, CA 90028.
Labels: Grunt, Millenium, Gold Seal,
Bluebird, Salsoul, Pablo, Planet, Total
Experience.

Reachout International Records (ROIR)
(212) 477-0563
611 Broadway
New York, NY 10012.

Rhino Records
(213) 450-6323
1201 Olympic Boulevard,
Santa Monica, CA 90404.

Rollin' Rock Records
(213) 781-4805
6918 Peach Avenue,
Van Nuys, CA 91406.
Labels: American Rhythm Music, Boppin'
Belle, California Rockabilly, Ray Campi,
Ollie, Ragin' Rockabilly, Rockabilly
Rebellion, Rockin' Ronny, Rockin' Weiser.

Rough Trade Inc.
(415) 621-4045
326 Sixth Street
San Francisco, CA 94103.
Label: Factory US.

Rounder Records
(617) 354-0700
1 Camp Street
Cambridge, MA 02140.

Shanachie Records Corp.
(201) 445-5561
1 Hollywood Ave.
HoHoKus, NJ 07423.

Slash Records
(213) 937-4660
7381 Beverly Boulevard,
Los Angeles, CA 90036.

Sounds Interesting Records
PO Box 54,
Stone Harbor, NJ 08247.

Subterranean Records
(415) 864-1649
577 Valencia
San Francisco, CA 94110.

Sugar Hill Records Inc.
(201) 569-5170
96 West Street
Englewood, NJ 07631.

Tommy Boy Records
(212) 722-2211
1747 First Ave.
New York, NY 10028

Twin Tone Records
(612) 872-0646
2541 Nicolette Ave.
Minneapolis, MN 55404

Vanguard Recording Society, Inc.
(212) 255-7732
71 West 23 Street
New York, NY 10010.
Labels: O, Flip.

Warner Bros Records Inc.
(213) 846-9090
3300 Warner Boulevard
Burbank, CA 91510.
New York office:
(212) 702-0318
3 East 54 Street
New York, NY 10022.
Labels: Sire, Bearsville, Slash, ECM,
Geffen, Reprise, Dark Horse.

Windham Records
(415) 329-0647
Box 9388
Stanford, CA 94305

ZE Records and Tapes
(212) 245-7233
850 7th Ave.
New York, NY 10019.

MUSIC PUBLISHERS/UK

Albion Music Ltd
(01) 243-0011
119/121 Freston Road
London W11 4BD

Ambassador Music Ltd
(01) 836-5996
22 Denmark Street
London WC2

April Music Ltd
(01) 439-1845
37 Soho Square
London W1V 5DG

Arnakata Music Ltd
(01) 723-8424
10L Oxford & Cambrdige Mansions
Transcept Street
London NW1

Arretta Music Ltd
(0689) 27000
Pinnacle House
1 Oasthouse Way
Orpington
Kent BR5 3QJ

Ash Music Publishers
(0623) 752448
Cropwell House
Salmon Lane
Kirkby-in-Ashfield
Notts

ASL Publishing
(0633) 856327
5 Ogmore Crescent
Bettws
Newport
Gwent NPT 6SP

Asterisk Music
(01) 397-9857
PO Box 18F
Chessington
Surrey KT9 1UZ

ATV Music Ltd
(01) 409-2211
19 Upper Brook Street
London W1Y 1PD

Automatic Music
5 Avery Row
London W1X 9HA

Balgier Ltd
(021) 643-7727
Room 32
Princes Chambers
6 Coronation Street
Birmingham B2 4RN

Banks Music Publications
(0904) 21818
139 Holgate Road
York YO2 4DF

Barn Publishing Ltd
(01) 637-2111
35 Portland Place
London W1

Beadle Music Ltd
(0444) 412284
Suite D
The Priory
Haywards Heath
Sussex

Belsize Music Ltd
(01) 491-3175
38 North Row
London W1R 1DH

Big Ben Music Ltd
(01) 723-4499
18 Lancaster Mews
London W2 3QE

Big Secret Music
(0735) 213623
Havoc House
Cods Hill
Beenham
Berkshire

Black Sheep Music Ltd UK
(395) 2109/2143
Fulmer Gardens House
Fulmer
Bucks.

Bocu Music Ltd
(01) 402-7433/4/5
1 Wyndham Yard
Wyndham Place
London W1H 1AR

Bourne Music Ltd
(01) 493-6412
34/36 Maddox Street
London W1R 9PD

Bread Lion Music
Lion Studios
Aire Street Workshops
31 Aire Street
Leeds LS1 4HT

Bridge House Music Ltd
(01) 476-9947
15 Tinto Road
Canning Town
London EJ6 4BB

Sydney Bron Music Co.Ltd
(01) 267-4499
100 Chalk Farm Road
London NW1 8EH

Brothers Music Ltd
(01) 794-9177
5 Hollycroft Avenue
London NW3 7QG

BTW (Music) Ltd
(01) 888-6655
125 Myddleton Road
Wood Green
London N22 4NG

Bullseye Music Ltd
(0388) 814632
AIR House
Spennymoor
Co.Durham DL16 7SE

Burlington Music Co.Ltd
(01) 499-0067
40 South Audley Street
London W1

Cambar Music Ltd
(01) 434-2525
17 Newburgh Street
London W1V 1LE

Carlin Music Corporation
(01) 734-3251
14 New Burlington Street
London W1X 2LR

CBS Songs
(01) 439 1845
37 Soho Square
London W1V SDG

Centridge Ltd
(01) 272-7501
PO Box 137
London N7 OEF

Chappell Music Ltd
(01) 629-7600
129 Park Street
London W1Y 3FA

Charly Publishing Ltd
(01) 732-5647
46-7 Pall Mall
London SW1 5JG

Cherry Music
(01) 437-7418/9
49 Greek Street
London W1

Chevron Music Publishing Ltd
(0532) 438283
The Television Centre
Leeds LS3 1JS

Christabel Music Ltd
(0532) 694105
358 Alwoody Lane
Leeds 17

Chrysalis Music Ltd
(01) 408-2359
12 Stratford Place
London W1N 9AF

Barry Cole Music Ltd
(02273) 67241
65/69 Mortimer Street
Herne Bay
Kent CT6 5PR

Collins Music Company
(01) 258-3891
38 Kendal street
London W2

Barry Collings Music Ltd
(0702) 43464
15 Claremont Road
Westcliffe-on-Sea
Essex

Creole Music Ltd
(01) 965-9223
91-93 High Street
Harlesden
London NW10

Eaton Music Ltd
(01) 235-9046
8 West Eaton Place
London SW1X 8LS

Ebony Music
(0482) 25850
18 Mayfield Street
Spring Bank
Hull HU3 1NS

John Edward Music Ltd
(01) 806-0071
38-40 Upper Clapton Road
London E5 8BQ

Edwardson Music Ltd
(01) 935-7615
106 Bickenhall Mansions
London W1H 3LB

EG Music Ltd
(01) 730-2162
63a King's Road
London SW3 4NT

EMI Music Publishing
(01) 836-6699
138-40 Charing Cross Road
London WC2H OLD

E & S Music Ltd
(01) 995-5432
20-24 Beaumont Road
London W4 5AP

TRO Essex Music Ltd
(01) 637-7665/6
85 Gower Street
London WC1

Faber Music Ltd
(01) 278-6881
3 Queen Square
London WC1N 3AU

Fast Western Ltd
(01) 723-9559, 402-4024
2 York House
Upper Montagu Street
London W1

Fentone Music Ltd
(05366) 60981
Fleming Road
Earlstrees
Corby
Northants.

Noel Gay Music Co.Ltd
(01) 836-3941
24 Denmark Street
London WC2H 8NJ

Graduate Music Ltd
(0384) 59048/211159
Chaddesley House
196 Wolverhampton Street
Dudley
West Midlands

Halcyon Music Ltd
(01) 586-0288
11 Howitt Road
London NW3

Handle Music Ltd
(01) 493-9637
1 Derby Street
London W1

Hansa Productions
(01) 402-2191
26 Castlereagh Street
London W1

Happy Face Music
(0905) 820569
The Old Smithy Recording Studio
Post Office Lane
Kempsey
Worcs.

Heath Levy Music Co.Ltd
(01) 439-7731
184-86 Regent Street
London W1R 5DF

Hedley Music
(0246) 79976
71 Rutland Road
Chesterfield
Derbys S40 1ND

Heisenberg Ltd
(01) 703-7677
18 Crofton Road
London SE5 8NB

Hensley Music Publishing Co.Ltd
(01) 727-5118
29 Clarendon Road
London W11 4JB

Hollywood Music
(01) 806-0071
38-40 Upper Clapton Road
London E5

Hub Music Ltd
(01) 891-3146
4-10 Queens Road
Twickenham TW1 4ES

Hush Music Ltd
(01) 589-6293
117c Fulham Road
London SW3

Intersong Music Ltd
(01) 499-0067
40 South Audley Street
London W1Y 5DH

Island Music Ltd
(01) 741-1511
22 St Peter's Square
Hammersmith
London W6 9NW

Ivory Coast Music Ltd
(01) 381-1393
452 Fulham Road
London SW6

Kamela Music Ltd
(061) 652-2491
225 Ripponden Road
Oldham
Lancs OL1 4HR

Edward Kassner Music Co.Ltd
(01) 839-4672
21 Panton Street
London SW1

Kenmar Music Company
(01) 437-3711/2
(2nd Floor Rear)
11 Great Marlborough Street
London W1A 4QD

Kennick Music
(01) 589-7711/8861
Flat 3
50 Cadogan Square
London SW1X OJW

Lantern Music Publishing Co.Ltd
(01) 828-4595
66 Roebuck House
Palace Street
London SW1

Logorhythm Music Ltd
(01) 734-7443/4
6-10 Lexington Street
London W1

Louvigny Music Co.Ltd
(01) 493-5961
38 Hertford Street
London W1Y 8BA

Magnet Music Ltd
(01) 486-8151
22 York Street
London W1H 1FD

MAM (Music Publishing) Ltd
(01) 629-9255
24-25 New Bond Street
London W1Y 9HD

Sue Manning Music Publishing Ltd
(01) 379-5920
31 Betterton Street
Covent Garden
London WC2

Martin-Coulter Music Ltd
(01) 582-7622
11th Floor
Alembic House
93 Albert Embankment
London SE1 7TY

MCA Music Ltd
(01) 629-7211
139 Piccadilly
London W1V 9FH

Midnight Music Ltd
(01) 845-1518
58 Islip Manor Road
Northolt
Middx.

Morrison Leahy Music Ltd
(01) 402-9238
Flat 3
1 Hyde Park Place
London W2 2LH

MPL Communications Ltd
(01) 439-6621
1 Soho Square
London W1V 6BQ

The Music Production Co.Ltd
(01) 567-7038
2 Springbridge Mews
London W5

Neptune Music Ltd
(01) 437-2066/7
31 Old Burlington Street
London W1X 1LB

No Future Music
(068 45) 68036
3 Adelaide House
21 Wells Road
Malvern
Worcs WR14 4RH

Orange Publishing Ltd
(01) 769-7517
C/o Oakwood House
92 Erdley Road
London SW16 6BL

Oval Music
(01) 622-0111
11 Liston Road
London SW4

Page One Music Ltd
(01) 221-7179/7381
29 Rushton Mews
London W11 1RB

Palace Music Co.Ltd
(01) 499-0067
40 South Audley Street
London W1

Paper Music Ltd
(01) 434-2882/3
112 Wardour Street
London W1V 3LD

Paragon Music Co.Ltd
(01) 681-6663
Park House
22 Park Street
Croydon
Surrey

Pattern Music Ltd
(01) 836-5996
22 Denmark Street
London WC2

Peers Music
(01) 836-6699
8 Denmark Place
London WC2

Pink Floyd Music Publishers Ltd
(01) 734-6892
27 Noel Street
London W1V 3RD

Plangent Visions Music Ltd
(01) 734-6892
27 Noel Street
London W1V 3RD

Point Music Ltd
(01) 730-9777
The Point
9 Eccleston Street
Victoria
London SW1W 9LX

RAK Publishing Ltd
(01) 586-2012
42-48 Charlbert Street
London NW8 7BU

The Really Useful Company Ltd
(01) 734-2114
20 Greek Street
London W1V 5LF

Red Bus Music (International) Ltd
(01) 258-0324/5/6/7/8
Red Bus House
48 Broadley Terrace
London NW1

RCA Music Ltd
(01) 437-2468
155-157 Oxford Street
London W1

Riva Music Ltd
(01) 731-4131
2 New King's Road
London SW6

Rock Music Co.Ltd
(01) 734-6892
27 Noel Street
London W1V 3RD

Rock City Music Ltd
(09328) 66531
Shepperton Studio Centre
Shepperton
Middx

Rocket Publishing
(01) 938-1741
125 Kensington High Street
London W8 5SN

Rondor Music (London) Ltd
(01) 731-4161/5
Rondor House
10a Parsons Green
London SW6 4TW

Sarm Songs Ltd
(01) 229-1229
8-10 Basing Street
London W11 1ET

Satril Music Ltd
(01) 435-8063/4/5
444 Finchley Road
London NW2 2HT

Scorpio Music
(01) 455-4556
9 Ravenscroft Avenue
London NW11 OSA

Shapiro Bernstein And Co.Ltd
(01) 439-7731
186 Regent Street
London W1R 5DF

Sonet Records & Publishing Ltd
(01) 229-7267
121 Ledbury Road
London W11 2AQ

Sound Diagrams Ltd
(031) 229-8946
21 Atholl Crescent
Edinburgh
Scotland EH3 8HQ

Southern Music Publishing Co.Ltd
(01) 836-4524)
8 Denmark Street
London WC2H 8LT

St Annes Music Ltd
(061) 941-5151
Kennedy House
31 Stamford Street
Altrincham
Cheshire WA14 1ES

Storm Music
(0253) 27357
133 Park Road
Blackpool FY1 4ET

Street Music Ltd
(01) 451-3044
Zomba House
165-67 Willesden High Road
London NW10

Summit Music Ltd
(01) 491-3175/409-0287
38 North Row
London W1R 1DH

Sunbury Music Ltd
(01) 437-2468
155-57 Oxford Street
London W1R 1TB

Tabitha Music Ltd
(0392) 79914
39 Cordery Road
St Thomas
Exeter
Devon EX2 9DJ

Tembo Music Ltd
(01) 586-5591/2
50 Regents Park Road
London NW1 7SX

Thames Music Ltd
(01) 741-2406
117 Church Road
Barnes
London SW13 9HL

Tristan Music Ltd
(01) 836-5996
22 Denmark Street
London WC2

United Music Publishers Ltd
(01) 729-4700
42 Rivington Street
London EC2A 3BN

Valentine Music Group
(01) 240-1628
7 Garrick Street
London WC2E 9AR

Valley Music Ltd
(01) 629-7211
138 Piccadilly
London W1V 9FH

Virgin Music Publishers Ltd
(01) 229-1282
95-99 Ladbroke Grove
London W11 1PG

Warner Brothers Music Ltd
(01) 637-3771
17 Berners Street
London W1P 3DD

Bruce Welch Music Ltd
(01) 434-1839
64 Stirling Court
Marshall Street
London W1V 1LG

Westminster Music Ltd
(01) 734-8121
19-20 Poland Street
London W1V 3DD

Zebra Publishing Songs Ltd
(01) 408-1611
243 Regent Street
London W1R 8PN

 # MUSIC PUBLISHERS/US

ATV Music Corp.
(213) 462-6933
6255 Sunset Boulevard
Hollywood, CA 90028.

Abkco Music Inc.
(212) 399-0300
1700 Broadway
New York, NY 10019.

Acuff-Rose Publications Inc.
(615) 385-3031
2510 Franklin Road
Nashville, TN 37204.

Allied Artists Music Co. Inc.
(212) 541-9200
15 Columbus Circle
New York, NY 10023.

April/Blackwood Music Inc.
(212) 975-4886
1350 Avenue of the Americas
New York, NY 10019.

Augsburg Publishing House
(612) 330-3300
426 South Fifth Street
Minneapolis, MN 55415.

Beechwood Music Corp.
(213) 469-8371
6920 Sunset Boulevard
Hollywood, CA 90028.

Beserkley
(415) 848-6701
2054 University Avenue,
Berkeley, CA 94704.

Big Music
(203) 269-4465
10 George Street
Wallingford, CT 06492.

Big Seven Music Corp.
(212) 582-4267
1790 Broadway
New York, NY 10019.

Buddah Music Inc.
(212) 582-6900
1790 Broadway
New York, NY 10019.

Bug Music
(213) 466 4352
6777 Hollywood Boulevard,
Hollywood, CA 90028.

Cameron Organisation Inc.
(312) 246-8222
822 Hillgrove Avenue
Western Springs, IL 60558.

Chappell/Intersong Music Co.
(212) 399-7373
810 Seventh Avenue
New York, NY 10019.

Chrysalis Music Group
(212) 758-3555
645 Madison Avenue
New York, NY 10022.

Cotillion Music Inc.
(212) 484-8132
75 Rockefeller Plaza
New York, NY 10019.

Crazy Cajun Music
(713) 926-4431
5626 Brock
Houston, TX 77023.

Cream Publishng Group
(818) 905-6344
13107 Ventura Blvd.
Studio City, CA 91604.

Duane Music Inc.
(408) 739-6133
382 Clarence Avenue
Sunnyvale, CA 94086.

Elm Publishng Co.
(714) 898-7317
14621 Allen Street
Westminster, CA 92683

Elvis Music Inc.
(212) 489-8170
1619 Broadway
New York, NY 10019.

Entertainment Company Music Group
(212) 265-2600
40 West 57 Street
New York, NY 10019

Evansongs Ltd.
(212) 765-8450
1790 Broadway
New York, NY 10019.

Famous Music Corp.
(213) 333-3433
1 Gulf and Western Plaza
New York, NY 10023.

Carl Fischer Inc.
(212) 777-0900
62 Cooper Square
New York, NY 10003.

Flying Fish Music
(312) 528-5455
1304 West Schubert
Chicago, IL 60614.

Fort Knox Music Co.
(212) 489-8170
1619 Broadway
New York, NY 10019.

Al Gallico Music Corp.
(212) 355-5980
120 East 56 Street
New York, NY 10022.

Garrett Music Enterprises
(213) 467-2181
6255 Sunset Boulevard
Hollywood, CA 90028.

Al Green
(901) 794-6220
P.O. Box 9485
Mephis, TN 38109

Hallnote Music Co.
(615) 790-1726
P.O. Box 40209
Nashville, TN 37204.

Hilaria Music Inc.
(608) 251-2644
315 West Gorham Street
Madison, WI 53703.

Home Grown Music Inc.
(213) 763-6323
4412 Whitsett
Studio City, CA 91606.

House Of Cash Inc.
(615) 824-5110
700 Johnny Cash Parkway
Hendersonville, TN 37115.

Intersong Music Inc.
(213) 469-5141
6255 Sunset Boulevard,
Hollywood, CA 90028.

Island Music
(213) 469-1285
6525 Sunset Boulevard
Hollywood, CA 90028.

Jobete Music Co. Inc.
(213) 468-3500
6255 Sunset Boulevard
Hollywood, CA 90028.

Laurie Publishing Group
(914) 425-7000
20-F Robert Pitt Drive
Monsey, NY 10952.

Largo Music Inc.
(212) 371-9400
425 Park Avenue
New York, NY 10022.

Hal Leonard Publishing Corp.
(414) 774-3630
8112 West Bluemound Road
Milwaukee, WI 53213.

MCA Music
(818) 508-4550
100 Universal City Plaza
Universal City, CA 91608.

MPL Communications Inc.
39 West 54 Street
New York, NY 10019.

Marsaint Music Inc.
(504) 949-8386
3809 Clematis Avenue
New Orleans, LA 70122.

Ivan Mogull Music Corp.
(212) 355-5636
625 Madison Avenue
New York, NY 10022.

Neil Music Inc.
(213) 656-2614
8400 Sunset Boulevard
Los Angeles, CA 90069.

Open End Music Inc.
(213) 855-7056
P.O. Box 69338
Los Angeles, CA 90069

Pale Pachyderm Publishing
(415) 543-4085
109 Minna Street
San Francisco, CA 94105.

Phenetones
(617) 744-7678
400 Essex Street
Salem, MA 01970

Rough Trade Inc.
(415) 621-4045
326 Sixth Street
San Francisco, CA 94103.

Salsoul Music Publishing Corp.
(212) 889-7340
401 Fifth Avenue,
New York, NY 10016.

Screen Gems-EMI Music Inc.
(213) 469-8371
6920 Sunset Boulevard
Hollywood, CA 90028.

Paul Simon
(212) 541-7571
1619 Broadway
New York, NY 10019.

Skyhill Publishing Co. Inc.
(213) 469 1285
6525 Sunset Boulevard
Hollywood, CA 90028

Special Rider Music
(212) 473-5900
P.O. Box 860
Cooper Station
New York, NY 10276.

The Richmond Organisation (TRO)
(212) 765-9889
10 Columbus Circle
New York, NY 10019.

20th Century Fox Music Corp.
(213) 203 1487
10201 West Pico
Los Angeles, CA 90035.

WPN Music Co. Inc.
(516) 796-3698
10 Swirl Lane
Levittown, NY 11756.

Warner Bros Music
(213) 273-3323
9000 Sunset Boulevard
Los Angeles, CA 90069.

Word Music
(817) 772-7650
4800 Waco Drive
Waco, TX 76796.

INDEPENDENT RECORD DISTRIBUTORS/UK

Arabesque Ltd
(01) 995-3023
Swan Works
Fishers Lane
London W4 1RX

Backs Records Ltd
(0603) 26221
St Mary's Works
St Mary's Plain
Norwich

Cadillac Music
(01) 836-3646
180 Shafesbury Avenue
London WC2H 8SJ

Caroline Exports Ltd
(01) 961-2919
56 Standard Road
London NW10

The Cartel
(See: Backs, Fast Product, Red Rhino,
Revolver, Rough Trade)

Conifer Records
(0895) 447707
Horton Road
West Drayton
Middx. UB7 8JL

Daddy Kool Records
(01) 437-3535
94 Dean Street
London W1

Discovery Records
(067285) 406
Broad Street
Beechingstoke
Pewsey
Wilts

and

24 Drury Lane
Solihull
West Midlands

**ESSP (Electronic Synthesizer Sound
Projects)**
(01) 979-9997
The Sound House
P.O.Box 37b
East Molesey
Surrey

Fast Product
(031) 661-5811/2
3-4 East Norton Place
Edinburgh

Graduate Records
(0384) 59048/21159
196 Wolverhampton Street
Dudley, West Midlands

Greensleeves Records Ltd
(01) 749-3277/8
Unit 7
Goldhawk Industrial Estate
2a Brackenbury Road
London W6

**IDS (Independent Distribution
Services Ltd)**
(01) 476-1476
7 Deanston Wharf
Badfield Road
London E16 2BJ

Independent Record Labels Association
(01) 935-2303
56-60 Wigmore Street
London W1

Jazz Horizon (Importers/Distributors)
(0279) 724572
102 London Road
Sawbridgeworth
Herts CMW1 9JJ

Jazz Music (Manchester)
(061) 794-3525
7 Kildare Road
Swinton
Manchester M27 3AB

JSU Distribution
(0422) 64773
21 Bull Green
Halifax
West Yorkshire HX1 2RZ

Jungle Records (Bravour Ltd)
(01) 359-8444/9161
24 Gaskin Street
Islington
London N1 2RY

Lasgo Exports Ltd
(01) 961-1333
Unit M
New Crescent Works
Nicholl Road
London NW10

Lightning Records And Video Ltd
(01) 969-5255
841 Harrow Road
London NW10 5NH

Lotus Records
(0782) 628916
23 High Street
Newcastle-Under-Lyme
Staffs ST5 1QZ

Making Waves Ltd
(01) 481-9917
6-8 Alie Street
London E1

Mirage
(0272) 691867
614 Southmead Road
Filton
Bristol BS12 7RF

Neumusik
12 Cedar Drive
Chichester
West Sussex

Nine Mile Distribution
(0926) 881211
Lower Avenue
Leamington Spa
Warwickshire

Oldies Unlimited
(0952) 612244
Dukes Way
St Georges
Telford
Shropshire

Pickwick International Inc.Ltd
(01) 200-7000
The Hyde Industrial Estate
The Hyde
London NW9 6JU

Pinnacle Records
(66) 27000
Pinnacle House
1 Oasthouse Way
Orpington, Kent

Pizza Express Music Distribution
(01) 734-6112
29 Romilly Street
London W1

Probe Records
(051) 227-5646
8-12 Rainford Gardens
Liverpool 2

Projection Records Distribution
(0702) 72281/714025
74 High Street
Old Town/Leigh-On-Sea
Essex

PRT Distribution
(01) 648-7000
132 Western Road
Mitcham
Surrey CR4 3UT

Recommended Distribution
(01) 622-8834
387 Wandsworth Road
London SW8

Red Lightnin' Records
(0379) 88693
The White House
North Lopham
Diss
Norfolk

Red Rhino Distribution Ltd
(0904) 641415
The Coach House
Fetter Lane
York YO1 1EM

Revolver Records
(0272) 299105/211115
1 Berkley Crescent
The Triangle
B58 1HA

Rose Records
(01) 609-8288
3 Ellington Street
Islington
London N7 8PP

Ross Record Distribution
(0888) 12403
29 Main Street
Turriff
Aberdeenshire

Rough Trade Distribution
(01) 833-2133
67/71 Collier Street
London N1

Scotia Distribution
(021) 557-0029
37 Jeffrey Street
Edinburgh

Small Wonder Records
(0787) 76206
P.O.Box 23
Sudbury
Suffolk

Stage One Records Ltd
(0428) 4001
Parshire House
2 Kings Road
Haslemere
Surrey

Wynd-Up Records
(061) 872-0170
2 Sable House
Guinness Road Trading Estate
Trafford Park
Manchester

DISTRIBUTORS/IMPORTERS/US

Dutch East India Trading
(516) 432-3500
45 Alabama Avenue
Island Park, NY 11558

Greenworld Distribution
(213) 533-8075
PO Box 2896
Torrance, CA 90509

Important Records
(212) 995-9200
149-03 New York Boulevard
Jamaica, NY 11434

Jem Records
(201) 753-6100
3619 Kennedy Road
South Plainfield, NJ 07080
West Coast office:
(213) 996-6754
18629 Topham
Reseda, CA 91335

Rough Trade
(415) 621-4307
326 Sixth Street
San Francisco, CA 93103

Rounder Records
(612) 354-0700
186 Willow Avenue
Somerville, MA 02144

Sounds Good Import Co
(213) 452-5949
1201 Olympic Boulevard
Santa Monica, CA 90404

Systematic Record Distributors
(415) 431-9377
1331 Fulsom Street
San Francisco, CA 94103

RECORDING STUDIOS/UK

Abbey Road Studios
(01) 286-1161
3 Abbey Road
London NW8 9AY

Alaska Rehearsal And Recording Studios
(01) 928-7440
127-29 Alaska Street
London SE1

Alvic Sound Studio
(01) 385-8244/0700
17 Barons Court Road
London W14 9DP

Amazon Recording Studios
(051) 546-6444/0434
LSD Stopgate Lane
Simonswood
Liverpool 33

Angel Recording Studios Ltd
(01) 354-2525
311 Upper Street
London N1

Aosis
(01) 267-4680
10a Belmont Street
London NW10

Arny's Shack
7c Bank Chambers
Penhill Avenue
Parkstone
Dorset

The Barge
(01) 289-6204
Opposite No.63 Blomfield Road
Little Venice
London W9

Basement Studio
(01) 734-5784
145 Wardour Street
London W1V 3YB

Berwick Street Recording Studios
(01) 734-5750
8 Berwick Street
Soho
London W1V 3RG

Britannia Row Recording Studios Ltd
(01) 226-3377, 354-3390
35 Britannia Row
Islington
London N1 8QH

Ca Va Sound Workshop
(041) 334-5099/6330
49 Derby Street
Kelvingrove
Glasgow G3 7TU

Cargo Studios
(0706) 524420
Kenion Street
Rochdale
Lancashire

Castle Recording Studio
(0942) 58777
The Castle
Castle Hill Road
Hindley
Wigan
Lancashire WN2 4BH

CBS Recording Studios
(01) 636-3434
31-37 Whitfield Street
London W1P 5RE

Chipping Norton Recording Studios
(0609) 3636, (01) 960-7192
28-30 New Street
Chipping Norton
Oxfordshire OX7 5JL

Craighall Studio
(031) 552-3685
68 Craighall Road
Edinburgh EH6 4RL

De Wolfe Ltd
(01) 437-4933, 439-8481
80-88 Wardour Street
London W1V 3LF

Decibel Studios
(01) 802-7868
19 Stamford Hill
London N16 5TU

Denmark Street Studios
(01) 836-6061
9 Denmark Street
London WC2

DJM Recording Stuios
(01) 242-6886
5-11 Theobalds Road
London WC1X 8SE

Duffy's Studio
(01) 737-0817, 703-9608
1-2 The Parade
Dog Kennel Hill
East Dulwich
London SE22

Easy Street Studios
(01) 739-1451/8887
45 Blythe Street
London E2

Eden Studios Ltd
(01) 995-5432
20-24 Beaumont Road
London W4 5AP

Eel Pie Studios
(01) 891-1266/7/8/9
The Boathouse
Ranleagh Drive
Twickenham TW1 1QZ

The Elephant Recording Studio
(01) 481-8615
Basement N
Metropolitan Wharf
Wapping Hill
London E1

The Factory, Sound (Woldingham) Ltd
(01) 905-2386
Toftrees Church Road
Woldingham
Surrey

Fairworld Recording Studio
(0385) 887811
West Lane
Chester Le Street
Co.Durham

Fallout Shelter (Island Studios London)
(01) 741-1511
47 British Grove
London W4 2NL

Farmyard Recording Stuios
(02404) 2912
Bendrose House East
White Lion Road
Little Chalfont
Buckinghamshire

Focus Studios
(01) 403-0007/0020
Vineyard off Sanctuary Lane
London SE1

Foel Recording Studio Ltd
(0938) 810758
Llanfair Caereinion
Powys
Mid. Wales

Good Earth Productions Ltd
(01) 734-0864, 434-1490
59 Dean Street
London W1

Gooseberry Gerrard Street Studios
(01) 437-6255
19 Gerrard Street
London W1

Gooseberry Hillside Road studios
(01) 674-0548
2 Hillside Road
Tulse Hill
London SW2

Grosvenor Recording Studios
(021) 356-9636
16 Grosvenor Road
Handsworth Wood
Birmingham B30 3NP

Herne Place Studios
(0990) 26639
Herne Place
London Road
Sunningdale
Ascot
Berkshire

Hollywood Studios
(01) 806-0071/4
38-40 Upper Clapton Road
London E5 8BQ

Horizon Recording Studios
(0203) 21000
Horizon House
Warwick Road
Coventry

Jacobs Studio
(0252) 723518
Ridgway House
Runwick
Nr. Farnham
Surrey

JAM Recording Ltd
(01) 272-7545
106 Tollington Park
London N4

Jamm Studios
(0204) 286040/493126
Flash Mills
Great Moor Street
Bolton

R.G.Jones Recording Studio
(01) 540-9881
Beulah Road
London SW10 3SB

Kirkland Park Studios
(0357) 21130, (0236) 821081
Lethame Road
Strathaven M40 6EE

Konk 'Kinks' Productions Ltd
(01) 340-7873/4757
84-86 Tottenham Lane
London N8 7EE

Lansdowne Recording Studios Ltd
(01) 727-0041/2/3
Lansdowne House
Lansdowne Road
London W11 3LP

Livingston Studios Ltd
(01) 889-6558
Brook Road
Wood Green
London N22

The Manor Studios
(08675) 77551
Shipton-On-Cherwell
Nr. Kidlington
Oxfordshire

Marcus Music
(01) 229-9599
49-53 Kensington Gardens Square
London W2

Marquee Studios
(01) 437-6731
10 Richmond Mews
Dean Street
London W1

Mayfair Recording Studios
(01) 586-7746
11a Sharpleshall Street
London NW1

Misty Recording Studio
(0202) 295961
24 Norwich Road
Bournemouth

Mushroom Studios
(0272) 735994/735867
18 West Mall
Clifton
Bristol BS8 4BQ

Music Works
(01) 609-0808, 607-9495/6/7
23 Benwell Road
London N7

The Nova Suite
(01) 493-7403
21-27 Bryanston Street
Marble Arch
London W1H 7AB

Odyssey Recording Studios
(01) 402-2191
26-27 Castlereagh Street
London W1

Old Barn Recorders
(01) 680-9222/4831
39 Croham Road
South Croydon CR2 7HD

One Two Three Music Studios
(0222) 222826
48 Smithfield Square
Belfast
Northern Ireland

Pathway
(01) 359-0970
2a Grosvenor Avenue
London N5

Pennine Studios
(061) 665-2278
225 Ripponden Road
Littlemoore
Oldham OL1 4HR

Pineapple Recording Studios
(01) 571-4591
Abbottsbury House
Priory Way
Southall
Middlesex

Pluto Recording Studios
(061) 228-2022
36 Granby Row
Manchester 1

PolyGram Studio
(01) 402-6121
Garden Entrance
Stanhope House
Stanhope Place
London W2 2HH

Portland Recording Studios Ltd
(01) 637-2111
35 Portland Place
London W1N 3AG

Producers Workshop
(01) 589-8341
117c Fulham Road
London SW3

PRT Studios
(01) 402-8114
40 Bryanstone Street
London W1

Q Studios
(0533) 608813
1487 Melton Road
Queniborough Industrial Estate
Queniborough
Leicester

RAK Studios
(01) 586-2012
42-48 Charlbert Street
London NW8 7BU

Redan Recorders Ltd
(01) 229-9054
23 Redan Place
Queensway
London W2

Regal Sound Recorders
(0462) 54332
50 Bancroft
Hitchin
Herts

REL Studios
(031) 229-9651
7a Atholl Place
Edinburgh EH3 8HP

Ridge Farm Studios
(0306) 711202
Ridge Farm
Capel
Surrey RH5 5HG

Riverside Recordings Ltd
(01) 994-3142
78 Church Path
London W4 5BJ

Rockfield Studios
(0600) 2449/3625
Amberley Court
Rockfield Road
Monmouth
Gwent

Roundhouse Recording Studio
(01) 485-0131
100 Chalk Farm Road
London NW1 8EH

Sain Recordian (Cyf)
(0285) 851111
Llandwrog
Caernarfon
Gwynedd
Cymru
Wales

Sarm Recording Studios (East)
(01) 247-1311
Osborn House
9-13 Osborn Street
London E1 6TD

Sarm Recording Studios (West)
(01) 229-1229
8-10 Basing Street
London W11 1ET

Satril Studio
(01) 435-8063
444 Finchley Road
London NW2

SAV Studios Ltd
(01) 278-7893/4/5
26 Harrison Street
London WC1H 8JG

Scorpio Sound
(01) 388-0263/4
19-20 Euston Centre
London NW1 3JH

September Sound Studios
(0484) 643211
38 Knowl Road
Golcar
Huddersfield DH7 4AN

Sin City Studios
(0602) 784714/708622
22a Forest Road West
Nottingham NG7 4EQ

Sirocco Recording Studio
(0563) 36377
1 Glencairn Square
Kilmarnock
Ayrshire
Scotland

Sound Suite Recording Studios
(01) 485-4881
92 Camden Mews
London NW1

Southern Studios
(01) 888-8949
10 Myddleton Road
London N22 4NS

Spaceward Recording Studios
(035) 389-600/776
The Old School
High Street
Stretham
Cambridge CB6 3LD

Surrey Sound Studio Ltd
(0372) 379444
70 Kingston Road
Leatherhead
Surrey

Tapestry Studio
(01) 878-3353
67 First Avenue
Mortlake
London SW14 8SP

Town House Studios
(01) 743-9313
150 Goldhawk Road
London W12

Trident Studios
(01) 734-9901
17 St Anne's Court
Wardour Street
London W1

Utopia Studios
(01) 586-3434
Utopia Village
7 Chalcot Road
London NW1 8LH

Wessex Studios
(01) 359-0051
106 Highbury New Park
London N5 2DW

Woodlands Recording Studio
(0924) 896293
6 Garden Street
Normanton
West Yorkshire

The Workhouse
(01) 237-1736/7/8
488 Old Kent Road
London SE1

RECORDING STUDIOS/US

Alpha Audio
(804) 358-3852
2049 West Broad Street
Richmond, VA 23220

A&M Recording Studios
(213) 469-2411
1416 North LaBrea
Hollywood, CA 90028

A&R Recording
(212) 397-0300
322 West 48th Street
New York, NY 10036

Audio Innovators
(412) 471-6220
216 Boulevard of the Allies
Pittsburgh, PA 15222

Bee Jay Recording Studios
(305) 293-1781
5000 Eggleston Avenue
Orlando, FL 32810

Bullet Recording
(615) 327-4621
49 Music Square West
Nashville, TN 37203

Caribou Ranch
(303) 258-3215
PO Box 310
Nederland, CO 80466

Capitol Studios
(213) 462-6252
1750 North Vine Street
Hollywood, CA 90028

Cherokee Recording Studios
(213) 653-3412
751 North Fairfax
Hollywood, CA 90046

Clover Recorders
(213) 463-2371
6232 Santa Monica Boulevard
Hollywood, CA 90038

Criteria Recording Studios
(305) 947-5611
1755 NE 149 Street
Miami, FL 33181

Different Fur Recording
(415) 864-1967
3470 19th Street
San Francisco, CA 94110

El Dorado Studios
(213) 467-6151
1717 North Vine Street
Los Angeles, CA 90028

Electric Lady Studios
(212) 677-4700
52 West 8th Street
New York, NY 10011

Fantasy Studios
(415) 549-2500
10th and Parker
Berkeley, CA 94710

Hit Factory
(212) 664-1000
237 West 54th Street
New York, NY 10019

House Of Music
(201) 736-3062
1400 Pleasant Valley Way
West Orange, NJ 07052

Image Studios
(213) 850-1030
1020 North Sycamore
Hollywood, CA 90038

Kendun Recorders
(213) 843-8096
619 South Glenwood Place
Burbank, CA 91506

Larrabee Sound
(213) 657-6750
8811 Santa Monica Boulevard
West Hollywood, CA 90069

Lion Share
(213) 658-5990
8255 Beverly Boulevard
Los Angeles, CA 90048

MCA/Whitney Recording Studios
(818) 507-1041
1516 West Glen Oaks Boulevard
Glendale, CA 91201

Media Sound
(212) 765-4700
311 West 57th Street
New York, NY 10019

Motown/Hitsville USA
(213) 850-1510
7317 Romaine Street
Los Angeles, CA 90046

Muscle Shoals Sound Studios
(205) 381-2060
1000 Alabama Avenue
Muscle Shoals, AL 35660

Music Mill
(615) 254-5925
1710 Roy Acuff Place
Nashville, TN

National Recording Studios
(212) 279-2000
460 West 42nd Street
New York, NY 10036

Ocean Way Recording
(213) 467-9375
6050 Sunset Boulevard
Los Angeles, CA 90028

Park South Studio
(212) 977-9800
231 West 58th Street
New York, NY 10019

Pierce Arrow Recorders
(312) 328-8950
1911 Ridge Avenue
Evanston, IL 60202

Power Station
(212) 246-2900
441 West 53rd Street
New York, NY 10019

RCA Studios
(212) 930-4062
110 West 44th Street
New York, NY 10036

Record Plant
(213) 653-0240
8456 West Third Street
Los Angeles, CA 90048
New York office:
(212) 582-6505
321 West 44th Street
New York, NY 10036

Reflection Sound
(704) 377-4596
1018 Central Avenue
Charlotte, NC 28204

Sheffield Recording
(301) 628-7260
13816 Sunnybrook Road
Phoenix, MD 21131

Sigma Sound Studios
(215) 561-3660
212 North 12th Street
Philadelphia, PA 19107

Sigma Sound Studios
(212) 582-5055
1697 Broadway
New York, NY 10019

Sound City
(213) 873-2842
15456 Cabrito Road
Van Nuys, CA 91406

Sound Emporium
(615) 383-1982
3102 Belmont Boulevard
Nashville, TN 37212

Sound 80
(612) 339-9313
2709 East 25th Street
Minneapolis, MN 55406

Sound Labs
(213) 466-3463
1800 North Argyle Street
Los Angeles, CA 90028

Suma Recording Studio
(216) 951-3955
5706 Vrooman Road
Cleveland, OH 44077

Syncro Sound
(617) 424-1062
331 Newbury Street
Boston, MA 02115

Technisonic Studios
(314) 727-1055
1201 South Brentwood Boulevard
St. Louis, MO 63117

Universal Recording
(312) 642-6465
46 East Walton
Chicago, IL 60611

Village Recorder
(213) 478-8227
1616 Butler Avenue
West Los Angeles, CA 90025

Warner Bros Recording Studios
(213) 980-5605
1114 Cumpston Avenue
North Hollywood, CA 91601

Westlake Studios
(213) 654-2155
8447 Beverly Boulevard
Los Angeles, CA 90048

Allen Zentz Recording
(213) 469-5855
7083 Hollywood Boulevard
Los Angeles, Ca 90028

ROCK PUBLICATIONS/UK

Beatbox
(01) 437-0626
1 Golden Square
London W1R 3AB
Monthly. "Britain's No.1 Pop Video Magazine" (it sez 'ere). Once more the great name of *Smash Hits* is invoked at the drawing board, a selection of promo pix and video stills are mixed in, add a competition, a centrefold and what do you have? Sadly nothing to keep the index finger from the fast forward button.

Black Beat International
(01) 533-1321
143 Mare Street,
Hackney
London E8 3RH
Monthly. Commendably wide coverage of all forms of black music, from soul through reggae to soca, gospel, jazz and African sounds. Presentation leaves much to be desired in many cases, but well worth checking the cover titles for items of interest.

Blitz
(01) 734-8311/3
1 Lower James Street
London W1
Monthly. Survived last year's critical mauling in these pages with some style. Comparisons with *The Face* can't be avoided even now, but if it hasn't quite got its rival's visual snap it's blossomed into a good read. Interesting free music-only spin-off, *The Beat* is set to give *Smash Hits* and clones a run for their readership. Looks better, too, with smaller A4 format – is big *always* beautiful?

Blues And Soul
(01) 402-6869
153 Praed Street
London W2
Fortnightly. It's always been something of a mystery why soul fans, traditionally the sharpest kids on the block, buy the strangely put-together mix of glossy colour and newsprint that is *B&S* in such numbers. A veritable curate's egg, good in parts. Whether the recent incorporation of wider-ranging sister mag *Black Music* will improve the dodgy bits or vice versa remains to be seen.

Blues Unlimited
38 Belmon Park
London SE13
Quarterly. Title says it all for a well-respected and long-running publication

Bucketfull Of Brains
(01) 809-0461
58a Abbotsford Avenue
London N15
Quarterly. Distinctively original fanzine that's deservedly increasing its readership in leaps and bounds, aided by

the occasional flexidisc. Has exchanged Soft Boys fixation for pro-American stance in recent issues. Worth sampling despite the title.

Chartbeat
(01) 992-3275
81 Rothschild Road
Acton Green
London W4
Monthly. The latest in a long line of glossy poster magazines for teens. Need I say more – indeed is there more to say? Good for walls with peeling paint or unsightly cracks, and still cheaper than polyfilla.

Collusion
(01) 486-3985
14 Peto Place
London NW1
Annually. Applies the widest and most international definitions of popular music to its performers, processes and history. That's what they say, and who is this compiler to argue? Recommended.

Comstock Lode
(01) 747-0916
6 Dewsbury Court
Chiswick Road
London W4
After a year's hiatus in which editor John Platt was engaged in more profitable activities (writing books and making videos) the return of this long-established West Coast-inspired quarterly is strongly rumoured.

Country Music Round-Up
(0522) 685507
Belgrave House
32 Shaftesbury Avenue
Forest Park
Lincoln
Monthly. Newspaper-format information for C&W aficionados.

Country Music People
(0689) 70433
28 Broomwood Road
Orpington
Kent
Monthly. Well-produced rundown on the personalities behind the country sounds.

Debut
(01) 723-1634
13 New Quebec Street
London W1
Monthly. Is it an album? Is it a magazine? No, it's both – or so we're assured Well-intentioned publication that's failed to convince as either paper or vinyl with its first few issues. Sadly, the time is not right for such a radical project, but the format will doubtless succeed one day – which is little compensation for the publishers.

Disco And Club Trade International
(01) 278-3591
410 St John Street
London EC1
Monthly. Fight through the seemingly endless pages of ads for lights, speakers, decks, microphones and artifical palm trees (artificial palm trees?) and you'll find news, features and reviews which are doubtless invaluable information for the discerning dee-jay or club owner in an ever-changing and specialised field. Much of it baffled this reviewer, but they're celebrating their 100th issue in February 1985, so they must be doing *something* right, Get down!

Echoes
(01) 253-6662
Rococo House
283 City Road
London EC1 1LA
Weekly. Despite dropping the 'Black' prefix, poor old tabloid-format *Echoes* needs an injection of cash and ideas to waken it from its slumber and start attracting a less specialised (and therefore more lucrative) readership. Dare one say it lacks colour?

Electronics & Music Maker
(0223) 313722
Alexander House
1 Milton Road
Cambridge CB4 1UY
Monthly. With all the computer-linked keyboards in circulation these days, it wouldn't be difficult to confuse this with another magazine completely. . . Design resembles a complex circuit-board diagram, too. But its been successful enough to spawn specialist mags on guitars and home recording (see elsewhere for details), confirming the impression that the information content-reviews, news, interviews and the aforementioned circuit diagrams and computer programs – represents good value for money.

The Face
(01) 580-6756
5-11 Mortimer Street
London W1
Monthly. Is it wishful thinking, or is *The Face's* crown beginning to slip ever so slightly? Whether that's fact or just familiarity, it's still a good-looking crash-course in the ever-changing world of youth culture, and is eminently collectable. Save 'em for your grandchildren.

Guitarist
(0223) 313722
Alexander House
1 Milton Road
Cambridge CB4 1UY
Monthly. Why should the Yanks have it

their own way? From the stable of *E&MM* charges a British rival to *Guitar Player*, *Frets* et al. But instead of challenging the established (i.e. American) papers on their own turf (in-depth interviews), the result is rather like an *International Musician* guitar special with truss rods and pickguards all over the shop. Design is appalling, but then one mustn't expect too much too soon. Keep practicin', boys!

History Of Rock
(01) 379 6711
Orbis House
20-22 Bedfordbury
London WC2
Weekly. Now on its second run, the *History Of Rock* starts with Presley and ends with Boy George. For anything in between, the theory goes, you have to buy the lot – which doesn't come cheap. The 120-part collection is particularly well illustrated, though, with many rare pictures, so worth enquiring for single issues of your own particular favourites.

Home Studio Recording
(0223) 313722
Alexander House
1 Milton Road
Cambridge CB4 1UY
Monthly. "Sergeant Pepper was recorded on four-track wasn't it – what do I need all this for?" If that's your reaction to anything more complex than a second hand reel-to-reel and a couple of old microphones, this isn't for you – or perhaps it is! Unlike sister paper *E&MM* it prefers hardware to mugshots on the cover, and that reflects the editorial treatment. But it *is* understandable to the non-technically minded, so if you *do* fancy recording *Abbey Road* in your garage, the reivews and tips offered will prove worth investigation for the technology if not the talent.

I-D
(01) 328-0917
71 Sheriff Road
West Hampstead
London NW6
Monthly. Now in larger-format, this 'underground' fashion mag has come up-market with a vengeance. Still worth chasing for cheap chic ideas.

In The City
c/o Compendium Books
234 Camden High Street
London NW1
Prematurely but understandably laid to rest by last year's compiler, up pops the self-confessed "world's most irregular quarterly" fanzine after an 18-month absence. With *Jamming* having grown up overnight *ITC* must now be considered an endangered species: the last true punk-era fanzine. Difficult to find for obvious reasons.

International Country Music News
(05097) 3224
18 Burley Rise
Kegworth
Derby DE7 2DZ
Monthly. Relative newcomer to the country scene, with coverage of UK country as well as the 'real thang'.

International Musician And Recording World
(01) 987-5090
P.O.Box 381
Mill Harbour
London E14
Monthly. Established if conservative read for the musician. Boasts some fairly useful freelance contributors, but whole rarely seems to live up to the sum of the parts.

Jamming
(01) 602-0048
45-53 Sinclair Road
London W14
Bi-monthly. *Jamming's* catchphrase 'A new Optimism for the Eighties' sets it aside from *Zigzag's* post-punk tail chasing and has remained with it in its graudation to the high street stores. The slogan's been discarded, but the spirit lives on. Please don't drop the poet's corner, though, chaps. . .

Jazz Journal International
(01) 580-7244
35 Great Russell Street
London WC1B 3PP
Monthly. Founded in 1948, *JJI* claims to be the oldest surviving jazz publication – and since *Down Beat's* slide down market into the rock sphere, the purists' choice.

Kerrang!
(01) 836-1522
40 Long Acre
London WC2
Fortnightly. With ex-*Sounds* editor Geoff Barton at the helm, the heavy metallurgists' bible continues to flourish. Colourful in visuals and phraseology, it's often been imitated but never surpassed. Those of a nervous disposition or disinclined to wade through a sea of outlandish adjectives are advised to avoid.

Melody Maker
(01) 379-3581
Berkshire House
168-73 High Holborn
London WC1
Weekly. The patient continues to improve, in spite of a nasty rash of pull-out/drop-out/fall-out teen specials on Duran Duran, Madness etc. some months back. Assitant ed Allan Jones' acession to the throne means that rock 'n' roll will never find itself edged out of feature space, which is some relief for us traditionalists. And of course there's still the small ads. . .

Music UK
(01) 460-4474
26-28 Addison Road
Bromley
Kent BR2 9RR
Monthly. musicians' mag that's not seen

as often as it deserves to be, probably due to its split between distribution newsagents and music shops. Recently dropped usual A5 format for larger size – less distinctive but arguably better looking (and more expensive!) Recently launched *Sound Engineer* (£1.20, monthly) spinoff worth a mention.

Music Week
(01) 836-1522
40 Long Acre
London WC2
Weekly. *The* trade paper, the innards of which pull out to become the Top 100 singles and album charts. Seeing as these are reproduced – in less attractive form, admittedly in – *Record Mirror*, at half the price, one must assume that those paying the premium have an all-consuming interest in the business side of things. And consumption, measured in £s, is what *Music Week* is all about.

New Kommotion
(01) 902-6417
3 Bowrons Avenue
Wembley, Middlesex
Quarterly. An old chestnut among fanzines, *NK* is something of a bible for those of a rock 'n' roll and rockabilly persuasion. Though it rarely reaches its planned schedule (in common with many other fanzines, it must be added), ambitious plans are afoot to launch *Rocket 88*, a sister 'zine concentrating on 'roots' music (R&B, doowop, hillbilly and swing) to alternate with the established title. Wish 'em well.

NME (The New Musical Express)
(01) 439-8761
5-7 Carnaby Street
London W1
Weekly. Despite recent valiant efforts from IPC stablemate/rival *Melody Maker*, the reign of *New Musical Express* continues by default as much as layout and design. It's nearly ten years since Parsons and Burchill – can the world hold its breath much longer?

No.1
(01) 251-6598
Kings Reach Tower
Stanford Street
London SE1 9LS
Weekly. While *Smash Hits* found time to spin off *Just Seventeen* (a companion publication for teenage girls with more fashion and less pop) without noticeably damaging its circulation, IPC's carbon-copy would be happy to add a few more girls, boys or don't knows to their readership. Difficult not to echo last years debut entry, that all the cash and talent involved couldn't have been put to more imaginative use, and wonder if it'll still be here next time around

Now Dig This
(01) 954-4518
50 Drummond Crescent
Simonside
South Shields
Tyne and Wear
Monthly. Now that *Not Fade Away* has, sadly, faded away, this is the one for Fifties enthusiasts to follow.

Omaha Rainbow
(01) 647-5491
10 Lesley Court
Harcourt Road
Wallington, Surrey
Quarterly. Unaccountably omitted from last year's listing, Omaha Rainbow recently celebrated its tenth anniversary. Inspired by John Stewart, concentrates on the US songwriter genre: boasted the first Springsteen front cover in Europe, but suvives unspoilt. Associated record label, Sunstorm, just launched.

One Two Testing
(01) 379-3581
Berkshire House
168-73 High Holborn
London WC1
Monthly. IPC's latest venture in the 'muso' stakes. Displays a remarkably adventurous approach for a hardware guide, and won this reviewer's heart by putting Nick Heyward on the cover of the second issue – credibility? What credibility? Touches of schoolboy humour notwithstanding, this is surprisingly readable.

Outlet
(01) 551-3346
Trev Faull
33 Aintree Crescent
Barkingside
Ilford, Essex
Occasional. Possibly the ultimate in non-specialist information-packed fanzines that boasts an even more occasional sister publication, the self-explanatory *Instrumental Review*. You'd think in these days of pre-packaged pap, sorry pop, there'd be a little enough to write about, but you'll find contemporary and historical items rubbing matrix numbers happily. Not easy to read, admittedly, but worth the effort.

Record Collector
45 St Mary's Road
London W5
Monthly. With its larger format now visible in many high-street newsagents, *Record Collector* is obviously onto a winner. No prizes for layout, cover design or zippy editorial, but it'll do nicely for those whose spare rooms are filled with collectable 45s. If you're buying or selling old records, this is the only place to be

Record Mirror
(01) 836-1522
40 Long Acre
London WC2
Weekly. *RM* has never seemed wholly suited to the small-format stolen from the all-conquering *Smash Hits*. A recent change of editorship has seen less concentration on chart acts, but when the *Music Week* Top Hundred is the paper's main selling point the policy seems a bit self-defeating. Addition of a video supplement may win new readers, but long-term prospects seem unclear

Smash Hits
(01) 439-8801
Lisa House
52-55 Carnaby Street

London W1
Fortnightly. Brand leader for the last five – is it really five? – years, *SHits* (as we jealous critics abbreviate it) outsells just about everything in sight by continuing its winning formula of song words, colourful yet distinctive design and undeniable class. Better than the traditional elder brother/sister with their record collections, with which teenagers previously had to make do. Trouble is, what does a generation weaned on *Smash Hits* graduate to?

Soul on Sound
(01) 240-7632
2nd Floor
5 Garrick Street
London WC2E 9AZ
Fortnightly. News, reviews, interviews and – the magic ingredient, music – on cassette, as the title suggests! Walkman fodder for jazz, soul'n'funk fans.

Soundcheck
(01) 437-8942
Downton House
103-09 Wardour Street
London W1
Free, weekly. Great idea – a music paper financed by advertising revenue and and distributed free of charge at major venues – that found more favour with readers than the holders of record company purse strings. Ambitious weekly relaunch (from fortnightly) attempted to balance books, but future far from assured.

Sounds
(01) 836-1522
40 Long Acre
London WC2
Weekly. Always the most street-level (if not credible) of the big three rock weeklies, *Sounds* has often confused the issue by starting trends (the New Wave of heavy metal, Oi! and most recently the insubstantial 'casual' movement). With Garry Bushell, Punk/HM guru, having departed to "write his book", discovery of new writing talent in the next year could be crucial – but the first priority must be design, which has declined to a new low in recent times.

Southern Rag
(0252) 724638
2 Eastdale
East Street
Farnham, Surrey GU9 7TB
Quarterly. Along with *Swing 51*, the mainstay of the UK folk magazine scene New larger format should pay dividends this year.

Stick It In Your Ear
(0703) 440313
Geoff Wall
9 Gladstone Road
Sholing
Southampton SO2 8GU
Bi-monthly. Slight confusion here – not a fanzine on cassette but a cassette fanzine, if you get my meaning. Pleasant, unpretentious and extremely informative on the ever-active world of alternative tapes. Same operation also markets

compilation tapes of South Coast bands, if such is your interest: SAE brings catalogue.

Swing 51
(01) 641-1308
41 Bushey Road
Sutton
Surrey SM1 1QR
Semi-Annual. Well produced fanzine that splits its options between this side of the Atlantic (traditional and electric folk) and the other (bluegrass, folk/blues and

singer-songwriters of the John Hiatt-Jerry Garcia ilk). Interviews still stuck in the traditional question-answer format lend a feeling of old-fashioned wholesomeness to a worthy if infrequent mag.

What Keyboard
(01) 898-5090
P.O.Box 381
Mill Harbour
London E14
Monthly. Self-explanatory sister title to *International Musician*.

The Wire
(01) 385-5313
72 Farm Lane
London SW6
Three times yearly. Absorbing volume billed as "jazz, improvised music and. . ." that's well worth investigation by avant-gardeists everywhere.

Zigzag
(01) 278-6615
24 Ray Street
London EC1R 3DJ

Monthly. Your perspective of *Zigzag*, Britain's oldest fanzine, will depend on how far back memory extends. These days *ZZ* jostles with the glossy monthlies on the newsagents shelf, just a little out of its depth. Editorial approach still engagingly down to earth, but design looks like someone had fun with a new paintbox – not always easy on the eye.

 # ROCK PUBLICATIONS/US

Austin Chronicle
(512) 473-8995
P.O. Box 49066
Austin, Texas 78765
Bi-weekly freesheet from deep in the heart of Texas.

BAM
(415) 652-3810
5951 Canning Street
Oakland, CA 94609

(213) 467-7878
1800 North Highland
Hollywood, CA 90028
Original *Rolling Stone*-format paper whose Northern/Southern California editions differ only marginally in content.

Billboard
(212) 764-7300
1515 Broadway
New York, NY 10036
Top of the trades, with the all important Hot One Hundred and specialist charts in its favour. An industry watchword.

Blitz
P.O. Box 48124
Los Angeles, CA 90048
Bi-monthly with an interest in contemporary and historical rock: where else would you find Dream Syndicate and Herman's Hermits between the same covers?

Bomp
(213) 227-4141
P.O. Box 7112
Burbank, CA 91510
Resurrected to fill the gap left by the 1984 demise of *Trouser Press*, Greg Shaw promises a more contemporary format than previously. Hallelujah! Bomp is back. . .

Boston Rock
(617) 266-8787
739 Boylston Street
Boston, MA 02116
Wide ranging, fast moving monthly in the same shitkickin' style as the late, lamented *New York Rocker*.

Buddy
(214) 826-8742
501n Good-Latimer Expwy.
Dallas, TX 75204
"The Original Texan Magazine", Holly-inspired and still rooted firmly in traditional rock.

Cash Box
(212) 586-2640
330 West 58th Street
New York, NY 10019
Colourfully presented weekly trade paper still ranked second to *Billboard* in a field of two. Strong on minority musics.

Circus
(212) 685-5050
419 Park Avenue South
New York, NY 10016
Creem substitute almost as popular as the real thing.

Country Rhythms
(212) 689 2830
475 Park Avenue South
New York NY 10016
Danny Fields' personality-packed monthly for country enthusiasts.

Creem
(313) 642-8833
187 South Woodward Avenue
Birmingham, MI 48011
Wacky monthly that continues to treat the big names of US music with the irreverence they undoubtedly deserve. Brits don't get off scot free, either. Past masters of the cringe-worthy headline. Special editions well worth investigation.

Down Beat
(312) 346-7811
222 West Adams Street
Chicago, IL 60606
Monthly jazzers' bible that's recently been creating nationwide indignation by allowing rock artists within its pages.

Flipside
P.O. Box 363
Whittier, CA 90608
Bi-monthly for those with a fascination for

the frenzied extremes of US punk. Fanzines listing an added attraction of more general interest.

Goldmine
(715) 445-2214
700 East State Street
Iola, WI 54990
A change of ownership around the time of the last listings and a subsequent change of editorship have seen this respected record collector-oriented magazine struggle to maintain readership.

Guitar Player
Frets
(408) 446-1105
20605 Lazaneo
Cupertino, CA 95014
It's the concentration on technique rather than hardware that's made *GP* the guitarist's read since 1967. UK publications please note and emulate. *Frets*, also monthly, is the accoustic guitarist's equivalent.

Guitar World
(212) 807-7100
1115 Broadway
New York, NY 10010
Flashy bi-monthly competitor to the above which features the ultimate in guitar hero-worship – the Collectors' Choice centrefold!

High Fidelity
(212) 887-8337
825 Seventh Avenue
New York, NY 10019
Monthly audiophile mag with occasional rock features.

Hit Parader
(203) 735-3381
Charlton Building
Derby, CT 06481
Monthly song lyric and news confection with a Top 40 bias. Sister publciation to *Smash Hits* and similar in content.

Illinois Entertainer
(312) 298-9333
P.O. Box 356
Mt. Prospect, IL 60056

As the title suggests, a somewhat parochial monthly music paper with some national interest stories.

International Musician and Recording World
(212) 947-6740
12 West 32nd Street
New York, NY 10001
Glossy monthly interespersing hardware reviews with interviews and news features. Not a million miles away from British sister publication of the same name; some commonality of material.

Jazz Times
(301) 588-4114
8055 13th Street
Silver Springs, MD 20910
Monthly of interest to beret-bearing be-bop fanatics.

Keyboard
(408) 446-1105
20605 Lazaneo
Cupertino, CA 95014
Sister publication to *Guitar* – why should axemen have it all their own way, after all?

Living Blues
(312) 281-3385
2615 North Wilton Avenue
Chicago, IL 60614
Self-explanatory quarterly, still alive and pickin'.

Master
(312) 491-9112
624 Davis Street
Evanston, IL 60201
A monthly fanzine that's intellectual, but in tune with contemporary rock 'n' roll. Worthwhile.

Musician
(617) 281-3110
31 Commercial Street
Gloucester, MA 01930
New York office:
(212) 764-7300
1515 Broadway
New York, NY 10036